The Oxford Dictionary of
Political Quotations

edited by **Antony Jay**

From *Panorama* in 1956 to *Annie's Bar* in 1996, Antony Jay has spent 40 years travelling in the realms of government and politics as a television writer and producer. The journey has included the editorship of *Tonight*, writing the two royal television documentaries *Royal Family* and *Elizabeth R*, and many programmes with David Frost, including the twelve interviews with Harold Wilson in *A Prime Minister on Prime Ministers*. His insights into bureaucracy come from an unhappy year as a senior executive in BBC TV and two and a half entertaining ones on a government committee, the Annan Committee on the Future of Broadcasting. He got it all out of his system in the 1980s with *Yes Minister* and *Yes Prime Minister*. Now, with *The Oxford Dictionary of Political Quotations*, he finally reveals his sources.

Oxford   New York

OXFORD UNIVERSITY PRESS

1997

Oxford University Press, Great Clarendon Street, Oxford OX2 6DP

Oxford New York

Athens Auckland Bangkok Bogota Bombay
Buenos Aires Calcutta Cape Town Dar es Salaam
Delhi Florence Hong Kong Istanbul Karachi
Kuala Lumpur Madras Madrid Melbourne
Mexico City Nairobi Paris Singapore
Taipei Tokyo Toronto Warsaw

and associated companies in
Berlin Ibadan

Oxford is a trade mark of Oxford University Press

Selection and arrangement © Antony Jay, Oxford University Press 1996
Introduction © Antony Jay 1996

First published 1996 by Oxford University Press
First issued as an Oxford University Press paperback 1997

British Library Cataloguing in Publication Data
Data available

Library of Congress Cataloging in Publication Data

ISBN 0–19–280071–X

10 9 8 7 6 5 4 3 2 1

Designed by Jane Stevenson

Printed in Great Britain by
Biddles Ltd
Guildford and King's Lynn

Project Team

Managing Editor	Elizabeth M. Knowles
Index Editors	Susan Ratcliffe
	Christina Malkowska Zaba
Library Research	Ralph Bates
	Marie G. Diaz
Reading Programme	Helen McCurdy
	Verity Mason
	Penelope Newsome
Data Capture	Sandra Vaughan
Proof-reading	Fabia Claris
	Penny Trumble

We are grateful to George Chowdharay-Best for contributions to our file of incoming quotations, and to Gerald Blick, Jon Ross Simon, and Jeanne Croft for additional research.

Introduction

'The hard pressed writer in turning over these pages may find and note many excellent phrases, whether to give a pleasing touch of erudition or to save the trouble of thinking for himself.' Bernard Darwin's words in his introduction to the first *Oxford Dictionary of Quotations* are as true today as they were fifty-five years ago. But there are more honourable reasons for using quotations, especially in the world of politics. In mobilizing support for a project or a policy it is especially agreeable to be able to call upon the distinguished dead; their distinction adds intellectual weight and moral force to the argument, and their death makes it impossible for them to appear on television later and say that they meant something completely different.

Even more important, perhaps, than the support of the eminent is the wisdom of the ages. New ideas in politics are always suspect, but recourse to quotation can show that your ideas, far from being new and tender shoots, are rooted deep in the history of political society. Those who argue for punishment as deterrent rather than rehabilitation may find themselves out of the fashion, but a quick look at Aeschylus will enable them to demonstrate the two and a half thousand year pedigree of their belief. Those who oppose closer ties with Europe can quote Bagehot, 'Are they [the English people] not above all nations divided from the rest of the world?... Are they not out of the current of common European causes and affairs?' from the nineteenth century, and Gibbon, 'The division of Europe into a number of independent states is productive of the most beneficial consequences to the liberty of mankind,' from the eighteenth, to show that there is nothing new in their belief that there is strength and logic in their resistance, while Europhiles can adduce the dictum of the nineteenth century Prime Minister Lord Salisbury: 'We are part of the community of Europe and we must do our duty as such.' Just occasionally, too, quotations can be used not just for intellectual support, but for dramatic effect, as if they carried some magical power. Two Prime Ministers in living memory have felt the force of it. The first was Chamberlain in 1940, when Leo Amery quoted Cromwell's historic words to the Rump Parliament 'You have sat too long for any good you have been doing. Depart, I say, and let us have done with you. In the name of God, go!' Chamberlain went. The second was Macmillan in 1963, when a fellow Conservative, Nigel Birch, quoted just as lethally from Browning's *The Lost Leader*:

> Life's night begins; let him never come back to us!
> There would be doubt, hesitation and pain,
> Forced praise on our part—the glimmer of twilight,
> Never glad confident morning again!

Perhaps Macmillan was doomed anyway, but Birch's quotation made certain of his fall as surely as Brutus' dagger.

This Dictionary, it is hoped, will be of service to those who want to support their arguments and opinions with evidence of their distinguished pedigree and ancient lineage, as well as those looking for no more than a pleasing touch of erudition or the avoidance of thought. It is not, however, simply an anthology of political wit and wisdom. It is, first, foremost, and above all, a work of reference. The primary qualification for an entry is not its antiquity or its profundity but its familiarity. There is a bank of political quotations which are part of the currency of political speeches and writings throughout the English-speaking world. All of them should be in these pages, and if they are not (and I am sure time and alert readers will expose some glaring omissions) then the editor is to blame.

Beyond the central core of universally recognized political quotations there is a much wider circle of entries which, while they are quoted from time to time, are not immediately recognizable to all of those to whom they are addressed. These are subject to editorial judgment, and here the editor might try to defend an omission rather than apologize for it. But in both cases the key question has been 'Should this be in a work of reference?' The two principal users for whom the book is intended are those who have encountered or partly recall a quotation and want to verify or source it, and those who are looking for a quotation on a particular subject or from a given writer.

Many works of reference, however, have an appeal to browsers and grazers as well as hunters, and a dictionary of political quotations must be very close to the top of the list; it offers the delight of discovery as well as confirmation and verification. While this one is not designed as an anthology, it is bound to give the reader most of the pleasure of an anthology, and so in many cases I have tried to supply more contextual information than might be necessary in a work of pure reference. Some quotations (for instance Wellington's 'If you believe that you'll believe anything') make little sense to any but the expert reader, unless accompanied by some indication of the context. Others, while intelligible (like Margaret Thatcher's 'Now it must be business as usual'), can become much more interesting with some knowledge of the circumstances in which they were uttered. For the same reason the Dictionary is organized not by theme but by the name of the speaker or writer. I have never myself been entirely at ease with thematic organization—I always have a niggling suspicion that any thematic entry could legitimately have been included under a different heading, and often under several—whereas entries grouped under the name of the source cannot suffer under this disability, and arrangement by source is just as helpful as arrangement by theme for reference purposes. In a collection of political quotations, this form is particularly advantageous, especially for the random dipper: reading through the citations from one individual—Lloyd George, de Tocqueville, Halifax—gives a quick but vivid sense not only of what he said but also of his quality and individuality. So although this is indeed a work of reference, it is hoped that many people will also use it as an illuminating, if wildly unsystematic, compendium of opinions, ideas, and personalities that have marked our progress towards the political society we live in today.

So what makes a quotation into a political quotation? Often, of course, the answer is obvious. General truths about politics are immediate candidates: Aeschylus's 'Everyone's quick to blame the alien', Bacon's 'All rising to great place is by a winding stair', and Burke's 'To tax and to please, no more than to love and be wise, is not given to men.' Then there are quotations specific to an event or an individual which have passed into the language: Disraeli's 'I have climbed to the top of the greasy pole' or Mary Tudor's 'When I am dead and opened, you shall find "Calais" lying in my heart', even though it is more often misquoted than quoted. Some quotations would not merit inclusion but for the source; if you or I had said 'No woman in my time will be Prime Minister' we would hardly expect to find ourselves in the Dictionary. The fact that Margaret Thatcher said it makes all the difference.

There is however a disputed territory between what is obviously a political quotation and what is obviously not. There is nothing remotely political about the words 'I can't tell a lie, Pa; you know I can't tell a lie. I did cut it with my hatchet,' but because it illuminates Washington's character, and because its frequent quotation testifies to his reputation, there can be no question of leaving it out. But what about the sayings of great men when they are writing fiction and the words come from the mouths of their characters, as in Macaulay's poems or Disraeli's novels? Surely it can not be cheating to include them if exclusion would mean omitting 'A Jacobite's Epitaph'? And the 'Two nations' speech in *Sybil* is currently at the heart of the Conservative Party's internal strife.

Another obscure territorial boundary is that which divides, or fails to divide, political quotations from those which, while having large areas that overlap politics, might more properly be classified under headings such as law, warfare, royalty, or economics. If these subjects had their own Oxford quotation dictionaries, there might have been some debate about where to place Adam Smith's observation that 'people of the same trade seldom meet together, even for merriment and diversion, but the conversation ends in a conspiracy against the public, or in some contrivance to raise prices.' Since there is however (as yet) no Oxford Dictionary of Economics Quotations, there was no argument. There is however an excellent *Oxford Book of Political Anecdotes* and, while some anecdotes are the source of quotation, anecdotes as such are not included. Obviously there were temptations. After losing office in 1964 Iain Macleod was a conspicuous absentee from the opposition front bench, which Wilson knew was a cause of much critical comment among Conservative back-benchers. One day however he did appear, to put a challenging question to the Prime Minister. Wilson rose, paused, and then said 'Do you come here often?' It produced one of the biggest laughs ever heard from a party against one of its own front-benchers. But somehow 'Do you come here often?' did not sound like a political quotation; it belongs only in that anecdote and had to be excluded.

Of course not all political quotations are either by politicians or about politics. Lewis Carroll was certainly not a politician and *Alice Through the Looking Glass* is equally certainly not a political work, but 'Jam tomorrow' and 'When I use a word it means just what I choose it to mean' are regularly quoted in political debate—as witness the quotation from Tony Benn, 'Some of that jam we thought was for tomorrow we have already eaten.' The Dictionary would be failing its readers if it left them out. Politicians may no longer quote poetry as freely as they used to, but students of the politics of the recent past will find many quotations from and references to poets, and even today they may encounter Kipling's 'Paying the Dane-geld', Chesterton's 'The Secret People', and copious allusions to the Vicar of Bray. And there is of course one poet who stands out above all the others for frequency of quotation: it is not just the power and range of Shakespeare's writing that makes him so quotable in a political context, it is the fact that so many of his plays are so intensely political in their themes, characters, and conflicts. If readers feel that he is over-represented here, I can only say that I have been acutely aware of the apparently excessive space he has been given, and that the original section was considerably longer. Much weeding has been done, and the surviving entries represent the editor's judgement of those that could not be omitted without loss.

Shakespeare is not the only writer (though he is the only poet) to occupy what might seem to be a disproportionate amount of space. Four great national leaders—Churchill, Disraeli, Jefferson, and Lincoln—have been endlessly quoted by their contemporaries and successors. Certainly they had the gift of language, but it also seems as if the fame they achieved during their lifetime may have led to their words being more diligently recorded and more frequently repeated than those of their less famous contemporaries. There are however two people who figure prominently in these pages without having achieved the same world wide fame. Burke, though he was indeed a statesman, was not in their class, and Bagehot was never even a member of parliament. Both, however, consistently found a way of expressing ideas and arguments that everyone could remember and no one could improve on. Some of their ideas were original, but even those that were not have proved to be endlessly quotable. They exemplify Pope's definition:

> True wit is Nature to advantage dressed,
> What oft was thought, but ne'er so well expressed.

The editor feels no need to apologize for the amount of space they command.

There is one particular danger which confronts all quotation dictionaries: the danger of including only those quotations which have already appeared in other dictionaries. It is of course inevitable that many of the quotations will be found in other collections, but it is equally important that lexicographers should not be endlessly recycling the same material. If quotations are to refresh and invigorate political communication, they should be drawn from a living stream and not a stagnant pond. So while the starting point for this Dictionary was the existing corpus of political quotations held on the files of the Oxford University Press, it was only the starting point. The principal means of bringing in new material was a team of researchers who combed the daily papers and the periodicals, and listened to radio and television programmes, to record every significant quotation they came across and submit it for consideration. Another important source has been correspondence. A living dictionary of quotations will necessarily include quotations from the living, and many of them have been kind enough not only to verify and source entries attributed to them, but also to supply other of their writings and sayings that they have found being quoted. The living have also interceded for the dead: for example, the first draft selection, like all the quotation dictionaries I have encountered, was disturbingly short of quotations from one of Britain's most distinguished Prime Ministers, Robert Peel. It was hard to believe that he had left so few quotable remarks behind him, and a letter to the leading authority on Peel, Professor Norman Gash, produced evidence that it was not Peel but the record that was at fault. Peel's entry is now of a respectable length. Equally, one of the most politically astute civil servants of the nineteenth century would have remained unrepresented if Lord Dacre had not directed me to Henry Taylor's *The Statesman*.

This leads to the final aspect of the question 'What is a political quotation?', namely does it have to have been quoted, or is it sufficient for it to be quotable? Once you accept quotability as the criterion, you are on a slippery slope, at the bottom of which lie the broad acres of anthologies and commonplace books. The compilers of the first edition of the *Oxford Dictionary of Quotations* were in no doubt: 'During the whole work of selection a great effort was made to restrict the entries to actual current quotations and not to include phrases which the various editors or contributors believed to be quotable or wanted to be quoted.' Of course they were right. And yet even they said only that a great effort was made, not that it was successful in every case. I must confess to not having been quite so purist. Certainly this is essentially a dictionary of what has been quoted, but here and there I have taken one or two small steps down the slippery slope and included lines that I believed modern readers would like to quote. After all, how can one know that they have not been quoted somewhere at some time? I took the liberty of including Laertes's advice to Ophelia about marriage to the heir to the throne:

> His greatness weighed, his will is not his own
> For he himself is subject to his birth.
> He may not, as unvalued persons do,
> Carve for himself, for on his choice depends
> The sanity and health of the whole state;
> And therefore must his choice be circumscribed
> Unto the voice and yielding of that body
> Whereof he is the head.

I had no record of its being politically quoted anywhere, but in view of the continuing current debate about the divorce and remarriage of the Prince of Wales it seemed to me that many people might like to be reminded of it. It was only after it had been passed for the press that I discovered that Stanley Baldwin had quoted that same speech in the House of Commons, in relation to the abdication of King Edward VIII. So the reader will find here a small number—and an exceedingly small percentage—of entries that I cannot swear have been previously quoted, though equally I cannot swear that they have not. They are also another way of stopping the pool of political quotation from stagnating. And another aspect of this question is, when does a political quotation stop being a political quotation? It would have been easy to decide that Bismarck's observation that the Balkan conflict was 'not worth the healthy bones of a single Pomeranian grenadier' had passed into history's out-tray; but it surfaced again in 1995 in a House of Commons debate on the role of the UN forces in Bosnia.

If I may have taken slight liberties with the quotable as opposed to the quoted, this has not been the case with verification and sourcing. My colleagues at the Press have been rigorous and scrupulous about the tracing of quotations, and many promising runners fell at this last fence. They include familiar lines like *Pas d'ennemi à gauche* and 'Whoever is in office, the Conservatives are always in power', but among the omissions are a few whose absence I particularly regret. I am sure Bacon said 'Councils to which Time hath not been called, Time will not ratify' (and I am absolutely certain I did not make it up), and I am fairly sure he said 'Great events may have small occasions, but seldom small causes', but no amount of research has been able to track either of them down. I also wish we could have found who it was who said of Gladstone that when making a speech he not only followed every bay and headland along the coastline of his argument, but also insisted on tracking every river to its source. And I believe it was the American scholar Donald Schon who said that government bureaux are memorials to dead problems, but alas I cannot prove it. Another source of regret is the quotations that appeared just too late for inclusion, in particular Shimon Peres's observation 'Television has made dictatorship impossible, but democracy unbearable.' But we were not too late for President Izetbegović's words after signing the Dayton Accord: 'And to my people I say, this may not be a just peace, but it is more just than a continuation of war.'

Perhaps the most problematic of all the quotations are the very recent ones. Ultimately, time is the judge of whether an observation can be accepted as a quotation, and whether 'Tough on crime and tough on the causes of crime' is a full member of the club or merely a short-term visitor, only time will tell. On the other hand, to set an arbitrary limit of ten or twenty years from the first citation as a qualifying period would mean excluding many quotations to which readers would want to refer. I suspect that in any future edition it will be the most topical recent entries that are the least likely to survive.

And what about speech-writers? This is surely a recent problem. It may be that politicians in the past had help from time to time, but it is hard to picture Lincoln or Disraeli or Lloyd George or Churchill asking the boys in the back room to come up with some ideas for the next speech. Today a team of speech writers is part of the standard entourage of an international leader, and on occasions we learn, at least informally, that some famous phrase or other was coined by a hand unconnected to the tongue that uttered it. Should we seek out the names of the writers and give them due recognition? It would be an impossible task, and moreover the reader would look for the phrase under the name of the politician who delivered it. This is also true of quotations that were in circulation some time before a politician gave them national or international currency. Where we can trace the original we attribute it, but it has to be accepted that some of the quotations attributed to politicians were probably not their own coinage. Nevertheless they will always be associated with the words, just as Clark Gable, and not Margaret Mitchell or Sidney Howard, will always be associated with the line 'Frankly, my dear, I don't give a damn' (which would probably be the politician's comment on this question).

The other difficulty presented by the most recent quotations is the possibility that in their original form they reached a national or international audience without ever appearing on a printed page. Radio and television archives are not always accessible, and slow to plough through even when you know exactly what you are looking for; but when you have only an imprecise recollection or reference it can be effectively impossible to locate what would be fairly easy to find in a newspaper or press cuttings library. Of course all the memorable quotations eventually find their way into print, but not always in their original form. The chief whip's famous phrase in Michael Dobbs's *House of Cards*, 'You might very well think that. I couldn't possibly comment', is taken from the television script; it does not appear in the book. Equally, transcripts from radio and television can miss important emphases and nuances: when Neil Kinnock spoke to the Labour Party Conference about Liverpool Council, his stress on 'Labour' in the phrase, 'the grotesque chaos of a Labour council—a *Labour* council—hiring taxis to scuttle round the city handing out redundancy notices to its own workers' did not come through in the press reports as it did in the television news bulletins. And the televising of parliamentary debates has exposed the difference between the semi-incoherence of some members' speeches and the comparative lucidity and logic of the phrasing that appears subsequently in the august pages of Hansard.

Finally I must acknowledge with gratitude the large number of people whose help has been invaluable. Christopher Booker, Simon Heffer, Nigel Rees, and Peter Hennessy all read the whole of the first draft and made numerous comments and suggestions of which many were immediately incorporated. All of them are extremely busy professionals and I was astonished as well as delighted at the amount of time and care they were willing to give to the task. Indeed one of the happiest aspects of an unusually happy assignment has been the willingness of almost everyone I contacted to give up time and take trouble to make the Dictionary as full and accurate as possible. Of those who helped out on specific topics or authors I would like to offer especial thanks to the following: Lord Bauer, Tony Benn, John Biffen, John Blundell, Dr Eamonn Butler, the Bishop of Coventry, Lord Dacre, Lord Deedes, Oliver Everett, Milton Friedman, Norman Gash, Martin Gilbert, Henry Hardy, Lord Healey, Sir Bernard Ingham, Simon Jenkins, Bernard Levin, Kenneth Morgan, Nigel Nicolson, Matthew Parris, Enoch Powell, Stanley Wells, and Chris Wrigley. Above all, I want to thank the editorial team of the Quotations Dictionaries department of the Oxford University Press. Not only have they done the bulk of the work; their knowledge, expertise, and scholarly rigour have contributed immeasurably to the quality of the book.

Any credit for the final result must be shared with all of the above; the blame remains exclusively the editor's.

ANTONY JAY

Somerset, January 1996

How to Use the Dictionary

The sequence of entries is by alphabetical order of author, usually by surname but with occasional exceptions such as imperial or royal titles, or authors known by a pseudonym ('**Saki**'), or a nickname (**Caligula**). In general authors' names are given in the form by which they are best known, so that we have **Harold Macmillan** (not Lord Stockton), **Lord Melbourne** (not William Lamb), **H. G. Wells** (not Herbert George Wells), and **Harold Wilson** (not James Harold Wilson). Collections such as **Anonymous** and the **Bible** are included in the alphabetical sequence.

Author names are followed by dates of birth and death (where known) and brief descriptions; where appropriate, cross-references are then given to quotations about that author elsewhere in the text (*on Acheson:* see **Pearson** 200:7). Within each author entry, quotations are arranged according to date, with material from novels, plays, letters, diaries, and speeches forming a single chronological sequence. (The **Anonymous** section is an exception to this rule: quotations under this heading are arranged alphabetically according to the first word of the quotation.) Foreign-language text is given where it is felt that the quotation is more familiar in the language of origin ('*L'État c'est moi*').

Where the information is available (the composition date of a letter or diary, the publication date of a book), a quotation can be accorded a precise date. Some quotations are dated according to the circumstances with which the remark or comment is associated (Stanton's comment following the assassination of Abraham Lincoln, 'Now he belongs to the ages', dates the quotation as 1865). When the date is uncertain or unknown, and the quotation cannot be related to a particular event, the author's date of death has been used to date the quotation. A few entries (such as that for Winston Churchill) have a number of such attributed items; they are arranged alphabetically ('a' and 'the' being ignored).

Contextual information regarded as essential to a full appreciation of the quotation precedes the relevant text in an italicized note; information seen as providing helpful information follows in an italicized note. Bibliographical information as to the source from which the quotation is taken appears in a marginal note; titles and dates of publication are supplied, but full finding references are not given. Every attempt has been made to trace quotations to citable sources, but where necessary 'attributed' is used to indicate that while attribution to a particular author is popularly made, a specific reference has not been traced. It is felt more helpful to include widely known material with an account of its status, than to omit the item because it is not susceptible of final verification.

Cross-references are made both to individual quotations (cf. **Disraeli** 121:1) and to whole entries. References to specific quotations consist of the author's name followed by the page number and the number of the quotation on the page (**Burke** 63:1). Authors who have their own entries are typographically distinguished by the

use of bold (epitaph for John **Adams,** of Lord **Halifax**) in context or source notes, or in
the author descriptions (son of Joseph **Kennedy**).

The Index

Both the keywords and the entries following each keyword, including those in
foreign languages, are in strict alphabetical order. Singular and plural nouns
(with their possessive forms) are grouped separately.

The references show the author's name, usually in abbreviated form
(SHAK/Shakespeare), followed by the page number and the number of the quotation
on that page: 183:8 therefore means quotation 8 on page 183.

Diane Abbott 1953–

British Labour politician

1 Being an MP is the sort of job all working-class parents want for their children—clean, indoors and no heavy lifting.

in *Independent* 18 January 1994

Bella Abzug 1920–

American politician

2 Richard Nixon impeached himself. He gave us Gerald Ford as his revenge.

in *Rolling Stone*; Linda Botts *Loose Talk* (1980)

Accius 170–c.86 BC

Latin poet and dramatist

3 Let them hate, so long as they fear.

Atreus

Dean Acheson 1893–1971

American statesman
on Acheson: see **Pearson** 287:5

4 I will undoubtedly have to seek what is happily known as gainful employment, which I am glad to say does not describe holding public office.

in *Time* 22 December 1952

5 Great Britain has lost an empire and has not yet found a role.

speech at the Military Academy, West Point, 5 December 1962

6 The first requirement of a statesman is that he be dull.

in *Observer* 21 June 1970

7 A memorandum is written not to inform the reader but to protect the writer.

in *Wall Street Journal* 8 September 1977

of President **Eisenhower**:
8 I doubt very much if a man whose main literary interests were in works by Mr Zane Grey, admirable as they may be, is particularly equipped to be the chief executive of this country, particularly where Indian Affairs are concerned.

attributed

Lord Acton 1834–1902

British historian

9 Power tends to corrupt and absolute power corrupts absolutely.
    often quoted as 'All power corrupts...'

letter to Bishop Mandell Creighton, 3 April 1887

10 Great men are almost always bad men, even when they exercise influence and not authority.

letter to Bishop Mandell Creighton, 3 April 1887

Abigail Adams 1744–1818

wife of John **Adams**, 2nd President of the USA, and mother of
John Quincy **Adams**

1   In the new code of laws which I suppose it will be   letter to John Adams, 31 March
    necessary for you to make I desire you would remember   1776
    the ladies, and be more generous and favourable to them
    than your ancestors. Do not put such unlimited power
    into the hands of the husbands. Remember all men
    would be tyrants if they could.

2   These are times in which a genius would wish to live. It   letter to John Quincy Adams, 19
    is not in the still calm of life, or the repose of a pacific January 1780
    station, that great characters are formed…Great
    necessities call out great virtues.

3   Patriotism in the female sex is the most disinterested of   letter to John Adams, 17 June 1782
    all virtues. Excluded from honours and from offices, we
    cannot attach ourselves to the State or Government from
    having held a place of eminence…Yet all history and
    every age exhibit instances of patriotic virtue in the
    female sex; which considering our situation equals the
    most heroic of yours.

Franklin P. Adams 1881–1960

American journalist and humorist

4   When the political columnists say 'Every thinking man'   *Nods and Becks* (1944)
    they mean themselves, and when candidates appeal to
    'Every intelligent voter' they mean everybody who is
    going to vote for them.

5   The trouble with this country is that there are too many   *Nods and Becks* (1944)
    politicians who believe, with a conviction based on
    experience, that you can fool all of the people all of the
    time.

6   Elections are won by men and women chiefly because   *Nods and Becks* (1944)
    most people vote against somebody rather than for
    somebody.

Henry Brooks Adams 1838–1918

American man of letters

7   Politics, as a practice, whatever its professions, has   *The Education of Henry Adams*
    always been the systematic organization of hatreds.   (1907)

8   A friend in power is a friend lost.   *The Education of Henry Adams*
                                                                  (1907)

9   [Charles] Sumner's mind had reached the calm of water   *The Education of Henry Adams*
    which receives and reflects images without absorbing   (1907)
    them; it contained nothing but itself.
      of the American politician and orator Charles **Sumner**

10 The progress of evolution from President Washington to   *The Education of Henry Adams*
    President Grant was alone evidence to upset Darwin.   (1907)

1 Practical politics consists in ignoring facts.

The Education of Henry Adams (1907)

John Adams 1735–1826

1st Vice-President of the United States and 2nd President; father of John Quincy **Adams** and husband of Abigail **Adams**

2 I always consider the settlement of America with reverence and wonder, as the opening of a grand scene and design in providence, for the illumination of the ignorant and the emancipation of the slavish part of mankind all over the earth.

notes for *A Dissertation on the Canon and Feudal Law* (1765)

3 The jaws of power are always opened to devour, and her arm is always stretched out, if possible, to destroy the freedom of thinking, speaking, and writing.

A Dissertation on the Canon and the Feudal Law (1765)

4 Liberty cannot be preserved without a general knowledge among the people, who have a right...and a desire to know; but besides this, they have a right, an indisputable, unalienable, indefeasible, divine right to that most dreaded and envied kind of knowledge, I mean of the characters and conduct of their rulers.

A Dissertation on the Canon and Feudal Law (1765)

5 There is danger from all men. The only maxim of a free government ought to be to trust no man living with power to endanger the public liberty.

Notes for an Oration at Braintree (Spring 1772)

of the Boston Tea Party:
6 There is a dignity, a majesty, a sublimity, in this last effort of the patriots that I greatly admire. The people should never rise without doing something to be remembered—something notable and striking.

diary 17 December 1773

7 A government of laws, and not of men.
later incorporated in the Massachusetts Constitution (1780)

in *Boston Gazette* (1774)

8 I agree with you that in politics the middle way is none at all.

letter to Horatio Gates, 23 March 1776

9 Yesterday, the greatest question was decided which ever was debated in America, and a greater perhaps never was nor will be decided among men. A resolution was passed without one dissenting colony, 'that these United Colonies are, and of right ought to be, free and independent States.'

letter to Abigail Adams, 3 July 1776

10 The happiness of society is the end of government.

Thoughts on Government (1776)

11 Fear is the foundation of most governments.

Thoughts on Government (1776)

12 The judicial power ought to be distinct from both the legislative and executive, and independent upon both, that so it may be a check upon both, as both should be checks upon that.

Thoughts on Government (1776)

13 I must study politics and war that my sons may have liberty to study mathematics and philosophy.

letter to Abigail Adams, 12 May 1780

of the vice-presidency:

1 My country has in its wisdom contrived for me the most insignificant office that ever the invention of man contrived or his imagination conceived.

letter to Abigail Adams, 19 December 1793

2 Democracy never lasts long. It soon wastes, exhausts, and murders itself. There never was a democracy that did not commit suicide.

letter to John Taylor, 15 April 1814

3 The fundamental article of my political creed is that despotism, or unlimited sovereignty, or absolute power, is the same in a majority of a popular assembly, an aristocratic council, an oligarchical junto, and a single emperor.

letter to Thomas Jefferson, 13 November 1815

4 Thomas—Jefferson—still surv—
   Jefferson *died on the same day*

last words, 4 July 1826

John Quincy Adams 1767–1848

6th President of the USA and son of the 2nd President, John **Adams**, and Abigail **Adams**

5 Think of your forefathers! Think of your posterity!

Oration at Plymouth 22 December 1802

6 *Fiat justitia, pereat coelum* [Let justice be done, though heaven perish]. My toast would be, may our country be always successful, but whether successful or otherwise, always right.

letter to John Adams, 1 August 1816; cf. **Decatur** 111:4, **Mansfield** 249:6, **Watson** 380:3

7 America, with the same voice which spoke herself into existence as a nation, proclaimed to mankind the inextinguishable rights of human nature, and the only lawful foundations of government.

address, 4 July 1821

8 America...well knows that by once enlisting under other banners than her own, were they even the banners of foreign independence, she would involve herself beyond the power of extraction, in all the wars of interest and intrigue, of individual avarice, envy, and ambition, which assume the colours and usurp the standard of freedom. The fundamental maxims of her policy would insensibly change from liberty to force...She might become dictatress of the world. She would be no longer the ruler of her own spirit.

address, 4 July 1821

9 Individual liberty is individual power, and as the power of a community is a mass compounded of individual powers, the nation which enjoys the most freedom must necessarily be in proportion to its numbers the most powerful nation.

letter to James Lloyd, 1 October 1822

10 His letter is a dissertation to prove that the whole science of diplomacy consists in giving dinners.
   of a letter sent by **Canning** *to Christopher Hughes, US minister to Sweden*

diary 1825; Charles Francis Adams *Memoirs of John Quincy Adams*

11 This house will bear witness to his piety; this town [Braintree, Massachusetts], his birthplace, to his

epitaph for John **Adams**, 1829

munificence; history to his patriotism; posterity to the
depth and compass of his mind.

*on collapsing in the Senate, 21 February 1848 (he died two
days later):*
1 This, this is the end of earth. I am content.

William H. Seward *Eulogy of John
Quincy Adams to Legislature of
New York* 1848

Samuel Adams 1722–1803

American revolutionary leader

2 Let us contemplate our forefathers, and posterity, and
resolve to maintain the rights bequeathed to us by the
former, for the sake of the latter.

speech, 1771

on hearing gunfire at Lexington, 19 April 1775:
3 What a glorious morning is this.
 traditionally quoted as 'What a glorious morning for America'

J. K. Hosmer *Samuel Adams* (1886)

4 A nation of shopkeepers are very seldom so disinterested.

Oration in Philadelphia 1 August
1776 (the authenticity of this
publication is doubtful); cf.
Napoleon 270:1, **Smith** 341:6

5 Driven from every other corner of the earth, freedom of
thought and the right of private judgement in matters of
conscience direct their course to this happy country as
their last asylum.

speech in Philadelphia, 1 August
1776

6 We cannot make events. Our business is wisely to
improve them…Mankind are governed more by their
feelings than by reason. Events which excite those
feelings will produce wonderful effects.

J. N. Rakove *The Beginnings of
National Politics* (1979)

Frank Ezra Adcock 1886–1968

British classicist and historian of Greece and Rome

7 Rome under Sulla was like a bus, with half the
passengers trying to drive, and the rest trying to collect
the fare.

lecture at Cambridge in the 1940s

Joseph Addison 1672–1719

English poet, playwright, and essayist; co-founder of *The
Spectator*

8 　　　　　What pity is it
　That we can die but once to serve our country!

Cato (1713)

9 From hence, let fierce contending nations know
What dire effects from civil discord flow.

Cato (1713)

Konrad Adenauer 1876–1967

German statesman, first Chancellor of the Federal Republic of
Germany, 1949–63

1   A thick skin is a gift from God.   in *New York Times* 30 December
                                                               1959

Aeschylus *c.*525–456 BC

Greek tragedian

2   Do not taint pure laws with mere expediency   *The Eumenides*
    Guard well and reverence that form of government
    Which will eschew alike licence and slavery.
    And from your policy do not wholly banish fear
    For what man living, freed from fear, will still be just?

3   Everyone's quick to blame the alien.   *The Suppliant Maidens*

Herbert Agar 1897–1980

American poet and writer

4   The truth which makes men free is for the most part the   *Time for Greatness* (1942)
    truth which men prefer not to hear.

Spiro T. Agnew 1918–96

American Republican politician, Vice-President 1968–73; he
resigned the vice-presidency on 10 October 1973 amid charges
of financial wrong-doing while Governor of Maryland

5   I didn't say I wouldn't go into ghetto areas. I've been in in *Detroit Free Press* 19 October
    many of them and to some extent I would say this: If   1968
    you've seen one city slum you've seen them all.

6   A spirit of national masochism prevails, encouraged by   speech in New Orleans, 19 October
    an effete corps of impudent snobs who characterize   1969
    themselves as intellectuals.

7   In the United States today, we have more than our share   speech in San Diego, 11 September
    of the nattering nabobs of negativism.   1970

Alcuin *c.*735–804

English scholar and theologian

8   And those people should not be listened to who keep   letter 164 in *Works* (1863)
    saying the voice of the people is the voice of God [*Vox
    populi, vox Dei*], since the riotousness of the crowd is
    always very close to madness.

Richard Aldington 1892–1962

English poet, novelist, and biographer

9   Patriotism is a lively sense of collective responsibility. *The Colonel's Daughter* (1931)
    Nationalism is a silly cock crowing on its own dunghill.

Cecil Frances Alexander 1818–95

Irish poet

1   The rich man in his castle,   'All Things Bright and Beautiful'
    The poor man at his gate,   (1848)
    God made them, high or lowly,
    And ordered their estate.

Henry Southworth Allen

American writer

2   America is like a bar-room drunk. One minute it brags   *Going Too Far Enough* (1994)
    about its money and muscle, and then for the next hour
    it bleats into its beer about failure and hopelessness...
    Right now, we're in a bleating phase.

William Allen 1803–1879

American Democratic politician; US Senator

3   Fifty-four forty, or fight!   speech in the US Senate, 1844
    *slogan of expansionist Democrats in the presidential campaign
    of 1844, in which the Oregon boundary definition was an issue
    (in 1846 the new Democratic president, James K. Polk,
    compromised on the 49th parallel with Great Britain)*

Woody Allen 1935–

American film director, writer, and actor

4   I believe there is something out there watching over us.   Peter McWilliams *Ain't Nobody's
    Unfortunately, it's the government.   Business If You Do* (1993);
                                                                   attributed

Joseph Alsop b. 1910

American journalist

5   Gratitude, like love, is never a dependable international   in *Observer* 30 November 1952
    emotion.

Leo Amery 1873–1955

British Conservative politician

of H. H. **Asquith**:
6   For twenty years he has held a season-ticket on the line   in *Quarterly Review* July 1914
    of least resistance and has gone wherever the train of
    events has carried him, lucidly justifying his position at
    whatever point he has happened to find himself.

7   Speak for England.   said to Arthur Greenwood in House
                                                                   of Commons, 2 September 1939, in
                                                                   My Political Life (1955) vol. 3; cf.
                                                                   Boothby 52:4

1 I will quote certain other words. I do it with great
reluctance, because I am speaking of those who are old
friends and colleagues of mine, but they are words
which, I think, are applicable to the present situation.
This is what Cromwell said to the Long Parliament when
he thought it was no longer fit to conduct the affairs of
the nation: 'You have sat too long here for any good you
have been doing. Depart, I say, and let us have done
with you. In the name of God, go.'

*in the House of Commons, 7 May
1940; cf.* **Cromwell** *105:8*

Fisher Ames 1758–1808

American politician

2 A monarchy is a merchantman which sails well, but will
sometimes strike on a rock, and go to the bottom; whilst
a republic is a raft which would never sink, but then
your feet are always in the water.

*attributed to Ames, speaking in the
House of Representatives, 1795;
quoted by R. W. Emerson in* Essays
*(2nd series, 1844), but not traced
in Ames's speeches*

Anacharsis

Scythian prince of the sixth century BC

3 Written laws are like spider's webs; they will catch, it is
true, the weak and poor, but would be torn in pieces by
the rich and powerful.

Plutarch *Parallel Lives* 'Solon'

Anonymous

4 All human beings are born free and equal in dignity and
rights.

*Universal Declaration of Human
Rights* (1948) article 1

5 All the 'isms are wasms.
*said to have been the comment of a Foreign Office spokesman
on the signing of the Molotov–Ribbentrop Pact in August 1939*

Peter Hennessy *Whitehall* (1990)

6 All the way with LBJ.
*US Democratic Party campaign slogan supporting Lyndon
Baines* **Johnson**

in Washington Post *4 June 1960*

7 *Arbeit macht frei.*
Work makes free.
*on the gates of Dachau concentration camp, and subsequently
on those of Auschwitz*

inscription, 1933

8 Bad money drives out good.

*proverbial expression of a principle
attributed to Sir Thomas Gresham
(c.1519–79), founder of the Royal
Exchange*

9 Ban the bomb.
US anti-nuclear slogan, 1953 onwards

adopted by the Campaign for
Nuclear Disarmament

10 A bayonet is a weapon with a worker at each end.

British pacifist slogan (1940)

11 The best defence against the atom bomb is not to be
there when it goes off.

contributor to *British Army Journal*,
in Observer *20 February 1949*

1 Better red than dead.

slogan of nuclear disarmament
campaigners, late 1950s

2 A bigger bang for a buck.

Charles E. **Wilson**'s defence policy,
in *Newsweek* 22 March 1954

3 Black is beautiful.

slogan of American civil rights
campaigners, mid-1960s

4 Browne was like a hawk, he swooped down upon us;
Grey was like a rat, he undermined us.
Maori comment on Thomas Gore Browne and George Grey,
successively Governors of New Zealand in the mid nineteenth
century

in *Dictionary of National Biography*

5 Burn, baby, burn.

Black extremist slogan in use
during the Los Angeles riots,
August 1965

6 But this is terrible—*they*'ve elected a Labour Government,
and *the country* will never stand for that!
unidentified lady diner in the Savoy Hotel, 26 July 1945

Michael Sissons and Philip French
(eds.) *The Age of Austerity*
1945–51 (1964)

7 Careless talk costs lives.

Second World War security poster

8 A Company for carrying on an undertaking of Great
Advantage, but no one to know what it is.

Company Prospectus at the time of
the South Sea Bubble (1711)

9 Confound their politics,
Frustrate their knavish tricks.

'God save the King', attributed to
various authors, including Henry
Carey

10 Crisis? What Crisis?
summarizing James **Callaghan**'s *remark of 10 January 1979: 'I*
don't think other people in the world would share the view [that]
there is mounting chaos'

Sun headline, 11 January 1979

11 *Ein Reich, ein Volk, ein Führer.*
One realm, one people, one leader.
Nazi Party slogan

early 1930s

12 Every country has its own constitution; ours is
absolutism moderated by assassination.
of Russia

Ernst Friedrich Herbert, Count
Münster, quoting 'an intelligent
Russian', in *Political Sketches of*
the State of Europe, 1814–1867
(1868)

13 Everyone has the right to freedom of movement and
residence within the borders of each state. Everyone has
the right to leave any country, including his own, and to
return to his country. Everyone has the right to seek and
to enjoy in other countries asylum from persecution.

Universal Declaration of Human
Rights (1948)

14 Expletive deleted.

Submission of Recorded
Presidential Conversations to the
Committee on the Judiciary of the
House of Representatives by
President Richard M. Nixon 30
April 1974

1 Exterminate...the treacherous English, walk over
   General French's contemptible little army.
      often attributed to Kaiser Wilhelm II, but most probably
      fabricated by the British; source of the nickname 'the Old
      Contemptibles'

   Annexe to British Expeditionary
   Force Routine Orders of 24
   September 1914; Arthur Ponsonby
   Falsehood in Wartime (1928)

2 For the sake of brevity we have followed the common
   practice of using the phrase 'Communists' throughout to
   include Fascists.

   Radcliffe Report 'Security
   Procedures in the Public Service'
   April 1962

3 Frederick the Great lost the battle of Jena.
      attributing the Prussians' defeat at Jena by **Napoleon** *in 1806 to*
      their rigid adherence to the strategy of **Frederick** *(who had died*
      in 1786)

   Walter Bagehot *The English
   Constitution* (1867)

4 Happy is that city which in time of peace thinks of war.
      inscription found in the armoury of Venice

   Robert Burton *The Anatomy of
   Melancholy* (1621–51)

5 Hark the herald angels sing
   Mrs Simpson's pinched our king.
      contemporary children's rhyme on the abdication of **Edward VIII**

   Clement Attlee letter 26 December
   1938; Kenneth Harris *Attlee* (1982)

6 Have you heard? The Prime Minister has resigned and
   Northcliffe has sent for the King.
      a joke (c.1919) suggesting that Lord **Northcliffe**, *the press baron*
      and **Lloyd George**'s *implacable enemy, would succeed him as*
      Prime Minister

   Hamilton Fyfe *Northcliffe, an
   Intimate Biography* (1930)

7 He talked shop like a tenth muse.
      of **Gladstone**'s *Budget speech*

   G. W. E. Russell *Collections and
   Recollections* (1898)

8 He who writes the minutes rules the roost.

   Civil Service maxim

9 *Ils ne passeront pas.*
   They shall not pass.
      slogan used by French army defence at Verdun in 1916

   variously attributed to Marshal
   Pétain and to General Robert
   Nivelle; cf. **Ibarruri** 186:6

10 I'm backing Britain.
      slogan coined by workers at the Colt factory, Surbiton, Surrey,
      and subsequently used in a national campaign

   in *The Times* 1 January 1968

11 I met wid Napper Tandy, and he took me by the hand,
   And he said, 'How's poor ould Ireland, and how does she
      stand?'
   She's the most disthressful country that iver yet was
      seen,
   For they're hangin' men an' women for the wearin' o'
      the Green.

   'The Wearin' o' the Green' (c.1795
   ballad)

12 In good King Charles's golden days,
   When loyalty no harm meant;
   A furious High-Churchman I was,
   And so I gained preferment.
   Unto my flock I daily preached,
   Kings are by God appointed,
   And damned are those who dare resist,
   Or touch the Lord's Anointed.
   And this is law, I will maintain,
   Unto my dying day, Sir,
   That whatsoever King shall reign,
   I will be the Vicar of Bray, sir!

   'The Vicar of Bray' in *British
   Musical Miscellany* (1734) vol. 1

1 I never vote. It only encourages them.

elderly American lady quoted by comedian Jack Parr; William Safire *The New Language of Politics* (1968)

2 The iron lady.
*name given to Margaret **Thatcher**, then Leader of the Opposition, by the Soviet Defence Ministry newspaper* Red Star, *which accused her of trying to revive the cold war*

in *Sunday Times* 25 January 1976

3 It became necessary to destroy the town to save it.
comment by unidentified US Army major on Ben Tre, Vietnam

in Associated Press Report, *New York Times* 8 February 1968

4 It'll play in Peoria.
*catch-phrase of the **Nixon** administration (early 1970s) meaning 'it will be acceptable to middle America'*

originating in a standard music hall joke of the 1930s

5 It's that man again...! At the head of a cavalcade of seven black motor cars Hitler swept out of his Berlin Chancellery last night on a mystery journey.

headline in *Daily Express* 2 May 1939; the acronym ITMA became the title of a BBC radio show, from September 1939

6 The King over the Water.
Jacobite toast to the deposed and exiled James II and his heirs

current in the 18th century

7 King's Moll Reno'd in Wolsey's Home Town.
US newspaper headline on Wallis Simpson's divorce proceedings in Ipswich

Frances Donaldson *Edward VIII* (1974)

8 Labour isn't working.
caption to Conservative Party poster, 1978–9, showing a long queue outside an unemployment office

Philip Kleinman *The Saatchi and Saatchi Story* (1987)

9 Lacking any capacity for political passion, he has made it as nearly an unpolitical office as any man could.
*of Walter **Monckton** as Minister of Labour*

in *New Statesman* 8 January 1954

10 The land for the people.

Communist slogan, *c.*1917

11 LBJ, LBJ, how many kids have you killed today?
*anti-Vietnam War marching slogan during the presidency of Lyndon **Johnson***

Jacquin Sanders *The Draft and the Vietnam War* (1966)

12 Let's run it up the flagpole and see if anyone salutes it.

Reginald Rose *Twelve Angry Men* (1955); recorded as an established advertising expression in the 1960s

13 *Liberté! Égalité! Fraternité!*
Freedom! Equality! Brotherhood!
motto of the French Revolution (though of earlier origin)

the Club des Cordeliers passed a motion, 30 June 1793, 'that owners should be urged to paint on the front of their houses, in large letters, the words: Unity, indivisibility of the Republic, Liberty, Equality, Fraternity or death'; in *Journal de Paris* no. 182 (from 1795 the words 'or death' were dropped)

14 Liberty is always unfinished business.

title of 36th Annual Report of the American Civil Liberties Union, 1 July 1955 – 30 June 1956

1 [Like] watching a stream of blood coming from beneath a closed door.
a contemporary expression of the feelings evoked by news of the executions after the Easter Rising

Robert Kee *Ourselves Alone* (1916)

2 Lloyd George knew my father,
My father knew Lloyd George.

two-line comic song, sung to the tune of 'Onward, Christian Soldiers' and possibly by Tommy Rhys Roberts (1910–75)

3 Lost is our old simplicity of times,
The world abounds with laws, and teems with crimes.

On the Proceedings Against America (1775)

4 CHILD: Mamma, are Tories born wicked, or do they grow wicked afterwards?
MOTHER: They are born wicked, and grow worse.

G. W. E. Russell *Collections and Recollections* (1898)

5 Men said openly that Christ and His saints slept.
of twelfth-century England during the civil war between Stephen and Matilda

Anglo-Saxon Chronicle for 1137

6 Ministers say one of two things in Cabinet. Some say, 'Look, Daddy, no hands.' Others say, 'Look, Daddy, me too.'
unidentified senior official to Sarah Hogg on her arrival to take over the Prime Minister's policy unit

in *Sunday Times* 9 April 1995

7 The ministry of all the talents.
name given ironically to William Grenville's coalition of 1806, and also applied to later coalitions

G. W. Cooke *The History of Party* (1837) vol. 3

8 The nearest thing to death in life
Is David Patrick Maxwell Fyfe,
Though underneath that gloomy shell
He does himself extremely well.
of David Maxwell Fyfe, later Lord **Kilmuir**, *and said to have been current on the Northern circuit in the late 1930s*

E. Grierson *Confessions of a Country Magistrate* (1972)

9 Never stand when you could sit, and never miss a chance to relieve yourself.

advice given by a private secretary or equerry to **George V** or **George VI**

10 No man's life, liberty or property are safe while the legislature is in session.
view of an unidentified New York State Surrogate Court Judge

in 1866; unattributed

the defenders of the besieged city of Derry to the Jacobite army of James II, April 1689:

11 No surrender!
adopted as a slogan of Protestant Ulster

Jonathan Bardon *A History of Ulster* (1992)

12 Now that the Cabinet's gone to its dinner,
The Secretary stays and gets thinner and thinner,
Racking his brains to record and report
What he thinks they think they ought to have thought.

anonymous verse, undated; S. S. Wilson *The Cabinet Office* (1975)

13 One Cartwright brought a Slave from Russia, and would scourge him, for which he was questioned: and it was resolved, That England was too pure an Air for Slaves to breathe in.

'In the 11th of Elizabeth' (17 November 1568–16 November 1569); John Rushworth *Historical Collections* (1680–1722)

1 Order reigns in Warsaw.
after the brutal suppression of an uprising

the newspaper *Moniteur* reported, 16 September 1831, 'Order and calm are completely restored in the capital'; on the same day Count Sebastiani, minister of foreign affairs, declared: 'Peace reigns in Warsaw'

2 Please to remember the Fifth of November,
Gunpowder Treason and Plot.
We know no reason why gunpowder treason
Should ever be forgot.

traditional rhyme on the Gunpowder Plot (1605)

3 *Plus royaliste que le roi.*
More of a royalist than the king.
noted as a current catch-phrase which was not in fact new; 'it was coined under Louis XVI: it chained up the hands of the loyal, leaving free only the arm of the hangman'

François René, Vicomte de Chateaubriand *De la monarchie selon la charte* (1816)

4 Power to the people.

slogan of the Black Panther movement, from c.1968 onwards

5 *Sic transit gloria mundi.*
Thus passes the glory of the world.
said during the coronation of a new Pope, while flax is burned to represent the transitoriness of earthly glory

used at the coronation of Alexander V in Pisa, 7 July 1409, but earlier in origin

6 The silly, flat, dishwatery utterances of the man who has to be pointed out to intelligent observers as the President of the United States.

review of **Lincoln**'s Gettysburg Address, in *Chicago Times* 20 November 1863; cf. **Everett** 134:4

7 *Tempora mutantur, et nos mutamur in illis.*
Times change, and we change with them.

William Harrison *Description of Britain* (1577); attributed to the Emperor Lothar I (795–855) in the form '*omnia mutantur, nos et mutamur in illis* [all things change, and we change with them]'

8 There is one thing stronger than all the armies in the world; and that is an idea whose time has come.

in *Nation* 15 April 1943; cf. **Hugo** 184:5

9 There's no such thing as a free lunch.
*colloquial axiom in US economics from the 1960s, much associated with Milton **Friedman***

first found in printed form in Robert Heinlein *The Moon is a Harsh Mistress* (1966)

*an unnamed Labour MP commenting on the unusually pale eyes of Hugh **Dalton**:*
10 They have a habit of looking at you intently and conveying unfathomable depths of insincerity.
sometimes quoted as 'eyes blazing with insincerity'

Patricia Strauss *Bevin and Co. The Leaders of British Labour* (1941)

annotation to a ministerial brief, said to have been read out inadvertently in the House of Lords:
11 This is a rotten argument, but it should be good enough for their lordships on a hot summer afternoon.

Lord Home *The Way the Wind Blows* (1976)

12 Though I yield to no one in my admiration for Mr Coolidge, I do wish he did not look as if he had been weaned on a pickle.
*of President Calvin **Coolidge***

anonymous remark, in Alice Roosevelt Longworth *Crowded Hours* (1933)

1 Three acres and a cow.
   *regarded as the requirement for self-sufficiency; associated with
   the radical politician Jesse Collings (1831–1920) and his land
   reform campaign begun in 1885*

Jesse Collings in the House of
Commons, 26 January 1886,
although used earlier by Joseph
Chamberlain in a speech at
Evesham (in *The Times* 17
November 1885), by which time it
was already proverbial

2 'Tis bad enough in man or woman
   To steal a goose from off a common;
   But surely he's without excuse
   Who steals the common from the goose.

'On Inclosures'; in *The Oxford
Book of Light Verse* (1938)

3 To secure for the workers by hand or by brain the full
   fruits of their industry and the most equitable distribution
   thereof that may be possible upon the basis of the
   common ownership of the means of production,
   distribution, and exchange.

Clause Four of the Labour Party's
Constitution, adopted 1918/26; cf.
Blair 49:2

4 Ulster says no.
   *slogan coined in response to the Anglo-Irish Agreement of 15
   November 1985*

in *Irish Times* 25 November 1985

5 Under capitalism man exploits man. And under
   Communism it is just the reverse.
   *joke told to J. K. **Galbraith** at a dinner given for him during his
   lecture tour of Poland by the Polish Economic Society, May 1958*

J. K. Galbraith *A Life in Our Times*
(1981)

6 War will cease when men refuse to fight.
   pacifist slogan (often quoted 'Wars will cease … ')

from *c*.1936

7 We hold these truths to be self-evident, that all men are
   created equal, that they are endowed by their Creator
   with certain unalienable rights, that among these are life,
   liberty and the pursuit of happiness.

The American Declaration of
Independence, 4 July 1776

8 We shall not be moved.

title of labour and civil rights song
(1931) adapted from an earlier
gospel hymn

9 We shall overcome.
   *revived in 1946 as a protest song by Black tobacco workers, and
   in 1963 during the Black Civil Rights Campaign*

title of song, originating from
before the American Civil War,
adapted as a Baptist hymn ('I'll
Overcome Some Day', 1901) by C.
Albert Tindley

10 We want eight, and we won't wait.
    on the construction of Dreadnoughts

George Wyndham's speech in *The
Times* 29 March 1909

11 A well-regulated militia, being necessary to the security
    of a free State, the right of the people to keep and bear
    arms, shall not be infringed.

Constitution of the United States
(Second Amendment, 1791)

12 What did the President know and when did he know it?

question current at the time of
Watergate, associated particularly
with Howard Baker, Vice-Chairman
of the Senate Watergate
Committee

13 When war enters a country
    It produces lies like sand.

epigraph to Arthur Ponsonby
Falsehood in Wartime (1920)

1 Whose finger do you want on the trigger?   in *Daily Mirror* 21 September 1951
  headline alluding to the atom bomb, apropos the failure of both
  the Labour and Conservative parties to purge their leaders of
  proven failures

2 Why is there only one Monopolies Commission?   British graffito; incorporated in the
                                                             Official Monster Raving Loony
                                                             Party Manifesto, 1987

3 A willing foe and sea room.   W. N. T. Beckett *A Few Naval*
  Naval toast in the time of Nelson   *Customs, Expressions, Traditions,*
                                                             and Superstitions (1931) 'Customs'

4 Winston is back.   Martin Gilbert *Winston S. Churchill*
  Board of Admiralty signal to the Fleet on Winston **Churchill**'s (1976) vol. 5
  reappointment as First Sea Lord, 3 September 1939

Susan Brownell Anthony 1820–1906

American feminist and political activist

5 The men and women of the North are slaveholders, those   *Speech on No Union with*
  of the South slaveowners. The guilt rests on the North   *Slaveholders* 1857
  equally with the South.

6 Join the union, girls, and together say *Equal Pay for Equal*   in *The Revolution* 8 October 1869
  Work.

7 Here, in the first paragraph of the Declaration [of   *Is It a Crime for a Citizen of the*
  Independence], is the assertion of the natural right of all *United States to Vote?*
  to the ballot; for how can 'the consent of the governed'
  be given, if the right to vote be denied?
  speech in 1873 before her trial for voting

John Arbuthnot 1667–1735

Scottish physician and pamphleteer

8 He [the writer] warns the heads of parties against   *The Art of Political Lying* (1712)
  believing their own lies.

9 All political parties die at last of swallowing their own   Richard Garnett *Life of Emerson*
  lies.   (1988)

Hannah Arendt 1906–75

American political philosopher

10 The most radical revolutionary will become   in *New Yorker* 12 September 1970
   a conservative on the day after the revolution.

11 Under conditions of tyranny it is far easier to act than to W. H. Auden *A Certain World* (1970)
   think.

Marquis d'Argenson 1694–1757

French politician and political essayist

1 *Laisser-faire.*
   No interference.
      term applied to the doctrine of minimum state intervention in
      economic affairs

Mémoires et Journal Inédit du
Marquis d'Argenson; cf. **Quesnay**
299:2

Aristotle 384–322 BC

Greek philosopher

2 Therefore, the good of man must be the objective of the
   science of politics.

Nicomachean Ethics

3 We make war that we may live in peace.

Nicomachean Ethics

4 Politicians also have no leisure, because they are always
   aiming at something beyond political life itself, power and
   glory, or happiness.

Nicomachean Ethics

5 Man is by nature a political animal.

Politics

6 He who is unable to live in society, or who has no need
   because he is sufficient for himself, must be either a beast
   or a god.

Politics

7 For that some should rule, and others be ruled, is a thing
   not only necessary but expedient, for from the hour of
   their birth some are marked for subjection, others for
   rule.

Politics

8 Poverty is the parent of revolution and crime.

Politics

9 Where some people are very wealthy and others have
   nothing, the result will be either extreme democracy or
   absolute oligarchy, or despotism will come from either of
   those excesses.

Politics

10 The most perfect political community is one in which the
   middle class is in control, and outnumbers both of the
   other classes.

Politics

11 No tyrant need fear till men begin to feel confident in
   each other.

Politics

Robert Armstrong 1927–

British civil servant, Head of the Civil Service, 1981–7

12 It contains a misleading impression, not a lie. It was
   being economical with the truth.
      referring to a letter during the 'Spycatcher' trial, Supreme Court,
      New South Wales, November 1986

in *Daily Telegraph* 19 November
1986; cf. **Burke** 68:2

William Armstrong 1915–80

British civil servant, Head of the Civil Service 1968–74
on Armstrong: see **Rothschild** 313:7

1   The business of the Civil Service is the orderly
    management of decline.

in 1973: Peter Hennessy *Whitehall*
(1990)

Matthew Arnold 1822–88

English poet and essayist; son of Thomas **Arnold**

2   Our society distributes itself into Barbarians, Philistines,
    and Populace; and America is just ourselves, with the
    Barbarians quite left out, and the Populace nearly.

Culture and Anarchy (1869) preface

3   The men of culture are the true apostles of equality.

Culture and Anarchy (1869)

4   When I want to distinguish clearly the aristocratic class
    from the Philistines proper, or middle class, [I] name the
    former, in my own mind *the Barbarians*.

Culture and Anarchy (1869)

5   That vast portion...of the working-class which, raw and
    half-developed, has long lain half-hidden amidst its
    poverty and squalor, and is now issuing from its hiding-
    place to assert an Englishman's heaven-born privilege of
    doing as he likes, and is beginning to perplex us by
    marching where it likes, meeting where it likes, bawling
    what it likes, breaking what it likes—to this vast
    residuum we may with great propriety give the name of
    Populace.

Culture and Anarchy (1869)

Thomas Arnold 1795–1842

English historian; Headmaster of Rugby School from 1828;
father of Matthew **Arnold**

6   As for rioting, the old Roman way of dealing with that is
    always the right one; flog the rank and file, and fling the
    ringleaders from the Tarpeian rock.

from an unpublished letter written
before 1828

Raymond Aron 1905–

French sociologist and political journalist

7   Political thought, in France, is retrospective or utopian.

L'opium des intellectuels (1955)

Henry Fountain Ashurst

American politician

8   I am not in Washington as a statesman. I am there as
    a very well paid messenger boy doing your errands. My
    chief occupation is going around with a forked stick
    picking up little fragments of patronage for my
    constituents.

Thomas C. Donnelly *Rocky
Mountain Politics* (1940);
attributed

Herbert Henry Asquith 1852–1928

British Liberal statesman; Prime Minister, 1908–16
on Asquith: see Churchill 88:2, **Hennessy** 175:2

1 We had better wait and see.
   phrase used repeatedly in speeches in 1910, referring to the
   rumour that the House of Lords was to be flooded with new
   Liberal peers to ensure the passage of the Finance Bill

   Roy Jenkins *Asquith* (1964)

2 Happily there seems to be no reason why we should be
   anything more than spectators [of the approaching war].

   Letters to Venetia Stanley (1982)
   24 July 1914

3 We shall never sheath the sword which we have not
   lightly drawn until Belgium recovers in full measure all
   and more than all that she has sacrificed, until France is
   adequately secured against the menace of aggression,
   until the rights of the smaller nationalities of Europe are
   placed upon an unassailable foundation, and until the
   military domination of Prussia is wholly and finally
   destroyed.

   speech at the Guildhall, London, 9
   November 1914

4 There is no more striking illustration of the immobility of
   British institutions than the House of Commons.

   Fifty Years of Parliament (1926)
   vol. 2

5 The office of the Prime Minister is what its holder chooses
   and is able to make of it.

   Fifty Years of Parliament (1926)
   vol. 2

6 [The War Office kept three sets of figures:] one to mislead
   the public, another to mislead the Cabinet, and the third
   to mislead itself.

   Alistair Horne *Price of Glory* (1962)

7 It is fitting that we should have buried the Unknown
   Prime Minister [Bonar Law] by the side of the Unknown
   Soldier.

   Robert Blake *The Unknown Prime
   Minister* (1955)

8 He is a Chimborazo or Everest among the sandhills of the
   Baldwin Cabinet.
   of Winston **Churchill**

   Roy Jenkins *Asquith* (1964)

Margot Asquith 1864–1945

political hostess; wife of Herbert **Asquith**

on hearing that **Campbell-Bannerman,** *in planning the Liberal*
administration of 1905, intended to make R. B. **Haldane** *Home*
Secretary instead of Lord Chancellor:

9 I was reminded of George Eliot's remark, 'When a man
   wants a peach it is no good offering him the largest
   vegetable marrow.'

   Roy Jenkins *Asquith* (1964)

10 Kitchener is a great poster.

   More Memories (1933)

11 No amount of education will make women first-rate
   politicians. Can you see a woman becoming a Prime
   Minister? I cannot imagine a greater calamity for these
   islands than to be put under the guidance of a woman in
   10 Downing Street.

   Off the Record (1943)

1 Lord Birkenhead is very clever but sometimes his brains go to his head.

in *Listener* 11 June 1953 'Margot Oxford' by Lady Violet Bonham Carter

2 He can't see a belt without hitting below it.
of **Lloyd George**

in *Listener* 11 June 1953 'Margot Oxford' by Lady Violet Bonham Carter

Nancy Astor 1879–1964

American-born British Conservative politician

3 NANCY ASTOR: If I were your wife I would put poison in your coffee.
WINSTON CHURCHILL: And if I were your husband I would drink it.

Consuelo Vanderbilt *Glitter and Gold* (1952)

Brooks Atkinson 1894–1984

American journalist and critic

4 After each war there is a little less democracy to save.

Once Around the Sun (1951) 7 January

5 In every age 'the good old days' were a myth. No one ever thought they were good at the time. For every age had consisted of crises that seemed intolerable to the people who lived through them.

Once Around the Sun (1951) 8 February

6 There is a good deal of solemn cant about the common interests of capital and labour. As matters stand, their only common interest is that of cutting each other's throat.

Once Around the Sun (1951) 7 September

Clement Attlee 1883–1967

British Labour statesman; Prime Minister, 1945–51
on Attlee: see **Churchill** 93:13, 94:17, **Hennessy** 175:2,
Nicolson 272:5, **Orwell** 278:8

7 Why does Mosley always speak to us as though he were a feudal landlord abusing tenants who are in arrears with their rent?
at a meeting of the Parliamentary Labour Party, 20 November 1930, a few months before Oswald Mosley was expelled from the Party

Hugh Dalton *Political Diary* (1986) 20 November 1930

8 A period of silence on your part would be welcome.
in reply to a letter from the Chairman of the Labour Party, Harold **Laski**, *asking (for the second time and at length) that Attlee should not form a new government until the Parliamentary Labour Party had had the chance to elect a new leader*

letter to Harold Laski, 20 August 1945; Francis Williams *A Prime Minister Remembers* (1961)

9 If the King asks you to form a Government you say 'Yes' or 'No', not 'I'll let you know later!'

Kenneth Harris *Attlee* (1982)

10 A monologue is not a decision.
to Winston **Churchill**, *who had complained that a matter had been raised several times in Cabinet*

Francis Williams *A Prime Minister Remembers* (1961)

1 The voice we heard was that of Mr Churchill but the mind was that of Lord Beaverbrook.

speech on radio, 5 June 1945; Francis Williams *A Prime Minister Remembers* (1961)

at a Cabinet Meeting, when Aneurin **Bevan** *as Minister of Housing complained that he could not get enough people for his building programme:*

2 BEVAN: Where are all the people I need for my programme?
ATTLEE: Looking for houses, Nye!

Michael Foot *Aneurin Bevan* (1973) vol. 2

3 Always was a loud-mouthed fellow.
of Hugh **Dalton,** *who had resigned as Chancellor of the Exchequer after a Budget leak*

Kenneth Harris *Attlee* (1982)

4 I should be a sad subject for any publicity expert. I have none of the qualities which create publicity.

Harold Nicolson *Diary* 14 January 1949

5 I think the British have the distinction above all other nations of being able to put new wine into old bottles without bursting them.

in the House of Commons, 24 October 1950

response to a memorandum from the Ministry of Works saying, 'We have read the Cabinet's proposals':

6 The Cabinet does not propose, it decides.

Tony Benn diary 20 May 1974

7 I believe that conscience is a still small voice and not a loudspeaker.

attributed, 1955

8 [Russian Communism is] the illegitimate child of Karl Marx and Catherine the Great.

speech at Aarhus University, 11 April 1956, in *The Times* 12 April 1956

9 Few thought he was even a starter
There were many who thought themselves smarter
But he ended PM
CH and OM
An earl and a knight of the garter.
describing himself in a letter to Tom Attlee, 8 April 1956

Kenneth Harris *Attlee* (1982)

10 Generally speaking the Press lives on disaster.

attributed, 1956

11 Democracy means government by discussion, but it is only effective if you can stop people talking.

speech at Oxford, 14 June 1957

12 Often the 'experts' make the worst possible Ministers in their own fields. In this country we prefer rule by amateurs.

speech at Oxford, 14 June 1957

13 It's a good maxim that if you have a good dog you don't bark yourself. I had a very good dog in Mr Ernest Bevin.

attributed, 1960

definition of the art of politics:
14 Judgement which is needed to make important decisions on imperfect knowledge in a limited time.

attributed

15 Queer bird, Halifax. Very humorous, all hunting and Holy Communion
of Lord **Halifax**

in an interview; Peter Hennessy *Never Again* (1992)

W. H. Auden 1907–73

English poet

1 Private faces in public places
Are wiser and nicer
Than public faces in private places.

Orators (1932) dedication

2 There is no such thing as the State
And no one exists alone;
Hunger allows no choice
To the citizen or the police;
We must love one another or die.

'September 1, 1939' (1940)

3 Our researchers into Public Opinion are content
That he held the proper opinions for the time of year;
When there was peace, he was for peace; when there
was war, he went.

'The Unknown Citizen' (1940)

4 This marble monument was erected by the state.
Was he free? Was he happy? The question is absurd:
Had anything been wrong, we should certainly have
heard.

'The Unknown Citizen' (1940)

5 He knew human folly like the back of his hand,
And was greatly interested in armies and fleets;
When he laughed, respectable senators burst with
laughter,
And when he cried the little children died in the streets.

'Epitaph on a Tyrant' (1940)

6 To save your world you asked this man to die:
Would this man, could he see you now, ask why?

'Epitaph for the Unknown Soldier'
(1955)

Augustus 63 BC–AD 14

first Roman emperor
on Augustus: see **Cicero** 95:13

7 Quintilius Varus, give me back my legions.
*after the annihilation by the German leader Arminius of three
Roman legions under Quintilius Varus*

Suetonius *Lives of the Caesars*

8 He could boast that he inherited it brick and left it
marble.
of the city of Rome

Suetonius *Lives of the Caesars*

Marcus Aurelius AD 121–80

Roman emperor from AD 161

9 Man, you have been a citizen in this world city, what
does it matter whether for five years or fifty?

Meditations

Jane Austen 1775–1817

English novelist

10 From politics, it was an easy step to silence.

Northanger Abbey (1818)

Francis Bacon 1561–1626

English lawyer, courtier, philosopher, and essayist

1 For also knowledge itself is power.   *Meditationes Sacrae* (1597) 'Of Heresies'

2 It is well to observe the force and virtue and consequence   *Novum Organum* (1620)
 of discoveries, and these are to be seen nowhere more
 conspicuously than in those three which were unknown
 to the ancients, and of which the origins, though recent,
 are obscure and inglorious; namely, printing,
 gunpowder, and the magnet [Mariner's Needle]. For these
 three have changed the whole face and state of things
 throughout the world.

3 To worship the people is to be worshipped.   *De Dignitate et Augmentis Scientiarum* (1623)

4 In civil business; what first? boldness; what second and   *Essays* (1625) 'Of Boldness'
 third? boldness: and yet boldness is a child of ignorance
 and baseness.

5 [Some] there be that can pack the cards and yet   *Essays* (1625) 'Of Cunning'
 cannot play well; so there are some that are good in
 canvasses and factions, that are otherwise weak men.

6 Nothing doth more hurt in a state than that cunning   *Essays* (1625) 'Of Cunning'
 men pass for wise.

7 There is surely no greater wisdom than well to time the   *Essays* (1625) 'Of Delays'
 beginnings and endings of things.

8 The difficulties in princes' business are many and great,   *Essays* (1625) 'Of Empire'
 but the greatest difficulty is often in their own mind.

9 Men in great place are thrice servants: servants of the   *Essays* (1625) 'Of Great Place'
 sovereign or state, servants of fame, and servants of
 business.

10 It is a strange desire to seek power and to lose liberty.   *Essays* (1625) 'Of Great Place'

11 The rising unto place is laborious, and by pains men   *Essays* (1625) 'Of Great Place'
 come to greater pains; and it is sometimes base, and by
 indignities men come to dignities. The standing is
 slippery, and the regress is either a downfall, or at least
 an eclipse.

12 Severity breedeth fear, but roughness breedeth hate. Even   *Essays* (1625) 'Of Great Place'
 reproofs from authority ought to be grave, and not
 taunting.

13 All rising to great place is by a winding stair.   *Essays* (1625) 'Of Great Place'

14 New nobility is but the act of power, but ancient nobility *Essays* (1625) 'Of Nobility'
 is the act of time.

15 Fame is like a river, that beareth up things light and   *Essays* (1625) 'Of Praise'
 swollen, and drowns things weighty and solid.

16 So when any of the four pillars of government are mainly   *Essays* (1625) 'Of Seditions and
 shakened or weakened (which are religion, justice,   Troubles'
 counsel, and treasure) men had need to pray for fair
 weather.

1 The surest way to prevent seditions (if the times do bear
   it) is to take away the matter of them.

Essays (1625) 'Of Seditions and
Troubles'

2 Suspicions amongst thoughts are like bats amongst birds,
   they ever fly by twilight.

Essays (1625) 'Of Suspicion'

3 Neither is money the sinews of war (as it is trivially said).

Essays (1625) 'Of the True
Greatness of Kingdoms'

4 Neither will it be, that a people overlaid with taxes
   should ever become valiant and martial.

Essays (1625) 'Of the True
Greatness of Kingdoms'

5 What is truth? said jesting Pilate; and would not stay for
   an answer.

Essays (1625) 'Of Truth'

6 All colours will agree in the dark.

Essays (1625) 'Of Unity in Religion'

7 In the youth of a state arms do flourish; in the middle
   age of a state, learning; and then both of them together
   for a time; in the declining age of a state, mechanical
   arts and merchandise.

Essays (1625) 'Of Vicissitude of
Things'

8 He is the fountain of honour.

An Essay of a King (1642);
attribution doubtful;
cf. **Bagehot** 24:12

9 There be three things which make a nation great and
   prosperous: a fertile soil, busy workshops, easy
   conveyance for men and goods from place to place.

attributed; S. Platt (ed.)
Respectfully Quoted (1989)

10 For my name and memory, I leave it to men's charitable
   speeches, and to foreign nations, and the next ages.

his last will, 19 December 1625

Joan Baez 1941–

American singer and songwriter

11 The only thing that's been a worse flop than the
   organization of non-violence has been the organization of
   violence.

Daybreak (1970) 'What Would You
Do If?'

Walter Bagehot 1826–77

English economist and essayist

12 Dullness in matters of government is a good sign, and
   not a bad one—in particular, dullness in Parliamentary
   government is a test of its excellence, an indication of its
   success.

in *Saturday Review* 16 February
1856

13 The English people never expect any one to be original.

in *Saturday Review* 19 April 1856

14 A constitutional statesman is in general a man of
   common opinion and uncommon abilities.

in *National Review* July 1856

15 The most influential of constitutional statesmen is the
   one who most felicitously expresses the creed of the
   moment, who administers it, who embodies it in laws
   and institutions, who gives it the highest life it is capable
   of, who induces the average man to think: 'I could not
   have done it any better if I had had time myself.'

in *National Review* July 1856

1 Public opinion is a permeating influence, and it exacts
obedience to itself; it requires us to think other men's
thoughts, to speak other men's words, to follow other
men's habits.

in National Review July 1856

2 The path of great principles is marked through history by
trouble, anxiety, and conflict.

in Saturday Review 16 February 1856

3 It has been the bane of many countries which have tried
to obtain freedom, but failed in the attempt, that they
have regarded popular government rather as a means of
intellectual excitement than as an implement of political
work.

in Saturday Review 16 February 1856

4 No real English gentleman, in his secret soul, was ever
sorry for the death of a political economist.

Estimates of some Englishmen and Scotchmen (1858)

5 He believes, with all his heart and soul and strength,
that there *is* such a thing as truth; he has the soul of
a martyr with the intellect of an advocate.
   of **Gladstone**

in National Review July 1860

6 There is no method by which men can be both free and
equal.

in The Economist 5 September 1863

7 The American nation has very much the sort of faults
which 'only children' are said to have. It has no correct
measure of its own strength. Having never entered into
close competition with any other nation, it indulges in
that infinite braggadocio which a public school so soon
rubs out of a conceited boy.

in The Economist 14 November 1863

8 Persecute a sect and it holds together, legalize it and it
splits and resplits, till its unity is either null or a non-
oppressive bond.

in The Economist 27 April 1867

9 The mystic reverence, the religious allegiance, which are
essential to a true monarchy, are imaginative sentiments
that no legislature can manufacture in any people.

The English Constitution (1867)

10 In such constitutions [as England's] there are two
parts...first, those which excite and preserve the
reverence of the population—the *dignified* parts...and
next, the *efficient* parts—those by which it, in fact, works
and rules.

The English Constitution (1867)

11 No orator ever made an impression by appealing to men
as to their plainest physical wants, except when he could
allege that those wants were caused by some one's
tyranny.

The English Constitution (1867)

12 The Crown is, according to the saying, the 'fountain of
honour'; but the Treasury is the spring of business.

The English Constitution (1867); cf.
Bacon 23:8

13 A cabinet is a combining committee—a *hyphen* which
joins, a *buckle* which fastens, the legislative part of the
state to the executive part of the state.

The English Constitution (1867)

14 It has been said that England invented the phrase, 'Her
Majesty's Opposition'; that it was the first government
which made a criticism of administration as much a part

The English Constitution (1867); cf.
Hobhouse 180:10

of the polity as administration itself. This critical
opposition is the consequence of cabinet government.

1 *The Times* has made many ministries.

The English Constitution (1867)
'The Cabinet'

2 The great qualities, the imperious will, the rapid energy,
the eager nature fit for a great crisis are not required—
are impediments—in common times.

The English Constitution (1867)
'The Cabinet'

3 By the structure of the world we often want, at the
sudden occurrence of a grave tempest, to change the
helmsman—to replace the pilot of the calm by the pilot
of the storm.

The English Constitution (1867)
'The Cabinet'

*of Queen **Victoria** and the future **Edward VII***
4 It is nice to trace how the actions of a retired widow and
an unemployed youth become of such importance.

The English Constitution (1867)
'The Monarchy'

5 The best reason why Monarchy is a strong government
is, that it is an intelligible government. The mass of
mankind understand it, and they hardly anywhere in the
world understand any other.

The English Constitution (1867)
'The Monarchy'

6 It is often said that men are ruled by their imaginations;
but it would be truer to say they are governed by the
weakness of their imaginations.

The English Constitution (1867)
'The Monarchy'

7 The characteristic of the English Monarchy is that it
retains the feelings by which the heroic kings governed
their rude age, and has added the feelings by which the
constitutions of later Greece ruled in more refined ages.

The English Constitution (1867)
'The Monarchy'

8 Women—one half the human race at least—care fifty
times more for a marriage than a ministry.

The English Constitution (1867)
'The Monarchy'

9 Royalty is a government in which the attention of the
nation is concentrated on one person doing interesting
actions. A Republic is a government in which that
attention is divided between many, who are all doing
uninteresting actions. Accordingly, so long as the human
heart is strong and the human reason weak, Royalty will
be strong because it appeals to diffused feeling, and
Republics weak because they appeal to the
understanding.

The English Constitution (1867)
'The Monarchy'

10 Throughout the greater part of his life George III was
a kind of 'consecrated obstruction'.

The English Constitution (1867)
'The Monarchy'

11 There are arguments for not having a Court, and there
are arguments for having a splendid Court; but there are
no arguments for having a mean Court.

The English Constitution (1867)
'The Monarchy'

12 The Queen...must sign her own death-warrant if the
two Houses unanimously send it up to her.

The English Constitution (1867)
'The Monarchy'

13 Above all things our royalty is to be reverenced, and if
you begin to poke about it you cannot reverence it...Its
mystery is its life. We must not let in daylight upon
magic.

The English Constitution (1867)
'The Monarchy'

1 The Sovereign has, under a constitutional monarchy
   such as ours, three rights—the right to be consulted, the
   right to encourage, the right to warn.

   The English Constitution (1867)
   'The Monarchy'

2 The only fit material for a constitutional king is a prince
   who begins early to reign—who in his youth is superior
   to pleasure—who in his youth is willing to labour—who
   has by nature a genius for discretion. Such kings are
   among God's greatest gifts, but they are also among His
   rarest.

   The English Constitution (1867)
   'The Monarchy'

3 The order of nobility is of great use, too, not only in
   what it creates, but in what it prevents. It prevents the
   rule of wealth—the religion of gold. This is the obvious
   and natural idol of the Anglo-Saxon.

   The English Constitution (1867)
   'The House of Lords'

4 A severe though not unfriendly critic of our institutions
   said that 'the cure for admiring the House of Lords was
   to go and look at it.'

   The English Constitution (1867)
   'The House of Lords'

5 Nations touch at their summits.

   The English Constitution (1867)
   'The House of Lords'

*a 'cynical politician''s view of the parliamentary county
members:*

6 The finest brute votes in Europe.

   The English Constitution (1867)
   'The House of Commons'

7 The House of Commons lives in a state of perpetual
   potential choice: at any moment it can choose a ruler
   and dismiss a ruler. And therefore party is inherent in it,
   is bone of its bone, and breath of its breath.

   The English Constitution (1867)
   'The House of Commons'

8 An Opposition, on coming into power, is often like
   a speculative merchant whose bills become due. Ministers
   have to make good their promises, and they find
   a difficulty in so doing.

   The English Constitution (1867)
   'The House of Commons'

9 It is an inevitable defect, that bureaucrats will care more
   for routine than for results.

   The English Constitution (1867)
   'On Changes of Ministry'

10 A bureaucracy is sure to think that its duty is to
   augment official power, official business, or official
   members, rather than to leave free the energies of
   mankind; it overdoes the quantity of government, as well
   as impairs its quality.

   The English Constitution (1867)
   'On Changes of Ministry'

11 But would it not have been a miracle if the English
   people, directing their own policy, and being what they
   are, had directed a good policy? Are they not above all
   nations divided from the rest of the world, insular both in
   situation and in mind, both for good and for evil? Are
   they not out of the current of common European causes
   and affairs? Are they not a race contemptuous of others?
   Are they not a race with no special education or culture
   as to the modern world, and too often despising such
   culture? Who could expect such a people to comprehend
   the new and strange events of foreign places?

   The English Constitution (1867)
   'On Changes of Ministry'

1 It has been said, not truly, but with a possible   *The English Constitution* (1867) 'Its
   approximation to truth, that in 1802 every hereditary   Supposed Checks and Balances'
   monarch was insane.

2 As soon as we see that England is a disguised republic we   *The English Constitution* (1867) 'Its
   must see too that the classes for whom the disguise is   History'
   necessary must be tenderly dealt with.

3 The natural impulse of the English people is to resist   *The English Constitution* (1867) 'Its
   authority.   History'

4 In plain English, what I fear is that both our political   *The English Constitution*:
   parties will bid for the support of the working man; that   introduction to the second edition
   both of them will promise to do as he likes, if he will only
   tell them what it is; that, as he now holds the casting
   vote in our affairs, both parties will beg and pray him to
   give that vote to them. I can conceive of nothing more
   corrupting or worse for a set of poor ignorant people
   than that two combinations of well-taught and rich men
   should constantly offer to defer to their decision, and
   compete for the office of executing it.

5 A political country is like an American forest: you only   *The English Constitution*:
   have to cut down the old trees, and immediately new   introduction to the second edition
   trees come up to replace them; the seeds were waiting in   (1872)
   the ground, and they began to grow as soon as the
   withdrawal of the old ones brought in light and air.

6 If we know that a nation is capable of enduring   *Physics and Politics* (1872)
   continuous discussion, we know that it is capable of
   practising with equanimity continuous tolerance.

7 In happy states, the Conservative party must rule upon   'The Chances for a Long
   the whole a much longer time than their adversaries. In   Conservative Régime in England'
   well-framed politics, innovation—great innovation that   (1874)
   is—can only be occasional. If you are always altering
   your house, it is a sign either that you have a bad house,
   or that you have an excessively restless disposition—
   there is something wrong somewhere.

8 A great Premier must add the vivacity of an idle man to   in *The Economist* 2 January 1875
   the assiduity of a very laborious one.

9 The being without an opinion is so painful to human   in *The Economist* 4 December 1875
   nature that most people will leap to a hasty opinion
   rather than undergo it.

10 Good government depends at least as much on an   in *The Economist* 27 May 1876
   impartial respect for the rights of all as it does on energy
   in enforcing respect for the authority which protects
   those rights.

11 In every country the extreme party is most irritated   in *The Economist* 22 April 1876
   against the party which comes nearest to itself, but does
   not go so far.

12 The characteristic danger of great nations, like the   in *Fortnightly Review* 1 November
   Romans or the English, which have a long history of   1876
   continuous creation, is that they may at last fail from not
   comprehending the great institutions which they have
   created.

1 There never was a worse blunder than the supposition that the more states there are to suffer by a sanguinary quarrel, the sooner will the motives prevail for bringing it to a conclusion.

in The Economist 17 March 1877

2 Capital must be propelled by self-interest; it cannot be enticed by benevolence.

Economic Studies (1880)

Jacques Bainville 1879–1936

French historian

of the Treaty of Versailles:
3 Written by Bible readers *for* Bible readers.

'Les Consequences Politiques de la Paix' (1920)

Michael Bakunin 1814–76

Russian revolutionary and anarchist

4 The urge for destruction is also a creative urge!

in Jahrbuch für Wissenschaft und Kunst (1842)

5 We wish, in a word, equality—equality in fact as corollary, or rather, as primordial condition of liberty. From each according to his faculties, to each according to his needs; that is what we wish sincerely and energetically.
   declaration signed by forty-seven anarchists on trial after the failure of their uprising at Lyons in 1870

J. Morrison Davidson *The Old Order and the New* (1890)

James Baldwin 1924–87

American novelist and essayist

6 It comes as a great shock around the age of 5, 6 or 7 to discover that the flag to which you have pledged allegiance, along with everybody else, has not pledged allegiance to you. It comes as a great shock to see Gary Cooper killing off the Indians and, although you are rooting for Gary Cooper, that the Indians are you.
   speaking for the proposition that 'The American Dream is at the expense of the American Negro' at the Cambridge Union, England, 17 February 1965

in New York Times Magazine 7 March 1965

7 Freedom is not something that anybody can be given; freedom is something people take and people are as free as they want to be.

Nobody Knows My Name (1961) 'Notes for a Hypothetical Novel'

8 At the root of the American Negro problem is the necessity of the American white man to find a way of living with the Negro in order to be able to live with himself.

in Harper's Magazine October 1953 'Stranger in a Village'

9 If they take you in the morning, they will be coming for us that night.

in New York Review of Books 7 January 1971 'Open Letter to my Sister, Angela Davis'

Stanley Baldwin 1867–1947

British Conservative statesman; Prime Minister, 1923–4,
1924–9, 1935–7
on Baldwin: see **Beaverbrook** 34:2, **Churchill** 92:13, 93:3,
Curzon 108:4, **Trevelyan** 368:3; cf. **Kipling** 214:1

1 They [parliament] are a lot of hard-faced men who look
as if they had done very well out of the war.

J. M. Keynes *Economic
Consequences of the Peace* (1919)

2 A platitude is simply a truth repeated until people get
tired of hearing it.

in the House of Commons, 29 May
1924

3 There are three classes which need sanctuary more than
others—birds, wild flowers, and Prime Ministers.

in *Observer* 24 May 1925

4 'Safety first' does not mean a smug self-satisfaction with
everything as it is. It is a warning to all persons who are
going to cross a road in dangerous circumstances.

in *The Times* 21 May 1929

5 Had the employers of past generations all of them dealt
fairly with their men there would have been no unions.

speech in Birmingham, 14 January
1931

6 I think it is well also for the man in the street to realize
that there is no power on earth that can protect him
from being bombed. Whatever people may tell him, the
bomber will always get through. The only defence is in
offence, which means that you have to kill more women
and children more quickly than the enemy if you want to
save yourselves.

in the House of Commons, 10
November 1932

7 Since the day of the air, the old frontiers are gone. When
you think of the defence of England you no longer think
of the chalk cliffs of Dover; you think of the Rhine. That
is where our frontier lies.

in the House of Commons, 30 July
1934

of his reasons for excluding **Churchill** *from the Cabinet:*
8 If there is going to be a war—and no one can say that
there is not—we must keep him fresh to be our war
Prime Minister.

letter 17 November 1935

9 I shall be but a short time tonight. I have seldom spoken
with greater regret, for my lips are not yet unsealed.
Were these troubles over I would make a case, and
I guarantee that not a man would go into the lobby
against us.
usually quoted as 'My lips are sealed'

in the House of Commons on the
Abyssinian crisis, 10 December
1935

10 Supposing I had gone to the country and said that
Germany was rearming and that we must rearm, does
anybody think that this pacific democracy would have
rallied to that cry at that moment? I cannot think of
anything that would have made the loss of the election
from my point of view more certain.

in the House of Commons, 12
November 1936

11 You will find in politics that you are much exposed to the
attribution of false motive. Never complain and never
explain.

Harold Nicolson *Diary* 21 July 1943

12 Do not run up your nose dead against the Pope or the
NUM!

Lord Butler *The Art of Memory*
(1982); cf. **Macmillan** 245:9

1 He spent his whole life in plastering together the true and the false and therefrom manufacturing the plausible.
of **Lloyd George**

attributed

2 The intelligent are to the intelligentsia what a gentleman is to a gent.

G. M. Young *Stanley Baldwin* (1952)

3 Then comes Winston with his hundred-horse-power mind and what can I do?

G. M. Young *Stanley Baldwin* (1952)

Arthur James Balfour 1848–1930

British Conservative statesman; Prime Minister, 1902–5; in 1917, as Foreign Secretary, Balfour issued the declaration in favour of a Jewish National Home in Palestine that came to be known as the Balfour Declaration.
on Balfour: see **Churchill** 88:2, 88:3, **Housman** 183:7, **Lloyd George** 229:1, 230:2

4 It is unfortunate, considering that enthusiasm moves the world, that so few enthusiasts can be trusted to speak the truth.

letter to Mrs Drew, 19 May 1891

5 Campbell-Bannerman is a mere cork, dancing on a torrent he cannot control.
of the election of 1906, which had produced a Liberal landslide and 50 Labour MPs, and in which Balfour, the former Tory Prime Minister, and six of his Cabinet colleagues had lost their seats

letter to Lady Salisbury, 1906; Blanche Dugdale *Arthur James Balfour* (1939)

6 His Majesty's Government view with favour the establishment in Palestine of a national home for the Jewish people, and will use their best endeavours to facilitate the achievement of this object, it being clearly understood that nothing shall be done which may prejudice the civil and religious rights of existing non-Jewish communities in Palestine, or the rights and political status enjoyed by Jews in any other country.

letter to Lord Rothschild, 2 November 1917

7 Zionism, be it right or wrong, good or bad, is rooted in age-long traditions, in present need, in future hopes, of far profounder import than the desires and prejudices of the seven hundred thousand Arabs who now inhabit that ancient land.

in August 1919; Max Egremont *Balfour* (1980)

on being asked what he thought of the behaviour of the German delegation at the signing of the Treaty of Versailles:
8 I make it a rule never to stare at people when they are in obvious distress.

Max Egremont *Balfour* (1980)

replying to Frank Harris, who had claimed that 'all the faults of the age come from Christianity and journalism':
9 Christianity, of course...but why journalism?

Margot Asquith *Autobiography* (1920) vol. 1

on the continuing financial dependence of **Curzon,** *who had failed to become Prime Minister in succession to* **Bonar Law,** *on his second wife Grace Duggan:*
10 He may have lost the hope of glory, but he still retains the means of Grace.

attributed

1   Biography should be written by an acute enemy.   in *Observer* 30 January 1927

2   [Our] whole political machinery pre-supposes a people so   introduction to Walter Bagehot *The*
    fundamentally at one that they can safely afford to   *English Constitution* (World
    bicker.   Classics ed., 1928)

    of an unwelcome supporter:
3   He pursues us with malignant fidelity.   Winston Churchill *Great*
                                              Contemporaries (1937)

4   I am more or less happy when being praised, not very   K. Young *A. J. Balfour* (1963)
    uncomfortable when being abused, but I have moments
    of uneasiness when being explained.

5   I never forgive but I always forget.   R. Blake *Conservative Party* (1970)

6   I thought he was a young man of promise, but it appears   Winston Churchill *My Early Life*
    he is a young man of promises.   (1930)
     describing Churchill

Lord Balogh 1905–85

Hungarian-born political economist and adviser to Harold
Wilson's Government

7   Blatant fallacies leading to inappropriate, indeed   *The Irrelevance of Conventional*
    catastrophic, policies can survive if a sufficient part of the   *Economics* (1982)
    profession [of economists] is committed to them.

8   Some people would believe anything, especially if it   *The Irrelevance of Conventional*
    eliminates awkward social and political problems.   *Economics* (1982)

E. Digby Baltzell 1915–

9   There is a crisis in American leadership in the middle of   *The Protestant Establishment*
    the twentieth century that is partly due, I think, to the   (1964)
    declining authority of an establishment which is now
    based on an increasingly castelike White-Anglo Saxon-
    Protestant (WASP) upper class.

Honoré de Balzac 1799–1850

French novelist

10   Despotism accomplishes great things illegally; liberty   *La Peau de Chagrin* (1831)
    doesn't even go to the trouble of accomplishing small
    things legally.

George Bancroft 1800–91

American historian and politician

11   Calvinism [in Switzerland]…established a religion   *History of the United States* (1855
    without a prelate, a government without a king.   ed.) vol. 3

Lord Bancroft 1922–96

British civil servant; Head of the Civil Service 1978–81

1 Conviction politicians, certainly: conviction civil servants, no.

'Whitehall: Some Personal Reflections', lecture at the London School of Economics 1 December 1983

Imamu Amiri Baraka 1934–

American poet and playwright

2 A man is either free or he is not. There cannot be any apprenticeship for freedom.

in *Kulchur* Spring 1962 'Tokenism'

Ernest Barker 1874–1960

British political scientist

3 Sovereignty is unlimited—unlimited and illimitable.

Principles of Social and Political Theory (1951)

Bernard Baruch 1870–1965

American financier and presidential adviser

4 Behind the black portent of a new atomic age lies a hope which, seized upon with faith, can work out salvation... Let us not deceive ourselves: we must elect world peace or world destruction.

address to the United Nations Atomic Energy Commission, 14 June 1946

5 Let us not be deceived—we are today in the midst of a cold war.

speech to South Carolina Legislature 16 April 1947; the expression 'cold war' was suggested to him by H. B. Swope, former editor of the *New York World*

6 We are in the midst of a cold war which is getting warmer.

speech before the Senate Committee, 1948

7 Vote for the man who promises least; he'll be the least disappointing.

Meyer Berger *New York* (1960)

8 You can talk about capitalism and communism and all that sort of thing, but the important thing is the struggle everybody is engaged in to get better living conditions, and they are not interested too much in government.

in *The Times* 20 August 1964

9 A political leader must keep looking over his shoulder all the time to see if the boys are still there. If they aren't still there, he's no longer a political leader.

in *New York Times* 21 June 1965

Lord Bauer 1915–

British economist

1 Foreign aid is a system of taking money from poor
people in rich countries and giving it to rich people in
poor countries.

*attributed; not recollected by
Lord Bauer but not repudiated
by him*

Beverley Baxter 1891–1964

British journalist and Conservative politician

2 Beaverbrook is so pleased to be in the Government that
he is like the town tart who has finally married the
Mayor!

*Henry ('Chips') Channon diary 12
June 1940*

Charles Austin Beard 1874–1948 and **Mary Ritter Beard** 1876–1958

3 At no time, at no place, in solemn convention assembled,
through no chosen agents, had the American people
officially proclaimed the United States to be
a democracy…When the Constitution was framed no
respectable person called himself or herself a democrat.

America in Midpassage (1939)

Lord Beaverbrook 1879–1964

Canadian-born British newspaper proprietor and Conservative
politician
on Beaverbrook: see **Baxter** 33:2, **Lloyd George** 230:12,
Wells 385:6; cf. also **Kipling** 214:1

4 I hope you will give up the New Party. If you must burn
your fingers in public life, go to a bright and big blaze.
    to Harold **Nicolson**

*letter 25 June 1931 in Harold
Nicolson Diaries (1980)*

5 Churchill on top of the wave has in him the stuff of
which tyrants are made.

Politicians and the War (1932)

6 Our cock won't fight.
    said to Winston **Churchill**, *of* **Edward VIII**, *during the abdication
crisis of 1936*

*Frances Donaldson Edward VIII
(1974)*

7 The Daily Express declares that Great Britain will not be
involved in a European war this year or next year either.

*in Daily Express 19 September
1938*

8 Now who is responsible for this work of development on
which so much depends? To whom must the praise be
given? To the boys in the back rooms. They do not sit in
the limelight. But they are the men who do the work.

in Listener 27 March 1941

9 I ran the paper [the *Daily Express*] purely for propaganda
and with no other purpose.
    evidence to the Royal Commission on the Press, 18 March 1948

A. J. P. Taylor Beaverbrook (1972)

10 Always threatening resignation, he never signed off.
    of Lord **Derby**

Men and Power (1956)

of Lord **Curzon**, *who had been created Viceroy of India at the age of thirty-nine:*

1 For all the rest of his life Curzon was influenced by his sudden journey to heaven at the age of thirty-nine, and then by his return seven years later to earth, for the remainder of his mortal existence.

Men and Power (1956)

2 His conversation turned on the beauty of the mountain rose, and the splendour of hawthorn buds in spring.
   of Stanley **Baldwin**

Men and Power (1956)

3 Often undecided whether to desert a sinking ship for one that might not float, he would make up his mind to sit on the wharf for a day.
   of Lord **Curzon**

Men and Power (1956)

4 With the publication of his Private Papers in 1952, he [Earl Haig] committed suicide 25 years after his death.
   of Earl **Haig**

Men and Power (1956)

5 [Lloyd George] did not seem to care which way he travelled providing he was in the driver's seat.

The Decline and Fall of Lloyd George (1963)

6 The British electors will not vote for a man who does not wear a hat.
   advice to Tom Driberg

Alan Watkins *Brief Lives* (1982)

of **Bonar Law** *and* **Churchill**:

7 I have had two masters and one of them betrayed me.

A. J. P. Taylor letter 16 December 1973; *Letters to Eva* (1991)

Henry Becque 1837–99

French dramatist and critic

8 What makes equality such a difficult business is that we only want it with our superiors.

Querelles littéraires (1890)

Brendan Behan 1923–64

Irish playwright

9 PAT: He was an Anglo-Irishman.
   MEG: In the blessed name of God what's that?
   PAT: A Protestant with a horse.

The Hostage (1958)

10 When I came back to Dublin, I was courtmartialled in my absence and sentenced to death in my absence, so I said they could shoot me in my absence.

The Hostage (1958)

Francis Bellamy 1856–1931

American clergyman and editor

11 I pledge allegiance to the flag of the United States of America and to the republic for which it stands, one nation under God, indivisible, with liberty and justice for all.

The Pledge of Allegiance to the Flag (1892)

Hilaire Belloc 1870–1953

British poet, essayist, historian, novelist, and Liberal politician

1 Whatever happens we have got
The Maxim Gun, and they have not.

The Modern Traveller (1898)

2 Gentlemen, I am a Catholic...If you reject me on
account of my religion, I shall thank God that He has
spared me the indignity of being your representative.

speech to voters of South Salford,
1906; Speaight *Life of Hilaire
Belloc* (1957)

3 Sir! you have disappointed us!
We had intended you to be
The next Prime Minister but three:
The stocks were sold; the Press was squared;
The Middle Class was quite prepared.
But as it is!...My language fails!
Go out and govern New South Wales!

Cautionary Tales (1907) 'Lord
Lundy'

of the House of Commons:
4 A man can no more make a good speech in such a place
than sing a song in it.

Hugh Dalton *Political Diary* (1986)
29 July 1930

5 Here richly, with ridiculous display,
The Politician's corpse was laid away.
While all of his acquaintance sneered and slanged
I wept: for I had longed to see him hanged.

'Epitaph on the Politician Himself'
(1923)

Julien Benda 1867–1956

French philosopher and novelist

6 *La trahison des clercs.*
The treachery of the intellectuals.

title of book, 1927

Ruth Fulton Benedict 1887–1948

American anthropologist

7 The tough-minded...respect difference. Their goal is
a world made safe for differences, where the United States
may be American to the hilt without threatening the
peace of the world, and France may be France, and
Japan may be Japan on the same conditions.

*The Chrysanthemum and the
Sword* (1946)

Ernest Benn 1875–1954

English publisher and economist

8 Politics is the art of looking for trouble, finding it
whether it exists or not, diagnosing it incorrectly, and
applying the wrong remedy.

attributed

Tony Benn 1925–

British Labour politician and sometime Viscount Stansgate,
who campaigned for the change in the law that made it
possible to renounce a hereditary peerage
on Benn: see **Levin** 222:4, **Wilson** 391:8

1 Not a reluctant peer but a persistent commoner.

at a Press Conference, 23
November 1960

2 Broadcasting is really too important to be left to the
broadcasters.
   as Minister of Technology in 1968

Anthony Sampson *The New
Anatomy of Britain* (1971)

3 Some of the jam we thought was for tomorrow, we've
already eaten.

attributed, 1969; cf. **Carroll** 77:2

4 The crisis that we inherit when we come to power will
be the occasion for fundamental change and not the
excuse for postponing it.

at the Labour Party Conference,
1973

5 In developing our industrial strategy for the period
ahead, we have the benefit of much experience. Almost
everything has been tried at least once.

speech in House of Commons, 13
March 1974

on seeing Harold **Wilson***, who had resigned as Prime Minister
in March, looking 'absolutely shrunk':*
6 Office is something that builds up a man only if he is
somebody in his own right.

diary 12 April 1976

7 Marxism is now a world faith and must be allowed to
enter into a continuous dialogue with other world faiths,
including religious faiths.

Karl Marx lecture, 16 March 1982

of the influence of Parliament:
8 Through talk, we tamed kings, restrained tyrants,
averted revolution.

Anthony Sampson *The Changing
Anatomy of Britain* (1982)

9 I did not enter the Labour Party forty-seven years ago to
have our manifesto written by Dr Mori, Dr Gallup and
Mr Harris.

in *Guardian* 13 June 1988

10 A faith is something you die for; a doctrine is something
you kill for: there is all the difference in the world.

in *Observer* 16 April 1989 'Sayings
of the Week'

*questions habitually asked by Tony Benn on meeting
somebody in power:*
11 What power have you got? Where did you get it from?
In whose interests do you exercise it? To whom are you
accountable? How do we get rid of you?

'The Independent Mind', lecture at
Nottingham, 18 June 1993

12 To understand how we're governed, and hence the
power of the Prime Minister, you have to understand the
power of the Crown. It's like the Trinity: God the Father
is the Queen—she's just there and nobody knows very
much about her; God the Son is the Prime Minister—
who exercises all the patronage and has all the real
power; and God the Holy Ghost is the Crown—the Royal
Prerogative—and the Crown in a state-within-a-state,
surrounded by barbed wire and covered in secrecy.

briefing for a 'Cabinet and
Premiership' course at Queen Mary
and Westfield College, 26 April
1994

1 The Civil Service is a bit like a rusty weathercock. It
   moves with opinion then it stays where it is until
   another wind moves it in a different direction.

briefing for 'Cabinet and
Premiership' course (Queen Mary
and Westfield College), held at the
House of Commons 1 March 1995

2 When you get to No. 10, you've climbed there on a little
   ladder called 'the status quo'. And, when you're there,
   the status quo looks very good.

at the House of Commons 1 March
1995

Arnold Bennett 1867–1931

English novelist

3 Examine the Honours List and you can instantly tell how
   the Government feels in its inside. When the Honours
   List is full of rascals, millionaires, and—er—chumps, you
   may be quite sure that the Government is dangerously ill.

The Title (1918)

4 Literature's always a good card to play for Honours. It
   makes people think that Cabinet ministers are educated.

The Title (1918)

5 Seventy minutes had passed before Mr Lloyd George
   arrived at his proper theme. He spoke for a hundred and
   seventeen minutes, in which period he was detected only
   once in the use of an argument.

Things that have Interested Me
(1921) 'After the March Offensive'

A. C. Benson 1862–1925

English writer

6 Land of Hope and Glory, Mother of the Free,
   How shall we extol thee who are born of thee?
   Wider still and wider shall thy bounds be set;
   God who made thee mighty, make thee mightier yet.

'Land of Hope and Glory' written to
be sung as the Finale to Elgar's
Coronation Ode (1902)

Jeremy Bentham 1748–1832

English philosopher

7 Right...is the child of law: from real laws come real
   rights; but from imaginary laws, from laws of nature,
   fancied and invented by poets, rhetoricians, and dealers
   in moral and intellectual poisons, come imaginary rights,
   a bastard brood of monsters.

Anarchical Fallacies (1843)

8 Natural rights is simple nonsense: natural and
   imprescriptible rights, rhetorical nonsense—nonsense
   upon stilts.

Anarchical Fallacies (1843)

9 The greatest happiness of the greatest number is the
   foundation of morals and legislation.
      *Bentham claims to have acquired the 'sacred truth' either from
      Joseph Priestley (1733–1804) or Cesare Beccaria (1738–94)*

The Commonplace Book (1843)

10 Every law is contrary to liberty.

Principles of the Civil Code (1843)

11 He rather hated the ruling few than loved the suffering
   many.
      of James Mill

H. N. Pym (ed.) *Memories of Old
Friends, being Extracts from the
Journals and Letters of Caroline
Fox* (1882)

Edmund Clerihew Bentley 1875–1956

English writer

1 When their lordships asked Bacon
   How many bribes he had taken
   He had at least the grace
   To get very red in the face.

Baseless Biography (1939) 'Bacon'

2 George the Third
   Ought never to have occurred.
   One can only wonder
   At so grotesque a blunder.

More Biography (1929) 'George the Third'

Lloyd Bentsen 1921–

American Democratic politician

*responding to Dan Quayle's claim to have 'as much experience in the Congress as Jack **Kennedy** had when he sought the presidency':*

3 Senator, I served with Jack Kennedy. I knew Jack
   Kennedy. Jack Kennedy was a friend of mine. Senator,
   you're no Jack Kennedy.

in the vice-presidential debate, 5 October 1988

George Berkeley 1685–1753

Irish philosopher and Anglican bishop

4 Westward the course of empire takes its way;
   The first four acts already past,
   A fifth shall close the drama with the day:
   Time's noblest offspring is the last.

'On the Prospect of Planting Arts and Learning in America' (1752); cf. John Quincy Adams *Oration at Plymouth* (1802): 'Westward the star of empire takes its way'

Peter Berger

political scientist

5 Capitalism, as an institutional arrangement, has been
   singularly devoid of plausible myths. By contrast,
   socialism, its major alternative under modern conditions,
   has been singularly blessed with myth-generating
   potency.

in 1986; Anthony Sampson *The Company Man* (1995)

Irving Berlin 1888–1989

American songwriter

6 God bless America,
   Land that I love,
   Stand beside her and guide her
   Thru the night with a light from above.
   From the mountains to the prairies,
   To the oceans white with foam,
   God bless America,
   My home sweet home.

'God Bless America' (1939)

Isaiah Berlin 1909–

British philosopher

1 Liberty is liberty, not equality or fairness or justice or human happiness or a quiet conscience.

Two Concepts of Liberty (1958)

2 It is this—the 'positive' conception of liberty: not freedom from, but freedom to—which the adherents of the 'negative' notion represent as being, at times, no better than a specious disguise for brutal tyranny.

Two Concepts of Liberty (1958)

3 The fundamental sense of freedom is freedom from chains, from imprisonment, from enslavement by others. The rest is extension of this sense, or else metaphor.

Four Essays on Liberty (1969); introduction

4 Injustice, poverty, slavery, ignorance—these may be cured by reform or revolution. But men do not live only by fighting evils. They live by positive goals, individual and collective, a vast variety of them, seldom predictable, at times incompatible.

Four Essays on Liberty (1969)

5 Those who have ever valued liberty for its own sake believed that to be free to choose, and not be chosen for, is an inalienable ingredient in what makes human beings human.

Four Essays on Liberty (1969)

6 Few new truths have ever won their way against the resistance of established ideas save by being overstated.

Vico and Herder (1976)

Daniel Berrigan

US anti-Vietnam War activist

7 This is a war run to show the world, and particularly the Third World, where exactly it stands in relation to our technology.

attributed, 1973

Theobald von Bethmann Hollweg
1856–1921

Chancellor of Germany, 1909–17

8 Just for a word 'neutrality'—a word which in wartime has so often been disregarded—just for a scrap of paper, Great Britain is going to make war on a kindred nation who desires nothing better than to be friends with her.

summary of a report by E. Goschen to Edward Grey in *British Documents on Origins of the War 1898–1914* (1926) vol. 11

Mary McLeod Bethune 1875–1955

American educator

9 If we accept and acquiesce in the face of discrimination, we accept the responsibility ourselves and allow those responsible to salve their conscience by believing that they have our acceptance and concurrence.

Rayford W. Logan (ed.) *What the Negro Wants* (1944) 'Certain Inalienable Rights'

John Betjeman 1906–84

English poet

1   Think of what our Nation stands for,   'In Westminster Abbey' (1940)
    Books from Boots' and country lanes,
    Free speech, free passes, class distinction,
    Democracy and proper drains.
    Lord, put beneath Thy special care
    One-eighty-nine Cadogan Square.

Aneurin Bevan 1897–1960

British Labour politician

2   The worst thing I can say about democracy is that it has   in the House of Commons, 23 July
    tolerated the Right Honourable Gentleman for four and   1929
    a half years.
    of Neville **Chamberlain**

3   Listening to a speech by Chamberlain is like paying   Michael Foot *Aneurin Bevan* vol. 1
    a visit to Woolworth's: everything in its place and   (1962)
    nothing above sixpence.

    taking over as Minister of Health in 1945, Bevan immediately
    banished a well-upholstered leather armchair:
4   This won't do. It drains all the blood from the head and   Michael Foot *Aneurin Bevan* vol. 2
    explains a lot about my predecessors.   (1973)

5   This island is made mainly of coal and surrounded by   speech at Blackpool 24 May 1945
    fish. Only an organizing genius could produce a shortage
    of coal and fish at the same time.

6   No amount of cajolery, and no attempts at ethical or   speech at Manchester, 4 July 1948,
    social seduction, can eradicate from my heart a deep   in *The Times* 5 July 1948
    burning hatred for the Tory Party...So far as I am
    concerned they are lower than vermin.

7   The language of priorities is the religion of Socialism.   speech at Labour Party Conference
                                                                in Blackpool, 8 June 1949

8   Why read the crystal when he can read the book?   in the House of Commons, 29
    referring to Robert **Boothby** *during a debate on the Sterling*   September 1949
    Exchange Rate

9   The Tories, every election, must have a bogy man. If you   speech in the general election
    haven't got a programme, a bogy man will do. In 1945   campaign at Stonehouse,
    it was Harold Laski, in 1951 it is me.   Gloucester, 13 October 1951

10 [Winston Churchill] does not talk the language of the   speech at Labour Party
    20th century but that of the 18th. He is still fighting   Conference, Scarborough, 2
    Blenheim all over again. His only answer to a difficult   October 1951
    situation is send a gun-boat.

11 Discontent arises from a knowledge of the possible, as   *In Place of Fear* (1952)
    contrasted with the actual.

12 He is a man suffering from petrified adolescence.   Vincent Brome *Aneurin Bevan*
    of Winston **Churchill**   (1953)

13 We know what happens to people who stay in the middle   in *Observer* 6 December 1953
    of the road. They get run down.

1 Damn it all, you can't have the crown of thorns *and* the thirty pieces of silver.
  on his position in the Labour Party, c.1956

Michael Foot *Aneurin Bevan* vol. 2 (1973)

2 I am not going to spend any time whatsoever in attacking the Foreign Secretary...If we complain about the tune, there is no reason to attack the monkey when the organ grinder is present.
  during a debate on the Suez crisis

in the House of Commons, 16 May 1957

3 If you carry this resolution you will send Britain's Foreign Secretary naked into the conference chamber.
  speaking against a motion proposing unilateral nuclear disarmament by the United Kingdom

speech at Labour Party Conference in Brighton, 3 October 1957

4 You call that statesmanship? I call it an emotional spasm.
  speaking against a motion proposing unilateral nuclear disarmament by the United Kingdom

speech at Labour Party Conference in Brighton, 3 October 1957

5 I know that the right kind of leader for the Labour Party is a desiccated calculating machine who must not in any way permit himself to be swayed by indignation. If he sees suffering, privation or injustice he must not allow it to move him, for that would be evidence of the lack of proper education or of absence of self-control. He must speak in calm and objective accents and talk about a dying child in the same way as he would about the pieces inside an internal combustion engine.
  frequently taken as referring to Hugh Gaitskell, although Bevan specifically denied it in an interview with Robin Day on 28 April 1959

Michael Foot *Aneurin Bevan* vol. 2 (1973)

6 The conquest of the commanding heights of the economy.
  recalling his own earlier use of the phrase (possibly originated by Lenin)

at the Labour Party Conference, November 1959

7 The Prime Minister has an absolute genius for putting flamboyant labels on empty luggage.
  of Harold Macmillan

in the House of Commons, 3 November 1959

8 Tory shame was only slightly alleviated by Walter Monckton—and then they didn't know whether to wear him as a gas-mask or a jock strap.
  of Walter Monckton at the time of Suez

Andrew Roberts *Eminent Churchillians* (1994)

9 I read the newspapers avidly. It is my one form of continuous fiction.

in *The Times* 29 March 1960

of his handling of the consultants during the establishment of the National Health Service:
10 I stuffed their mouths with gold.

Brian Abel-Smith *The Hospitals 1800–1948* (1964)

11 There are only two ways of getting into the Cabinet. One way is to crawl up the staircase of preferment on your belly; the other way is to kick them in the teeth.

Richard Crossman *Inside View* (1972)

Albert Jeremiah Beveridge 1862–1927

American Republican politician and member of the Senate, who in 1912 chaired the convention that organized the Progressive party and nominated Theodore **Roosevelt** for President

1   This party comes from the grass roots. It has grown from the soil of the people's hard necessities.

address at the Bull Moose Convention in Chicago, 5 August 1912

William Henry Beveridge 1879–1963

British economist

2   The object of government in peace and in war is not the glory of rulers or of races, but the happiness of the common man.

Social Insurance and Allied Services (1942)

3   Want is one only of five giants on the road of reconstruction...the others are Disease, Ignorance, Squalor and Idleness.

Social Insurance and Allied Services (1942)

4   Ignorance is an evil weed, which dictators may cultivate among their dupes, but which no democracy can afford among its citizens.

Full Employment in a Free Society (1944)

5   The state is or can be master of money, but in a free society it is master of very little else.

Voluntary Action (1948)

Ernest Bevin 1881–1951

British Labour politician and trade unionist

6   The most conservative man in this world is the British Trade Unionist when you want to change him.

speech, 8 September 1927

7   I hope you will carry no resolution of an emergency character telling a man with a conscience like Lansbury what he ought to do...It is placing the Executive in an absolutely wrong position to be taking your conscience round from body to body to be told what you ought to do with it.

often quoted as 'hawking his conscience round the Chancellories of Europe'

in *Labour Party Conference Report* (1935)

the scientist Patrick Blackett had questioned the wisdom of trying to manufacture a British atomic bomb:

8   Stick to science.

Henry Pelling *The Labour Governments, 1945–51* (1984)

9   I am not one of those who decry Eton and Harrow. I was very glad of them in the Battle of Britain.

speech at Blackpool, 1945; D. Healey *The Time of My Life* (1989)

10   There never has been a war yet which, if the facts had been put calmly before the ordinary folk, could not have been prevented. The common man, I think, is the great protection against war.

in the House of Commons, 23 November 1945

as Minister of Labour to his Civil Servants:

1 You've just given me twenty reasons why I can't do this;
I'm sure that clever chaps like you can go away and
produce twenty good reasons why I can.

oral tradition; Peter Hennessy
Whitehall (1990)

*on being told, at the ending of the British Mandate, that the Air
Staff wanted to stay in Palestine:*

2 If they want to stay, they'll have to stay up in
helicopters.

Hugh Dalton diary *Political Diary*
(1986) 20 September 1947

*someone had remarked that Aneurin **Bevan** was his own worst
enemy:*

3 Not while I'm alive 'e ain't.
*also attributed to Bevin of Herbert **Morrison***

Roderick Barclay *Ernest Bevin and
the Foreign Office* (1975)

4 My [foreign] policy is to be able to take a ticket at
Victoria Station and go anywhere I damn well please.

in *Spectator* 20 April 1951

5 If you open that Pandora's Box, you never know what
Trojan 'orses will jump out.
on the Council of Europe

Roderick Barclay *Ernest Bevin and
the Foreign Office* (1975)

6 I didn't ought never to have done it. It was you, Willie,
what put me up to it.
to Lord Strang, after officially recognizing Communist China

C. Parrott *Serpent and Nightingale*
(1977)

The Bible (Authorized Version)

7 Let my people go.

Exodus

8 Let them live; but let them be hewers of wood and
drawers of water unto all the congregation.

Joshua

9 He smote them hip and thigh.

Judges

10 And she named the child I-chabod, saying, The glory is
departed from Israel.

I Samuel

11 And Saul said, God hath delivered him into mine hand.

I Samuel

12 He shall know that there is a prophet in Israel.

II Kings

13 Thus shall it be done to the man whom the king
delighteth to honour.

Esther

14 Great men are not always wise.

Job

15 Where there is no vision, the people perish.

Proverbs

16 The race is not to the swift, nor the battle to the strong.

Ecclesiastes

17 Woe to thee, O land, when thy king is a child.

Ecclesiastes

18 They shall beat their swords into plowshares, and their
spears into pruninghooks: nation shall not lift up sword
against nation, neither shall they learn war any more.

Isaiah; cf. **Rendall** 303:1

19 Of the increase of his government and peace there shall
be no end.

Isaiah

20 Now, O king, establish the decree, and sign the writing,
that it be not changed, according to the law of the Medes
and Persians, which altereth not.

Daniel

1	They have sown the wind, and they shall reap the whirlwind.	Hosea
2	Let us now praise famous men, and our fathers that begat us.	Ecclesiasticus
3	Such as did bear rule in their kingdoms.	Ecclesiasticus
4	Judge not, that ye be not judged.	St Matthew
5	I came not to send peace, but a sword.	St Matthew
6	He that is not with me is against me.	St Matthew; St Luke
7	Render therefore unto Caesar the things which are Caesar's; and unto God the things that are God's.	St Matthew
8	Ye shall hear of wars and rumours of wars: see that ye be not troubled: for all these things must come to pass but the end is not yet.	St Matthew
9	For nation shall rise against nation, and kingdom against kingdom.	St Matthew, St John
10	Those that have turned the world upside down are come hither also.	Acts of the Apostles
11	But Paul said, I am a man which am a Jew of Tarsus, a city in Cilicia, a citizen of no mean city.	Acts of the Apostles
12	Hast thou appealed unto Caesar? unto Caesar shalt thou go.	Acts of the Apostles
13	For where no law is, there is no transgression.	Romans

Georges Bidault 1899–1983

French statesman; Prime Minister, 1946, 1949–50

| 14 | The weak have one weapon: the errors of those who think they are strong. | in *Observer* 15 July 1962 'Sayings of the Week' |

Ambrose Bierce 1842–c.1914

American writer

15	BATTLE, *n.* A method of untying with the teeth a political knot that would not yield to the tongue.	*The Cynic's Word Book* (1906)
16	CONSERVATIVE, *n.* A statesman who is enamoured of existing evils, as distinguished from the Liberal, who wishes to replace them with others.	*The Cynic's Word Book* (1906)
17	PEACE, *n.* In international affairs, a period of cheating between two periods of fighting.	*The Devil's Dictionary* (1911)

John Biffen 1930–

British Conservative politician

commenting on a critical remark from the Downing Street Press Secretary, Bernard **Ingham**:

| 18 | He was the sewer and not the sewage. | recorded for a television interview, c.1988, but not broadcast |

of Margaret **Thatcher** *as Prime Minister:*

1 She was a tigress surrounded by hamsters.

in Observer 9 December 1990

2 In politics I think it is wiser to leave five minutes too
soon than to continue for five years too long.
resignation letter

in Daily Telegraph 5 January 1995

John Biggs-Davison 1918–88

British Conservative politician

3 I have never conceived it my duty as a Member of
Parliament to seek to amend the Ten Commandments.

speech at Chelmsford, 7 November
1976

Steve Biko 1946–77

South African anti-apartheid campaigner

4 The most potent weapon in the hands of the oppressor is
the mind of the oppressed.

statement as witness, 3 May 1976

Josh Billings 1818–85

American humorist

5 It is better to know nothing than to know what ain't so.

Proverb (1874)

Nigel Birch 1906–81

British Conservative politician

on hearing of the resignation of Hugh **Dalton**, *Chancellor of the
Exchequer in the Labour Government, 13 November 1947:*
6 My God! They've shot our fox!

Harold Macmillan *Tides of Fortune*
(1969)

as Minister of Works in 1951, Birch said that he had enjoyed:
7 Gardening with a staff of three thousand.

in Dictionary of National Biography

8 For the second time the Prime Minister has got rid of
a Chancellor of the Exchequer who tried to get
expenditure under control. Once is more than enough.
after Harold **Macmillan**'s *dismissal of Selwyn* **Lloyd** *in favour of
Reginald Maudling*

letter to *The Times*, 14 July 1962

9 I must say that he never struck me as a man at all like
a cloistered monk; and Miss Keeler was a professional
prostitute...There seems to me to be a certain basic
improbability about the proposition that their relationship
was purely platonic.
of John Profumo, during the Profumo debate

in the House of Commons, 17 June
1963

10 On the question of competence and good sense I cannot
think that the verdict can be favourable.
of Harold **Macmillan** *and his handling of the Profumo affair;
Birch's peroration for this speech was from Browning's 'The Lost
Leader': 'Let him never come back to us...never glad confident
morning again'*

in the House of Commons, 17 June
1963

1 No one could accuse himself of courage more often than
the Prime Minister.
  of Harold **Wilson**

in the House of Commons, 2
August 1965

Lord Birkenhead see **F. E. Smith**

Augustine Birrell 1850–1933

British essayist and politician

at a dinner in Trinity College, Cambridge, in 1902, the Master in
proposing the health of the college pointed out that at that
moment the Sovereign and the Prime Minister were both
Trinity men:

2 The Master should have added that he can go further, for
it is obvious that the affairs of the world are built upon
the momentous fact that God also is a Trinity man.

Harold Laski letter to Oliver
Wendell Holmes 4 December 1926

Otto von Bismarck 1815–98

German statesman, and the driving force behind the unification
of Germany; Chancellor of the new German Empire 1871–90
on Bismarck: see **Taylor** 356:9, **Tenniel** 359:6

3 The secret of politics? Make a good treaty with Russia.
  in 1863, when first in power

A. J. P. Taylor *Bismarck* (1955)

4 Politics is not an exact science.

speech to the Prussian legislature,
18 December 1863

after the Austro-Prussian war of 1866, there were calls in
Prussia for punishment of the defeated Austrians:

5 Austria was no more in the wrong in opposing our
claims than we were in making them.

A. J. P. Taylor *Bismarck* (1955)

6 Politics is the art of the possible.

in conversation with Meyer von
Waldeck, 11 August 1867

7 The politician has not to revenge what has happened but
to ensure that it does not happen again.
  in 1867, following public criticism of courtesy shown to the
  defeated Napoleon III after the battle of Sedan

A. J. P. Taylor *Bismarck* (1955)

8 Let us...put Germany in the saddle! She will know well
enough how to ride!

in 1867; Alan Palmer *Bismarck*
(1976)

9 Whoever speaks of Europe is wrong, [it is] a geographical
concept.

marginal note on a letter from the
Russian Chancellor Gorchakov,
November 1876; cf.
Metternich 257:7

10 I have always found the word Europe on the lips of those
politicians who wanted something from other Powers
which they dared not demand in their own names.
  to the Russian Chancellor Gorchakov, who had urged that
  a rising in Bosnia in 1878 was a European, rather than a German
  or Russian, question

A. J. P. Taylor *Bismarck* (1955)

1 I do not regard the procuring of peace as a matter in which we should play the role of arbiter between different opinions...more that of an honest broker who really wants to press the business forward.
before the Congress of Berlin

speech to the Reichstag, 19 February 1878

2 A lath of wood painted to look like iron.
*of Lord **Salisbury** at the Congress of Berlin in 1878*

attributed, but vigorously denied by Sidney Whitman in *Personal Reminiscences of Prince Bismarck* (1902)

3 The old Jew! That is the man.
*of **Disraeli** at the Congress of Berlin*

attributed

4 Place in the hands of the King of Prussia the strongest possible military power, then he will be able to carry out the policy you wish; this policy cannot succeed through speeches, and shooting-matches, and songs; it can only be carried out through blood and iron.

in the Prussian House of Deputies, 28 January 1886; in a speech on 30 September 1862, Bismarck had used the form 'iron and blood'

5 I am bored; the great things are done. The German *Reich* is made.

A. J. P. Taylor *Bismarck* (1955)

6 Jena came twenty years after the death of Frederick the Great; the crash will come twenty years after my departure if things go on like this.
*to Kaiser **Wilhelm II** at their last meeting in 1895*

A. J. P. Taylor *Bismarck* (1955)

of the English political system:
7 If reactionary measures are to be carried, the Liberal party takes the rudder, from the correct assumption that it will not overstep the necessary limits; if liberal measures are to be carried, the Conservative party takes office in its turn for the same consideration.

A. J. P. Taylor *Bismarck* (1955)

8 If there is ever another war in Europe, it will come out of some damned silly thing in the Balkans.

reported by the shipping magnate Herr Ballen as being said by Bismarck in his later years; quoted in the House of Commons, 16 August 1945

9 Man cannot create the current of events. He can only float with it and steer.

A. J. P. Taylor *Bismarck* (1955)

of possible German involvement in the Balkans:
10 Not worth the healthy bones of a single Pomeranian grenadier.

George O. Kent *Bismarck and his Times* (1978)

11 A statesman...must wait until he hears the steps of God sounding through events; then leap up and grasp the hem of his garment.

A. J. P. Taylor *Bismarck* (1955)

12 There is a providence that protects idiots, drunkards, children, and the United States of America.

attributed, perhaps apocryphal

13 The tongue in the balance.
of Germany's position in relation to other European states

A. J. P. Taylor *Bismarck* (1955)

14 What is an opportunist? He is a man who uses the most favourable opportunity to carry through what he regards as useful and appropriate.

A. J. P. Taylor *Bismarck* (1955)

1 When a man says he approves of something in principle, it means he hasn't the slightest intention of putting it into practice.

attributed

Hugo La Fayette Black 1886–1971
American judge

2 The First Amendment has erected a wall between church and state. That wall must be kept high and impregnable. We could not approve the slightest breach.

in *Emerson v. Board of Education* 1947

3 It is my belief that there *are* absolutes in our Bill of Rights, and that they were put there on purpose by men who knew what words meant and meant their prohibitions to be 'absolutes'.

interview before the American Jewish Congress, 14 April 1962

4 An unconditional right to say what one pleases about public affairs is what I consider to be the minimum guarantee of the First Amendment.

in *New York Times Company v. Sullivan* 1964

5 In revealing the workings of government that led to the Vietnam War, the newspapers nobly did precisely that which the Founders hoped and trusted they would do.

concurring opinion on the publication of the Pentagon Papers, 1971

William Blackstone 1723–80
English jurist

6 The king never dies.

Commentaries on the Laws of England (1765)

7 The royal navy of England hath ever been its greatest defence and ornament; it is its ancient and natural strength; the floating bulwark of the island.

Commentaries on the Laws of England (1765)

8 That the king can do no wrong, is a necessary and fundamental principle of the English constitution.

Commentaries on the Laws of England (1765)

9 In all tyrannical governments the supreme magistracy, or the right both of making and of enforcing the laws, is vested in one and the same man, or one and the same body of men; and wherever these two powers are united together, there can be no public liberty.

Commentaries on the Laws of England (1765)

10 Herein indeed consists the excellence of the English government, that all parts of it form a mutual check upon each other.

Commentaries on the Laws of England (1765)

Tony Blair 1953–
British Labour statesman, Prime Minister since 1997

11 Labour is the party of law and order in Britain today. Tough on crime and tough on the causes of crime.
   as Shadow Home Secretary

speech at the Labour Party Conference, 30 September 1993

12 The art of leadership is saying no, not yes. It is very easy to say yes.

in *Mail on Sunday* 2 October 1994

1 It has surely come to something when a government can   in *Independent* 17 November 1994
   only secure the passage of its own legislative programme
   by threatening its own demise.
   of John **Major***'s warning to Conservative rebels*

2 Those who seriously believe we cannot improve on words   in *Independent* 11 January 1995;
   written for the world of 1918 when we are now in 1995   cf. **Anonymous** 14:3
   are not learning from our history but living it.
   on the proposed revision of Clause IV

William Blake 1757–1827

English poet

3 The strongest poison ever known   'Auguries of Innocence' (*c.*1803)
   Came from Caesar's laurel crown.

4 The whore and gambler by the State   'Auguries of Innocence' (*c.*1803)
   Licensed build that nation's fate
   The harlot's cry from street to street
   Shall weave old England's winding sheet.

5 And was Jerusalem builded here   *Milton* (1804–10) preface 'And
   Among these dark Satanic mills?   did those feet in ancient time'

6 I will not cease from mental fight,   *Milton* (1804–10) preface 'And
   Nor shall my sword sleep in my hand,   did those feet in ancient time'
   Till we have built Jerusalem,
   In England's green and pleasant land.

Alfred Blunt, Bishop of Bradford
1879–1957

English clergyman

7 The benefit of the King's Coronation depends, under God,   speech to Bradford Diocesan
   upon two elements: First on the faith, prayer, and self-   Conference, 1 December 1936
   dedication of the King himself, and on that it would be
   improper for me to say anything except to commend
   him, and ask you to commend him, to God's grace,
   which he will so abundantly need...if he is to do his
   duty faithfully. We hope that he is aware of his need.
   Some of us wish that he gave more positive signs of his
   awareness.
   it was this speech that broke the story of **Edward VIII** *and Mrs
   Simpson which the media had been voluntarily suppressing until
   then*

William Joseph Blyton 1887–1944

English journalist and author

8 Winston [Churchill] is so wonderfully eloquent,   Andrew Roberts *Eminent
   impressive and wrong.   Churchillians* (1994)
   letter to his publisher on his book Arrows of Desire

David Boaz 1953–
American foundation executive

1 Alcohol didn't cause the high crime rates of the '20s and '30s, Prohibition did. Drugs don't cause today's alarming crime rates, but drug prohibition does.
'The Legalization of Drugs' 27 April 1988

2 Trying to wage war on 23 million Americans who are obviously very committed to certain recreational activities is not going to be any more successful than Prohibition was.
'The Legalization of Drugs' 27 April 1988

Allan Boesak 1945–
South African politician and clergyman, anti-apartheid campaigner

3 My humanity is not dependent on the acceptance of white people.
after losing in Western Cape, April 1994, as an African National Congress candidate
in *The New York Review of Books* 20 October 1994 'The Election Mandela Lost'

Ivan Boesky 1937–
American financier, imprisoned in 1987 for insider dealing

4 Greed is all right...Greed is healthy. You can be greedy and still feel good about yourself.
commencement address at the University of California, Berkeley, 18 May 1986; cf. **Weiser** 383:6

Curtis Bok 1897–1962
American federal judge

5 It has been said that a judge is a member of the Bar who once knew a Governor.
The Backbone of the Herring (1941)

Henry St John, Lord Bolingbroke
1678–1751
English statesman

6 The great mistake is that of looking upon men as virtuous, or thinking that they can be made so by laws.
comment (c.1728) in Joseph Spence *Observations, Anecdotes, and Characters* (1820)

7 The greatest art of a politician is to render vice serviceable to the cause of virtue.
comment (c.1728) in Joseph Spence *Observations, Anecdotes, and Characters* (1820)

8 Nations, like men, have their infancy.
On the Study of History letter 5, in *Works* (1809) vol. 3

Simón Bolívar 1783–1830
Venezuelan patriot and statesman

1 A state too extensive in itself, or by virtue of its
dependencies, ultimately falls into decay; its free
government is transformed into a tyranny; it disregards
the principles which it should preserve, and finally
degenerates into despotism. The distinguishing
characteristic of small republics is stability: the character
of large republics is mutability.

Letter from Jamaica Summer 1815

2 Those who have served the cause of the revolution have
ploughed the sea.

attributed

Robert Bolt 1924–95
English playwright

3 THOMAS MORE: This country's planted thick with laws
from coast to coast—Man's laws, not God's—and if
you cut them down—and you're just the man to do
it—d'you really think you could stand upright in the
winds that would blow then?

A Man for All Seasons (1960)

Andrew Bonar Law 1858–1923
Canadian-born British Conservative statesman; Prime Minister
1922–3
on Bonar Law: see **Asquith** 18:7, **Beaverbrook** 34:7

4 If, therefore, war should ever come between these two
countries [Great Britain and Germany], which Heaven
forbid! it will not, I think, be due to irresistible natural
laws, it will be due to want of human wisdom.

in the House of Commons, 27
November 1911

5 In war it is necessary not only to be active but to seem active.

letter, 1916; Robert Blake *The
Unknown Prime Minister* (1955)

6 If I am a great man, then all great men are frauds.

Lord Beaverbrook *Politicians and
the War* (1932)

The Book of Common Prayer 1662

7 The Bishop of Rome hath no jurisdiction in this Realm of
England.

Articles of Religion (1562) no. 37

Christopher Booker 1937–
English author and journalist

8 In the life of any government, however safe its majority,
there comes a moment when the social movements of
which it had once been the expression turn inexorably
against it.... After that moment, every mistake it makes
becomes magnified; indeed blunders multiply as if feeding on
themselves; and both outwardly

The Neophiliacs (1969)

and inwardly the Government appears to be at the mercy of every wind.

1 It is a familiar pattern of history that, on the eve of revolutionary crises, the established order veers erratically between liberal concessions and recklessly reactionary steps which seem calculated to cast it in the most unfavourable light and to hasten its own destruction.

The Neophiliacs (1969)

2 Our government has recently unleashed the greatest avalanche of regulations in peacetime history; and wherever we examine their working we see that they are using a sledgehammer to miss a nut.

speech, 1995

John Wilkes Booth 1838–65

American assassin

3 *Sic semper tyrannis!* The South is avenged.
   having shot President Lincoln, 14 April 1865 ('Sic semper tyrannis [Thus always to tyrants]' — motto of the State of Virginia; the second part of the statement is possibly apocryphal)

in *New York Times* 15 April 1865

Robert Boothby 1900–86

British Conservative politician

4 *You* speak for Britain!
   to Arthur Greenwood, acting Leader of the Labour Party, after Neville Chamberlain had failed to announce an ultimatum to Germany; perhaps taking up an appeal already voiced by Leo Amery

Harold Nicolson diary 2 September 1939; cf. **Amery** 7:7

Betty Boothroyd 1929–

Labour politician; Speaker of the House of Commons since 1992

5 My desire to get here [Parliament] was like miners' coal dust, it was under my fingers and I couldn't scrub it out.

Glenys Kinnock and Fiona Millar (eds.) *By Faith and Daring* (1993)

James H. Boren 1925–

American bureaucrat

6 Guidelines for bureaucrats: (1) When in charge, ponder. (2) When in trouble, delegate. (3) When in doubt, mumble.

in *New York Times* 8 November 1970

Jorge Luis Borges 1899–1986

Argentinian writer

7 The Falklands thing was a fight between two bald men over a comb.

application of a proverbial phrase; in *Time* 14 February 1983

Cesare Borgia 1476–1507

Italian statesman

1 *Aut Caesar, aut nihil.*
Caesar or nothing.
   motto inscribed on his sword

John Leslie Garner *Caesar Borgia* (1912)

Robert H. Bork 1927–

American judge and educationalist

2 One of the uses of history is to free us of a falsely imagined past. The less we know of how ideas actually took root and grew, the more apt we are to accept them unquestioningly, as inevitable features of the world in which we move.

The Antitrust Paradox (1978)

George Borrow 1803–81

English writer

3 I am invariably of the politics of the people at whose table I sit, or beneath whose roof I sleep.

The Bible in Spain (1843)

James Boswell 1740–95

Scottish lawyer; biographer of Samuel Johnson

4 We [Boswell and Johnson] are both *Tories*; both convinced of the utility of monarchical power, and both lovers of that reverence and affection for a sovereign which constitute loyalty, a principle which I take to be absolutely extinguished in Britain.

Journal of a Tour to the Hebrides 13 September 1773

Antoine Boulay de la Meurthe 1761–1840

French statesman

on hearing of the execution of the Duc d'Enghien, 1804:
5 It is worse than a crime, it is a blunder.

C.-A. Sainte-Beuve *Nouveaux Lundis* (1870) vol. 12

Pierre Boulez 1925–

French conductor and composer

6 Revolutions are celebrated when they are no longer dangerous.

in *Guardian* 13 January 1989

Randolph Silliman Bourne 1886–1918

7 War is the health of the state. It automatically sets in motion throughout society those irresistible forces for uniformity, for passionate cooperation with the Government in coercing into obedience the minority groups and individuals which lack the larger herd sense.

The State (1918)

Lord Bowen 1835–94

British judge

1 The man on the Clapham omnibus.   in *Law Reports* (1903); attributed
   the average man

Edward Boyle 1923–81

British Conservative politician

2 Nothing in politics is ever as good or as bad as it first   William Whitelaw *Memoirs* (1989)
   appears.

Omar Bradley 1893–1981

American general

3 The way to win an atomic war is to make certain it   speech to Boston Chamber of
   never starts.   Commerce, 10 November 1948

4 We have grasped the mystery of the atom and rejected   speech on Armistice Day, 1948
   the Sermon on the Mount.

5 The world has achieved brilliance without wisdom,   speech on Armistice Day, 1948
   power without conscience. Ours is a world of nuclear
   giants and ethical infants.

6 In war there is no second prize for the runner-up.   in *Military Review* February 1950

7 This strategy would involve us in the wrong war, at the   in *US Congressional Senate
   wrong place, at the wrong time, and with the wrong   Committee on Armed Service*
   enemy.   (1951) vol. 2
   *on General Macarthur's wish to extend the Korean War into
   China*

John Bradshaw 1602–59

English judge at the trial of Charles I

8 Rebellion to tyrants is obedience to God.   suppositious epitaph; Henry S.
                                                            Randall *Life of Thomas Jefferson*
                                                            (1865) vol. 3

Edward Stuyvesant Bragg 1827–1912

American politician

9 They love him most for the enemies he has made.   speech 9 July 1884
   seconding the presidential nomination of Grover **Cleveland**

Louis D. Brandeis 1856–1941

Justice of the US Supreme Court

10 Those who won our independence believed that the final   in *Whitney v. California* (1927)
    end of the State was to make men free to develop their
    faculties; and that in its government the deliberative
    forces should prevail over the arbitrary. They valued
    liberty both as an end and as a means. They believed

liberty to be the secret of happiness and courage to be
the secret of liberty.

1 Fear of serious injury cannot alone justify suppression of
free speech and assembly. Men feared witches and burned
women. It is the function of speech to free men from the
bondage of irrational fears.

in Whitney v. California (1927)

2 They [the makers of the Constitution] conferred, as
against the Government, the right to be let alone—the
most comprehensive of rights and the right most valued
by civilized men.

in Olmstead v. United States (1928)

3 Experience should teach us to be most on our guard to
protect liberty when the government's purposes are
beneficent...the greatest dangers to liberty lurk in
insidious encroachment by men of zeal, well-meaning but
without understanding.

*dissenting opinion in Olmstead v.
United States (1928)*

4 There is in most Americans some spark of idealism,
which can be fanned into a flame. It takes sometimes
a divining rod to find what it is; but when found, and
that means often, when disclosed to the owners, the
results are often most extraordinary.

*The Words of Justice Brandeis
(1951)*

William Cowper Brann 1855–98

5 No man can be a patriot on an empty stomach.

*The Iconoclast, Old Glory 4 July
1893*

Bertolt Brecht 1898–1956

German playwright

6 ANDREA: Unhappy the land that has no heroes!...
GALILEO: No. Unhappy the land that needs heroes.

Life of Galileo (1939)

7 One observes, they have gone too long without a war
here. Where is morality to come from in such a case,
I ask? Peace is nothing but slovenliness, only war creates
order.

Mother Courage (1939)

8 The finest plans are always ruined by the littleness of
those who ought to carry them out, for the Emperors can
actually do nothing.

Mother Courage (1939)

9 War always finds a way.

Mother Courage (1939)

10 Don't tell me peace has broken out, when I've just
bought some new supplies.

Mother Courage (1939)

William Joseph Brennan Jr. 1906–

American judge

11 Debate on public issues should be uninhibited, robust,
and wide open, and that...may well include vehement,
caustic, and sometimes unpleasantly sharp attacks on
government and public officials.

*in New York Times Co. v. Sullivan
(1964)*

1 If the right of privacy means anything, it is the right of the individual, married or single, to be free from unwarranted governmental intrusion into matters so fundamentally affecting a person as the decision whether to bear or beget a child.

in Eisenstadt v. Baird (1972)

Aristide Briand 1862–1932
French statesman

2 The high contracting powers solemnly declare...that they condemn recourse to war and renounce it...as an instrument of their national policy towards each other... The settlement or the solution of all disputes or conflicts of whatever nature or of whatever origin they may be which may arise...shall never be sought by either side except by pacific means.

draft, 20 June 1927, later incorporated into the Kellogg Pact, 1928, in *Le Temps* 13 April 1928

Edward Bridges 1892–1969
British Cabinet Secretary and Head of the Civil Service

3 I confidently expect that we [civil servants] shall continue to be grouped with mothers-in-law and Wigan Pier as one of the recognized objects of ridicule.

Portrait of a Profession (1950)

John Bright 1811–89
English Liberal politician and reformer

4 The angel of death has been abroad throughout the land; you may almost hear the beating of his wings.
on the effects of the war in the Crimea

in the House of Commons, 23 February 1855

5 I am for 'Peace, retrenchment, and reform', the watchword of the great Liberal party 30 years ago.

speech at Birmingham, 28 April 1859, in *The Times* 29 April 1859; the phrase quoted may be found in Samuel Warren's novel *Ten Thousand a Year* (1841)

6 My opinion is that the Northern States will manage somehow to muddle through.
said during the American Civil War

Justin McCarthy *Reminiscences* (1899) vol. 1

7 England is the mother of Parliaments.

speech at Birmingham, 18 January 1865

of Robert Lowe, leader of the dissident Whigs opposed to the Reform Bill of 1866:
8 The right hon Gentleman...has retired into what may be called his political Cave of Adullam—and he has called about him every one that was in distress and every one that was discontented.

in the House of Commons, 13 March 1866; cf. I Samuel ch. 22

of Robert Lowe and Edward Horsman:
9 This party of two is like the Scotch terrier that was so covered with hair that you could not tell which was the head and which was the tail.

in the House of Commons, 13 March 1866

1 Force is not a remedy.

speech to the Birmingham Junior
Liberal Club, 16 November 1880, in
The Times 17 November 1880

of British foreign policy:
2 A gigantic system of outdoor relief for the aristocracy of
Great Britain.

speech at Birmingham, 29 October
1858

Vera Brittain 1893–1970

English writer

3 Politics are usually the executive expression of human
immaturity.

Rebel Passion (1964)

David Broder 1929–

American columnist

4 Anybody that wants the presidency so much that he'll
spend two years organizing and campaigning for it is not
to be trusted with the office.

in *Washington Post* 18 July 1973

D. W. Brogan 1900–74

Scottish historian

5 A people that has licked a more formidable enemy than
Germany or Japan, primitive North America...a country
whose national motto has been 'root, hog, or die.'

The American Character (1944)

6 Any well-established village in New England or the
northern Middle West could afford a town drunkard,
a town atheist, and a few Democrats.

The American Character (1944)

Henry Brooke 1703–83

Irish poet and playwright

7 For righteous monarchs,
Justly to judge, with their own eyes should see;
To rule o'er freemen, should themselves be free.

Earl of Essex (performed 1750,
published 1761)

Robert Barnabas Brough 1828–60

English satirical writer

8 My Lord Tomnoddy is thirty-four;
The Earl can last but a few years more.
My Lord in the Peers will take his place:
Her Majesty's councils his words will grace.
Office he'll hold and patronage sway;
Fortunes and lives he will vote away;
And what are his qualifications?—ONE!
He's the Earl of Fitzdotterel's eldest son.

Songs of the Governing Classes
(1855) 'My Lord Tomnoddy'

Lord Brougham 1778–1868

Scottish lawyer and politician; Lord Chancellor 1830–4
on Brougham: see **Melbourne** 255:6, 255:7

1 In my mind, he was guilty of no error—he was
chargeable with no exaggeration—he was betrayed by
his fancy into no metaphor, who once said, that all we
see about us, King, Lords, and Commons, the whole
machinery of the State, all the apparatus of the system,
and its varied workings, end in simply bringing twelve
good men into a box.

in the House of Commons, 7 February 1828

2 Education makes a people easy to lead, but difficult to
drive; easy to govern, but impossible to enslave.

attributed

Heywood Broun 1888–1939

American journalist

3 Just as every conviction begins as a whim so does every
emancipator serve his apprenticeship as a crank. A
fanatic is a great leader who is just entering the room.

in New York World 6 February 1928

4 Appeasers believe that if you keep on throwing steaks to
a tiger, the tiger will turn vegetarian.

attributed

George Brown 1914–85

British Labour politician

5 I've seen MPs on both sides of the House obviously
having to create a sensation on Thursday in order to
have a peg on which to hang an article for Sunday.
  on Members of Parliament who were also journalists

In My Way (1971)

Gordon Brown 1951–

British Labour politician

6 Ideas which stress the growing importance of
international cooperation and new theories of economic
sovereignty across a wide range of areas—
macroeconomics, the environment, the growth of post
neo-classical endogenous growth theory and the
symbiotic relationships between growth and investment
in people and infrastructure.

New Labour Economics speech, September 1994, 'winner' of the ironic Plain English No Nonsense Award for 1994

H. Rap Brown 1943–

American Black Power leader

7 I say violence is necessary. It is as American as cherry
pie.

speech at Washington, 27 July 1967, in Washington Post 28 July 1967

John Brown 1800–59

American abolitionist

1 Had I so interfered in behalf of the rich, the powerful, the intelligent, the so-called great, or in behalf of any of their friends...every man in this court would have deemed it an act worthy of reward rather than punishment.
   last speech to the court at his trial

on 2 November 1859

2 I am yet too young to understand that God is any respecter of persons.
   last speech to the court at his trial

on 2 November 1859

3 If it is deemed necessary that I should forfeit my life for the furtherance of the ends of justice, and mingle my blood further with the blood of my children, and with the blood of millions in this slave country whose rights are disregarded by wicked, cruel, and most unjust enactments, I submit: so let it be done!
   last speech to the court at his trial

on 2 November 1859

4 This *is* a beautiful country!
   as he rode to the gallows, seated on his coffin

at his execution on 2 December 1859

Joseph Brown 1821–94

American politician; Confederate Governor of Georgia during the Civil War

refusing to accept the Confederate President Jefferson **Davis***'s call for a day of national fasting:*
5 I entered into this Revolution to contribute my mite to sustain the rights of states and prevent the consolidation of the Government, and I am *still* a rebel...no matter who may be in power.

in 1863; Geoffrey C. Ward *The Civil War* (1991)

William Browne 1692–1774

English physician and writer

6 The King to Oxford sent a troop of horse,
   For Tories own no argument but force:
   With equal skill to Cambridge books he sent,
   For Whigs admit no force but argument.

reply to Trapp's epigram, in J. Nichols *Literary Anecdotes* vol. 3; cf. **Trapp** 367:6

Frederick 'Boy' Browning 1896–1965

British soldier and courtier; husband of Daphne du Maurier

expressing reservations about the Arnhem 'Market Garden' operation to Field Marshal Montgomery on 10 September 1944:
7 I think we might be going a bridge too far.

R. E. Urquhart *Arnhem* (1958)

Robert Browning 1812–89

English poet

1 Just for a handful of silver he left us,
Just for a riband to stick in his coat.
of **Wordsworth**'s *implied abandonment of radical principles by*
his acceptance of the Laureateship

'The Lost Leader' (1845)

2 Life's night begins: let him never come back to us!
There would be doubt, hesitation and pain,
Forced praise on our part—the glimmer of twilight,
Never glad confident morning again!

'The Lost Leader' (1845); cf.
Birch 45:10

Louis Brownlow 1879–1963

of presidential aides (from advice given by Stanley **Baldwin**'s
private secretary Tom Jones):

3 They should be possessed of high competence, great
physical vigour, and a passion for anonymity.

in *Administrative Management in
the Government of the United
States: Report of the President's
Committee on Administrative
Management* January 1937

William Jennings Bryan 1860–1925

American Democratic politician; a fervent proponent of
bimetallism as an alternative to the gold standard

4 The humblest citizen of all the land, when clad in the
armour of a righteous cause, is stronger than all the
hosts of error.

speech at the Democratic National
Convention, Chicago, 1896

5 Destroy our farms and the grass will grow in the streets
of every city in the country.

speech at the Democratic National
Convention, Chicago 1896; cf.
Hoover 182:10

6 You shall not press down upon the brow of labour this
crown of thorns, you shall not crucify mankind upon
a cross of gold.

speech at the Democratic National
Convention, Chicago, 1896

Arthur Bryant 1899–1985

English historical writer

7 The great German whom fate has raised up to rescue his
people.
of Adolf **Hitler**

Andrew Roberts *Eminent
Churchillians* (1994)

8 Liberty does not consist merely of denouncing Tyranny,
any more than horticulture does of deploring and
abusing weeds, or even pulling them out.

in *Illustrated London News* 24 June
1939

of England in 1699:
9 A world of hedges, squires and parsons, of yeomen,
cottages and ragged squatters, making their wares and
pleasures after the manner of their forefathers.

Protestant Island (1967)

James Bryce 1838–1922

British historian and diplomat

1 Europeans often ask, and Americans do not often explain, how it happens that this great office [the presidency], the greatest in the world, unless we except the Papacy, to which any man can rise by his own merits, is not more frequently filled by great and striking men.

The American Commonwealth (1888) vol. 1

2 The government of cities is the one conspicuous failure of the United States.

The American Commonwealth (1888) vol. 1

Zbigniew Brzezinski 1928–

US Secretary of State and National Security Advisor

3 Russia can be an empire or a democracy, but it cannot be both.

in *Foreign Affairs* March/April 1994 'The Premature Partnership'

Frank Buchman 1878–1961

American evangelist; founder of the Moral Re-Armament movement

4 I thank heaven for a man like Adolf Hitler, who built a front line of defence against the anti-Christ of Communism.

in *New York World-Telegram* 26 August 1936

Gerald Bullett

British writer

5 My Lord Archbishop, what a scold you are!
And when your man is down how bold you are!
Of charity how oddly scant you are!
How Lang, O Lord, how full of Cantuar!
  on the role of Cosmo Gordon Lang, Archbishop of Canterbury, in the abdication of Edward VIII

in 1936

Ivor Bulmer-Thomas 1905–93

British Conservative politician

of Harold **Wilson**:

6 If he ever went to school without any boots it was because he was too big for them.

speech at the Conservative Party Conference, in *Manchester Guardian* 13 October 1949

Prince Bernhard von Bülow 1849–1929

Chancellor of Germany, 1900–9

7 In a word, we desire to throw no one into the shade [in East Asia], but we also demand our own place in the sun.

speech in the Reichstag, 6 December 1897; cf. **Wilhelm II** 388:9

Edward George Bulwer-Lytton 1803–73

British novelist and politician

1   Here Stanley meets,—how Stanley scorns, the glance!   *The New Timon* (1846); cf. **Disraeli**
    The brilliant chief, irregularly great,   117:14
    Frank, haughty, rash,—the Rupert of Debate!
    on Edward Stanley, 14th Earl of **Derby**

Samuel Dickinson Burchard 1812–91

American Presbyterian minister

2   We are Republicans and don't propose to leave our party   speech at the Fifth Avenue Hotel,
    and identify ourselves with the party whose antecedents   New York, 29 October 1884
    are rum, Romanism, and rebellion.

Edmund Burke 1729–97

Irish-born Whig politician and man of letters
on Burke: see **Gibbon** 151:14, **Johnson** 198:11, **O'Brien** 276:5,
Paine 282:4, 283:4

3   No passion so effectually robs the mind of all its powers   *On the Sublime and Beautiful*
    of acting and reasoning as fear.   (1757)

4   In all forms of Government the people is the true   *A Tract on the Popery Laws*
    legislator.   (planned c.1765)

5   Laws, like houses, lean on one another.   *A Tract on the Popery Laws*
                                                                 (planned c.1765)

6   People must be governed in a manner agreeable to their   *Observation on a Late Publication
    temper and disposition; and men of free character and   entitled 'The Present State of the
    spirit must be ruled with, at least, some condescension to   Nation'* (1769)
    this spirit and this character.

7   It is a general popular error to imagine the loudest   *Observations on a late Publication
    complainers for the public to be the most anxious for its   on the Present State of the Nation*
    welfare.   (2nd ed., 1769)

8   There is, however, a limit at which forbearance ceases to   *Observations on a late Publication
    be a virtue.   on the Present State of the Nation*
                                                                 (2nd ed., 1769)

9   If ever there was in all the proceedings of government   in the House of Commons, 9 May
    a rule that is fundamental, universal, invariable it is this: 1770
    that you ought never to attempt a measure of authority
    you are not morally sure you can go through with.

10 To complain of the age we live in, to murmur at the   *Thoughts on the Cause of the
    present possessors of power, to lament the past, to   Present Discontents* (1770)
    conceive extravagant hopes of the future, are the
    common dispositions of the greatest part of mankind.

11 I am not one of those who think that the people are   *Thoughts on the Cause of the
    never in the wrong. They have been so, frequently and   Present Discontents* (1770)
    outrageously, both in other countries and in this. But
    I do say, that in all disputes between them and their
    rulers, the presumption is at least upon a par in favour of
    the people.

1 The power of the crown, almost dead and rotten as
   Prerogative, has grown up anew, with much more
   strength, and far less odium, under the name of
   Influence.

   Thoughts on the Cause of the
   Present Discontents (1770)

2 We must soften into a credulity below the milkiness of
   infancy to think all men virtuous. We must be tainted
   with a malignity truly diabolical, to believe all the world
   to be equally wicked and corrupt.

   Thoughts on the Cause of the
   Present Discontents (1770)

3 When ... [people] imagine that their food is only a cover
   for poison, and when they neither love nor trust the
   hand that serves it, it is not the name of the roast beef of
   old England that will persuade them to sit down to the
   table that is spread for them.

   Thoughts on the Cause of the
   Present Discontents (1770)

4 When bad men combine, the good must associate; else
   they will fall, one by one, an unpitied sacrifice in
   a contemptible struggle.

   Thoughts on the Cause of the
   Present Discontents (1770)

5 Of this stamp is the cant of *Not men, but measures*; a sort
   of charm by which many people get loose from every
   honourable engagement.

   Thoughts on the Cause of the
   Present Discontents (1770); cf.
   Canning 74:9

6 It is therefore our business carefully to cultivate in our
   minds, to rear to the most perfect vigour and maturity,
   every sort of generous and honest feeling that belongs to
   our nature. To bring the dispositions that are lovely in
   private life into the service and conduct of the
   commonwealth; so to be patriots, as not to forget we are
   gentlemen.

   Thoughts on the Cause of the
   Present Discontents (1770)

7 The greater the power, the more dangerous the abuse.

   speech on the Middlesex Election,
   7 February 1771

8 Your representative owes you, not his industry only, but
   his judgement; and he betrays, instead of serving you, if
   he sacrifices it to your opinion.

   speech, 3 November 1774, in
   Speeches at his Arrival at Bristol
   (1774)

9 Abstract liberty, like other mere abstractions, is not to be
   found.

   On Conciliation with America
   (1775)

10 All Protestantism, even the most cold and passive, is
   a sort of dissent. But the religion most prevalent in our
   northern colonies is a refinement on the principle of
   resistance; it is the dissidence of dissent, and the
   Protestantism of the Protestant religion.

   On Conciliation with America
   (1775)

11 By adverting to the dignity of this high calling, our
   ancestors have turned a savage wilderness into a glorious
   empire: and have made the most extensive, and the only
   honourable conquests; not by destroying, but by
   promoting the wealth, the number, the happiness of the
   human race.

   On Conciliation with America
   (1775)

12 Deny them this participation of freedom, and you break
   that sole bond, which originally made, and must still
   preserve the unity of the empire.

   On Conciliation with America
   (1775)

1 Freedom and not servitude is the cure of anarchy; as religion, and not atheism, is the true remedy for superstition.

On Conciliation with America (1775)

2 I do not know the method of drawing up an indictment against an whole people.

On Conciliation with America (1775)

3 I have in general no very exalted opinion of the virtue of paper government.

On Conciliation with America (1775)

4 Instead of a standing revenue, you will have therefore a perpetual quarrel.

On Conciliation with America (1775)

5 It is not, what a lawyer tells me I *may* do; but what humanity, reason, and justice, tells me I ought to do.

On Conciliation with America (1775)

6 It is the love of the people; it is their attachment to their government, from the sense of the deep stake they have in such a glorious institution, which gives you your army and your navy, and infuses into both that liberal obedience, without which your army would be a base rabble, and your navy nothing but rotten timber.

On Conciliation with America (1775)

7 Magnanimity in politics is not seldom the truest wisdom; and a great empire and little minds go ill together.

On Conciliation with America (1775)

8 Nothing less will content me, than *whole America.*

On Conciliation with America (1775)

9 Parties must ever exist in a free country.

On Conciliation with America (1775)

10 Slavery they can have anywhere. It is a weed that grows in every soil.

On Conciliation with America (1775)

11 The concessions of the weak are the concessions of fear.

On Conciliation with America (1775)

12 The use of force alone is but *temporary.* It may subdue for a moment; but it does not remove the necessity of subduing again; and a nation is not governed, which is perpetually to be conquered.

On Conciliation with America (1775)

13 When we speak of the commerce with our colonies, fiction lags after truth; invention is unfruitful, and imagination cold and barren.

On Conciliation with America (1775)

14 It is the nature of all greatness not to be exact; and great trade will always be attended with considerable abuses.

On American Taxation (1775)

15 To tax and to please, no more than to love and to be wise, is not given to men.

On American Taxation (1775)

16 Bodies tied together by so unnatural a bond of union as mutual hatred are only connected to their ruin.

Letter to the Sheriffs of Bristol (1777)

17 I was persuaded that government was a practical thing made for the happiness of mankind, and not to furnish out a spectacle of uniformity to gratify the schemes of visionary politicians.

Letter to the Sheriffs of Bristol (1777)

18 Among a people generally corrupt, liberty cannot long exist.

Letter to the Sheriffs of Bristol (1777)

1 Liberty too must be limited in order to be possessed.   *Letter to the Sheriffs of Bristol*
                                                                (1777)

2 Nothing in progression can rest on its original plan. We   *Letter to the Sheriffs of Bristol*
   may as well think of rocking a grown man in the cradle   (1777)
   of an infant.

3 People crushed by law have no hopes but from power. If   letter to Charles James Fox, 8
   laws are their enemies, they will be enemies to laws; and   October 1777
   those, who have much to hope and nothing to lose, will
   always be dangerous, more or less.

4 Bad laws are the worst sort of tyranny.   *Speech at Bristol, previous to the
                                                                Late Election* (1780)

5 The people are the masters.   in the House of Commons, 11
                                                                February 1780

   of the younger **Pitt***'s maiden speech, February 1781:*
6 Not merely a chip of the old 'block', but the old block   N. W. Wraxall *Historical Memoirs of
   itself.   My Own Time* (1904 ed.)

7 I feel an insuperable reluctance in giving my hand to   in the House of Commons on Fox's
   destroy any established institution of government, upon   East India Bill, 1 December 1783
   a theory, however plausible it may be.

8 Men will not look to acts of parliament, to regulations, to in the House of Commons on Fox's
   declarations, to votes, and resolutions. No, they are not   East India Bill, 1 December 1783
   such fools. They will ask, what is the road to power,
   credit, wealth, and honours. They will ask, what conduct
   ends in neglect, disgrace, poverty, exile, prison, and
   gibbet? These will teach them the course which they are
   to follow. It is your distribution of these that will give the
   character and tone to your government. All the rest is
   miserable grimace.

9 Every other conqueror of every other description has left   in the House of Commons, 1
   some monument, either of state or beneficence, behind   December 1783
   him. Were we to be driven out of India this day, nothing
   would remain to tell that it had been possessed, during
   the inglorious period of our dominion, by anything better
   than the orang-outang or the tiger.
   speech on Fox's East India Bill

10 The people never give up their liberties but under some   speech at County Meeting of
   delusion.   Buckinghamshire, 1784, attributed
                                                                in E. Latham *Famous Sayings*
                                                                (1904), with 'except' substituted
                                                                for 'but'

11 The laws of morality are the same everywhere, and...   opening speech at impeachment of
   there is no action which would pass for an act of   Warren Hastings, 16 February 1788
   extortion, of peculation, of bribery, and of oppression in
   England, that is not an act of extortion, of peculation, of
   bribery and oppression in Europe, Asia, Africa, and all
   the world over.

12 Where two motives, neither of them perfectly justifiable,   opening speech, impeachment of
   may be assigned, the worst has the chance of being   Warren Hastings, House of
   preferred.   Commons 13 February 1788

1 You strike at the whole corps, if you strike at the head.

opening speech, impeachment of Warren Hastings, House of Commons 13 February 1788

2 Never wholly separate in your mind the merits of any political question from the men who are concerned in it. You will be told, that if a measure is good, what have you [to] do with the character and views of those who bring it forward. But designing men never separate their plans from their interests.

letter to Charles-Jean-François Depont, November 1789

3 There is a mob of their constituents ready to hang them if they should deviate into moderation.

letter 27 September 1789

4 An event has happened, upon which it is difficult to speak, and impossible to be silent.

speech, 5 May 1789; E. A. Bond (ed.) *Speeches...in the Trial of Warren Hastings* (1859) vol. 2

5 At last dying in the last dyke of prevarication.

speech, 7 May 1789; E. A. Bond (ed.) *Speeches...in the Trial of Warren Hastings* (1859) vol. 2

6 I flatter myself that I love a manly, moral, regulated liberty as well as any gentleman.

Reflections on the Revolution in France (1790)

7 Whenever our neighbour's house is on fire, it cannot be amiss for the engines to play a little on our own.

Reflections on the Revolution in France (1790)

8 A state without the means of some change is without the means of its conservation.

Reflections on the Revolution in France (1790)

9 Make the Revolution a parent of settlement, and not a nursery of future revolutions.

Reflections on the Revolution in France (1790)

10 People will not look forward to posterity, who never look backward to their ancestors.

Reflections on the Revolution in France (1790)

11 Those who attempt to level never equalize.

Reflections on the Revolution in France (1790)

12 Government is a contrivance of human wisdom to provide for human *wants*. Men have a right that these wants should be provided for by this wisdom.

Reflections on the Revolution in France (1790)

13 Flattery corrupts both the receiver and the giver.

Reflections on the Revolution in France (1790)

14 This sort of people are so taken up with their theories about the rights of man, that they have totally forgotten his nature.

Reflections on the Revolution in France 1790

of **Marie-Antoinette**:
15 I thought ten thousand swords must have leapt from their scabbards to avenge even a look that threatened her with insult.

Reflections on the Revolution in France (1790)

16 The age of chivalry is gone.—That of sophisters, economists, and calculators, has succeeded; and the glory of Europe is extinguished for ever.

Reflections on the Revolution in France (1790)

17 This barbarous philosophy, which is the offspring of cold hearts and muddy understandings.

Reflections on the Revolution in France (1790)

1 In the groves of *their* academy, at the end of every vista, *Reflections on the Revolution in*
   you see nothing but the gallows.   *France* (1790)

2 Kings will be tyrants from policy when subjects are rebels *Reflections on the Revolution in*
   from principle.   *France* (1790)

3 Because half a dozen grasshoppers under a fern make the *Reflections on the Revolution in*
   field ring with their importunate chink, whilst thousands *France* (1790)
   of great cattle, reposed beneath the shadow of the British
   oak, chew the cud and are silent, pray do not imagine
   that those who make the noise are the only inhabitants
   of the field.

4 A perfect democracy is therefore the most shameless *Reflections on the Revolution in*
   thing in the world.   *France* (1790)

5 Society is indeed a contract...it becomes a partnership *Reflections on the Revolution in*
   not only between those who are living, but between   *France* (1790)
   those who are living, those who are dead, and those who
   are to be born.

6 Nobility is a graceful ornament to the civil order. It is the *Reflections on the Revolution in*
   Corinthian capital of polished society.   *France* (1790)

7 History consists, for the greater part, of the miseries *Reflections on the Revolution in*
   brought upon the world by pride, ambition, avarice, *France* (1790)
   revenge, lust, sedition, hypocrisy, ungoverned zeal, and
   all the train of disorderly appetites...these vices are the
   causes of those storms. Religion, morals, laws,
   prerogatives, privileges, liberties, rights of men, are the
   pretexts.

8 By hating vices too much, they come to love men too *Reflections on the Revolution in*
   little.   *France* (1790)

9 We begin our public affections in our families. No cold *Reflections on the Revolution in*
   relation is a zealous citizen.   *France* (1790)

10 Good order is the foundation of all good things.   *Reflections on the Revolution in*
                                                       France (1790)

11 Every politician ought to sacrifice to the graces; and to *Reflections on the Revolution in*
   join compliance with reason.   *France* (1790)

12 Nothing turns out to be so oppressive and unjust as *Reflections on the Revolution in*
   a feeble government.   *France* (1790)

13 The conduct of a losing party never appears right: at *Letter to a Member of the National*
   least it never can possess the only infallible criterion of *Assembly* (1791)
   wisdom to vulgar judgements—success.

14 Those who have been once intoxicated with power, and *Letter to a Member of the National*
   have derived any kind of emolument from it, even   *Assembly* (1791)
   though for but one year, can never willingly abandon it.

15 Tyrants seldom want pretexts.   *Letter to a Member of the National*
                                                       Assembly (1791)

16 You can never plan the future by the past.   *Letter to a Member of the National*
                                                       Assembly (1791)

17 Somebody has said, that a king may make a nobleman letter to William Smith, 29 January
   but he cannot make a gentleman.   1795

1 All men that are ruined are ruined on the side of their natural propensities.

Two Letters on the Proposals for Peace with the Regicide Directory (9th ed., 1796)

2 Falsehood and delusion are allowed in no case whatsoever: But, as in the exercise of all the virtues, there is an economy of truth.

Two Letters on the Proposals for Peace with the Regicide Directory (9th ed., 1796); cf. **Armstrong** 16:12

3 The king, and his faithful subjects, the lords and commons of this realm,—the triple cord, which no man can break.

A Letter to a Noble Lord (1796)

4 To innovate is not to reform.

A Letter to a Noble Lord (1796)

5 Well is it known that ambition can creep as well as soar.

Third Letter... on the Proposals for Peace with the Regicide Directory (1797)

6 And having looked to government for bread, on the very first scarcity they will turn and bite the hand that fed them.

Thoughts and Details on Scarcity (1800)

7 It is necessary only for the good man to do nothing for evil to triumph.

attributed (in a number of forms) to Burke, but not found in his writings.

8 It is the interest of the commercial world that wealth should be found everywhere.

The Correspondence of Edmund Burke (1958–78) vol. 3

John Burns 1858–1943

British Labour politician

9 I have seen the Mississippi. That is muddy water. I have seen the St Lawrence. That is crystal water. But the Thames is liquid history.

in *Daily Mail* 25 January 1943

Robert Burns 1759–96

Scottish poet

10 The rank is but the guinea's stamp,
The man's the gowd for a' that!

'For a' that and a' that' (1790)

11 A fig for those by law protected!
LIBERTY's a glorious feast!
Courts for cowards were erected,
Churches built to please the PRIEST.

'The Jolly Beggars' (1799)

12 Liberty's in every blow!
Let us do—or die!!!

'Robert Bruce's March to Bannockburn' (1799)

13 We labour soon, we labour late,
To feed the titled knave, man;
And a' the comfort we're to get,
Is that ayont the grave, man.

'The Tree of Liberty' (1838)

Aaron Burr 1756–1836

American politician

1 Law is whatever is boldly asserted and plausibly   attributed
  maintained.

Ian Buruma 1951–

2 She did much to replace birth as a mark of distinction   in *The New York Review of Books*
  with money.   20 October 1994 'Action Anglaise'
  of Margaret **Thatcher**

Barbara Bush 1925–

wife of George **Bush**; First Lady 1989–93

3 Somewhere out in this audience may even be someone   at Wellesley College
  who will one day follow in my footsteps, and preside over Commencement, 1 June 1990
  the White House as the President's spouse. I wish him
  well!

  asked why she thought she was a popular First Lady:
4 It was because I threatened no one. I was old, white-   in *Independent on Sunday* 4
  headed and large.   December 1994 'Quotes of the
                                                             Week'

George Bush 1924–

American Republican statesman; 41st President of the US,
1989–93
on Bush: see **Richards** 305:2

5 Oh, the vision thing.   in *Time* 26 January 1987
  responding to the suggestion that he turn his attention from
  short-term campaign objectives and look to the longer term.

6 We are a nation of communities, of tens and tens of   acceptance speech at the
  thousands of ethnic, religious, social, business, labour   Republican National Convention in
  union, neighbourhood, regional and other organizations,   New Orleans, 18 August 1988
  all of them varied, voluntary, and unique...a brilliant
  diversity spread like stars, like a thousand points of light
  in a broad and peaceful sky.

7 Read my lips: no new taxes.   in *New York Times* 19 August 1988
  accepting the Republican nomination

8 Giving peace a chance does not mean taking a chance on   in *Guardian* 21 August 1990
  peace.
  to the Veterans of Foreign Wars Convention in Baltimore, 20
  August 1990

9 The continent, frozen in hostility for so long, has become in *Guardian* 23 November 1990
  a continent of revolutionary change.

David Butler 1924–

British political scientist

1 Has he got a resignation in him?
of James **Callaghan**, *to Hugh* **Dalton**

Hugh Dalton *Political Diary* (1986)
13 July 1960

R. A. ('Rab') Butler 1902–82

British Conservative politician
on Butler: see **Hennessy** 175:1, **Macmillan** 245:12

on hearing of the appointment of Winston **Churchill** *as Prime
Minister in succession to Neville* **Chamberlain**:
2 The good clean tradition of English politics, that of Pitt as
opposed to Fox, has been sold to the greatest adventurer
of modern political history.

John Colville *The Fringes of Power,
Downing Street Diaries
1939–1955* (1985) 10 May 1940

3 REPORTER: Mr Butler, would you say that this [Anthony
Eden] is the best Prime Minister we have?
R A BUTLER: Yes.
interview at London Airport, 8 January 1956

R. A. Butler *The Art of the Possible*
(1971)

4 The Civil Service is a bit like a Rolls-Royce—you know
it's the best machine in the world, but you're not quite
sure what to do with it.

Anthony Sampson *Anatomy of
Britain* (1962)

5 I think a Prime Minister has to be a butcher and know
the joints. That is perhaps where I have not been quite
competent, in knowing all the ways that you can cut up
a carcass.

in *Listener* 28 June 1966

6 I cannot help feeling that a man who always held all the
bridge scores in his head, who seemed to know all the
numbers, and played *vingt et un* so successfully would
have been useful.
on Iain **Macleod***'s likely success as Chancellor*

The Art of Memory (1982)

7 I especially like Gibbon on the Christians. They really had
nothing to offer except bishops and the after-life, but they
pushed on and came through rather well.

John Mortimer *In Character*
'Remember Compassion'

8 Politics is largely a matter of heart.

Peter Hennessy in *Independent* 8
May 1987

9 In politics you must always keep running with the pack.
The moment that you falter and they sense that you are
injured, the rest will turn on you like wolves.

Dennis Walters *Not Always with
the Pack* (1989)

John Byrom 1692–1763

English poet

10 God bless the King, I mean the Faith's Defender;
God bless—no harm in blessing—the Pretender;
But who Pretender is, or who is King,
God bless us all—that's quite another thing.

'To an Officer in the Army,
Extempore, Intended to allay the
Violence of Party-Spirit' (1773)

Lord Byron 1788–1824

English poet

1 I have no consistency, except in politics; and *that*   letter 16 January 1814
   probably arises from my indifference on the subject
   altogether.

2 The Cincinnatus of the West.   'Ode to Napoleon Bonaparte'
   of George **Washington**   (1814)

3 The arbiter of others' fate   'Ode to Napoleon Bonaparte'
   A suppliant for his own!   (1814)

4 So he has cut his throat at last!—He! Who?   'Epigram on Lord Castlereagh'
   The man who cut his country's long ago.
   on Castlereagh's suicide, c.1822

5 For what were all these country patriots born?   'The Age of Bronze' (1823)
   To hunt, and vote, and raise the price of corn?

6 Year after year they voted cent per cent   'The Age of Bronze' (1823)
   Blood, sweat, and tear-wrung millions—why? for rent!

Julius Caesar 100–44 BC

Roman general and statesman

7 *Gallia est omnis divisa in partes tres.*   *De Bello Gallico*
   Gaul as a whole is divided into three parts.

8 Men are nearly always willing to believe what they wish.   *De Bello Gallico*

9 Caesar's wife must be above suspicion.   oral tradition, based on Plutarch
                                                                  Parallel Lives 'Julius Caesar'

10 Caesar, when he first went into Gaul, made no scruple to   Francis Bacon *The Advancement of
   profess 'That he had rather be first in a village than   Learning* (based on Plutarch
   second at Rome'.   *Parallel Lives* 'Julius Caesar')

11 The die is cast.   Suetonius *Lives of the Caesars*
   at the crossing of the Rubicon   'Divus Julius' (often quoted in Latin
                                                                  'Iacta alea est' but originally
                                                                  spoken in Greek)

12 *Veni, vidi, vici.*   inscription displayed in Caesar's
   I came, I saw, I conquered.   Pontic triumph, according to
                                                                  Suetonius *Lives of the Caesars*
                                                                  'Divus Julius'; or, according to
                                                                  Plutarch *Parallel Lives* 'Julius
                                                                  Caesar', written in a letter by
                                                                  Caesar, announcing the victory of
                                                                  Zela which concluded the Pontic
                                                                  campaign

13 *Et tu, Brute?*   traditional rendering of Suetonius
   You too, Brutus?   *Lives of the Caesars* 'Divus Julius':
                                                                  'Some have written that when
                                                                  Marcus Brutus rushed at him, he
                                                                  said in Greek, "You too, my child?"'

Joseph Cairns 1920–

British industrialist and politician

1 The betrayal of Ulster, the cynical and entirely
undemocratic banishment of its properly elected
Parliament and a relegation to the status of a fuzzy
wuzzy colony is, I hope, a last betrayal contemplated by
Downing Street because it is the last that Ulster will
countenance.
speech on retiring as Lord Mayor of Belfast, 31 May 1972

in Daily Telegraph 1 June 1972

John Caldwell Calhoun 1782–1850

American politician
on Calhoun: see Jackson 189:5

2 The very essence of a free government consists in
considering offices as public trusts, bestowed for the good
of the country, and not for the benefit of an individual or
party.

speech 13 February 1835

3 A power has risen up in the government greater than the
people themselves, consisting of many and various and
powerful interests, combined into one mass, and held
together by the cohesive power of the vast surplus in the
banks.

speech 27 May 1836

4 The surrender of life is nothing to sinking down into
acknowledgement of inferiority.

speech in the Senate, 19 February 1847

Caligula (Gaius Julius Caesar Germanicus) AD 12–41

Roman emperor from AD 37

5 Would that the Roman people had but one neck!

Suetonius Lives of the Caesars 'Gaius Caligula'

James Callaghan 1912–

British Labour statesman; Prime Minister 1976–9
on Callaghan: see Butler 70:1, Jenkins 194:2; cf. also Anonymous 9:10

6 Leaking is what you do; briefing is what I do.
when giving evidence to the Franks Committee on Official Secrecy in 1971

Franks Report (1972); oral evidence

7 We say that what Britain needs is a new social contract.
That is what this document [Labour's Programme for Britain] is about.

speech at Labour Party Annual Conference, 2 October 1972

8 You cannot now, if you ever could, spend your way out
of a recession.

speech at Labour Party Conference, 28 September 1976

9 You never reach the promised land. You can march
towards it.

in a television interview, 20 July 1978

1   It's the first time in recorded history that turkeys have   in the House of Commons, 28
    been known to vote for an early Christmas.   March 1979
      in the debate resulting in the fall of the Labour government,
      when the pact between Labour and the Liberals had collapsed,
      and the Nationalists also withdrew their support in the wake of
      the failure of the devolution bills

    of the popularity of Mrs **Thatcher**:
2   The further you got from Britain, the more admired you   in *Spectator* 1 December 1990
    found she was.

3   Well, it works, doesn't it? So I think that's the answer,   Peter Hennessy and Simon Coates
    even if it is on the back of an envelope and doesn't have   *The Back of the Envelope* (1991)
    a written constitution with every comma and every semi-
    colon in place. Because sometimes they can make for
    difficulties that common sense can overcome.

Italo Calvino 1923–85

Italian novelist and short-story writer

4   Revolutionaries are more formalistic than conservatives.   *Il Barone Rampante* (1957)

Lord Camden 1714–94

British Whig politician; Lord Chancellor, 1766–70

5   Taxation and representation are inseparable…whatever   in the House of Lords, 10 February
    is a man's own, is absolutely his own; no man hath   1766
    a right to take it from him without his consent either
    expressed by himself or representative; whoever attempts
    to do it, attempts an injury; whoever does it, commits
    a robbery; he throws down and destroys the distinction
    between liberty and slavery.
      on the taxation of Americans by the British parliament

Simon Cameron 1799–1889

American politician

6   An honest politician is one who when he's bought stays   attributed
    bought.

Lord Campbell of Eskan 1912–

British industrialist

7   The only justification of the [House of] Lords is its   Anthony Sampson *The Changing*
    irrationality: once you try to make it rational, you satisfy   *Anatomy of Britain* (1982)
    no one.

Thomas Campbell 1777–1844

Scottish poet

8   What millions died—that Caesar might be great!   *Pleasures of Hope* (1799)

Timothy Campbell 1840–1904

American politician

1 What's the Constitution between friends?   attributed, c.1885
   reported response to President **Cleveland***'s refusing to support
   a bill on the grounds of its being unconstitutional*

Henry Campbell-Bannerman 1836–1908

British Liberal statesman, Prime Minister 1905–8
on Campbell-Bannerman: see **Asquith** 18:9, **Balfour** 30:5

2 There is a phrase which seems in itself somewhat self-   speech to National Reform Union,
   evident, which is often used to account for a good deal—   14 June 1901
   that 'war is war' But when you come to ask about it,
   then you are told that the war now going on is not war.
   [Laughter] When is a war not a war? When it is carried
   on by methods of barbarism in South Africa.

3 Good government could never be a substitute for   speech at Stirling, 23 November
   government by the people themselves.   1905

4 No more tact than a hippopotamus...Haldane always   attributed
   prefers the backstairs. But it does not matter. The clatter
   can be heard all over the house.
   of R. B. **Haldane**

Albert Camus 1913–60

French novelist, playwright, and essayist

5 Politics and the fate of mankind are formed by men   *Carnets, 1935–42* (1962)
   without ideals and without greatness. Those who have
   greatness within them do not go in for politics.

6 What is a rebel? A man who says no.   *L'Homme révolté* (1951)

7 All modern revolutions have ended in a reinforcement of   *L'Homme révolté* (1951)
   the State.

8 Every revolutionary ends as an oppressor or a heretic.   *L'Homme révolté* (1951)

George Canning 1770–1827

British Tory statesman; Prime Minister, 1827

9 Away with the cant of 'Measures not men'!—the idle   *Speeches of... Canning* (1828) vol.
   supposition that it is the harness and not the horses that   2; the phrase 'measures not men'
   draw the chariot along. If the comparison must be made,   may be found as early as 1742 (in
   if the distinction must be taken, men are everything,   a letter from Chesterfield to Dr
   measures comparatively nothing.   Chevenix, 6 March); also in
   speech on the Army estimates, 8 December 1802   Goldsmith *The Good Natured Man*
                                                                (1768), 'Measures not men, have
                                                                always been my mark'; cf.
                                                                Burke 63:5

10 Pitt is to Addington   'The Oracle' (c.1803)
   As London is to Paddington.

1   A steady patriot of the world alone,   'New Morality' (1821)
    The friend of every country but his own.
      on the Jacobin

2   And finds, with keen discriminating sight,   'New Morality' (1821)
    Black's not so black;—nor white so very white.

3   In matters of commerce the fault of the Dutch   dispatch, in cipher, to the English
    Is offering too little and asking too much.   ambassador at the Hague, 31
    The French are with equal advantage content,   January 1826; Harry Poland *Mr*
    So we clap on Dutch bottoms just twenty per cent.   *Canning's Rhyming 'Dispatch' to*
                                                             Sir Charles Bagot (1905)

4   I called the New World into existence, to redress the   in the House of Commons, 12
    balance of the Old.   December 1826
      speech on the affairs of Portugal

5   [The Whip's duty is] to make a House, and keep   J. E. Ritchie *Modern Statesmen*
    a House, and cheer the minister.   (1861)

Al Capone 1899–1947

Italian-born American gangster, notorious for his domination of
organized crime in Chicago in the 1920s

6   Don't you get the idea I'm one of these goddam radicals. interview, *c.*1929; Claud Cockburn
    Don't get the idea I'm knocking the American system.   *In Time of Trouble* (1956)

Benjamin Nathan Cardozo 1870–1938

American judge

7   [The Constitution] was framed upon the theory that the   in *Baldwin v. Seelig* (1935)
    peoples of the several states must sink or swim together,
    and that in the long run prosperity and salvation are in
    union and not division.

Thomas Carlyle 1795–1881

Scottish historian and political philosopher

8   Two centuries; hardly less; before Democracy go through *History of the French Revolution*
    its due, most baleful, stages of *Quackocracy*.   (1837) vol. 1

9   The seagreen Incorruptible.   *History of the French Revolution*
      describing **Robespierre**   (1837) vol. 2

10 Aristocracy of the Moneybag.   *History of the French Revolution*
                                                             (1837) vol. 3

11 France was long a despotism tempered by epigrams.   *History of the French Revolution*
                                                             (1837) vol. 3

12 The three great elements of modern civilization,   *Critical and Miscellaneous Essays*
    Gunpowder, Printing, and the Protestant Religion.   (1838) 'The State of German
                                                             Literature'

13 To the very last he [Napoleon] had a kind of idea; that, *Critical and Miscellaneous Essays*
    namely, of *La carrière ouverte aux talents*, The tools to him (1838) 'Sir Walter Scott'
    that can handle them.

1 A witty statesman said, you might prove anything by   *Chartism* (1839)
   figures.

2 In epochs when cash payment has become the sole nexus   *Chartism* (1839)
   of man to man.

3 Surely of all 'rights of man', this right of the ignorant   *Chartism* (1839)
   man to be guided by the wiser, to be, gently or forcibly,
   held in the true course by him, is the indisputablest.

4 A Hell in England—the Hell of not making money.   *Past and Present* (1843)

   on parliamentarians:
5 Windbag, weak in the faith of a God, which he believes   *Past and Present* (1843)
   only at church on Sundays, if even then; strong only in
   the faith that paragraphs and plausibilities bring votes;
   that force of public opinion, as he calls it, is the primal
   necessity of things, and highest God we have.

6 Despotism is essential in most enterprises.   *Past and Present* (1843)

7 A Parliament speaking through reporters to Buncombe   *Latter-Day Pamphlets* (1850)
   and the twenty-seven millions mostly fools.   'Parliaments'; cf. **Walker** 376:8

   of himself:
8 Little other than a redtape talking-machine, and unhappy   *Latter-Day Pamphlets* (1850) 'The
   bag of parliamentary eloquence.   Present Time'

   of political economy:
9 The Dismal Science.   *Latter-Day Pamphlets* (1850) 'The
                                                                Present Time'

10 Councillors of state sit plotting, and playing their high   *Sartor Resartus* (1858)
   chess-game, whereof the pawns are men.

11 These ballot-boxing, Nigger-emancipating, empty, dirt-   *Shooting Niagara: and After?*
   eclipsed days.   (1867)
   *in an anti-liberal polemic which caused great offence by its mode
   of expression*

   of **Disraeli**:
12 A superlative Hebrew conjuror.   *Shooting Niagara: and After?*
                                                                (1867)

13 Cobden is an inspired bagman, who believes in a calico   T. W. Reid *Life, Letters and
   millenium.   Friendships of Richard Monckton*
                                                                (1890) vol. 1

14 Democracy, which means despair of finding any heroes   attributed
   to govern you.

15 Vote by ballot is the dyspepsia of the society.   Simon Heffer *Moral Desperado*
                                                                (1995)

Stokely Carmichael 1941– and Charles Vernon Hamilton 1929–

16 Black power...is a call for black people in this country to *Black Power* (1967)
   unite, to recognize their heritage, to build a sense of
   community.

17 Before a group can enter the open society, it must first   *Black Power* (1967)
   close ranks.

Lewis Carroll 1832–98

English writer and logician

1 'When *I* use a word,' Humpty Dumpty said in a rather scornful tone, 'it means just what I choose it to mean— neither more nor less.'

Through the Looking-Glass (1872); cf. **Shawcross** 337:4

2 The rule is, jam to-morrow and jam yesterday—but never jam today.

Through the Looking-Glass (1872); cf. **Benn** 36:3

Edward Carson 1854–1935

British lawyer and politician, Ulster leader and Unionist

3 My only great qualification for being put at the head of the Navy is that I am very much at sea.

Ian Colvin *Life of Lord Carson* (1936) vol. 3

4 From the day I first entered parliament up to the present, devotion to the union has been the guiding star of my political life.

in *Dictionary of National Biography*

Jimmy Carter 1924–

American Democratic statesman, 39th President of the US, 1977–81

5 We should live our lives as though Christ were coming this afternoon.
    to a Bible class at Plains, Georgia, March 1976

in *Boston Sunday Herald Advertiser* 11 April 1976

6 We are of course a nation of differences. Those differences don't make us weak. They're the source of our strength…The question is not when we came here…but why our families came here. And what we did after we arrived.

speech at Al Smith dinner in New York City, 21 October 1976

7 I've looked on a lot of women with lust. I've committed adultery in my heart many times. This is something that God recognizes I will do—and I have done it—and God forgives me for it.

in *Playboy* November 1976

8 Two problems of our country—energy and malaise.

at town meeting in Bardstown, Kentucky, 31 July 1979

John Cartwright 1740–1824

English political reformer

9 One man shall have one vote.

The People's Barrier Against Undue Influence (1780) 'Principles, maxims, and primary rules of politics' no. 68

Thomas Nixon Carver

American conservative, who had previously given the course in agricultural economics at Harvard taken over by Galbraith in 1934

1 The trouble with radicals is that they only read radical literature, and the trouble with conservatives is that they don't read anything.

'Carver's Law'; J. K. Galbraith *A Life in Our Times* (1981)

Roger Casement 1864–1916

Irish nationalist; executed for treason in 1916

2 Where all your rights become only an accumulated wrong; where men must beg with bated breath for leave to subsist in their own land, to think their own thoughts, to sing their own songs, to garner the fruits of their own labours...then surely it is a braver, a saner and truer thing, to be a rebel in act and deed against such circumstances as these than tamely to accept it as the natural lot of men.

statement from prison, 29 June 1916

Ted Castle 1907–79

British journalist

3 In place of strife.

title of Labour Government White Paper, 17 January 1969; suggested by Castle to his wife, Barbara Castle, then Secretary of State for Employment

Catherine the Great 1729–96

Empress of Russia from 1762

4 I shall be an autocrat: that's my trade. And the good Lord will forgive me: that's his.

attributed

Wyn Catlin

5 Diplomacy is saying 'Nice doggie' until you find a rock.

Laurence J. Peter (ed.) *Quotations for our Time* (1977)

Carrie Chapman Catt 1859–1947

American feminist

6 No written law has ever been more binding than unwritten custom supported by popular opinion.
  speech at Senate hearing on woman's suffrage, 13 February 1900

Why We Ask for the Submission of an Amendment (1900)

7 When a just cause reaches its flood-tide...whatever stands in the way must fall before its overwhelming power.

speech at Stockholm, *Is Woman Suffrage Progressing?* (1911)

Cato the Elder (or 'the Censor') 234–149 BC

Roman statesman, orator, and writer

1 *Delenda est Carthago.*   Pliny the Elder *Naturalis Historia*
  Carthage must be destroyed.

Constantine Cavafy 1863–1933

Greek poet

2 What are we waiting for, gathered in the market-place?   'Waiting for the Barbarians' (1904)
  The barbarians are to arrive today.

3 And now, what will become of us without the   'Waiting for the Barbarians' (1904)
    barbarians?
  Those people were a kind of solution.

Count Cavour 1810–61

Italian statesman

4 We are ready to proclaim throughout Italy this great   speech, 27 March 1861
  principle: a free church in a free state.

Lord Edward Cecil 1867–1918

British soldier and civil servant; chief British adviser in the
Egyptian government

definition of a compromise:
5 An agreement between two men to do what both agree   letter 3 September 1911
  is wrong.

Lord Hugh Cecil 1869–1956

British Conservative politician and Provost of Eton

6 There is no more ungraceful figure than that of   in *The Times* 24 June 1901
  a humanitarian with an eye to the main chance.
    dismissal of a manoeuvre by **Campbell-Bannerman**

7 The socialist believes that it is better to be rich than poor,   *Conservatism* (1912)
  the Christian that it is better to be poor than rich.

8 Losses to a nation may be so great that they change the   *Conservatism* (1912)
  character of the nation itself. It would be so with us if we
  lost our dominions beyond the sea.

Robert Cecil 1563–1612

English courtier and statesman, son of William Cecil, Lord
Burghley

9 Rest content, and give heed to one that hath sorrowed in   letter to Sir John Harington;
  the bright lustre of a court, and gone heavily even on the Algernon Cecil *A Life of Robert
  best-seeming fair ground…I know it bringeth little   Cecil* (1915)
  comfort on earth; and he is, I reckon, no wise man that
  looketh this way to Heaven.

Joseph Chamberlain 1836–1914

British Liberal politician; father of Neville **Chamberlain**
on Chamberlain: see **Housman** 183:7

1 In politics, there is no use looking beyond the next
   fortnight.

A. J. Balfour letter to Lord
Salisbury, 24 March 1886; cf.
Wilson 390:8

2 It is not to your interest to arouse the prejudices of the
   society in which you hope one day again to take your
   place...Therefore my advice is: Be as Radical as you like.
   Be Home Ruler if you must. But be a little Jingo if you
   can.
   *to his friend Charles Dilke, who was hoping to make a political
   comeback*

Roy Jenkins *Sir Charles Dilke* (1958)

3 It is no use blowing the trumpet for the charge, and then
   looking around to find nobody following.
   discussing negotiations with President **Kruger** *prior to the
   Second Boer War*

Winston Churchill *Great
Contemporaries* (1937)

4 Provided that the City of London remains, as it is at
   present, the clearing-house of the world, any other
   nation may be its workshop.

speech at the Guildhall, 19 January
1904

5 Learn to think Imperially.
   with reference to Alexander **Hamilton**'s *advice to the newly
   independent United States*

speech at the Guildhall, 19 January
1904; cf. **Hamilton** 167:7

6 The day of small nations has long passed away. The day
   of Empires has come.

speech at Birmingham, 12 May
1904

7 We are not downhearted. The only trouble is we cannot
   understand what is happening to our neighbours.
   *referring to a constituency which had remained unaffected by an
   electoral landslide*

speech at Smethwick, 18 January
1906

Neville Chamberlain 1869–1940

British Conservative statesman; Prime Minister, 1937–40; son
of Joseph **Chamberlain**
on Chamberlain: see **Bevan** 40:2, **Channon** 81:7, **Churchill**
90:2, **Lloyd George** 230:7, **Nicolson** 272:1, 272:2

8 In war, whichever side may call itself the victor, there
   are no winners, but all are losers.

speech at Kettering, 3 July 1938

9 How horrible, fantastic, incredible it is that we should be
   digging trenches and trying on gas-masks here because of
   a quarrel in a far away country between people of whom
   we know nothing.
   on Germany's annexation of the Sudetenland

radio broadcast, 27 September
1938

10 This morning I had another talk with the German
   Chancellor, Herr Hitler, and here is the paper which
   bears his name upon it as well as mine...'We regard the
   agreeement signed last night and the Anglo-German
   Naval Agreement, as symbolic of the desire of our two
   peoples never to go to war with one another again.'

speech at Heston Airport, 30
September 1938

1　This is the second time in our history that there has
　come back from Germany to Downing Street peace with
　honour. I believe it is peace for our time.
　　speech from the window of 10 Downing Street, 30 September
　　1938

in *The Times* 1 October 1938

2　It's no part of a Prime Minister's duty to take a country
　into a war which he thinks you can't win.
　　shortly before Munich, as recalled by Lord **Home**

attributed

the British Ambassador in Berlin had handed the German
government a final note stating that unless the British
government had heard by eleven o'clock that Germany was
prepared to withdraw her troops from Poland, a state of war
would exist between the two countries:

3　I have to tell you now that no such undertaking has
　been received, and that consequently this country is at
　war with Germany.

radio broadcast, 3 September 1939

4　Whatever may be the reason—whether it was that Hitler
　thought he might get away with what he had got
　without fighting for it, or whether it was that after all
　the preparations were not sufficiently complete—
　however, one thing is certain—he missed the bus.

speech at Central Hall,
Westminster, 4 April 1940

Henry ('Chips') Channon 1897–1958

American-born British Conservative MP and diarist

5　I personally think...that there will be an unheaval, that
　the Throne will sway a little, but that it will survive and
　that the King will get away with it. We are working up
　to something terrific. What is history unfolding?
　　during the Abdication crisis of 1936

diary 22 November 1936

6　There is nowhere in the world where sleep is so deep as
　in the libraries of the House of Commons.

diary 17 December 1937

7　He is winning through and will probably be Premier for
　years to come.
　　of Neville **Chamberlain**

diary 15 January 1939

8　I gather it has now been decided not to embrace the
　Russian bear, but to hold out a hand and accept its paw
　gingerly. No more. The worst of both worlds.

diary 16 May 1939

Rab **Butler** *had asked whether he and Ivan Maisky could use*
Channon's house in Belgrave Square for a secret meeting:

9　I never thought that the Russian Ambassador would ever
　cross my threshold; I checked up on the snuff-boxes on
　my return but did not notice anything missing.

diary 28 November 1939

on hearing Lady Mountbatten expounding her anti-
monarchical views:

10　How easy it seems for a semi-royal millionairess, who has
　exhausted all the pleasures of money and position, to
　turn almost Communist!

diary 19 September 1944

John Jay Chapman 1862–1933

1 Everybody in America is soft, and hates conflict. The cure   *Practical Agitation* (1898)
for this, both in politics and social life, is the same—
hardihood. Give them raw truth.

Charles I 1600–49

King of England, Scotland, and Ireland from 1625
on Charles I: see **Marvell** 251:7

2 Never make a defence or apology before you be accused.   letter to Lord Wentworth, 3
September 1636

3 I see all the birds are flown.   in the House of Commons, 4
after attempting to arrest the Five Members   January 1642

4 You manifestly wrong even the poorest ploughman, if   S. R. Gardiner *Constitutional*
you demand not his free consent.   *Documents of the Puritan*
rejecting the jurisdiction of the High Court of Justice, 21 January   *Revolution* (1906 ed.)
1649

5 Sweet-heart, now they will cut off thy father's head.   in *Reliquiae Sacrae Carolinae*
Mark, child, what I say: they will cut off my head, and   (1650)
perhaps make thee a king. But mark what I say: you
must not be a king, so long as your brothers Charles and
James do live.
said to Prince Henry

6 As to the King, the laws of the land will clearly instruct   J. Rushworth *Historical Collections*
you for that…For the people; and truly I desire their   vol. 2 (1701)
liberty and freedom, as much as any body: but I must
tell you, that their liberty and freedom consists in having
the government of those laws, by which their life and
their goods may be most their own; 'tis not for having
share in government [sirs] that is nothing pertaining to
'em. A subject and a sovereign are clean different
things…If I would have given way to an arbitrary way,
for to have all laws changed according to the power of
the sword, I needed not to have come here; and therefore
I tell you (and I pray God it be not laid to your charge)
that I am the martyr of the people.
speech on the scaffold, 30 January 1649

7 I die a Christian, according to the profession of the   J. Rushworth *Historical Collections*
Church of England, as I found it left me by my father.   vol. 2 (1701)

Charles II 1630–85

King of England, Scotland and Ireland from 1660
on Charles II: see **Rochester** 307:5

8 It is upon the navy under the good Providence of God   'Articles of War' preamble
that the safety, honour, and welfare of this realm do   (probably a popular paraphrase);
chiefly depend.   Geoffrey Callender *The Naval Side*
of British History (1952)

1   This is very true: for my words are my own, and my   in *Thomas Hearne: Remarks and*
    actions are my ministers'.   *Collections* (1885–1921) 17
    reply to Lord **Rochester***'s epitaph on him*   November 1706; cf.
                                                                   Rochester 307:5

2   Better than a play.   A. Bryant *King Charles II* (1931)
    on the debates in the House of Lords on Lord Ross's Divorce Bill

3   I am sure no man in England will take away my life to   William King *Political & Literary*
    make you King.   *Anecdotes* (1818)
    to his brother James, afterwards James II

4   I am weary of travelling and am resolved to go abroad   attributed
    no more. But when I am dead and gone I know not what
    my brother will do: I am much afraid that when he
    comes to wear the crown he will be obliged to travel
    again.
    on the difference between himself and his brother

5   I, who will never use arbitrary government myself, am   attributed
    resolved not to suffer it in others.
    to the Whigs

6   He had been, he said, an unconscionable time dying; but   Lord Macaulay *History of England*
    he hoped that they would excuse it.   (1849) vol. 1

Salmon Portland Chase 1808–73

American lawyer and politician

7   The Constitution, in all its provisions, looks to an   decision in Texas v. White, 1868
    indestructible Union composed of indestructible States.

Mary Chesnut 1823–86

American diarist and Confederate supporter

8   The Confederacy has been done to death by politicians.   in 1863; Ken Burns *The Civil War*
                                                                   (documentary, 1989) episode 4

9   Atlanta is gone. That agony is over. There is no hope but   Geoffrey C. Ward *The Civil War*
    we will try to have no fear.   (1991)
    after the fall of Atlanta to Sherman's army in 1864

Lord Chesterfield 1694–1773

English writer and politician
on Chesterfield: see **Johnson** 197:1, **Walpole** 377:6

10 Women, then, are only children of a larger growth: they   letter 5 September 1748
    have an entertaining tattle, and sometimes wit; but for
    solid, reasoning good sense, I never knew in my life one
    that had it, or who reasoned or acted consequentially for
    four and twenty hours together.

11 Politicians neither love nor hate. Interest, not sentiment,   *Letters* 1748
    directs them.

12 I...could not help reflecting in my way upon the   in *The World* 7 October 1756
    singular ill-luck of this my dear country, which, as long

as ever I remember it, and as far back as I have read,
has always been governed by the only two or three
people, out of two or three millions, totally incapable of
governing, and unfit to be trusted.

G. K. Chesterton 1874–1936

English essayist, novelist, and poet

1 'My country, right or wrong' is a thing no patriot would   *The Defendant* (1901)
   ever think of saying except in a desperate case. It is like
   saying, 'My mother, drunk or sober.'

2 Tradition means giving votes to the most obscure of all   *Orthodoxy* (1908)
   classes, our ancestors. It is the democracy of the dead.

3 Democrats object to men being disqualified by the   *Orthodoxy* (1908)
   accident of birth; tradition objects to their being
   disqualified by the accident of death. Tradition refuses to
   submit to the small and arrogant oligarchy of those who
   merely happen to be walking around.

4 All conservatism is based upon the idea that if you leave   *Orthodoxy* (1908)
   things alone you leave them as they are. But you do not.
   If you leave a thing alone you leave it to a torrent of
   change.

5 Are they clinging to their crosses, F. E. Smith?   'Antichrist' (1912)
   satirizing F. E. **Smith**'s response to the Welsh Disestablishment
   Bill

6 Talk about the pews and steeples   'Antichrist' (1912)
   And the Cash that goes therewith!
   But the souls of Christian peoples...
   Chuck it, Smith!

7 Smile at us, pay us, pass us; but do not quite forget.   'The Secret People' (1915)
   For we are the people of England, that never have spoken
   yet.

8 We only know the last sad squires ride slowly towards   'The Secret People' (1915)
   the sea,
   And a new people takes the land: and still it is not we.

9 They have given us into the hand of new unhappy lords,   'The Secret People' (1915)
   Lords without anger and honour, who dare not carry
   their swords.
   They fight us by shuffling papers; they have bright dead
   alien eyes;
   And they look at our labour and laughter as a tired man
   looks at flies.
   And the load of their loveless pity is worse than the
   ancient wrongs,
   Their doors are shut in the evening; And they know no
   songs.

10 They died to save their country and they only saved the   'English Graves' (1922)
   world.

11 Lancashire merchants whenever they like   'Songs of Education: II Geography'
   Can water the beer of a man in Klondike   (1922)

Or poison the meat of a man in Bombay;
And that is the meaning of Empire Day.

1 Democracy means government by the uneducated, while   in *New York Times* 1 February 1931
  aristocracy means government by the badly educated.

Lydia Maria Child 1802–80

American abolitionist and suffragist

2 We first crush people to the earth, and then claim the   *An Appeal on Behalf of That Class*
  right of trampling on them forever, because they are   *of Americans Called Africans* (1833)
  prostrate.

3 Woman stock is rising in the market. I shall not live to   letter to Sarah Shaw, 3 August
  see women vote, but I'll come and rap at the ballot box.   1856

Erskine Childers 1870–1922

Anglo-Irish writer and political activist

to the firing squad at his execution:
4 Come closer, boys. It will be easier for you.   Burke Wilkinson *The Zeal of the*
                                                                 Convert (1976)

Lawton Chiles 1930–

American politician

5 You are misunderstood, maligned, viewed by the press as   in *St Petersburg (Florida) Times* 6
  a Pulitzer Prize ready to be won.   March 1991
    on the problems of investigative journalism for politicians

Rufus Choate 1799–1859

American lawyer and politician

6 The courage of New England was the 'courage of   address at Ipswich,
  conscience'. It did not rise to that insane and awful   Massachusetts, Centennial, 1834
  passion, the love of war for itself.

7 We join ourselves to no party that does not carry the flag   letter to the Whig Convention,
  and keep step to the music of the Union.   Worcester, Massachusetts, 1
                                                                 October 1855

8 Its constitution the glittering and sounding generalities of   letter to the Maine Whig State
  natural right which make up the Declaration of   Central Committee, 9 August 1856
  Independence.

Frank Chodorov 1887–1966

American economist and writer

9 [When people] say 'let's do something about it,' they   'Freedom is Better' (1949)
  mean 'let's get hold of the political machinery so that we
  can do something to somebody else.' And that somebody
  is invariably you.

10 The only way to a world society is through free trade.   'One Worldism' (1950)

David Christy 1802–c.68

1 Cotton is King; or, the economical relations of slavery.   title of book, 1855

Clementine Churchill 1885–1977

wife of Winston **Churchill**

2 Winston...has the supreme quality which I venture to   Martin Gilbert *In Search of*
say very few of your present or future Cabinet possess,   *Churchill* (1994)
the power, the imagination, the deadliness to fight
Germany.
*letter to **Asquith** on Winston **Churchill**'s dismissal from the
Admiralty, May 1915*

Lord Randolph Churchill 1849–94

British Conservative politician; father of Winston **Churchill**
on Churchill: see **Gladstone** 155:2; **Rosebery** 312:6

3 To tell the truth I don't know myself what Tory   Elizabeth Longford *A Pilgrimage of*
Democracy is. But I believe it is principally opportunism.   *Passion* (1979)
*having urged Wilfrid Scawen Blunt in 1885 to stand for
Parliament as a Tory Democrat*

4 For the purposes of recreation he [Gladstone] has selected   speech on Financial Reform,
the felling of trees, and we may usefully remark that his   delivered in Blackpool, 24 January
amusements, like his politics, are essentially   1884
destructive...The forest laments in order that Mr
Gladstone may perspire.

5 He [Gladstone] told them that he would give them and   speech on Financial Reform,
all other subjects of the Queen much legislation, great   delivered in Blackpool, 24 January
prosperity, and universal peace, and he has given them   1884
nothing but chips. Chips to the faithful allies in
Afghanistan, chips to the trusting native races of South
Africa, chips to the Egyptian fellah, chips to the British
farmer, chips to the manufacturer and the artisan, chips
to the agricultural labourer, chips to the House of
Commons itself.

6 Ulster will fight; Ulster will be right.   public letter, 7 May 1886

7 An old man in a hurry.   in an address to the electors of
*of **Gladstone***   South Paddington, 19 June 1886

8 I decided some time ago that if the G.O.M. [Gladstone]   letter to Lord Justice FitzGibbon, 16
went for Home Rule, the Orange card would be the one   February 1886
to play. Please God it may turn out the ace of trumps
and not the two.
*often quoted as 'Play the Orange card'; cf. **Shapiro** 335:12*

9 All great men make mistakes. Napoleon forgot Blücher,   in *Leaves from the Notebooks of*
I forgot Goschen.   *Lady Dorothy Nevill* (1907)
*when Lord Randolph suddenly resigned the position of
Chancellor of the Exchequer in 1886, **Goschen** had been
appointed in his place*

1 I never could make out what those damned dots meant.   Winston Churchill *Lord Randolph*
    of decimal points   *Churchill* (1906) vol. 2

Winston Churchill 1874–1965

British Conservative statesman; Prime Minister, 1940–5,
1951–5
on Churchill: see **Asquith** 18:8, **Baldwin** 29:8, **Bevan** 40:10,
40:12, **Butler** 70:2, **Headlam** 172:1, **Laski** 218:5, **Lloyd
George** 230:9, 230:16, **Morton** 266:8, **Nicolson** 272:5,
Webb 381:2, **Wilson** 391:10

2 It may be that vengeance is sweet, and that the gods   *The River War* (1899)
    forbade vengeance to men because they reserved for
    themselves so delicious and intoxicating a drink. But no
    one should drain the cup to the bottom. The dregs are
    often filthy-tasting.

3 Corruption at home, aggression abroad to cover it up…   Andrew Roberts *Eminent*
    Sentiment by the bucketful, patriotism by the imperial   *Churchillians* (1994)
    pint; the open hand at the public exchequer, the open
    door at the public house; dear food for the millions,
    cheap labour for the millionaire.
    *of the Conservatives in 1904 as the Party of great vested
    interests*

4 A labour contract into which men enter voluntarily for   in the House of Commons, 22
    a limited and for a brief period, under which they are   February 1906
    paid wages which they consider adequate, under which
    they are not bought or sold and from which they can
    obtain relief…on payment of £17.10s, the cost of their
    passage, may not be a healthy or proper contract, but it
    cannot in the opinion of His Majesty's Government be
    classified as slavery in the extreme acceptance of the
    word without some risk of terminological inexactitude.

5 He [Lord Charles Beresford] is one of those orators of   in the House of Commons, 20
    whom it was well said, 'Before they get up, they do not   December 1912
    know what they are going to say; when they are
    speaking, they do not know what they are saying; and
    when they have sat down, they do not know what they
    have said.'

6 Business carried on as usual during alterations on the   speech at Guildhall, 9 November
    map of Europe.   1914
    on the self-adopted 'motto' of the British people

7 I am never going to have anything more to do with   Martin Gilbert *In Search of*
    politics or politicians. When this war is over I shall   *Churchill* (1994)
    confine myself entirely to writing and painting.
    to a fellow officer on the Western Front, 1915

8 We live very simply—but with all the essentials of life   Martin Gilbert *In Search of*
    well understood and well provided for—hot baths, cold   *Churchill* (1994)
    champagne, new peas, and old brandy.
    *of life at his country bolthole, Hoe Farm, after his dismissal from
    the Admiralty in 1915*

1 A drizzle of Empires...falling through the air.
of the Austro-Hungarian and Ottoman empires in 1918

Martin Gilbert *In Search of Churchill* (1994)

comparing H. H. **Asquith** *with Arthur* **Balfour:**
2 The difference between him and Arthur is that Arthur is wicked and moral, Asquith is good and immoral.

E. T. Raymond *Mr Balfour* (1920)

of **Balfour**'*s moving from* **Asquith**'*s Cabinet to that of* **Lloyd George:**
3 Like a powerful graceful cat walking delicately and unsoiled across a rather muddy street.

Great Contemporaries (1937)

4 The whole map of Europe has been changed...but as the deluge subsides and the waters fall short we see the dreary steeples of Fermanagh and Tyrone emerging once again.

in the House of Commons, 16 February 1922

5 Anyone can rat, but it takes a certain amount of ingenuity to re-rat.
on rejoining the Conservatives twenty years after leaving them for the Liberals, c.1924

Kay Halle *Irrepressible Churchill* (1966)

of a meeting in 1926 with **Lloyd George,** *by then out of office:*
6 Within five minutes the old relationship between us was completely re-established. The relationship between Master and Servant. And I was the Servant.

Lord Boothby *Recollections of a Rebel* (1978)

7 I decline utterly to be impartial as between the fire brigade and the fire.
replying to complaints of his bias in editing the British Gazette *during the General Strike*

in the House of Commons, 7 July 1926

8 If you strike at savings you at once propagate the idea of 'Let us eat, drink and be merry, for tomorrow we die.' That is at once the inspiration and the mortal disease by which the Socialist philosophy is affected.

in the House of Commons, 19 May 1927

9 Cultured people are merely the glittering scum which floats upon the deep river of production.
on hearing his son Randolph criticize the lack of culture of the Calgary oil magnates, probably c.1929

Martin Gilbert *In Search of Churchill* (1994)

when taking the entrance examination for Harrow, Churchill's answer paper consisted of his own name and a bracketed figure 1 for the first question:
10 It was from these slender indications of scholarship that Mr Welldon drew the conclusion that I was worthy to pass into Harrow. It is very much to his credit.

My Early Life (1930)

11 Headmasters have powers at their disposal with which Prime Ministers have never yet been invested.

My Early Life (1930)

12 I am biased in favour of boys learning English. I would make them all learn English: and then I would let the clever ones learn Latin as an honour, and Greek as a treat.

My Early Life (1930)

13 Mr Gladstone read Homer for fun, which I thought served him right.

My Early Life (1930)

14 I had no idea [in 1894] of the enormous and unquestionably helpful part that humbug plays in the

My Early Life (1930)

social life of great peoples dwelling in a state of democratic freedom.

1 I remember, when I was a child, being taken to the celebrated Barnum's circus, which contained an exhibition of freaks and monstrosities, but the exhibit on the programme which I most desired to see was the one described as 'The Boneless Wonder'. My parents judged that that spectacle would be too revolting and demoralizing for my youthful eyes, and I have waited 50 years to see the boneless wonder sitting on the Treasury Bench.
    of Ramsay **MacDonald**

in the House of Commons, 28 January 1931

2 I do not like elections, but it is in my many elections that I have learnt to know and honour the people of this island. They are good through and through.

Thoughts and Adventures (1932)

of the General Election of 1922:
3 In the twinkling of an eye I found myself without an office, without a seat, without a party, and without an appendix.

Thoughts and Adventures (1932)

4 Tell your boss from me that anti-Semitism may be a good starter, but it is a bad sticker.
    in 1932, having been asked by a German friend of his son Randolph whether he would be willing to meet **Hitler**

Martin Gilbert *In Search of Churchill* (1994)

5 A gigantic quilt of jumbled crochet work, a monstrous monument of shame built by pigmies.
    on the Government of India Bill, 1935

Kenneth Rose *The Later Cecils* (1975)

6 There is not much collective security in a flock of sheep on the way to the butcher.

speech at the New Commonwealth Society luncheon, Dorchester Hotel, 25 November 1936

7 So they [the Government] go on in strange paradox, decided only to be undecided, resolved to be irresolute, adamant for drift, solid for fluidity, all-powerful to be impotent.

in the House of Commons, 12 November 1936

8 Dictators ride to and fro upon tigers which they dare not dismount. And the tigers are getting hungry.

letter, 11 November 1937

of the career of Lord **Curzon**:
9 The morning had been golden; the noontide was bronze; and the evening lead. But all were solid, and each was polished till it shone after its fashion.

Great Contemporaries (1937)

10 No part of the education of a politician is more indispensable than the fighting of elections.

Great Contemporaries (1937)

11 The utmost he [Neville Chamberlain] has been able to gain for Czechoslovakia and in the matters which were in dispute has been that the German dictator, instead of snatching his victuals from the table, has been content to have them served to him course by course.

in the House of Commons, 5 October 1938

1 I cannot forecast to you the action of Russia. It is a riddle wrapped in a mystery inside an enigma.

radio broadcast, 1 October 1939

on being asked where to set the podium from which Neville **Chamberlain** *was to give an address to local Conservatives:*

2 It doesn't matter where you put it as long as he has the sun in his eyes and the wind in his teeth.

Martin Gilbert *In Search of Churchill* (1994)

3 An appeaser is one who feeds a crocodile hoping it will eat him last.

in the House of Commons, January 1940

as Prime Minister:

4 [I was] conscious of a profound source of relief. I felt as if I was walking with destiny, and that all my past life had been but a preparation for this hour and this trial.

on 10 May 1940

5 I have nothing to offer but blood, toil, tears and sweat.

in the House of Commons, 13 May 1940

6 What is our policy?...to wage war against a monstrous tyranny, never surpassed in the dark, lamentable catalogue of human crime.

in the House of Commons, 13 May 1940

7 We shall not flag or fail. We shall go on to the end. We shall fight in France, we shall fight on the seas and oceans, we shall fight with growing confidence and growing strength in the air, we shall defend our island, whatever the cost may be. We shall fight on the beaches, we shall fight on the landing grounds, we shall fight in the fields and in the streets, we shall fight in the hills; we shall never surrender.

in the House of Commons, 4 June 1940

8 Let us therefore brace ourselves to our duty, and so bear ourselves that, if the British Commonwealth and its Empire lasts for a thousand years, men will still say, 'This was their finest hour.'

in the House of Commons, 18 June 1940

on being bombed:

9 Learn to get used to it. Eels get used to skinning.

notes for a speech, 20 June 1940

10 Never in the field of human conflict was so much owed by so many to so few.
on the skill and courage of British airmen

in the House of Commons, 20 August 1940

11 Death and sorrow will be the companions of our journey; hardship our garment; constancy and valour our only shield. We must be united, we must be undaunted, we must be inflexible.

in the House of Commons, 8 October 1940

comment allegedly made on a long-winded report submitted by Anthony **Eden** *on his tour of the Near East:*

12 As far as I can see you have used every cliché except 'God is Love' and 'Please adjust your dress before leaving.'

in *Life* December 1940

13 I well appreciate the necessity of preserving the piebald complexion of my pony.
on a proposed appointment likely to upset the balance of his coalition

Andrew Roberts *Eminent Churchillians* (1994)

14 What I want is for you to keep the flies off the meat. It becomes bad if they are allowed to settle even for

Andrew Roberts *Eminent Churchillians* (1994)

a moment. I am the meat and you must show me the
warning light when troubles arise in the Parliamentary
and political scene.
to his newly appointed Parliamentary Private Secretary, c.1941

1 What could you hope to achieve except to be sunk in
a bigger and more expensive ship this time?
*to **Mountbatten** in November 1941, overriding his protests at
being appointed to a desk job as Adviser on Combined
Operations rather than being allowed to remain on active service
in the Navy*

Andrew Roberts *Eminent
Churchillians* (1994)

2 A medal glitters, but it also casts a shadow.
a reference to the envy caused by the award of honours

in 1941; Kenneth Rose *King George
V* (1983)

3 It becomes still more difficult to reconcile Japanese action
with prudence or even with sanity. What kind of
a people do they think we are?

speech to US Congress, 26
December 1941

4 The British nation is unique in this respect. They are the
only people who like to be told how bad things are, who
like to be told the worst.

in the House of Commons, 10 June
1941

5 The people of London with one voice would say to Hitler:
'You have committed every crime under the sun...We
will have no truce or parley with you, or the grisly gang
who work your wicked will. You do your worst—and we
will do our best.

speech at County Hall, London, 14
July 1941

6 Here is the answer which I will give to President
Roosevelt...Give us the tools and we will finish the job.

radio broadcast 9 February 1941

7 When I warned them [the French Government] that
Britain would fight on alone whatever they did, their
generals told their Prime Minister and his divided
Cabinet, 'In three weeks England will have her neck
wrung like a chicken.' Some chicken! Some neck!

speech to Canadian Parliament, 30
December 1941

8 There you are, fixed, old cock.
*note sent to the Minister of Education, Rab **Butler**, who was
working on the Education Act in 1942 when the Cardinal
Archbishop of Westminster publicly asserted the independence
of Roman Catholic education*

R. A. Butler *The Art of Memory*
(1982)

9 I have not become the King's First Minister in order to
preside over the liquidation of the British Empire.

speech in London, 10 November
1942

10 Now this is not the end. It is not even the beginning of
the end. But it is, perhaps, the end of the beginning.
on British success in the North African campaign

speech at the Mansion House,
London, 10 November 1942

11 We make this wide encircling movement in the
Mediterranean, having for its primary object the recovery
of the command of that vital sea, but also having for its
object the exposure of the under-belly of the Axis,
especially Italy, to heavy attack.
often misquoted as 'the soft under-belly of the Axis'

in the House of Commons, 11
November 1942

12 National compulsory insurance for all classes for all
purposes from the cradle to the grave.

radio broadcast 21 March 1943

1 There is no finer investment for any community than putting milk into babies.

radio broadcast, 21 March 1943

2 The empires of the future are the empires of the mind.

speech at Harvard, 6 September 1943

on rebuilding the Houses of Parliament:
3 We shape our dwellings, and afterwards our dwellings shape us.

in the House of Commons, 28 October 1944

4 I do not see any other way of realizing our hopes about World Organization in five or six days. Even the Almighty took seven.
    *to Franklin **Roosevelt** on the likely duration of the Yalta conference with **Stalin** in 1945*

The Second World War (1954) vol. 6

5 He devised the extraordinary measure of assistance called Lend-Lease, which will stand forth as the most unselfish and unsordid financial act of any country in all history.
    *of President **Roosevelt***

in the House of Commons, 17 April 1945

6 One day President Roosevelt told me that he was asking publicly for suggestions about what the war should be called. I said at once, 'The Unnecessary War'.

The Second World War (1948) vol. 1

after the General Election of 1945:
7 Why should I accept the Order of the Garter from His Majesty when the people have just given me the order of the boot?

D. Bardens *Churchill in Parliament* (1967)

*of Aneurin **Bevan**:*
8 Unless the right hon. gentleman changes his policy and methods and moves without the slightest delay, he will be as great a curse to this country in time of peace, as he was a squalid nuisance in time of war.

in the House of Commons, 6 December 1945

9 The Prime Minister has nothing to hide from the President of the United States
    *on stepping from his bath in the presence of a startled President **Roosevelt***

as recalled by Roosevelt's son in *Churchill* (BBC television series presented by Martin Gilbert, 1992) pt. 3

10 From Stettin in the Baltic to Trieste in the Adriatic an iron curtain has descended across the Continent.
    the expression 'iron curtain' previously had been applied by others to the Soviet Union or her sphere of influence, e.g. Ethel Snowden Through Bolshevik Russia *(1920), Dr Goebbels* Das Reich, *25 February 1945, and by Churchill himself in a cable to President Truman, 4 June 1945*

speech at Westminster College, Fulton, Missouri, 5 March 1946

11 We must build a kind of United States of Europe.

in Zurich, 19 September 1946

after the Nuremberg war trials:
12 From now on I shall have to take care not to lose wars.

attributed

13 I wish Stanley Baldwin no ill, but it would have been much better if he had never lived.
    *on being asked to send **Baldwin** an 80th birthday tribute*

Martin Gilbert *In Search of Churchill* (1994)

14 It would be a great reform in politics if wisdom could be made to spread as easily and as rapidly as folly.

speech at the Guildhall, London, 10 September 1947

1 No one pretends that democracy is perfect or all-wise. Indeed, it has been said that democracy is the worst form of Government except all those other forms that have been tried from time to time.

in the House of Commons, 11 November 1947

2 When I am abroad I always make it a rule never to criticize or attack the Government of my country. I make up for lost time when I am at home.

in the House of Commons, 18 April 1947

3 The candle in that great turnip has gone out.
on Stanley **Baldwin** *in his last years*

Harold Nicolson diary 17 August 1950

4 This is the sort of English up with which I will not put.
after an official had gone through one of his papers moving prepositions away from the ends of sentences

Ernest Gowers *Plain Words* (1948) 'Troubles with Prepositions'

5 In war: resolution. In defeat: defiance. In victory: magnanimity. In peace: goodwill.

The Second World War vol. 1 (1948) epigraph, which according to Edward Marsh in *A Number of People* (1939), occurred to Churchill shortly after the conclusion of the First World War

6 The loyalties which centre upon number one are enormous. If he trips he must be sustained. If he makes mistakes they must be covered. If he sleeps he must not be wantonly disturbed. If he is no good he must be pole-axed. But this last extreme process cannot be carried out every day; and certainly not in the days just after he has been chosen.

The Second World War vol. 2 (1949)

7 Naval tradition? Monstrous. Nothing but rum, sodomy, prayers, and the lash.
often quoted as, 'rum, sodomy, and the lash', as in Peter Gretton Former Naval Person *(1968)*

Harold Nicolson diary 17 August 1950

8 When the English history of the first quarter of the twentieth century is written, it will be seen that the greater part of our fortunes in peace and in war were shaped by this one man.
of **Lloyd George**

in *Evening Standard* 4 October 1951

9 It is an error to believe that the world began when any particular party or statesman got into office. It has all been going on quite a long time.

speech at the Guildhall, London, 9 November 1951

10 It may almost be said, 'Before Alamein we never had a victory. After Alamein we never had a defeat.'

The Second World War (1951) vol. 4

11 I did not suffer from any desire to be relieved of my responsibilities. All I wanted was compliance with my wishes after reasonable discussion.

The Second World War vol. 4 (1951)

12 There but for the grace of God, goes God.
of Stafford Cripps

P. Brendon *Churchill* (1984)

13 A modest man who has much to be modest about.
of Clement **Attlee**

in *Chicago Sunday Tribune Magazine of Books* 27 June 1954

14 I am prepared to meet my Maker. Whether my Maker is prepared for the great ordeal of meeting me is another matter.

at a news conference in Washington in 1954

1 It was the nation and the race dwelling all round the globe that had the lion's heart. I had the luck to be called upon to give the roar.

speech at Westminster Hall, 30 November 1954

2 To jaw-jaw is always better than to war-war.

speech at the White House, 26 June 1954

to Hugh Foot, Governor of Jamaica, in the early 1950s, on the prospect of immigration continuing unabated:

3 We would have a magpie society: that would never do.

Andrew Roberts *Eminent Churchillians* (1994)

4 I still have the ideas, Walter, but I can't find the words to clothe them.
   to Walter **Monckton**

Tony Benn diary 15 December 1956

of Lord **Montgomery**:

5 In defeat unbeatable: in victory unbearable.

Edward Marsh *Ambrosia and Small Beer* (1964)

of the qualifications desirable in a prospective politician:

6 The ability to foretell what is going to happen tomorrow, next week, next month, and next year. And to have the ability afterwards to explain why it didn't happen.

B. Adler *Churchill Wit* (1965)

7 As to freedom of the press, why should any man be allowed to buy a printing press and disseminate pernicious opinions calculated to embarrass the government?

Piers Brendon *Winston Churchill* (1984)

of his recurring depression:

8 Black dog is back again.

attributed

9 An empty taxi arrived at 10 Downing Street, and when the door was opened Attlee got out.
   attributed to Churchill, but strongly repudiated by him

Kenneth Harris *Attlee* (1982)

of Stanley **Baldwin**:

10 He occasionally stumbled over the truth, but hastily picked himself up and hurried on as if nothing had happened.

attributed

11 I am fond of pigs. Dogs look up to us. Cats look down on us. Pigs treat us as equals.

Martin Gilbert *Never Despair* (1988); attributed

12 I have taken more out of alcohol than alcohol has taken out of me.

Quentin Reynolds *By Quentin Reynolds* (1964)

13 I know of no case where a man added to his dignity by standing on it.

attributed

14 If you have ten thousand regulations you destroy all respect for the law.

attributed

15 In the course of my life I have often had to eat my words, and I must confess that I have always found it a wholesome diet.

W. Manchester *The Caged Lion* (1988)

16 Most wars in history have been avoided simply by postponing them.

J. K. Galbraith *A Life in Our Times* (1981)

17 A sheep in sheep's clothing.
   of Clement **Attlee**

Lord Home *The Way the Wind Blows* (1976)

1 Take away that pudding—it has no theme.

Lord Home *The Way the Wind Blows* (1976)

2 There he stalks, that Wuthering Height.
  of John Reith

Andrew Boyle *Only the Wind Will Listen*

of Alfred Bossom:
3 Who is this man whose name is neither one thing nor the other?

attributed

Count Galeazzo Ciano 1903–44

Italian fascist politician; son-in-law of Mussolini

4 Victory has a hundred fathers, but defeat is an orphan.

Diary (1946) vol. 2, 9 September 1942 (literally 'no-one wants to recognise defeat as his own')

Cicero (Marcus Tullius Cicero) 106–43 BC

Roman orator and statesman
on Cicero: see **Plutarch** 294:9, **Stevenson** 350:13

5 For he delivers his opinions as though he were living in Plato's Republic rather than among the dregs of Romulus.
  of M. Porcius Cato, the Younger

Ad Atticum

6 *Salus populi suprema est lex.*
  The good of the people is the chief law.

De Legibus

7 Let war yield to peace, laurels to paeans.

De Officiis

8 In men of the highest character and noblest genius there is to be found an insatiable desire for honour, command, power, and glory.

De Officis

9 *O tempora, O mores!*
  Oh, the times! Oh, the manners!

In Catilinam

10 *Civis Romanus sum.*
   I am a Roman citizen.

In Verrem

11 The sinews of war, unlimited money.

Fifth Philippic

12 Laws are silent in time of war.

Pro Milone

13 The young man should be praised, decorated, and got rid of.
   of Octavian, the future Emperor **Augustus**

referred to in a letter from Decimus Brutus to Cicero; *Epistulae ad Familiares*

Lord Clare 1749–1802

Lord Chancellor of Ireland from 1789

14 Make him a bishop, or even an archbishop, but not a Chief Justice.
   an Irish Lord Chancellor's view of the proposed appointment of Lord Norbury as Lord Chief Justice

in *Dictionary of National Biography*

Edward Hyde, Lord Clarendon 1609–74

English statesman and historian

1 Without question, when he first drew the sword, he threw away the scabbard.
   of John Hampden

   The History of the Rebellion (1703) vol. 3

2 He had a head to contrive, a tongue to persuade, and a hand to execute any mischief.
   of Hampden

   The History of the Rebellion (1703) vol. 3

3 He...would, with a shrill and sad accent, ingeminate the word *Peace, Peace*.
   of **Falkland**

   The History of the Rebellion (1703) vol. 3

4 So enamoured on peace that he would have been glad the King should have bought it at any price.
   of **Falkland**

   The History of the Rebellion (1703) vol. 3

5 He will be looked upon by posterity as a brave bad man.
   of **Cromwell**

   The History of the Rebellion (1703) vol. 6

Alan Clark 1928–

British Conservative politician

6 In the end we are all sacked and it's always awful. It is as inevitable as death following life. If you are elevated there comes a day when you are demoted. Even Prime Ministers.

   diary 21 June 1983

7 Give a civil servant a good case and he'll wreck it with clichés, bad punctuation, double negatives and convoluted apology.

   diary 22 July 1983

8 Like most Chief Whips he knew who the shits were.
   of Michael Jopling

   diary 17 June 1987

9 There's nothing so improves the mood of the Party as the imminent execution of a senior colleague.

   diary 13 July 1990

10 There are no true friends in politics. We are all sharks circling, and waiting, for traces of blood to appear in the water.

   diary 30 November 1990

Karl von Clausewitz 1780–1831

Prussian soldier and military theorist

11 War is nothing but a continuation of politics with the admixture of other means.
   commonly rendered 'War is the continuation of politics by other means'

   On War (1832–4)

Henry Clay 1777–1852

American politician
on Clay: see **Glascock** 156:4, **Jackson** 189:5

1 I am for resistance by the *sword*. No man in the nation
desires peace more than I. But I prefer the troubled ocean
of war...to the tranquil, putrescent pool of ignominious
peace.

speech in the US Senate on the
Macon Bill, 22 February 1810

2 If you wish to avoid foreign collision, you had better
abandon the ocean.

in the House of Representatives,
22 January 1812

3 The gentleman [Josiah Quincy] can not have forgotten
his own sentiment, uttered even on the floor of this
House, 'peaceably if we can, forcibly if we must'.

speech in Congress, 8 January 1813

Clay had been shown a letter from **Canning** *to Christopher
Hughes, US minister to Sweden:*
4 I should fall in love with Mr Canning, if I were to read
many more of such letters from him...Under his
ministry...Mr Canning is placing England in her natural
attitude, that of being the head of European liberal
principles, political and commercial.

letter to Samuel Smith, 4 May 1825

of the Native American peoples:
5 Their disappearance from the human family will be no
great loss to the world.

at a cabinet meeting in 1825;
Robert V. Remini *Henry Clay*

6 [Andrew Jackson] is ignorant, passionate, hypocritical,
corrupt, and easily swayed by the basest men who
surround him.

letter to Francis T. Brooke, 2
August 1833

7 The arts of power and its minions are the same in all
countries and in all ages. It marks a victim; denounces
it; and excites the public odium and the public hatred, to
conceal its own abuses and encroachments.

speech in the Senate, 14 March
1834

8 I had rather be right than be President.

to Senator Preston of South
Carolina, 1839; S. W. McCall *Life of
Thomas Brackett Reed* (1914)

9 It has been my invariable rule to do all for the Union. If
any man wants the key of my heart, let him take the key
of the Union, and that is the key to my heart.

speech in Norfolk, 22 April 1844

*when Speaker of the US Senate, Clay was seen leaving a party
at sunrise, and asked how he could expect to preside over the
House that day:*
10 Come up, and you shall see how I will throw the reins
over their necks.

Robert V. Remini *Henry Clay* (1991)

*to Madame de Staël, expressing his regret that the British
forces in America had not been commanded by* **Wellington**:
11 Had we beaten the Duke, we should have gained
immortal honour, whilst we should have lost none, had
we been defeated by the Conqueror of Napoleon.

Robert V. Remini *Henry Clay* (1991)

12 I have heard something said about allegiance to the
South. I know no South, no North, no East, no West, to

speech in the US Senate, 1848

which I owe any allegiance…The Union, sir, is my
country.

1 The Constitution of the United States was made not
merely for the generation that then existed, but for
posterity—unlimited, undefined, endless, perpetual
posterity.

speech in the US Senate, 1850

Eldridge Cleaver 1935–

American political activist

2 What we're saying today is that you're either part of the
solution or you're part of the problem.

speech in San Francisco, 1968; R.
Scheer *Eldridge Cleaver, Post
Prison Writings and Speeches*
(1969)

Sarah Norcliffe Cleghorn 1876–1959

3 The golf-links lie so near the mill
That almost every day
The labouring children can look out
And watch the men at play.

'For Some Must Watch, While —'
(1914)

Georges Clemenceau 1841–1929

French statesman; Prime Minister of France, 1906–9,
1917–20
on Clemenceau: see **Keynes** 207:3, **Lloyd George** 229:10

4 My home policy: I wage war; my foreign policy: I wage
war. All the time I wage war.

speech to French Chamber of
Deputies, 8 March 1918

to André Tardieu, on being asked why he always gave in to
Lloyd George *at the Paris Peace Conference, 1918*
5 What do you expect when I'm between two men of
whom one [Lloyd George] thinks he is Napoleon and the
other [Woodrow Wilson] thinks he is Jesus Christ?

James Lees-Milne *Harold Nicolson*
(1980) vol. 1, letter from Nicolson
to his wife, 20 May 1919

6 It is easier to make war than to make peace.

speech at Verdun, 20 July 1919

7 War is too serious a matter to entrust to military men.

attributed to Clemenceau, e.g. in
Hampden Jackson *Clemenceau and
the Third Republic* (1946), but also
to Briand and Talleyrand

on seeing a pretty girl on his eightieth birthday:
8 Oh, to be seventy again!

James Agate diary 19 April 1938;
has also been attributed to Oliver
Wendell **Holmes** Jr.

Grover Cleveland 1837–1908

American Democratic statesman, 22nd and 24th President of
the US, 1885–9 and 1893–7
on Cleveland: see **Bragg** 54:9

1 Your every voter, as surely as your chief magistrate,   inaugural address, 4 March 1885
   exercises a public trust.
     'public office is a public trust' was used as the motto of the
     Cleveland administration

2 I have considered the pension list of the republic a roll of   veto of Dependent Pension Bill, 5
   honour.   July 1888

3 The lessons of paternalism ought to be unlearned and the   inaugural address, 4 March 1893
   better lesson taught that, while the people should
   patriotically and cheerfully support their government, its
   functions do not include the support of the people.

Harlan Cleveland 1918–

American government official

4 The revolution of rising expectations.   phrase coined, 1950; see Arthur
                                                                        Schlesinger *A Thousand Days*
                                                                        (1965)

William Jefferson ('Bill') Clinton 1946–

American Democratic statesman; 42nd President of the US
from 1993
on Clinton: see **Jackson** 189:8

5 I experimented with marijuana a time or two. And   in *Washington Post* 30 March 1992
   I didn't like it, and I didn't inhale.

6 The comeback kid!   Michael Barone and Grant Ujifusa
     description of himself after coming second in the New   *The Almanac of American Politics*
     Hampshire primary in the 1992 presidential election (since 1952, 1994
     no presidential candidate had won the election without first
     winning in New Hampshire)

7 The urgent question of our time is whether we can make   inaugural address, 1993
   change our friend and not our enemy.

Lord Clive 1725–74

British general; Governor of Bengal

while attempting to take his own life, his pistol twice failed to
fire:
8 I feel that I am reserved for some end or other.   G. R. Gleig *The Life of Robert, First*
                                                                        Lord Clive (1848)

9 By God, Mr Chairman, at this moment I stand astonished   G. R. Gleig *The Life of Robert, First*
   at my own moderation!   *Lord Clive* (1848)
     reply during Parliamentary cross-examination, 1773

Thomas W. Cobb

American politician

1 If you persist, the Union will be dissolved. You have   Robert V. Remini *Henry Clay* (1991)
   kindled a fire which all the waters of the ocean cannot
   put out, which seas of blood can only extinguish.
   *to James Tallmadge, on his amendment to the bill to admit
   Missouri to the Union as a slave state in 1820*

William Cobbett 1762–1835

English political reformer and radical journalist

2 Nouns of number, or multitude, such as Mob,   *English Grammar* (1817)
   Parliament, Rabble, House of Commons, Regiment, Court
   of King's Bench, Den of Thieves, and the like.

3 But what is to be the fate of the great wen of all? The   *Rural Rides: The Kentish Journal* 5
   monster, called... 'the metropolis of the empire'?   January 1822
   of London

4 From a very early age, I had imbibed the opinion, that it   *Political Register* 22 December
   was every man's duty to do all that lay in his power to   1832
   leave his country as good as he had found it.

Lord Cobbold 1904–87

Lord Chamberlain, 1963–71

5 All ceremonial is ridiculous unless it is perfect.   attributed

Claud Cockburn 1904–81

British left-wing journalist

6 Believe nothing until it has been officially denied.   *In Time of Trouble* (1956)
   advice frequently given to the young Claud Cockburn

7 I am prepared to believe that a lot of the people I had   *Crossing the Line* (1958)
   cast as principal figures were really mere cat's-paws. But
   then a cat's-paw is a cat's-paw and must expect to be
   treated as part of the cat.
   of his writing about the 'Cliveden Set'

8 Discipline, unless operated by very remote control, gives   *Crossing the Line* (1958)
   me claustrophobia.
   of his membership of the Communist Party

9 A war-time Minister of Information is compelled, in the   *Crossing the Line* (1958)
   national interest, to such continuous acts of duplicity
   that even his natural hair must grow to resemble a wig.
   *of Brendan **Bracken***

Edward Coke 1552–1634

English jurist

1   Magna Charta is such a fellow, that he will have no
sovereign.
on the Lords' Amendment to the Petition of Right, 17 May 1628

J. Rushworth *Historical Collections*
(1659) vol. 1

Samuel Taylor Coleridge 1772–1834

English poet, critic, and philosopher

2   In politics, what begins in fear usually ends in folly.

Table Talk (1835) 5 October 1830

3   State policy, a cyclops with one eye, and that in the back
of the head!

*On the Constitution of the Church
and State* (1839)

Michael Collins 1890–1922

Irish nationalist leader and politician; on the death of Arthur
Griffith in 1922, he became head of state, but was shot in an
ambush ten days later

4   I tell you—early this morning I signed my death
warrant.
on signing the Anglo-Irish Treaty of 1921

letter 6 December 1921

*on arriving at Dublin Castle for the handover by British forces
on 16 January 1922, and being told that he was seven minutes
late:*
5   We've been waiting 700 years, you can have the seven
minutes.

Tim Pat Coogan *Michael Collins*
(1990); attributed

Barber B. Conable Jr. 1922–

American Republican politician and banker

6   I guess we have found the smoking pistol, haven't we?
*on hearing a tape of President **Nixon**'s discussion with H. R.
Haldeman, on 23 June 1972, as to how the FBI's investigation of
the Watergate burglary could be limited*

Nigel Rees *Brewer's Quotations*
(1994)

James M. Connell 1852–1929

Irish socialist songwriter

7   The people's flag is deepest red;
It shrouded oft our martyred dead,
And ere their limbs grew stiff and cold,
Their heart's blood dyed its every fold.
Then raise the scarlet standard high!
Within its shade we'll live or die.
Tho' cowards flinch and traitors sneer,
We'll keep the red flag flying here.

'The Red Flag' (1889)

Cyril Connolly 1903–74

English writer

1 M is for Marx   'Where Engels Fears to Tread'
   And Movement of Masses
   And Massing of Arses.
   And Clashing of Classes.

James Connolly 1868–1916

Irish labour leader; executed after the Easter Rising, 1916

2 The worker is the slave of capitalist society, the female   *The Re-conquest of Ireland* (1915)
   worker is the slave of that slave.

Joseph Conrad 1857–1924

Polish-born English novelist

3 The terrorist and the policeman both come from the   *The Secret Agent* (1907)
   same basket.

4 The scrupulous and the just, the noble, humane, and   *Under Western Eyes* (1911)
   devoted natures; the unselfish and the intelligent may
   begin a movement—but it passes away from them. They
   are not the leaders of a revolution. They are its victims.

A. J. Cook 1885–1931

English labour leader; Secretary of the Miners' Federation of
Great Britain, 1924–31

5 Not a penny off the pay, not a second on the day.   speech at York, 3 April 1926
   often quoted with 'minute' substituted for 'second'

Peter Cook 1937–95

British satirist and performer

6 I have recently been travelling round the world—on your   *Beyond the Fringe* (1961)
   behalf, and at your expense—visiting some of the chaps
   with whom I hope to be shaping your future. I went first
   to Germany, and there I spoke with the German Foreign
   Minister, Herr...Herr and there, and we exchanged
   many frank words in our respective languages.
   sketch satirizing the Prime Minister, Harold **Macmillan**

7 The people who went into politics were those who   in *Guardian* 10 January 1995
   couldn't get in the Footlights or were no good at
   journalism.
   of his Cambridge contemporaries

Calvin Coolidge 1872–1933

American Republican statesman, 30th President of the US
1923–9
on Coolidge: see **Anonymous** 13:12, **Mencken** 256:13,
Parker 285:3

1 There is no right to strike against the public safety by
   anybody, anywhere, any time.

telegram to Samuel Gompers, 14
September 1919

2 Civilization and profits go hand in hand.

speech in New York, 27 November
1920

3 The chief business of the American people is business.

speech in Washington, 17 January
1925

4 They hired the money, didn't they?
   on the subject of war debts incurred by England and others

John H. McKee *Coolidge: Wit and
Wisdom* (1933)

*account (probably apocryphal) supposedly given by Coolidge
to his wife of what a preacher had said about sin:*
5 He was against it.

John H. McKee *Coolidge: Wit and
Wisdom* (1933)

6 Nothing is easier than spending the public money. It does
   not appear to belong to anybody. The temptation is
   overwhelming to bestow it on somebody.

attributed

7 When a great many people are unable to find work,
   unemployment results.

attributed

Francis M. Cornford 1874–1943

English classical scholar

8 Every public action, which is not customary, either is
   wrong, or, if it is right, is a dangerous precedent. It
   follows that nothing should ever be done for the first
   time.

Microcosmographia Academica
(1908)

of propaganda:
9 That branch of the art of lying which consists in very
   nearly deceiving your friends without quite deceiving
   your enemies.

Microcosmographia Academica
(1922 ed.)

Coronation Service

10 We present you with this Book, the most valuable thing
    that this world affords. Here is wisdom; this is the royal
    Law; these are the lively Oracles of God.

'The Presenting of the Holy Bible';
L. G. Wickham Legge *English
Coronation Records* (1901)

Thomas Coventry 1578–1640

English judge

11 The dominion of the sea, as it is an ancient and
    undoubted right of the crown of England, so it is the best
    security of the land…The wooden walls are the best
    walls of this kingdom.

speech to the Judges, 17 June 1635

Michel Guillaume Jean de Crèvecoeur
1735–1813

French-born immigrant to America

1 What then is the American, this new man? He is either *Letters from an American Farmer*
a European, or the descendant of a European, hence that (1782)
strange mixture of blood, which you will find in no other
country...Here individuals of all nations are melted into
a new race of men, whose labours and posterity will one
day cause great changes in the world.

Ivor Crewe 1945–
British political scientist

2 The British public has always displayed a healthy *in Guardian* 18 January 1995
cynicism of MPs. They have taken it for granted that MPs
are self-serving impostors and hypocrites who put party
before country and self before party.
   addressing the Nolan inquiry into standards in public life

George Washington Crile 1864–1943
American surgeon and physiologist

3 France...a nation of forty millions with a deep-rooted *A Mechanistic View of War and*
grievance and an iron curtain at its frontier. *Peace* (1915)

Julian Critchley 1930–
British Conservative politician and journalist

4 The only safe pleasure for a parliamentarian is a bag of *in Listener* 10 June 1982
boiled sweets.

5 She cannot see an institution without hitting it with her *in The Times* 21 June 1982
handbag.
   of Margaret **Thatcher**

6 Humming, Hawing and Hesitation are the three Graces of *Westminster Blues* (1985)
contemporary Parliamentary oratory.

7 He could not see a parapet without ducking beneath it. *Heseltine* (1987)
   of Michael **Heseltine**

8 Like Marxism, Thatcherism is, in fact, riddled with *Palace of Varieties* (1989)
contradictions. Mrs Thatcher, on the other hand, is free
of doubt, she is the label on the can of worms.

9 Disloyalty is the secret weapon of the Tory Party. *in Observer* 11 November 1990

Oliver Cromwell 1599–1658

English soldier, politician, and general; Lord Protector from
1653

on being asked by **Lord Falkland** *what he would have done if
the Grand Remonstrance of 1641 against the King had not
passed:*

1 I would have sold all I had the next morning, and never
have seen England more.

Clarendon *History of the Rebellion*
(1826)

2 A few honest men are better than numbers.

letter to William Spring, September
1643

3 I would rather have a plain russet-coated captain that
knows what he fights for, and loves what he knows,
than that which you call 'a gentleman' and is nothing
else.

letter to William Spring, September
1643

4 Cruel necessity.
on the execution of **Charles I**

Joseph Spence *Anecdotes* (1820)

5 For that which you mention concerning liberty of
conscience, I meddle not with any man's conscience.
letter to the Governor of Ross in Ireland, 19 October 1649

W. C. Abbott *Writings and
Speeches of Oliver Cromwell*
(1939) vol. 3

6 I beseech you, in the bowels of Christ, think it possible
you may be mistaken.

letter to the General Assembly of
the Kirk of Scotland, 3 August 1650

7 The dimensions of this mercy are above my thoughts. It
is, for aught I know, a crowning mercy.

letter to William **Lenthall**, Speaker
of the Parliament of England, 4
September 1651

8 You have sat too long here for any good you have been
doing. Depart, I say, and let us have done with you. In
the name of God, go!
*addressing the Rump Parliament, 20 April 1653 (oral tradition;
quoted by Leo* **Amery** *to Neville* **Chamberlain** *in the House of
Commons, 7 May 1940)*

Bulstrode Whitelock *Memorials of
the English Affairs* (1732 ed.)

9 Take away that fool's bauble, the mace.
*at the dismissal of the Rump Parliament, 20 April 1653; often
quoted as 'Take away these baubles'*

Bulstrode Whitelock *Memorials of
the English Affairs* (1732 ed.)

10 It's a maxim not to be despised, 'Though peace be made,
yet it's interest that keeps peace.'

speech to Parliament, 4 September
1654

11 Necessity hath no law. Feigned necessities, imaginary
necessities...are the greatest cozenage that men can put
upon the Providence of God, and make pretences to
break known rules by.

speech to Parliament, 12
September 1654

12 Your poor army, those poor contemptible men, came up
hither.

speech to Parliament, 21 April 1657

13 You have accounted yourselves happy on being
environed with a great ditch from all the world besides.

speech to Parliament, 25 January
1658

14 Mr Lely, I desire you would use all your skill to paint my
picture truly like me, and not flatter me at all; but
remark all these roughnesses, pimples, warts, and
everything as you see me; otherwise I will never pay

Horace Walpole *Anecdotes of
Painting in England* vol. 3 (1763)

a farthing for it.
commonly quoted as 'warts and all'

1 None climbs so high as he who knows not whither he is   attributed
   going.

2 There is no one I am more at a loss how to manage than   B. Martyn and Dr Kippis *The Life of*
   that Marcus Tullius Cicero, the little man with three   *the First Earl of Shaftesbury* (1836)
   names.
   of Anthony Ashley Cooper, Lord **Shaftesbury**

3 My design is to make what haste I can to be gone.   John Morley *Oliver Cromwell* (1900)
   last words

Anthony Crosland 1918–77

British Labour politician; Foreign Secretary 1976–7

4 Total abstinence and a good filing system are not now   *The Future of Socialism* (1956)
   the right signposts to the socialist Utopia; or at least, if
   they are, some of us will fall by the wayside.

5 If it's the last thing I do, I'm going to destroy every   Susan Crosland *Tony Crosland*
   fucking grammar school in England. And Wales, and   (1982)
   Northern Ireland.
   c.1965, while Secretary of State for Education and Science

6 The party's over.   Anthony Sampson *The Changing*
   cutting back central government's support for rates, as Minister   *Anatomy of Britain* (1982)
   of the Environment in the 1970's

7 In the blood of the socialist there should always run   Susan Crosland *Tony Crosland*
   a trace of the anarchist and the libertarian, and not too   (1982)
   much of the prig and the prude.

Lord Cross 1823–1914

British Conservative politician

8 I hear a smile.   G. W. E. Russell *Collections and*
   when the House of Lords laughed at his speech in favour of   *Recollections* (1898)
   Spiritual Peers

Richard Crossman 1907–74

British Labour politician
on Crossman: see **Dalton** 109:2

9 While there is death there is hope.   Tam Dalyell *Dick Crossman* (1989)
   on the death of Hugh **Gaitskell** *in 1963*

10 The Civil Service is profoundly deferential—'Yes,   *Diaries of a Cabinet Minister* vol. 1
   Minister! No, Minister! If you wish it, Minister!'   (1975) 22 October 1964

11 There is a cracking sound in the political atmosphere: the   in 1970; Anthony Sampson *The*
   sound of the consensus breaking up.   *Changing Anatomy of Britain*
                                                                (1982)

12 [To strip away] the thick masses of foliage which we call   introduction to *Diaries of a Cabinet*
   the myth of democracy.   *Minister* vol. 1 (1975)

Robert Crouch

British Conservative politician

*criticizing the conduct of Ministry of Agriculture officials in the
Crichel Down affair, when landowners were not permitted to
buy back land compulsorily purchased for a wartime airfield:*
1   Charles I lost his head for no less than this.

in the House of Commons, 20 July
1954

E. E. Cummings 1894–1962

American poet

2   a politician is an arse upon
which everyone has sat except a man.

1 x 1 (1944) no. 10

Mario Cuomo 1932–

American Democratic politician, former Governor of New York

3   You campaign in poetry. You govern in prose.

in *New Republic*, Washington, DC,
8 April 1985

John Philpot Curran 1750–1817

Irish judge

4   The condition upon which God hath given liberty to man
is eternal vigilance; which condition if he break,
servitude is at once the consequence of his crime, and
the punishment of his guilt.

speech on the right of election of
the Lord Mayor of Dublin, 10 July
1790

of Robert Peel's smile:
5   Like the silver plate on a coffin.

quoted by Daniel O'Connell in the
House of Commons, 26 February
1835

Edwina Currie 1946–

British Conservative politician

6   I honestly don't think that problem has anything to do
with poverty…The problem very often for people is,
I think, just ignorance.
  on problems of high smoking and alcoholism

speech at Newcastle upon Tyne,
23 September 1986

7   My message to the businessmen of this country when
they go abroad on business is that there is one thing
above all they can take with them to stop them catching
Aids—and that is the wife.

speech at Runcorn, 12 February
1987

Lord Curzon 1859–1925

British Conservative politician; Viceroy of India 1898–1905
on Curzon: **Beaverbrook** 34:1, 34:3; **Churchill** 89:9,
Nehru 270:12

1 Other countries have but one capital—Paris, Berlin,
Madrid. Great Britain has a series of capitals all over the
world, from Ottawa to Shanghai.

notebook, 1887; Kenneth Rose
Superior Person (1969)

2 I never knew that the lower classes had such white skins.
*supposedly said when watching troops bathing during the First
World War*

Kenneth Rose *Superior Person*
(1969)

3 When a group of Cabinet Ministers begins to meet
separately and to discuss independent action, the death-
tick is audible in the rafters.
*in November 1922, shortly before the fall of **Lloyd George**'s
Coalition Government*

David Gilmour *Curzon* (1994)

4 Not even a public figure. A man of no experience. And of
the utmost insignificance.
*of Stanley **Baldwin**, appointed Prime Minister in 1923 in
succession to **Bonar Law***

Harold Nicolson *Curzon: the Last
Phase* (1934)

5 Gentlemen do not take soup at luncheon.

E. L. Woodward *Short Journey*
(1942)

Astolphe Louis Léonard, Marquis de Custine 1790–1857

French author and traveller

6 This empire, vast as it is, is only a prison to which the
emperor holds the key.
of Russia

La Russie en 1839; at Peterhof, 23
July 1839

7 Whoever has really seen Russia will find himself content
to live anywhere else. It is always good to know that
a society exists where no happiness is possible because,
by a law of nature, man cannot be happy unless he is
free.

La Russie en 1839; at Peterhof, 23
July 1839; conclusion

Richard J. Daley 1902–76

American Democratic politician and Mayor of Chicago

8 The policeman isn't there to create disorder; the
policeman is there to preserve disorder.
*to the press, on the riots during the Democratic Convention in
1968*

Milton N. Rakove *Don't Make No
Waves: Don't Back No Losers*
(1975)

Hugh Dalton 1887–1962

British Labour politician
on Dalton: see **Anonymous** 13:10; **Attlee** 20:3; **Birch** 45:6

9 It is very difficult for anybody outside the cage of the
Parliamentary Labour Party to measure up the

Political Diary (1986) 15 June 1938

inclinations of the inmates.
on support for a challenge by Herbert **Morrison** *to* **Attlee***'s leadership*

1 The King says that he has to remind Winston that he is only PM in England and not in France as well.

diary 31 May 1940

2 I view this able and energetic man with some detachment. He is loyal to his own career but only incidentally to anything or anyone else.
of Richard **Crossman**

diary 17 September 1941

3 How I love a colleague-free day! Then I can really get on with the job.
as Chancellor of the Exchequer

Political Diary (1986) 15 May 1946

George Dangerfield

4 To reform the House of Lords [in 1910] meant to set down in writing a Constitution which for centuries had remained happily unwritten, to conjure a great ghost into the narrow and corruptible flesh of a code.

The Strange Death of Liberal England (1936)

Samuel Daniel 1563–1619

English poet and playwright

5   Princes in this case
Do hate the traitor, though they love the treason.

The Tragedy of Cleopatra (1594)

Georges Jacques Danton 1759–94

French revolutionary

6 *De l'audace, et encore de l'audace, et toujours de l'audace!*
Boldness, and again boldness, and always boldness!

speech to the Legislative Committee of General Defence, 2 September 1792

7 Thou wilt show my head to the people: it is worth showing.
to his executioner, 5 April 1794

Thomas Carlyle *History of the French Revolution* (1837) vol. 3

Clarence Darrow 1857–1938

American lawyer

8 When I was a boy I was told that anybody could become President. I'm beginning to believe it.

Irving Stone *Clarence Darrow for the Defence* (1941)

Harry Daugherty 1860–1941

American Republican supporter

9 Some twelve or fifteen men, worn out and bleary-eyed for lack of sleep, will sit down about two o'clock in the morning around a table in a smoke-filled room in some hotel and decide the nomination.
the way in which the Republican Party's presidential candidate

attributed (although subsequently denied by Daugherty); William Safire *The New Language of Politics* (1968) *for 1920 would be selected if (as in fact happened) no clear nomination emerged from the convention; cf. **Simpson** 340:7*

Charles D'Avenant 1656–1714

English playwright and political economist

1 Custom, that unwritten law,
By which the people keep even kings in awe.

Circe (1677)

David Davis 1815–86

American judge

2 The Constitution of the United States is a law for rulers and people, equally in war and in peace, and covers with the shield of its protection all classes of men, at all times, and under all circumstances. No doctrine, involving more pernicious consequences, was ever invented by the wit of man than that any of its provisions can be suspended during any of the great exigencies of government.

in *Ex Parte Milligan* (1866)

Jefferson Davis 1808–89

American statesman; President of the Confederate states 1861–5
on Davis: see **Yancey** 395:3

3 If the Confederacy fails, there should be written on its tombstone: *Died of a Theory.*

in 1865; Geoffrey C. Ward *The Civil War* (1991)

Christopher Dawson 1889–1970

4 As soon as men decide that all means are permitted to fight an evil, then their good becomes indistinguishable from the evil that they set out to destroy.

The Judgment of the Nations (1942)

Lord Dawson of Penn 1864–1945

British doctor; physician to King **George V**

5 The King's life is moving peacefully towards its close.
bulletin, drafted on a menu card at Buckingham Palace on the eve of the king's death, 20 January 1936

Kenneth Rose *King George V* (1983)

John Dean 1938–

American lawyer and White House counsel during the Watergate affair

6 We have a cancer within, close to the Presidency, that is growing.

from the [Nixon] Presidential Transcripts, 21 March 1973

Régis Debray 1940–

French Marxist theorist

1 International life is right-wing, like nature. The social   *Charles de Gaulle* (1994)
   contract is left-wing, like humanity.

Eugene Victor Debs 1855–1926

founder of the Socialist Party of America

2 When great changes occur in history, when great   *Speeches* (1928)
   principles are involved, as a rule the majority are wrong.
   The minority are right.
   *speech at his trial for sedition in Cleveland, Ohio, 11 September
   1918*

3 While there is a lower class, I am in it; while there is   in *Liberator* November 1918
   a criminal element, I am of it; while there is a soul in
   prison, I am not free.
   *speech at his trial for sedition in Cleveland, Ohio, 11 September
   1918*

Stephen Decatur 1779–1820

American naval officer

4 Our country! In her intercourse with foreign nations,   A. S. Mackenzie *Life of Stephen
   may she always be in the right; but our country, right or   Decatur* (1846); cf. **Adams** 4:6
   wrong.
   Decatur's toast at Norfolk, Virginia, April 1816

Daniel Defoe 1660–1731

English novelist and journalist

5 Fools out of favour grudge at knaves in place.   *The True-Born Englishman* (1701)
                                                                    introduction

6 From this amphibious ill-born mob began   *The True-Born Englishman* (1701)
   That vain, ill-natured thing, an Englishman.

7 Your Roman-Saxon-Danish-Norman English.   *The True-Born Englishman* (1701)

8 His lazy, long, lascivious reign.   *The True-Born Englishman* (1701)
   of **Charles II**

9 Great families of yesterday we show,   *The True-Born Englishman* (1701)
   And lords whose parents were the Lord knows who.

10 And of all plagues with which mankind are curst,   *The True-Born Englishman* (1701)
   Ecclesiastic tyranny's the worst.

11 When kings the sword of justice first lay down,   *The True-Born Englishman* (1701)
   They are no kings, though they possess the crown.
   Titles are shadows, crowns are empty things,
   The good of subjects is the end of kings.

12 Nature has left this tincture in the blood,   *The History of the Kentish Petition*
   That all men would be tyrants if they could.   (1712–13)

Charles de Gaulle 1890–1970

French general; President of France, 1959–69

1 Authority doesn't work without prestige, or prestige without distance.

Le Fil de l'épée (1932) 'Du caractère'

2 The sword is the axis of the world and its power is absolute.

Vers l'armée de métier (1934) 'Comment?' Commandement 3

3 France has lost a battle. But France has not lost the war!

proclamation, 18 June 1940

4 Since they whose duty it was to wield the sword of France have let it fall shattered to the ground, I have taken up the broken blade.

speech, 13 July 1940

5 When I am right, I get angry. Churchill gets angry when he is wrong. We are angry at each other much of the time.

attributed

on the death of his daughter, who had been born with Down's Syndrome:

6 And now she is like everyone else.

in 1948; Jean Lacouture *De Gaulle* (1965)

7 Is it credible that at the age of sixty-seven I am going to begin a career as a dictator?

attibuted, 1958

8 Yes, it is Europe, from the Atlantic to the Urals, it is Europe, it is the whole of Europe, that will decide the fate of the world.

speech to the people of Strasbourg, 23 November 1959

9 Politics are too serious a matter to be left to the politicians.
    *replying to Clement **Attlee**'s remark that 'De Gaulle is a very good soldier and a very bad politician'*

Clement Attlee *A Prime Minister Remembers* (1961)

10 *Europe des patries.*
   A Europe of nations.

widely associated with De Gaulle and taken as encapsulating his views, although perhaps not coined by him; J. Lacouture *De Gaulle: the Ruler* (1991)

11 How can you govern a country which has 246 varieties of cheese?

Ernest Mignon *Les Mots du Général* (1962)

12 Since a politician never believes what he says, he is quite surprised to be taken at his word.

Ernest Mignon *Les Mots du Général* (1962)

13 Treaties, you see, are like girls and roses: they last while they last.

speech at Elysée Palace, 2 July 1963

14 *Vive Le Québec Libre.*
   Long Live Free Quebec.
     quoting the slogan of the separatist movement for an independent Quebec

speech in Montreal, 24 July 1967

Vine Victor Deloria Jr. 1933–

Standing Rock Sioux

15 Tribalism is the strongest force at work in the world today.

Custer Died for Your Sins (1969)

1 This country was a lot better off when the Indians were
   running it.

in *New York Times Magazine* 3
March 1970

Demosthenes *c.*384 – *c.*322 BC

Athenian orator and statesman

2 There is one safeguard known generally to the wise,
   which is an advantage and security to all, but especially
   to democracies against despots—suspicion.

Philippic

Jack Dempsey 1895–1983

American boxer

3 Honey, I just forgot to duck.
     *to his wife, on losing the World Heavyweight title, 23 September
     1926; after a failed attempt on his life in 1981, Ronald* **Reagan**
     quipped to his wife 'Honey, I forgot to duck'

J. and B. P. Dempsey *Dempsey*
(1977)

Deng Xiaoping 1904–97

Chinese Communist statesman, Vice-Premier 1973–6 and
1977–80; Vice-Chairman of the Central Committee of the
Chinese Communist Party 1977–80, and from that period
paramount leader of China

4 The colour of the cat doesn't matter as long as it catches
   the mice.

proverbial expression; in *Financial
Times* 18 December 1986

Lord Denning 1899–

British judge

5 The Treaty [of Rome] is like an incoming tide. It flows
   into the estuaries and up the rivers. It cannot be held
   back.

in 1975; Anthony Sampson *The
Essential Anatomy of Britain* (1992)

6 To every subject of this land, however powerful, I would
   use Thomas Fuller's words over three hundred years ago,
   'Be ye never so high, the law is above you.'

in a High Court ruling against the
Attorney-General, January 1977; cf.
Fuller 144:6

7 The keystone of the rule of law in England has been the
   independence of judges. It is the only respect in which we
   make any real separation of powers.

The Family Story (1981)

8 Properly exercised the new powers of the executive lead
   to the welfare state; but abused they lead to the
   totalitarian state.

Anthony Sampson *The Changing
Anatomy of Britain* (1982)

Edward Stanley, 14th Earl of Derby

1799–1869

British Conservative statesman; Prime Minister, 1852,
1858–9, 1866–8
on Derby: see **Bulwer-Lytton** 62:1; **Disraeli** 117:14

1 The duty of an Opposition [is] very simple...to oppose
everything, and propose nothing.

quoting 'Mr Tierney, a great Whig authority', in the House of Commons, 4 June 1841

2 Meddle and muddle.
   *summarizing Lord John **Russell**'s foreign policy*

speech on the Address, in the House of Lords 4 February 1864

Edward Stanley, 15th Earl of Derby

1826–93

British Conservative politician

3 She is civil to persons in power under her, whose good
will contributes to her comfort (and not always to them):
but sees no reason for wasting civility on those who can
no longer be of use to her.
   *of Queen **Victoria**, as seen in her relations with her former Prime
   Minister, the fourteenth earl of **Derby**, in his last illness*

Political Journals of Lord Stanley 1849–69

Camille Desmoulins 1760–94

French revolutionary

4 My age is that of the *bon Sansculotte Jésus*; an age fatal to
Revolutionists.
   reply given at his trial

Thomas Carlyle History of the French Revolution (1837)

Thomas E. Dewey 1902–71

American politician and presidential candidate

5 That's why it's time for a change!
   phrase used extensively in campaigns of 1944, 1948, and 1952

campaign speech in San Francisco, 21 September 1944

Porfirio Diaz 1830–1915

President of Mexico, 1877–80, 1884–1911

6 Poor Mexico, so far from God and so close to the United
States.

attributed

A. V. Dicey 1835–1922

British jurist

7 The beneficial effect of state intervention, especially in the
form of legislation, is direct, immediate, and, so to speak,
visible, while its evil effects are gradual and indirect, and
lie out of sight...Hence the majority of mankind must

Lectures on the Relation between Law and Public Opinion (1914)

almost of necessity look with undue favour upon
government intervention.

Charles Dickens 1812–70

English novelist

1 'It's always best on these occasions to do what the mob
do.' 'But suppose there are two mobs?' suggested Mr
Snodgrass. 'Shout with the largest,' replied Mr Pickwick.

Pickwick Papers (1837)

2 O let us love our occupations,
Bless the squire and his relations,
Live upon our daily rations,
And always know our proper stations.

The Chimes (1844) 'The Second
Quarter'

3 Annual income twenty pounds, annual expenditure
nineteen nineteen six, result happiness. Annual income
twenty pounds, annual expenditure twenty pounds ought
and six, result misery.

David Copperfield (1850)

4 It was the best of times, it was the worst of times, it was
the age of wisdom, it was the age of foolishness, it was
the epoch of belief, it was the epoch of incredulity, it was
the season of Light, it was the season of Darkness, it was
the spring of hope, it was the winter of despair, we had
everything before us, we had nothing before us, we were
all going direct to Heaven, we were all going direct the
other way.
     of the French Revolution

A Tale of Two Cities (1859)

5 'It is possible—that it may not come, during our lives…
We shall not see the triumph.' 'We shall have helped it,'
returned madame.

A Tale of Two Cities (1859)

6 Detestation of the high is the involuntary homage of the
low.

A Tale of Two Cities (1859)

7 My faith in the people governing is, on the whole,
infinitesimal; my faith in The People governed is, on the
whole, illimitable.

speech at Birmingham and
Midland Institute, 27 September
1869

John Dickinson 1732–1808

American politician

8 Then join hand in hand, brave Americans all,—
By uniting we stand, by dividing we fall.

'The Liberty Song' (1768)

9 We have counted the cost of this contest, and find
nothing so dreadful as voluntary slavery…Our cause is
just, our union is perfect.
     *declaration of reasons for taking up arms against England,
     presented to Congress, 8 July 1775*

C. J. Stillé *The Life and Times of
John Dickinson* (1891)

Denis Diderot 1713–84

French philosopher and man of letters

1 And [with] the guts of the last priest
   Let's shake the neck of the last king.

Dithrambe sur fete de rois; cf.
Meslier 257:6

Joan Didion 1934–

American writer

2 When we start deceiving ourselves into thinking not that
   we want something or need something, not that it is
   a pragmatic necessity for us to have it, but that it is
   a *moral imperative* that we have it, then is when we join
   the fashionable madmen, and then is when the thin
   whine of hysteria is heard in the land, and then is when
   we are in bad trouble.

Slouching towards Bethlehem
(1968) 'On Morality'

Benjamin Disraeli 1804–81

British Tory statesman, Prime Minister 1868 and 1874–80
on Disraeli: see **Bismarck** 47:3, **Carlyle** 76:12, **Foot** 138:6,
Palmerston 284:3

3 I repeat...that all power is a trust—that we are
   accountable for its exercise—that, from the people, and
   for the people, all springs, and all must exist.

Vivian Grey (1826)

4 Experience is the child of thought and thought is the
   child of action. We cannot learn men from books.

Vivian Grey (1826)

5 There is no act of treachery or meanness of which
   a political party is not capable; for in politics there is no
   honour.

Vivian Grey (1826)

6 The Lords do not encourage wit, and so are obliged to
   put up with pertness.

The Young Duke (1831)

7 Read no history: nothing but biography, for that is life
   without theory.

Contarini Fleming (1832)

8 The practice of politics in the East may be defined by one
   word—dissimulation.

Contarini Fleming (1832)

9 Between ourselves I could floor them all. This *entre nous*.
   I was never more confident of anything than that I could
   carry everything before me in that House. The time will
   come.
   four years before he entered Parliament

letter 7 February 1833

10 In the 'Town' yesterday, I am told 'some one asked
   Disraeli, in offering himself for Marylebone, on what he
   intended *to stand*. "On my head," was the reply.'

letter 8 April 1833

11 What we anticipate seldom occurs; what we least
   expected generally happens.

Henrietta Temple (1837)

12 Though I sit down now, the time will come when you
   will hear me.
   maiden speech

in the House of Commons, 7
December 1837

1 The Continent will [not] suffer England to be the   in the House of Commons, 15
   workshop of the world.   March 1838

2 The House of Commons is absolute. It is the State. 'L'État *Coningsby* (1844)
   c'est moi.'

3 What by way of jest they call the Lower House.   *Coningsby* (1844)
   of the House of Commons

4 A government of statesmen or of clerks? Of Humbug or   *Coningsby* (1844)
   Humdrum?

5 We owe the English peerage to three sources: the   *Coningsby* (1844)
   spoliation of the Church; the open and flagrant sale of
   honours by the elder Stuarts; and the borough-
   mongering of our own time.

6 Conservatism discards Prescription, shrinks from   *Coningsby* (1844)
   Principle, disavows Progress; having rejected all respect
   for antiquity, it offers no redress for the present, and
   makes no preparation for the future.

7 'A sound Conservative government,' said Taper,   *Coningsby* (1844)
   musingly. 'I understand: Tory men and Whig measures.'

8 Youth is a blunder; Manhood a struggle; Old Age   *Coningsby* (1844)
   a regret.

9 It seems to me a barren thing this Conservatism—an   *Coningsby* (1844); cf.
   unhappy cross-breed, the mule of politics that engenders   **Donnelly** 122:7, **Power** 298:1
   nothing.

10 The depositary of power is always unpopular.   *Coningsby* (1844)

11 Where can we find faith in a nation of sectaries?   *Coningsby* (1844)

12 No Government can be long secure without a formidable   *Coningsby* (1844)
   Opposition.

13 Thus you have a starving population, an absentee   in the House of Commons, 16
   aristocracy, and an alien Church, and in addition the   February 1844
   weakest executive in the world. That is the Irish
   Question.

14 The noble Lord is the Prince Rupert of Parliamentary   in the House of Commons, 24 April
   discussion.   1844; cf. **Bulwer-Lytton** 62:1
   of Lord Stanley, later the 14th Earl of **Derby**

15 The right hon. Gentleman caught the Whigs bathing,   in the House of Commons, 28
   and walked away with their clothes.   February 1845
   on Robert **Peel***'s abandoning protection in favour of free trade,*
   traditionally the policy of the [Whig] Opposition

16 Protection is not a principle, but an expedient.   in the House of Commons, 17
                                                              March 1845

17 A Conservative Government is an organized hypocrisy.   in the House of Commons, 17
                                                              March 1845, (Bagehot, quoting
                                                              Disraeli in *The English Constitution*
                                                              (1867) 'The House of Lords',
                                                              elaborated on the theme with the
                                                              words 'so much did the ideas of its
                                                              "head" differ from the sensations
                                                              of its "tail" ')

1 He traces the steam-engine always back to the tea-kettle. | in the House of Commons, 11 April
   of Robert **Peel** | 1845

2 'Two nations; between whom there is no intercourse and | *Sybil* (1845)
   no sympathy; who are as ignorant of each other's habits,
   thoughts, and feelings, as if they were dwellers in
   different zones, or inhabitants of different planets; who
   are formed by a different breeding, are fed by a different
   food, are ordered by different manners, and are not
   governed by the same laws.' 'You speak of—' said
   Egremont, hesitatingly, 'THE RICH AND THE POOR'

3 I was told that the Privileged and the People formed Two | *Sybil* (1845)
   Nations.

4 Pretending that people can be better off than they are is | *Sybil* (1845)
   radicalism and nothing else.

5 'Frank and explicit'—that is the right line to take when | *Sybil* (1845)
   you wish to conceal your own mind and to confuse the
   minds of others.

6 The Youth of a Nation are the trustees of Posterity. | *Sybil* (1845)

7 That fatal drollery called a representative government. | *Tancred* (1847)

8 A majority is always the best repartee. | *Tancred* (1847)

9 Progress to what and from where...The European talks | *Tancred* (1847)
   of progress because by an ingenious application of some
   scientific acquirements he has established a society which
   has mistaken comfort for civilization.

10 London is a modern Babylon. | *Tancred* (1847)

11 We should never lose an occasion. Opportunity is more | *Tancred* (1847)
   powerful even than conquerors and prophets.

12 The grovelling tyranny of self-government. | *Tancred* (1847)

   of Robert **Peel**:
13 He is a burglar of others' intellect...There is no | W. Monypenny and G. Buckle *Life*
   statesman who has committed political petty larceny on | *of Benjamin Disraeli* vol. 2 (1912)
   so great a scale.

14 Justice is truth in action. | in the House of Commons, 11
   | February 1851

15 I read this morning an awful, though monotonous, | in the House of Commons, 13
   manifesto in the great organ of public opinion, which | February 1851
   always makes me tremble: Olympian bolts; and yet
   I could not help fancying amid their rumbling terrors
   I heard the plaintive treble of the Treasury Bench.

16 He has to learn that petulance is not sarcasm, and that | in the House of Commons, 16
   insolence is not invective. | December 1852
   of Charles Wood

17 England does not love coalitions. | in the House of Commons, 16
   | December 1852

18 An aristocracy is rather apt to exaggerate the qualities | *Lord George Bentinck* (1852)
   and magnify the importance of a plebeian leader.

of Robert **Peel**:

1 Wanting imagination he lacked prescience...His *Lord George Bentinck* (1852)
judgement was faultless provided he had not to deal with
the future.

2 These wretched colonies will all be independent, too, in letter to Lord Malmesbury, 13
a few years, and are a millstone round our necks. August 1852

3 Finality is not the language of politics. in the House of Commons, 28
February 1859

4 He seems to think that posterity is a pack-horse, always speech, 3 June 1862; attributed
ready to be loaded.

5 It is, I say, in the noble Lord's power to come to some in the House of Commons, 8 May
really cordial understanding...between this country and 1862
France...and to put an end to these bloated armaments
which only involve states in financial embarrassment.

6 Colonies do not cease to be colonies because they are in the House of Commons, 5
independent. February 1863

7 You are not going, I hope, to leave the destinies of the in the House of Commons, 5
British Empire to prigs and pedants. February 1863

8 I hold that the characteristic of the present age is craving speech at Oxford, 25 November
credulity. 1864

9 Party is organized opinion. speech at Oxford, 25 November
1864

10 Is man an ape or an angel? Now I am on the side of the speech at Oxford, 25 November
angels. 1864

11 Assassination has never changed the history of the in the House of Commons, 1 May
world. 1865

12 I had to prepare the mind of the country, and...to speech at Edinburgh, 29 October
educate our party. 1867

13 Change is inevitable in a progressive country. Change is speech at Edinburgh, 29 October
constant. 1867

14 There can be no economy where there is no efficiency. address to his Constituents, 1
October 1868

to Queen Victoria after the publication of Leaves from the
Journal of our Life in the Highlands *in 1868:*

15 We authors, Ma'am. Elizabeth Longford *Victoria R.I.*
(1964)

16 We have legalized confiscation, consecrated sacrilege, and in the House of Commons, 27
condoned high treason. February 1871
on **Gladstone**'s *Irish policy*

17 I look upon Parliamentary Government as the noblest speech at Manchester, 3 April 1872
government in the world.

18 I believe that without party Parliamentary government is speech at Manchester, 3 April 1872
impossible.

19 You behold a range of exhausted volcanoes. speech at Manchester, 3 April 1872
of the Liberal Government

20 Increased means and increased leisure are the two speech at Manchester, 3 April 1872
civilizers of man.

1 The very phrase 'foreign affairs' makes an Englishman convinced that I am about to treat of subjects with which he has no concern.

speech at Manchester, 3 April 1872

2 A University should be a place of light, of liberty, and of learning.

in the House of Commons, 11 March 1873

3 An author who speaks about his own books is almost as bad as a mother who talks about her own children.
   at a banquet given in Glasgow on his installation as Lord Rector, 19 November 1873

in The Times 20 November 1873

4 King Louis Philippe once said to me that he attributed the great success of the British nation in political life to their talking politics after dinner.

in Glasgow, 19 November 1873

5 He is a great master of gibes and flouts and jeers.
   *of Lord **Salisbury***

in the House of Commons, 5 August 1874

6 Upon the education of the people of this country the fate of this country depends.

in the House of Commons, 15 June 1874

7 Coffee house babble.
   on the Bulgarian Atrocities, 1876

R. W. Seton-Watson *Britain in Europe 1789–1914* (1955)

8 Cosmopolitan critics, men who are the friends of every country save their own.

speech at Guildhall, 9 November 1877

9 Lord Salisbury and myself have brought you back peace—but a peace I hope with honour.
   speech on returning from the Congress of Berlin, 16 July 1878

in The Times 17 July 1878

10 A series of congratulatory regrets.
    of Lord Harrington's Resolution on the Berlin Treaty

at a banquet, Knightsbridge, 27 July 1878

11 A sophistical rhetorician, inebriated with the exuberance of his own verbosity.
    *of **Gladstone***

in The Times 29 July 1878

12 I admit that there is gossip...But the government of the world is carried on by sovereigns and statesmen, and not by anonymous paragraph writers...or by the hare-brained chatter of irresponsible frivolity.

speech at Guildhall, London, 9 November 1878

13 One of the greatest of Romans, when asked what were his politics, replied, *Imperium et Libertas*. That would not make a bad programme for a British Ministry.

speech at Mansion House, London, 10 November 1879, paraphrasing Tacitus *Agricola*

14 the transient and embarrassed phantom of Lord Goderich.
    of Lord Goderich as Prime Minister

Endymion (1880)

15 An insular country, subject to fogs, and with a powerful middle class, requires grave statesmen.

Endymion (1880)

16 I look upon the House of Commons as a mere vestry. Reform has dished it.

Endymion (1880)

17 As for our majority...one is enough.

Endymion (1880)

18 The greatest opportunity that can be offered to an Englishman—a seat in the House of Commons.

Endymion (1880)

19 The sweet simplicity of the three per cents.

Endymion (1880); cf. **Stowell** 352:2

1 I believe they went out, like all good things, with the
   Stuarts.

   Endymion (1880)

2 The key of India is London.

   in the House of Commons, 4 March
   1881

3 Damn your principles! Stick to your party.

   attributed to Disraeli and believed
   to have been said to Edward
   Bulwer-Lytton; E. Latham *Famous
   Sayings and their Authors* (1904)

4 Everyone likes flattery; and when you come to Royalty
   you should lay it on with a trowel.

   to Matthew **Arnold**, in G. W. E.
   Russell *Collections and
   Recollections* (1898) ch. 23

5 I have climbed to the top of the greasy pole.
   on becoming Prime Minister

   W. Monypenny and G. Buckle *Life
   of Benjamin Disraeli* vol. 4 (1916)

6 I am dead; dead, but in the Elysian fields.
   to a peer, on his elevation to the House of Lords

   W. Monypenny and G. Buckle *Life
   of Benjamin Disraeli* vol. 5 (1920)

7 I never deny; I never contradict; I sometimes forget.
   said to Lord Esher of his relations with Queen Victoria

   Elizabeth Longford *Victoria R. I*
   (1964)

8 Never complain and never explain.

   J. Morley *Life of William Ewart
   Gladstone* (1903) vol. 1; cf.
   Fisher 137:4

9 Posterity will do justice to that unprincipled maniac
   Gladstone—extraordinary mixture of envy,
   vindictiveness, hypocrisy and superstition; and with one
   commanding characteristic—whether Prime Minister or
   Leader of the Opposition, whether preaching, praying,
   speechifying or scribbling—never a gentleman.

   W. Monypenny and G. Buckle *Life
   of Benjamin Disraeli* vol. 6 (1920)

10 Pray remember, Mr Dean, no dogma, no Dean.

   W. Monypenny and G. Buckle *Life
   of Benjamin Disraeli* vol. 4 (1916)

11 Protection is not only dead, but damned.

   W. Monypenny and G. Buckle *Life
   of Benjamin Disraeli* vol. 3 (1914)

   on being offered an air cushion to sit on:
12 Take away that emblem of mortality.

   Robert Blake *Disraeli* (1966)

13 The palace is not safe when the cottage is not happy.

   Robert Blake *Disraeli* (1966)

14 The school of Manchester.
   of the free trade politics of Cobden and **Bright**

   Robert Blake *Disraeli* (1966)

15 There are three kinds of lies: lies, damned lies and
   statistics.

   attributed to Disraeli in Mark Twain
   Autobiography (1924) vol. 1

16 We came here for fame.
   to John **Bright**, *in the House of Commons*

   Robert Blake *Disraeli* (1966)

17 When Gentlemen cease to be returned to Parliament this
   Empire will perish.

   W. Fraser *Disraeli and His Day*
   (1891)

18 When I want to read a novel, I write one.

   W. Monypenny and G. Buckle *Life
   of Benjamin Disraeli* vol. 6 (1920)

19 You will find as you grow older that courage is the rarest
   of all qualities to be found in public life.
   to Lady Gwendolen Cecil, telling her that her father Lord

   Lady Gwendolen Cecil *Life of
   Robert Marquis of Salisbury* (1931)

Salisbury *was the only man of real courage with whom Disraeli had worked*

1 I will not go down to posterity talking bad grammar.
while correcting proofs of his last Parliamentary speech, 31 March 1881

Robert Blake *Disraeli* (1966)

on his death-bed, declining a proposed visit from Queen Victoria:

2 No it is better not. She would only ask me to take a message to Albert.

Robert Blake *Disraeli* (1966)

Milovan Djilas 1911–

political writer and former member of the Yugoslav Communist Party (from which he resigned in April 1954)

3 The Party line is that there is no Party line.
comment on reforms of the Yugoslavian Communist Party, November 1952

Fitzroy Maclean *Disputed Barricade* (1957)

Michael Dobbs 1948–

British writer

4 You might very well think that. I couldn't possibly comment.
the Chief Whip's habitual response to questioning

House of Cards (as dramatized for television, 1990)

Bubb Dodington 1691–1762

English politician

5 Love thy country, wish it well,
Not with too intense a care,
'Tis enough, that when it fell,
Thou its ruin didst not share.

'Ode' (written 1761) in Joseph Spence *Anecdotes* (1820)

Robert Dole 1923–

American Republican politician
on Dole: see **Gingrich** 153:2

6 A little gridlock might be good from time to time.
as Senate Republican leader, immediately after the election of President Clinton ('gridlock', a traffic jam affecting a network of streets, being the term used in Washington for the situation in which legislation makes no progress because of conflicts between Congress and the Administration)

Michael Barone and Grant Ujifusa *The American Political Almanac* 1994

Ignatius Donnelly 1831–1901

American politician

7 The Democratic Party is like a mule—without pride of ancestry or hope of posterity.

attributed; cf. **Disraeli** 117:9, **Power** 298:1

Reginald Dorman-Smith 1899–1977

British politician; Minister of Agriculture and Fisheries,
1939–40

1 Let 'Dig for Victory' be the motto of every one with
a garden and of every able-bodied man and woman
capable of digging an allotment in their spare time.

radio broadcast, 3 October 1939, in
The Times 4 October 1939

John Dos Passos 1896–1970

American novelist, noted for his collage-like portrayal of the
energy and diversity of American life in the first decades of the
20th century

2 America our nation has been beaten by strangers who
have bought the laws and fenced off the meadows and
cut down the woods for pulp and turned our pleasant
cities into slums and sweated the wealth out of our
people and when they want to they hire the executioner
to throw the switch.

The Big Money (1936)

William O. Douglas 1898–1980

US Justice of the Supreme Court

3 The Fifth Amendment is an old friend and a good friend.
It is one of the great landmarks in man's struggle to be
free of tyranny, to be decent and civilized.

An Almanac of Liberty (1954)

4 The search…for ways and means to make the
machine—and the vast bureaucracy of the corporation
state and of government that runs that machine—the
servant of man. That is the revolution that is coming.

in 1970; Anthony Sampson *The
Company Man* (1995)

Alec Douglas-Home see Home

Caroline Douglas-Home 1937–

daughter of Lord **Home**

5 He is used to dealing with estate workers. I cannot see
how anyone can say he is out of touch.
   *on Lord **Home**'s becoming Prime Minister in succession to
   Harold **Macmillan***

in *Daily Herald* 21 October 1963

Frederick Douglass *c.*1818–95

American former slave and Civil Rights campaigner

6 What, to the American slave, is your Fourth of July?
I answer: A day that reveals to him, more than all other
days in the year, the gross injustice and cruelty to which
he is the constant victim. To him your celebration is
a sham.

speech at Rochester, New York, 4
July 1852

1 The ground which a coloured man occupies in this country is, every inch of it, sternly disputed.

speech at the American and Foreign Anti-Slavery Society annual meeting in New York City, May 1853

2 In all the relations of life and death, we are met by the colour line.

speech at the Convention of Coloured Men, Louisville, Kentucky, 24 September 1883

3 No man can put a chain about the ankle of his fellow man without at last finding the other end fastened about his own neck.

speech at Civil Rights Mass Meeting, Washington, DC, 22 October 1883

4 Where justice is denied, where poverty is enforced, where ignorance prevails, and where any one class is made to feel that society is in an organized conspiracy to oppress, rob, and degrade them, neither persons nor property will be safe.

speech on the twenty-fourth anniversary of Emancipation in the District of Columbia, Washington, DC, April 1886

Margaret Drabble 1939–

English novelist

5 England's not a bad country... It's just a mean, cold, ugly, divided, tired, clapped-out, post-imperial, post-industrial slag-heap covered in polystyrene hamburger cartons.

A Natural Curiosity (1989)

Francis Drake c.1540–96

English sailor and explorer

6 The singeing of the King of Spain's Beard.
   on the expedition to Cadiz, 1587

Francis Bacon *Considerations touching a War with Spain* (1629)

7 There is plenty of time to win this game, and to thrash the Spaniards too.

attributed, in *Dictionary of National Biography* (1917–) vol. 5

Joseph Rodman Drake 1795–1820

American poet

8 Forever float that standard sheet!
   Where breathes the foe but falls before us,
   With Freedom's soil beneath our feet,
   And Freedom's banner streaming o'er us?

'The American Flag' in *New York Evening Post*, 29 May 1819 (also attributed to Fitz-Greene Halleck)

William Driver 1803–86

9 I name thee Old Glory.
   as the flag was hoisted to the masthead of his ship (Driver was captain of the Charles Doggett, *the ship on which the Bounty mutineers were returned from Tahiti to Pitcairn, and was presented with a large American flag by a band of women in recognition of this)*

attributed

John Dryden 1631–1700

English poet, critic, and playwright

1   If by the people you understand the multitude, the *hoi*
    polloi, 'tis no matter what they think; they are sometimes
    in the right, sometimes in the wrong: their judgement is
    a mere lottery.

An Essay of Dramatic Poesy (1668)

2   But 'tis the talent of our English nation,
    Still to be plotting some new reformation.

'The Prologue at Oxford, 1680'
(prologue to Nathaniel Lee
Sophonisba, 2nd ed., 1681)

3   Plots, true or false, are necessary things,
    To raise up commonwealths and ruin kings.

Absalom and Achitophel (1681)

4   Of these the false Achitophel was first,
    A name to all succeeding ages curst.
    For close designs and crooked counsels fit,
    Sagacious, bold, and turbulent of wit,
    Restless, unfixed in principles and place,
    In power unpleased, impatient of disgrace.
      in Dryden's political satire relating to the Protestant succession
      'Achitophel' represented **Shaftesbury**, *and 'Absalom' the Duke*
      of **Monmouth**

Absalom and Achitophel (1681)

5   A daring pilot in extremity;
    Pleased with the danger, when the waves went high
    He sought the storms; but for a calm unfit,
    Would steer too nigh the sands to boast his wit.

Absalom and Achitophel (1681)

6   In friendship false, implacable in hate:
    Resolved to ruin or to rule the state.

Absalom and Achitophel (1681)

7   The people's prayer, the glad diviner's theme,
    The young men's vision and the old men's dream!

Absalom and Achitophel (1681)

8   All empire is no more than power in trust.

Absalom and Achitophel (1681)

9   Better one suffer, than a nation grieve.

Absalom and Achitophel (1681)

10 Youth, beauty, graceful action seldom fail:
    But common interest always will prevail:
    And pity never ceases to be shown
    To him, who makes the people's wrongs his own.

Absalom and Achitophel (1681)

11 For who can be secure of private right,
    If sovereign sway may be dissolved by might?
    Nor is the people's judgement always true:
    The most may err as grossly as the few.

Absalom and Achitophel (1681)

12 Never was patriot yet, but was a fool.

Absalom and Achitophel (1681)

13 But treason is not owned when 'tis descried;
    Successful crimes alone are justified.

The Medal (1682)

14 Freedom which in no other land will thrive,
    Freedom an English subject's sole prerogative.

Threnodia Augustalis (1685)

15 Reason to rule, but mercy to forgive:
    The first is law, the last prerogative.

The Hind and the Panther (1687)

16 Either be wholly slaves or wholly free.

The Hind and the Panther (1687)

1 T''abhor the makers, and their laws approve,   *The Hind and the Panther* (1687)
   Is to hate traitors and the treason love.

2 War is the trade of kings.   *King Arthur* (1691)

Alexander Dubček 1921–92

Czechoslovak statesman, First Secretary of the Czechoslovak
Communist Party 1968–9

3 In the service of the people we followed such a policy   in *Rudé Právo* 19 July 1968
   that socialism would not lose its human face.

Joachim Du Bellay 1522–60

French poet

4 France, mother of arts, of warfare, and of laws.   *Les Regrets* (1558) Sonnet no. 9

W. E. B. Du Bois 1868–1963

American social reformer and political activist

5 The problem of the twentieth century is the problem of   *The Souls of Black Folk* (1905)
   the colour line—the relation of the darker to the lighter
   races of men in Asia and Africa, in America and the
   islands of the sea.

6 Herein lies the tragedy of the age: not that men are   *The Souls of Black Folk* (1905)
   poor...not that men are wicked...but that men know so
   little of men.

7 The cost of liberty is less than the price of repression.   *John Brown* (1909)

John Foster Dulles 1888–1959

American international lawyer and politician

8 If...the European Defence Community should not become   speech to NATO Council in Paris, 14
   effective; if France and Germany remain apart...That   December 1953
   would compel an agonizing reappraisal of basic United
   States policy.

9 You have to take chances for peace, just as you must   in *Life* 16 January 1956; cf.
   take chances in war. Some say that we were brought to   **Stevenson** 350:10
   the verge of war. Of course we were brought to the verge
   of war. The ability to get to the verge without getting
   into the war is the necessary art. If you cannot master it,
   you inevitably get into war. If you try to run away from
   it, if you are scared to go to the brink, you are lost.
   We've had to look it square in the face—on the question
   of enlarging the Korean war, on the question of getting
   into the Indochina war, on the question of Formosa. We
   walked to the brink and we looked it in the face.
   this policy became known as 'brinkmanship'

John Dunning, Lord Ashburton 1731–83

English lawyer and politician

1 The influence of the Crown has increased, is increasing, and ought to be diminished.

resolution passed in the House of Commons, 6 April 1780

Eric Dupin

journalist

2 His inconstancy is his great constant.
    of François **Mitterrand**

in *The New York Review of Books* 3 November 1994

Lillian K. Dykstra

3 He is just about the nastiest little man I've ever known. He struts sitting down.
    of Thomas **Dewey**

letter to Franz Dykstra, 8 July 1952; James T. Patterson *Mr Republican* (1972)

Stephen T. Early 1889–1951

4 Don't Worry Me—I am an 8 Ulcer Man on 4 Ulcer Pay.
    card received by Harry Truman

William Hillman *Mr President: the First Publication from the Personal Diaries, Private Letters, Papers and Revealing Interviews of Harry S. Truman* (1952)

Abba Eban 1915–

Israeli diplomat

5 History teaches us that men and nations behave wisely once they have exhausted all other alternatives.

speech in London, 16 December 1970

of the British Foreign Office:
6 A hotbed of cold feet.

in conversation with Antony Jay

Anthony Eden 1897–1977

British Conservative statesman, Prime Minister 1955–7
on Eden: see **Butler** 70:3, **McLachlan** 242:5, **Monkton** 261:11, **Muggeridge** 268:1

7 We are in an armed conflict; that is the phrase I have used. There has been no declaration of war.
    on the Suez crisis

in the House of Commons, 1 November 1956

8 Everyone is always in favour of general economy and particular expenditure.

in *Observer* 17 June 1956

Clarissa Eden 1920–

wife of Anthony Eden

1 For the past few weeks I have really felt as if the Suez
Canal was flowing through my drawing room.

speech at Gateshead, 20
November 1956

Edward VII 1841–1910

King of the United Kingdom from 1901

2 Because a man has a black face and a different religion
from our own, there is no reason why he should be
treated as a brute.

letter to Lord Granville, 30
November 1875

3 The last King of England.
*introducing his son, the future George V, to Lord Haldane,
expressing his pessimism for the survival of the British monarchy*

Andrew Roberts *Eminent
Churchillians* (1994)

Edward VIII 1894–1972

King of the United Kingdom, 1936; afterwards Duke of Windsor
on Edward VIII: see **George V** 149:10, **Thomas** 363:5

4 These works brought all these people here. Something
should be done to get them at work again.
*speaking at the derelict Dowlais Iron and Steel Works, 18
November 1936 (generally quoted 'Something must be done')*

in *Western Mail* 19 November 1936

5 At long last I am able to say a few words of my own...
you must believe me when I tell you that I have found it
impossible to carry the heavy burden of responsibility and
to discharge my duties as King as I would wish to do
without the help and support of the woman I love.
radio broadcast following his abdication, 11 December 1936

in *The Times* 12 December 1936

John Ehrlichman 1925–

Presidential assistant to Richard Nixon

6 I think we ought to let him hang there. Let him twist
slowly, slowly in the wind.
*speaking of Patrick Gray (regarding his nomination as director of
the FBI) in a telephone conversation with John Dean*

in *Washington Post* 27 July 1973

Albert Einstein 1879–1955

German-born American theoretical physicist, founder of the
theory of relativity

7 The prestige of government has undoubtedly been
lowered considerably by the Prohibition laws. For
nothing is more destructive of respect for the government
and the law of the land than passing laws which cannot
be enforced. It is an open secret that the dangerous
increase of crime in this country is closely connected
with this.

after visiting America in 1921; *The
World As I See It* (1935)

1 Nationalism is an infantile sickness. It is the measles of
   the human race.

Helen Dukas and Banesh Hoffman
Albert Einstein, the Human Side
(1979)

explaining why equations mattered more to him than politics:
2 Politics is for the present, but an equation is something
   for eternity.

Stephen Hawking *A Brief History of Time* (1988)

Dwight D. Eisenhower 1890–1969

American general and Republican statesman, 34th President of
the US, 1953–61
on Eisenhower: see **Acheson** 1:8

3 People of Western Europe: A landing was made this
   morning on the coast of France by troops of the Allied
   Expeditionary Force. This landing is part of the concerted
   United Nations plan for the liberation of Europe, made in
   conjunction with our great Russian allies...I call upon
   all who love freedom to stand with us now. Together we
   shall achieve victory.

broadcast on D-Day, 6 June 1944

4 Every gun that is made, every warship launched, every
   rocket fired signifies, in the final sense, a theft from those
   who hunger and are not fed, those who are cold and are
   not clothed. This world in arms is not spending money
   alone. It is spending the sweat of its labourers, the genius
   of its scientists, the hopes of its children.

speech in Washington, 16 April
1953

5 You have broader considerations that might follow what
   you might call the 'falling domino' principle. You have
   a row of dominoes set up. You knock over the first one,
   and what will happen to the last one is that it will go
   over very quickly. So you have the beginning of
   a disintegration that would have the most profound
   influences.

speech at press conference, 7 April
1954

6 Governments are far more stupid than their people.

attributed, 1958

7 I think that people want peace so much that one of these
   days governments had better get out of the way and let
   them have it.

broadcast discussion, 31 August
1959

8 In the councils of government, we must guard against
   the acquisition of unwarranted influence, whether sought
   or unsought, by the military-industrial complex. The
   potential for the disastrous rise of misplaced power exists
   and will persist.
   farewell broadcast, 17 January 1961

in *New York Times* 18 January 1961

9 Biggest damfool mistake I ever made.
   of his appointment, in 1953, of Earl **Warren** *as Chief Justice of the
   United States*

attributed

George Eliot 1819-80

English novelist

1 An election is coming. Universal peace is declared, and   *Felix Holt* (1866)
   the foxes have a sincere interest in prolonging the lives of
   the poultry.

T. S. Eliot 1888-1965

Anglo-American poet, critic, and playwright

2 This is the way the world ends   'The Hollow Men' (1925)
   Not with a bang but a whimper.

Queen Elisabeth of Belgium 1876-1965

German-born consort of King Albert of the Belgians

3 Between them [Germany] and me there is now a bloody   attributed
   curtain which has descended forever.
   on Germany's invasion of Belgium in 1914

Elizabeth I 1533-1603

Queen of England and Ireland from 1558

4 I am your anointed Queen. I will never be by violence   speech to Members of Parliament,
   constrained to do anything. I thank God that I am   5 November 1566
   endued with such qualities that if I were turned out of
   the Realm in my petticoat, I were able to live in any
   place in Christome.

5 The queen of Scots is this day leichter of a fair son, and   Sir James Melville *Memoirs of His*
   I am but a barren stock.   *Own Life* (1827 ed.)

6 As for me, I assure you I find no great cause I should be   J. E. Neale *Elizabeth I and her*
   fond to live. I take no such pleasure in it that I should   *Parliaments 1584–1601* (1957),
   much wish it, nor conceive such terror in death that   from a report 'which the Queen
   I should greatly fear it...I have had good experience and   herself heavily amended in her
   trial of this world. I know what it is to be a subject, what   own hand'
   to be a Sovereign, what to have good neighbours, and
   sometimes meet evil-willers.
   speech to a Parliamentary deputation at Richmond, 12
   November 1586; the traditional version concludes: 'In trust
   I have found treason'

7 I will make you shorter by the head.   F. Chamberlin *Sayings of Queen*
   to the leaders of her Council, who were opposing her course   *Elizabeth* (1923)
   towards Mary Queen of Scots

8 The daughter of debate, that eke discord doth sow.   George Puttenham (ed.) *The Art of*
   on Mary Queen of Scots   *English Poesie* (1589)

9 I know I have the body of a weak and feeble woman, but   Lord Somers *A Third Collection of*
   I have the heart and stomach of a king, and of a king of   *Scarce and Valuable Tracts* (1751)
   England too; and think foul scorn that Parma or Spain,
   or any prince of Europe, should dare to invade the
   borders of my realm.

speech to the troops at Tilbury on the approach of the Armada,
1588

1 I will have here but one Mistress, and no Master.
   reproving the presumption of the Earl of Leicester

   Robert Naunton *Fragmenta Regalia*
   (1641)

2 I do entreat heaven daily for your longer life, else will my
   people and myself stand in need of cordials too. My
   comfort hath been in my people's happiness and their
   happiness in thy discretion.
   to William Cecil on his death-bed

   F. Chamberlin *Sayings of Queen*
   Elizabeth (1923)

3 My lord, we make use of you, not for your bad legs, but
   for your good head.
   to William Cecil, who suffered from gout

   F. Chamberlin *Sayings of Queen*
   Elizabeth (1923)

   on being asked her opinion of Christ's presence in the
   Sacrament:
4 'Twas God the word that spake it,
   He took the bread and brake it;
   And what the word did make it;
   That I believe, and take it.

   S. Clarke *The Marrow of*
   Ecclesiastical History (1675) 'The
   Life of Queen Elizabeth'

5 God may pardon you, but I never can.
   to the dying Countess of Nottingham, who was said to have
   prevented a last appeal by the Earl of Essex from reaching the
   Queen

   David Hume *The History of*
   England under the House of Tudor
   (1759) vol. 2

6 I think that, at the worst, God has not yet ordained that
   England shall perish.

   F. Chamberlin *Sayings of Queen*
   Elizabeth (1923)

7 I would not open windows into men's souls.

   oral tradition, in J. B. Black *Reign*
   of Elizabeth 1558–1603 (1936)
   (the words very possibly
   originating in a letter drafted by
   Bacon)

8 If thy heart fails thee, climb not at all.
   lines after Walter **Ralegh**, *written on a window-pane*

   Thomas Fuller *Worthies of England*
   vol. 1; cf. **Ralegh** 300:3

9 Like strawberry wives, that laid two or three great
   strawberries at the mouth of their pot, and all the rest
   were little ones.
   describing the tactics of the Commission of Sales, in their
   dealings with her

   Francis Bacon *Apophthegms New*
   and Old (1625)

10 Madam I may not call you; mistress I am ashamed to
   call you; and so I know not what to call you; but
   howsoever, I thank you.
   to the wife of the Archbishop of Canterbury, the Queen
   disapproving of marriage among the clergy

   John Harington *A Brief View of the*
   State of the Church of England
   (1653)

   welcoming Edward de Vere, Earl of Oxford, on his return from
   seven years self-imposed exile, occasioned by the acute
   embarrassment to himself of breaking wind in the presence of
   the Queen:
11 My Lord, I had forgot the fart.

   John Aubrey *Brief Lives* 'Edward de
   Vere'

1 Though God hath raised me high, yet this I count the glory of my crown: that I have reigned with your loves.
    the Golden Speech, 1601

in *The Journals of All the Parliaments ... Collected by Sir Simonds D'Ewes* (1682)

2 Must! Is *must* a word to be addressed to princes? Little man, little man! thy father, if he had been alive, durst not have used that word.
    to Robert Cecil, on his saying in her last illness that she must go to bed

J. R. Green *A Short History of the English People* (1874); *Dodd's Church History of England* vol. 3 (ed. M. A. Tierney, 1840) adds, 'but thou knowest I must die, and that maketh thee so presumptuous'

3 All my possessions for a moment of time.
    last words

attributed, but almost certainly apocryphal

Elizabeth II 1926–

Queen of the United Kingdom from 1952

4 I declare before you all that my whole life, whether it be long or short, shall be devoted to your service and the service of our great Imperial family to which we all belong.
    broadcast speech, as Princess Elizabeth, to the Commonwealth from Cape Town, 21 April 1947

in *The Times* 22 April 1947

speech at Guildhall, London, on her 25th wedding anniversary:
5 I think everybody really will concede that on this, of all days, I should begin my speech with the words 'My husband and I'.

in *The Times* 21 November 1972

6 In the words of one of my more sympathetic correspondents, it has turned out to be an 'annus horribilis'.

speech at Guildhall, London, 24 November 1992

7 The British Constitution has always been puzzling and always will be.

Peter Hennessy *The Hidden Wiring* (1995)

Queen Elizabeth, the Queen Mother

1900–

Queen Consort of **George VI** and mother of **Elizabeth II**

8 I'm glad we've been bombed. It makes me feel I can look the East End in the face.
    to a London policeman, 13 September 1940

John Wheeler-Bennett *King George VI* (1958)

on the suggestion that the royal family be evacuated during the Blitz:
9 The Princesses would never leave without me and I couldn't leave without the King, and the King will never leave.

Penelope Mortimer *Queen Elizabeth* (1986)

Alf Ellerton

10 Belgium put the kibosh on the Kaiser.

title of song

Ebenezer Elliott 1781–1849

English poet known as the 'Corn Law Rhymer'

1 What is a communist? One who hath yearnings   'Epigram' (1850)
   For equal division of unequal earnings.

Ralph Waldo Emerson 1803–82

American philosopher and poet

2 The two parties which divide the state, the party of   'The Conservative' (lecture, 1841)
   Conservatism and that of Innovation, are very old, and
   have disputed the possession of the world ever since it
   was made.

3 There is always a certain meanness in the argument of   *The Conservative* (1842)
   conservatism, joined with a certain superiority in its fact.

4 The louder he talked of his honour, the faster we counted   *The Conduct of Life* (1860)
   our spoons.   'Worship'

5 When you strike at a king, you must kill him.   attributed to Emerson by Oliver
                                                          Wendell **Holmes** Jr.; Max Lerner
                                                          *The Mind and Faith of Justice
                                                          Holmes* (1943)

Friedrich Engels 1820–95

German socialist; founder, with Karl Marx, of modern
Communism

6 The State is not 'abolished', *it withers away.*   *Anti-Dühring* (1878)

7 Naturally, the workers are perfectly free; the   *The Condition of the Working Class
   manufacturer does not force them to take his materials   in England in 1844* (1892)
   and his cards, but he says to them … 'If you don't like to
   be frizzled in my frying-pan, you can take a walk into the
   fire'.

Friedrich Engels see also **Marx** and **Engels**

Ennius 239–169 BC

Roman writer

8 The Roman state survives by its ancient customs and its   *Annals*
   manhood.

9 One man by delaying put the state to rights for us.   *Annals*
   referring to the Roman general Fabius Cunctator ('The Delayer')

Erasmus c.1469–1536

Dutch Christian humanist

10 In the country of the blind the one-eyed man is king.   *Adages*

Dudley Erwin 1917–84

Australian politician

Claiming that the 'political manoeuvre' which had cost him his job in the reshuffled Government was actually the Prime Minister's secretary:

1 It wiggles, it's shapely and its name is Ainsley Gotto

in *The Times* 14 November 1969

Robert Devereux, Lord Essex 1566–1601

English soldier and courtier, executed for treason

2 Reasons are not like garments, the worse for wearing.

letter to Lord Willoughby, 4 January 1599

William Maxwell Evarts 1818–83

American politician and lawyer

3 The pious ones of Plymouth, who, reaching the Rock, first fell upon their own knees and then upon the aborigines.

in *Louisville Courier-Journal* 4 July 1913; a pun which has been variously attributed

Edward Everett 1794–1865

American orator and politician

4 I should be glad if I could flatter myself that I came as near the central idea of the occasion in two hours as you did in two minutes.
   to Abraham **Lincoln** *on the Gettysburg address, which had been publicly criticized while Everett's two hour speech had received adulatory attention in the press*

letter to Lincoln, 20 November 1863; cf. **Anonymous** 13:6

William Norman Ewer 1885–1976

British writer

5 I gave my life for freedom—This I know:
   For those who bade me fight had told me so.

'Five Souls' (1917)

Quintus Fabius Maximus c.275–203 BC

Roman politician and general

6 To be turned from one's course by men's opinions, by blame, and by misrepresentation shows a man unfit to hold an office.

Plutarch *Parallel Lives* 'Fabius Maximus'

Émile Faguet 1847–1916

French writer and critic

commenting on Rousseau's 'Man was born free, and everywhere he is in chains':

1 It would be equally correct to say that sheep are born carnivorous, and everywhere they nibble grass.

paraphrasing Joseph de Maistre; *Politiques et Moralistes du Dix-Neuvième Siècle* (1899)

Thomas Fairfax 1621–71

English Parliamentary general, appointed commander of the New Model Army in 1645, and replaced in 1650 by Oliver **Cromwell** for refusing to march against the Scots, who had proclaimed the future **Charles II** king

2 Human probabilities are not sufficient grounds to make war upon a neighbour nation.
   to the proposal in 1650 that the expected attack by the Scots should be anticipated by the invasion of Scotland

in *Dictionary of National Biography*

Lucius Cary, Lord Falkland 1610–43

English royalist politician

3 When it is not necessary to change, it is necessary not to change.

Discourses of Infallibility (1660) 'A Speech concerning Episcopacy' delivered in 1641

Michael Faraday 1791–1867

English chemist and physicist

to **Gladstone**, *when asked about the usefulness of electricity:*

4 Why sir, there is every possibility that you will soon be able to tax it!

W. E. H. Lecky *Democracy and Liberty* (1899 ed.)

James A. Farley 1888–1976

American Democratic politician

5 As Maine goes, so goes Vermont.
   after predicting correctly that Franklin **Roosevelt** *would carry all but two states in the election of 1936 (reworking an American political maxim of c.1888, 'as Maine goes, so goes the nation')*

statement to the press, 4 November 1936

Farouk 1920–65

King of Egypt, 1936–52

6 The whole world is in revolt. Soon there will be only five Kings left—the King of England, the King of Spades, the King of Clubs, the King of Hearts and the King of Diamonds.

Lord Boyd-Orr *As I Recall* (1966), addressed to the author at a conference in Cairo, 1948

Guy Fawkes 1570–1606

conspirator in the Gunpowder Plot, 1605

1 A desperate disease requires a dangerous remedy.

on 6 November 1605, in *Dictionary of National Biography* (1917–) vol. 6

Dianne Feinstein 1933–

American Democratic politician, Mayor of San Francisco

2 Toughness doesn't have to come in a pinstripe suit.

in *Time* 4 June 1984

3 There was a time when you could say the least government was the best—but not in the nation's most populous state.

campaign speech, 15 March 1990

Ferdinand I 1503–64

Holy Roman Emperor from 1558

4 *Fiat justitia et pereat mundus.*
Let justice be done, though the world perish.

motto; see Johannes Manlius *Locorum Communium Collectanea* (1563) vol. 2 'De Lege: Octatum Praeceptum'

Eric Field

5 Your King and Country need you.
First World War recruiting poster

Advertising (1959)

Frank Field 1942–

British Labour politician

6 Democracy no longer works for the poor if politicians treat them as a separate race.

in *Independent* 29 October 1994

L'Abbé Edgeworth de Firmont 1745–1807

Irish-born confessor to Louis XVI

7 Son of Saint Louis, ascend to heaven.
to Louis XVI as he mounted the steps of the guillotine, 1793

attributed

H. A. L. Fisher 1856–1940

English historian

8 Men wiser and more learned than I have discerned in history a plot, a rhythm, a predetermined pattern. These harmonies are concealed from me. I can see only one emergency following upon another as wave follows upon wave, only one great fact with respect to which, since it is unique, there can be no generalizations, only one safe rule for the historian: that he should recognize in the

A History of Europe (1935)

development of human destinies the play of the
contingent and the unforeseen.

1 Purity of race does not exist. Europe is a continent of   *A History of Europe* (1935)
  energetic mongrels.

2 Nothing commends a radical change to an Englishman   *A History of Europe* (1935)
  more than the belief that it is really conservative.

John Arbuthnot Fisher 1841–1920

British admiral

3 Sack the lot!   letter to *The Times*, 2 September
   on overmanning and overspending within government   1919
   departments

4 Never contradict   letter to *The Times*, 5 September
  Never explain   1919; cf. **Disraeli** 121:8
  Never apologize.

John Fiske 1842–1901

5 The United States—bounded on the north by the Aurora   *Bounding the United States*
  Borealis, on the south by the precession of the equinoxes,
  on the east by the primeval chaos, and on the west by
  the Day of Judgement.

Gerry Fitt 1926–

Northern Irish politician

6 People [in Northern Ireland] don't march as an   in *The Times* 5 August 1994
  alternative to jogging. They do it to assert their
  supremacy. It is pure tribalism, the cause of troubles all
  over the world.

Robert, Marquis de Flers 1872–1927 and
Arman de Caillavet 1869–1915

French playwrights

7 Democracy is the name we give the people whenever we   *L'habit vert*, in *La petite illustration*
  need them.   *série théâtre* 31 May 1913

Andrew Fletcher of Saltoun 1655–1716

Scottish patriot and anti-Unionist

8 I knew a very wise man so much of Sir Chr—'s   'An Account of a Conversation
  sentiment, that he believed if a man were permitted to   concerning a Right Regulation of
  make all the ballads, he need not care who should make   Government for the Good of
  the laws of a nation.   Mankind. In a Letter to the Marquis
                                                               of Montrose' (1704) in *Political
                                                               Works* (1732)

Ferdinand Foch 1851–1929

French general

1 My centre is giving way, my right is retreating, situation   R. Recouly *Foch* (1919)
excellent, I am attacking.
*message sent during the first Battle of the Marne, September
1914*

2 This is not a peace treaty, it is an armistice for twenty   Paul Reynaud *Mémoires* (1963)
years.   vol. 2
at the signing of the Treaty of Versailles, 1919

Michael Foot 1913–

British Labour politician

of Iain **Macleod**:
3 A perspiration of firm confidence exudes from every   in *Daily Herald* 8 October 1962
political pore.

4 A speech from Ernest Bevin on a major occasion had all   *Aneurin Bevan* (1962) vol. 1
the horrific fascination of a public execution. If the mind
was left immune, eyes and ears and emotions were
riveted.

5 Think of it! A second Chamber selected by the Whips. A   in the House of Commons, 3
seraglio of eunuchs.   February 1969

6 Disraeli was my favourite Tory. He was an adventurer   in *Observer* 16 March 1975
pure and simple, or impure and complex. I'm glad to say   'Sayings of the Week'
Gladstone got the better of him.

7 It is not necessary that every time he rises he should give   in the House of Commons, 2 March
his famous imitation of a semi-house-trained polecat.   1978
of Norman **Tebbit**

of David **Steel**, *Leader of the Liberal Party:*
8 He's passed from rising hope to elder statesman without   in the House of Commons, 28
any intervening period whatsoever.   March 1979

9 If democratic socialism cannot secure the right answer at   Anthony Sampson *The Changing*
the next parliamentary opportunity, we may not be   *Anatomy of Britain* (1982)
asked again, or rather this old famous socialist stream
could perish in sectarian bogs and sands.

Gerald Ford 1909–

American Republican statesman, 38th President of the US
1974–7
on Ford: see **Abzug** 1:2, **Johnson** 196:10, **Morton** 267:1

10 If the Government is big enough to give you everything   John F. Parker *If Elected* (1960);
you want, it is big enough to take away everything you   a similar remark has been
have.   attributed to Barry **Goldwater**

11 I am a Ford, not a Lincoln.   in *Washington Post* 7 December
on taking the vice-presidential oath, 6 December 1973   1973

12 Our long national nightmare is over. Our Constitution   speech on 9 August 1974
works; our great Republic is a Government of laws and

not of men.
on being sworn in as President in succession to Richard **Nixon**

1 I believe that truth is the glue that holds Government   speech on 9 August 1974
together, not only our Government, but civilization itself.
on being sworn in as President

2 There is no Soviet domination of Eastern Europe and   S. Kraus *Great Debates* (1979)
there never will be under a Ford administration.
in a television debate with Jimmy Carter, 6 October 1976

Howell Forgy 1908–83

American naval chaplain

3 Praise the Lord and pass the ammunition.   in *New York Times* 1 November
at Pearl Harbor, 7 December 1941, as Forgy moved along a line   1942
of sailors passing ammunition by hand to the deck (later the title
of a song by Frank Loesser, 1942)

E. M. Forster 1879–1970

English novelist

4 If I had to choose between betraying my country and   *Two Cheers for Democracy* (1951)
betraying my friend, I hope I should have the guts to   'What I Believe'
betray my country.

5 So Two cheers for Democracy: one because it admits   *Two Cheers for Democracy* (1951)
variety and two because it permits criticism. Two cheers   'What I Believe' ('Love, the beloved
are quite enough: there is no occasion to give three. Only   republic' borrowed from
Love the Beloved Republic deserves that.   Swinburne's poem 'Hertha')

Harry Emerson Fosdick 1878–1969

American Baptist minister

6 I renounce war for its consequences, for the lies it lives   Armistice Day Sermon in New York,
on and propagates, for the undying hatred it arouses, for   1933, in *The Secret of Victorious*
the dictatorships it puts in the place of democracy, for   *Living* (1934)
the starvation that stalks after it.

Charles Foster 1828–1904

American politician

7 Isn't this a billion dollar country?   also attributed to Thomas B. Reed,
at the 51st Congress, responding to a Democratic gibe about   who reported the exchange in
a 'million dollar Congress'   *North American Review* March
                                                                1892, vol. 154

George Foster 1847–1931

Canadian politician

1 In these somewhat troublesome days when the great
Mother Empire stands splendidly isolated in Europe.

in *Official Report of the Debates of the House of Commons of the Dominion of Canada* (1896) vol. 41, for 16 January 1896; on 22 January 1896, *The Times* referred to this speech under the heading 'Splendid Isolation'

Charles Fourier 1772–1837

French social theorist

2 The extension of women's rights is the basic principle of
all social progress.

Théorie des Quatre Mouvements (1808) vol. 2

Norman Fowler 1938–

British Conservative politician

3 I have a young family and for the next few years
I should like to devote more time to them.
   often quoted as 'spend more time with my family'

resignation letter to the Prime Minister, in *Guardian* 4 January 1990; cf. **Thatcher** 362:8

Caroline Fox d. 1774

wife of Henry Fox, Lord **Holland**, and mother of Charles James **Fox**

4 That little boy will be a thorn in Charles's side as long as
he lives.
   seeing in the young William **Pitt** *a prospective rival for her son Charles James* **Fox**

attributed

Charles James Fox 1749–1806

English Whig politician, son of Henry Fox, Lord **Holland** and Caroline **Fox**
on *Fox*: see **Gibbon** 152:1, **Holland** 181:4, **Johnson** 198:12, **Shaw-Lefevre** 337:5

5 He [Pitt the Younger] was uniformly of an opinion
which, though not a popular one, he was ready to aver,
that the right of governing was not property but a trust.
   on **Pitt**'s *scheme of Parliamentary Reform, 1785*

J. L. Hammond *Charles James Fox* (1903)

6 How much the greatest event it is that ever happened in
the world! and how much the best!
   on the fall of the Bastille

letter to Richard Fitzpatrick, 30 July 1789

*In the last year of his life Fox's friends suggested that he
should accept a peerage:*

7 I will not close my politics in that foolish way.

in *Dictionary of National Biography*

1 I die happy.
last words

Lord John Russell *Life and Times of C. J. Fox* vol. 3 (1860)

Henry Fox see Holland

Anatole France 1844–1924

French novelist and man of letters

2 They [the poor] have to labour in the face of the majestic equality of the law, which forbids the rich as well as the poor to sleep under bridges, to beg in the streets, and to steal bread.

Le Lys rouge (1894)

3 In every well-governed state, wealth is a sacred thing; in democracies it is the only sacred thing.

L'Île des pingouins (1908)

Francis I 1494–1547

King of France from 1515

4 Of all I had, only honour and life have been spared.
letter to his mother following his defeat at Pavia, 1525, usually quoted as 'All is lost, save honour'

in *Collection des Documents Inédits sur l'Histoire de France* (1847) vol. 1

Barney Frank

American Democratic politician

5 He doesn't have ideas. He has ideas about how nice it would be to have ideas...He's operating on the level of abstraction and generality.
of the new Republican Speaker, Newton **Gingrich**

in *Daily Telegraph* 5 January 1995

Felix Frankfurter 1882–1965

American judge

6 The history of liberty has largely been the history of the observance of procedural standards.

in *McNabb v. the United States* (1943)

7 One who belongs to the most vilified and persecuted minority in history is not likely to be insensitive to the freedoms guaranteed by our Constitution...But as judges we are neither Jew nor Gentile, neither Catholic nor agnostic.

in *Flag Salute Cases* (1943)

8 It is a fair summary of history to say that the safeguards of liberty have been forged in controversies involving not very nice people.

dissenting opinion in *United States v. Rabinowitz* (1950)

Benjamin Franklin 1706–90

American politician, inventor, and scientist
on Franklin: see **Turgot** 372:7

9 They that can give up essential liberty to obtain a little temporary safety deserve neither liberty nor safety.

Historical Review of Pennsylvania (1759)

1 Idleness and pride tax with a heavier hand than kings   letter 11 July 1765
  and parliaments. If we can get rid of the former, we may
  easily bear the latter.
  on the Stamp Act

2 We must indeed all hang together, or, most assuredly,   P. M. Zall *Ben Franklin* (1980)
  we shall all hang separately.
  at the signing of the Declaration of Independence, 4 July 1776
  (possibly not original)

3 Here [in France] you would know and enjoy what   letter to Washington, 5 March 1780
  posterity will say of Washington. For a thousand leagues
  have nearly the same effect with a thousand years.

4 There never was a good war, or a bad peace.   letter to Josiah Quincy, 11
                                                   September 1783

5 George Washington, Commander of the American   attributed
  Armies, who, like Joshua of old, commanded the sun and
  the moon to stand still, and they obeyed him.
  toast given at a dinner at Versailles, when the British minister
  had proposed a toast to **George III***, likening him to the sun, and*
  the French minister had likened **Louis XVI** *to the moon*

6 No nation was ever ruined by trade.   *Thoughts on Commercial Subjects*

7 I wish the bald eagle had not been chosen as the   letter to Sarah Bache, 26 January
  representative of our country; he is a bird of bad moral   1784
  character...like those among men who live by sharping
  and robbing, he is generally poor, and often very lousy.
    The turkey...is a much more respectable bird, and
  withal a true original native of America.

  on being asked, 'have we got a republic or a monarchy?':
8 A republic, if you can keep it.   in conversation, 18 September
                                      1787

9 In this world nothing can be said to be certain, except   letter to Jean Baptiste Le Roy, 13
  death and taxes.   November 1789; cf. Daniel Defoe
                      History of the Devil (1726) 'Things
                      as certain as death and taxes, can
                      be more firmly believed'

Lord Franks 1905–92

British philosopher and administrator

10 The Pentagon, that immense monument to modern   in *Observer* 30 November 1952
   man's subservience to the desk.

11 A secret in the Oxford sense: you may tell it to only one   in *Sunday Telegraph* 30 January
   person at a time.   1977

   on the composition of such bodies as royal commissions and
   committees of inquiry:
12 There is a fashion in these things and when you are in   in conversation, 24 January 1977;
   fashion you are asked to do a lot.   Peter Hennessy *Whitehall* (1990)

Michael Frayn 1933–

British writer

1 To be absolutely honest, what I feel really bad about is   *in Observer* 8 August 1965
  that I don't feel worse. That's the ineffectual liberal's
  problem in a nutshell.

Frederick the Great 1712–86

King of Prussia from 1740

2 Rascals, would you live for ever?   attributed
  to hesitant Guards at Kolin, 18 June 1757

3 Drive out prejudices through the door, and they will   letter to Voltaire, 19 March 1771
  return through the window.

4 My people and I have come to an agreement which   attributed
  satisfies us both. They are to say what they please, and
  I am to do what I please.
  his interpretation of benevolent despotism

E. A. Freeman 1823–92

English historian

5 History is past politics, and politics is present history.   *Methods of Historical Study* (1886)

John Freeth c.1731–1808

English poet

6 The loss of America what can repay?   'Botany Bay' in *New London*
  New colonies seek for at Botany Bay.   *Magazine* (1786)

Milton Friedman 1912–

American economist and exponent of monetarism; policy
adviser to President Reagan 1981–9

7 Few trends could so thoroughly undermine the very   *Capitalism and Freedom* (1962)
  foundations of our free society as the acceptance by
  corporate officials of a social responsibility other than to
  make as much money for their stockholders as possible.

8 Economists may not know how to run the economy, but   in 1962, attributed
  they do know how to create shortages or gluts simply by
  regulating prices below the market, or artificially
  supporting them from above.

9 There's only one place where inflation is made: that's in   in 1977; attributed
  Washington.

10 A society that puts equality—in the sense of equality of   *Free to Choose* (1980)
   outcome—ahead of freedom will end up with neither
   equality nor freedom.

11 The high rate of unemployment among teenagers, and   *Free to Choose* (1980)
   especially black teenagers, is both a scandal and a serious

source of social unrest. Yet it is largely a result of minimum wage laws...We regard the minimum wage law as one of the most, if not the most, antiblack laws on the statute books.

1 There is an invisible hand in politics that operates in the opposite direction to the invisible hand in the market. In politics, individuals who seek to promote only the public good are led by an invisible hand to promote special interests that it was no part of their intention to promote.

Bright Promises, Dismal Performance: An Economist's Protest (1983)

2 Thank heavens we do not get all of the government that we are made to pay for.

attributed; quoted by Lord Harris in the House of Lords, 24 November 1994

Robert Frost 1874–1963

American poet

3 I never dared be radical when young
For fear it would make me conservative when old.

'Desert Places' (1936)

J. William Fulbright 1905–95

American Senator

4 A policy that can be accurately, though perhaps not prudently, defined as one of 'peaceful coexistence'.

speech in the US Senate, 27 March 1964

5 We must dare to think 'unthinkable' thoughts. We must learn to explore all the options and possibilities that confront us in a complex and rapidly changing world. We must learn to welcome and not to fear the voices of dissent. We must dare to think about 'unthinkable things' because when things become unthinkable, thinking stops and action becomes mindless.

speech in the US Senate, 27 March 1964

Thomas Fuller 1654–1734

English writer and physician

6 Be you never so high, the law is above you.

Gnomologia (1732); cf. **Denning** 113:6

Alfred Funke b. 1869

German writer

7 *Gott strafe England!*
God punish England!

Sword and Myrtle (1914)

David Maxwell Fyfe see **Kilmuir**

Hugh Gaitskell 1906–63

British Labour politician; Leader of the Labour Party from 1955
on Gaitskell: see **Bevan** 41:5, **Crossman** 106:9

1 There are some of us...who will fight and fight and fight
again to save the Party we love.
   opposing the vote in favour of unilateral disarmament

speech at Labour Party
Conference, 5 October 1960

2 It means the end of a thousand years of history.
   on a European federation

speech at Labour Party
Conference, 3 October 1962

John Kenneth Galbraith 1908–

Canadian-born American economist, noted for his criticism of
a perceived preoccupation in Western society with economic
growth for its own sake; US Ambassador to India 1961–3

of the defeat of Germany in World War Two:
3 That they were defeated is conclusive testimony to the
inherent inefficiencies of dictatorship, the inherent
efficiencies of freedom.

in *Fortune* December 1945

4 It is not necessary to advertise food to hungry people,
fuel to cold people, or houses to the homeless.

American Capitalism (1952)

5 [Intellectual torpor is] the disease of opposition parties,
for initiative and imagination ordinarily lie with
responsibility for action.

letter to Adlai Stevenson,
September 1953

6 The affluent society.

title of book (1958)

7 The conventional wisdom.
   *ironic term for 'the beliefs that are at any time assiduously,
   solemnly and mindlessly traded between the conventionally
   wise'*

The Affluent Society (1958)

8 These are the days when men of all social disciplines and
all political faiths seek the comfortable and the accepted;
when the man of controversy is looked upon as
a disturbing influence; when originality is taken to be
a mark of instability; and when, in minor modification of
the scriptural parable, the bland lead the bland.

The Affluent Society (1958)

9 It is a far, far better thing to have a firm anchor in
nonsense than to put out on the troubled seas of
thought.

The Affluent Society (1958)

10 In a community where public services have failed to keep
abreast of private consumption things are very different.
Here, in an atmosphere of private opulence and public
squalor, the private goods have full sway.

The Affluent Society (1958)

11 The greater the wealth, the thicker will be the dirt.

The Affluent Society (1958)

12 Politics is not the art of the possible. It consists in
choosing between the disastrous and the unpalatable.

letter to President **Kennedy**, 2
March 1962; cf. **Bismarck** 46:6

13 You cannot know the intentions of a government that
doesn't know them itself.
   'Galbraith's First Law of Intelligence', formulated in early 1960s

J. K. Galbraith *A Life in Our Times*
(1981)

1 There are times in politics when you must be on the right side and lose.

attributed, 1968

2 Galbraith's law states that anyone who says he won't resign four times, will.

attributed, 1973

3 I have never understood why one's affections must be confined, as once with women, to a single country.

A Life in Our Times (1981)

4 The reduction of politics to a spectator sport...has been one of the more malign accomplishments of television. Television newsmen are breathless on how the game is being played, largely silent on what the game is all about.

A Life in Our Times (1981)

5 The experience of being disastrously wrong is salutary; no economist should be denied it, and not many are.

A Life in Our Times (1981)

6 In public administration good sense would seem to require the public expectation be kept at the lowest possible level in order to minimize eventual disappointment.

A Life in Our Times (1981)

7 After a lifetime in public office, self-censorship becomes not only automatic but a part of one's personality.

A Life in Our Times (1981)

8 Nothing is so firmly established in Puritan and Presbyterian belief as that people cannot be suffering very much if they are out in healthy fresh air—and also safely out of sight.
   of the public view of rural as opposed to urban poverty

A Life in Our Times (1981)

9 Of all the races on earth, the Indians have the most nearly inexhaustible appetite for oratory.

A Life in Our Times (1981)

10 From the fact of general well-being came the new position of the poor. They were now in most communities a minority. The voice of the people was now the voice of relative affluence. Politicians in pursuit of votes could be expected to have a diminishing concern for the very poor. Compassion would have to serve instead—an uncertain substitute.

A Life in Our Times (1981)

11 Civilian administration is by discussion and consensus; military action is by information and command. The latter has a rewarding simplicity for all civilians and especially for anyone from the discursive tradition of academic life. This is why few men become as dangerously warlike as the academic figure who is plunged into military affairs.

A Life in Our Times (1981)

12 One of the recurrent and dangerous influences on our foreign policy—fear of the political consequences of doing the sensible thing, which in many cases is nothing much at all.

A Life in Our Times (1981)

13 One of the little-celebrated powers of Presidents (and other high government officials) is to listen to their critics with just enough sympathy to ensure their silence.

A Life in Our Times (1981)

1 Trickle-down theory—the less than elegant metaphor
that if one feeds the horse enough oats, some will pass
through to the road for the sparrows.

The Culture of Contentment (1992)

Indira Gandhi 1917–84

Indian stateswoman and daughter of Jawaharlal **Nehru**, Prime
Minister of India 1966–77 and 1980–4

2 Politics is the art of acquiring, holding, and wielding
power.

attributed, 1975

Mahatma Gandhi 1869–1948

Indian nationalist and spiritual leader
on Gandhi: see **Naidu** 268:9, **Nehru** 270:8

3 Non-violence is the first article of my faith. It is also the
last article of my creed.
   speech at Shahi Bag, 18 March 1922, on a charge of sedition

in *Young India* 23 March 1922

on being asked what he thought of modern civilization:
4 That would be a good idea.
   while visiting England in 1930

E. F. Schumacher *Good Work*
(1979)

5 What difference does it make to the dead, the orphans
and the homeless, whether the mad destruction is
wrought under the name of totalitarianism or the holy
name of liberty or democracy?

Non-Violence in Peace and War
(1942) vol. 1

6 Please go on. It is my day of silence.
   note passed to the British Cabinet Mission at a meeting in 1942

Peter Hennessy *Never Again* (1992)

7 The moment the slave resolves that he will no longer be
a slave, his fetters fall. He frees himself and shows the
way to others. Freedom and slavery are mental states.

Non-Violence in Peace and War
(1949) vol. 2

James A. Garfield 1831–81

American Republican statesman, 20th President of the US, who
was assassinated within months of taking presidential office

8 Fellow-citizens: God reigns, and the Government at
Washington lives!
   *speech on the assassination of President **Lincoln**, 1865*

in *Death of President Garfield*
(1881)

9 I am not willing that this discussion should close without
any mention of the value of a true teacher. Give me a log
hut, with only a simple bench, Mark Hopkins [president
of Williams College] on one end and I on the other, and
you may have all the buildings, apparatus and libraries
without him.

address to Williams College
Alumni, New York, 28 December
1871

Giuseppe Garibaldi 1807–82

Italian patriot and military leader

1 Men, I'm getting out of Rome. Anyone who wants to
carry on the war against the outsiders, come with me.
I can offer you neither honours nor wages; I offer you
hunger, thirst, forced marches, battles and death.
Anyone who loves his country, follow me.

Giuseppe Guerzoni *Garibaldi*
(1882) vol. 1 (not a verbatim
record)

John Nance Garner 1868–1967

American politician

2 The vice-presidency isn't worth a pitcher of warm piss.

O. C. Fisher *Cactus Jack* (1978)

William Lloyd Garrison 1805–79

American anti-slavery campaigner

3 I am in earnest—I will not equivocate—I will not
excuse—I will not retreat a single inch—and I will be
heard!

in *The Liberator* 1 January 1831
'Salutatory Address'

4 The compact which exists between the North and the
South is 'a covenant with death and an agreement with
hell'.

resolution adopted by the
Massachusetts Anti-Slavery
Society, 27 January 1843

5 With reasonable men, I will reason; with humane men
I will plead; but to tyrants I will give no quarter, nor
waste arguments where they will certainly be lost.

W. P. and F. J. T. Garrison *William
Lloyd Garrison* (1885–89) vol. 1

James Louis Garvin 1868–1947

British journalist and editor of the *Observer*

6 He spoke for an hour and put the house in his pocket.
   *of F. E. Smith's maiden speech in the House of Commons, 12
   May 1906*

attributed

Eric Geddes 1875–1937

British politician and administrator

7 The Germans, if this Government is returned, are going
to pay every penny; they are going to be squeezed as
a lemon is squeezed—until the pips squeak.

speech at Cambridge, 10 December
1918

George II 1683–1760

King of Great Britain and Ireland from 1727

8 We are come for your good, for all your goods.

speech at Portsmouth, probably
1716, in Joseph Spence *Anecdotes*
(ed. J. M. Osborn, 1966)

George III 1738–1820

King of Great Britain and Ireland from 1760
on George III: see **Walpole** 377:13

1 Born and educated in this country, I glory in the name of Briton.

The King's Speech on Opening the Session 18 November 1760

2 When he has wearied me for two hours he looks at his watch, to see if he may not tire me for an hour more.
   of George **Grenville**

in 1765; Horace Walpole *The Reign of George III* (1845)

3 I would sooner meet Grenville at the point of the sword than let him into my closet.
   of George **Grenville**

Lord Hardwicke letter 10 July 1767

of America:
4 Knavery seems to be so much the striking feature of its inhabitants that it may not in the end be an evil that they become aliens to this kingdom.

draft of letter to Lord Shelburne, 10 November 1782

George V 1865–1936

King of Great Britain and Ireland from 1910

5 I venture to allude to the impression which seemed generally to prevail among their brethren across the seas, that the Old Country must wake up if she intends to maintain her old position of pre-eminence in her Colonial trade against foreign competitors.

speech at Guildhall, 5 December 1901 (the speech was reprinted in 1911 with the title 'Wake up, England')

6 I have many times asked myself whether there can be more potent advocates of peace upon earth through the years to come than this massed multitude of silent witnesses to the desolation of war.
   message read at Terlincthun Cemetery, Boulogne, 13 May 1922

in *The Times* 15 May 1922

7 You have kept up the dignity of the office without using it to give you dignity.
   to the outgoing Prime Minister, **Ramsay MacDonald**

Ramsay MacDonald diary 7 June 1934

8 I will not have another war. *I will not.* The last one was none of my doing and if there is another one and we are threatened with being brought into it, I will go to Trafalgar Square and wave a red flag myself sooner than allow this country to be brought in.

Andrew Roberts *Eminent Churchillians* (1994)

in conversation with Anthony **Eden,** *23 December 1935, following Samuel Hoare's resignation as Foreign Secretary:*
9 I said to your predecessor: 'You know what they're all saying, no more coals to Newcastle, no more Hoares to Paris.' The fellow didn't even laugh.

Earl of Avon *Facing the Dictators* (1962)

10 After I am dead, the boy will ruin himself in twelve months.
   on his son, the future **Edward VIII**

Keith Middlemas and John Barnes *Baldwin* (1969)

11 Bugger Bognor.
   comment made either in 1929, when it was proposed that the town be named Bognor Regis on account of the king's convalescence there after a serious illness; or on his deathbed in

Kenneth Rose *King George V* (1983)

1936, when someone remarked 'Cheer up, your Majesty, you will soon be at Bognor again.'

1 How's the Empire?
   to his private secretary on the morning of his death, probably prompted by an article in The Times, *which he held open at the imperial and foreign page*

   Kenneth Rose *King George V* (1983)

2 Gentlemen, I am so sorry for keeping you waiting like this. I am unable to concentrate.
   on his deathbed

   Lord Wigram memorandum 20 January 1936

George VI 1895–1952

King of Great Britain and Northern Ireland from 1936

3 It [is] utterly damnable that that villain Hitler has upset everything.
   on hearing of the Nazi-Soviet pact of 1940

   Andrew Roberts *Eminent Churchillians* (1994)

4 Personally I feel happier now that we have no allies to be polite to and to pamper.
   to Queen Mary, 27 June 1940

   John Wheeler-Bennett *King George VI* (1958)

5 ATTLEE: I've won the election.
   GEORGE VI: I know. I heard it on the Six O'Clock News.
   first exchange between the King and his newly elected Labour Prime Minister, 26 July 1945; perhaps apocryphal

   Peter Hennessy *Never Again* (1992)

6 Well the Prime Minister has had a very difficult time, I'm sure. What I say is 'Thank God for the Civil Service.'
   shortly after Labour's election victory

   Hugh Dalton *Political Diary* (1986) 28 July 1945

7 HARRY TRUMAN: You've had a revolution.
   GEORGE VI: Oh no! we don't have those here.
   during President **Truman***'s visit to Britain just after Labour's election victory.*

   Hugh Dalton *Political Diary* (1986) 28 July 1945

8 Everything is going nowadays. Before long, I shall have to go myself.
   on hearing, c.1949, that the Sackville-West family home, Knole Park, was to be sold to the National Trust

   Andrew Roberts *Eminent Churchillians* (1994)

Daniel George

English writer

9 O Freedom, what liberties are taken in thy name!

   The Perpetual Pessimist (1963)

Henry George 1839–97

American economist and social reformer

10 So long as all the increased wealth which modern progress brings goes to build up great fortunes, to increase luxury and make sharper the contrast between the House of Have and the House of Want, progress is not real and cannot be permanent.

   Progress and Poverty (1879); introduction

Edward Gibbon 1737–94

English historian

1 In elective monarchies, the vacancy of the throne is a moment big with danger and mischief.

The Decline and Fall of the Roman Empire (1776–88)

2 The division of Europe into a number of independent states connected, however, with each other, by the general resemblance of religion, language, and manners, is productive of the most beneficial consequences to the liberty of mankind.

The Decline and Fall of the Roman Empire (1776–88)

3 The various modes of worship, which prevailed in the Roman world, were all considered by the people as equally true; by the philosopher, as equally false; and by the magistrate, as equally useful. And thus toleration produced not only mutual indulgence, but even religious concord.

The Decline and Fall of the Roman Empire (1776–88)

4 The principles of a free constitution are irrecoverably lost, when the legislative power is nominated by the executive.

The Decline and Fall of the Roman Empire (1776–88)

5 The ascent to greatness, however steep and dangerous, may entertain an active spirit with the consciousness and exercise of its own powers; but the possession of a throne could never yet afford a lasting satisfaction to an ambitious mind.

The Decline and Fall of the Roman Empire (1776–88)

6 History...is, indeed, little more than the register of the crimes, follies, and misfortunes of mankind.

The Decline and Fall of the Roman Empire (1776–88)

7 In every age and country, the wiser, or at least the stronger, of the two sexes, has usurped the powers of the state, and confined the other to the cares and pleasures of domestic life.

The Decline and Fall of the Roman Empire (1776–88)

8 According to the reasoning of tyrants, those who have been esteemed worthy of the throne deserve death, and those who deliberate have already rebelled.

The Decline and Fall of the Roman Empire (1776–88)

9 Corruption, the most infallible symptom of constitutional liberty.

The Decline and Fall of the Roman Empire (1776–88)

10 In every deed of mischief he had a heart to resolve, a head to contrive, and a hand to execute.
   of Comnenus

The Decline and Fall of the Roman Empire (1776–88)

11 Our sympathy is cold to the relation of distant misery.

The Decline and Fall of the Roman Empire (1776–88)

12 Persuasion is the resource of the feeble; and the feeble can seldom persuade.

The Decline and Fall of the Roman Empire (1776–88)

13 All that is human must retrograde if it does not advance.

The Decline and Fall of the Roman Empire (1776–88)

14 I admire his eloquence, I approve his politics, I adore his chivalry, and I can even forgive his superstition.
   of Edmund **Burke**

letter to Lord Sheffield, 5 February 1791

1 Let him do what he will I must love the dog.   letter to Lord Sheffield, 6 January
   of Charles James **Fox**   1793

2 The satirist may laugh, the philosopher may preach, but   *Memoirs of My Life* (1796)
   Reason herself will respect the prejudices and habits
   which have been consecrated by the experience of
   mankind.

Kahlil Gibran 1883–1931

Syrian writer and painter

3 Are you a politician who says to himself: 'I will use my   *The New Frontier* (1931)
   country for my own benefit'?…Or are you a devoted
   patriot, who whispers in the ear of his inner self: 'I love
   to serve my country as a faithful servant.'

W. S. Gilbert 1836–1911

English writer of comic and satirical verse

4 I always voted at my party's call,   *HMS Pinafore* (1878)
   And I never thought of thinking for myself at all.

5 No Englishman unmoved that statement hears,   *The Pirates of Penzance* (1879)
   Because, with all our faults, we love our House of Peers.

6 I often think it's comical   *Iolanthe* (1882)
   How Nature always does contrive
   That every boy and every gal,
   That's born into the world alive,
   Is either a little Liberal,
   Or else a little Conservative!

7 The House of Peers, throughout the war,   *Iolanthe* (1882)
   Did nothing in particular,
   And did it very well.

8 When in that House MPs divide,   *Iolanthe* (1882)
   If they've a brain and cerebellum too,
   They have to leave that brain outside,
   And vote just as their leaders tell 'em to.

9 The prospect of a lot   *Iolanthe* (1882)
   Of dull MPs in close proximity,
   All thinking for themselves is what
   No man can face with equanimity.

10 The idiot who praises, with enthusiastic tone,   *Mikado* (1885)
   All centuries but this, and every country but his own.

11 All shall equal be.   *The Gondoliers* (1889)
   The Earl, the Marquis, and the Dook,
   The Groom, the Butler, and the Cook,
   The Aristocrat who banks with Coutts,
   The Aristocrat who cleans the boots.

Ian Gilmour 1926–

British Conservative politician

1 Unfortunately monetarism, like Marxism, suffered the   *Dancing with Dogma* (1992)
  only fate that for a theory is worse than death: it was
  put into practice.

Newton Gingrich 1943–

American Republican politician; Speaker of the House of
Representatives from 1995
on Gingrich: see **Frank** 141:5

of Senator Robert **Dole**:
2 The tax collector for the welfare state.   in *New York Times* 9 September
                                                                 1984

3 One of the greatest intellectual failures of the welfare   in *USA Today* 16 January 1995
  state is the penchant for sacrifice, so long as the only
  people being asked to sacrifice are working, tax-paying
  Americans.

4 No society can survive, no civilization can survive, with   in *The Times* 9 February 1995
  12-year-olds having babies, with 15-year-olds killing
  each other, with 17-year-olds dying of Aids, with 18-
  year-olds getting diplomas they can't read.
    in December 1994, after the Republican electoral victory

George Gipp d. 1920

American footballer

5 Win just one for the Gipper.   catch-phrase later associated with
                                                                 Ronald **Reagan**, who uttered the
                                                                 immortal words in the 1940 film
                                                                 Knute Rockne, All American

Valéry Giscard d'Estaing 1926–

French statesman, President 1974–81

explaining why he should not stand again for the presidency:
6 Too old, too bourgeois, too distant from the average   in *Independent on Sunday* 5 March
  man, not supported by my political friends, too low in   1995 'Quotes of the Week'
  the opinion polls, and having already been sampled
  nobody wants to repeat the experience.

William Ewart Gladstone 1809–98

British Liberal statesman; Prime Minister, 1868–74, 1880–5, 1886, 1892–4

on Gladstone: see **Bagehot** 24:5, **Churchill** 86:4, 86:7, **Churchill** 88:13, **Disraeli** 120:11, 121:9, **Foot** 138:6, **Hennessy** 175:2, **King** 210:1, **Labouchere** 216:1, **Macaulay** 238:1, **Salisbury** 318:9, **Victoria** 374:6, 374:8

1 Ireland, Ireland! that cloud in the west, that coming storm.

letter to his wife, 12 October 1845

2 This is the negation of God erected into a system of Government.

A Letter to the Earl of Aberdeen on the State Prosecutions of the Neapolitan Government (1851)

3 Finance is, as it were, the stomach of the country, from which all the other organs take their tone.
article on finance, 1858

H. C. G. Matthew *Gladstone 1809–1874* (1986)

4 Your business is not to govern the country but it is, if you think fit, to call to account those who do govern it.

speech to the House of Commons, 29 January 1869

5 I am come among you 'unmuzzled'.
speech in Manchester, 18 July 1865, after his parliamentary defeat at Oxford University

John Morley *Life of Gladstone* (1903) vol. 2

6 You cannot fight against the future. Time is on our side.
speech on the Reform Bill

in the House of Commons, 27 April 1866

7 My mission is to pacify Ireland.
on receiving the news that he was to form his first cabinet, 1st December 1868

H. C. G. Matthew *Gladstone 1809–1874* (1986)

8 Swimming for his life, a man does not see much of the country through which the river winds.

diary 31 December 1868

9 We have been borne down in a torrent of gin and beer.

letter to his brother, 6 February 1874

10 Human justice is ever lagging after wrong, as the prayers in Homer came limping after sin.

in *Contemporary Review* December 1876

11 The love of freedom itself is hardly stronger in England than the love of aristocracy.

in *Nineteenth Century* 1877

12 Let the Turks now carry away their abuses in the only possible manner, namely by carrying off themselves... one and all, bag and baggage, shall I hope clear out from the province they have desolated and profaned.

Bulgarian Horrors and the Question of the East (1876)

13 [The British Constitution] presumes more boldly than any other the good sense and the good faith of those who work it.

Gleanings of Past Years (1879) vol. 1

14 [An] Established Clergy will always be a Tory Corps d'Armée.

letter to Bishop Goodwin, 8 September 1881

15 The resources of civilization against its enemies are not yet exhausted.
on the Irish Land League

speech at Leeds, 7 October 1881

16 It is perfectly true that these gentlemen wish to march through rapine to disintegration and dismemberment of

speech at Knowsley, 27 October 1881

the Empire, and, I am sorry to say, even to the placing of different parts of the Empire in direct hostility one with the other.
on the Irish Land League

1 To the actual, as distinct from the reported, strength of the Empire, India adds nothing. She immensely adds to the responsibility of Government.

H. C. G. Matthew *Gladstone 1875–1898* (1995)

2 There never was a Churchill from John of Marlborough down that had either morals or principles.

in conversation in 1882, recorded by Captain R. V. Briscoe; R. F. Foster *Lord Randolph Churchill* (1981)

3 Ideal perfection is not the true basis of English legislation. We look at the attainable; we look at the practical, and we have too much English sense to be drawn away by those sanguine delineations of what might possibly be attained in Utopia, from a path which promises to enable us to effect great good for the people of England.
on the Reform Bill

in the House of Commons, 28 February 1884

4 Our first site in Egypt, be it by larceny or be it by emption, will be the almost certain egg of a North African Empire, that will grow and grow...till we finally join hands across the Equator with Natal and Cape Town, to say nothing of the Transvaal and the Orange River on the south, or of Abyssinia or Zanzibar to be swallowed by way of *viaticum* on our journey.

Aggression on Egypt and Freedom in the East (1884)

5 I will venture to say, that upon the one great class of subjects, the largest and the most weighty of them all, where the leading and determining considerations that ought to lead to a conclusion are truth, justice, and humanity—upon these, gentlemen, all the world over, I will back the masses against the classes.

speech in Liverpool, 28 June 1886

6 I would tell them of my own intention to keep my counsel...and I will venture to recommend them, as an old Parliamentary hand, to do the same.

in the House of Commons, 21 January 1886

7 This, if I understand it, is one of those golden moments of our history, one of those opportunities which may come and may go, but which rarely returns.
on the Second Reading of the Home Rule Bill

in the House of Commons, 7 June 1886

8 One prayer absorbs all others: Ireland, Ireland, Ireland.

diary 10 April 1887

9 The blubbering Cabinet.
of the colleagues who wept at his final Cabinet meeting

diary 1 March 1894; note

10 What that Sicilian mule was to me, I have been to the Queen.
memorandum on relations with Queen **Victoria**, *20 March 1894*

Autobiographical Memoranda 1868–94 (1981)

11 I absorb the vapour and return it as a flood.
– on public speaking

Lord Riddell *Some Things That Matter* (1927 ed.)

12 It is not a Life at all. It is a Reticence, in three volumes.
on J. W. Cross's Life of George Eliot

E. F. Benson *As We Were* (1930)

1 We are bound to lose Ireland in consequence of years of cruelty, stupidity and misgovernment and I would rather lose her as a friend than as a foe.

Margot Asquith *More Memories* (1933)

2 [Money should] fructify in the pockets of the people.

H. C. G. Matthew *Gladstone 1809–1874* (1986)

3 There is scarcely a single moral action of a single man of which other men can have such a knowledge, in its ultimate grounds, its surrounding incidents, and the real determining cause of its merits, as to warrant their pronouncing a conclusive judgement upon it.

H. C. G. Matthew *Gladstone 1875–1898* (1995)

Thomas Glascock

US Senator

when General Thomas Glascock of Georgia took his seat in the US Senate, a mutual friend expressed the wish to introduce him to Henry **Clay** *of Virginia:*

4 No, sir! I am his adversary, and choose not to subject myself to his fascination.

Robert V. Remini *Henry Clay* (1991)

Joseph Goebbels 1897–1945

German Nazi leader

5 We can manage without butter but not, for example, without guns. If we are attacked we can only defend ourselves with guns not with butter.

speech in Berlin, 17 January 1936; cf. **Goering** 156:6

Hermann Goering 1893–1946

German Nazi leader

6 We have no butter...but I ask you—would you rather have butter or guns?...preparedness makes us powerful. Butter merely makes us fat.

speech at Hamburg, 1936; W. Frischauer *Goering* (1951); cf. **Goebbels** 156:5

7 I herewith commission you to carry out all preparations with regard to...a *total solution* of the Jewish question in those territories of Europe which are under German influence.
   instructions to Heydrich, 31 July 1941

W. L. Shirer *The Rise and Fall of the Third Reich* (1962)

Nikolai Gogol 1809–52

Russian writer

8 [Are not] you too, Russia, speeding along like a spirited *troika* that nothing can overtake?...Everything on earth is flying past, and looking askance, other nations and states draw aside and make way.

Dead Souls (1842)

Isaac Goldberg 1887–1938

9 Diplomacy is to do and say
   The nastiest thing in the nicest way.

The Reflex October 1927

Ludwig Max Goldberger 1848–1913

1 America, the land of unlimited possibilities.

Land of Unlimited Possibilities: Observations on Economic Life in the United States of America (1903)

Emma Goldman 1869–1940

American anarchist

2 Anarchism, then, really, stands for the liberation of the human mind from the dominion of religion; the liberation of the human body from the dominion of property; liberation from the shackles and restraints of government.

Anarchism and Other Essays (1910)

Oliver Goldsmith 1730–74

Anglo-Irish writer, poet, and playwright

3 Such is the patriot's boast, where'er we roam,
His first, best country ever is, at home.

The Traveller (1764)

4 Laws grind the poor, and rich men rule the law.

The Traveller (1764)

5 How small, of all that human hearts endure,
That part which laws or kings can cause or cure!

The Traveller (1764); cf.
Johnson 197:7

6 Ill fares the land, to hast'ning ills a prey,
Where wealth accumulates, and men decay;
Princes and lords may flourish, or may fade;
A breath can make them, as a breath has made;
But a bold peasantry, their country's pride,
When once destroyed, can never be supplied.
A time there was, ere England's griefs began,
When every rood of ground maintained its man;
For him light labour spread her wholesome store,
Just gave what life required, but gave no more;
His best companions, innocence and health;
And his best riches, ignorance of wealth.

The Deserted Village (1770)

7   How wide the limits stand
Between a splendid and a happy land.

The Deserted Village (1770)

Barry Goldwater 1909–

American Republican politician

8 I would remind you that extremism in the defence of liberty is no vice! And let me remind you also that moderation in the pursuit of justice is no virtue!
   speech accepting the presidential nomination, 16 July 1964

in *New York Times* 17 July 1964

Richard Goodwin

1   People come to Washington believing it's the centre of   Peter McWilliams *Ain't Nobody's*
    power. I know I did. It was only much later that   *Business If You Do* (1993)
    I learned that Washington is a steering wheel that's not
    connected to the engine.

Mikhail Sergeevich Gorbachev 1931–

Soviet statesman, General Secretary of the Communist Party of
the USSR 1985–91 and President 1988–91
on Gorbachev: see **Gromyko** 162:4, **Thatcher** 361:11

2   The guilt of Stalin and his immediate entourage before   speech on the seventieth
    the Party and the people for the mass repressions and   anniversary of the Russian
    lawlessness they committed is enormous and   Revolution, 2 November 1987
    unforgivable.

3   The idea of restructuring [*perestroika*]... combines   speech on the seventieth
    continuity and innovation, the historical experience of   anniversary of the Russian
    Bolshevism and the contemporaneity of socialism.   Revolution, 2 November 1987

George Joachim, Lord Goschen

1831–1907

British Liberal Unionist politician, appointed Chancellor of the
Exchequer in 1886 on the sudden resignation of Lord Randolph
Churchill
on Goschen: see **Churchill** 86:9

4   I have the courage of my opinions, but I have not the   in the House of Commons, 19
    temerity to give a political blank cheque to Lord   February 1884
    Salisbury.

Ernest Gowers 1880–1966

British public servant

5   It is not easy nowadays to remember anything so   *Plain Words* (1948)
    contrary to all appearances as that officials are the
    servants of the public; and the official must try not to
    foster the illusion that it is the other way round.

D. M. Graham 1911–

6   That this House will in no circumstances fight for its   motion worded by Graham when
    King and Country.   Librarian of the Oxford Union
    motion for a debate at the Oxford Union, 9 February 1933
    (passed by 275 votes to 153)

James Graham, Marquess of Montrose
1612–50
Scottish royalist general and poet

1   Great, Good and Just, could I but rate
    My grief to thy too rigid fate!

    'Epitaph on King Charles I'

2   Let them bestow on every airth a limb;
    Then open all my veins, that I may swim
    To thee, my Maker! in that crimson lake;
    Then place my parboiled head upon a stake—
    Scatter my ashes—strew them in the air;—
    Lord! since thou know'st where all these atoms are,
    I'm hopeful thou'lt recover once my dust,
    And confident thou'lt raise me with the just.

    'Lines written on the Window of his
    Jail the Night before his Execution'

Phil Gramm 1942–
American Republican politician

3   Balancing the budget is like going to heaven. Everybody
    wants to do it, but nobody wants to do what you have to
    do to get there.

    in a television interview, 16
    September 1990

4   I did not come to Washington to be loved, and I have
    not been disappointed.

    Michael Barone and Grant Ujifusa
    The American Political Almanac
    1994

Bernie Grant 1944–
British Labour politician

5   The police were to blame for what happened on Sunday
    night and what they got was a bloody good hiding.
    after the Broadwater Farm riots in which a policeman was killed

    as leader of Haringey Council
    outside Tottenham Town Hall, 8
    October 1985

Ulysses S. Grant 1822–85
American Union general and 18th President of the US
on Grant: see **Sherman** 339:2

6   No terms except unconditional and immediate surrender
    can be accepted. I propose to move immediately upon
    your works.
    *to Simon Bolivar Buckner, under siege at Fort Donelson, 16
    February 1862*

    P. C. Headley *The Life and
    Campaigns of General U. S. Grant*
    (1869)

7   I purpose to fight it out on this line, if it takes all
    summer.
    *dispatch to Washington, from headquarters in the field, 11 May
    1864*

    P. C. Headley *The Life and
    Campaigns of General U. S. Grant*
    (1869)

8   The war is over—the rebels are our countrymen again.
    *preventing his men from cheering after Lee's surrender at
    Appomattox*

    on 9 April, 1865

1 Let us have peace.
letter to General Joseph R. Hawkey, 29 May 1868, accepting the presidential nomination

P. C. Headley *The Life and Campaigns of General U. S. Grant* (1869)

2 I know no method to secure the repeal of bad or obnoxious laws so effective as their stringent execution.

inaugural address, 4 March 1869

3 Leave the matter of religion to the family altar, the church, and the private school, supported entirely by private contributions. Keep the church and state forever separate.

speech at Des Moines, Iowa, 1875

4 Labour disgraces no man; unfortunately you occasionally find men disgrace labour.

speech at Midland International Arbitration Union, Birmingham, England, 1877

Henry Grattan 1746–1820

Irish nationalist leader

5 The thing he proposes to buy is what cannot be sold—liberty.
speech in the Irish Parliament against the proposed union, 16 January 1800

in Dictionary of National Biography

John Chipman Gray 1839–1915

American lawyer

6 Dirt is only matter out of place; and what is a blot on the escutcheon of the Common Law may be a jewel in the crown of the Social Republic.

Restraints on the Alienation of Property (2nd ed., 1895) preface

Patrick, Lord Gray d. 1612

7 A dead woman bites not.
*oral tradition, Gray being said to have pressed hard for the execution of **Mary** Queen of Scots in 1587, with the words 'Mortua non mordet [Being dead, she will bite no more]'*

A. Darcy's 1625 translation of William Camden's *Annals of the Reign of Queen Elizabeth* (1615) vol. 1

Thomas Gray 1716–71

English poet

8 Some village-Hampden, that with dauntless breast
The little tyrant of his fields withstood;
Some mute inglorious Milton here may rest,
Some Cromwell guiltless of his country's blood.

Th'applause of list'ning senates to command
The threats of pain and ruin to despise,
To scatter plenty o'er a smiling land,
And read their history in a nations eyes,

Their lot forbad: nor circumscribed alone
Their growing virtues, but their crimes confined;
Forbad to wade through slaughter to a throne,
And shut the gates of mercy on mankind.

Elegy Written in a Country Churchyard (1751)

Horace Greeley 1811–72
American editor and politician

1   The illusion that times that were are better than those   *The American Conflict* (1864-6)
    that are, has probably pervaded all ages.

2   I never said all Democrats were saloon keepers. What   attributed
    I said was that all saloon keepers were Democrats.

Gregory VII *c.*1020–85
Pope from 1073

3   I have loved justice and hated iniquity: therefore I die in   J. W. Bowden *The Life and*
    exile.   *Pontificate of Gregory VII* (1840)
    last words   vol. 2

George Grenville 1712–70
British Whig statesman; Prime Minister 1763–5
on Grenville: see **George III** 149:2, 149:3, **Walpole** 377:12

4   A wise government knows how to enforce with temper,   in the House of Commons, 3
    or to conciliate with dignity.   February 1769
    speaking against the expulsion of John **Wilkes**

Lord Grey of Fallodon 1862–1933
British Liberal politician

5   The lamps are going out all over Europe; we shall not   *25 Years* (1925) vol. 2
    see them lit again in our lifetime.
    on the eve of the First World War

John Grey Griffith 1918–
British lawyer and academic

6   The Constitution is what happens.   to Peter Hennessy during the
                                                                     Westland affair, 5 February 1986;
                                                                     Peter Hennessy *Whitehall* (1990)

Roy Griffiths

7   If Florence Nightingale were carrying her lamp through   in *Report of the NHS Management*
    the corridors of the NHS today she would almost   *Inquiry*, DHSS, 1983
    certainly be searching for the people in charge.

John Grigg 1924–
British writer and journalist

8   Lloyd George would have a better rating in British   attributed, 1963
    mythology if he had shared the fate of Abraham Lincoln.

9   Politicians are exiles from the normal, private world.   attributed, 1964

Joseph ('Jo') Grimond 1913–93

British Liberal politician, Leader of the Liberal Party
1956–67

1 In bygone days, commanders were taught that when in
doubt, they should march their troops towards the sound
of gunfire. I intend to march my troops towards the
sound of gunfire.

*speech to the Liberal Party
Assembly, 14 September 1963*

on the chance of a pact with the Labour Government:
2 Our teeth are in the real meat.

*speech to the Liberal Party
Assembly, 1965*

3 The trouble with the Labour Party is that they don't
really believe in Socialism, but they cannot
wholeheartedly approve of private enterprise either.

attributed, 1965

Andrei Gromyko 1909–89

Soviet statesman, President of the USSR 1985–8

4 Comrades, this man has a nice smile, but he's got iron
teeth.
   of Mikhail Gorbachev

*speech to Soviet Communist Party
Central Committee, 11 March 1985*

Philip Guedalla 1889–1944

British historian and biographer

of the Admiralty committee to examine inventions:
5 There they sit, like inverted Micawbers, waiting for
something to turn down.

*in a speech at the Oxford Union,
1912; a similar comment has
also been attributed to Winston
Churchill of Treasury staff (Anthony
Sampson The Anatomy of Britain
Today)*

Henry Gurney 1898–1951

Colonial civil servant and last Chief Secretary of the British
Administration in Palestine

*on the last day of the British Mandate, Gurney was allegedly
asked to whom he intended to give the keys of his office:*
6 To Nobody. I shall put them under the mat.
   *apocryphal; Gurney's diary records that having had the stores
   locked up he informed the initially unwilling United Nations that
   if they did not accept the keys, the British would 'leave the
   keys on their doorstep'*

Peter Hennessy Never Again (1992)

Nell Gwyn 1650–87

English actress and courtesan

7 Pray, good people, be civil. I am the Protestant whore.
   at Oxford, during the Popish Terror, 1681

B. Bevan Nell Gwyn (1969)

Earl Haig 1861–1928

Commander of British armies in France, 1915–18

1 A very weak-minded fellow I am afraid, and, like the
feather pillow, bears the marks of the last person who
has sat on him!
*describing the 17th Earl of Derby, in a letter to Lady Haig, 14
January 1918*

R. Blake *Private Papers of Douglas
Haig* (1952)

2 Every position must be held to the last man: there must
be no retirement. With our backs to the wall, and
believing in the justice of our cause, each one of us must
fight on to the end.
order to British troops, 12 April 1918

A. Duff Cooper *Haig* (1936) vol. 2

Lord Hailsham 1907–

British Conservative politician

3 Conservatives do not believe that the political struggle is
the most important thing in life...The simplest of them
prefer fox-hunting—the wisest religion.

The Case for Conservatism (1947)

4 The responsibility of a political party is in inverse
proportion to its chances of getting office.

in the House of Lords, 13 February
1961

5 A great party is not to be brought down because of
a squalid affair between a woman of easy virtue and
a proved liar.
on the Profumo affair

in a television interview, 13 June
1963

6 If the British public falls for this, I think it will be stark,
raving bonkers.
on the Labour Party programme

at a press conference at
Conservative Central Office, 12
October 1964

7 I believe there is a golden thread which alone gives
meaning to the political history of the West, from
Marathon to Alamein, from Solon to Winston Churchill
and after. This I chose to call the doctrine of liberty
under the law.

in 1975; Anthony Sampson *The
Changing Anatomy of Britain*
(1982)

8 The elective dictatorship.

title of the Dimbleby Lecture, 19
October 1976

9 In a confrontation with the politics of power, the soft
centre has always melted away.

in October 1981; Anthony Sampson
The Changing Anatomy of Britain
(1982)

of Denis **Healey**:
10 A piratical old bruiser with a first-class mind and very
bad manners.

interview in *The Times* 2 June 1987

11 Nations begin by forming their institutions, but in the
end, are continuously formed by them or under their
influence.

'The Granada Guildhall Lecture
1987' 10 November 1987

12 The English and, more latterly, the British, have the
habit of acquiring their institutions by chance or
inadvertence, and shedding them in a fit of absent-
mindedness.

'The Granada Guildhall Lecture
1987' 10 November 1987; cf.
Seeley 322:6

1 We are a democratically governed republic with a wholly admirable head of state.

Values: Collapse and Cure (1994)

Richard Burdon Haldane 1856–1928

British politician, lawyer, and philosopher
on Haldane: see **Asquith** 18:9, **Campbell-Bannerman** 74:4

2 We have come to the conclusion…that in the sphere of civil government the duty of investigation and thought, as preliminary to action, might with great advantage be more definitely added.

Peter Hennessy *Whitehall* (1990)

H. R. Haldeman 1929–93

Presidential assistant to Richard **Nixon**

3 Once the toothpaste is out of the tube, it is awfully hard to get it back in.
on the Watergate affair, to John Dean, 8 April 1973

in *Hearings Before the Select Committee on Presidential Campaign Activities of US Senate: Watergate and Related Activities* (1973) vol. 4

Edward Everett Hale 1822–1909

American clergyman

4 'Do you pray for the senators, Dr Hale?' 'No, I look at the senators and I pray for the country.'

Van Wyck Brooks *New England Indian Summer* (1940)

Matthew Hale 1609–76

English judge

5 Christianity is part of the laws of England.

William Blackstone's summary of Hale's words (Taylor's case, 1676) in *Commentaries* (1769) vol. 4; the origin of the expression has been traced to Sir John Prisot (d. 1460)

Nathan Hale 1755–76

American revolutionary

6 I only regret that I have but one life to lose for my country.
prior to his execution by the British for spying, 22 September 1776

Henry Phelps Johnston *Nathan Hale, 1776* (1914)

William Haley 1901–87

British journalist

7 It *is* a moral issue.
heading of leading article on the Profumo affair

in *The Times* 11 June 1963

Lord Halifax ('the Trimmer') 1633–95

English politician and essayist

1 Lord Rochester was made Lord president: which being
a post superior in rank, but much inferior both in
advantage and credit to that he held formerly, drew
a jest from Lord Halifax...he had heard of many kicked
down stairs, but never of any that was kicked up stairs
before.

Gilbert Burnet *History of My Own Time* (written 1683–6) vol. 1 (1724)

2 This innocent word *Trimmer* signifieth no more than this,
that if men are together in a boat, and one part of the
company would weigh it down on one side, another
would make it lean as much to the contrary.

Character of a Trimmer (1685, printed 1688)

3 To the question, What shall we do to be saved in this
World? there is no other answer but this, Look to your
Moat.

A Rough Draft of a New Model at Sea (1694)

4 Men in business are in as much danger from those that
work under them, as from those that work against them.

Political, Moral, and Miscellaneous Thoughts and Reflections (1750) 'Instruments of State Ministers'

5 The best way to suppose what may come, is to remember
what is past.

Political, Moral, and Miscellaneous Thoughts and Reflections (1750) 'Miscellaneous: Experience'

6 A known liar should be outlawed in a well-ordered
government.

Political, Moral, and Miscellaneous Thoughts and Reflections (1750) 'Miscellaneous: Lying'

7 Anger is never without an argument, but seldom with
a good one.

Political, Moral, and Miscellaneous Thoughts and Reflections (1750) 'Of Anger'

8 After a revolution, you see the same men in the drawing-
room, and within a week the same flatterers.

Political, Moral, and Miscellaneous Thoughts and Reflections (1750) 'Of Courts'

9 Most men make little other use of their speech than to
give evidence against their own understanding.

Political, Moral, and Miscellaneous Thoughts and Reflections (1750) 'Of Folly and Fools'

10 There is...no fundamental, but that *every supreme power
must be arbitrary.*

Political, Moral, and Miscellaneous Thoughts and Reflections (1750) 'Of Fundamentals'

11 The people are never so perfectly backed, but that they
will kick and fling if not stroked at seasonable times.

Political, Moral, and Miscellaneous Thoughts and Reflections (1750) 'Of Fundamentals'

12 In corrupted governments the place is given for the sake
of the man; in good ones the man is chosen for the sake
of the place.

Political, Moral, and Miscellaneous Thoughts and Reflections (1750) 'Of Fundamentals'

13 It is in a disorderly government as in a river, the lightest
things swim at the top.

Political, Moral, and Miscellaneous Thoughts and Reflections (1750) 'Of Government'

14 The best definition of the best government is, that it has
no inconveniences but such as are supportable; but
inconveniences there must be.

Political, Moral, and Miscellaneous Thoughts and Reflections (1750) 'Of Government'

1 If the laws could speak for themselves, they would complain of the lawyers in the first place.

Political, Moral, and Miscellaneous Thoughts and Reflections (1750) 'Of Laws'

2 Malice is of a low stature, but it hath very long arms.

Political, Moral, and Miscellaneous Thoughts and Reflections (1750) 'Of Malice and Envy'

3 In parliaments, men wrangle in behalf of liberty, that do as little care for it, as they deserve it.

Political, Moral, and Miscellaneous Thoughts and Reflections (1750) 'Of Parliaments'

4 The best party is but a kind of conspiracy against the rest of the nation.

Political, Moral, and Miscellaneous Thoughts and Reflections (1750) 'Of Parties'

5 There are men who shine in a faction, and make a figure by opposition, who would stand in a worse light, if they had the preferments they struggle for.

Political, Moral, and Miscellaneous Thoughts and Reflections (1750) 'Of Parties'

6 Party is little less than an inquisition, where men are under such a discipline in carrying on the common cause, as leaves no liberty of private opinion.

Political, Moral, and Miscellaneous Thoughts and Reflections (1750) 'Of Parties'

7 When the people contend for their liberty, they seldom get anything by their victory but new masters.

Political, Moral, and Miscellaneous Thoughts and Reflections (1750) 'Of Prerogative, Power and Liberty'

8 Power is so apt to be insolent and Liberty to be saucy, that they are very seldom upon good terms.

Political, Moral, and Miscellaneous Thoughts and Reflections (1750) 'Of Prerogative, Power and Liberty'

9 If none were to have liberty but those who understand what it is, there would not be many freed men in the world.

Political, Moral, and Miscellaneous Thoughts and Reflections (1750) 'Of Prerogative, Power and Liberty'

10 Men are not hanged for stealing horses, but that horses may not be stolen.

Political, Moral, and Miscellaneous Thoughts and Reflections (1750) 'Of Punishment'

11 Wherever a knave is not punished, an honest man is laughed at.

Political, Moral, and Miscellaneous Thoughts and Reflections (1750) 'Of Punishment'

12 State business is a cruel trade; good nature is a bungler in it.

Political, Moral, and Miscellaneous Thoughts and Reflections (1750) 'Wicked Ministers'

Lord Halifax 1881–1959

British Conservative politician and Foreign Secretary

On being asked immediately after the Munich crisis if he were not worn out by the late nights:

13 No, not exactly. But it spoils one's eye for the high birds.   attributed

Alexander Hamilton c.1755–1804

American Federalist politician, killed in a duel by Aaron **Burr**
on Hamilton: see **Webster** 382:6

1   A national debt, if it is not excessive, will be to us
     a national blessing.

                letter to Robert Morris, 30 April 1781

2   I believe the British government forms the best model the
     world ever produced…This government has for its object
     public strength and individual security.

                in Debates of the Federal Convention 18 June 1787

3   All communities divide themselves into the few and the
     many. The first are the rich and wellborn, the other the
     mass of the people…The people are turbulent and
     changing; they seldom judge or determine right. Give
     therefore to the first class a distinct, permanent share in
     the government. They will check the unsteadiness of the
     second, and as they cannot receive any advantage by
     a change, they therefore will ever maintain good
     government.

                in Debates of the Federal Convention 18 June 1787

4   We are now forming a republican government. Real
     liberty is neither found in despotism or the extremes of
     democracy, but in moderate government.

                in Debates of the Federal Convention 26 June 1787

5   Let Americans disdain to be the instruments of European
     greatness. Let the thirteen States, bound together in
     a strict and indissoluble Union, concur in erecting one
     great American system, superior to the control of all
     transatlantic force or influence, and able to dictate the
     terms of the connection between the old and the new
     world!

                in The Federalist (1787–8) no. 11

6   Why has government been instituted at all? Because the
     passions of men will not conform to the dictates of reason
     and justice, without constraint.

                in The Federalist (1787–8) no. 15

7   Learn to think continentally.
     advice to the newly independent United States

                attributed; cf. **Chamberlain** 80:5

8   To admit foreigners indiscriminately to the rights of
     citizens…would be nothing less than to admit the
     Grecian horse into the citadel of our liberty and
     sovereignty.

                Works (1886) vol.7

Richard Hampden 1631–95

Parliamentary supporter, Chancellor of the Exchequer
1690–94

9   To tie a popish successor with laws for the preservation
     of the Protestant religion was binding Samson with
     withes.
     *moving a bill to exclude the Duke of York by name from the
     succession, 11 May 1679*

                in Dictionary of National Biography

Mark Hanna 1837–1904

American politician and businessman

on Theodore **Roosevelt***'s acceding to the Presidency on the*
assassination of William McKinley

1 Now look, that damned cowboy is President of the United   in September 1901
   States.

William Harcourt 1827–1904

British Liberal politician; Chancellor of the Exchequer

2 We are all socialists now.   G. B. Shaw (ed.) *Fabian Essays in*
   during the passage of Lord **Goschen***'s 1888 budget, noted for*   *Socialism* (1889)
   the reduction of the national debt

3 The value of the political heads of departments is to tell   A. G. Gardiner *The Life of Sir*
   the permanent officials what the public will not stand.   *William Harcourt* (1923) vol. 2

Keir Hardie 1856–1915

Scottish Labour politician

4 From his childhood onward this boy [the future Edward   in the House of Commons, 28 June
   VIII] will be surrounded by sycophants and flatterers by   1894
   the score—[*Cries of* 'Oh, oh!']—and will be taught to
   believe himself as of a superior creation. [*Cries of* 'Oh,
   oh!'] A line will be drawn between him and the people
   whom he is to be called upon some day to reign over. In
   due course, following the precedent which has already
   been set, he will be sent on a tour round the world, and
   probably rumours of a morganatic alliance will follow—
   [*Loud cries of* 'Oh, oh!' *and* 'Order!']—and the end of it all
   will be that the country will be called upon to pay the
   bill. [*Cries of* Divide!]

Warren G. Harding 1865–1923

American Republican statesman, 29th President of the US
1921–3

5 In the great fulfillment we must have a citizenship less   speech at the Republican National
   concerned about what the government can do for it and   Convention, 7 June 1916; cf.
   more anxious about what it can do for the nation.   **Kennedy** 204:7

6 America's present need is not heroics, but healing; not   speech at Boston, 14 May 1920
   nostrums but normalcy; not revolution, but restoration.

Thomas Hardy 1840–1928

English novelist and poet

7 The offhand decision of some commonplace mind high in   Florence Hardy *The Early Life of*
   office at a critical moment influences the course of events   *Thomas Hardy 1840–91* (1928)
   for a hundred years.

John Harington 1561–1612

English writer and courtier

1 Treason doth never prosper, what's the reason?
For if it prosper, none dare call it treason.

Epigrams (1618)

John Marshall Harlan 1833–1911

American judge

2 Our Constitution is colour-blind, and neither knows nor
tolerates classes among citizens. In respect of civil rights,
all citizens are equal before the law. The humblest is the
peer of the most powerful.

dissenting opinion in *Plessy v.
Ferguson* (1896)

Lord Harlech 1918–85

British Ambassador to Washington, 1961–5

3 Britain will be honoured by historians more for the way
she disposed of an empire than for the way in which she
acquired it.

in *New York Times* 28 October
1962

Harold II *c.*1019–66

King of England, 1066

4 He will give him seven feet of English ground, or as
much more as he may be taller than other men.
   his offer to Harald Sigurdson, invading England

Snorri Sturluson *King Harald's
Saga* (*c.*1260)

Robert Goodloe Harper 1765–1825

5 Millions for defence, but not one cent for tribute.

toast at a banquet for John
Marshall, 18 June 1798

Michael Harrington 1928–89

American writer and sociologist

6 For the urban poor the police are those who arrest you.
In almost any slum there is a vast conspiracy against the
forces of law and order.

*The Other America: Poverty in the
United States* (1962)

William Henry Harrison 1773–1841

American Whig statesman and soldier, noted for his victory at
the battle of Tippecanoe in 1811, and 9th President of the US,
1841, who died of pneumonia one month after his inauguration
on Harrison: see **Morris** 266:4, **Ross** 313:3

7 We admit of no government by divine right...the only
legitimate right to govern is an express grant of power
from the governed.

inaugural address, 4 March 1841

1 A decent and manly examination of the acts of government should be not only tolerated, but encouraged.

inaugural address, 4 March 1841

Minnie Louise Haskins 1875–1957

English teacher and writer

2 And I said to the man who stood at the gate of the year: 'Give me a light that I may tread safely into the unknown.'
    And he replied:
    'Go out into the darkness and put your hand into the Hand of God. That shall be to you better than light and safer than a known way.'
    quoted by King **George VI** *in his Christmas broadcast, 25 December 1939*

Desert (1908) 'God Knows'

Roy Hattersley 1932–

British Labour politician

3 Opposition is four or five years' humiliation in which there is no escape from the indignity of no longer controlling events.

in Independent 25 March 1995 'Quote Unquote'

Václav Havel 1936–

Czech dramatist and statesman; President of Czechoslovakia 1989–92 and of the Czech Republic since 1993

4 A spectre is haunting eastern Europe: the spectre of what in the West is called 'dissent'.

The Power of the Powerless (1978)

5 I see a renewed focus of politics on real people as something far more profound than merely returning to the everyday mechanisms of western (or if you like bourgeois) democracy.

Václav Havel et al. The Power of the Powerless (1985)

6 To respond to evil by committing another evil does not eliminate evil but allows it to go on forever.

letter 5 November 1989

R. S. Hawker 1803–75

English clergyman and poet

7 And have they fixed the where and when?
And shall Trelawny die?
Here's twenty thousand Cornish men
Will know the reason why!
    the last three lines are taken from a traditional rhyme dating from the imprisonment by James II, in 1688, of the seven Bishops, including Trelawny, Bishop of Bristol

'The Song of the Western Men'

John Milton Hay 1838–1905

American politician

1 It has been a splendid little war, begun with the highest
motives, carried on with magnificent intelligence and
spirit, favoured by that fortune which loves the brave.
on the Spanish-American War of 1898

letter to Theodore Roosevelt, 27
July 1898

2 The open door.
*on the completion of the trade policy he had negotiated with
China*

letter to the Cabinet, 2 January
1900

Bill Hayden 1933–

Australian Labor politician

*Hayden had resigned as Opposition leader in 1983 as Malcolm
Fraser was in the process of calling the election, but remained
convinced that he would have won:*

3 I am not convinced the Labor Party could not win under
my leadership. I believe a drover's dog could lead the
Labor Party to victory the way the country is.

John Stubbs *Hayden* (1989)

Friedrich August von Hayek 1899–1992

Austrian-born economist

4 The system of private property is the most important
guarantee of freedom, not only for those who own
property, but scarcely less for those who do not.

The Road to Serfdom (1944)

5 Probably nothing has done so much harm to the liberal
cause as the wooden insistence of some liberals on
certain rough rules of thumb, above all the principle of
laissez-faire.

The Road to Serfdom (1944)

6 Although the professed aims of planning would be that
man should cease to be a mere means, in fact...the
individual would more than ever become a mere means,
to be used by the authority in the service of such
abstractions as the 'social welfare' or the 'good of the
community'

The Road to Serfdom (1944)

7 In any society freedom of thought will probably be of
direct significance only for a small minority. But this does
not mean that anyone is competent, or ought to have
power, to select those to whom this freedom is to be
reserved.

The Road to Serfdom (1944)

8 We need good principles rather than good people. We
need fixed rules, not fixers.

*Studies in Philosophy, Politics and
Economics* (1967)

9 I am certain that nothing has done so much to destroy
the juridical safeguards of individual freedom as the
striving after this miracle of social justice.

*Economic Freedom and
Representative Government* (1973)

10 One cannot help a country to maintain its standard of life
by assisting people to consume more than they produce.

in *Daily Telegraph* 26 August 1976

Cuthbert Morley Headlam 1876–1964

British Conservative politician

1 He is a terrible burden for any Govt. to carry—someone   diary 20 July 1927
said of Randolph Churchill that he was the kind of man
who would like to be the bride at a wedding, and the
corpse at the funeral—the same applies to his more
brilliant son.
  of Winston **Churchill**

2 He is very clever and takes infinite pains to make himself   diary 31 January 1932
well informed—but somehow I doubt whether he will
ever make much political progress. He bores people too
quickly and has little or no sense of humour. However, it
is never safe to prophesy about anyone's political
prospects and Harold may yet come out on top.
  of Harold **Macmillan**

3 This Parliament is enough to discourage anyone from   diary 27 March 1933
entering political life—a vast untutored majority with
a helpless minority and an extremely uninteresting
Government.

4 We ought to have made up more to the political leaders   diary 28 July 1933
and their wives—the latter are an unattractive lot, but
their influence is greater than one supposes.

5 In politics only one thing really counts and that is   diary 2 April 1934
a power of decision: a policy is all that is required...
Better to break your party on a matter of principle than
to let it fall to pieces because you cannot yourself make
up your mind what you want to do.

Denis Healey 1917–

British Labour politician
on Healey: see **Hailsham** 163:10

6 The Fabians...found socialism wandering aimlessly in   *New Fabian Essays* (1952)
Cloud-cuckoo-land and set it working on the gas and
water problems of the nearest town or village.
  of the parochialism of the Fabians

7 There are going to be howls of anguish from the 80,000   speech at the Labour Party
people who are rich enough to pay over 75% [tax] on   Conference, 1 October 1973
the last slice of their income.

8 It's no good ceasing to become the world's policeman in   at a meeting of the Cabinet at
order to become the world's parson instead.   Chequers, 17 November 1974;
                                                               Peter Hennessy *Whitehall* (1990)

9 We should not allow middle-class guilt to blind us to   Anthony Sampson *The Changing*
what's going on.   *Anatomy of Britain*
  of the susceptibility of ministers, in the Labour Cabinet of 1974,
  to the charge that they did not understand the problems of the
  workers or the unemployed

  of being criticized by Geoffrey **Howe** *in the House of Commons:*
10 Like being savaged by a dead sheep.   in the House of Commons, 14 June
                                                               1978

of Margaret **Thatcher**:

1 And who is the Mephistopheles behind this shabby Faust   in the House of Commons, 27
[the Foreign Secretary, Geoffrey Howe]?...To quote her   February 1984
own backbenchers, the Great She-elephant, She-Who-
Must-Be-Obeyed, the Catherine the Great of Finchley, the
Prime Minister herself.

2 La Passionaria of middle-class privilege.   Kenneth Minogue and Michael
of Margaret **Thatcher**   Biddiss *Thatcherism* (1987)

3 Healey's first law of politics: when you're in a hole, stop attributed
digging.

4 While the rest of Europe is marching to confront the new   in the House of Commons, 22
challenges, the Prime Minister is shuffling along in the   February 1990
gutter in the opposite direction, like an old bag lady,
muttering imprecations at anyone who catches her eye.

William Randolph Hearst 1863–1951

American newspaper publisher and tycoon

5 You furnish the pictures and I'll furnish the war.   attributed
message to the artist Frederic Remington in Havana, Cuba,
during the Spanish-American War of 1898

Edward Heath 1916–

British Conservative statesman; Prime Minister 1970–4
on Heath: see **Hennessy** 175:2, **Jenkins** 194:8, **Thatcher** 360:9

6 This would, at a stroke, reduce the rise in prices, increase from Conservative Central Office,
productivity and reduce unemployment.   16 June 1970
press release, never actually spoken by Heath

7 I entered the House in 1950 having fought an election   speech at the Conservative Party
on Mr Churchill's theme that Conservatives were to set   Conference, October 1970
the people free. It was not a theme that we were to set
the people free to do what we tell them.

8 The unpleasant and unacceptable face of capitalism.   in the House of Commons, 15 May
on the Lonrho affair   1973

9 If politicians lived on praise and thanks they'd be forced attributed, 1973
into some other line of business.

10 I am not a product of privilege. I am a product of   attributed, 1974
opportunity.

11 Out go the estate-owners, in come the estate agents.   in *Observer* 30 September 1990

G. W. F. Hegel 1770–1831

German idealist philosopher

12 What experience and history teach is this—that nations   *Lectures on the Philosophy of*
and governments have never learned anything from   *World History: Introduction* (1830)
history, or acted upon any lessons they might have
drawn from it.

Heinrich Heine 1797–1856

German poet

1   Wherever books will be burned, men also, in the end, are   *Almansor* (1823)
    burned.

Joseph Heller 1923–

American novelist

2   If I'm going to be trivial, inconsequential, and deceitful...   *Closing Time* (1994)
    then I might as well be in government.

Lillian Hellman 1905–84

American playwright

3   I cannot and will not cut my conscience to fit this year's   letter to John S. Wood, 19 May
    fashions.   1952

Leona Helmsley *c.*1920–

American hotelier

4   Only the little people pay taxes.   to her housekeeper; in *New York*
    reported at her trial for tax evasion   *Times* 12 July 1983

Arthur Henderson 1863–1935

British Labour politician and from 1931 Party Leader

to critics in his own party, when as adviser on labour matters
he was made minister without portfolio in **Lloyd George***'s War*
Cabinet (December 1916):

5   I am not here either to please myself or you; I am here   in *Dictionary of National Biography*
    to see the war through.

6   The first forty-eight hours decide whether a Minister is   Susan Crosland *Tony Crosland*
    going to run his office or whether his office is going to   (1982)
    run him.

Leon Henderson 1895–1956

American economist; appointed by Roosevelt to the National
Defense Advisory Commission in 1940

7   Having a little inflation is like being a little pregnant.   J. K. Galbraith *A Life in Our Times*
                                                                  (1981)

Peter Hennessy 1947–

English historian and writer

8   MI5 is a job creation scheme for muscular   in *The Times* 1981, profile of Roger
    underachievers from the ancient universities.   Hollis

of Rab **Butler** *in his last years:*

1 He seemed like a benign and decent beached whale   *in Independent* 8 May 1987
   washed up on the harder shores of modern Conservatism.

2 The model of a modern Prime Minister would be a kind   *The Hidden Wiring* (1995)
   of grotesque composite freak—someone with the
   dedication to duty of a Peel, the physical energy of
   a Gladstone, the detachment of a Salisbury, the brains of
   an Asquith, the balls of a Lloyd George, the word-power
   of a Churchill, the administrative gifts of an Attlee, the
   style of a Macmillan, the managerialism of a Heath, and
   the sleep requirements of a Thatcher. Human beings do
   not come like that.

Henri IV (of Navarre) 1553–1610

King of France from 1589

3 Hang yourself, brave Crillon; we fought at Arques and   traditional form given by Voltaire
   you were not there.   to a letter from Henri to Crillon, 20
                                                             September 1597; Henri's actual
                                                             words were: 'My good man, Crillon,
                                                             hang yourself for not having been
                                                             at my side last Monday at the
                                                             greatest event that's ever been
                                                             seen and perhaps ever will be
                                                             seen'

4 The wisest fool in Christendom.   attributed both to Henri IV and
   of **James I** *of England*   **Sully**

5 I want there to be no peasant in my kingdom so poor   In Hardouin de Péréfixe *Histoire de
   that he is unable to have a chicken in his pot every   Henry le Grand* (1681); cf.
   Sunday.   **Hoover** 182:9

6 Paris is well worth a mass.   attributed to Henri IV; alternatively
   when told that, though a Protestant, he must hear mass at   to his minister Sully, in
   Notre-Dame Cathedral to be consecrated king   conversation with Henri

Henry II 1133–89

King of England from 1154

7 Will no one rid me of this turbulent priest?   oral tradition, conflating a number
   of Thomas Becket, Archbishop of Canterbury, murdered in   of variant forms, including G.
   Canterbury Cathedral, December 1170   Lyttelton *History of the Life of King
                                                             Henry the Second* (1769): 'so many
                                                             cowardly and ungrateful men in his
                                                             court, none of whom would
                                                             revenge him of the injuries he
                                                             sustained from one turbulent
                                                             priest'

Henry VIII 1491–1547

King of England from 1509

1   The King found her [Anne of Cleves] so different from her
    picture...that...he swore they had brought him
    a Flanders mare.

    *Tobias Smollett A Complete
    History of England (3rd ed., 1759)*

2   This man hath the right sow by the ear.
    of Thomas Cranmer, June 1529

    in *Acts and Monuments of John
    Foxe* ['Fox's Book of Martyrs']
    (1570)

Patrick Henry 1736–99

American statesman

3   Caesar had his Brutus—Charles the First, his Cromwell—
    and George the Third—('Treason,' cried the Speaker)...
    may profit by their example. If *this* be treason, make the
    most of it.

    speech in the Virginia assembly,
    May 1765

4   I am not a Virginian, but an American.

    in [John Adams's] Notes of Debates
    in the Continental Congress,
    Philadelphia, 6 September 1774

5   I know not what course others may take; but as for me,
    give me liberty, or give me death!

    speech in Virginia Convention, 23
    March 1775

6   I have but one lamp by which my feet are guided, and
    that is the lamp of experience. I know no way of judging
    the future but by the past.

    speech in Virginia Convention,
    Richmond, 23 March 1775

7   We are not weak if we make a proper use of those means
    which the God of Nature has placed in our power...The
    battle, sir, is not to the strong alone; it is to the vigilant,
    the active, the brave.

    speech in Virginia Convention,
    Richmond, 23 March 1775

8   Guard with jealous attention the public liberty. Suspect
    everyone who approaches that jewel. Unfortunately,
    nothing will preserve it but downright force. Whenever
    you give up that force, you are inevitably ruined.

    attributed

A. P. Herbert 1890–1971

English writer and humorist

9   This high official, all allow,
    Is grossly overpaid;
    There wasn't any Board, and now
    There isn't any Trade.

    'The President of the Board of
    Trade' (1922)

10 Testators would do well to provide some indication of the
    particular Liberal Party which they have in mind, such
    as a telephone number or a Christian name.

    Misleading Cases (1935)

11 People must not do things for fun. We are not here for
    fun. There is no reference to fun in any Act of
    Parliament.

    Uncommon Law (1935) 'Is it a Free
    Country?'

1 The Common Law of England has been laboriously built   *Uncommon Law* (1935) 'The
   about a mythical figure—the figure of 'The Reasonable   Reasonable Man'
   Man'.

Frank Herbert 1920–86

American writer of science fiction

2 If you think of yourselves as helpless and ineffectual, it is   *The Dosadi Experiment* (1978)
   certain that you will create a despotic government to be
   your master. The wise despot, therefore, maintains
   among his subjects a popular sense that they are helpless
   and ineffectual.

Herodotus *c.*485–*c.*425 BC

Greek historian

3 In peace, children inter their parents; war violates the   *Histories*
   order of nature and causes parents to inter their children.

4 The most hateful torment for men is to have knowledge   *Histories*
   of everything but power over nothing.

Lord Hervey 1696–1743

English politician and writer

5 Whoever would lie usefully should lie seldom.   *Memoirs of the Reign of George II*
                                                              (ed. J. W. Croker, 1848) vol. 1

6 I am fit for nothing but to carry candles and set chairs all   letter to Sir Robert Walpole, 1737
   my life.

Alexander Ivanovich Herzen 1812–70

Russian author and revolutionary

7 Communism is a Russian autocracy turned upside down.   *The Development of Revolutionary
                                                              Ideas in Russia* (1851)

8 Russia's future will be a great danger for Europe and   *The Development of Revolutionary
   a great misfortune for Russia if there is no emancipation   Ideas in Russia* (1851)
   of the individual. One more century of present despotism
   will destroy all the good qualities of the Russian people.

Michael Heseltine 1933–

British Conservative politician
on Heseltine: see **Critchley** 104:7

9 I knew that, 'He who wields the knife never wears the   in *New Society* 14 February 1986
   crown.'

10 There are those who never stretch out the hand for fear   *Where There's a Will* (1987)
   it will be bitten. But those who never stretch out the
   hand will never feel it clasped in friendship.

11 The market has no morality.   on *Panorama* BBC1 27 June 1988

1 The biggest headline is always the last headline. I don't want the last headline. You don't if you want a future in politics. Which I suppose I have.
   on why he avoided criticism of Mrs **Thatcher**'s *anti-Europeanism during the Euro Elections*

interview in *The Spectator* 16 September 1989

2 Polluted rivers, filthy streets, bodies bedded down in doorways are no advertisement for a prosperous or caring society.

speech at Conservative Party Conference 10 October 1989

3 The Tory recognizes the contrast between laissez-faire and noblesse oblige.

in *Observer* 18 March 1990 'Sayings of the Week'

4 If I have to intervene to help British companies...I'll intervene—before breakfast, before lunch, before tea and before dinner. And I'll get up the next morning and I'll start all over again.
   of his role as President of the Board of Trade

to the Conservative Party Conference, 7 October 1992

Gordon Hewart 1870–1943

British lawyer and politician

5 A long line of cases shows that it is not merely of some importance, but is of fundamental importance that justice should not only be done, but should manifestly and undoubtedly be seen to be done.

in *Rex v Sussex Justices* 9 November 1923

J. R. Hicks 1904–89

British economist

6 The best of all monopoly profits is a quiet life.

Econometrica (1935) 'The Theory of Monopoly'

Charles Hill 1904–89

British Conservative politician, doctor, and broadcaster

7 It does not do to appear clever. Advancement in this man's party is due entirely to alcoholic stupidity.
   advice given in 1959 to the newly elected MP, Julian **Critchley**, *whom he had seen reading in the Smoking Room of the House of Commons*

Julian Critchley *A Bag of Boiled Sweets* (1994)

Joe Hill 1879–1915

American labour leader and songwriter

8 You will eat, bye and bye,
   In that glorious land above the sky;
   Work and pray, live on hay,
   You'll get pie in the sky when you die.

'Preacher and the Slave' in *Songs of the Workers* (Industrial Workers of the World, 1911)

9 I will die like a true-blue rebel. Don't waste any time in mourning—organize.
   farewell telegram to Bill Haywood, 18 November 1915, prior to his death by firing squad

in *Salt Lake* (Utah) *Tribune* 19 November 1915

Emperor Hirohito 1901–89

Emperor of Japan 1926–89

1 The war situation has developed not necessarily to   on 15 August 1945
   Japan's advantage.
   announcing Japan's surrender, in a broadcast to his people after
   atom bombs had destroyed Hiroshima and Nagasaki

2 Certainly things happened during the Second World War   attributed, 1971
   for which I feel personally sorry.

Adolf Hitler 1889–1945

German dictator

3 The broad mass of a nation...will more easily fall victim   *Mein Kampf* (1925) vol. 1
   to a big lie than to a small one.

4 The night of the long knives.   speech in the Reichstag, 13 July
   applied to the massacre of Ernst Roehm and his associates by   1934
   Hitler on 29–30 June 1934, though taken from an early Nazi
   marching song; the phrase was subsequently associated with
   *Harold **Macmillan**'s Cabinet dismissals of 13 July 1962*

5 I go the way that Providence dictates with the assurance   speech in Munich, 15 March 1936
   of a sleepwalker.

6 It is the last territorial claim which I have to make in   speech at Berlin Sportpalast, 26
   Europe, but it is the claim from which I will not recede   September 1938
   and which, God-willing, I will make good.
   on the Sudetenland

7 With regard to the problem of the Sudeten Germans, my   speech at Berlin Sportpalast, 26
   patience is now at an end!   September 1938

   to Mussolini, having spent nine hours intermittently in Franco's
   company:
8 Rather than go through that again, I would prefer to   Paul Preston *Franco* (1993)
   have three or four teeth taken out.

Thomas Hobbes 1588–1679

English philosopher

9 By art is created that great Leviathan, called   *Leviathan* (1651); introduction
   a commonwealth or state, (in Latin *civitas*) which is but
   an artificial man...and in which, the sovereignty is an
   artificial soul.

10 I put for a general inclination of all mankind, a perpetual   *Leviathan* (1651)
   and restless desire of power after power, that ceaseth
   only in death.

11 They that approve a private opinion, call it opinion; but   *Leviathan* (1651)
   they that mislike it, heresy: and yet heresy signifies no
   more than private opinion.

12 During the time men live without a common power to   *Leviathan* (1651)
   keep them all in awe, they are in that condition which is

called war; and such a war as is of every man against every man.

1 For as the nature of foul weather, lieth not in a shower or two of rain; but in an inclination thereto of many days together: so the nature of war consisteth not in actual fighting, but in the known disposition thereto during all the time there is no assurance to the contrary.

Leviathan (1651)

2 No arts; no letters; no society; and which is worst of all, continual fear and danger of violent death; and the life of man, solitary, poor, nasty, brutish, and short.

Leviathan (1651)

3 Force, and fraud, are in war the two cardinal virtues.

Leviathan (1651)

4 There is written on the turrets of the city of Lucca...the word *libertas*: yet no man can thence infer, that a particular man has more liberty, or immunity from the service of the commonwealth there, than in Constantinople. Whether a commonwealth be monarchical or popular, the freedom is still the same.

Leviathan (1651)

5 Liberties...depend on the silence of the law.

Leviathan (1651)

6 The obligation of subjects to the sovereign, is understood to last as long, and no longer, than the power lasteth, by which he is able to protect them.

Leviathan (1651)

7 I put down for one of the most effectual seeds of the death of any state, that the conquerors require not only a submission of men's actions to them for the future, but also an approbation of all their actions past.

Leviathan (1651)

8 They that are discontented under *monarchy*, call it *tyranny*; and they that are displeased with *aristocracy*, call it *oligarchy*: so also, they which find themselves grieved under a *democracy*, call it *anarchy*, which signifies the want of government; and yet I think no man believes, that want of government, is any new kind of government.

Leviathan (1651)

9 The papacy is not other than the ghost of the deceased Roman Empire, sitting crowned upon the grave thereof.

Leviathan (1651)

John Cam Hobhouse 1786–1869

English politician

10 When I invented the phrase 'His Majesty's Opposition' [Canning] paid me a compliment on the fortunate hit.

Recollections of a Long Life (1865) vol. 2; cf. **Bagehot** 24:14

August Heinrich Hoffman 1798–1874

German poet

11 *Deutschland über alles.*
Germany above all.

Title of poem (1841)

Lancelot Hogben 1895–1975

English scientist

1 This is not the age of pamphleteers. It is the age of the engineers. The spark-gap is mightier than the pen. Democracy will not be salvaged by men who talk fluently, debate forcefully and quote aptly.

Science for the Citizen (1938) epilogue

James Hogg 1770–1835

Scottish poet

2 God bless our lord the king!
God save our lord the king!
God save the king!
Make him victorious,
Happy, and glorious,
Long to reign over us:
God save the king!

'The King's Anthem' in *Jacobite Relics of Scotland* Second Series (1821)

Sarah Hogg 1946–

former head of John Major's policy unit

3 So much of cabinet consists of reporting, rather than debating; congratulating, rather than arguing.
   on leaving the Prime Minister's policy unit

in *Sunday Times* 9 April 1995

Henry Fox, Lord Holland 1705–74

English Whig politician, father of Charles James **Fox**
on Holland: see **Walpole** 377:8

4 Let nothing be done to break his spirit. The world will do that business fast enough.
   of his son Charles James **Fox** *as a child*

attributed

5 If Mr Selwyn calls again, shew him up: if I am alive I shall be delighted to see him; and if I am dead he would like to see me.
   during his last illness

J. H. Jesse *George Selwyn and his Contemporaries* (1844) vol. 3

Oliver Wendell Holmes Jr. 1841–1935

Justice of the US Supreme Court

6 Men must turn square corners when they deal with the Government.

in *Rock Island, Arkansas & Louisiana Ry. v. United States* (1920)

7 I pay my tax bills more readily than any others—for whether the money is well or ill spent I get civilized society for it.

letter to Harold Laski, 12 May 1930

8 A second-class intellect. But a first-class temperament!
   of Franklin **Roosevelt**

on 8 March 1933

1 The mind of a bigot is like the pupil of the eye; the more   attributed
   light you pour upon it, the more it will contract.

Alec Douglas-Home, Lord Home 1903–95

British Conservative statesman; Prime Minister, 1963–4

2 When I have to read economic documents I have to have   in *Observer* 16 September 1962
   a box of matches and start moving them into position to
   simplify and illustrate the points to myself.

3 As far as the fourteenth earl is concerned, I suppose Mr   in *Daily Telegraph* 22 October 1963
   Wilson, when you come to think of it, is the fourteenth
   Mr Wilson.
     *replying to Harold **Wilson**'s remark (on Home's becoming*
     Prime Minister in 1963) that 'the whole [democratic]
     process has ground to a halt with a fourteenth Earl'

4 There are two problems in my life. The political ones are   attributed, 1964
   insoluble and the economic ones are incomprehensible.

Richard Hooker c.1554–1600

English theologian

5 He that goeth about to persuade a multitude, that they   *Of the Laws of Ecclesiastical Polity*
   are not so well governed as they ought to be, shall never   (1593)
   want attentive and favourable hearers.

6 Alteration though it be from worse to better hath in it   *Of the Laws of Ecclesiastical Polity*
   inconveniences, and those weighty.   (1593)

Herbert Hoover 1874–1964

American Republican statesman; 31st President of the US
1929–33

7 Our country has deliberately undertaken a great social   letter to Senator W. H. Borah, 23
   and economic experiment, noble in motive and far-   February 1928
   reaching in purpose.
     on the Eighteenth Amendment enacting Prohibition, often
     referred to as 'the noble experiment'

8 The American system of rugged individualism.   speech in New York City, 22
     October 1928

9 The slogan of progress is changing from the full dinner   speech in New York, 22 October
   pail to the full garage.   1928; cf. **Henri IV** 175:5
     sometimes paraphrased as, 'a car in every garage and a chicken
     in every pot'

10 The grass will grow in the streets of a hundred cities,   speech, 31 October 1932; cf.
   a thousand towns.   **Bryan** 60:5
     on proposals 'to reduce the protective tariff to a competitive
     tariff for revenue'

11 A good many things go around in the dark besides Santa   address to the John Marshall
   Claus.   Republican Club, St Louis,
     Missouri, 16 December 1935

1 Older men declare war. But it is youth who must fight
and die.

speech at the Republican National
Convention, Chicago, 27 June 1944

Bob Hope 1903–

American comedian

2 I must say the Senator's victory in Wisconsin was
a triumph for democracy. It proves that a millionaire has
just as good a chance as anybody else.
  of John Fitzgerald **Kennedy**'s *electoral victory*

in 1960; William Robert Faith *Bob
Hope* (1983)

Horace 65–8 BC

Roman poet

3 O citizens, first acquire wealth; you can practise virtue
afterwards

Satires; cf. **Pope** 295:6

Samuel Horsley 1733–1806

English bishop

4 In this country…the individual subject…'has nothing to
do with the laws but to obey them.'
  defending a maxim he had used earlier in committee

in the House of Lords, 13
November 1795

John Hoskyns 1927–

British businessman; head of the Prime Minister's Policy Unit
1979–82

5 The House of Commons is the greatest closed shop of
all…For the purposes of government, a country of 55
million people is forced to depend on a talent pool which
could not sustain a single multinational company.

'Conservatism is Not Enough'
(Institute of Directors Annual
Lecture) 25 September 1983

6 The Tory party never panics, except in a crisis.

in *Sunday Times* 19 February 1989

A. E. Housman 1859–1936

English poet and classicist

7 To represent [Joseph] Chamberlain as an injured man,
and Balfour as the man who injured him, is like saying
that Christ crucified Pontius Pilate.

letter 7 December 1922

Samuel Houston 1793–1863

American politician and military leader who led the struggle to
win control of Texas (1834–6) and make it part of the US

8 The North is determined to preserve this Union. They are
not a fiery, impulsive people as you are, for they live in
colder climates. But when they begin to move in a given
direction…they move with the steady momentum and
perseverance of a mighty avalanche.
  in 1861, warning the people of Texas against secession

Geoffrey C. Ward *The Civil War*
(1991)

Geoffrey Howe 1926–

British Conservative politician; Foreign Secretary 1983-9
on Howe: see **Healey** 172:10

1 It is rather like sending your opening batsmen to the
crease only for them to find, the moment the first balls
are bowled, that their bats have been broken before the
game by the team captain.
  resignation speech which precipitated the fall of Margaret
  Thatcher

*in the House of Commons, 13
November 1990*

2 The time has come for others to consider their own
response to the tragic conflict of loyalties with which
I have myself wrestled for perhaps too long.
  resignation speech

*in the House of Commons, 13
November 1990*

Julia Ward Howe 1819–1910

American Unitarian lay preacher

3 Mine eyes have seen the glory of the coming of the Lord:
He is trampling out the vintage where the grapes of
  wrath are stored;
He hath loosed the fateful lightning of his terrible swift
  sword:
His truth is marching on.

*'Battle Hymn of the Republic'
(1862)*

4 As He died to make men holy, let us die to make men
  free.

*'Battle Hymn of the Republic'
(1862)*

Victor Hugo 1802–85

French poet, novelist, and playwright

5 A stand can be made against invasion by an army; no
stand can be made against invasion by an idea.

Histoire d'un Crime (written
1851–2, published 1877)

6 Take away *time is money*, and what is left of England?
take away *cotton is king*, and what is left of America?

Les Misérables (1862)

David Hume 1711–76

Scottish philosopher

7 Money...is none of the wheels of trade: it is the oil
which renders the motion of the wheels more smooth
and easy.

Essays: Moral and Political
(1741–2) 'Of Money'

8 That policy is violent, which aggrandizes the public by
the poverty of individuals.

Essays: Moral and Political
(1741–2) 'Of Money'

9 Should it be said, that, by living under the dominion of
a prince, which one might leave, every individual has
given a tacit assent to his authority...We may as well
assert, that a man by remaining in a vessel, freely
consents to the dominion of the master; though he was
carried on board while asleep, and must leap into the
ocean, and perish, the moment he leaves her.

'Of the Original Contract' (1748)

1 In all ages of the world, priests have been enemies of   'Of the Parties of Great Britain'
   liberty.   (1741–2)

2 It is a just political maxim, that every man must be   *Political Discourses* (1751)
   supposed a knave.

Hubert Humphrey 1911–78

American Democratic politician

3 There are not enough jails, not enough policemen, not   speech at Williamsburg, 1 May
   enough courts to enforce a law not supported by the   1965
   people.

4 The right to be heard does not automatically include the   speech to National Student
   right to be taken seriously.   Association at Madison, 23 August
                                                                1965

5 Here we are the way politics ought to be in America, the   speech in Washington, 27 April
   politics of happiness, the politics of purpose and the   1968
   politics of joy.

6 Compassion is not weakness, and concern for the   attributed
   unfortunate is not socialism.

Lord Hunt of Tanworth 1919–

British civil servant; Secretary of the Cabinet 1973–9

of British Cabinet government, described as 'a shambles':
7 It has got to be, so far as possible, a democratic and   at a seminar at the Institute of
   accountable shambles.   Historical Research, 20 October
                                                                1993

Douglas Hurd 1930–

British conservative politician; Foreign Secretary

8 Lord Rothschild roamed like a condottiere through   *An End to Promises* (1979)
   Whitehall, laying an ambush here, there breaching some
   crumbling fortress which had outlived its usefulness...He
   respected persons occasionally but rarely policies.
     of Lord **Rothschild** *as first Director of the Central Policy Review*
     Staff

9 If President Clinton decides to accelerate the run-down in   speech at Chatham House; in
   US forces in Europe—and by implication the priority   *Financial Times* 4 February 1993
   Washington attaches to Nato—that wedge will be
   removed. With it will go one of the principal props which
   have allowed Britain to punch above its weight in the
   world.

Saddam Hussein 1937–

President of Iraq from 1979

1 The mother of battles.
   popular interpretation of his description of the approaching Gulf War, given in a speech in Baghdad, 6 January 1991

in *The Times* 7 January 1991 it was reported that Saddam had no intention of relinquishing Kuwait and was ready for the 'mother of all wars'

Robert Maynard Hutchins 1899–1977

2 The death of democracy is not likely to be an assassination from ambush. It will be a slow extinction from apathy, indifference, and undernourishment.

Great Books (1954)

Aldous Huxley 1894–1963

English novelist

3 So long as men worship the Caesars and Napoleons, Caesars and Napoleons will duly arise and make them miserable.

Ends and Means (1937)

4 Idealism is the noble toga that political gentlemen drape over their will to power.

in *New York Herald Tribune* 25 November 1963

5 The propagandist's purpose is to make one set of people forget that certain other sets of people are human.

attributed

Dolores Ibarruri ('La Pasionaria') 1895–1989

Spanish Communist leader

6 It is better to die on your feet than to live on your knees.

speech in Paris, 3 September 1936; also attributed to Emiliano Zapata; cf. **Roosevelt** 309:12

7 *No pasarán.*
   They shall not pass.

radio broadcast, Madrid, 19 July 1936; cf. **Anonymous** 10:9

Henrik Ibsen 1828–1906

Norwegian playwright

8 The majority never has right on its side. Never I say! That is one of the social lies that a free, thinking man is bound to rebel against. Who makes up the majority in any given country? Is it the wise men or the fools? I think we must agree that the fools are in a terrible overwhelming majority, all the wide world over. But, damn it, it can surely never be right that the stupid should rule over the clever!

An Enemy of the People (1882)

9 You should never have your best trousers on when you go out to fight for freedom and truth.

An Enemy of the People (1882)

Harold L. Ickes 1874–1952

American lawyer and administrator

1 The trouble with Senator Long...is that he's suffering
from halitosis of the intellect. That's presuming Emperor
Long has an intellect.

speech, 1935; G. Wolfskill and J. A.
Hudson *All But the People:
Franklin D. Roosevelt and his
Critics, 1933–39* (1969)

2 Dewey threw his diaper into the ring.
on the Republican candidate for the presidency

in *New York Times* 12 December
1939

3 I am against government by crony.
on resigning as secretary of the interior

in February 1946

Ivan Illich 1926–

American sociologist

4 In a consumer society there are inevitably two kinds of
slaves: the prisoners of addiction and the prisoners of
envy.

Tools for Conviviality (1973)

William Ralph Inge 1860–1954

English writer; Dean of St. Paul's, 1911–34

5 It takes in reality only one to make a quarrel. It is useless
for the sheep to pass resolutions in favour of
vegetarianism, while the wolf remains of a different
opinion.

Outspoken Essays: First Series
(1919)

6 The nations which have put mankind and posterity most
in their debt have been small states—Israel, Athens,
Florence, Elizabethan England.

Outspoken Essays: Second Series
(1922) 'State, visible and invisible'

7 A man may build himself a throne of bayonets, but he
cannot sit on it.

Philosophy of Plotinus (1923) vol.
2, quoted by Boris **Yeltsin** at the
time of the failed military coup in
Russia, August 1991

8 The enemies of Freedom do not argue; they shout and
they shoot.

End of an Age (1948)

9 The effect of boredom on a large scale in history is
underestimated. It is a main cause of revolutions, and
would soon bring to an end all the static Utopias and the
farmyard civilization of the Fabians.

End of an Age (1948)

Bernard Ingham 1932–

British journalist and public relations specialist, Chief Press
Secretary to the Prime Minister, 1979–90
on Ingham: see **Biffen** 44:18

10 Blood sport is brought to its ultimate refinement in the
gossip columns.

speech, 5 February 1986

1 The media, I tell pedants in the Government, is like an oil painting. Close up, it looks like nothing on earth. Stand back and you get the drift.

at a meeting of the Parliamentary Lobby, noticing that he had a spot of blood on his shirt:

2 My God, I've been stabbed in the front.

speech to the Parliamentary Press Gallery, February 1990

recalled in a letter to Antony Jay, January 1995

Eugène Ionesco 1912–94

French playwright

3 A civil servant doesn't make jokes.

The Killer (1958)

Hastings Lionel ('Pug') Ismay 1887–1965

British general and Secretary to the Committee of Imperial Defence; first Secretary-General of Nato

4 NATO exists for three reasons—to keep the Russians out, the Americans in and the Germans down.
   to a group of British Conservative backbenchers in 1949

Peter Hennessy *Never Again* (1992); oral tradition

Alija Izetbegović 1925–

Bosnian statesman; President of Bosnia and Herzegovina since 1990

5 And to my people I say, this may not be a just peace, but it is more just than a continuation of war.
   after signing the Dayton accord with representatives of Serbia and Croatia

in Dayton, Ohio, 21 November 1995

Andrew Jackson 1767–1845

American general and Democratic statesman, 7th President of the US 1829–37
on Jackson: see **Clay** 97:6

6 The individual who refuses to defend his rights when called by his Government, deserves to be a slave, and must be punished as an enemy of his country and friend to her foe.

proclamation to the people of Louisiana from Mobile, 21 September 1814

7 The brave man inattentive to his duty, is worth little more to his country, than the coward who deserts her in the hour of danger.
   to troops who had abandoned their lines during the battle of New Orleans, 8 January 1815

attributed

8 Our Federal Union: it must be preserved.
   toast given on the Jefferson Birthday Celebration, 13 April 1830

Thomas Hart Benton *Thirty Years' View* (1856) vol. 1

9 Each public officer who takes an oath to support the constitution swears that he will support it as he understands it, and not as it is understood by others.
   presidential message vetoing the bill to re-charter the Bank of the United States, 10 July 1832

H. S. Commager (ed.) *Documents of American History* vol. 1 (1963)

1 Every man is equally entitled to protection by law; but   veto of the Bank Bill, 10 July 1832
  when the laws undertake to add...artificial distinctions,
  to grant titles, gratuities, and exclusive privileges, to
  make the rich richer and the potent more powerful, the
  humble members of society—the farmers, mechanics, and
  labourers—who have neither the time nor the means of
  securing like favours to themselves, have a right to
  complain of the injustice of their government.

2 There are no necessary evils in government. Its evils exist   veto of the Bank Bill, 10 July 1832
  only in its abuses. If it would confine itself to equal
  protection, and, as Heaven does its rains, shower its
  favours alike on the high and the low, the rich and the
  poor, it would be an unqualified blessing.

3 You are uneasy; you never sailed with *me* before, I see.   James Parton *Life of Jackson* (1860)
                                                                 vol. 3

4 One man with courage makes a majority.   attributed

  shortly before his death, Jackson was asked if he had left
  anything undone:
5 I didn't shoot Henry Clay, and I didn't hang John C.   Robert V. Remini *Henry Clay* (1991);
  Calhoun.   attributed

Jesse Jackson 1941–
American Democratic politician and clergyman

6 My right and my privilege to stand here before you has   speech at Democratic National
  been won—won in my lifetime—by the blood and the   Convention, Atlanta, 19 July 1988
  sweat of the innocent.

7 When I look out at this convention, I see the face of   speech at Democratic National
  America, red, yellow, brown, black, and white. We are   Convention, Atlanta, 19 July 1988
  all precious in God's sight—the real rainbow coalition.

8 You can't keep on running from labour, running from   in *Guardian* 28 November 1994
  blacks, running from cities and expect to inspire them to
  vote.
  on President **Clinton,** *after the results of the 1994 election*

James I (James VI of Scotland) 1566–1625
King of Scotland from 1567 and of England from 1603

9 No bishop, no King.   W. Barlow *Sum and Substance of*
  to a deputation of Presbyterians from the Church of Scotland,   *the Conference* (1604)
  seeking religious tolerance in England

10 The king is truly *parens patriae*, the polite father of his   speech to Parliament, 21 March
   people.   1610

11 The state of monarchy is the supremest thing upon   speech to Parliament, 21 March
   earth; for kings are not only God's lieutenants upon   1610
   earth, and sit upon God's throne, but even by God
   himself they are called gods.

1 That which concerns the mystery of the king's power is
   not lawful to be disputed; for that is to wade into the
   weakness of Princes and to take away the mystical
   reverence, that belongs unto them that sit in the throne
   of God.

'A Speech in the Star Chamber'
[speech to the judges] 20 June 1616

2 I will govern according to the common weal, but not
   according to the common will.

in December, 1621; J. R. Green
History of the English People vol. 3
(1879)

James V 1512–42
King of Scotland from 1513

*of the crown of Scotland (which had come to the Stuarts
through the female line), on learning of the birth of Mary
Queen of Scots, December 1542:*

3 It came with a lass, and it will pass with a lass.

Robert Lindsay of Pitscottie
(*c*.1500–65) *History of Scotland*
(1728)

Antony Jay see Lynn and Jay

Douglas Jay 1907–96
British Labour politician

4 In the case of nutrition and health, just as in the case of
   education, the gentleman in Whitehall really does know
   better what is good for people than the people know
   themselves.

The Socialist Case (1939)

5 Fair shares for all, is Labour's call.
   slogan devised for the North Battersea by-election, 1946

Change and Fortune (1980)

Thomas Jefferson 1743–1826
American Democratic Republican statesman, 3rd President of
the US 1801–9
on Jefferson: see **Adams** 4:4, **Kennedy** 205:1

6 We must therefore…hold them [the British] as we hold
   the rest of mankind, enemies in war, in peace friends.

Declaration of Independence 4 July
1776

7 When in the course of human events, it becomes
   necessary for one people to dissolve the political bonds
   which have connected them with another, and to assume
   among the powers of the earth the separate and equal
   station to which the laws of nature and of Nature's God
   entitle them, a decent respect to the opinions of mankind
   requires that they should declare the causes which impel
   them to the separation.

American Declaration of
Independence, 4 July 1776
(preamble)

1 We hold these truths to be sacred and undeniable; that all men are created equal and independent, that from that equal creation they derive rights inherent and inalienable, among which are the preservation of life, and liberty, and the pursuit of happiness.

'Rough Draft' of the American Declaration of Independence; J. P. Boyd et al. *Papers of Thomas Jefferson* vol. 1 (1950)

2 Millions of innocent men, women, and children, since the introduction of Christianity, have been burnt, tortured, fined, imprisoned; yet we have not advanced one inch towards uniformity [of opinion]. What has been the effect of coercion? To make one half the world fools, and the other half hypocrites.

Notes on the State of Virginia (1781–5)

3 Indeed I tremble for my country when I reflect that God is just.

Notes on the State of Virginia (1781–5)

4 The basis of our government being the opinion of the people, the very first object should be to keep that right; and were it left to me to decide whether we should have a government without newspapers or newspapers without a government, I should not hesitate for a moment to prefer the latter.

letter to Colonel Edward Carrington, 16 January 1787

5 Experience declares that man is the only animal which devours its own kind, for I can apply no milder term to the governments of Europe, and to the general prey of the rich on the poor.

letter to Colonel Edward Carrington, 16 January 1787

6 A little rebellion now and then is a good thing.

letter to James Madison, 30 January 1787

7 The tree of liberty must be refreshed from time to time with the blood of patriots and tyrants. It is its natural manure.

letter to W. S. Smith, 13 November 1787

8 The natural progress of things is for liberty to yield and governments to gain ground.

letter to Colonel Edward Carrington, 27 May 1788

9 If I could not go to Heaven but with a party, I would not go there at all.

letter to Francis Hopkinson, 13 March 1789

10 The republican is the only form of government which is not eternally at open or secret war with the rights of mankind.

letter to William Hunter, 11 March 1790

11 We are not to expect to be translated from despotism to liberty in a featherbed.

letter to Lafayette, 2 April 1790

12 No government ought to be without censors: and where the press is free, no one ever will.

letter to George Washington, 9 September 1792

13 The second office of government is honourable and easy, the first is but a splendid misery.

letter to Elbridge Gerry, 13 May 1797

14 Offices are acceptable here as elsewhere, and whenever a man has cast a longing eye on them [official positions], a rottenness begins in his conduct.

letter to Tench Coxe, 21 May 1799

15 To the press alone, chequered as it is with abuses, the world is indebted for all the triumphs which have been gained by reason and humanity over error and oppression.

Virginia and Kentucky Resolutions (1799)

1   What an augmentation of the field for jobbing,   letter 13 August 1800
    speculating, plundering, office-building and office-hunting
    would be produced by an assumption of all the state
    powers into the hands of the general government.

2   If the principle were to prevail, of a common law [i.e.   letter to Gideon Granger, 13 August
    a single government] being in force in the U.S....it would   1800
    become the most corrupt government on the earth.

3   Still one thing more, fellow citizens—a wise and frugal   first inaugural address, 4 March
    government, which shall restrain men from injuring one   1801
    another, which shall leave them otherwise free to
    regulate their own pursuits of industry and improvement,
    and shall not take from the mouth of labour the bread it
    has earned. This is the sum of good government, and this
    is necessary to close the circle of our felicities.

4   We are all Republicans—we are all Federalists. If there be   first inaugural address, 4 March
    any among us who would wish to dissolve this Union or   1801
    to change its republican form, let them stand undisturbed
    as monuments of the safety with which error of opinion
    may be tolerated where reason is left free to combat it.

5   All, too, will bear in mind this sacred principle, that   first inaugural address, 4 March
    though the will of the majority is in all cases to prevail,   1801
    that will to be rightful must be reasonable; that the
    minority possess their equal rights, which equal law
    must protect, and to violate would be oppression.

6   Would the honest patriot, in the full tide of successful   first inaugural address, 4 March
    experiment, abandon a government which has so far   1801
    kept us free and firm?

7   Peace, commerce, and honest friendship with all   first inaugural address, 4 March
    nations—entangling alliances with none.   1801

8   Freedom of religion; freedom of the press, and freedom of   first inaugural address, 4 March
    person under the protection of *habeas corpus*, and trial by   1801
    juries impartially selected. These principles form the
    bright constellation which has gone before us, and
    guided our steps through an age of revolution and
    reformation.

9   If a due participation of office is a matter of right, how   letter to E. Shipman and others, 12
    are vacancies to be obtained? Those by death are few; by   July 1801
    resignation none.
    usually quoted as: 'Few die and none resign'

10 If we can prevent the government from wasting the   letter to Thomas Cooper, 29
    labours of the people, under the pretence of taking care   November 1802
    of them, they must become happy.

11 Whensoever hostile aggressions...require a resort to war,   letter to Andrew Jackson, 3
    we must meet our duty and convince the world that we   December 1806
    are just friends and brave enemies.

12 When a man assumes a public trust, he should consider   B. L. Rayner *Life of Jefferson* (1834)
    himself as public property.
    to Baron von Humboldt, 1807

1 The care of human life and happiness, and not their
   destruction, is the first and only legitimate object of good
   government.

   to the Republican Citizens of
   Washington County, Maryland, 31
   March 1809

2 A strict observance of the written law is doubtless one of
   the high duties of a good citizen, but it is not the highest.
   The laws of necessity, of self-preservation, of saving our
   country when in danger, are of higher obligation.

   letter to John B. Colvin, 20
   September 1810

3 Politics, like religion, hold up the torches of martyrdom
   to the reformers of error.

   letter to James Ogilvie, 4 August
   1811

4 I agree with you that there is a natural aristocracy
   among men. The grounds of this are virtue and talents.

   letter to John Adams, 28 October
   1813

5 Merchants have no country. The mere spot they stand on
   does not constitute so strong an attachment as that from
   which they draw their gains.

   letter to Horatio G. Spafford, 17
   March 1814

6 If a nation expects to be ignorant and free, in a state of
   civilization, it expects what never was and never will be.

   letter to Colonel Charles Yancey, 6
   January 1816

7 But this momentous question [the Missouri Compromise],
   like a firebell in the night awakened and filled me with
   terror. I considered it the knell of the Union.

   letter to John Holmes, 22 April
   1820

8 I know no safe depository of the ultimate powers of the
   society but the people themselves; and if we think them
   not enlightened enough to exercise their control with
   a wholesome discretion, the remedy is not to take it from
   them, but to inform their discretion by education.

   letter to William Charles Jarvis, 28
   September 1820

9 We have the wolf by the ears; and we can neither hold
   him, nor safely let him go. Justice is in one scale, and
   self-preservation in the other.
   on slavery

   letter to John Holmes, 22 April
   1820

10 That one hundred and fifty lawyers should do business
   together ought not to be expected.
   on the United States Congress

   Autobiography 6 January 1821

11 To attain all this [universal republicanism], however,
   rivers of blood must yet flow, and years of desolation pass
   over; yet the object is worth rivers of blood, and years of
   desolation.

   letter to John Adams, 4 September
   1823

12 The good old Dominion, the blessed mother of us all.

   Thoughts on Lotteries (1826)

13 The legitimate powers of government extend to such acts
   only as are injurious to others. But it does me no injury
   for my neighbour to say there are twenty gods, or no
   God. It neither picks my pocket nor breaks my leg.

   attributed

14 No duty the Executive had to perform was so trying as to
   put the right man in the right place.

   J. B. MacMaster *History of the
   People of the United States*
   (1883–1913) vol. 2

15 The policy of the American government is to leave their
   citizens free, neither restraining nor aiding them in their
   pursuits.

   attributed

16 Were we directed from Washington when to sow, and
   when to reap, we should soon want bread.

   Autobiography

1 This is the Fourth?   on 4 July 1826
   last words

Roy Jenkins 1920–

British politician; co-founder of the Social Democratic Party,
1981

of James **Callaghan**:

2 There is nobody in politics I can remember and no case   Richard Crossman diary 5
   I can think of in history where a man combined such   September 1969
   a powerful political personality with so little intelligence.

3 He simply stopped the engine in its tracks, lifted it up,   Roy Jenkins *Nine Men of Power*
   and put it back facing in the other direction.   (1974)
   of Ernest **Bevin** *changing the course of a Cabinet meeting*

4 The politics of the left and centre of this country are   speech to Parliamentary Press
   frozen in an out-of-date mould which is bad for the   Gallery, 9 June 1980
   political and economic health of Britain and increasingly
   inhibiting for those who live within the mould. Can it be
   broken?

of the Labour Party:

5 A dead or dying beast lying across a railway line and   in *Guardian* 16 May 1987
   preventing other trains from getting through.

of Margaret **Thatcher**:

6 A First Minister whose self-righteous stubbornness has   in *Observer* 11 March 1990
   not been equalled, save briefly by Neville Chamberlain,
   since Lord North.

7 The record does not provide much sustenance for the   in *Guardian* 14 April 1990
   view that limpet-like Prime Ministers can be easily
   disposed of by their parties.

of Edward **Heath**:

8 A great lighthouse which stands there, flashing out   in *Independent* 22 September 1990
   beams of light, indifferent to the waves which beat
   against him.

Simon Jenkins 1943–

British political journalist

9 A belief in ever-rising crime seems to answer a deep   in *Sunday Times* 22 March 1987
   social need: spurious proof that all bad news must be
   true. It is statistics as pornography.

10 A truth not universally acknowledged is that every   interview with Margaret **Thatcher**
   politician not in Government must needs be in   in *The Times* 29 June 1991
   Opposition.

W. Stanley Jevons 1835–82

English economist

11 All classes of society are trades unionists at heart, and   *The State in Relation to Labour*
   differ chiefly in the boldness, ability, and secrecy with   (1882)
   which they pursue their respective interests.

John XXIII 1881–1963

Pope from 1958

1 If civil authorities legislate for or allow anything that is contrary to that order and therefore contrary to the will of God, neither the laws made or the authorizations granted can be binding on the consciences of the citizens, since God has more right to be obeyed than man.

Pacem in Terris (1963)

2 The social progress, order, security and peace of each country are necessarily connected with the social progress, order, security and peace of all other countries.

Pacem in Terris (1963)

3 [In the universal *Declaration of Human Rights* (December, 1948)] in most solemn form, the dignity of a person is acknowledged to all human beings; and as a consequence there is proclaimed, as a fundamental right, the right of free movement in search for truth and in the attainment of moral good and of justice, and also the right to a dignified life.

Pacem in Terris (1963)

Lyndon Baines Johnson 1908–73

American Democratic statesman, 36th President of the US 1963–9
on Johnson: see White 387:1

to a reporter who had queried his embracing Richard **Nixon** *on the vice-president's return from a controversial tour of South America in 1958:*

4 Son, in politics you've got to learn that overnight chicken shit can turn to chicken salad.

Fawn Brodie *Richard Nixon* (1983)

5 I am a free man, an American, a United States Senator, and a Democrat, in that order.

in *Texas Quarterly* Winter 1958

6 I'll tell you what's at the bottom of it. If you can convince the lowest white man that he's better than the best coloured man, he won't notice you're picking his pocket. Hell, give him someone to look down on and he'll empty his pockets for you.
during the 1960 Presidential campaign, to Bill Moyers

Robert Dallek *Lone Star Rising* (1991)

7 All I have I would have given gladly not to be standing here today.
following the assassination of J. F. **Kennedy**

first speech to Congress as President, 27 November 1963

8 We have talked long enough in this country about equal rights. We have talked for a hundred years or more. It is time now to write the next chapter, and to write it in the books of law.

speech to Congress, 27 November 1963

9 We hope that the world will not narrow into a neighbourhood before it has broadened into a brotherhood.
speech at the lighting of the Nation's Christmas Tree

on 22 December 1963

10 This administration, here and now declares unconditional war on poverty in America.

State of the Union address to Congress, 8 January 1964

1 For the first time in our history, it is possible to conquer poverty.

speech to Congress, 16 March 1964

2 In your time we have the opportunity to move not only toward the rich society and the powerful society, but upward to the Great Society.

speech at University of Michigan, 22 May 1964

3 We Americans know, although others appear to forget, the risks of spreading conflict. We still seek no wider war.

speech on radio and television, 4 August 1964

4 We are not about to send American boys 9 or 10,000 miles away from home to do what Asian boys ought to be doing for themselves.

speech at Akron University, 21 October 1964

5 Extremism in the pursuit of the Presidency is an unpardonable vice. Moderation in the affairs of the nation is the highest virtue.

speech in New York, 31 October 1964

6 A President's hardest task is not to *do* what is right, but to *know* what is right.

State of the Union address to Congress, 4 January 1965

7 It is not enough to open the gates of opportunity. All of our citizens must have the ability to walk through those gates.
   speech at Harvard in 1965

Paul L. Fisher and Ralph L. Lavenstein (eds.) *Race and the News Media* (1967)

8 I don't want loyalty. I want *loyalty*. I want him to kiss my ass in Macy's window at high noon and tell me it smells like roses. I want his pecker in my pocket.
   discussing a prospective assistant

David Halberstam *The Best and the Brightest* (1972)

9 Better to have him inside the tent pissing out, than outside pissing in.
   of J. Edgar Hoover

David Halberstam *The Best and the Brightest* (1972)

10 So dumb he can't fart and chew gum at the same time.
   of Gerald **Ford**

Richard Reeves *A Ford, not a Lincoln* (1975)

11 Come now, let us reason together.

habitual saying

12 Did you ever think that making a speech on economics is a lot like pissing down your leg? It seems hot to you, but it never does to anyone else.
   to J. K. **Galbraith**

J. K. Galbraith *A Life in Our Times* (1981)

Paul Johnson 1928–

British journalist

13 Tories, in short, are atrophied Englishmen, lacking certain moral and intellectual reflexes. They are recognizable, homely—even, on occasions, endearing—but liable to turn very nasty at short notice.

in *New Statesman* 18 October 1958 'Rule Like Pigs'

Samuel Johnson 1709–84

English poet, critic, and lexicographer

14 Superfluous lags the vet'ran on the stage.

The Vanity of Human Wishes (1749)

1   This man [Lord Chesterfield] I thought had been a Lord
    among wits; but, I find, he is only a wit among Lords.

James Boswell *Life of Samuel Johnson* (1791) 1754

2   If the changes we fear be thus irresistible, what remains
    but to acquiesce with silence, as in the other
    insurmountable distresses of humanity? It remains that
    we retard what we cannot repel, that we palliate what
    we cannot cure.

A Dictionary of the English Language (1755) preface

3   *Pension.* Pay given to a state hireling for treason to his
    country.

A Dictionary of the English Language (1755)

4   Among the calamities of war may be jointly numbered
    the diminution of the love of truth, by the falsehoods
    which interest dictates and credulity encourages.

The Idler 11 November 1758; possibly the source, in essence, of 'When war is declared, Truth is the first casualty', epigraph to Arthur Ponsonby's *Falsehood in Wartime* (1928) (in this form, it has been attributed also to Hiram Johnson, speaking in the US Senate, 1918, but is not recorded in his speech)

5   In all pointed sentences, some degree of accuracy must
    be sacrificed to conciseness.

'The Bravery of the English Common Soldier' in *The British Magazine* January 1760

6   Liberty is, to the lowest rank of every nation, little more
    than the choice of working or starving.

'The Bravery of the English Common Soldier' in *The British Magazine* January 1760

7   How small of all that human hearts endure,
    That part which laws or kings can cause or cure.

lines added to Oliver Goldsmith's *The Traveller* (1764); cf. **Goldsmith** 157:5

8   Your levellers wish to level *down* as far as themselves;
    but they cannot bear levelling *up* to themselves.

James Boswell *Life of Samuel Johnson* (1791) 21 July 1763

9   A woman's preaching is like a dog's walking on his
    hinder legs. It is not done well; but you are surprised to
    find it done at all.

James Boswell *Life of Samuel Johnson* (1791) 31 July 1763

10 BOSWELL: So, Sir, you laugh at schemes of political
    improvement.
    JOHNSON: Why, Sir, most schemes of political
    improvement are very laughable things.

James Boswell *Life of Samuel Johnson* (1791) 26 October 1769

11 So many objections may be made to everything, that
    nothing can overcome them but the necessity of doing
    something.

James Boswell *Life of Samuel Johnson* (1791) 1770

12 A decent provision for the poor, is the true test of
    civilization.

James Boswell *Life of Samuel Johnson* (1791) 1770

13 I would not give half a guinea to live under one form of
    government rather than another. It is of no moment to
    the happiness of an individual.

James Boswell *Life of Samuel Johnson* (1791) 31 March 1772

14 I do not much like to see a Whig in any dress; but I hate
    to see a Whig in a parson's gown.

James Boswell *Journal of a Tour to the Hebrides* (1785) 24 September 1773

1 There are few ways in which a man can be more innocently employed than in getting money.

James Boswell *Life of Samuel Johnson* (1791) 27 March 1775

2 George the First knew nothing, and desired to know nothing; did nothing, and desired to do nothing; and the only good thing that is told of him is, that he wished to restore the crown to its hereditary successor.

James Boswell *Life of Samuel Johnson* (1791) 6 April 1775

3 Patriotism is the last refuge of a scoundrel.

James Boswell *Life of Samuel Johnson* (1791) 7 April 1775

4 Politics are now nothing more than means of rising in the world.

James Boswell *Life of Samuel Johnson* (1791) 18 April 1775

5 Every man who attacks my belief, diminishes in some degree my confidence in it, and therefore makes me uneasy; and I am angry with him who makes me uneasy.

James Boswell *Life of Samuel Johnson* (1791) 3 April 1776

6 It is better that some should be unhappy than that none should be happy, which would be the case in a general state of equality.

James Boswell *Life of Samuel Johnson* (1791) 7 April 1776

7 Though we cannot out-vote them we will out-argue them.

James Boswell *Life of Samuel Johnson* (1791) 3 April 1778

8 I have always said, the first Whig was the Devil.

James Boswell *Life of Samuel Johnson* (1791) 28 April 1778

9 How is it that we hear the loudest yelps for liberty among the drivers of negroes?

Taxation No Tyranny (1775)

10 A wise Tory and a wise Whig, I believe, will agree. Their principles are the same, though their modes of thinking are different.

James Boswell *Life of Samuel Johnson* (1791) May 1781; written statement given to Boswell

11 If a man were to go by chance at the same time with Burke under a shed, to shun a shower, he would say—'this is an extraordinary man.'
   on Edmund **Burke**

James Boswell *Life of Samuel Johnson* (1791) 15 May 1784

12 Fox divided the kingdom with Caesar; so that it was a doubt whether the nation should be ruled by the sceptre of George III or the tongue of Fox.
   on the Parliamentary defeat of Charles James **Fox**, *and the subsequent dissolution, in 1784*

in *Dictionary of National Biography*

13 Mankind are happier in a state of inequality and subordination. Were they to be in this pretty state of equality, they would soon degenerate into brutes.

attributed

Hanns Johst 1890–1978

German playwright

14 Whenever I hear the word culture...I release the safety-catch of my Browning!
   often quoted as: 'Whenever I hear the word culture, I reach for my pistol!', and attributed to Hermann **Goering**

Schlageter (1933)

John Paul Jones 1747–92

American admiral

1 I have not yet begun to fight.   Mrs Reginald De Koven *Life and*
   as his ship was sinking, 23 September 1779, having been asked   *Letters of John Paul Jones* (1914)
   whether he had lowered his flag   vol. 1

William Jones 1746–94

English jurist

2 My opinion is, that power should always be distrusted, in   letter to Lord Althorpe, 5 October
   whatever hands it is placed.   1782

Ben Jonson c.1573–1637

English playwright and poet

3 PEOPLE: The Voice of Cato is the voice of Rome.   *Catiline his Conspiracy* (1611)
   CATO: The voice of Rome is the consent of heaven!

Barbara Jordan

American Democratic politician

4 The Bill of Rights was not ordained by nature or God. It's   in *New York Times Magazine* 21
   very human, very fragile.   October 1990

Thomas Jordan c.1612–85

English poet and playwright

5 They plucked communion tables down   'How the War began' (1664)
   And broke our painted glasses;
   They threw our altars to the ground
   And tumbled down the crosses.
   They set up Cromwell and his heir—
   The Lord and Lady Claypole—
   Because they hated Common Prayer,
   The organ and the maypole.

Keith Joseph 1918–94

British Conservative politician

6 Problems reproduce themselves from generation to   speech in London to the Pre-
   generation...I refer to this as a 'cycle of deprivation'.   School Playgroups Association, 29
                                                               June 1972

7 We [the Conservative Party] found it hard to avoid the   Peter Jenkins *Mrs Thatcher's*
   feeling that somehow the lean and tight-lipped mufflered   *Revolution* (1987)
   men in the 1930s dole queue were at least partly our
   fault.
   reflection occasioned by the national euphoria in 1945 on the
   outcome of the Second World War

1 People who could not tell a lathe from a lawn mower and have never carried the responsibilities of management never tire of telling British management off for its alleged inefficiency.

in The Times 9 August 1974

2 Incomes policy alone as a way to abate inflation caused by excessive money supply is like trying to stop water coming out of a leaky hose without turning off the tap.

speech at Preston, 5 September 1974

3 The balance of our population, our human stock, is threatened...a high and rising proportion of children are being born to mothers least fitted to bring children into the world and bring them up.

speech in Birmingham, 19 October 1974

4 If we are to be prosperous we need more millionaires and more bankrupts.

maiden speech in the House of Lords, 19 February 1988

5 There are no illegitimate children, only illegitimate parents.
   in Kiss Hollywood Good-Bye *(1978), Anita Loos attributes an earlier coinage of this statement to the American philanthropist Edna Gladney*

speech to National Children's Home, 6 November 1991

Joseph Joubert 1754–1824

French essayist and moralist

6 One of the surest ways of killing a tree is to lay bare its roots. It is the same with institutions. We must not be too ready to disinter the origins of those we wish to preserve. All beginnings are small.

Pensées (1842)

7 It's better to debate a question without settling it than to settle a question without debating it.

attributed

William Joyce ('Lord Haw-Haw') 1906–46

Fascist supporter and wartime broadcaster from Nazi Germany; executed for treason in 1946

8 Germany calling! Germany calling!
   habitual introduction to propaganda broadcast

broadcasts from Germany to Britain during the Second World War

'Junius'

18th-century pseudonymous writer, probably Philip Francis (1740–1818)

9 The right of election is the very essence of the constitution.

in Public Advertiser 24 April 1769, letter 11

10 Is this the wisdom of a great minister? or is it the ominous vibration of a pendulum?

in Public Advertiser 30 May 1769, letter 12

11 There is a holy mistaken zeal in politics as well as in religion. By persuading others, we convince ourselves.

in Public Advertiser 19 December 1769, letter 35

12 However distinguished by rank or property, in the rights of freedom we are all equal.

in Public Advertiser 19 March 1770, letter 37

1 The injustice done to an individual is sometimes of service to the public.

in Public Advertiser 14 November 1770, letter 41

2 As for Mr Wedderburne, there is something about him, which even treachery cannot trust.

in Public Advertiser 22 June 1771, letter 49

3 The liberty of the press is the *Palladium* of all the civil, political, and religious rights of an Englishman.

The Letters of Junius (1772 ed.) 'Dedication to the English Nation'

John Junor 1919–97

British Journalist

4 Such a graceful exit. And then he had to go and do this on the doorstep.

on Harold **Wilson***'s 'Lavender List', the honours list he drew up on resigning the British premiership in 1976*

in Observer 23 January 1990

Juvenal AD 483–565

Roman satirist

5 Who would put up with the Gracchi complaining about subversion?

referring to the Roman tribune Tiberius Sempronius Gracchus (163–133 BC) and his brother Gaius Sempronius Gracchus (c.153–121 BC), who were responsible for radical social and economic legislation, passed against the wishes of the senatorial class

Satires

6   *Sed quis custodiet ipsos Custodes?*
But who is to guard the guards themselves?

Satires

7 A huge wordy letter came from Capri.

on the Emperor Tiberius's letter to the Senate, which caused the downfall of Sejanus in AD 31

Satires

8 Only two things does he [the modern citizen] anxiously wish for—bread and circuses.

Satires

Franz Kafka 1883–1924

Czech novelist

9 It's often better to be in chains than to be free.

The Trial (1925)

Nicholas Kaldor 1908–86

British economist

10 There is no need for the economist to prove...that as a result of the adoption of a certain measure nobody is going to suffer. In order to establish his case, it is quite sufficient for him to show that even if all those who suffer as a result are fully compensated for their loss, the rest of the community will still be better off than before.

'Welfare Propositions of Economics' in *Economic Journal* September 1939

Immanuel Kant 1724–1804

German philosopher

1 Out of the crooked timber of humanity no straight thing
was ever made.

*Idee zu einer allgemeinen
Geschichte in weltbürgerliche
Absicht (1784)*

2 There is, therefore, only one categorical imperative. It is:
Act only according to that maxim by which you can at
the same time will that it should become a universal law.

*Fundamental Principles of the
Metaphysics of Ethics (1785)*

Gerald Kaufman 1930–

British Labour politician

3 Cabinet minutes are studied in Government Departments
with the reverence generally reserved for sacred texts,
and can be triumphantly produced conclusively to settle
any arguments.

How to be a Minister (1980)

4 The longest suicide note in history.
on the Labour Party's New Hope for Britain (1983)

Denis Healey *The Time of My Life*
(1989)

John Keane 1949–

Australian political scientist

5 Sovereign state power is an indispensable condition of the
democratization of civil society... a more democratic
order cannot be built *through* state power, it cannot be
built *without* state power.

Democracy and Civil Society (1988)

Paul Keating 1944–

Australian Labor statesman; Prime Minister 1991–6

6 You look like an Easter Island statue with an arse full of
razor blades.
*in the Australian Parliament to the then Prime Minister, Malcolm
Fraser*

Michael Gordon *A Question of
Leadership* (1993)

7 Even as it [Great Britain] walked out on you and joined
the Common Market, you were still looking for your
MBEs and your knighthoods, and all the rest of the
regalia that comes with it. You would take Australia
right back down the time tunnel to the cultural cringe
where you have always come from.
*addressing Australian Conservative supporters of Great Britain
in the Australian Parliament, 27 February 1992*

in *House of Representatives
Weekly Hansard* [Australia] (1992)
no. 1

8 These are the same old fogies who doffed their lids and
tugged the forelock to the British establishment.
*of Australian Conservative supporters of Great Britain, 27
February 1992*

in *House of Representatives
Weekly Hansard* [Australia] (1992)
no. 1

9 This little flower, this delicate little beauty, this cream
puff, is supposed to be beyond personal criticism...He is

attributed

simply a shiver looking for a spine to run up.
of the then Australian Liberal leader, John Hewson

1 I'm a bastard. But I'm a bastard who gets the mail   in *Sunday Telegraph* 20 November
   through. And they appreciate that.   1994
   in 1994, to a senior colleague

2 Leadership is not about being nice. It's about being right   in *Time* 9 January 1995
   and being strong.

Garrison Keillor 1942–

American writer

3 Ronald Reagan, the President who never told bad news   *We Are Still Married* (1989),
   to the American people.   introduction

4 My ancestors were Puritans from England. They arrived   attributed, 1993
   here in 1648 in the hope of finding greater restrictions
   than were permissible under English law at that time.

George F. Kennan 1904–

American diplomat and historian

5 There is no political or ideological difference between the   *The Cloud of Danger* (1977)
   Soviet Union and the United States—nothing which
   either side would like, or would hope, to achieve at the
   expense of the other—that would be worth the risks and
   sacrifices of a military encounter.

6 A war regarded as inevitable or even probable, and   *The Cloud of Danger* (1977)
   therefore much prepared for, has a very good chance of
   being eventually fought.

7 Government...is simply not the channel through which   *Around the Cragged Hill* (1993)
   men's noblest impulses are to be realized. Its task, on the
   contrary, is largely to see to it that the ignoble ones are
   kept under restraint and not permitted to go too far.

John F. Kennedy 1917–63

American Democratic statesman, 35th President of the US
1961–3, son of Joseph and Rose **Kennedy** and brother of
Robert **Kennedy**
on Kennedy: see **Bentsen** 38:3, **Hope** 183:2, **Kennedy** 206:1,
Stevenson 350:13

8 Don't buy a single vote more than necessary. I'll be   J. F. Cutler *Honey Fitz* (1962)
   damned if I'm going to pay for a landslide.
   *telegraphed message from his father, read at a Gridiron dinner
   in Washington, 15 March 1958, and almost certainly JFK's
   invention*

9 We stand today on the edge of a new frontier...But the   speech in Los Angeles, 15 July 1960
   New Frontier of which I speak is not a set of promises—it
   is a set of challenges. It sums up not what I intend to
   offer the American people, but what I intend to ask of

them.
accepting the Democratic nomination

1 I am not the Catholic candidate for President. I am the
Democratic Party's candidate for President, who happens
also to be a Catholic.

speech to Greater Houston
Ministerial Association, 12
September 1960

2 Let the word go forth from this time and place, to friend
and foe alike, that the torch has been passed to a new
generation of Americans—born in this century, tempered
by war, disciplined by a hard and bitter peace, proud of
our ancient heritage—and unwilling to witness or permit
the slow undoing of those human rights to which this
nation has always been committed, and to which we are
committed today at home and around the world.
    Let every nation know, whether it wishes us well or ill,
that we shall pay any price, bear any burden, meet
any hardship, support any friend, oppose any foe to
assure the survival and the success of liberty.

inaugural address, 20 January 1961

3 If a free society cannot help the many who are poor, it
cannot save the few who are rich.

inaugural address, 20 January 1961

4 Let us never negotiate out of fear. But let us never fear to
negotiate.

inaugural address, 20 January 1961

5 All this will not be finished in the first 100 days. Nor will
it be finished in the first 1,000 days, nor in the life of
this Administration, nor even perhaps in our lifetime on
this planet. But let us begin.

inaugural address, 20 January 1961

6 Now the trumpet summons us again—not as a call to
bear arms, though arms we need—not as a call to battle,
though embattled we are—but a call to bear the burden
of a long twilight struggle, year in and year out,
'rejoicing in hope, patient in tribulation'—a struggle
against the common enemies of man: tyranny, poverty,
disease and war itself.

inaugural address, 20 January 1961

7 And so, my fellow Americans: ask not what your
country can do for you—ask what you can do for your
country. My fellow citizens of the world: ask not what
America will do for you, but what together we can do for
the freedom of man.

inaugural address, 20 January
1961; Oliver Wendell **Holmes** Jr.,
speaking at Keene, New
Hampshire, 30 May 1884 said: 'We
pause to...recall what our country
has done for each of us and to ask
ourselves what we can do for our
country in return'

8 I believe that this Nation should commit itself to
achieving the goal, before this decade is out, of landing
a man on the Moon and returning him safely to earth.

supplementary State of the Union
message to Congress, 25 May 1961

9 When we got into office, the thing that surprised me
most was to find that things were just as bad as we'd
been saying they were.

speech at the White House, 27
May 1961

10 Mankind must put an end to war or war will put an end
to mankind.

speech to United Nations General
Assembly, 25 September 1961

11 Those who make peaceful revolution impossible will
make violent revolution inevitable.

speech at the White House, 13
March 1962

1 Probably the greatest concentration of talent and genius in this house except for perhaps those times when Thomas Jefferson ate alone.
   of a dinner for the Nobel prizewinners at the White House

   in *New York Times* 30 April 1962

2 My father always told me that all businessmen were sons of bitches, but I never believed it till now.
   on the price increases proposed by US Steel

   in April 1962

3 Liberty without learning is always in peril and learning without liberty is always in vain.

   said on the ninetieth anniversary of Vanderbilt University, 18 March 1963

4 If we cannot end now our differences, at least we can help make the world safe for diversity.

   address at American University, Washington, DC, 10 June 1963

5 No one has been barred on account of his race from fighting or dying for America—there are no 'white' or 'coloured' signs on the foxholes or graveyards of battle.

   message to Congress on proposed Civil Rights Bill, 19 June 1963

   speaking in the then newly divided city of West Berlin:
6 All free men, wherever they may live, are citizens of Berlin, and therefore, as a free man, I take pride in the words *Ich bin ein Berliner* [I am a Berliner].
   in 1963, expressing the USA's commitment to the support and defence of West Berlin (it was later the cause of some hilarity, as ein Berliner *is the German name for a doughnut)*

   speech in West Berlin, 26 June 1963

7 Yesterday, a shaft of light cut into the darkness...For the first time, an agreement has been reached on bringing the forces of nuclear destruction under international control.

   television address in Washington, 26 July 1963

8 When power leads man toward arrogance, poetry reminds him of his limitations. When power narrows the areas of man's concern, poetry reminds him of the richness and diversity of his existence. When power corrupts, poetry cleanses. For art establishes the basic human truths which must serve as the touchstone of our judgement.

   speech at Amherst College, Massachusetts, 26 October 1963

9 In free society art is not a weapon...Artists are not engineers of the soul.

   speech at Amherst College, Massachusetts, 26 October 1963

10 I'm an idealist without illusions.

   attributed; cf. **Macleod** 243:4

   on being asked how he became a war hero:
11 It was involuntary. They sank my boat.

   Arthur M. Schlesinger Jr. *A Thousand Days* (1965)

12 Washington is a city of southern efficiency and northern charm.

   Arthur M. Schlesinger Jr. *A Thousand Days* (1965)

Joseph P. Kennedy 1888–1969

American financier and diplomat; father of John Fitzgerald **Kennedy** and Robert **Kennedy**; husband of Rose **Kennedy**

13 This is a hell of a long way from East Boston.
   to his wife Rose, on a visit to Windsor Castle two weeks after his arrival as Ambassador

   in *The Times* 24 January 1995 (obituary of Rose **Kennedy***)*

1 We're going to sell Jack like soapflakes.
   when his son John F. **Kennedy** *made his bid for the Presidency*

   John H. Davis *The Kennedy Clan*
   (1984)

2 When the going gets tough, the tough get going.

   J. H. Cutler *Honey Fitz* (1962); also
   attributed to Knute Rockne

Robert F. Kennedy 1925–68

American democratic politician; son of Joseph and Rose
Kennedy and brother of John Fitzgerald **Kennedy**

3 About one-fifth of the people are against everything all
   the time.

   speech at University of
   Pennsylvania, 6 May 1964

Rose Kennedy 1890–1995

wife of Joseph **Kennedy**, mother of John Fitzgerald and Robert
Kennedy

4 It's our money, and we're free to spend it any way we
   please...If you have money you spend it, and win.
   in response to criticism of overlavish funding of her son Robert
   Kennedy's *1968 presidential campaign*

   in *Daily Telegraph* 24 January 1995
   (obituary)

5 Now Teddy must run.
   to her daughter, on hearing of the assassination of Robert
   Kennedy

   in *The Times* 24 January 1995
   (obituary); attributed, perhaps
   apocryphal

Jomo Kenyatta 1891–1978

Kenyan statesman, Prime Minister of Kenya 1963 and President
1964–78

6 The African is conditioned, by the cultural and social
   institutions of centuries, to a freedom of which Europe
   has little conception, and it is not in his nature to accept
   serfdom forever. He realizes that he must fight
   unceasingly for his own emancipation; for without this
   he is doomed to remain the prey of rival imperialisms.

   Facing Mount Kenya (1938);
   conclusion

Philip Henry Kerr, Lord Lothian
1882–1940

British journalist and politician, ambassador to the United
States from 1939

of German troops re-entering the Rhineland in 1936:
7 After all, they are only going into their own back garden.

   A. Lentin *Lloyd George, Woodrow
   Wilson and the Guilt of Germany*
   (1984)

8 If you back us you won't be backing a quitter.
   address to the American people, read for him on the day before
   his death

   in *Dictionary of National Biography*

Francis Scott Key 1779–1843

American lawyer and verse-writer

1 'Tis the star-spangled banner; O long may it wave   'The Star-Spangled Banner' (1814)
O'er the land of the free, and the home of the brave!

John Maynard Keynes 1883–1946

English economist

2 I work for a Government I despise for ends I think   letter to Duncan Grant, 15
criminal.   December 1917

of **Clemenceau**:
3 He felt about France what Pericles felt of Athens—unique   *The Economic Consequences of the*
value in her, nothing else mattering; but his theory of   *Peace* (1919)
politics was Bismarck's. He had one illusion—France;
and one disillusion—mankind, including Frenchmen, and
his colleagues not least.

4 Like Odysseus, the President looked wiser when he was   *The Economic Consequences of the*
seated.   *Peace* (1919)
     of Woodrow **Wilson**

5 Lenin was right. There is no subtler, no surer means of   *The Economic Consequences of the*
overturning the existing basis of society than to debauch   *Peace* (1919)
the currency. The process engages all the hidden forces of
economic law on the side of destruction, and does it in
a manner which not one man in a million is able to
diagnose.

6 But this *long run* is a misleading guide to current affairs.   *A Tract on Monetary Reform* (1923)
In the long run we are all dead.

7 Capitalism, wisely managed, can probably be made more   *The End of Laissez-Faire* (1926)
efficient for attaining economic ends than any alternative
system yet in sight, but...in itself it is in many ways
extremely objectionable.

8 Marxian Socialism must always remain a portent to the   *The End of Laissez-Faire* (1926)
historians of Opinion—how a doctrine so illogical and so
dull can have exercised so powerful and enduring an
influence over the minds of men, and, through them, the
events of history.

9 I do not know which makes a man more conservative—   *The End of Laissez-Faire* (1926)
to know nothing but the present, or nothing but the
past.

10 The important thing for Government is not to do things   *The End of Laissez-Faire* (1926)
which individuals are doing already, and to do them
a little better or a little worse; but to do those things
which at present are not done at all.

of **Lloyd George**:
11 This extraordinary figure of our time, this syren, this   *Essays in Biography* (1933) 'Mr
goat-footed bard, this half-human visitor to our age from   Lloyd George'
the hag-ridden magic and enchanted woods of Celtic
antiquity.

of **Lloyd George**:

1 Who shall paint the chameleon, who can tether
a broomstick?

Essays and Biography (1933) 'Mr
Lloyd George'

2 It is better that a man should tyrannize over his bank
balance than over his fellow-citizens.

General Theory (1936)

3 We take it as a fundamental psychological rule of any
modern community that, when its real income is
increased, it will not increase its consumption by an
equal *absolute* amount.

General Theory (1936)

4 If the Treasury were to fill old bottles with banknotes,
bury them at suitable depths in disused coalmines which
are then filled up to the surface with town rubbish, and
leave it to private enterprise on well-tried principles of
laissez-faire to dig the notes up again (the right to do so
being obtained, of course, by tendering for leases of the
note-bearing territory) there need be no more
unemployment and, with the help of the repercussions,
the real income of the community, and its capital wealth
also, would probably become a good deal greater than it
actually is. It would, indeed, be more sensible to build
houses and the like; but as there are political and
practical difficulties in the way of this, the above would
be better than nothing.

General Theory (1936)

5 I evidently knew more about economics than my
examiners.
*explaining why he performed badly in the Civil Service
examinations*

Roy Harrod *Life of John Maynard
Keynes* (1951)

6 The ideas of economists and political philosophers, both
when they are right and when they are wrong, are more
powerful than is commonly understood...Practical men,
who believe themselves to be quite exempt from any
intellectual influences, are usually the slaves of some
defunct economist. Madmen in authority, who hear
voices in the air, are distilling their frenzy from some
academic scribbler of a few years back.

General Theory (1947 ed.)

7 We threw good housekeeping to the winds. But we saved
ourselves and helped save the world.
of Britain in the Second World War

A. J. P. Taylor *English History,
1914–1945* (1965)

8 LADY VIOLET BONHAM CARTER: What do you think happens
to Mr Lloyd George when he is alone in the room?
MAYNARD KEYNES: When he is alone in the room there is
nobody there.

Lady Violet Bonham Carter *The
Impact of Personality in Politics*
(Romanes Lecture, 1963)

Ayatollah Ruhollah Khomeini 1900–89

Iranian Shiite Muslim leader, who returned to Iran from exile in
1979 to lead an Islamic revolution which overthrew the Shah

9 If laws are needed, Islam has established them all.There
is no need...after establishing a government, to sit down
and draw up laws.

*Islam and Revolution: Writings and
Declarations of Imam Khomeini*
(1981) ' Islamic Government'

Nikita Khrushchev 1894–1971

Soviet statesman; Premier, 1958–64

1 If anyone believes that our smiles involve abandonment
of the teaching of Marx, Engels and Lenin he deceives
himself. Those who wait for that must wait until
a shrimp learns to whistle.

speech in Moscow, 17 September
1955

2 We must abolish the cult of the individual decisively,
once and for all.

speech to secret session of the
20th Congress of the Communist
Party, 25 February 1956

3 We say this not only for the socialist states, who are
more akin to us. We base ourselves on the idea that we
must peacefully co-exist. About the capitalist States, it
doesn't depend on you whether or not we exist. If you
don't like us, don't accept our invitations and don't
invite us to come to see you. Whether you like it or not,
history is on our side. We will bury you.
    speech to Western diplomats at reception in Moscow for Polish
    leader Mr Gomulka, 18 November 1956; 'We will bury you' in this
    context means 'we will outlive you'

in *The Times* 19 November 1956

4 If one cannot catch the bird of paradise, better take a wet
hen.

in *Time* 6 January 1958

5 We are going to make the imperialists dance like fishes in
a saucepan, even without war.

in Vienna, 2 July 1960

6 Politicians are the same all over. They promise to build
a bridge where there is no river.

at a press conference in New York,
October 1960

7 If you start throwing hedgehogs under me, I shall throw
a couple of porcupines under you.

in *New York Times* 7 November
1963

8 Anyone who believes that the worker can be lulled by
fine revolutionary phrases is mistaken…If no concern is
shown for the growth of material and spiritual riches, the
people will listen today, they will listen tomorrow, and
then they may say: 'Why do you promise us everything
for the future? You are talking, so to speak, about life
beyond the grave. The priest has already told us about
this.'

speech at World Youth Forum, 19
September 1964

David Maxwell Fyfe, Lord Kilmuir

1900–67

British Conservative politician and lawyer
on Kilmuir: see **Anonymous** 12:8

9 Loyalty is the Tory's secret weapon.

Anthony Sampson *Anatomy of
Britain* (1962); cf. **Critchley** 104:9

10 Gratitude is not a normal feature of political life.

Political Adventure (1964)

Edward King 1829–1910

English clergyman, the first Professor of Pastoral Theology at Oxford

1 I have been voting against Gladstone all my life, and   *in Dictionary of National Biography*
   now he makes me a bishop.
   view of a staunch Conservative on being appointed Bishop of
   Lincoln in 1885

Martin Luther King 1929–68

American civil rights leader

2 I want to be the white man's brother, not his brother-in-   *in New York Journal-American* 10
   law.   September 1962

3 If we assume that mankind has a right to survive, then   *Strength to Love* (1963)
   we must find an alternative to war and destruction. In
   our day of space vehicles and guided ballistic missiles, the
   choice is either nonviolence or nonexistence.

4 Jesus eloquently affirmed from the cross a higher law. He   *Strength to Love* (1963)
   knew that the old eye-for-an-eye philosophy would leave
   everyone blind. He did not seek to overcome evil with
   evil. He overcame evil with good.

5 Nothing in all the world is more dangerous than sincere   *Strength to Love* (1963)
   ignorance and conscientious stupidity.

6 The ultimate measure of a man is not where he stands in   *Strength to Love* (1963)
   moments of comfort and convenience, but where he
   stands at times of challenge and controversy.

7 Injustice anywhere is a threat to justice everywhere.   letter from Birmingham Jail,
                                                                  Alabama, 16 April 1963

8 The Negro's great stumbling block in the stride toward   letter from Birmingham Jail,
   freedom is not the White Citizens Councillor or the Ku   Alabama, 16 April 1963
   Klux Klanner but the white moderate who is more
   devoted to order than to justice; who prefers a negative
   peace which is the absence of tension to a positive peace
   which is the presence of justice.

9 I submit to you that if a man hasn't discovered   speech in Detroit, 23 June 1963
   something he will die for, he isn't fit to live.

10 I have a dream that one day on the red hills of Georgia   speech at Civil Rights March in
   the sons of former slaves and the sons of former slave   Washington, 28 August 1963
   owners will be able to sit down together at the table of
   brotherhood...
      I have a dream that my four little children will one
   day live in a nation where they will not be judged by the
   colour of their skin but by the content of their character.

11 When we let freedom ring, when we let it ring from   speech at Civil Rights March in
   every village and every hamlet, from every state and   Washington, 28 August 1963
   every city, we will be able to speed up that day when all
   of God's children, black men and white men, Jews and
   Gentiles, Protestants and Catholics, will be able to join
   hands and sing in the words of the old Negro spiritual,

'Free at last! Free at last! Thank God Almighty, we are free at last!'

1 The means by which we live have outdistanced the ends for which we live. Our scientific power has outrun our spiritual power. We have guided missiles and misguided men.	*Strength to Love* (1963)
2 We must learn to live together as brothers or perish together as fools.	speech at St Louis, 22 March 1964
3 A riot is at bottom the language of the unheard.	*Where Do We Go From Here?* (1967)
4 I just want to do God's will. And he's allowed me to go up to the mountain. And I've looked over, and I've seen the promised land...So I'm happy tonight. I'm not worried about anything. I'm not fearing any man. *speech in Memphis, 3 April 1968, the day before his assassination*	in *New York Times* 4 April 1968

David Kingsley, Dennis Lyons, and Peter Lovell-Davis

5 Yesterday's men (they failed before!). *advertising slogan for the Labour Party, referring to the Conservatives*	David Butler and Michael Pinto-Duschinsky *The British General Election of 1970* (1971)

Hugh Kingsmill 1889–1949

English man of letters

6 A nation is only at peace when it's at war.	attributed

Neil Kinnock 1942–

British Labour politician; Leader of the Labour Party 1983–92

7 Loyalty is a fine quality but in excess it fills political graveyards. *in June 1976, in opposition to Conference decisions on devolution*	G. M. F. Drower *Neil Kinnock* (1984)
8 They want a kindly capitalism, a gentle market economy, an air-conditioned jungle. *of the Council for Social Democracy*	in *Guardian* 6 February 1981

of servicemen in the Falklands War, when replying to a heckler who said that Mrs **Thatcher** *'showed guts':*

9 It's a pity others had to leave theirs on the ground at Goose Green to prove it.	television interview, 6 June 1983
10 If Margaret Thatcher wins on Thursday, I warn you not to be ordinary, I warn you not to be young, I warn you not to fall ill, and I warn you not to grow old. *on the prospect of a Conservative re-election*	speech at Bridgend, 7 June 1983
11 The grotesque chaos of a Labour council hiring taxis to scuttle round the city handing out redundancy notices to	speech at the Labour Party Conference, 1 October 1985

its own workers.
of the actions of the Labour city council in Liverpool

1 I would die for my country but I could never let my country die for me.

speech at Labour Party Conference, 30 September 1986

2 Why am I the first Kinnock in a thousand generations to be able to get to university?
later plagiarized by the American politician Joe Biden

speech at Llandudno, 15 May 1987

3 There are lots of ways to get socialism, but I think trying to fracture the Labour party by incessant contest cannot be one of them.

in *Guardian* 29 January 1988

4 I don't think anyone could accuse someone who has been leader of the Labour party for more than seven years of being impulsive.

in *Sunday Times* 5 August 1990

5 I'm not going to be bloody kebabbed by you.
when being interviewed by James Naughtie (the comment was not broadcast, but became widely known through unofficial circulation)

in *Sunday Times* 14 October 1990

Rudyard Kipling 1865–1936

English writer and poet, cousin of Stanley **Baldwin**

6 Oh, East is East, and West is West, and never the twain shall meet.

'The Ballad of East and West' (1892)

7 Winds of the World, give answer! They are whimpering to and fro—
And what should they know of England who only England know?—
The poor little street-bred people that vapour and fume and brag.

'The English Flag' (1892)

8 Ship me somewheres east of Suez, where the best is like the worst,
Where there aren't no Ten Commandments an' a man can raise a thirst.

'Mandalay' (1892)

9 Now this is the Law of the Jungle—as old and as true as the sky;
And the Wolf that shall keep it may prosper, but the Wolf that shall break it must die.

'The Law of the Jungle' (1895)

10 We have fed our sea for a thousand years
And she calls us, still unfed,
Though there's never a wave of all her waves
But marks our English dead:
We have strawed our best to the weed's unrest
To the shark and sheering gull.
If blood be the price of admiralty,
Lord God, we ha' paid in full!

'The Song of the Dead' (1896)

11 God of our fathers, known of old,
Lord of our far-flung battle-line,
Beneath whose awful Hand we hold
Dominion over palm and pine—
Lord God of Hosts, be with us yet,

'Recessional' (1897)

Lest we forget—lest we forget!

The tumult and the shouting dies—
The captains and the kings depart—
Still stands Thine ancient Sacrifice,
An humble and a contrite heart.
Lord God of Hosts, be with us yet,
Lest we forget—lest we forget!

1 A Nation spoke to a Nation,   'Our Lady of the Snows' (1898)
   A Throne sent word to a Throne:
   'Daughter am I in my mother's house,
   But mistress in my own.
   The gates are mine to open,
   As the gates are mine to close,
   And I abide by my Mother's House.'
   Said our Lady of the Snows.

2 Take up the White Man's burden—   'The White Man's Burden' (1899)
   Send forth the best ye breed—
   Go, bind your sons to exile
   To serve your captives' need.

3 If you can keep your head when all about you   'If —' (1910)
   Are losing theirs and blaming it on you;
   If you can trust yourself when all men doubt you,
   But make allowance for their doubting too;
   If you can wait and not be tired by waiting,
   Or being lied about, don't deal in lies,
   Or being hated, don't give way to hating,
   And yet don't look too good, nor talk too wise;
   If you can dream—and not make dreams your master;
   If you can think—and not make thoughts your aim,
   If you can meet with triumph and disaster
   And treat those two imposters just the same...

4 It is always a temptation to a rich and lazy nation,   'What Dane-geld means' (1911)
   To puff and look important and to say:-
   'Though we know we should defeat you, we have not
       the time to meet you,
   We will therefore pay you cash to go away.'

   And that is called paying the Dane-geld;
   But we've proved it again and again,
   That if once you have paid him the Dane-geld
   You never get rid of the Dane.

5 All Power, each Tyrant, every Mob   'The Benefactors' (1919)
   Whose head has grown too large,
   Ends by destroying its own job
   And works its own discharge.

6 I could not dig: I dared not rob: 'Epitaphs of the War: A Dead
   Therefore I lied to please the mob.   Statesman' (1919)
   Now all my lies are proved untrue
   And I must face the men I slew.
   What tale shall serve me here among
   Mine angry and defrauded young?

1 Power without responsibility: the prerogative of the harlot throughout the ages.

   summing up Lord **Beaverbrook**'s *political standpoint* vis-à-vis *the* Daily Express, *after he had said to Kipling, 'What I want is power. Kiss 'em one day and kick 'em the next'; Stanley* **Baldwin,** *Kipling's cousin, subsequently obtained permission to use the phrase in a speech in London on 18 March 1931*

in *Kipling Journal* December 1971

Henry Kissinger 1923–

American politician

2 There cannot be a crisis next week. My schedule is already full.

in *New York Times Magazine* 1 June 1969

3 Power is the great aphrodisiac.

in *New York Times* 19 January 1971

4 We are the President's men and we must behave accordingly.

M. and B. Kalb *Kissinger* (1974)

5 The illegal we do immediately. The unconstitutional takes a little longer.

in *Washington Post* 20 January 1977; attributed

6 Ninety percent of the politicians give the other ten percent a bad name.

in 1978, attributed

7 History knows no resting places and no plateaus.

White House Years (1979)

8 The management of a balance of power is a permanent undertaking, not an exertion that has a foreseeable end.

White House Years (1979)

9 An Iranian moderate is one who has run out of ammunition.

in *Today* 23 July 1987

10 History has so far shown us only two roads to international stability: domination and equilibrium.

in *The Times* 12 March 1991

11 For other nations, Utopia is a blessed past never to be recovered; for Americans it is just beyond the horizon.

attributed

12 For [Woodrow] Wilson, the justification of America's international role was messianic: America had an obligation not to the balance of power, but to spread its principles throughout the world.

Diplomacy (1994)

13 It combined legitimacy and equilibrium, shared values, and balance-of-power diplomacy. Common values restrained the scope of nations' demands while equilibrium limited the capacity to insist upon them.

   of the Congress of Vienna

Diplomacy (1994)

14 The main advantage of being famous is that when you bore people at dinner parties they think it is their fault.

James Naughtie in *Spectator* 1 April 1995; attributed

Lord Kitchener 1850–1916

British soldier and politician
on Kitchener: see **Asquith** 18:10, **Lloyd George** 231:1

15 You are ordered abroad as a soldier of the King to help our French comrades against the invasion of a common enemy...In this new experience you may find

in *The Times* 19 August 1914

temptations both in wine and women. You must entirely resist both temptations, and, while treating all women with perfect courtesy, you should avoid any intimacy. Do your duty bravely. Fear God. Honour the King.
message to soldiers of the British Expeditionary Force (1914)

1 I don't mind your being killed, but I object to your being taken prisoner.
*to the Prince of Wales (later **Edward VIII**) on his asking to be allowed to the Front during the First World War*

in *Journals and Letters of Reginald Viscount Esher* vol. 3 (1938) 18 December 1914

Philander C. Knox 1853–1921

US Attorney-General

*Theodore **Roosevelt** had requested a legal justification for his acquisition of the Panama Canal:*
2 Oh, Mr. President, do not let so great an achievement suffer from any taint of legality.

Tyler Dennett *John Hay: From Poetry to Politics* (1933)

Helmut Kohl 1930–

Chancellor of West Germany (1982–90) and first postwar Chancellor of united Germany (1990–)

3 I have been underestimated for decades. I have done very well that way.

in *New York Times* 25 January 1987

4 My goal, when the historical hour allows it, is the unity of the nation.
to crowds in Dresden on the occasion of his first official visit to East Germany, 19 December 1989

in *The Times* 20 December 1989

5 We Germans now have the historic chance to realize the unity of our fatherland.

in *Guardian* 15 February 1990

Paul Kruger 1825–1904

South African soldier and statesman

6 A bill of indemnity...for raid by Dr Jameson and the British South Africa Company's troops. The amount falls under two heads—first, material damage, total of claim, £677,938 3s. 3d.—second, moral or intellectual damage, total of claim, £1,000,000.
*telegram from the South African Republic, communicated to the House of Commons by Joseph **Chamberlain***

in the House of Commons 18 February 1897

Stanley Kubrick 1928–

American film director and screenwriter

7 The great nations have always acted like gangsters, and the small nations like prostitutes.

in *Guardian* 5 June 1963

Henry Labouchere 1831–1912

British politician

1 I do not object to the old man always having a card up his sleeve, but I do object to his insinuating that the Almighty has placed it there.
 on **Gladstone**'s *'frequent appeals to a higher power'*

Earl Curzon *Modern Parliamentary Eloquence* (1913)

Jean de la Bruyère 1645–96

French satiric moralist

2 When the populace is excited, one cannot conceive how calm can be restored; and when it is peaceful, one cannot see how calm can be disturbed.

Characters (1688) 'Of the Sovereign and the State'

Fiorello La Guardia 1882–1947

American politician, mayor of New York City

3 When I make a mistake, it's a beaut!
 on the appointment of Herbert O'Brien as a judge in 1936

William Manners *Patience and Fortitude* (1976)

4 Ticker tape ain't spaghetti.

speech to the United Nations Relief and Rehabilitation Administration, 29 March 1946

5 There is no Democratic or Republican way of cleaning the streets.

Charles Garrett *The La Guardia Years, Machine and Reform Politics in New York City* (1961)

John Lambert 1619–83

English soldier and Parliamentary supporter

6 The quarrel is now between light and darkness, not who shall rule, but whether we shall live or be preserved or no. Good words will not do with the cavaliers.
 speech in the Parliament of 1656 supporting the rule of the major-generals

in *Dictionary of National Biography*

John George Lambton, Lord Durham
1792–1840

English Whig politician

7 £40,000 a year a moderate income—such a one as a man *might jog on with.*

Thomas Creevey letter to Elizabeth Ord, 13 September 1821

Norman Lamont 1942–

British Conservative politician

8 A price worth paying.
 as Chancellor, responding to criticism on the rise in unemployment

in the House of Commons, 16 May 1991

1 The turn of the tide is sometimes difficult to discern.   speech at the Conservative Party
What we are seeing is the return of that vital   Conference, 9 October 1991
ingredient—confidence. The green shoots of economic
spring are appearing once again.
  often quoted as 'the green shoots of recovery'

2 We give the impression of being in office but not in   speech in House of Commons, 9
power.   June 1993
  'in office, but not in power' had earlier been used by A. J. P.
  Taylor *of Ramsay* **Macdonald***'s minority government of 1924*

Bert Lance 1931–

American government official

3 If it ain't broke, don't fix it.   in *Nation's Business* May 1977

Walter Savage Landor 1775–1864

English poet

4 The wise become as the unwise in the enchanted   *Imaginary Conversations*
chambers of Power, whose lamps make every face the   (1824–9)
same colour.

5 George the First was always reckoned   epigram in *The Atlas*, 28 April 1855
Vile, but viler George the Second;
And what mortal ever heard
Any good of George the Third?
When from earth the Fourth descended
God be praised the Georges ended!

Andrew Lang 1844–1912

Scottish man of letters

6 He uses statistics as a drunken man uses lampposts—for   Alan L. Mackay *Harvest of a Quiet*
support rather than illumination.   *Eye* (1977); attributed

William Langland c.1330–c.1400

English poet

7 Brewesters and baksters, bochiers and cokes—   *The Vision of Piers Plowman*
For thise are men on this molde that moost harm
    wercheth
To the povere peple.
  in an alternative text, 'As bakeres and breweres, bocheres and
  cokes; /For thyse men don most harm to the mene peple'

Lao-tzu c.604–c.531 BC

Chinese philosopher; founder of Taoism

8 Of the best rulers,   *The Wisdom of Laotse* (1948)
The people only know that they exist;
The next best they love and praise;
The next they fear;

And the next they revile...
But of the best when their task is accomplished, their
   work done,
The people all remark, 'We have done it ourselves.'

Duc de la Rochefoucauld-Liancourt
1747–1827
French social reformer

1 LOUIS XVI: It is a big revolt.   F. Dreyfus *La Rochefoucauld-*
LA ROCHEFOUCAULD-LIANCOURT: No, Sire, a big revolution.   *Liancourt* (1903)
on a report reaching Versailles of the Fall of the Bastille, 1789

Harold Laski 1893–1950
British Labour politician and academic

2 I read Hobbes again with a hopeless sense of despairing   letter to Oliver Wendell **Holmes** Jr.
infirmity. The others in English theory I would have a shot at   29 January 1919
equalling, but that old rascal leaves me with a sense of how
high above all others he is.

3 Shaw, with incredibly brilliant insolence, began to prove   letter to Oliver Wendell **Holmes** Jr.
that Foreign Secretaries are by definition cynical and   3 July 1926
corrupt. Poor Austen, of course, tried to riposte; but he
was like an elephant trying to catch an exceedingly agile
wasp.
*of an encounter between Bernard **Shaw** and Austen Chamberlain*

4 I respect fidelity to colleagues even though they are fit for   letter to Oliver Wendell **Holmes** Jr.
the hangman.   4 December 1926

5 He searched always to end a sentence with a climax. He   letter to Oliver Wendell **Holmes** Jr.
looked for antithesis like a monkey looking for fleas.   7 May 1927
*of Winston **Churchill** at a dinner at the London School of
Economics*

Hugh Latimer c.1485–1555
English Protestant martyr

6 Be of good comfort Master Ridley, and play the man. We   John Foxe *Actes and Monuments*
shall this day light such a candle by God's grace in   (1570 ed.)
England, as (I trust) shall never be put out.
prior to being burned for heresy, 16 October 1555

Richard Law 1901–80

British Conservative politician, son of Andrew **Bonar Law**

1 We do not ask of Mr Chamberlain that he should be Pitt   in *Time and Tide* 30 September
or Chatham—only that he should seem a little less like   1939
an alderman exposing a sewage scandal.
of Neville **Chamberlain**

Mark Lawson 1962–

British writer and journalist

2 Office tends to confer a dreadful plausibility on even the   Joe Queenan *Imperial Caddy*
most negligible of those who hold it.   (1992); introduction

Nigel Lawson 1932–

British Conservative politician; Chancellor of the Exchequer
1983–9

3 The Conservative Party has never believed that the   in the House of Commons, 10
business of government is the government of business.   November 1981

4 Teenage scribblers.   in *Financial Times* 28 September
of the financial press   1985; coinage attributed to one of
                                                             Nigel Lawson's Treasury aides

5 It represented the tip of a singularly ill-concealed iceberg, in the House of Commons
with all the destructive potential that icebergs possess.   following his resignation as
of an article by Alan Walters, the Prime Minister's economic   Chancellor, 31 October 1989
adviser, criticizing the Exchange Rate Mechanism

6 When I was a minister I always looked forward to the   'Cabinet Government in the
Cabinet meeting immensely because it was, apart from   Thatcher Years' (1994)
the summer holidays, the only period of real rest I got in
what was a very heavy job.

Emma Lazarus 1849–87

American poet

7 Give me your tired, your poor,   'The New Colossus' (1883)
Your huddled masses yearning to breathe free,
The wretched refuse of your teeming shore,
Send these, the homeless, tempest-tossed, to me:
I lift my lamp beside the golden door.
inscription on the Statue of Liberty, New York

Alexandre Auguste Ledru-Rollin 1807–74

French politician

8 Ah well! I am their leader, I really had to follow them!   E. de Mirecourt *Les Contemporains*
                                                             vol. 14 (1857) 'Ledru-Rollin'

Charles Lee 1731–82

American soldier

1 Beware that your Northern laurels do not change to   on 17 October 1777
  Southern willows.
  *to General Horatio Gates after the surrender of Burgoyne at
  Saratoga*

Henry ('Light-Horse Harry') Lee
1756–1818

American soldier and politician

2 A citizen, first in war, first in peace, and first in the   *Funeral Oration on the death of
  hearts of his countrymen.   General Washington* (1800)
  of George Washington

Richard Henry Lee 1732–94

American politician

3 That these united colonies are, and of right ought to be,   resolution moved at the
  free and independent states; that they are absolved from   Continental Congress on 7 June
  all allegiance to the British crown; and that all political   1776; adopted 2 July 1776
  connection between them and the State of Great Britain
  is, and ought to be, totally dissolved.

Robert E. Lee 1807–70

American Confederate general

4 It is well that war is so terrible. We should grow too fond   attributed
  of it.
  after the battle of Fredericksburg, December 1862

5 There is nothing left for me to do but to go and see   Geoffrey C. Ward *The Civil War*
  General Grant and I would rather die a thousand deaths.   (1991)
  just before the Confederate surrender at Appomattox in 1865

6 I have fought against the people of the North because   Geoffrey C. Ward *The Civil War*
  I believed they were seeking to wrest from the South its   (1991)
  dearest rights. But I have never cherished toward them
  bitter or vindictive feelings, and I have never seen the
  day when I did not pray for them.

7 Strike the tent.   on 12 October 1870
  last words

Curtis E. LeMay 1906–90

US air-force officer

8 They've got to draw in their horns and stop their   *Mission with LeMay* (1965)
  aggression, or we're going to bomb them back into the
  Stone Age.
  on the North Vietnamese

Lenin 1870–1924

Russian revolutionary, first Premier (Chairman of the Council of People's Commissars) of the Soviet Union 1918–24

1 What is to be done?

title of pamphlet (1902); originally the title of a novel (1863) by N. G. Chernyshevsky

2 One step forward two steps back

title of book 1904

3 Imperialism is the monopoly stage of capitalism.

Imperialism as the Last Stage of Capitalism (1916) 'Briefest possible definition of imperialism'

4 We must now set about building a proletarian socialist state in Russia.

speech in Petrograd, 7 November 1917

5 A good man fallen among Fabians.
of George Bernard **Shaw**

Arthur Ransome *Six Weeks in Russia in 1919* (1919) 'Notes of Conversations with Lenin'

6 No, Democracy is *not* identical with majority rule. Democracy is a *State* which recognizes the subjection of the minority to the majority, that is, an organization for the systematic use of *force* by one class against the other, by one part of the population against another.

State and Revolution (1919)

7 While the State exists, there can be no freedom. When there is freedom there will be no State.

State and Revolution (1919)

8 Communism equals Soviet power plus the electrification of the whole country.

report to 8th Congress, 1920

9 Who? Whom?
definition of political science, meaning 'Who will outstrip whom?'

in *Polnoe Sobranie Sochinenii* (1970) 17 October 1921

10 An end to bossing.

Neil Harding *Lenin's Political Thought* (1981) vol.2

11 Liberty is precious—so precious that it must be rationed.

Sidney and Beatrice Webb *Soviet Communism* (1935) vol. 2

William Lenthall 1591–1662

Speaker of the House of Commons

12 I have neither eye to see, nor tongue to speak here, but as the House is pleased to direct me.
to **Charles I,** *4 January 1642, on being asked if he had seen any of the five MPs whom the King had ordered to be arrested*

John Rushworth *Historical Collections. The Third Part* vol. 2 (1692)

Doris Lessing 1919–

British novelist and short-story writer, brought up in Rhodesia

13 When old settlers say 'One has to understand the country,' what they mean is, 'You have to get used to our ideas about the native.'

The Grass is Singing (1950)

1 When a white man in Africa by accident looks into the   *The Grass is Singing* (1950)
   eyes of a native and sees the human being (which it is
   his chief preoccupation to avoid), his sense of guilt,
   which he denies, fumes up in resentment and he brings
   down the whip.

Leslie Lever 1905–77

British Labour politician

2 Generosity is part of my character, and I therefore hasten   Leon Harris *The Fine Art of Political*
   to assure this Government that I will never make an   *Wit* (1964)
   allegation of dishonesty against it wherever a simple
   explanation of stupidity will suffice.

Bernard Levin 1928–

British journalist

3 Whom the mad would destroy, they first make gods.   in *The Times* 21 September 1987
   of **Mao** *Zedong in 1967*

4 [Tony] Benn flung himself into the Sixties technology   *The Pendulum Years* (1970)
   with the enthusiasm (not to say language) of a newly
   enrolled Boy Scout demonstrating knot-tying to his
   indulgent parents.

   of Harold **Macmillan** *and Harold* **Wilson**:
5 Between them, then, Walrus and Carpenter, they divided   *The Pendulum Years* (1970)
   up the Sixties.

6 The Stag at Bay with the mentality of a fox at large.   *The Pendulum Years* (1970)
   of Harold **Macmillan**

7 Inflation in the Sixties was a nuisance to be endured, like *The Pendulum Years* (1970);
   varicose veins or French foreign policy.   epilogue

8 Once, when a British Minister sneezed, men half a world   in *The Times* 1976
   away would blow their noses. Now when a British Prime
   Minister sneezes nobody else will even say, 'Bless You.'

9 What has happened to architecture since the second   in *The Times* 1983
   world war that the only passers-by who can contemplate
   it without pain are those equipped with a white stick and
   a dog?

10 Since when was fastidiousness a quality useful for   *If You Want My Opinion* (1992)
   political advancement?

11 Harold Macmillan, whose elevation was achieved by   *If You Want My Opinion* (1992); cf.
   a brutality, cunning and greed for power normally met   **Macmillan** 245:7
   only in the conclaves of Mafia *capi*, said, after he had
   climbed the greasy pole and pushed all his rivals off (*takes
   out handkerchief containing concealed onion*) that the whole
   thing was Dead Sea Fruit.

12 The less the power, the greater the desire to exercise it. in *The Times* 21 September 1993

13 I have more than once pointed out that no organization   in *Times* 14 April 1995
   with 'Liberation' in its title has ever, or ever will, liberate
   anyone or anything.

Duc de Lévis 1764–1830

French soldier and writer

1 To govern is to choose.   *Maximes et Réflexions* (1812 ed.)
                                                        'Politique: Maximes de Politique'

Willmott Lewis 1877–1950

British journalist and *Times* correspondent in Washington

2 One should perhaps avoid being hypercritical of acts of   Claud Cockburn *In Time of Trouble*
   high policy. Take the charitable view, bearing in mind   (1957)
   that every government will do as much harm as it can
   and as much good as it must.
     to Claud **Cockburn**

   the leader of the French delegation to the Disarmament
   Conference in Washington after the First World War had
   described the city as un Versailles nègre:
3 Thus (for you figure to yourself the reactions of Southern   Claud Cockburn *In Time of Trouble*
   senators to whom his ill-timed if apt remark was, I need   (1957)
   hardly tell you, instantly communicated) stabbing himself
   in the back, a performance singularly otiose in a city
   where so many stand only too eagerly ready to do it for
   you.
     to Claud **Cockburn**

Robert Ley 1890–1945

German Nazi; head of the Labour Front from 1933

4 Strength through joy.   German Labour Front slogan from
                                                        1933

Basil Henry Liddell Hart 1895–1970

British military historian and strategist

5 Keep strong, if possible. In any case, keep cool. Have   *Deterrent or Defence* (1960)
   unlimited patience. Never corner an opponent, and
   always assist him to save his face. Put yourself in his
   shoes—so as to see things through his eyes. Avoid self-
   righteousness like the devil—nothing so self-blinding.
     'Advice to Statesmen'

Abbott Joseph Liebling 1904–63

6 Freedom of the press is guaranteed only to those who   in *New Yorker* 14 May 1960
   own one.

Charles-Joseph, Prince de Ligne
1735–1814·
Belgian soldier

1   The Congress makes no progress; it dances.
    of the Congress of Vienna

Auguste de la Garde-Chambonas
Souvenirs du Congrès de Vienne
(1820)

Abraham Lincoln 1809–65
American Republican statesman, 16th President of the US
1861–5
on Lincoln: see **Stanton** 348:9, **Whitman** 387:9

2   Politicians [are] a set of men who have interests aside
    from the interests of the people, and who, to say the
    most of them, are, taken as a mass, at least one long step
    removed from honest men. I say this with the greater
    freedom because, being a politician myself, none can
    regard it as personal.

speech in the Illinois Legislature,
11 January 1837

3   There is no grievance that is a fit object of redress by
    mob law.

address at the Young Men's
Lyceum, Springfield, Illinois, 27
January 1838

4   Prohibition...goes beyond the bounds of reason in that it
    attempts to control a man's appetite by legislation, and
    makes a crime out of things that are not crimes. A
    Prohibition law strikes a blow at the very principles upon
    which our government was founded.

speech in the Illinois House of
Representatives, 18 December
1840

5   Any people anywhere, being inclined and having the
    power, have the *right* to rise up, and shake off the
    existing government, and form a new one that suits
    them better.

in the House of Representatives,
12 January 1848

6   No man is good enough to govern another man without
    that other's consent.

speech at Peoria, Illinois, 16
October 1854

7   To give victory to the right, not bloody bullets, but
    peaceful ballots only, are necessary.
    usually quoted as, 'The ballot is stronger than the bullet'

speech, 18 May 1858

8   As I would not be a *slave*, so I would not be a *master*.
    This expresses my idea of democracy. Whatever differs
    from this, to the extent of the difference, is no
    democracy.

fragment, 1 August 1858?

9   When...you have succeeded in dehumanizing the Negro,
    when you have put him down and made it forever
    impossible for him to be but as the beasts of the field;
    when you have extinguished his soul and placed him
    where the ray of hope is blown out in darkness like that
    which broods over the spirits of the damned, are you
    quite sure that the demon you have roused will not turn
    and rend you?

speech at Edwardsville, Illinois, 11
September 1858

1 'A house divided against itself cannot stand.' I believe   speech, 16 June 1858
this government cannot endure permanently, half slave
and half free.

2 I have no purpose to introduce political and social   speech, 21 August 1858
equality between the white and black races. There is
a physical difference between the two which, in my
judgement, will probably for ever forbid their living
together upon the footing of perfect equality; and
inasmuch as it becomes a necessity that there must be
a difference, I...am in favour of the race to which
I belong having the superior position.

3 What is conservatism? Is it not adherence to the old and   speech, 27 February 1860
tried, against the new and untried?

4 If we do not make common cause to save the good old   address at Cleveland, Ohio, 15
ship of the Union on this voyage, nobody will have   February 1861
a chance to pilot her on another voyage.

5 It is safe to assert that no government proper ever had   first inaugural address, 4 March
a provision in its organic law for its own termination.   1861

6 I take the official oath to-day with no mental   first inaugural address, 4 March
reservations, and with no purpose to construe the   1861
Constitution or laws by any hypercritical rules.

7 This country, with its institutions, belongs to the people   first inaugural address, 4 March
who inhabit it. Whenever they shall grow weary of the   1861
existing government, they can exercise their
constitutional right of amending it, or their revolutionary
right to dismember or overthrow it.

8 The mystic chords of memory, stretching from every   first inaugural address, 4 March
battlefield and patriot grave to every living heart and   1861
heartstone all over this broad land, will yet swell the
chorus of the Union when again touched, as surely they
will be, by the better angels of our nature.

9 I think the necessity of being *ready* increases. Look to it.   the whole of a letter to Governor
Andrew Curtin of Pennsylvania, 8
April 1861

when asked how he felt about the New York elections:
10 Somewhat like the boy in Kentucky who stubbed his toe   in *Frank Leslie's Illustrated Weekly*
while running to see his sweetheart. The boy said he was   22 November 1862
too big to cry, and far too badly hurt to laugh.

11 On the first day of January in the year of our Lord, one   *Preliminary Emancipation*
thousand eight hundred and sixty-three, all persons held   *Proclamation*, 22 September 1862
as slaves within any state, or designated part of a state,
the people whereof shall then be in rebellion against the
United States shall be then, thenceforward, and forever
free.

12 Fellow citizens, we cannot escape history...No personal   annual message to Congress, 1
significance or insignificance can spare one or another of   December 1862
us. The fiery trial through which we pass will light us
down in honour or dishonour to the last generation.

1 In giving freedom to the slave, we assure freedom to the free—honourable alike in what we give and what we preserve. We shall nobly save, or meanly lose, the last, best hope of earth.

annual message to Congress, 1 December 1862

2 My paramount object in this struggle is to save the Union...If I could save the Union without freeing any slave, I would do it; and if I could save it by freeing all the slaves, I would do it; and if I could save it by freeing some and leaving others alone, I would also do that...I have here stated my purpose according to my views of official duty and I intend no modification of my oft-expressed personal wish that all men everywhere could be free.

letter to Horace **Greeley**, 22 August 1862

3 Fourscore and seven years ago our fathers brought forth upon this continent a new nation, conceived in liberty, and dedicated to the proposition that all men are created equal...In a larger sense we cannot dedicate, we cannot consecrate, we cannot hallow this ground. The brave men, living and these dead, who struggled here, have consecrated it far above our power to add or detract. The world will little note, nor long remember, what we say here, but it can never forget what they did here. It is for us, the living, rather to be dedicated here to the unfinished work which they who fought here have thus far so nobly advanced...we here highly resolve that the dead shall not have died in vain, that this nation, under God, shall have a new birth of freedom; and that government of the people, by the people, and for the people, shall not perish from the earth.

address at the Dedication of the National Cemetery at Gettysburg, 19 November 1863, as reported the following day; the Lincoln Memorial inscription reads 'by the people, for the people'; cf. **Anonymous** 13:6, **Everett** 134:4; cf. also **Parker** 285:6

4 Only those generals who gain success can set up dictators. What I ask of you is military success, and I will risk the dictatorship.
   letter appointing Joseph Hooker to command of the Army of the Potomac in 1863

Shelby Foote *The Civil War: Fredericksburg to Meridian* (1991)

5 I claim not to have controlled events, but confess plainly that events have controlled me.

letter to A. G. Hodges, 4 April 1864

6 It is not best to swap horses when crossing streams.

reply to National Union League, 9 June 1864

7 It has long been a grave question whether any government, not too strong for the liberties of its people, can be strong enough to maintain its existence in great emergencies.

response to a serenade, 10 November 1864

8 I desire so to conduct the affairs of this administration that if at the end, when I come to lay down the reins of power, I have lost every other friend on earth, I shall at least have one friend left, and that friend shall be down inside me.

reply to the Missouri Committee of Seventy, 1864

9 Fondly do we hope, fervently do we pray, that this mighty scourge of war may speedily pass away. Yet, if God wills that it continue until all the wealth piled by the bond-man's two hundred and fifty years of unrequited

second inaugural address, 4 March 1865

toil shall be sunk, and until every drop of blood drawn with the lash shall be paid by another drawn with the sword, as was said three thousand years ago, so still it must be said, 'The judgements of the Lord are true and righteous altogether.'

1 With malice toward none; with charity for all; with firmness in the right, as God gives us to see the right, let us strive on to finish the work we are in: to bind up the nation's wounds; to care for him who shall have borne the battle, and for his widow and his orphan, to do all which may achieve and cherish a just and lasting peace among ourselves, and with all nations.

second inaugural address, 4 March 1865

2 As President, I have no eyes but constitutional eyes; I cannot see you.
reply to the South Carolina Commissioners

attributed

3 People who like this sort of thing will find this the sort of thing they like.
judgement of a book

G. W. E. Russell *Collections and Recollections* (1898)

4 So you're the little woman who wrote the book that made this great war!
on meeting Harriet Beecher Stowe, author of Uncle Tom's Cabin *(1852)*

Carl Sandburg *Abraham Lincoln: The War Years* (1936) vol. 2

5 The Lord prefers common-looking people. That is why he makes so many of them.

attributed; James Morgan Our Presidents *(1928)*

6 Whenever I hear anyone arguing for slavery, I feel a strong impulse to see it tried on him personally.

address to an Indiana Regiment, 17 March 1865

7 You cannot help the poor by destroying the rich. You cannot lift the wage earner by pulling down the wage payer.

attributed, but probably apocryphal

8 You may fool all the people some of the time; you can even fool some of the people all the time; but you can't fool all of the people all the time.

Alexander K. McClure *Lincoln's Yarns and Stories* (1904); also attributed to Phineas Barnum

Eric Linklater 1899–1974

Scottish novelist

9 'There won't be any revolution in America,' said Isadore. Nikitin agreed. 'The people are all too clean. They spend all their time changing their shirts and washing themselves. You can't feel fierce and revolutionary in a bathroom.'

Juan in America (1931)

George Linley 1798–1865

English songwriter

10 Among our ancient mountains,
And from our lovely vales,
Oh, let the prayer re-echo:
'God bless the Prince of Wales!'

'God Bless the Prince of Wales' (1862 song)

Walter Lippmann 1889–1974

American journalist

1 Mr Coolidge's genius for inactivity is developed to a very *Men of Destiny* (1927)
high point. It is far from being an indolent activity. It is
a grim, determined, alert inactivity which keeps Mr
Coolidge occupied constantly. Nobody has ever worked
harder at inactivity, with such force of character, with
such unremitting attention to detail, with such
conscientious devotion to the task.

2 Private property was the original source of freedom. It *The Good Society* (1937)
still is its main bulwark.

3 The final test of a leader is that he leaves behind him in in *New York Herald Tribune* 14 April
other men the conviction and the will to carry on. 1945

4 A free press is not a privilege but an organic necessity in address at the International Press
a great society. Institute Assembly in London, 27
  May 1965

5 The will to be free is perpetually renewed in every Arthur Seldon *The State is Rolling*
individual who uses his faculties and affirms his *Back* (1994)
manhood.

Maxim Litvinov 1876–1951

Soviet diplomat

6 Peace is indivisible. A. U. Pope *Maxim Litvinoff* (1943)
   note to the Allies, 25 February 1920

Ken Livingstone 1945–

British Labour politician

7 The problem is that many MPs never see the London that in *The Times* 19 February 1987
exists beyond the wine bars and brothels of Westminster.

Livy 59 BC–AD 17

Roman historian

8 *Vae victis.* *Ab Urbe Condita*
   Down with the defeated!
   cry (already proverbial) of the Gallic King, Brennus, on capturing
   Rome in 390 BC

9 We have been defeated in a great battle. *Ab Urbe Condita*
   the announcement of disaster for the Romans in Hannibal's
   ambush at Lake Trasimene in 217 BC

Selwyn Lloyd 1904–78

British Conservative politician

10 I do not speak any foreign language. Except in war, *Suez 1956* (1978)
I have never visited any foreign country. I do not like
foreigners.

David Lloyd George 1863–1945

British Liberal politician; Prime Minister, 1916–22
on Lloyd George: see **Asquith** 19:2, **Baldwin** 30:1, **Bennett**
37:5, **Churchill** 88:6, **Clemenceau** 98:5, **Grigg** 161:8,
Keynes 207:11, 208:1, **Massingham** 254:3, **Taylor** 357:12

1 The leal and trusty mastiff which is to watch over our
interests, but which runs away at the first snarl of the
trade unions...A mastiff? It is the right hon. Gentleman's
poodle.
on the House of Lords and Arthur **Balfour** *respectively*

in the House of Commons, 26 June
1907

2 I have no nest-eggs. I am looking for someone else's hen-
roost to rob next year.
in 1908, as Chancellor

Frank Owen *Tempestuous Journey*
(1954)

3 A fully-equipped duke costs as much to keep up as two
Dreadnoughts; and dukes are just as great a terror and
they last longer.

speech at Newcastle, 9 October
1909

4 The best example of the unearned increment is the
hyphen in the Hon. Member's name.
*of William Joynson-Hicks, who had married the daughter of a silk
manufacturer and added her name to his own.*

c.1909, attributed

of the House of Lords, c.1911:

5 A body of five hundred men chosen at random from
amongst the unemployed.

speech at Newcastle, 9 October
1909

6 The great peaks of honour we had forgotten—Duty,
Patriotism, and—clad in glittering white—the great
pinnacle of Sacrifice, pointing like a rugged finger to
Heaven.

speech at Queen's Hall, London, 19
September 1914

7 I would as soon go for a sunny evening stroll round
Walton Heath with a grasshopper, as try to work with
Northcliffe.
of Lord **Northcliffe**, *c.1916*

Frank Owen *Tempestuous Journey*
(1954)

8 At eleven o'clock this morning came to an end the
cruellest and most terrible war that has ever scourged
mankind. I hope we may say that thus, this fateful
morning, came to an end all wars.

in the House of Commons, 11
November 1918

9 What is our task? To make Britain a fit country for
heroes to live in.

speech at Wolverhampton, 23
November 1918

10 M. Clemenceau...is one of the greatest living orators, but
he knows that the finest eloquence is that which gets
things done and the worst is that which delays them.
speech at Paris Peace Conference, 18 January 1919

in *The Times* 20 January 1919

11 Wild men screaming through the keyholes.
of the Versailles Peace Conference

in the House of Commons, 16 April
1919

12 If you want to succeed in politics, you must keep your
conscience well under control.

Lord Riddell diary 23 April 1919

13 Death is the most convenient time to tax rich people.

in *Lord Riddell's Intimate Diary of
the Peace Conference and After,
1918–23* (1933)

1 Unless I am mistaken, by the steps we have taken [in Ireland] we have murder by the throat.

speech at the Mansion House, 9 November 1920

of Arthur **Balfour***'s impact on history:*

2 No more than the whiff of scent on a lady's pocket handkerchief.

Thomas Jones diary 9 June 1922

3 Negotiating with de Valera...is like trying to pick up mercury with a fork.
    to which de Valera replied, 'Why doesn't he use a spoon?'

M. J. MacManus *Eamon de Valera* (1944)

4 Of all the bigotries that savage the human temper there is none so stupid as the anti-Semitic.

Is It Peace? 1923

5 The world is becoming like a lunatic asylum run by lunatics.

in *Observer* 8 January 1933

6 A politician was a person with whose politics you did not agree. When you did agree, he was a statesman.

speech at Central Hall, Westminster, 2 July 1935

7 Neville has a retail mind in a wholesale business.
    of Neville **Chamberlain**

in 1935; David Dilks *Neville Chamberlain* (1984)

after meeting **Hitler** *in 1936:*

8 Führer is the proper name for him. He is a great and wonderful leader.

Frank Owen *Tempestuous Journey* (1954)

9 Winston would go up to his Creator and say that he would very much like to meet His Son, of Whom he had heard a great deal and, if possible, would like to call on the Holy Ghost. Winston *loves* meeting people.
    of Winston **Churchill**

A. J. Sylvester diary 2 January 1937

10 The Government are behaving like a bevy of maiden aunts who have fallen among buccaneers.
    during the Spanish Civil War, when British merchant seamen off the east coast of Spain had been bombed

on 21 June 1938; Peter Rowland *Lloyd George* (1975)

11 The Prime Minister should give an example of sacrifice, because there is nothing which can contribute more to victory than that he should sacrifice the seals of office.
    of Neville **Chamberlain**

in the House of Commons, 7 May 1940

on being told by Lord **Beaverbrook***'s butler that, 'The Lord is out walking':*

12 Ah, on the water, I presume.

Lord Cudlipp letter in *Daily Telegraph* 13 September 1993

13 There is no friendship at the top.

habitual remark, said to be quoting **Gladstone**; A. J. P. Taylor *Lloyd George, Rise and Fall* (1961)

14 Truth against the world.
    Welsh proverb; motto taken on becoming Earl Lloyd-George of Dwyfor, January 1945

Donald McCormick *The Mask of Merlin* (1963)

15 He has sat on the fence so long the iron has entered into his soul.
    of John Simon

attributed

16 He would make a drum out of the skin of his mother in order to sound his own praises.
    of Winston **Churchill**

Peter Rowland *Lloyd George* (1975)

1 One of those revolving lighthouses which radiate   attributed
   momentary gleams of light far out into the surrounding
   gloom, and then suddenly relapse into complete darkness.
   There were no intermediate stages.
   of Kitchener as War Minister

2 Sufficient conscience to bother him, but not sufficient to   A. J. Sylvester *Life with Lloyd*
   keep him straight.   *George* (1975)
   of Ramsay **MacDonald**

Gwilym Lloyd George, Lord Tenby
1894–1967

British Liberal politician, younger son of David **Lloyd George**

3 Politicians are like monkeys. The higher they climb, the   *c.* 1954, attributed; Peter Hennessy
   more revolting are the parts they expose.   at the Annual Dinner of the Fabian
                                                                       Society, 25 November 1995

John Locke 1632–1704
English philosopher

4 Whatsoever...[man] removes out of the state that nature   *Second Treatise of Civil*
   hath provided and left it in, he hath mixed his labour   *Government* (1690)
   with, and joined to it something that is his own, and
   thereby makes it his property.

5 Man...hath by nature a power...to preserve his   *Second Treatise of Civil*
   property—that is, his life, liberty, and estate—against the   *Government* (1690)
   injuries and attempts of other men.

6 Man being...by nature all free, equal, and independent,   *Second Treatise of Civil*
   no one can be put out of this estate, and subjected to the   *Government* (1690)
   political power of another, without his own consent.

7 The great and chief end, therefore, of men's uniting into   *Second Treatise of Civil*
   commonwealths, and putting themselves under   *Government* (1690)
   government, is the preservation of their property.

8 The only way by which any one divests himself of his   *Second Treatise of Civil*
   natural liberty and puts on the bonds of civil society is by   *Government* (1690)
   agreeing with other men to join and unite into
   a community.

9 This power to act according to discretion for the public   *Second Treatise of Civil*
   good, without the prescription of the law, and sometimes   *Government* (1690)
   even against it, is that which is called prerogative.

Henry Cabot Lodge Snr. 1850–1924
American Republican politician

10 Let us have done with British-Americans and Irish-   *The Day We Celebrate (Forefathers'*
   Americans and German-Americans, and so on, and all be   *Day) Address*, New England
   Americans...If a man is going to be an American at all   Society of Brooklyn, 21 December
   let him be so without any qualifying adjectives; and if he   1888; cf. **Roosevelt** 311:14
   is going to be something else, let him drop the word
   American from his person description.

1 It is the flag just as much of the man who was   address, 1915
   naturalized yesterday as of the man whose people have
   been here many generations.

Henry Cabot Lodge Jr. 1902–85

American Republican politician

2 It was those damned tea parties that beat me!   in obituary of Rose **Kennedy** in
     attributing the loss of his 1952 senatorial campaign, against the   *Guardian* 24 January 1995
     national Republican trend, to the tea parties given by Rose
     Kennedy *on behalf of her son, the Democratic candidate John F.*
     Kennedy

Huey Long 1893–1935

American Democratic politician; Governor of Louisiana

3 For the present you can just call me the Kingfish.   *Every Man a King* (1933)

     answering his opponent's supporters, who said their candidate
     had gone barefoot as a boy:
4 I can go Mr Wilson one better; I was born barefoot.   T. Harry Williams *Huey Long* (1969)

5 Oh hell, say that I am *sui generis* and let it go at that.   T. Harry Williams *Huey Long* (1969)
     to journalists attempting to analyse his political personality

6 Bible's the greatest book ever written. But I sure don't   T. Harry Williams *Huey Long* (1969)
   need anybody I can buy for six bits and a chew of
   tobacco to explain it to me. When I need preachers I buy
   'em cheap.

7 The time has come for all good men to rise above   attributed
   principle.

Alice Roosevelt Longworth 1884–1980

daughter of Theodore **Roosevelt**

8 Harding was not a bad man. He was just a slob.   *Crowded Hours* (1933)
     of US President Warren G. **Harding**

Louis XIV (the 'Sun King') 1638–1715

King of France from 1643

9 *L'État c'est moi.*   J. A. Dulaure *Histoire de Paris*
   I am the State.   (1834) vol. 6
     before the Parlement de Paris, 13 April 1655 (probably
     apocryphal)

10 I was nearly kept waiting.   attribution queried, among others,
                                                                     by E. Fournier in *L'Esprit dans
                                                                     l'Histoire* (1857)

11 Every time I create an appointment, I create a hundred   Voltaire *Siècle de Louis XIV* (1768
   malcontents and one ingrate.   ed.) vol. 2

1 The Pyrenees are no more.
   on the accession of his grandson to the throne of Spain, 1700

attributed to Louis by Voltaire in *Siècle de Louis XIV* (1753), but to the Spanish Ambassador to France in the *Mercure Galant* (Paris) November 1700

Louis XVI 1754–93

King of France from 1774; deposed in 1789 on the outbreak of the French Revolution and executed in 1793

diary entry for 14 July 1789, the day of the storming of the Bastille:

2 *Rien.*
   Nothing.

Simon Schama *Citizens* (1989)

Louis XVIII 1755–1824

King of France from 1814; titular king from 1795

3 Remember that there is not one of you who does not carry in his cartridge-pouch the marshal's baton of the duke of Reggio; it is up to you to bring it forth.
   speech to Saint-Cyr cadets, 9 August 1819

in *Moniteur Universel* 10 August 1819

4 Punctuality is the politeness of kings.

in *Souvenirs de J. Lafitte* (1844), attributed

David Low 1891–1963

British political cartoonist and creator of 'Colonel Blimp', proponent of reactionary establishment opinions

5 I have never met anyone who wasn't against war. Even Hitler and Mussolini were, according to themselves.

in *New York Times Magazine* 10 February 1946

Robert Lowe, Viscount Sherbrooke 1811–92

British Liberal politician

6 I believe it will be absolutely necessary that you should prevail on our future masters to learn their letters.
   on the passing of the Reform Bill, popularized as 'We must educate our masters'

in the House of Commons, 15 July 1867

7 The Chancellor of the Exchequer is a man whose duties make him more or less of a taxing machine. He is intrusted with a certain amount of misery which it is his duty to distribute as fairly as he can.

in the House of Commons, 11 April 1870

James Russell Lowell 1819–91

American poet

8 We've a war, an' a debt, an' a flag; an' ef this
   Ain't to be inderpendunt, why, wut on airth is?

The Biglow Papers (Second Series, 1867) no. 4 'A Message of Jeff. Davis in Secret Session'

1 Once to every man and nation comes the moment to decide,
  In the strife of Truth with Falsehood, for the good or evil side.

'The Present Crisis' (1845)

2 Truth forever on the scaffold, Wrong forever on the throne,—
  Yet that scaffold sways the future, and, behind the dim unknown,
  Standeth God within the shadow, keeping watch above his own.

'The Present Crisis' (1845)

Lucan AD 39–65

Roman poet

3 It is not granted to know which man took up arms with more right on his side. Each pleads his cause before a great judge: the winning cause pleased the gods, but the losing one pleased Cato.

Pharsalia

4 There stands the ghost of a great name.
    of Pompey

Pharsalia

5 Thinking nothing done while anything remained to be done.

Pharsalia

Martin Luther 1483–1546

German Protestant theologian

6 Here stand I. I can do no other. God help me. Amen.

speech at the Diet of Worms, 18 April 1521; attributed

7 If I had heard that as many devils would set on me in Worms as there are tiles on the roofs, I should none the less have ridden there.

to the Princes of Saxony, 21 August 1524

Rosa Luxemburg 1871–1919

German revolutionary

8 Freedom is always and exclusively freedom for the one who thinks differently.

Die Russische Revolution (1918)

Robert Lynd 1879–1949

Anglo-Irish essayist and journalist

9 The belief in the possibility of a short decisive war appears to be one of the most ancient and dangerous of human illusions.

attributed

Jonathan Lynn 1943– and Antony Jay 1930–

10 Years of political training and experience had taught him to use twenty words where one would do, to write

editors' note, *Yes Minister* vol. 1 (1981)

millions of words where thousands would suffice, to use
language to blur and fudge the issues and events so that
they become incomprehensible to others. When
incomprehensibility has been achieved by a politician, so
has safety.
   of 'Jim Hacker'

1 'Opposition's about asking awkward questions.' 'Yes...   *Yes Minister* vol. 1 (1981)
   and government's about not answering them.'

2 'Under consideration' means we've lost the file. 'Under   *Yes Minister* vol. 1 (1981)
   active consideration' means we're trying to find it.

3 Ministers need activity. It's their substitute for   *Yes Minister* vol. 1 (1981)
   achievement.

4 The PM—whose motto is...'In Defeat, Malice—in   *Yes Minister* vol. 1 (1981)
   Victory, Revenge!'

5 If you wish to describe a proposal in a way that   *Yes Minister* vol. 1 (1981)
   guarantees that a Minister will reject it, describe it as
   courageous.

6 The Official Secrets Act is not to protect secrets but to   *Yes Minister* vol. 1 (1981)
   protect officials.

7 *Restricted* means it was in the papers yesterday.   *Yes Minister* vol. 2 (1982)
   Confidential means it won't be in the papers till today.

8 Diplomacy is about surviving till the next century—   *Yes Prime Minister* vol. 1 (1986)
   politics is about surviving till Friday afternoon.

9 Collective responsibility means that when we do   *Yes Prime Minister* vol. 2 (1987)
   something popular they all leak the fact that it was their
   idea, and when we do something unpopular they leak
   the fact that they were against it.

10 That's another of those irregular verbs, isn't it? I give   *Yes Prime Minister* vol. 2 (1987)
   confidential briefings; you leak; he has been charged
   under Section 2a of the Official Secrets Act.

   what is known to the Civil Service as the Politicians' Syllogism:
11 Step One: We must do something.   *Yes Prime Minister* vol. 2 (1987)
   Step Two: This is something.
   Step Three: Therefore we must do it.

Douglas MacArthur 1880–1964

American general

12 I came through and I shall return.   in *New York Times* 21 March 1942
   *on reaching Australia, 20 March 1942, having broken through
   Japanese lines en route from Corregidor*

13 In war, indeed, there can be no substitute for victory.   in *Congressional Record* 19 April
                                                            1951, vol. 97

14 I still remember the refrain of one of the most popular   address to a Joint Meeting of
   barracks ballads of that day, which proclaimed most   Congress, 19 April 1951
   proudly that old soldiers never die; they just fade away.
   I now close my military career and just fade away.

Lord Macaulay 1800–59

English Whig politician, historian, and poet
on Macaulay: see **Melbourne** 255:10, **Smith** 344:9

1 Thank you, madam, the agony is abated.
   aged four, having had hot coffee spilt over his legs

   G. O. Trevelyan *Life and Letters of Lord Macaulay* (1876)

2 Obadiah Bind-their-kings-in-chains-and-their-nobles-with-links-of-iron.

   'The Battle of Naseby' (1824)
   fictitious author's name

3 Oh, wherefore come ye forth in triumph from the north,
   With your hands, and your feet, and your raiment all
      red?
   And wherefore doth your rout send forth a joyous shout?
   And whence be the grapes of the wine-press which ye
      tread?

   'The Battle of Naseby' (1824)

4 And the Man of Blood was there, with his long essenced
      hair,
   And Astley, and Sir Marmaduke, and Rupert of the
      Rhine.

   'The Battle of Naseby' (1824)

5 The object of oratory alone is not truth, but persuasion.

   'Essay on Athenian Orators' in *Knight's Quarterly Magazine* August 1824

6 This province of literature [history] is a debatable line. It
   lies on the confines of two distinct territories. It is under
   the jurisdiction of two hostile powers; and like other
   districts similarly situated it is ill-defined, ill-cultivated,
   and ill-regulated. Instead of being equally shared between
   its two rulers, the Reason and the Imagination, it falls
   alternately under the sole and absolute dominion of each.
   It is sometimes fiction. It is sometimes theory.

   'History' (1828)

7 Nothing is so galling to a people not broken in from the
   birth as a paternal, or in other words a meddling
   government, a government which tells them what to
   read and say and eat and drink and wear.

   in *Edinburgh Review* January 1830

8 He has one eminent merit—that of being an enthusiastic
   admirer of mine—so that I may be the Hero of a novel
   yet, under the name of Delamere or Mortimer. Only think
   what an honour.
   of the novelist and politician **Bulwer Lytton**

   letter 5 August 1831

9 He took the praise as a greedy boy takes apple pie, and
   the criticism as a good dutiful boy takes senna-tea.
   of **Bulwer Lytton***, whose novels he had criticized*

   letter 5 August 1831

10 I detest him more than cold boiled veal.
   of the Tory essayist and politician John Wilson Croker

   letter 5 August 1831

11 We must at present do our best to form a class who may
   be interpreters between us and the millions whom we
   govern; a class of persons, Indian in blood and colour,
   but English in taste, in opinions, in morals, and in
   intellect.

   minute, as Member of Supreme Council of India, 2 February 1835

1 Then none was for a party;
   Then all were for the state;
   Then the great man helped the poor,
   And the poor man loved the great:
   Then lands were fairly portioned;
   Then spoils were fairly sold:
   The Romans were like brothers
   In the brave days of old.

Lays of Ancient Rome (1842)
'Horatius'

2 The business of everybody is the business of nobody.

*Essays Contributed to the
Edinburgh Review* (1843) vol. 1
'Hallam'

3 The gallery in which the reporters sit has become
   a fourth estate of the realm.

*Essays Contributed to the
Edinburgh Review* (1843) vol. 1
'Hallam'

4 He knew that the essence of war is violence, and that
   moderation in war is imbecility.

*Essays Contributed to the
Edinburgh Review* (1843) vol. 1
'John Hampden'

of Niccolò **Machiavelli**:

5 Out of his surname they have coined an epithet for
   a knave, and out of his Christian name a synonym for
   the Devil.

*Essays Contributed to the
Edinburgh Review* (1843) vol. 1
'Machiavelli'

6 Many politicians of our time are in the habit of laying it
   down as a self-evident proposition, that no people ought
   to be free till they are fit to use their freedom. The maxim
   is worthy of the fool in the old story, who resolved not to
   go into the water till he had learnt to swim. If men are
   to wait for liberty till they become wise and good in
   slavery, they may indeed wait for ever.

*Essays Contributed to the
Edinburgh Review* (1843) vol. 1
'Milton'

7 On the rich and the eloquent, on nobles and priests, they
   [the Puritans] looked down with contempt: for they
   esteemed themselves rich in a more precious treasure,
   and eloquent in a more sublime language, nobles by the
   right of an earlier creation, and priests by the imposition
   of a mightier hand.

*Essays Contributed to the
Edinburgh Review* (1843) vol. 1
'Milton'

8 We know no spectacle so ridiculous as the British public
   in one of its periodical fits of morality.

*Essays Contributed to the
Edinburgh Review* (1843) vol. 1
'Moore's *Life of Lord Byron*'

9 We have heard it said that five per cent is the natural
   interest of money.

*Essays Contributed to the
Edinburgh Review* (1843) vol. 1
'Southey's Colloquies'

10 With the dead there is no rivalry. In the dead there is no
   change. Plato is never sullen. Cervantes is never petulant.
   Demosthenes never comes unseasonably. Dante never
   stays too long. No difference of political opinion can
   alienate Cicero. No heresy can excite the horror of
   Bossuet.

*Essays Contributed to the
Edinburgh Review* (1843) vol. 2
'Lord Bacon'

11 An acre in Middlesex is better than a principality in
   Utopia.

*Essays Contributed to the
Edinburgh Review* (1843) vol. 2
'Lord Bacon'

1 The rising hope of those stern and unbending Tories.
   of **Gladstone**

*Essays Contributed to the
Edinburgh Review* (1843) vol. 2
'Gladstone on Church and State'

2 The highest intellects, like the tops of mountains, are the
   first to catch and to reflect the dawn.

*Essays Contributed to the
Edinburgh Review* (1843) vol. 2 'Sir
James Mackintosh'

3 The history of England is emphatically the history of
   progress.

*Essays Contributed to the
Edinburgh Review* (1843) vol. 2 'Sir
James Mackintosh'

4 On the day of the accession of George the Third, the
   ascendancy of the Whig party terminated; and on that
   day the purification of the Whig party began.

*Essays Contributed to the
Edinburgh Review* (1843) vol. 2
'William Pitt, Earl of Chatham'

5 The reluctant obedience of distant provinces generally
   costs more than it [the territory] is worth.

*Essays Contributed to the
Edinburgh Review* (1843) vol. 2
'The War of Succession in Spain'

6 Every schoolboy knows who imprisoned Montezuma, and
   who strangled Atahualpa.

*Essays Contributed to the
Edinburgh Review* (1843) vol. 3
'Lord Clive'

7 The Chief Justice was rich, quiet, and infamous.

*Essays Contributed to the
Edinburgh Review* (1843) vol. 3
'Warren Hastings'

of Westminster Abbey:
8 That temple of silence and reconciliation where the
   enmities of twenty generations lie buried.

*Essays Contributed to the
Edinburgh Review* (1843) vol. 3
'Warren Hastings'

9 To my true king I offered free from stain
   Courage and faith; vain faith, and courage vain.

'A Jacobite's Epitaph' (1845)

10 By those white cliffs I never more must see,
   By that dear language which I spake like thee,
   Forget all feuds, and shed one English tear
   O'er English dust. A broken heart lies here.

'A Jacobite's Epitaph' (1845)

11 I shall cheerfully bear the reproach of having descended
   below the dignity of history.

History of England vol. 1 (1849)

12 Thus our democracy was, from an early period, the most
   aristocratic, and our aristocracy the most democratic in
   the world.

History of England vol. 1 (1849)

13 Persecution produced its natural effect on them [Puritans
   and Calvinists]. It found them a sect; it made them
   a faction.

History of England vol. 1 (1849)

14 [Louis XIV] had shown, in an eminent degree, two
   talents invaluable to a prince, the talent of choosing his
   servants well, and the talent of appropriating to himself
   the chief part of the credit of their acts.

History of England vol. 1 (1849)

15 No man is fit to govern great societies who hesitates
   about disobliging the few who have access to him for the
   sake of the many he will never see.

History of England vol. 1 (1849)

1 It was a crime in a child to read by the bedside of a sick parent one of those beautiful collects which had soothed the griefs of forty generations of Christians.

History of England vol. 1 (1849)

2 The Puritan hated bear-baiting, not because it gave pain to the bear, but because it gave pleasure to the spectators.

History of England vol. 1 (1849)

3 It has often been found that profuse expenditure, heavy taxation, absurd commercial restrictions, corrupt tribunals, disastrous wars, seditions, persecutions, conflagrations, inundations, have not been able to destroy capital so fast as the exertions of private citizens have been able to create it.

History of England vol. 1 (1849)

4 In order that he might rob a neighbour whom he had promised to defend, black men fought on the coast of Coromandel, and red men scalped each other by the Great Lakes of North America.

Biographical Essays (1857) 'Frederic the Great'

Eugene McCarthy 1916–

American Democratic politician

5 Being in politics is like being a football coach. You have to be smart enough to understand the game, and dumb enough to think it's important.
   while campaigning for the presidency

in an interview, 1968

Joseph McCarthy 1908–57

American politician and anti-Communist agitator

6 I have here in my hand a list of two hundred and five [people] that were known to the Secretary of State as being members of the Communist Party and who nevertheless are still working and shaping the policy of the State Department.

speech at Wheeling, West Virginia, 9 February 1950

7 McCarthyism is Americanism with its sleeves rolled.

speech in Wisconsin, 1952; Richard Rovere *Senator Joe McCarthy* (1973)

Mary McCarthy 1912–89

American writer

8 Bureaucracy, the rule of no one, has become the modern form of despotism.

in *New Yorker* 18 October 1958

George B. McClellan 1826–85

American soldier and politician

9 All quiet along the Potomac.
   said at the time of the American Civil War

attributed

Colonel McCormick
of the *Chicago Tribune*

1 The British are no longer important enough for me to
dislike.
   *explaining his willingness to give an interview to the British
   journalist Woodrow Wyatt*

J. K. Galbraith *A Life in Our Times*
(1981)

John McCrae 1872–1918
Canadian poet and military physician

2 To you from failing hands we throw
The torch; be yours to hold it high.
If ye break faith with us who die
We shall not sleep, though poppies grow
In Flanders fields.

'In Flanders Fields' (1915)

Ramsay MacDonald 1866–1937
British Labour statesman, Prime Minister 1924, 1929–31, and
1931–5
on MacDonald: see **George V** 149:7, **Lloyd George** 231:2,
Nicolson 272:4; see also **Lamont** 217:2

3 Wars are popular. Contractors make profits; the
aristocracy glean honour.

in *Labour Leader* 11 March 1915

4 A terror decreed by a Secret Committee is child's play
compared with a terror instituted by 'lawful authority'.

in *Socialist Review* January-March
1921

5 We hear war called murder. It is not: it is suicide.

in *Observer* 4 May 1930

6 Tomorrow every Duchess in London will be wanting to
kiss me!
   after forming the National Government, 25 August 1931

Viscount Snowden *An
Autobiography* (1934) vol. 2

7 A body representing the citizenship of the whole nation is
charged with so much that it can do nothing swiftly and
well.

Carl Cohen *Parliament and
Democracy* (1962)

Mick McGahey
British miner and trade unionist

8 He mistakes a mass meeting for a mass movement.
   of the President of the NUM, Arthur Scargill

in *Independent* 10 March 1990

George McGovern 1922–
American Democratic politician, presidential candidate in 1972

9 Sometimes, when they say you're ahead of your time, it's
just a polite way of saying you have a real bad sense of
timing.

in *Observer* 18 March 1990
'Sayings of the Week'

Lord McGregor 1921–

British sociologist

1　An odious exhibition of journalists dabbling their fingers　*in The Times* 9 June 1992
　 in the stuff of other people's souls.
　　　on press coverage of the marriage of the Prince and Princess of
　　　Wales, speaking as Chairman of the Press Complaints
　　　Commission

Niccolò Machiavelli 1469–1527

Florentine statesman and political philosopher

2　Men should be either treated generously or destroyed,　*The Prince* (1513)
　 because they take revenge for slight injuries—for heavy
　 ones they cannot.

3　This leads to a debate: is it better to be loved than feared,　*The Prince* (1513)
　 or the reverse? The answer is that it is desirable to be
　 both, but because it is difficult to join them together, it is
　 much safer for a prince to be feared than loved, if he is to
　 fail in one of the two.

4　Let no one oppose this belief of mine with that well-worn　*The Prince* (written 1513)
　 proverb: 'He who builds on the people builds on mud.'

5　Since, then, a prince is necessitated to play the animal　*The Prince* (1513)
　 well, he chooses among the beasts the fox and the lion,
　 because the lion does not protect himself from traps; the
　 fox does not protect himself from wolves. The prince
　 must be a fox, therefore, to recognize the traps and a lion
　 to frighten the wolves.

6　So long as the great majority of men are not deprived of　*The Prince* (1513)
　 either property or honour, they are satisfied.

7　There is no other way for securing yourself against　*The Prince* (1513)
　 flatteries except that men understand that they do not
　 offend you by telling you the truth; but when everybody
　 can tell you the truth, you fail to get respect.

8　In seizing a state, the usurper ought to examine closely　*The Prince* (1513)
　 into all those injuries which it is necessary for him to
　 inflict, and to do them all at one stroke, so as not to have
　 to repeat them daily; and thus by not unsettling men he
　 will be able to reassure them, and win them to himself
　 by benefits. He who does otherwise, either from timidity
　 or evil advice, is always compelled to keep the knife in
　 his hand.

9　Princes ought to leave affairs of reproach to the　*The Prince* (1513)
　 management of others, and keep those of grace in their
　 own hands.

10　It is necessary for him who lays out a state and arranges　*Discorsi Supra la Prima Deca di*
　 laws for it to presuppose that all men are evil and that　*Tito Livio* (1513–17)
　 they are always going to act according to the wickedness
　 of their spirits whenever they have free scope.

11　Success or failure lies in conforming to the times.　*Discourse on Livy* (1518)

1 And if, to be sure, sometimes you need to conceal a fact
   with words, do it in such a way that it does not become
   known, or, if it does become known, that you have
   a ready and quick defence.

   'Advice to Raffaello Girolami when
   he went as Ambassador to the
   Emperor' (October 1522)

2 Wars begin when you will, but they do not end when
   you please.

   History of Florence (1521–4)

James Mackintosh 1765–1832

Scottish philosopher and historian

3 Men are never so good or so bad as their opinions.

   *Dissertation on the Progress of
   Ethical Philosophy* (1830) 'Jeremy
   Bentham'

4 The Commons, faithful to their system, remained in
   a wise and masterly inactivity.
   of the French Commons

   Vindiciae Gallicae (1791)

Donald McLachlan

first Editor of the *Sunday Telegraph*

on the government of Anthony Eden:
5 Most Conservatives, and almost certainly some of the
   wiser Trade Union leaders, are waiting to feel the *smack
   of firm government*.

   editorial comment in *Sunday
   Telegraph* 3 January 1956

Iain Macleod 1913–70

British Conservative politician
on Macleod: see **Butler** 70:6, **Foot** 138:3, **Salisbury** 319:3

6 I want to deal closely and with relish with the vulgar,
   crude and intemperate speech to which the House of
   Commons has just listened.
   *of Aneurin **Bevan**'s speech during the second reading debate on
   the National Health Service Bill*

   in the House of Commons, 27
   March 1952

7 To have a debate on the National Health Service without
   the right hon. Gentleman [Aneurin Bevan] would be like
   putting on Hamlet with no one in the part of the First
   Gravedigger.

   in the House of Commons, 27
   March 1952

8 It is some measure of the tightness of the magic circle on
   this occasion that neither the Chancellor of the
   Exchequer nor the Leader of the House of Commons had
   any inkling of what was happening.
   *of the 'evolvement' of Alec **Douglas-Home** as Conservative
   leader after the resignation of Harold **Macmillan***

   in *The Spectator* 17 January 1964

9 One does not expect to have many people with one in the
   last ditch.
   *on remaining firm in his refusal to serve in Lord **Home**'s
   government of 1963 after his support of Rab **Butler**, despite
   seeing others retract or waver*

   in *Dictionary of National Biography*

1 The Conservative Party always in time forgives those   in *The Spectator* 21 February 1964
  who were wrong. Indeed often, in time, they forgive
  those who were right.

2 Revolutions in this country, and especially within the   in *Spectator* 30 July 1965
  Tory party, are rarely plotted. They just happen.
   of the Conservative leadership election of 1965

   comparing his political approach with that of Enoch **Powell**:
3 I am a fellow-traveller but sometimes I leave Powell's   in 1965; Nigel Fisher *Iain Macleod*
  train a few stations down the line before it reaches, and   (1973)
  sometimes crashes into, the terminal buffers.

4 John Fitzgerald Kennedy described himself, in a brilliant   in the House of Commons, 1 March
  phrase, as an idealist without illusions. I would describe   1966; cf. **Kennedy** 205:10
  the Prime Minister as an illusionist without ideals.

5 In Parliament it should not only be the duty but the   in *The Spectator* 26 August 1966
  pleasure of the Opposition to oppose whenever they
  reasonably can.

6 I like seeing my political opponents standing shoulder to   attributed, 1967
  shoulder on a burning deck.

7 I cannot help it if every time the Opposition are asked to   in *Dictionary of National Biography*
  name their weapons they pick boomerangs.

8 I don't run in a race to run second.   Nigel Fisher *Iain Macleod* (1973)

Marshall McLuhan 1911–80

Canadian communications scholar

9 Television brought the brutality of war into the comfort   in *Montreal Gazette* 16 May 1975
  of the living room. Vietnam was lost in the living rooms
  of America—not the battlefields of Vietnam.

Comte de Macmahon 1808–93

French military commander; President of the Third Republic,
1873–9

10 *J'y suis, j'y reste.*   G. Hanotaux *Histoire de la France*
   Here I am, and here I stay.   *Contemporaine* (1903–8) vol. 2
    at the taking of the Malakoff fortress during the Crimean War, 8
    September 1855

William McMahon 1908–88

Australian statesman, Prime Minister 1971–2

11 Politics is trying to get into office.   L. Oakes and D. Solomon *The*
                                                                 Making of an Australian Prime
                                                                 Minister (1973)

Harold Macmillan 1894–1986

British Conservative statesman, Prime Minister 1957–63
on Macmillan: see **Bevan** 41:7, **Birch** 45:8, 45:10, **Headlam**
172:2, **Hennessy** 175:2, **Levin** 222:5, 222:6, 222:11,
Macleod 242:8, **Thorpe** 364:7

1 Toryism has always been a form of paternal socialism.
   in 1936

Anthony Sampson *Macmillan* (1967)

2 We...are Greeks in this American empire...We must
run the Allied Forces HQ as the Greeks ran the
operations of the Emperor Claudius.
   to Richard **Crossman** *in 1944, after French North Africa had*
   become an American sphere of influence, with **Eisenhower** *as*
   Supreme Allied Commander

in *Sunday Telegraph* 9 February 1964

3 Germany, now cast down, despised, shunned like an
unclean thing, will once more be courted by each of the
two groups, and from a starving outcast she will become
the pampered courtesan of Europe, selling her favours to
the highest bidder.

in the House of Commons, 20 February 1946

4 We have not overthrown the divine right of Kings to fall
down before the divine right of experts.

in 1950; Peter Hennessy *Whitehall* (1990)

5 There ain't gonna be no war.
   at a London press conference, 24 July 1955, following the
   Geneva summit

in *News Chronicle* 25 July 1955

6 Forever poised between a cliché and an indiscretion.
   on the life of a Foreign Secretary

in *Newsweek* 30 April 1956

7 Let us be frank about it: most of our people have never
had it so good. Go around the country, go to the
industrial towns, go to the farms, and you'll see a state
of prosperity such as we have never had in my lifetime—
nor indeed ever in the history of this country. What is
beginning to worry some of us is 'Is it too good to be
true?' or perhaps I should say 'Is it too good to last?'
   'You Never Had It So Good' was the Democratic Party slogan
   during the 1952 US election campaign

speech at Bedford, 20 July 1957

8 I thought the best thing to do was to settle up these little
local difficulties, and then turn to the wider vision of the
Commonwealth.
   statement at London airport on leaving for a Commonwealth
   tour, 7 January 1958, following the resignation of the Chancellor
   of the Exchequer and others

in *The Times* 8 January 1958

9 Do not be impatient with the majors in the party; all
regiments have need of majors.
   advice to newly elected MPs, at an East India Club dinner in 1959

Julian Critchley *A Bag of Boiled Sweets* (1994)

10 Revolt by all means; but only on one issue at a time; to
do more would be to confuse the whips.
   advice to newly elected MPs

Julian Critchley *A Bag of Boiled Sweets* (1994)

11 He [Aneurin Bevan] enjoys prophesying the imminent fall
of the capitalist system and is prepared to play a part,
any part, in its burial, except that of mute.

Michael Foot *Aneurin Bevan* (1962)

1 The wind of change is blowing through this continent, and, whether we like it or not, this growth of [African] national consciousness is a political fact.

speech at Cape Town, 3 February 1960

2 Can we say that with fifteen representatives, Ambassadors or Ministers, in Nato acting in unanimity, the deterrent would continue to be credible? There might be one finger on the trigger. There would be fifteen fingers on the safety catch.

attributed, 1960

3 As usual the Liberals offer a mixture of sound and original ideas. Unfortunately none of the sound ideas is original and none of the original ideas is sound.

speech to London Conservatives, 7 March 1961

4 A successful [political] television show seems to be more and more a cross between a music-hall turn and a scene in a torture-chamber.

speech to the Parliamentary Press Gallery, 14 March 1962

5 [They are a] strange people, tortured by material success and affluence.
   of the British, in a confidential memorandum on his possible successors, 1963

in *Independent* 1 January 1995

6 I was determined that no British government should be brought down by the action of two tarts.
   comment on the Profumo affair, July 1963

Anthony Sampson *Macmillan* (1967)

7 Power? It's like a Dead Sea fruit. When you achieve it, there is nothing there.

Anthony Sampson *The New Anatomy of Britain* (1971); cf. **Levin** 222:11

8 Churchill was fundamentally what the English call unstable—by which they mean anybody who has that touch of genius which is inconvenient in normal times.

attributed, 1975

9 There are three bodies no sensible man directly challenges: the Roman Catholic Church, the Brigade of Guards and the National Union of Mineworkers.

in *Observer* 22 February 1981; cf. **Baldwin** 29:12

of the office of Prime Minister:
10 Sometimes the strain is awful, you have to resort to Jane Austen.

in the Butler Papers; Peter Hennessy *The Hidden Wiring* (1995)

11 First of all the Georgian silver goes, and then all that nice furniture that used to be in the saloon. Then the Canalettos go.
   speech on privatization to the Tory Reform Group, 8 November 1985; often quoted as 'selling the family silver'

in *The Times* 9 November 1985

12 He would have been marvellous in medieval politics, creeping about the Vatican; a tremendous intriguer, he always had some marvellous plan...and he loved the press.
   of Rab **Butler**

Alistair Horne *Macmillan* (1988) vol. 1

13 The only quality needed for an MP is the ability to write a good letter.

Julian Critchley *A Bag of Boiled Sweets* (1994)

14 It has always seemed to me more artistic, when the curtain falls on the last performance, to accept the inevitable *E finita la commedia*. It is tempting, perhaps,

At the End of the Day (1973)

but unrewarding to hang about the greenroom after final
retirement from the stage.

James Madison 1751–1836

American Democratic Republican statesman, 4th President of
the US 1809–17

1 Liberty is to faction what air is to fire, an ailment   *The Federalist* (1787)
without which it instantly expires. But it could not be
less folly to abolish liberty, which is essential to political
life, because it nourishes faction than it would be to wish
the annihilation of air, which is essential to animal life,
because it imparts to fire its destructive agency.

2 The diversity in the faculties of men, from which the   *The Federalist* (1787)
rights of property originate, is not less an insuperable
obstacle to a uniformity of interests. The protection of
these faculties is the first object of government. From the
protection of different and unequal faculties of acquiring
property, the possession of different degrees and kinds of
property immediately results.

3 By a faction, understand a number of citizens, whether   *The Federalist* (1787)
amounting to a majority or minority of the whole, who
are united and actuated by some common impulse of
passion, or of interest, adverse to the rights of other
citizens, or to the permanent and aggregate interests of
the community.

4 The most common and durable source of factions has   *The Federalist* (1787)
been the various and unequal distribution of property.

5 The accumulation of all powers, legislative, executive,   *The Federalist* (1787)
and judiciary, in the same hands, whether of one, a few,
or many, and whether hereditary, self-appointed, or
elective, may justly be pronounced the very definition of
tyranny.

6 I believe there are more instances of the abridgement of   speech in the Virginia Convention,
the freedom of the people by gradual and silent   16 June 1788
encroachment of those in power than by violent and
sudden usurpations.

7 In framing a government, which is to be administered by   attributed
men over men, the great difficulty lies in this: you must
first enable the government to control the governed, and
in the next place oblige it to control itself.

John Maffey 1877–1969

British diplomat

as British Ambassador to Dublin:
8 Phrases make history here.   letter 21 May 1945

William Connor Magee 1821–91

English prelate

1   It would be better that England should be free than that   in the House of Lords, 2 May 1872
    England should be compulsorily sober.
    on the Intoxicating Liquor Bill

Magna Carta

Political charter signed by King John at Runnymede, 1215

2   That the English Church shall be free.   Clause 1

3   No free man shall be taken or imprisoned or dispossessed,   Clause 39
    or outlawed or exiled, or in any way destroyed, nor will
    we go upon him, nor will we send against him except by
    the lawful judgement of his peers or by the law of the
    land.

4   To no man will we sell, or deny, or delay, right or   Clause 40
    justice.

Alex Magowan

Councillor for Newtonabbey, Northern Ireland

5   A councillor is like a mushroom. You're kept in the dark   attributed, 1974
    and now and again manure is thrown over you.

Alfred T. Mahan 1840–1914

American naval officer and historian

6   Those far distant, storm-beaten ships, upon which the   *The Influence of Sea Power upon*
    Grand Army never looked, stood between it and the   *the French Revolution and Empire*
    dominion of the world.   *1793–1812* (1892) vol. 2

Norman Mailer 1923–

American novelist and essayist

7   All the security around the American President is just to   in *Sunday Telegraph* 4 March 1990
    make sure the man who shoots him gets caught.

John Major 1943–

British Conservative statesman, Prime Minister 1990–7
on Major: see **Blair** 49:1, **Thatcher** 362:11

8   The first requirement of politics is not intellect or stamina   in *Daily Express* 25 July 1989
    but patience. Politics is a very long-run game and the
    tortoise will usually beat the hare.

9   If the policy isn't hurting, it isn't working.   speech in Northampton, 27
                                                                      October 1989

10 If I sounded lukewarm about our commitment to enter   in *Independent* 24 March 1990
    the European exchange rate mechanism it was because of
    a frog in my throat.

1 Society needs to condemn a little more and understand a little less.

interview with Mail on Sunday 21 February 1993

2 Fifty years on from now, Britain will still be the country of long shadows on county [cricket] grounds, warm beer, invincible green suburbs, dog lovers, and—as George Orwell said—old maids bicycling to Holy Communion through the morning mist.

speech to the Conservative Group for Europe, 22 April 1993; cf. Orwell 278:7

3 It is time to get back to basics: to self-discipline and respect for the law, to consideration for others, to accepting responsibility for yourself and your family, and not shuffling it off on the state.

speech to the Conservative Party Conference, 8 October 1993

4 I could name eight people—half of those eight are barmy. How many apples short of a picnic?
    of Conservative critics

on 19 September 1993

Joseph de Maistre 1753–1821
French writer and diplomat

5 Every country has the government it deserves.

letter 15 August 1811

Bernard Malamud 1914–86
American novelist and short-story writer

6 There's no such thing as an unpolitical man, especially a Jew.

The Fixer (1966)

Malcolm X 1925–65
American civil rights campaigner

7 If you're born in America with a black skin, you're born in prison.

in an interview, June 1963

8 We are not fighting for integration, nor are we fighting for separation. We are fighting for recognition as human beings. We are fighting for...human rights.

Black Revolution, speech in New York, 1964

Thomas Robert Malthus 1766–1834
English political economist

9 Population, when unchecked, increases in a geometrical ratio. Subsistence only increases in an arithmetical ratio.

Essay on the Principle of Population (1798)

10 The perpetual struggle for room and food.

Essay on the Principle of Population (1798)

11 A man who is born into a world already possessed, if he cannot get subsistence from his parents on whom he has a just demand, and if the society do not want his labour, has no claim of *right* to the smallest portion of food, and, in fact, has no business to be where he is. At Nature's mighty feast there is no vacant cover for him.

Essay on the Principle of Population (1803 ed.)

Earl of Manchester 1602–71

politician and Parliamentary commander in the Civil War

1 If we beat the King ninety-nine times, yet he is king still
and so will his posterity be after him; but if the king beat
us once we shall all be hanged, and our posterity made
slaves.
 at a Parliamentary Council-of-War, 10 November 1644

in *Calendar of State Papers,
Domestic* 1644–5

Lord Mancroft 1914–87

British Conservative politician

2 Cricket—a game which the English, not being a spiritual
people, have invented in order to give themselves some
conception of eternity.

Bees in Some Bonnets (1979)

Nelson Mandela 1918–

South African politician and African National Congress activist;
President since 1994

3 Through its imperialist system Britain brought about
untold suffering of millions of people. And this is an
historical fact. To be able to admit this would increase
the respect, you know, which we have for British
institutions.

in *Guardian* 2 April 1990

Winnie Mandela 1934–

South African political activist

4 With that stick of matches, with our necklace, we shall
liberate this country.
 *speech in black townships, 14 April 1986; a 'necklace' was a tyre
 soaked or filled with petrol, placed around a victim's neck, and
 set alight*

in *Guardian* 15 April 1986

John Manners, Duke of Rutland 1818–1906

English Tory politician and writer

5 Let wealth and commerce, laws and learning die,
But leave us still our old nobility!

England's Trust (1841)

Lord Mansfield 1705–93

Scottish lawyer and politician

6 The constitution does not allow reasons of state to
influence our judgements: God forbid it should! We must
not regard political consequences; however formidable
soever they might be: if rebellion was the certain
consequence, we are bound to say '*fiat justitia, ruat
caelum*'.

Rex v. Wilkes, 8 June 1768, in *The
English Reports* (1909) vol. 98; cf.
Adams 4:6

1 Consider what you think justice requires, and decide accordingly. But never give your reasons; for your judgement will probably be right, but your reasons will certainly be wrong.

advice to a newly appointed colonial governor ignorant in the law

Lord Campbell *The Lives of the Chief Justices of England* (1849) vol. 2

Mao Zedong 1893–1976

Chinese statesman, chairman of the Communist Party of the Chinese People's Republic 1949–76 and head of state 1949–59

2 A revolution is not the same as inviting people to dinner, or writing an essay, or painting a picture.

report, March 1927

3 Politics is war without bloodshed while war is politics with bloodshed.

lecture, 1938

4 Every Communist must grasp the truth, 'Political power grows out of the barrel of a gun'.

speech, 6 November 1938

5 The atom bomb is a paper tiger which the United States reactionaries use to scare people. It looks terrible, but in fact it isn't...All reactionaries are paper tigers.

interview, 1946

6 Letting a hundred flowers blossom and a hundred schools of thought contend is the policy for promoting progress in the arts and the sciences and a flourishing socialist culture in our land.

speech in Peking, 27 February 1957

7 People of the world, unite and defeat the US aggressors and all their running dogs!

'Statement Supporting the People of the Congo against US Aggression' 28 November 1964

William Learned Marcy 1786–1857

American politician

8 The politicians of New York...see nothing wrong in the rule, that to the victor belong the spoils of the enemy.

speech to the Senate, 25 January 1832

Marie-Antoinette 1755–93

Queen consort of Louis XVI

9 Let them eat cake.

on being told that her people had no bread

attributed; in *Confessions* (1740) Rousseau refers to a similar remark being a well-known saying; in *Relation d'un Voyage à Bruxelles et à Coblentz en 1791* (1823), Louis XVIII attributes 'Why don't they eat pastry?' to Marie-Thérèse (1638–83), wife of Louis XIV

George C. Marshall 1880–1959

American general and statesman, who as US Secretary of State (1947–9) initiated the programme of economic aid to European countries known as the Marshall Plan

1 If man does find the solution for world peace it will be the most revolutionary reversal of his record we have ever known.

biennal report of the Chief of Staff, United States Army, 1 September 1945

2 Our policy is directed not against any country or doctrine but against hunger, poverty, desperation and chaos. Its purpose should be the revival of a working economy in the world so as to permit the emergence of political and social conditions in which free institutions can exist.
   announcing the Marshall Plan

address at Harvard, 5 June 1947

John Marshall 1755–1835

American jurist

3 The power to tax involves the power to destroy.

in *McCulloch v. Maryland* (1819)

4 The people made the Constitution, and the people can unmake it. It is the creature of their own will, and lives only by their will.

in *Cohens v. Virginia* (1821)

Thomas R. Marshall 1854–1925

American politician

5 What this country needs is a really good 5-cent cigar.

in *New York Tribune* 4 January 1920

José Martí 1853–95

6 The spirit of a government must be that of the country. The form of a government must come from the make-up of the country. Government is nothing but the balance of the natural elements of a country.

Our America (1891)

Andrew Marvell 1621–78

English poet

7 *He* nothing common did or mean
Upon that memorable scene:
But with his keener eye
The axe's edge did try:
Nor called the gods with vulgar spite
To vindicate his helpless right,
But bowed his comely head,
Down as upon a bed.
   on the execution of **Charles I**

'An Horatian Ode upon Cromwell's Return from Ireland' (written 1650)

8 And now the Irish are ashamed
To see themselves in one year tamed:

'An Horatian Ode upon Cromwell's Return from Ireland' (written 1650)

So much one man can do,
That does both act and know.

1 Choosing each stone, and poising every weight,
Trying the measures of the breadth and height;
Here pulling down, and there erecting new,
Founding a firm state by proportions true.

'The First Anniversary of the
Government under His Highness
the Lord Protector, 1655'

Karl Marx 1818–83

German political philosopher; founder of modern Communism

2 Religion...is the opium of the people.

*A Contribution to the Critique of
Hegel's Philosophy of Right*
(1843–4) introduction

3 The philosophers have only interpreted the world in
various ways; the point is to change it.

Theses on Feuerbach (written
1845)

4 Hegel says somewhere that all great events and
personalities in world history reappear in one fashion or
another. He forgot to add: the first time as tragedy, the
second as farce.

*The Eighteenth Brumaire of Louis
Bonaparte* (1852)

5 What I did that was new was to prove...that the class
struggle necessarily leads to the dictatorship of the
proletariat.
*the phrase 'dictatorship of the proletariat' had been used earlier
in the Constitution of the World Society of Revolutionary
Communists (1850), signed by Marx and others*

letter to Georg Weydemeyer 5
March 1852; Marx claimed that the
phrase had been coined by
Auguste Blanqui (1805–81), but it
has not been found in this form in
Blanqui's work

6 Mankind always sets itself only such problems as it can
solve; since, looking at the matter more closely, it will
always be found that the task itself arises only when the
material conditions for its solution already exist or are at
least in the process of formation.

*A Contribution to the Critique of
Political Economy* (1859) preface

7 It is not the consciousness of men that determines their
being, but, on the contrary, their social being that
determines their consciousness.

*A Contribution to the Critique of
Political Economy* (1859) preface

8 It is the ultimate aim of this work, to lay bare the
economic law of motion of modern society.

Das Kapital (1st German ed., 1867)
preface (25 July 1865)

9 From each according to his abilities, to each according to
his needs.

Critique of the Gotha Programme
(written 1875, but of earlier origin);
see Morelly *Code de la nature*
(1755) , and J. J. L. Blanc
Organisation du travail (1839)
(who, in quoting Saint-Simon,
rejects the notion) for possible
sources

10 All I know is that I am not a Marxist.

attributed in a letter from Friedrich
Engels to Conrad Schmidt, 5
August 1890

Karl Marx 1818–83 and **Friedrich Engels**
1820–95

Co-founders of modern Communism

1   A spectre is haunting Europe—the spectre of   *The Communist Manifesto* (1848)
    Communism.   opening words

2   The history of all hitherto existing society is the history   *The Communist Manifesto* (1848)
    of class struggles.

3   In place of the old bourgeois society, with its classes and   *The Communist Manifesto* (1848)
    class antagonists, we shall have an association, in which
    the free development of each is the free development of
    all.

4   The proletarians have nothing to lose but their chains.   *The Communist Manifesto* (1848)
    They have a world to win. WORKING MEN OF ALL   *ad fin.*
    COUNTRIES UNITE
      often quoted as 'Workers of the world, unite!'

Queen Mary 1867–1953

Queen Consort of George V

5   *This* is a pretty kettle of fish!   James Pope-Hennessy *Life of*
      to the Prime Minister, Stanley **Baldwin***, after* **Edward VIII** *had*   *Queen Mary* (1959)
      told her that he was prepared to give up the throne to marry Mrs
      Simpson

6   All *this* thrown away for *that.*   David Duff *George and Elizabeth*
      on returning home to Marlborough House, London after the   (1983)
      abdication of her son, King **Edward VIII***, December 1936*

7   I do not think you have ever realised the shock, which   letter to the Duke of Windsor, the
    the attitude you took up caused your family and the   former **Edward VIII**, July 1938
    whole nation. It seemed inconceivable to those who had
    made such sacrifices during the war that you, as their
    King, refused a lesser sacrifice.

Mary, Queen of Scots 1542–87

Queen of Scotland, 1542–67

8   *En ma fin git mon commencement.*   quoted in a letter from William
    In my end is my beginning.   Drummond of Hawthornden to Ben
      motto embroidered with an emblem of her mother, Mary of   Jonson in 1619
      Guise

Mary Tudor 1516–58

Queen of England from 1553

9   When I am dead and opened, you shall find 'Calais' lying   in *Holinshed's Chronicles* vol. 4
    in my heart.   (1808)

Philip Massinger 1583–1640

English playwright

1 Ambition, in a private man a vice,
Is in a prince the virtue.

The Bashful Lover (licensed 1636, published 1655)

2   Greatness, with private men
Esteemed a blessing, is to me a curse;
And we, whom, for our high births, they conclude
The only freemen, are the only slaves.
Happy the golden mean!

The Great Duke of Florence (licensed 1627, printed 1635)

Henry William Massingham 1860–1924

British journalist; Editor of the *Nation*

3 To me there are few spectacles more melancholy than that of dear old C. P. Scott wearily dredging in a foul pool for the soul of Lloyd George.
of the attempts by C. P. Scott, editor of the Manchester Guardian, *to find a saving word for* Lloyd George *during the last days of the Coalition in 1922*

Vivian Phillipps *My Days and Ways* (1943)

W. Somerset Maugham 1874–1965

British novelist, short-story writer, and dramatist

4 The geniality of the politician who for years has gone out of his way to be cordial with everyone he meets.

A Writer's Notebook (1949) written in 1938

James Maxton 1885–1946

British Labour politician

5 All I say is, if you cannot ride two horses you have no right in the circus.
opposing disaffiliation of the Scottish Independent Labour Party from the Labour Party, often quoted as 'no right in the bloody circus'

in *Daily Herald* 12 January 1931

Horace Maybray-King 1901–86

British Labour politician; Speaker of the House of Commons

6 One of the myths of the British Parliament is that there are three parties there. I can assure you from bitter personal experience there are 629.

in *Observer* 9 October 1966 'Sayings of the Week'

Jonathan Mayhew 1720–66

American divine

7 Rulers have no authority from God to do mischief.

A Discourse Concerning Unlimited Submission and Non-Resistance to the Higher Powers (1750)

1 As soon as the prince sets himself up above the law, he loses the king in the tyrant; he does to all intents and purpose unking himself…And in such cases, has no more right to be obeyed, than any inferior officer who acts beyond his commission.

A Discourse Concerning Unlimited Submission and Non-Resistance to the Higher Powers (1750)

Catherine de' Medici 1518–89

Queen Consort of France, wife of Henri II

2 A false report, if believed during three days, may be of great service to a government.

Isaac D'Israeli *Curiosities of Literature* 2nd series (1849) vol. 2; perhaps apocryphal

Robert Megarry 1910–

3 Whereas in England all is permitted that is not expressly prohibited, it has been said that in Germany all is prohibited unless expressly permitted and in France all is permitted that is expressly prohibited. In the European Common Market (as it then was) no-one knows what is permitted and it all costs more.

'Law and Lawyers in a Permissive Society' (5th Riddell Lecture delivered in Lincoln's Inn Hall 22 March 1972)

Lord Melbourne 1779–1848

British Whig politician; Prime Minister 1834, 1835–41

4 What all the wise men promised has not happened, and what all the d—d fools said would happen has come to pass.
    of the Catholic Emancipation Act (1829)

H. Dunckley *Lord Melbourne* (1890)

5 I have always thought complaints of ill-usage contemptible, whether from a seduced disappointed girl or a turned-out Prime Minister.
    on being dismissed by William IV

Emily Eden letter to Mrs Lister, 23 November 1834

6 If left out he would be dangerous, but if taken in, he would be simply destructive.
    when forming his second administration, Melbourne omitted the former Lord Chancellor, **Brougham**

Lord David Cecil *Lord M* (1954)

7 You domineered too much, you interfered too much with other departments, you encroached upon the provinces of the Prime Minister, you worked, as I believe, with the Press in a manner unbecoming to the dignity of your station.
    letter to the former Lord Chancellor, **Brougham**, *explaining why he had been omitted from Melbourne's second administration*

Lord David Cecil *Lord M* (1954)

8 Damn it! Another Bishop dead! I believe they die to vex me.

Lord David Cecil *Lord M* (1954)

9 God help the Minister that meddles with art!

Lord David Cecil *Lord M* (1954)

10 I wish I was as cocksure of anything as Tom Macaulay is of everything.

Earl Cowper *Preface to Lord Melbourne's Papers* (1889)

1 Nobody ever did anything very foolish except from some strong principle.

Lord David Cecil *The Young Melbourne* (1939)

2 Now, is it to lower the price of corn, or isn't it? It is not much matter which we say, but mind, we must all say *the same*.

at the end of a Cabinet meeting to agree a fixed tariff for corn; Melbourne is said to have put his back to the door and only opened it when they agreed

Walter Bagehot *The English Constitution* (1867)

3 Things have come to a pretty pass when religion is allowed to invade the sphere of private life.

on hearing an evangelical sermon

G. W. E. Russell *Collections and Recollections* (1898)

4 What I want is men who will support me when I am in the wrong.

replying to a politician who said 'I will support you as long as you are in the right'

Lord David Cecil *Lord M* (1954)

5 When in doubt what should be done, do nothing.

Lord David Cecil *Lord M* (1954)

6 The whole duty of government is to prevent crime and to preserve contracts.

Lord David Cecil *Lord M* (1954)

David Mellor 1949–

British Conservative politician

7 I do believe the popular press is drinking in the last chance saloon.

interview on *Hard News* (Channel 4), 21 December 1989

H. L. Mencken 1880–1956

American journalist and literary critic

8 Democracy is the theory that the common people know what they want, and deserve to get it good and hard.

A Little Book in C major (1916)

9 The whole aim of practical politics is to keep the populace alarmed (and hence clamorous to be led to safety) by menacing it with an endless series of hobgoblins, all of them imaginary.

In Defence of Women (1923)

10 A good politician is quite as unthinkable as an honest burglar.

Prejudices 4th series (1925)

11 No one in this world, so far as I know—and I have searched the records for years, and employed agents to help me—has ever lost money by underestimating the intelligence of the great masses of the plain people.

in *Chicago Tribune* 19 September 1926

12 The saddest life is that of a political aspirant under democracy. His failure is ignominious and his success is disgraceful.

in *Baltimore Evening Sun* 9 December 1929

13 He [Calvin Coolidge] slept more than any other President, whether by day or by night. Nero fiddled, but Coolidge only snored.

in *American Mercury* April 1933

14 If there had been any formidable body of cannibals in the country he would have promised to provide them with

in *Baltimore Sun* 7 November 1948

free missionaries fattened at the taxpayer's expense.
of Harry **Truman***'s success in the 1948 presidential campaign*

1 Nothing is so abject and pathetic as a politician who has
   lost his job, save only a retired stud-horse.   *Chrestomathy* (1949)

2 Puritanism. The haunting fear that someone, somewhere,   *Chrestomathy* (1949)
   may be happy.

3 A government can never be the impersonal thing   *Minority Report* (1956)
   described in text-books. It is simply a group of men like
   any other. In every 100 of the men composing it there
   are two who are honest and intelligent, ten obvious
   scoundrels, and 88 poor fish.

4 Under democracy one party always devotes its chief   *Minority Report* (1956)
   energies to trying to prove that the other party is unfit to
   rule—and both commonly succeed, and are right.

5 The worst government is often the most moral. One   *Minority Report* (1956)
   composed of cynics is often very tolerant and humane.
   But when fanatics are on top there is no limit to
   oppression.

Jean Meslier *c.*1664–1733

French priest

6 I remember, on this matter, the wish made once by an   *Testament* (1864); cf.
   ignorant, uneducated man...He said he wished...that all   **Diderot** 116:1
   the great men in the world and all the nobility could be
   hanged, and strangled with the guts of priests. For
   myself...I wish I could have the strength of Hercules to
   purge the world of all vice and sin, and to have the
   pleasure of destroying all those monsters of error and sin
   [priests] who make all the peoples of the world groan so
   pitiably.
   often quoted as, 'I should like...the last king to be strangled
   with the guts of the last priest'

Prince Metternich 1773–1859

Austrian statesman

7 Italy is a geographical expression.   *Mémoires, Documents, etc. de*
   discussing the Italian question with **Palmerston** *in 1847*   *Metternich publiés par son fils*
                                                                    (1883) vol. 7; cf. **Bismarck** 46:9

   of his own downfall:
8 I feel obliged to call to the supporters of the social   *Aus Metternich's Nachgelassenen*
   uprising: Citizens of a dream-world, nothing is altered.   *Papieren* (ed. A. von Klinkowström,
   On 14 March 1848, there was merely one man fewer.   1880) vol. 8

9 Error has never approached my spirit.   François Pierre G. Guizot *Mémoires*
   addressed to Guizot in 1848   (1858–67) vol. 4

10 The Emperor is everything, Vienna is nothing.   letter to Count Bombelles, 5 June
                                                                    1848

1   The greatest gift of any statesman rests not in knowing
    what concessions to make, but recognising when to
    make them.

    Concessionen und
    Nichtconcessionen (1852)

2   The word 'freedom' means for me not a point of
    departure but a genuine point of arrival. The point of
    departure is defined by the word 'order'. Freedom cannot
    exist without the concept of order.

    Mein Politisches Testament

Anthony Meyer 1920–

British Conservative politician

3   I question the right of that great Moloch, national
    sovereignty, to burn its children to save its pride.
       speaking against the Falklands War, 1982

    in *Listener* 27 September 1990

Jules Michelet 1798–1874

French historian

4   What is the first part of politics? Education. The second?
    Education. And the third? Education.

    Le Peuple (1846)

5   England is an empire, Germany is a nation, a race,
    France is a person.

    Histoire de France (1833–1867)

William Porcher Miles 1822–96

6   'Vote early and vote often,' the advice openly displayed
    on the election banners in one of our northern cities.

    in the House of Representatives,
    31 March 1858

John Stuart Mill 1806–73

English philosopher and economist

7   The great majority of those who speak of perfectibility as
    a dream, do so because they feel that it is one which
    would afford them no pleasure if it were realized.

    Speech on Perfectibility (1828)

8   The sole end for which mankind are warranted,
    individually or collectively, in interfering with the liberty
    of action of any of their number, is self-protection.

    On Liberty (1859)

9   The only freedom worth the name, is that of pursuing
    our own good in our own way.

    On Liberty (1859)

10 The only purpose for which power can be rightfully
    exercised over any member of a civilized community,
    against his will, is to prevent harm to others. His own
    good, either physical or moral, is not a sufficient
    warrant.

    On Liberty (1859)

11 If all mankind minus one were of one opinion, and only
    one person were of the contrary opinion, mankind would
    be no more justified in silencing that one person, than
    he, if he had the power, would be justified in silencing
    mankind.

    On Liberty (1859)

1 A party of order or stability, and a party of progress or reform, are both necessary elements of a healthy state of political life.

On Liberty (1859)

2 The liberty of the individual must be thus far limited; he must not make himself a nuisance to other people.

On Liberty (1859)

3 I am not aware that any community has a right to force another to be civilized.

On Liberty (1859)

4 Liberty consists in doing what one desires.

On Liberty (1859)

5 A State which dwarfs its men, in order that they may be more docile instruments in its hands even for beneficial purposes, will find that with small men no great thing can really be accomplished.

On Liberty (1859)

6 When society requires to be rebuilt, there is no use in attempting to rebuild it on the old plan.

Dissertations and Discussions vol. 1 (1859) 'Essay on Coleridge'

7 The Conservatives...being by the law of their existence the stupidest party.

Considerations on Representative Government (1861)

8 The principle which regulates the existing social relations between the two sexes—the legal subordination of one sex to the other—is wrong in itself, and now one of the chief hindrances to human improvement.

The Subjection of Women (1869)

9 Laws and systems of polity always begin by recognising the relations they find already existing between individuals. They convert what was a mere physical fact into a legal right, give it the sanction of society, and principally aim at the substitution of public and organised means of asserting and protecting these rights, instead of the irregular and lawless conflict of physical strength.

The Subjection of Women (1869)

10 Everyone who desires power, desires it most over those who are nearest to him, with whom his life is passed, with whom he has most concerns in common, and in whom any independence of his authority is oftenest likely to interfere with his individual preferences.

The Subjection of Women (1869)

11 The laws of most countries are far worse than the people who execute them, and many of them are only able to remain laws by being seldom or never carried into effect. If married life were all that it might be expected to be, looking to the laws alone, society would be a hell upon earth.

The Subjection of Women (1869)

12 No great improvements in the lot of mankind are possible, until a great change takes place in the fundamental constitution of their modes of thought.

Autobiography (1873)

13 Detention by the State of the unearned increment of rent.

Dissertations and Discussions

14 In the case of most men the only inducement which has been found sufficiently constant and unflagging to overcome the ever-present influence of indolence and love of ease, and induce men to apply themselves unrelaxingly to work for the most part in itself dull and unexciting, is

in *Fortnightly Review* April 1879

the prospect of bettering their own economic condition
and that of their family.

Alice Duer Miller 1874–1942

American writer

1   I am American bred,   *The White Cliffs* (1940)
    I have seen much to hate here—much to forgive,
    But in a world where England is finished and dead,
    I do not wish to live.

Charles Wright Mills 1916–62

American sociologist

2   By the power elite, we refer to those political, economic,   *The Power Elite* (1956)
    and military circles which as an intricate set of
    overlapping cliques share decisions having at least
    national conseqences. In so far as national events are
    decided, the power elite are those who decide them.

Lord Milner 1854–1925

British colonial administrator

3   If we believe a thing to be bad, and if we have a right to   speech in Glasgow, 26 November
    prevent it, it is our duty to try to prevent it and to damn   1909
    the consequences.

John Milton 1608–74

English poet, who became a politically active Parliamentarian
during the Civil War, publishing the *Areopagitica* (1644) which
demanded a free press, and writing a defence of republicanism
on the eve of the Restoration (1660)

4   The land had once enfranchised herself from this   *The Reason of Church Government*
    impertinent yoke of prelaty, under whose inquisitorious   (1642) bk. 2, introduction
    and tyrannical duncery no free and splendid wit can
    flourish.

5   Let not England forget her precedence of teaching nations   *The Doctrine and Discipline of*
    how to live.   *Divorce* (1643) 'To the Parliament
                                                                 of England'

6   I cannot praise a fugitive and cloistered virtue,   *Areopagitica* (1644)
    unexercised and unbreathed, that never sallies out and
    sees her adversary, but slinks out of the race, where that
    immortal garland is to be run for, not without dust and
    heat.

7   Here the great art lies, to discern in what the law is to be *Areopagitica* (1644)
    to restraint and punishment, and in what things
    persuasion only is to work.

8   None can love freedom heartily, but good men; the rest   *The Tenure of Kings and*
    love not freedom, but licence.   *Magistrates* (1649)

1 No man who knows aught, can be so stupid to deny that   *The Tenure of Kings and*
   all men naturally were born free.   *Magistrates* (1649)

2 Cromwell, our chief of men.   'To the Lord General Cromwell'
                                                              (written 1652)

3 ...Peace hath her victories   'To the Lord General Cromwell'
   No less renowned than war.   (written 1652)

4 What I have spoken, is the language of that which is not   *The Ready and Easy Way to*
   called amiss *The good old Cause.*   *Establish a Free Commonwealth*
                                                              (2nd ed., 1660)

5 They also serve who only stand and wait.   'When I consider how my light is
                                                              spent' (1673)

Comte de Mirabeau 1749–91

French revolutionary

6 War is the national industry of Prussia.   attributed to Mirabeau by Albert
                                                              Sorel (1842–1906), based on
                                                              Mirabeau's introduction to *De la*
                                                              monarchie prussienne sous
                                                              Frédéric le Grand (1788)

Joni Mitchell 1943–

Canadian singer and songwriter

7 Lord, there's danger in this land.   Peter McWilliams *Ain't Nobody's*
   You get witch-hunts and wars when church and state   *Business If You Do* (1993)
      hold hands.

François Mitterrand 1916–96

French socialist statesman; President of France 1981–95

8 She has the eyes of Caligula, but the mouth of Marilyn   in *Observer* 25 November 1990
   Monroe.
      of Margaret **Thatcher***, briefing his new European Minister*
      Roland Dumas

Walter Monckton 1891–1965

British lawyer and Conservative politician

when offered the post of Minister of Labour, Monckton
hesitated on the grounds of inexperience:
9 CHURCHILL: Your qualification is that you have no   in *Dictionary of National Biography*
      political past.
   MONCKTON: I take it you do not expect me to have any
      political future.

asking his wife to curtsey to the Duchess of Windsor:
10 It does no harm, and makes the little man so happy.   Andrew Roberts *Eminent*
                                                              Churchillians (1994)

11 Too conventional a thinker to make a great leader.   Andrew Roberts *Eminent*
      of Anthony **Eden**   *Churchillians* (1994)

Walter Mondale 1928–

American Democratic politician and Vice-President

1 When I hear your new ideas I'm reminded of that ad, 'Where's the beef?'

alluding to an advertising slogan which made an unfavourable comparison between the relative sizes of a small hamburger and a large bun

in a televised debate with Gary Hart, 11 March 1984

2 Political image is like mixing cement. When it's wet, you can move it around and shape it, but at some point it hardens and there's almost nothing you can do to reshape it.

in *Independent on Sunday* 12 May 1991

Duke of Monmouth 1649–85

illegitimate son of Charles II; focus of the supporters of the Protestant succession in the Exclusion crisis of 1681 (cf. **Dryden**) and leader of the failed Monmouth rebellion against James II

3 Do not hack me as you did my Lord Russell.

words addressed to his executioner; according to a contemporary account five blows were needed

T. B. Macaulay *History of England* vol. 1 (1849)

Jean Monnet 1888–1979

French economist and diplomat; founder of the European Community

of American foreign policy in relation to European integration:

4 It is the first time in history that a great power, instead of basing its policy on ruling by dividing, has consistently and resolutely backed the creation of a large Community uniting peoples previously apart.

in 1953; François Duchêne *Jean Monnet* (1994)

5 Europe has never existed. It is not the addition of national sovereignties in a conclave which creates an entity. One must genuinely *create* Europe.

Anthony Sampson *The New Europeans* (1968)

6 The common market is a process, not a product.

Anthony Sampson *The New Europeans* (1968)

7 I did not understand the politics of Versailles, only the economics.

of the Treaty of Versailles

in an interview in 1971; François Duchêne *Jean Monnet* (1994)

8 It is astonishing how little the word 'alliance', which people find so reassuring, really means in practice if all it implies is the traditional machinery of cooperation… where national sovereignty is ultimately vested in points of prestige and solutions are compromises between them.

in an interview in 1971; François Duchêne *Jean Monnet* (1994)

9 A great statesman is one who can work for long-term goals which eventually suit situations as yet unforeseen.

Memoirs (1978)

10 Each man begins the world afresh. Only institutions grow wiser; they store up the collective experience; and, from this experience and wisdom, men subject to the same

François Duchêne *Jean Monnet* (1994)

laws will gradually find, not that their natures change
but that their experience does.
   a favourite sentiment ascribed by Monnet to the nineteenth-
   century Genevese diarist Henri Frédéric Amiel

1 Institutions govern relationships between people. They   François Duchêne *Jean Monnet*
  are the real pillars of civilization.   (1994)

2 We should not create a nation Europe instead of a nation   François Duchêne *Jean Monnet*
  France.   (1994)

James Monroe 1758–1831

American Democratic Republican statesman, 5th President of
the US 1817–25, who in 1803 negotiated the Lousiana
Purchase, and who formulated the Monroe Doctrine

3 National honour is national property of the highest   first inaugural address, 4 March
  value.   1817

4 The American continents...are henceforth not to be   annual message to Congress, 2
  considered as subjects for future colonization by any   December 1823
  European powers.
   first expression of what became the Monroe Doctrine

5 In the wars of the European powers in matters relating to   annual message to Congress, 2
  themselves we have never taken any part, nor does it   December 1823
  comport with our policy to do so.

6 With the existing colonies or dependencies of any   annual message to Congress, 2
  European power we...shall not interfere. But with the   December 1823
  governments...whose independence we have...
  acknowledged, we could not view any interposition for
  the purpose of oppressing them, or controlling, in any
  other manner, their destiny, by any European power, in
  any other light than as a manifestation of an unfriendly
  disposition toward the United States.

Montaigne 1533–92

French moralist and essayist

7 There is scarcely any less bother in the running of   *Essais* (1580)
  a family than in that of an entire state. And domestic
  business is no less importunate for being less important.

8 Fame and tranquillity can never be bedfellows.   *Essais* (1580)

9 On the highest throne in the world, we still sit only on   *Essais* (1580)
  our own bottom.

Montesquieu 1689–1755

French political philosopher

10 Ever since the invention of gunpowder...I continually   *Lettres Persanes* (1721)
   tremble lest men should, in the end, uncover some secret
   which would provide a short way of abolishing mankind,
   of annihilating peoples and nations in their entirety.

1   Just as the sea, which seems to want to cover the whole   *The Spirit of the Laws* (1748)
    earth, is checked by the grasses and the smallest bits of
    gravel on the shore, so monarchs, whose power seems
    boundless, are checked by the slightest obstacles and
    submit their natural pride to supplication and prayer.

2   When the savages of Louisiana want fruit, they cut down   *The Spirit of the Laws* (1748)
    the tree and gather the fruit. There you have despotic
    government.

3   Republics end in luxury; monarchies, in poverty.   *The Spirit of the Laws* (1748)

4   The corruption of each government almost always begins   *The Spirit of the Laws* (1748)
    with that of its principles.

5   The principle of democracy is corrupted not only when   *The Spirit of the Laws* (1748)
    the spirit of equality is lost but also when the spirit of
    extreme equality is taken up and each one wants to be
    the equal of those chosen to command.

6   If a republic is small, it is destroyed by a foreign force; if   *The Spirit of the Laws* (1748)
    it is large, it is destroyed by an internal vice.

7   When a neighbouring state is in decline, one should take   *The Spirit of the Laws* (1748)
    care not to hasten its ruin, because this is the most
    fortunate situation possible; there is nothing more
    suitable for a prince than to be close to another who
    receives in his stead all the blows and outrages of
    fortune.

8   Liberty is the right to do everything the laws permit.   *The Spirit of the Laws* (1748)

9   It has eternally been observed that any man who has   *The Spirit of the Laws* (1748)
    power is led to abuse it.

10 Political liberty in a citizen is that tranquillity of spirit   *The Spirit of the Laws* (1748)
    which comes from the opinion each one has of his
    security, and in order for him to have this liberty the
    government must be such that one citizen cannot fear
    another citizen.

11 The English have taken their idea of political government   *The Spirit of the Laws* (1748)
    from the Germans. This fine system was found in the
    forests.

12 This state [England] will perish when legislative power is   *The Spirit of the Laws* (1748)
    more corrupt than executive power.

13 States are often more flourishing during the imperceptible   *The Spirit of the Laws* (1748)
    shift from one constitution to another than they are
    under either constitution. At that time all the springs of
    the government are stretched...and there is a noble
    rivalry between those who defend the declining
    constitution and those who put forward the one that
    prevails.

14 Royal authority is a great spring that should move easily   *The Spirit of the Laws* (1748)
    and noiselessly.

15 In moderate states, there is a compensation for heavy   *The Spirit of the Laws* (1748)
    taxes; it is liberty. In despotic states, there is an
    equivalent for liberty; it is the modest taxes.

1 Lands produce less by reason of their fertility than by   Alexis de Tocqueville *The Ancien*
  reason of the liberty of their inhabitants.   *Régime* (1856); attributed

Lord Montgomery 1887–1976

British field marshal

2 War is a very rough game, but I think that politics is   attributed, 1956
  worse.

3 Rule 1, on page 1 of the book of war, is: 'Do not march   in the House of Lords, 30 May 1962
  on Moscow'...[Rule 2] is: 'Do not go fighting with your
  land armies in China.'

4 I have spent much of my life fighting the Germans and   in *The Times* 15 May 1967
  fighting the politicians. It is much easier to fight the
  Germans.
    lecture given in Cairo as part of the 25th anniversary
    commemoration of Alamein, 13 May 1967

Thomas More 1478–1535

English scholar and saint; Lord Chancellor of England,
1529–32
on More: see **Whittington** 388:6; see also **Bolt** 51:3

5 Your sheep, that were wont to be so meek and tame, and   *Utopia* (1516); following the
  so small eaters, now, as I hear say, be become so great   marginal précis 'The Disaster
  devourers, and so wild, that they eat up and swallow   Produced by Standing Military
  down the very men themselves.   Garrisons'

6 If the parties will at my hands call for justice, then, all   William Roper *Life of Sir Thomas*
  were it my father stood on the one side, and the Devil on   *More*
  the other, his cause being good, the Devil should have
  right.

7 'By god's body, master More, *Indignatio principis mors est*   William Roper *Life of Sir Thomas*
  [The anger of the sovereign is death].' 'Is that all, my   *More*
  Lord?' quoth he [to the Duke of Norfolk]. 'Then in good
  faith is there no more difference between your grace and
  me, but that I shall die to-day, and you to-morrow.'

8 Is not this house [the Tower of London] as nigh heaven   William Roper *Life of Sir Thomas*
  as my own?   *More*

9 I pray you, master Lieutenant, see me safe up, and my   William Roper *Life of Sir Thomas*
  coming down let me shift for my self.   *More*
    on mounting the scaffold

John Morley 1838–1923

British Liberal politician and writer

10 You have not converted a man, because you have   *On Compromise* (1874)
   silenced him.

11 The golden Gospel of Silence is effectively compressed in   *Critical Miscellanies* (1886) 'Carlyle'
   thirty fine volumes.
     on **Carlyle**'s History of Frederick the Great *(1858–65), Carlyle*
     having written of his subject as 'that strong, silent man'

1 Although in Cabinet all its members stand on an equal footing, speak with equal voices and, on the rare occasions when a division is taken, are counted on the fraternal principle of one man, one vote, yet the head of the Cabinet is *primus inter pares*, and occupies a position which, so long as it lasts, is one of exceptional and peculiar authority.

Walpole (1889)

2 Simplicity of character is no hindrance to subtlety of intellect.

Life of Gladstone (1903)

3 The proper memory for a politician is one that knows what to remember and what to forget.

Recollections (1917)

George Pope Morris 1802–64

4 The iron-armed soldier, the true-hearted soldier,
The gallant old soldier of Tippecanoe.
  campaign song for William Henry **Harrison**, *1840*

attributed; cf. **Ross** 313:3

William Morris 1834–96

English writer, artist, and designer

5 What is this, the sound and rumour? What is this that all men hear,
Like the wind in hollow valleys when the storm is drawing near,
Like the rolling on of ocean in the eventide of fear?
'Tis the people marching on.

Chants for Socialists (1885) 'The March of the Workers'

Herbert Morrison 1888–1965

British Labour politician

6 Work is the call. Work at war speed. Good-night—and go to it.

broadcast as Minister of Supply, 22 May 1940

Wayne Lyman Morse 1900–74

7 The liberal, emphasizing the civil and property rights of the individual, insists that the individual must remain so supreme as to make the state his servant.

in *New Republic* 22 July 1946

Desmond Morton 1891–1971

British soldier, intelligence officer, and public servant

of **Churchill**'s *love for Combined Operations:*

8 He addressed his mind to them as the Managing Director of a vast railway might have, as a hobby, a miniature railway in his garden.

Andrew Roberts *Eminent Churchillians* (1994)

Rogers Morton 1914–79

American public relations officer

1 I'm not going to rearrange the furniture on the deck of   *in Washington Post* 16 May 1976
the Titanic.
  having lost five of the last six primaries as President Ford's
  campaign manager

Oswald Mosley 1896–1980

English politician and Fascist leader
on Mosley: see **Attlee** 19:7

2 I am not, and never have been, a man of the right. My   letter to *The Times* 26 April 1968
position was on the left and is now in the centre of
politics.

John Lothrop Motley 1814–77

American historian

3 As long as he lived, he was the guiding-star of a whole   *The Rise of the Dutch Republic*
brave nation, and when he died the little children cried   (1856)
in the streets.
  of William of Orange

Lord Mountbatten 1900–79

British sailor, soldier, and statesman
on Mountbatten: see **Churchill** 91:1, **Whinney** 386:5,
Ziegler 397:2

4 The nuclear arms race has no military purpose. Wars   speech at Strasbourg, 11 May 1979
cannot be fought with nuclear weapons. Their existence
only adds to our perils.

Daniel P. Moynihan 1927–

American Democratic politician

5 Welfare became a term of opprobrium—a contentious,   in *The Washington Post* 25
often vindictive area of political conflict in which liberals   November 1994
and conservatives clashed and children were lost sight of.

Robert Mugabe 1924–

African politician; Prime Minister of Zimbabwe, 1980–7

6 Cricket civilizes people and creates good gentlemen.   in *Sunday Times* 26 February 1984
I want everyone to play cricket in Zimbabwe; I want
ours to be a nation of gentlemen.

Malcolm Muggeridge 1903–90

British journalist

1 He was not only a bore; he bored for England.   *Tread Softly* (1966)
    of Anthony **Eden**

2 To succeed pre-eminently in English public life it is   *The Infernal Grove* (1973)
    necessary to conform either to the popular image of
    a bookie or of a clergyman; Churchill being a perfect
    example of the former, Halifax of the latter.

Ed Murrow 1908–65

American broadcaster and journalist

3 I admired your history, doubted your future.   radio broadcast; in *Listener* 28
    of Britain in the 1930s   February 1946

4 Future generations who bother to read the official record   radio broadcast; in *Listener* 28
    of proceedings in the House of Commons will discover   February 1946
    that British armies retreated from many places, but that
    there was no retreat from the principles for which your
    ancestors fought.

   of **Winston Churchill**:
5 He mobilized the English language and sent it into battle   broadcast, 30 November 1954; *In*
    to steady his fellow countrymen and hearten those   *Search of Light* (1967)
    Europeans upon whom the long dark night of tyranny
    had descended.

6 When the politicians complain that TV turns their   attributed, 1959
    proceedings into a circus, it should be made plain that
    the circus was already there, and that TV has merely
    demonstrated that not all the performers are well trained.

7 Anyone who isn't confused doesn't really understand the   Walter Bryan *The Improbable Irish*
    situation.   (1969)
    on the Vietnam War

Benito Mussolini 1883–1945

Italian Fascist statesman, Prime Minister 1922–43

8 We must leave exactly on time...From now on   Giorgio Pini *Mussolini* (1939) vol. 2
    everything must function to perfection.
    to a stationmaster

Sarojini Naidu 1879–1949

Indian politician

9 If only Bapu [Gandhi] knew the cost of setting him up in   A. Campbell-Johnson *Mission with*
    poverty!   *Mountbatten* (1951)

Lewis Namier 1888–1960

Polish-born British historian

1 No number of atrocities however horrible can deprive   in 1919; Julia Namier *Lewis Namier*
   a nation of its right to independence, nor justify its being   (1971)
   put under the heel of its worst enemies and persecutors.

2 What matters most about political ideas is the underlying   *Personalities and Powers* (1955)
   emotions, the music, to which ideas are a mere libretto,
   often of very inferior quality.

Napoleon I 1769–1821

Emperor of France, 1804–15

3 Think of it, soldiers; from the summit of these pyramids,   Gaspard Gourgaud *Mémoires*
   forty centuries look down upon you.   (1823) vol. 2 'Égypte — Bataille des
   speech to the Army of Egypt on 21 July 1798, before the Battle of   Pyramides'
   the Pyramids

4 It [the Channel] is a mere ditch, and will be crossed as   letter to Consul Cambacérès, 16
   soon as someone has the courage to attempt it.   November 1803

5 It is easier to put up with unpleasantness from a man of   letter to J. Finckenstein, 14 April
   one's own way of thinking than from one who takes an   1807
   entirely different point of view.

6 A prince who gets a reputation for good nature in the   letter to the King of Holland, 4 April
   first year of his reign, is laughed at in the second.   1807

7 In war, three-quarters turns on personal character and   'Observations sur les affaires
   relations; the balance of manpower and materials counts   d'Espagne, Saint-Cloud, 27 août
   only for the remaining quarter.   1808'

8 It is a matter of great interest what sovereigns are doing;   letter 17 December 1811
   but as to what Grand Duchesses are doing—Who cares?

9 There is only one step from the sublime to the ridiculous.   D. G. De Pradt *Histoire de*
   to De Pradt, Polish ambassador, after the retreat from Moscow   *l'Ambassade dans le grand-duché*
   in 1812   *de Varsovie en 1812* (1815)

10 As to moral courage, I have very rarely met with two   E. A. de Las Cases *Mémorial de*
   o'clock in the morning courage: I mean instantaneous   *Ste-Hélène* (1823) vol. 1, 4–5
   courage.   December 1815

11 An army marches on its stomach.   attributed, but probably
                                                                  condensed from a long passage in
                                                                  E. A. de Las Cases *Mémorial de*
                                                                  Ste-Hélène (1823) vol. 4, 14
                                                                  November 1816; also attributed to
                                                                  Frederick the Great

   when asked how to deal with the Pope:
12 As though he had 200,000 men.   J. M. Robinson *Cardinal Consalvi*
                                                                  (1987)

13 The career open to the talents.   Barry E. O'Meara *Napoleon in Exile*
                                                                  (1822) vol. 1

1 England is a nation of shopkeepers.

Barry E. O'Meara *Napoleon in Exile*
(1822) vol. 2; cf. **Adams** 5:4,
Smith 341:6

2 Nothing is more contrary to the organization of the
mind, of the memory, and of the imagination...The new
system of weights and measures will be a stumbling
block and the source of difficulties for several
generations...It's just tormenting the people with
trivia!!!
    on the introduction of the metric system

Mémoires... écrits à Ste-Hélène
(1823–5)

3 Not tonight, Josephine.

attributed, but probably
apocryphal; R. H. Horne *The
History of Napoleon* (1841) vol. 2
describes the circumstances in
which the affront may have
occurred

of **Talleyrand**:
4 A pile of shit in a silk stocking.

attributed

Jawaharlal Nehru 1889–1964

Indian statesman, Prime Minister 1947–64
on Nehru: see **Patil** 287:2

5 There is no easy walk-over to freedom anywhere, and
many of us will have to pass through the valley of the
shadow again and again before we reach the mountain-
tops of our desire.

'From Lucknow to Tripuri' (1939)

6 History is almost always written by the victors and
conquerors and gives their viewpoint.

The Discovery of India (1946)

7 At the stroke of the midnight hour, while the world
sleeps, India will awake to life and freedom.
    immediately prior to Independence

speech to the Indian Constituent
Assembly, 14 August 1947

8 The light has gone out of our lives and there is darkness
everywhere.
    broadcast, 30 January 1948, following **Gandhi**'s *assassination*

Richard J. Walsh *Nehru on Gandhi*
(1948)

9 I may lose many things including my temper, but I do
not lose my nerve.

at a press conference in Delhi, 4
June 1958

10 Democracy and socialism are means to an end, not the
end itself.

'Basic Approach'; written for
private circulation and reprinted in
Vincent Shean *Nehru: the Years of
Power* (1960)

11 Normally speaking, it may be said that the forces of
a capitalist society, if left unchecked, tend to make the
rich richer and the poor poorer and thus increase the gap
between them.

'Basic Approach' in Vincent Shean
Nehru... (1960)

12 After every other Viceroy has been forgotten, Curzon will
be remembered because he restored all that was beautiful
in India.
    in conversation with Lord Swinton

Kenneth Rose *Superior Person*
(1969)

1 I shall be the last Englishman to rule in India.   J. K. Galbraith *A Life in Our Times* (1981)

Allan Nevins 1890–1971

American historian

2 The former Allies had blundered in the past by offering   in *Current History* (New York) May
Germany too little, and offering even that too late, until   1935
finally Nazi Germany had become a menace to all
mankind.

Huey Newton 1942–

American political activist

3 I suggested [in 1966] that we use the panther as our   *Revolutionary Suicide* (1973)
symbol and call our political vehicle the Black Panther
Party. The panther is a fierce animal, but he will not
attack until he is backed into a corner; then he will
strike out.

Nicholas I 1796–1855

Russian emperor from 1825

4 Turkey is a dying man. We may endeavour to keep him   F. Max Müller (ed.) *Memoirs of*
alive, but we shall not succeed. He will, he must die.   *Baron Stockmar* (1873)
   origin of the expression 'the sick man of Europe' referring to
   Ottoman Turkey

5 Russia has two generals in whom she can confide—   attributed; in *Punch* 10 March 1855
Generals Janvier [January] and Février [February].

Nicias *c.*470–413 BC

Athenian politician and general

6 For a city consists in men, and not in walls nor in ships   Thucydides *History of the*
empty of men.   *Peloponnesian Wars*
   speech to the defeated Athenian army at Syracuse, 413 BC

Harold Nicolson 1886–1968

English diplomat, politician, and writer; father of Nigel
Nicolson

7 Ponderous and uncertain is that relation between   *Public Faces* (1932)
pressure and resistance which constitutes the balance of
power. The arch of peace is morticed by no iron
tendons...One night a handful of dust will patter from
the vaulting: the bats will squeak and wheel in sudden
panic: nor can the fragile fingers of man then stay the
rush and rumble of destruction.

of the Duke of York (the future **George VI***), c.1936:*
8 Just a snipe from the great Windsor marshes.   Andrew Roberts *Eminent*
                                                                Churchillians (1994)

1 Chamberlain (who has the mind and manner of a clothes-brush) aims only at assuring temporary peace at the price of ultimate defeat.

of Neville **Chamberlain**

diary 6 June 1938

on being asked by C. E. Joad if he did not think that Neville **Chamberlain***'s mind had broadened recently:*

2 Yes, in the same way that a darning needle is broader than a sewing-needle.

Nigel Nicolson (ed.) *Diaries and Letters of Harold Nicolson* vol 1 (1966); introduction

3 We shall have to walk and live a Woolworth life hereafter.

anticipating the aftermath of the Second World War

diary 4 June 1941

4 I am haunted by mental decay such as I saw creeping over Ramsay MacDonald. A gradual dimming of the lights.

diary 28 April 1947

comparing **Attlee** *as a public speaker with Winston* **Churchill***:*

5 Like a village fiddler after Paganini.

diary 10 November 1947

6 I do not think it is quite fair to say that the British businessman has trampled on the faces of the poor. But he has sometimes not been very careful where he put his feet.

replying to a heckler in the North Croydon by-election, 1948

Nigel Nicolson (ed.) *Diaries and Letters of Harold Nicolson 1945–1962* vol. 3 (1968)

7 For seventeen years he did nothing at all but kill animals and stick in stamps.

of **George V** *as a subject for biography*

letter to Vita Sackville-West, 17 August 1949

8 Suez—a smash and grab raid that was all smash and no grab.

in conversation with Antony Jay, November 1956; see also letter to Vita Sackville-West, 8 November 1956, 'Our smash-and-grab raid got stuck at the smash'

Nigel Nicolson 1917–

British Conservative politician and writer; son of Harold **Nicolson**

9 One final tip to rebels: always have a second profession in reserve.

reflecting on the vote on the Maastricht Treaty in the House of Commons, in the light of having abstained from voting with the Government on the Suez Crisis in 1956 and subsequently lost his seat

in *The Spectator* 7 November 1992

Reinhold Niebuhr 1892–1971

American theologian

10 Man's capacity for justice makes democracy possible, but man's inclination to injustice makes democracy necessary.

Children of Light and Children of Darkness (1944) foreword

Martin Niemöller 1892–1984

German theologian

1 When Hitler attacked the Jews I was not a Jew, therefore,
I was not concerned. And when Hitler attacked the
Catholics, I was not a Catholic, and therefore, I was not
concerned. And when Hitler attacked the unions and the
industrialists, I was not a member of the unions and
I was not concerned. Then, Hitler attacked me and the
Protestant church—and there was nobody left to be
concerned.

    *often quoted in the form 'In Germany they came first for the
Communists, and I didn't speak up because I wasn't
a Communist...' and so on*

in Congressional Record 14
October 1968

Friedrich Nietzsche 1844–1900

German philosopher and writer

2 Morality is the herd-instinct in the individual.

Die fröhliche Wissenschaft (1882)

3 I teach you the superman. Man is something to be
surpassed.

Also Sprach Zarathustra (1883)
prologue

4 Master-morality and slave-morality.

Jenseits von Gut und Böse (1886)

5 At the base of all these aristocratic races the predator is
not to be mistaken, the splendorous *blond beast*, avidly
rampant for plunder and victory.

Zur Genealogie der Moral (1887)

Richard Milhous Nixon 1913–94

American Republican statesman, 37th President of the US
1969–74; re-elected for a second term in November 1972, it
soon became clear that he was implicated in the Watergate
scandal, and in 1974 he became the first President to resign
from office
on Nixon: see **Abzug** 1:2, **Anonymous** 9:14, 11:4, 14:12,
Conable 101:6, **Johnson** 195:4, **Stevenson** 350:8,
Ziegler 397:3

6 Pat and I have the satisfaction that every dime that
we've got is honestly ours...Pat doesn't have a mink
coat. But she does have a respectable Republican cloth
coat. And I always tell her that she'd look good in
anything.

    *having been elected as Vice-President in 1952, in response to
criticisms of his electoral campaign*

speech on television, 23
September 1952

*of the post-election gift of a cocker spaniel, named Checkers by
his small daughter:*

7 One other thing I probably should tell you, because if
I don't they'll probably be saying this about me too, we
did get something—a gift—after the election...It was
a little cocker-spaniel dog...The kids love that dog and
I just want to say this right now, that regardless of what
they say about it, we're going to keep it.

speech on television, 23
September 1952

1 There is no such thing as a nonpolitical speech by a politician.

address to Radio-Television Executives Society, New York City, 14 September 1955

2 You won't have Nixon to kick around any more.
at a press conference after losing the election for Governor of California, 5 November 1962

in *New York Times* 8 November 1962

3 Let us begin by committing ourselves to the truth, to see it like it is and tell it like it is, to find the truth, to speak the truth and to live the truth. That's what we will do.
nomination acceptance speech in Miami, 1968

in *New York Times* 9 August 1968

4 There is nothing wrong with this country which a good election can't fix.
at a campaign meeting during the Presidential election

in Syracuse, New York, 29 October 1968

5 This is the greatest week in the history of the world since the Creation.
welcoming the return of the first men to land on the moon

speech, 24 July 1969

6 The great silent majority.

broadcast, 3 November 1969

7 The Chinese are a great and vital people who should not remain isolated from the international community...It is certainly in our interest, and in the interest of peace and stability in Asia and the world, that we take what steps we can toward improved practical relations with Peking.

first foreign policy report to Congress, February 1970

8 In our own lives, let each of us ask—not just what government will do for me, but what can I do for myself?

second inaugural address, 20 January 1973

9 There can be no whitewash at the White House.

television speech on Watergate, 30 April 1973

10 I made my mistakes, but in all my years of public life, I have never profited, never profited from public service. I've earned every cent. And in all of my years in public life I have never obstructed justice...I welcome this kind of examination because people have got to know whether or not their President is a crook. Well, I'm not a crook.

speech at press conference, 17 November 1973

11 This country needs good farmers, good businessmen, good plumbers, good carpenters.
farewell address at White House, 9 August 1974

in *New York Times* 10 August 1974

12 My own view is that taping of conversations for historical purposes was a bad decision.

attributed, 1974

13 When the President does it, that means that it is not illegal.

in conversation; David Frost *I Gave Them a Sword* (1978)

14 I brought myself down. I gave them a sword. And they stuck it in.

television interview, 19 May 1977; David Frost *I Gave Them a Sword* (1978)

15 Foreign aid is the most unpopular damn thing in the world. It is a loser politically.

in *Observer* 21 April 1985 'Sayings of the Week'

16 Finishing second in the Olympics gets you silver. Finishing second in politics gets you oblivion.

in *Sunday Times* 13 November 1988

of the defeat of Michael Dukakis by George **Bush** *in the 1988
presidential election*

1   I played by the rules of politics as I found them. Not   *In the Arena* (1990)
taking a higher road than my predecessors and my
adversaries was my central mistake.

Charles Howard, Duke of Norfolk

1746–1815

English nobleman

2   I cannot be a good Catholic; I cannot go to heaven; and   Henry Best *Personal and Literary*
if a man is to go to the devil, he may as well go thither   *Memorials* (1829)
from the House of Lords as from any other place on
earth.

Christopher North 1785–1854

Scottish literary critic

3   His Majesty's dominions, on which the sun never sets.   in *Blackwood's Magazine* (April
1829) 'Noctes Ambrosianae'

4   Laws were made to be broken.   in *Blackwood's Magazine* (May
1830) 'Noctes Ambrosianae'

5   I cannot sit still, James, and hear you abuse the   in *Blackwood's Magazine*
shopocracy.   (February 1835) 'Noctes
Ambrosianae'

Lord Northcliffe 1865–1922

British newspaper proprietor
on Northcliffe: see **Taylor** 357:9

6   When I want a peerage, I shall buy it like an honest   Tom Driberg *Swaff* (1974)
man.

7   The power of the press is very great, but not so great as   Reginald Rose and Geoffrey
the power of suppress.   Harmsworth *Northcliffe* (1959)
office message, Daily Mail *1918*

Earl of Northumberland 1564–1632

English nobleman

*in a letter to the Council, 11 November 1605, adducing his
habits of life as proof that his interests lay elsewhere than in
political conspiracy:*

8   Examine but my humours in buildings, gardenings, and   in *Dictionary of National Biography*
private expenses these two years past.

Julius Nyerere 1922–

Tanzanian statesman, President of Tanganyika 1962–4 and of
Tanzania 1964–85

1 Should we really let our people starve so we can pay our
debts?

in *Guardian* 21 March 1985

2 We are a poor country and we opted for socialist policies,
but to build a socialist society you have to have
a developed society.

in *Observer* 28 July 1985 'Sayings
of the Week'

Michael Oakeshott 1901–91

British academic

3 A plan to resist all planning may be better than its
opposite, but it belongs to the same style of politics.
  of **Hayek***'s* The Road to Serfdom

Rationalism in Politics (1962)

Conor Cruise O'Brien 1917–

Irish politician, writer, and journalist

4 If I saw Mr Haughey buried at midnight at a crossroads,
with a stake driven through his heart—politically
speaking—I should continue to wear a clove of garlic
round my neck, just in case.

in *Observer* 10 October 1982

5 The first great act of intellectual resistance to the first
great experiment in totalitarian innovation.
  of **Burke***'s writings on the French Revolution*

The Great Melody (1992)

Daniel O'Connell 1775–1847

Irish nationalist leader and social reformer, elected to
Parliament in 1828

6 I have given my advice to my countrymen, and
whenever I feel it necessary I shall continue to do so,
careless whether it pleases or displeases this house or any
mad person out of it.

in *Dictionary of National Biography*

James Ogilvy, Lord Seafield 1664–1730

Lord Chancellor of Scotland

7 Now there's ane end of ane old song.
  as he signed the engrossed exemplification of the Act of Union,
  1706

in *The Lockhart Papers* (1817)

Thomas ('Tip') O'Neill 1912–94

American Democratic politician; Speaker of the House of
Representatives 1977–87

8 All politics is local.

in *New York Review of Books* 13
March 1989

P. J. O'Rourke 1947–

American humorous writer and journalist

1 Giving money and power to government is like giving whisky and car keys to teenage boys.

Parliament of Whores (1991)

2 Politics are, like God's infinite mercy, a last resort.

Parliament of Whores (1991)

3 I have only one firm belief about the American political system, and that is this: God is a Republican and Santa Claus is a Democrat.

Parliament of Whores (1991)

4 The Constitution is an equally forthright piece of work and quite succinct...giving the complete operating instructions for a nation of 250 million people. The manual for a Toyota Camry, which only seats five, is four times as long.

Parliament of Whores (1991)

5 Washington has lots of those Greek- and Roman-style buildings that practically make you feel like a senator just walking up the steps of them. Senators, in particular, are fond of this feeling, and this is one reason official Washington escaped the worst effects of modern architecture.

Parliament of Whores (1991)

6 The actual work of government is too unglamorous for the people who govern us to do. Important elected office-holders and high appointed officials create bureaucratic departments to perform the humdrum tasks of national supervision.

Parliament of Whores (1991)

7 Whatever it is that the government does, sensible Americans would prefer that the government does it to somebody else. This is the idea behind foreign policy.

Parliament of Whores (1991)

8 Every government is a parliament of whores. The trouble is, in a democracy the whores are us.

Parliament of Whores (1991)

George Orwell 1903–50

English novelist

9 A person of bourgeois origin goes through life with some expectation of getting what he wants, within reasonable limits. Hence the fact that in times of stress 'educated' people tend to come to the front.

The Road to Wigan Pier (1937)

10 In a Lancashire cotton-town you could probably go for months on end without once hearing an 'educated' accent, whereas there can hardly be a town in the South of England where you could throw a brick without hitting the niece of a bishop.

The Road to Wigan Pier (1937)

11 The typical Socialist is...a prim little man with a white-collar job, usually a secret teetotaller and often with vegetarian leanings, with a history of Nonconformity behind him, and, above all, with a social position which he has no intention of forfeiting.

The Road to Wigan Pier (1937)

1 To the ordinary working man, the sort you would meet
   in any pub on Saturday night, Socialism does not mean
   much more than better wages and shorter hours and
   nobody bossing you about.

   The Road to Wigan Pier (1937)

2 We of the sinking middle class...may sink without
   further struggles into the working class where we belong,
   and probably when we get there it will not be so dreadful
   as we feared, for, after all, we have nothing to lose but
   our aitches.

   The Road to Wigan Pier (1937)

3 Down here it was still the England I had known in my
   childhood: the railway cuttings smothered in wild
   flowers...the red buses, the blue policemen—all sleeping
   the deep, deep sleep of England, from which I sometimes
   fear that we shall never wake till we are jerked out of it
   by the roar of bombs.

   Homage to Catalonia (1938)

4 Most revolutionaries are potential Tories, because they
   imagine that everything can be put right by altering the
   shape of society; once that change is effected, as it
   sometimes is, they see no need for any other.

   Inside the Whale (1940) 'Charles
   Dickens'

5 England...resembles a family, a rather stuffy Victorian
   family, with not many black sheep in it but with all its
   cupboards bursting with skeletons. It has rich relations
   who have to be kowtowed to and poor relations who are
   horribly sat upon, and there is a deep conspiracy of
   silence about the source of the family income. It is
   a family in which the young are generally thwarted and
   most of the power is in the hands of irresponsible uncles
   and bed-ridden aunts. Still, it is a family. It has its private
   language and its common memories, and at the
   approach of an enemy it closes its ranks. A family with
   the wrong members in control.

   The Lion and the Unicorn (1941) pt.
   1 'England Your England'

6 Probably the battle of Waterloo *was* won on the playing-
   fields of Eton, but the opening battles of all subsequent
   wars have been lost there.

   The Lion and the Unicorn (1941) pt.
   1 'England Your England'; cf.
   Wellington 384:11

7 Old maids biking to Holy Communion through the mists
   of the autumn mornings...these are not only fragments,
   but *characteristic* fragments, of the English scene.

   The Lion and the Unicorn (1941) pt.
   1 'England Your England'; cf.
   Major 248:2

8 Attlee reminds me of nothing so much as a recently dead
   fish, before it has had time to stiffen.

   diary 19 May 1942

9 Man is the only creature that consumes without
   producing.

   Animal Farm (1945)

10 Four legs good, two legs bad.

    Animal Farm (1945)

11 All animals are equal but some animals are more equal
    than others.

    Animal Farm (1945)

12 The Catholic and the Communist are alike in assuming
    that an opponent cannot be both honest and intelligent.

    in *Polemic* January 1946 'The
    Prevention of Literature'

13 The quickest way of ending a war is to lose it.

    in *Polemic* May 1946 'Second
    Thoughts on James Burnham'

14 BIG BROTHER IS WATCHING YOU.

    Nineteen Eighty-Four (1949)

1 War is peace. Freedom is slavery. Ignorance is strength.   *Nineteen Eighty-Four* (1949)

2 Who controls the past controls the future: who controls   *Nineteen Eighty-Four* (1949)
   the present controls the past.

3 Don't you see that the whole aim of Newspeak is to   *Nineteen Eighty-Four* (1949)
   narrow the range of thought? In the end we shall make
   thoughtcrime literally impossible, because there will be
   no words in which to express it.

4 Freedom is the freedom to say that two plus two make   *Nineteen Eighty-Four* (1949)
   four. If that is granted, all else follows.

5 Syme was not only dead, he was abolished, an un-   *Nineteen Eighty-Four* (1949)
   person.

6 *Doublethink* means the power of holding two   *Nineteen Eighty-Four* (1949)
   contradictory beliefs in one's mind simultaneously, and
   accepting both of them.

7 Power is not a means, it is an end. One does not   *Nineteen Eighty-Four* (1949)
   establish a dictatorship in order to safeguard
   a revolution; one makes the revolution in order to
   establish the dictatorship.

8 If you want a picture of the future, imagine a boot   *Nineteen Eighty-Four* (1949)
   stamping on a human face—for ever.

9 In our time, political speech and writing are largely the   *Shooting an Elephant* (1950)
   defence of the indefensible.   'Politics and the English Language'

10 The great enemy of clear language is insincerity. When   *Shooting an Elephant* (1950)
   there is a gap between one's real and one's declared   'Politics and the English Language'
   aims, one turns as it were instinctively to long words and
   exhausted idioms, like a cuttlefish squirting out ink.

11 Political language...is designed to make lies sound   *Shooting an Elephant* (1950)
   truthful and murder respectable, and to give an   'Politics and the English Language'
   appearance of solidity to pure wind.

John L. O'Sullivan 1813–95

American journalist and diplomat

12 Understood as a central consolidated power, managing   in *United States Magazine and*
   and directing the various general interests of the society,   *Democratic Review* (1837)
   all government is evil, and the parent of evil...The best   introduction
   government is that which governs least.

13 A spirit of hostile interference against us...checking the   in *United States Magazine and*
   fulfilment of our manifest destiny to overspread the   *Democratic Review* (1845)
   continent allotted by Providence for the free development
   of our yearly multiplying millions.
   on opposition to the annexation of Texas

James Otis 1725–83

American politician

14 Taxation without representation is tyranny.   in *Dictionary of American*
   watchword (c.1761) of the American Revolution   *Biography*

1 An act against the Constitution is void; an act against natural equity is void.

Argument Against the Writs of Assistance (1763)

2 Where liberty is, there is my country.

motto used by James Otis; also attributed to Benjamin **Franklin**; cf. **Paine** 283:11

Ovid 43 BC–AD *c.*17
Roman poet

3 I see the better things, and approve; I follow the worse.

Metamorphoses

4 How you, rebellious Germany, laid your wretched head beneath the feet of the great general.

Tristia

Robert Owen 1771–1858
Welsh-born socialist and philanthropist

5 All the world is queer save thee and me, and even thou art a little queer.
    to his partner W. Allen, on severing business relations at New Lanark, 1828

attributed

Count Oxenstierna 1583–1654
Swedish statesman

6 Dost thou not know, my son, with how little wisdom the world is governed?

letter to his son, 1648; John Selden, in *Table Talk* (1689) 'Pope', quotes 'a certain Pope' (possibly Julius III) saying 'Thou little thinkest what *a little foolery governs the whole world!*'

William Tyler Page 1868–1942

7 I believe in the United States of America as a government of the people, by the people, for the people, whose just powers are derived from the consent of the governed; a democracy in a republic; a sovereign Nation of many sovereign States; a perfect Union, one and inseparable, established upon those principles of freedom, equality, justice, and humanity for which American patriots sacrificed their lives and fortunes. I therefore believe it is my duty to my country to love it, to support its Constitution, to obey its laws, to respect its flag, and to defend it against all enemies.

American's Creed (prize-winning competition entry, 1918) in *Congressional Record* vol. 56

Thomas Paine 1737–1809
English political theorist

8 Though we have been wise enough to shut and lock a door against absolute Monarchy, we at the same time

Common Sense (1776)

have been foolish enough to put the crown in possession of the key.

1 Government, even in its best state, is but a necessary evil; in its worst state, an intolerable one. Government, like dress, is the badge of lost innocence; the palaces of kings are built upon the ruins of the bowers of paradise.

Common Sense (1776)

2 One of the strongest natural proofs of the folly of hereditary right in kings, is that nature disapproves it, otherwise she would not so frequently turn it into ridicule, by giving mankind an *ass for a lion*.

Common Sense (1776)

3 Monarchy and succession have laid...the world in blood and ashes.

Common Sense (1776)

4 Of more worth is one honest man to society, and in the sight of God, than all the crowned ruffians that ever lived.

Common Sense (1776)

5 'Tis not the affair of a city, a county, a province, or a kingdom—but of a continent—of at least one eighth part of the habitable globe. 'Tis not the concern of a day, a year, or an age; posterity are virtually involved in the contest. Now is the seed-time of continental union.

Common Sense (1776)

6 Any submission to, or dependence on, Great Britain, tends directly to involve this continent in European wars and quarrels, and set us at variance with nations who would otherwise seek our friendship, and against whom we have neither anger nor complaint.

Common Sense (1776)

to America:
7 Freedom hath been hunted round the globe. Asia and Africa have long expelled her. Europe regards her like a stranger, and England hath given her warning to depart. O! receive the fugitive, and prepare in time an asylum for mankind.

Common Sense (1776)

8 We have it in our power to begin the world over again.

Common Sense (1776)

9 As to religion, I hold it to be the indispensable duty of government to protect all conscientious professors thereof, and I know of no other business which government hath to do therewith.

Common Sense (1776)

10 These are the times that try men's souls. The summer soldier and the sunshine patriot will, in this crisis, shrink from the service of their country; but he that stands it *now*, deserves the love and thanks of men and women.

The Crisis (December 1776) introduction

11 What we obtain too cheap, we esteem too lightly.

The Crisis (December 1776) introduction

of Great Britain:
12 Blessed with all the commerce she could wish for, and furnished, by a vast extension of dominion, with the means of civilizing both the eastern and the western world, she has made no use of both than proudly to idolize her own 'thunder', and rip up the bowels of whole countries for what she could get.

The American Crisis pt 2 (1777)

1 I am a farmer of thoughts, and all the crops I raise I give away.

letter to Henry Laurens, c. spring 1778

2 A rich man makes a bonny traitor.

letter to Joseph Reed, 4 June 1780

3 A total reformation is wanted in England. She wants an expanded mind—a heart which embraces the universe. Instead of shutting herself up in an island, and quarrelling with the world, she would derive more lasting happiness, and acquire more real riches, by generously mixing with it, and bravely saying, I am the enemy of none.

Letter to the Abbé Raynal (1782)

4 [Edmund Burke] is not affected by the reality of distress touching his heart, but by the showy resemblance of it striking his imagination. He pities the plumage, but forgets the dying bird.
   *on **Burke**'s Reflections on the Revolution in France, 1790*

The Rights of Man (1791)

5 Lay then the axe to the root, and teach governments humanity. It is their sanguinary punishments which corrupt mankind.

The Rights of Man (1791)

6 [In France] all that class of equivocal generation, which in some countries is called *aristocracy,* and in others *nobility,* is done away, and the peer is exalted into MAN.

The Rights of Man (1791)

7 Titles are but nick-names, and every nick-name is a title.

The Rights of Man (1791)

8 The idea of hereditary legislators is as inconsistent as that of hereditary judges, or hereditary juries; and as absurd as an hereditary mathematician, or an hereditary wise man; and as ridiculous as an hereditary poet laureate.

The Rights of Man (1791)

9 Persecution is not an original feature of *any* religion; but it is always the strongly marked feature of all law-religions, or religions established by law.

The Rights of Man (1791)

10 The candidates were not men but principles.

The Rights of Man (1791)

11 What were formerly called revolutions were little more than a change of persons...what we now see in the world, from the revolutions of America and France, is a renovation of the natural order of things.

The Rights of Man (1791)

12 With respect to the two Houses, of which the English Parliament is composed, they appear to be effectually influenced into one, and as a legislature, to have no temper of its own. The Minister, whoever he at any time may be, touches it as with an opium wand, and it sleeps obedience.

The Rights of Man pt. 2 (1792)

13 All hereditary government is in its nature tyranny...To inherit a government, is to inherit the people, as if they were flocks and herds.

The Rights of Man pt. 2 (1792)

14 The instant formal government is abolished, society begins to act. A general association takes place, and common interest produces common security.

The Rights of Man pt. 2 (1792)

of monarchy:
15 I compare it to something kept behind a curtain, about

The Rights of Man pt. 2 (1792)

which there is a great deal of bustle and fuss, and
a wonderful air of seeming solemnity; but when, by any
accident, the curtain happens to be open, and the
company see what it is, they burst into laughter.

1 When, in countries that are called civilized, we see age
going to the workhouse and youth to the gallows,
something must be wrong in the system of government.

The Rights of Man pt. 2 (1792)

2 My country is the world, and my religion is to do good.

The Rights of Man pt. 2 (1792)

3 I do not believe that any two men, on what are called
doctrinal points, think alike who think at all. It is only
those who have not thought that appear to agree.

The Rights of Man pt. 2 (1792)

4 As he rose like a rocket, he fell like the stick.
on Edmund **Burke***'s losing the parliamentary debate on the
French Revolution to Charles James* **Fox**

*Letter to the Addressers on the late
Proclamation* (1792)

5 It is necessary to the happiness of man that he be
mentally faithful to himself. Infidelity does not consist in
believing, or in disbelieving, it consists in professing to
believe what one does not believe.

The Age of Reason pt. 1 (1794)

6 Revelation is necessarily limited to the first
communication—after that it is only an account of
something which that person says was a revelation made
to him; and though he may find himself obliged to
believe it, it cannot be incumbent on me to believe it in
the same manner; for it was not a revelation made to
me, and I have only his word for it that it was made to
him.

The Age of Reason pt. 1 (1794)

7 To elect, and to reject, is the prerogative of a free people.

in *National Intelligencer* 29
November 1802

8 When moral principles, rather than persons, are
candidates for power, to vote is to perform a moral duty,
and not to vote is to neglect a duty.

in *Trenton True-American* April
1803

9 The religion of humanity.

*Letter... on the Invasion of
England* (1804)

10 A share in two revolutions is living to some purpose.

Eric Foner *Tom Paine and
Revolutionary America* (1976)

11 Where Liberty is not, there is my country.

John Keane *Tom Paine* (1995); cf.
Otis 280:2

12 When it shall be said in any country in the world, 'My
poor are happy; neither ignorance nor distress is to be
found among them; my jails are empty of prisoners, my
streets of beggars; the aged are not in want, the taxes
are not oppressive; the rational world is my friend,
because I am the friend of its happiness': when these
things can be said, then may that country boast of its
constitution and its government.

John Keane *Tom Paine* (1995)

Lord Palmerston 1784–1865

British Whig statesman, Prime Minister 1855–8 and
1859–65

1 We have no eternal allies and we have no perpetual
enemies. Our interests are eternal and perpetual, and
those interests it is our duty to follow.

in the House of Commons, 1 March
1848

2 I therefore fearlessly challenge the verdict which this
House…is to give…whether, as the Roman, in days of
old, held himself free from indignity, when he could say
Civis Romanus sum; so also a British subject, in whatever
land he may be, shall feel confident that the watchful eye
and the strong arm of England will protect him against
injustice and wrong.

in the House of Commons, 25 June
1850

*speech in the debate on the protection afforded to the Greek
trader David Pacifico (1784–1854), who had been born a British
subject at Gibraltar*

3 You may call it combination, you may call it the
accidental and fortuitous concurrence of atoms.
on a projected coalition with **Disraeli**

in the House of Commons, 5 March
1857

4 We do not want Egypt any more than any rational man
with an estate in the north of England and a residence in
the south, would have wished to possess the inns on the
north road. All he could want would have been that the
inns should be well kept, always accessible, and
furnishing him, when he came, with mutton chops and
post horses.

letter to Earl Cowley, 25 November
1859

5 The function of a government is to calm, rather than to
excite agitation.

P. Guedalla *Gladstone and
Palmerston* (1928)

6 What is merit? The opinion one man entertains of
another.

T. Carlyle *Shooting Niagara: and
After?* (1867)

7 Lord Palmerston, with characteristic levity had once said
that only three men in Europe had ever understood [the
Schleswig-Holstein question], and of these the Prince
Consort was dead, a Danish statesman (unnamed) was in
an asylum, and he himself had forgotten it.

R. W. Seton-Watson *Britain in
Europe 1789–1914* (1937)

*on being told that English has no word equivalent to
sensibilité:*

8 Yes we have. Humbug.

attributed

9 Die, my dear Doctor, that's the last thing I shall do!
last words

E. Latham *Famous Sayings and
their Authors* (1904)

Christabel Pankhurst 1880–1958

English suffragette; daughter of Emmeline **Pankhurst**

10 We are here to claim our right as women, not only to be
free, but to fight for freedom. That it is our right as well
as our duty.

in *Votes for Women* 31 March 1911

11 Never lose your temper with the Press or the public is
a major rule of political life.

Unshackled (1959)

Emmeline Pankhurst 1858–1928

English suffragette leader; founder of the Women's Social and
Political Union, 1903

1 There is something that Governments care far more for
than human life, and that is the security of property, and
so it is through property that we shall strike the
enemy...I say to the Government: You have not dared
to take the leaders of Ulster for their incitement to
rebellion. Take me if you dare.

*speech at Albert Hall, 17 October
1912*

2 The argument of the broken window pane is the most
valuable argument in modern politics.

*George Dangerfield The Strange
Death of Liberal England (1936)*

Dorothy Parker 1893–1967

American critic and humorist

on being told that Calvin **Coolidge** *was dead:*

3 How do they know?

*Malcolm Cowley Writers at Work
1st Series (1958)*

Martin Parker d. c.1656

English balladmonger

4 But all's to no end, for the times will not mend
Till the King enjoys his own again.

'Upon Defacing of Whitehall' (1671)

Theodore Parker 1810–60

5 Truth never yet fell dead in the streets; it has such
affinity with the soul of man, the seed however broadcast
will catch somewhere and produce its hundredfold.

*A Discourse of Matters Pertaining
to Religion (1842)*

6 A democracy—that is a government of all the people, by
all the people, for all the people; of course, a government
of the principles of eternal justice, the unchanging law
of God; for shortness' sake I will call it the idea of Freedom.

The American Idea 29 May 1850

C. Northcote Parkinson 1909–

English writer

7 Expenditure rises to meet income.

Parkinson's Law (1958)

8 Work expands so as to fill the time available for its
completion.

Parkinson's Law (1958)

9 A committee is organic rather than mechanical in its
nature: it is not a structure but a plant. It takes root and
grows, it flowers, wilts, and dies, scattering the seed from
which other committees will bloom in their turn.

Parkinson's Law (1958)

10 Time spent on any item of the agenda will be in inverse
proportion to the sum involved.

Parkinson's Law (1958)

1 The man who is denied the opportunity of taking decisions of importance begins to regard as important the decisions he is allowed to take.

Parkinson's Law (1958)

2 Men enter local politics solely as a result of being unhappily married.

Parkinson's Law (1958)

Francis Parkman 1823–93

3 The growth of New England was a result of the aggregate efforts of a busy multitude, each in his narrow circle toiling for himself, to gather competence or wealth. The expansion of New France was the achievement of a gigantic ambition striving to grasp a continent. It was a vain attempt.

Pioneers of France in the New World (1865); introduction

4 The most momentous and far-reaching question ever brought to issue on this continent [North America] was: Shall France remain here or shall she not?

Montcalm and Wolfe (1884); introduction

Charles Stewart Parnell 1846–91

Irish nationalist leader
on Parnell: see **Yeats** 396:1

5 Why should Ireland be treated as a geographical fragment of England...Ireland is not a geographical fragment, but a nation.

in the House of Commons, 26 April 1875

6 My policy is not a policy of conciliation, but a policy of retaliation.

in 1877, on his parliamentary tactics in the House of Commmons as leader of the Irish party

in *Dictionary of National Biography*

7 None of us, whether we are in America or Ireland, or wherever we may be, will be satisfied until we have destroyed the last link which keeps Ireland bound to England.

speech at Cincinnati, 20 February 1880

8 No man has a right to fix the boundary of the march of a nation; no man has a right to say to his country—thus far shalt thou go and no further.

speech at Cork, 21 January 1885

9 Get the advice of everybody whose advice is worth having—they are very few—and then do what you think best yourself.

Conor Cruise O'Brien *Parnell*

Matthew Parris 1949–

British journalist and former Conservative politician

of Lady **Thatcher** *in the House of Lords:*

10 A big cat detained briefly in a poodle parlour, sharpening her claws on the velvet.

Look Behind You! (1993)

11 Being an MP feeds your vanity and starves your self-respect.

in *The Times* 9 February 1994

Blaise Pascal 1623–62

French mathematician, physicist, and moralist

1   Had Cleopatra's nose been shorter, the whole face of the   *Pensées* (1909)
world would have changed.

Sadashiv Kanoji Patil

Indian politician; Minister for Food and Agriculture in **Nehru**'s
government

2   The Prime Minister is like the great banyan tree.   J. K. Galbraith *A Life in Our Times*
Thousands shelter beneath it, but nothing grows.   (1981)
  *when asked in an interview who would be **Nehru**'s successor*

Patrick Pearse 1879–1916

Irish nationalist leader; executed after the Easter Rising
*on Pearse: see **Yeats** 395:8*

3   The fools, the fools, the fools, they have left us our   oration over the grave of the
Fenian dead, and while Ireland holds these graves Ireland   Fenian Jeremiah O'Donovan Rossa,
unfree shall never be at peace.   1 August 1915

Lester Pearson 1897–1972

Canadian diplomat and Liberal statesman, Prime Minister
1963–8

4   The grim fact is that we prepare for war like precocious   speech in Toronto, 14 March 1955
giants and for peace like retarded pygmies.

5   Not only did he not suffer fools gladly, he did not suffer   in *Time* 25 October 1971
them at all.
  *of Dean **Acheson***

6   The chief distinction of a diplomat is that he can say no   Geoffrey Pearson *Seize the Day*
in such a way that it sounds like yes.   (1993)

7   Canada was supposed to get British government, French   in *The Economist* 27 July 1991
culture, and American know-how. Instead it got French
government, American culture, and British know-how.

Robert Peel 1788–1850

British Conservative statesman, Prime Minister 1834–5 and
1841–6
*on Peel: see **Curran** 107:5, **Disraeli** 117:15, 118:1, 118:13,*
Hennessy 175:2, **Wellington** 384:13

8   What is right must unavoidably be politic.   to Goulburn, 23 September 1822

9   I may be a Tory. I may be an illiberal—but…Tory as   in the House of Commons, 1 May
I am, I have the further satisfaction of knowing that   1827
there is not a single law connected with my name which
has not had as its object some mitigation of the severity
of the criminal law; some prevention of abuse in the

exercise of it; or some security for its impartial
administration.

1 There is no appetite for truth in Ireland.   to Leveson Gower in 1828

2 As minister of the Crown...I reserve to myself, distinctly   in the House of Commons, 30
and unequivocally, the right of adapting my conduct to   March 1829
the exigency of the moment, and to the wants of the
country.

3 All my experience in public life is in favour of the   to Wellington in 1829
employment of what the world would call young men
instead of old ones.

4 The longer I live, the more clearly do I see the folly of   in the House of Commons, 1830
yielding a rash and precipitate assent to any political
measure.

5 Men, if in office, seemed really to be like the Indians—   in the House of Commons,1831
they inherited all the qualities of those enemies they
killed.

6 We are here to consult the interests and not to obey the   in the House of Commons, 1831
will of the people, if we honestly believe that that will
conflicts with those interests.

7 No man attached to his country could always acquiesce   in the House of Commons, 1831
in the opinions of the majority.

8 No government can exist which does not control and   in the House of Commons, 1832
restrain the popular sentiments.

9 There will always be found a permanent fund of   in the House of Commons, 1832
discontent and dissatisfaction in every country.

10 The hasty inordinate demand for peace might be just as   in the House of Commons, 1832
dangerous as the clamour for war.

11 I see no dignity in persevering in error.   in the House of Commons, 1833

of Robert **Walpole**:
12 So far as the great majority of his audience was   to Mahon in 1833
concerned, he had blocks to cut, and he chose a fitter
instrument than a razor to cut them with.

13 I am not sure that those who clamour most, suffer most.   in the House of Commons, 1834

14 Of all vulgar arts of government, that of solving every   in the House of Commons, 1834
difficulty which might arise by thrusting the hand into
the public purse is the most delusory and contemptible.

15 English grouse are to Scotch what Scotchmen are to   to Aberdeen in 1836
Englishmen. They are much more wary and provident
birds more given to locomotion.

16 The true policy in public life is to act with decision and   to Graham in 1841
as far as possible to adhere to what is decided, but not to
decide before the time for decision shall have arrived, and
carefully to consider in the interval every mode of solving
a difficulty.

17 The distinction of being without an honour is becoming   to Graham in 1841
a rare and valuable one and should not become extinct.

1 A cordial and good understanding between France and   in the House of Commons, 1841
England is essential to the peace and welfare of Europe.

2 Speaking with that caution with which I am sometimes   in the House of Commons, 1842
taunted but which I find a great convenience.

3 There are those who seem to have nothing else to do but   in the House of Commons, 1842
to suggest modes of taxation to men in office.

4 The great art of government is to work by such   in Cabinet, 1844
instruments as the world supplies.

5 There are many parties in Ireland who desire to have   to the Queen, 1844
a grievance and prefer the grievance to the remedy.

6 Philosophers are very regardless of expense when the   to Haddington in 1844
public has to bear it.

7 Priests are not above sublunary considerations. Priests   to Graham, 13 August 1845
have nephews.

8 An Irishman has no sense of the ridiculous when office is   to Graham, 28 December 1845
in question.

9 There seem to me very few facts, at least ascertainable   to Lord **Brougham** in 1846
facts, in politics.

10 Great public measures cannot be carried by the influence   to Lord Radnor in 1846
of mere reason.

Charles Péguy 1873–1914

French poet and essayist

11 Tyranny is always better organized than freedom.   *Basic Verities* (1943) 'War and
Peace'

Henry Herbert, Lord Pembroke

*c.*1534–1601

12 A parliament can do any thing but make a man   quoted by his son, the 4th Earl, in
a woman, and a woman a man.   a speech on 11 April 1648, proving
himself Chancellor of Oxford

William Penn 1644–1718

English Quaker; founder of Pennsylvania

13 It is a reproach to religion and government to suffer so   *Some Fruits of Solitude* (1693)
much poverty and excess.

14 The taking of a bribe or gratuity, should be punished   *Some Fruits of Solitude* (1693)
with as severe penalties as the defrauding of the State.

Samuel Pepys 1633–1703

English diarist

15 I went out to Charing Cross, to see Major-general   diary 13 October 1660
Harrison hanged, drawn, and quartered; which was done

there, he looking as cheerful as any man could do in that condition.

1 But methought it lessened my esteem of a king, that he should not be able to command the rain.

diary 19 July 1662

2 I see it is impossible for the King to have things done as cheap as other men.

diary 21 July 1662

3 While we were talking came by several poor creatures carried by, by constables, for being at a conventicle...I would to God they would either conform, or be more wise, and not be catched!

diary 7 August 1664

4 Pretty witty Nell.
of Nell Gwyn

diary 3 April 1665

Pericles *c.*495–429 BC

Athenian statesman

5 For famous men have the whole earth as their memorial.

Thucydides *History of the Peloponnesian War*

Juan Perón 1895–1974

Argentinian soldier and statesman, President 1946–55 and 1973–4

6 If I had not been born Perón, I would have liked to be Perón.

in *Observer* 21 February 1960

H. Ross Perot 1930–

American businessman; independent presidential candidate in the 1992 election

7 After the election people like us to go back to work. We have to go back to work because we've got to work five months just to pay our taxes.

speech to the Symposium for Better Government, 2 November 1991

8 An activist is the guy who cleans the river, not the guy who concludes it's dirty.

a favourite saying; Ken Gross *Ross Perot* (1992)

after George **Bush** *had laid stress on the value of experience in the 1992 presidential debates:*

9 I don't have any experience in running up a $4 trillion debt.

in *Newsweek* 19 October 1992

on his political future:

10 Look, I would like to go away, but if I go away, the odds we'll get reforms are zero, so I kind of have to stay around.

in *Observer* 20 August 1995 'Sayings of the Week'

Henri Philippe Pétain 1856–1951

French general and statesman, head of state 1940–2

11 To write one's memoirs is to speak ill of everybody except oneself.

in *Observer* 26 May 1946

Mike Peters
American cartoonist

1 When I go into the voting booth, do I vote for the person who is the best President? Or the slime bucket who will make my life as a cartoonist wonderful?
in Wall Street Journal 20 January 1993

Roger Peyrefitte 1907–
French writer

2 The ideal civil servant should always be colourless, odourless and tasteless.
Diplomatic Diversions (1953)

Edward John Phelps 1822–1900
American lawyer and diplomat

3 The man who makes no mistakes does not usually make anything.
speech at the Mansion House, London, 24 January 1889

Kim Philby 1912–88
British intelligence officer and Soviet spy

4 To betray, you must first belong.
in Sunday Times 17 December 1967

Prince Philip 1921–
husband of **Elizabeth II**

5 Just at this moment we are suffering a national defeat comparable to any lost military campaign, and what is more it is self-inflicted…I think it is about time we pulled our finger out.
speech to businessmen, 17 October 1961

6 If at any stage people feel that the Monarchy has no further part to play, then for goodness sake let's end the thing on amicable grounds without having a row.
to the Canadians
attributed, 1969

Morgan Phillips 1902–63
British Labour politician

7 The Labour Party owes more to Methodism than to Marxism.
James Callaghan *Time and Chance* (1987)

Wendell Phillips 1811–84
American abolitionist and orator

8 Revolutions are not made; they come. A revolution is as natural a growth as an oak. It comes out of the past. Its foundations are laid far back.
speech 8 January 1852

9 The best use of laws is to teach men to trample bad laws under their feet.
speech 12 April 1852

1 One on God's side is a majority.   speech 1 November 1859

2 Every man meets his Waterloo at last.   speech 1 November 1859

3 Whether in chains or in laurels, Liberty knows nothing   speech 1 November 1859
  but victories.

4 Truth is one forever absolute, but opinion is truth filtered   in *Idols* 4 October 1859
  through the moods, the blood, the disposition of the
  spectator.

Phocion *c.*402–317 BC

Athenian soldier

5 DEMOSTHENES: The Athenians will kill thee, Phocion,   Plutarch *Parallel Lives* 'Phocion'
     should they go crazy.
  PHOCION: But they will kill thee, should they come to
     their senses.

Kenneth Pickthorn 1892–1975

British Conservative politician and historian

6 Procedure is all the poor Briton has, now that any   in the House of Commons, 8
  Government which commands 51 per cent of the House   February 1960
  can at any moment do anything they like with
  retrospective or prospective intention.

William Pitt, Earl of Chatham 1708–78

British Whig statesman; he became Secretary of State
(effectively Prime Minister) in 1756 and headed coalition
governments 1756–61 and 1766–8; father of William **Pitt**
(1759–1806)
on Pitt: see **Walpole** 378:4

7 The atrocious crime of being a young man...I shall   in the House of Commons, 2 March
  neither attempt to palliate nor deny.   1741

8 I must now address a few words to the Solicitor; they   Basil Williams *William Pitt, Earl of
  shall be few, but they shall be daggers.   Chatham* (1913)
     *to William Murray, the Attorney-General, in the House of
     Commons*

9 The poorest man may in his cottage bid defiance to all   speech, *c.* March 1763
  the forces of the Crown. It may be frail—its roof may
  shake—the wind may blow through it—the storm may
  enter—the rain may enter—but the King of England
  cannot enter!

10 Confidence is a plant of slow growth in an aged bosom: in the House of Commons, 14
   youth is the season of credulity.   January 1766

11 Unlimited power is apt to corrupt the minds of those who   in the House of Lords, 9 January
   possess it.   1770

12 There is something behind the throne greater than the   in the House of Lords, 2 March
   King himself.   1770

1 We have a Calvinistic creed, a Popish liturgy, and an   in the House of Lords, 19 May 1772
  Arminian clergy.

2 You cannot conquer America.   in the House of Lords, 18
    November 1777

3 I invoke the genius of the Constitution!   in the House of Lords, 18
    November 1777

4 Shall a people that fifteen years ago was the terror of the   Basil Williams *William Pitt, Earl of*
  world now stoop so low as to tell its ancient inveterate   *Chatham* (1913)
  enemy, 'Take all we have, only give us peace?'
    in his last speech in the Lords, shortly before his death,
    opposing a surrender to the American colonists and their ally
    France

5 Our watchword is security.   attributed

6 The parks are the lungs of London.   quoted in the House of Commons
    by William Windham, 30 June 1808

William Pitt 1759–1806

British statesman, Prime Minister 1783–1801 and 1804–6;
second son of William **Pitt**, Earl of Chatham
on Pitt: see **Burke** 65:6, **Fox** 140:4, **Fox** 140:5

7 Necessity is the plea for every infringement of human   in the House of Commons, 18
  freedom: it is the argument of tyrants; it is the creed of   November 1783
  slaves.

8 We must anew commence the salvation of Europe.   in 1795; in *Dictionary of National*
    Biography

9 We must recollect . . . what it is we have at stake, what it   *Speeches of the Rt. Hon. William*
  is we have to contend for. It is for our property, it is for   *Pitt* (1806)
  our liberty, it is for our independence, nay, for our
  existence as a nation; it is for our character, it is for our
  very name as Englishmen, it is for everything dear and
  valuable to man on this side of the grave.
    on the rupture of the Peace of Amiens and the resumption of war
    with Napoleon, 22 July 1803

10 England has saved herself by her exertions, and will, as   R. Coupland *War Speeches of*
   I trust, save Europe by her example.   *William Pitt* (1915)
    replying to a toast in which he had been described as the
    saviour of his country in the wars with France

11 Roll up that map; it will not be wanted these ten years.   Earl Stanhope *Life of the Rt. Hon.*
   *of a map of Europe, on hearing of **Napoleon**'s victory at*   *William Pitt* (1862)
   Austerlitz, December 1805

12 Oh, my country! how I leave my country!   Earl Stanhope *Life of the Rt. Hon.*
   last words; oral tradition reports 'I think I could eat one of   *William Pitt* vol. 3 (1879) ('How
   Bellamy's veal pies'   I love my country' in the 1st ed.,
    vol. 4 (1862) ch. 43); G. Rose
    Diaries and Correspondence (1860)
    vol. 2, 23 January 1806, cites 'My
    country! oh, my country!'

Pius VII 1742–1823

Pope from 1800

1 We are prepared to go to the gates of Hell—but no further.

attempting to reach an agreement with **Napoleon**, *c.1800–1*

J. M. Robinson *Cardinal Consalvi* (1987)

Plato 429–347 BC

Greek philosopher

2 What I say is that 'just' or 'right' means nothing but what is in the interest of the stronger party.

spoken by Thrasymachus in *The Republic*

3 One of the penalties for refusing to participate in politics is that you end up being governed by your inferiors.

The Republic

4 When the tyrant has disposed of foreign enemies by conquest or treaty, and there is nothing to fear from them, then he is always stirring up some war or other, in order that the people may require a leader.

'foreign enemies' here means 'exiled opponents'

The Republic

Pliny the Elder AD 23–79

Roman statesman and scholar

5 *Ex Africa semper aliquid novi.*
Always something new out of Africa.

traditional form of *Semper aliquid novi Africam adferre*; *Historia Naturalis*

George Washington Plunkitt 1842–1924

American politician

6 I seen my opportunities and I took 'em.

William L. Riordan *Plunkitt of Tammany Hall* (1905)

7 The politician who steals is worse than a thief. He is a fool. With all the grand opportunities around for the man with a political pull, there's no excuse for stealin' a cent.

William L. Riordan *Plunkitt of Tammany Hall* (1905)

Plutarch AD c.46–c.120

Greek philosopher and biographer

8 For we are told that when a certain man was accusing both of them to him, he [Caesar] said that he had no fear of those fat and long-haired fellows, but rather of those pale and thin ones.

Parallel Lives 'Anthony'

9 The man who is thought to have been the first to see beneath the surface of Caesar's public policy and to fear it, as one might fear the smiling surface of the sea.

of **Cicero**

Parallel Lives 'Julius Caesar'

Georges Pompidou 1911–74

French statesman, Prime Minister 1962–8 and President
1969–74

1 A statesman is a politician who places himself at the   in 1973, attributed
service of the nation. A politician is a statesman who
places the nation at his service.

Alexander Pope 1688–1744

English poet

2 Here thou, great Anna! whom three realms obey,   *The Rape of the Lock* (1714)
Dost sometimes counsel take—and sometimes tea.

3 Statesman, yet friend to Truth! of soul sincere,   *Epistles to Several Persons* 'To Mr
In action faithful, and in honour clear;   Addison' (1720)
Who broke no promise, served no private end,
Who gained no title, and who lost no friend.

4 For forms of government let fools contest;   *An Essay on Man* Epistle 3 (1733)
Whate'er is best administered is best.

5 If parts allure thee, think how Bacon shined,   *An Essay on Man* Epistle 4 (1734)
The wisest, brightest, meanest of mankind:
Or ravished with the whistling of a name,
See Cromwell, damned to everlasting fame!

6 Old politicians chew on wisdom past,   *Epistles to Several Persons* 'To
And totter on in business to the last.   Lord Cobham' (1734)

7 Get place and wealth, if possible, with grace;   *Imitations of Horace* Horace bk. 1,
If not, by any means get wealth and place.   Epistle 1 (1738); cf. **Horace** 183:3

8 Lo! thy dread empire, Chaos! is restored;   *The Dunciad* (1742)
Light dies before thy uncreating word:
Thy hand, great Anarch! lets the curtain fall;
And universal darkness buries all.

John Popham 1531?–1607

Speaker of the House of Commons and Chief Justice

*on being asked by the Queen what had passed in the Lower
House in the Parliament of 1581:*
9 If it please your Majesty, seven weeks.   Bacon *Apophthegms*

Karl Popper 1902–95

Austrian-born philosopher

10 We may become the makers of our fate when we have   *The Open Society and its Enemies*
ceased to pose as its prophets.   (1945) introduction

11 We must plan for freedom, and not only for security, if *The Open Society and its Enemies*
for no other reason than that only freedom can make   (1945)
security secure.

12 There is no history of mankind, there are only many   *The Open Society and its Enemies*
histories of all kinds of aspects of human life. And one of (1945)

these is the history of political power. This is elevated
into the history of the world.

1 Marxism is only an episode—one of the many mistakes   *The Open Society and its Enemies*
   we have made in the perennial and dangerous struggle   (rev. ed., 1952)
   for building a better and a freer world.

2 Piecemeal social engineering resembles physical   *The Poverty of Historicism* (1957)
   engineering in regarding the *ends* as beyond the province
   of technology.

David Morris Potter 1901–71

3 Democracy is clearly most appropriate for countries   *People of Plenty* (1954)
   which enjoy an economic surplus and least appropriate
   for countries where there is an economic insufficiency.

Henry Codman Potter 1835–1908

Bishop of New York from 1887

4 We have exchanged the Washingtonian dignity for the   *Bishop Potter's Address* (1890)
   Jeffersonian simplicity, which was, in truth, only another
   name for the Jacksonian vulgarity.

Colin Powell 1937–

American general

5 My philosophy in all this is rather simple: match political   in *The National Interest* Spring
   expectations to military means in a wholly realistic way.   1994
   Don't slide in, don't mislead yourself.
      speech at the National Press Club luncheon, 28 September 1993

Enoch Powell 1912–

British Conservative politician
on Powell: see **Macleod** 243:3

6 In politics it is more blessed not to take than to give.   in *Daily Telegraph* 31 January 1964

7 A little nonsense now and then is not a bad thing.   attributed, 1964
   Where would we politicians be if we were not allowed to
   talk it sometimes.?

8 The professional politician can sympathize with the   attributed, 1965
   professional advertiser...both must resign themselves to
   a low public estimation of their veracity and sincerity.

9 History is littered with the wars which everybody knew   speech to the Conservative Party
   would never happen.   Conference, 19 October 1967

10 Those whom the gods wish to destroy, they first make   speech at Birmingham, 20 April
   mad. We must be mad, literally mad, as a nation to be   1968
   permitting the annual inflow of some 50,000 dependents,
   who are for the most part the material of the future
   growth of the immigrant descended population. It is like
   watching a nation busily engaged in heaping up its own
   funeral pyre.

1 As I look ahead, I am filled with foreboding. Like the   speech at Birmingham, 20 April
Roman, I seem to see 'the River Tiber foaming with   1968; cf. **Virgil** 375:6
much blood'.

2 'Helping industry' is the elephant pit of socialism, a deep   speech in Eastbourne, 24
hole with sharp spikes at the bottom, covered over with   September 1969
twigs and fresh grass.

3 No one is forced to be a politician. It can only compare   attributed, 1973
with fox-hunting and writing poetry. These are two
things that men do for sheer enjoyment too.

4 There is a mania in legislation in detecting   attributed, 1975
discrimination. But all life is about discrimination.

5 A party...is not a faction or club of individuals who   speech 30 September 1976
associate for mutual assistance in acquiring and retaining
office. It is a body of persons who hold, advocate and
desire to bring into effect certain political principles and
policies.

6 Office before honour was the password of Conservative   in *Spectator* 15 October 1977
government.
   of the 1970–4 Conservative administration

7 All political lives, unless they are cut off in midstream at   *Joseph Chamberlain* (1977);
a happy juncture, end in failure, because that is the   epilogue
nature of politics and of human affairs.

8 Take Parliament out of the history of England and that   in 'The Parliamentarians' (BBC TV),
history itself becomes meaningless.   a discussion between Enoch
   Powell and Robin Day, 4 February
   1979

9 For a politician to complain about the press is like   in *Guardian* 3 December 1984
a ship's captain complaining about the sea.

10 A Tory is someone who thinks institutions are wiser than   in *Daily Telegraph* 31 March 1986
those who operate them.

11 ANNE BROWN: How would you like to be remembered?   in a radio interview, 13 April 1986
ENOCH POWELL: I should like to have been killed in the
   war.

12 The politician has to simplify in order to do his business   in *Spectator* 26 November 1988
with his public: but the historian can be so obsessed with
the falsity of simplification as to qualify his subject out of
recognizability.

13 To pretend that you cannot exchange goods and services   in *Guardian* 22 May 1990
freely with a Frenchman or an Italian, unless there is an
identical standard of bathing beaches or tap water in the
different countries is not logic. It is naked aggression.

14 To be and to remain a member of the House of Commons   'Theory and Practice' 1990
was the overriding and undiscussable motivation of my
life as a politician.

15 What is history except a nation's collective memory?   on BBC Radio 4 10 February 1991

16 Lift the curtain and 'the State' reveals itself as a little   attributed
group of fallible men in Whitehall, making guesses about
the future, influenced by political prejudices and partisan

prejudices, and working on projections drawn from the
past by a staff of economists.

John O'Connor Power b. 1846

Irish lawyer and politician

of the Liberal Unionists:

1 The mules of politics: without pride of ancestry, or hope   H. H. Asquith *Memories and*
   of posterity.   *Reflections* (1928); cf. **Disraeli**
                                                                      117:9, **Donnelly** 122:7

John Prescott 1938–

British Labour politician; Deputy Leader of the Labour Party
from 1994

on the contest for the Labour leadership, during a debate
between himself, Tony **Blair**, *and Margaret Beckett:*
2 We're in danger of loving ourselves to death.   in *Observer* 19 June 1994 'Sayings
                                                                      of the Week'

Richard Price 1723–91

English nonconformist minister

3 Now, methinks, I see the ardour for liberty catching and   *A Discourse on the Love of our*
   spreading; a general amendment beginning in human   *Country* (1790)
   affairs; the dominion of kings changed for the dominion
   of laws, and the dominion of priests giving way to the
   dominion of reason and conscience.

Matthew Prior 1664–1721

English poet

4 What is a King?—a man condemned to bear   *Solomon* (1718)
   The public burden of the nation's care.

Pierre-Joseph Proudhon 1809–65

French social reformer

5 Property is theft.   *Qu'est-ce que la propriété?* (1840)

John Pym 1584–1643

English Parliamentary leader

6 To have granted liberties, and not to have liberties in   in *Dictionary of National Biography*
   truth and realities, is but to mock the kingdom.
   after the battle of Edgehill, in a speech at Guildhall to the
   citizens of London pointing out the illusory nature of **Charles I**'s
   promises

Pyrrhus 319–272 BC

King of Epirus from 306 BC

1 One more such victory and we are lost.   Plutarch *Parallel Lives* 'Pyrrhus'
   on defeating the Romans at Asculum, 279 BC; origin of the
   phrase 'Pyrrhic victory'

François Quesnay 1694–1774

French political economist

2 *Vous ne connaissez qu'une seule règle du commerce; c'est*   letter from M. Alpha to de
   (pour me servir de vos propres termes) de laisser passer et de   Quesnay, 1767, in L. Salleron
   laisser faire tous les acheteurs et tous les vendeurs   *François Quesnay et la*
   quelconques.   *Physiocratie* (1958) vol. 2, but not
   You recognize but one rule of commerce; that is (to avail   found in de Quesnay's writings; cf.
   myself of your own terms) to allow free passage and   **Argenson** 16:1
   freedom of action to all buyers and sellers whoever they
   may be.

Josiah Quincy 1772–1864

American Federalist politician

3 As it will be the right of all, so it will be the duty of   in *Abridgement of Debates of*
   some, definitely to prepare for a separation, amicably if   *Congress* 14 January 1811
   they can, violently if they must.

Yitzhak Rabin 1922–95

Israeli statesman and military leader, Prime Minister 1974–7
and 1992–5

4 We say to you today in a loud and a clear voice: enough   in Washington, 13 September
   of blood and tears. Enough.   1993
   to the Palestinians, at the signing of the Israel–Palestine
   Declaration

Lord Radcliffe 1899–1977

British lawyer and public servant

5 Society has become used to the standing armies of   *Power and the State* (BBC Reith
   power—the permanent Civil Service, the police force, the   Lectures, 1951)
   tax-gatherer—organized on a scale which was unknown
   to earlier centuries.

6 Governments always tend to want not really a free press   in 1967; Peter Hennessy *What the*
   but a managed or well-conducted one.   *Papers Never Said* (1985)

Thomas Rainborowe d. 1648

English soldier and parliamentarian

1 The poorest he that is in England hath a life to live as the greatest he.
during the Army debates at Putney, 29 October 1647

C. H. Firth (ed.) *The Clarke Papers* vol. 1 (1891)

Milton Rakove 1918–83

2 The second law, Rakove's law of principle and politics, states that the citizen is influenced by principle in direct proportion to his distance from the political situation.

in *Virginia Quarterly Review* (1965)

Walter Ralegh c.1552–1618

English explorer and courtier

3 Fain would I climb, yet fear I to fall.
line written on a window-pane; cf. **Elizabeth I** 131:8

Thomas Fuller *History of the Worthies of England* (1662) 'Devonshire'

4 Say to the court, it glows
And shines like rotten wood;
Say to the church, it shows
What's good, and doth no good:
If church and court reply,
Then give them both the lie.

'The Lie' (1608)

5 'Tis a sharp remedy, but a sure one for all ills.
on feeling the edge of the axe prior to his execution

D. Hume *History of Great Britain* (1754)

6 So the heart be right, it is no matter which way the head lies.
at his execution, on being asked which way he preferred to lay his head

W. Stebbing *Sir Walter Raleigh* (1891)

7 I have a long journey to take, and must bid the company farewell.
parting words

E. Thompson *Sir Walter Raleigh* (1935)

John Randolph 1773–1833

American politician

8 The surest way to prevent war is not to fear it.

in the House of Representatives, 5 March 1806

9 God has given us Missouri, and the devil shall not take it from us.
in the debate in the US Senate in 1820 on the admission of Missouri to the Union as a slave state

Robert V. Remini *Henry Clay* (1991)

10 Never were abilities so much below mediocrity so well rewarded; no, not when Caligula's horse was made Consul.
on John Quincy **Adams**'s *appointment of Richard Rush as Secretary of the Treasury*

speech 1 February 1828

1 He is a man of splendid abilities but utterly corrupt. He
   shines and stinks like rotten mackerel by moonlight.
      of Edward Livingston

   W. Cabell Bruce *John Randolph of
   Roanoke* (1923) vol. 2

2 He rowed to his object with muffled oars.
      of Martin Van Buren

   W. Cabell Bruce *John Randolph of
   Roanoke* (1923) vol. 2

3 That most delicious of all privileges—spending other
   people's money.

   William Cabell Bruce *John
   Randolph of Roanoke* (1923) vol. 2

Sam Rayburn 1882–1961

American politician

4 If you want to get along, go along.

   Neil MacNeil *Forge of Democracy*
   (1963)

Ronald Reagan 1911–

American Republican statesman, 40th President of the US
1981–9; former Hollywood actor
on Reagan: see **Keillor** 203:3, **Schroeder** 321:8, **Vidal** 375:2;
see also **Dempsey** 113:3, **Gipp** 153:5

5 Government is like a big baby—an alimentary canal with
   a big appetite at one end and no responsibility at the
   other.
      campaigning for the governorship of California, 1965

   attributed

6 Politics is just like show business, you have a hell of an
   opening, coast for a while and then have a hell of
   a close.

   in 1966; Mark Green and Gail
   MacColl (eds.) *There He Goes
   Again* (1983)

7 Government does not solve problems; it subsidizes them.

   speech 11 December 1972

8 Politics is supposed to be the second oldest profession.
   I have come to realize that it bears a very close
   resemblance to the first.

   at a conference in Los Angeles, 2
   March 1977

9 I've noticed that everybody who is for abortion has
   already been born.

   presidential campaign debate, 21
   September 1980

10 You can tell a lot about a fellow's character by his way
   of eating jellybeans.

   in *New York Times* 15 January 1981

11 We're the party that wants to see an America in which
   people can still get rich.

   at a Republican congressional
   dinner, 4 May 1982

12 So in your discussions of the nuclear freeze proposals,
   I urge you to beware the temptation of pride—the
   temptation blithely to declare yourselves above it all and
   label both sides equally at fault, to ignore the facts of
   history and the aggressive impulses of an evil empire.

   speech to the National Association
   of Evangelicals, 8 March 1983

13 My fellow Americans, I am pleased to tell you I just
   signed legislation which outlaws Russia forever. The
   bombing begins in five minutes.
      said during radio microphone test, 11 August 1984

   in *New York Times* 13 August 1984

14 The taxpayer—that's someone who works for the federal
   government but doesn't have to take a Civil Service
   examination.

   attributed, 1985

1 We are especially not going to tolerate these attacks from   in *New York Times* 9 July 1985
outlaw states run by the strangest collection of misfits,
Looney Tunes, and squalid criminals since the advent of
the Third Reich.
speech following the hijack of a US plane, 8 July 1985

2 This mad dog of the Middle East.   in *New York Times* 10 April 1986
of Colonel Gadaffi of Libya, 9 April 1986

3 It's difficult to believe that people are starving in this   at a press conference, 11 June 1986
country because food isn't available.

4 The nine most terrifying words in the English language   at a press conference in Chicago, 2
are, 'I'm from the government and I'm here to help.'   August 1986
on assistance to farmers

5 Mr Gorbachev, tear down this wall.   in Berlin, 12 June 1987

6 I don't resent his popularity or anything else. Good Lord,   address to schoolchildren in
I co-starred with Errol Flynn once.   Jacksonville, Florida, 1 December
*of Mikhail **Gorbachev***   1987

7 To grasp and hold a vision, that is the very essence of   in *The Wilson Quarterly* Winter
successful leadership—not only on the movie set where   1994; attributed
I learned it, but everywhere.

8 I now begin the journey that will lead me into the sunset   in *Daily Telegraph* 5 January 1995
of my life.
statement to the American people revealing that he had
Alzheimer's disease, 1994

John Redmond 1856–1918

Irish politician and nationalist leader

in the Spring of 1914 Redmond was asked by a friend, a priest
from Tipperary, if anything could now rob them of Home Rule:
9 A European war might do it.   in *Dictionary of National Biography*

Joseph Reed 1741–85

American Revolutionary politician

10 I am not worth purchasing, but such as I am, the King   W. B. Read *Life and*
of Great Britain is not rich enough to do it.   *Correspondence of Joseph Reed*
replying to an offer from Governor George Johnstone of £10,000, (1847)
and any office in the Colonies in the King's gift, if he were able
successfully to promote a Union between the United Kingdom
and the American Colonies

Thomas Brackett Reed 1839–1902

American politician and member of Congress

of two fellow congressmen:
11 They never open their mouths without subtracting from   Samuel W. McCall *The Life of*
the sum of human knowledge.   *Thomas Brackett Reed* (1914)

Montague John Rendall 1862–1950

member of the first BBC Board of Governors

1   Nation shall speak peace unto nation.   motto of the BBC; cf. **Bible** 43:18

James Reston 1909–95

American journalist

2   This is the devilish thing about foreign affairs: they are foreign and will not always conform to our whim.   in *New York Times* 16 December 1964

3   All politics, however, are based on the indifference of the majority.   in *New York Times* 12 June 1968

Walter Reuther 1907–70

American labour leader

4   If it looks like a duck, walks like a duck and quacks like a duck, then it just may be a duck.   attributed
    as a test, during the McCarthy era, of Communist affiliations

5   Injustice was as common as streetcars. When men walked into their jobs, they left their dignity, their citizenship and their humanity outside.   attributed
    on working life in America before the Wagner Act

Paul Revere 1735–1818

American patriot

6   To the memory of the glorious Ninety-two: members of the Honorable House of Representatives of the Massachusetts Bay who, undaunted by the insolent menaces of villains in power, from a strict regard to conscience and the liberties of their constituents on the 30th June 1768 voted NOT TO RESCIND.   attributed
    inscription on Revere's silver 'Liberty' bowl, 1768

7   If the British went out by water, to show two lanterns in the North Church steeple; and if by land, one as a signal, for we were apprehensive it would be difficult to cross the Charles River or get over Boston Neck.   letter to Jeremy Belknap
    signal code arranged with Colonel Conant of the Charlestown Committee of Safety, 16 April 1775

Joshua Reynolds 1723–92

English painter

8   The House of Commons resembles a private company. How seldom is any man convinced by another's argument; passion and pride rise against it.   James Boswell *Life of Samuel Johnson* (1791) 3 April 1778

Cecil Rhodes 1853–1902

British-born South African diamond prospector and statesman,
Prime Minister of Cape Colony 1890–6

1 Ask any man what nationality he would prefer to be,
and ninety-nine out of a hundred will tell you that they
would prefer to be Englishmen.

Gordon Le Sueur *Cecil Rhodes*
(1913)

2 Being an Englishman is the greatest prize in the lottery of
life.

A. W. Jarvis *Jottings from an Active
Life* (1928)

3 So little done, so much to do.
said on the day of his death

Lewis Michell *Life of Rhodes* (1910)

David Ricardo 1772–1823

British economist

4 Rent is that portion of the earth, which is paid to the
landlord for the use of the original and indestructible
powers of the soil.

*On the Principles of Political
Economy and Taxation* (1817)

Grantland Rice 1880–1954

American sportswriter

5 All wars are planned by old men
In council rooms apart.

'The Two Sides of War' (1955)

Stephen Rice 1637–1715

Irish lawyer

6 I will drive a coach and six horses through the Act of
Settlement.

W. King *State of the Protestants of
Ireland* (1672)

Tim Rice 1944–

English lyricist

7 Don't cry for me, Argentina.
from the musical Evita, *based on the life of Eva Perón*

title of song (1976)

Mandy Rice-Davies 1944–

English courtesan

*at the trial of Stephen Ward, 29 June 1963, on being told that
Lord Astor claimed that her allegations, concerning himself
and his house parties at Cliveden, were untrue:*

8 He would, wouldn't he?

in *Guardian* 1 July 1963

Ann Richards 1933–

American Democratic politician; State Treasurer, and later
Governor, of Texas

1 That dog won't hunt.
   of Republican policies

keynote speech at the Democratic
convention, 1988; Wallace O.
Chariton *This Dog'll Hunt* (1989)

2 Poor George, he can't help it—he was born with a silver
   foot in his mouth.
   of George **Bush**

keynote speech at the Democratic
convention, 1988; in *Independent*
20 July 1988

Johann Paul Friedrich Richter ('Jean Paul')
1763–1825

German novelist

3 Providence has given to the French the empire of the
   land, to the English that of the sea, and to the Germans
   that of—the air!

Thomas Carlyle 'Jean Paul Friedrich
Richter' in *Edinburgh Review* no.
91 (1827)

Adam Ridley 1942–

British economist, former Director of the Conservative
Research Department

4 Parties come to power with silly, inconsistent and
   impossible policies because they have spent their whole
   period in opposition forgetting about the real world,
   destroying the lessons they learnt in government and
   clambering slowly back on to the ideological plain where
   they feel happiest.

in *RIPA Report* Winter 1985

Nicholas Ridley 1929–93

British Conservative politician

5 The last thing I want is to spend more time with my
   family.
   *as Trade and Industry Secretary, replying to taunts that he had
   more past than future as a minister*

in *Independent* 10 March 1990

of the European monetary union:
6 This is all a German racket designed to take over the
   whole of Europe.
   *in an interview with Dominic Lawson, in the aftermath of which
   Ridley resigned from the Government*

in *Spectator* 14 July 1990

7 Seventeen unelected reject politicians with no
   accountability to anybody, who are not responsible for
   raising taxes, just spending money, who are pandered to
   by a supine parliament which also is not responsible for
   raising taxes.
   of the European Community

in *Spectator* 14 July 1990

8 I'm not against giving up sovereignty in principle, but
   not to this lot. You might just as well give it to Adolf

in *Spectator* 14 July 1990

Hitler, frankly.
of the European Community

Hal Riney 1932–

American advertising executive

1   It's morning again in America.   in *Newsweek* 6 August 1984
    slogan for Ronald **Reagan**'s *1984 election campaign*

Geoffrey Rippon 1924–

British Conservative politician

2   The world is divided into three classes. The Haves, the   attributed, May 1987
    Have-nots, and the Haves but Have not Paid.

3   An opposition politician must at all times avoid being   attributed, May 1987
    contaminated by the truth.

Maximilien Robespierre 1758–94

French revolutionary
on Robespierre: see **Carlyle** 75:9

4   I am no courtesan, nor moderator, nor Tribune, nor   speech at the Jacobin Club, 27
    defender of the people: I am myself the people.   April 1792

5   The general will rules in society as the private will   *Lettres à ses commettans* (2nd
    governs each separate individual.   series) 5 January 1793

6   Any law which violates the inalienable rights of man is   *Déclaration des droits de l'homme*
    essentially unjust and tyrannical; it is not a law at all.   24 April 1793, article 6; this article,
                                                               in slightly different form, is
                                                               recorded as having figured in
                                                               Robespierre's *Projet* of 21 April
                                                               1793

7   Any institution which does not suppose the people good,   *Déclaration des droits de l'homme*
    and the magistrate corruptible, is evil.   24 April 1793, article 25

8   The revolutionary government is the despotism of liberty   speech 5 February 1794
    against tyranny.

9   Wickedness is the root of despotism as virtue is the   in the Convention, 7 May 1794
    essence of the Republic.

10 One single will is necessary.   private note; S, A. Berville and J. F.
                                                      Barrière *Papiers inédits trouvés
                                                      chez Robespierre* vol. 2 (1828)

11 If the basis of popular government in time of peace is   J. M. Thompson *The French
    virtue, its basis in a time of revolution is both virtue and   Revolution*; attributed
    intimidation. Intimidation without virtue is disastrous;
    virtue without intimidation is powerless.

James Harvey Robinson 1863–1936

12 Political campaigns are designedly made into emotional   *The Human Comedy* (1937)
    orgies which endeavour to distract attention from the

real issues involved, and they actually paralyze what
slight powers of cerebration man can normally muster.

1 With supreme irony, the war to 'make the world safe for
   democracy' ended by leaving democracy more unsafe in
   the world than at any time since the collapse of the
   revolutions of 1848.

The Human Comedy (1937)

Joan Robinson 1903–

British economist

2 Current experience suggests that socialism is not a stage
   beyond capitalism but a substitute for it—a means by
   which the nations which did not share in the Industrial
   Revolution can imitate its technical achievements;
   a means to achieve rapid accumulation under a different
   set of rules of the game.

'Marx, Marshall and Keynes' (1955)

Mary Robinson 1944–

Irish Labour stateswoman; President from 1990

3 Instead of rocking the cradle, they rocked the system.
     in her victory speech, paying tribute to the women of Ireland

in *The Times* 10 November 1990

Boyle Roche 1743–1807

Irish politician

4 Mr Speaker, I smell a rat; I see him forming in the air
   and darkening the sky; but I'll nip him in the bud.

attributed

Lord Rochester 1647–80

English poet

5 Here lies a great and mighty king
   Whose promise none relies on;
   He never said a foolish thing,
   Nor ever did a wise one.
     of **Charles II***; an alternative first line reads: 'Here lies our
     sovereign lord the King'*

'The King's Epitaph'; C. E. Doble et
al. *Thomas Hearne: Remarks and
Collections* (1885–1921) 17
November 1706; cf. **Charles II** 83:1

6 A merry monarch, scandalous and poor.

'A Satire on King Charles II' (1697)

Will Rogers 1879–1935

American humorist

7 The more you read and observe about this Politics thing,
   you got to admit that each party is worse than the other.
   The one that's out always looks the best.

Illiterate Digest (1924)

8 Communism is like prohibition, it's a good idea but it
   won't work.

in 1927; *Weekly Articles* (1981) vol.
3

9 I don't know jokes—I just watch the government and
   report the facts.

'A Rogers Thesaurus' in *Saturday
Review* 25 August 1962

Mme Roland 1754–93

French revolutionary

1 O liberty! O liberty! what crimes are committed in thy name!

A. de Lamartine *Histoire des Girondins* (1847)

Oscar Romero 1917–80

Salvadorean Roman Catholic priest, Archbishop of San Salvador

2 When a dictatorship seriously violates human rights and attacks the common good of the nation, when it becomes unbearable and closes all channels of dialogue, of understanding, of rationality, when this happens, the Church speaks of the legitimate right of insurrectional violence.

Alan Riding 'The Cross and the Sword in Latin America' (1981)

Eleanor Roosevelt 1884–1962

American humanitarian and diplomat, wife of Franklin
Roosevelt
on Roosevelt: see **Stevenson** 350:14

3 No one can make you feel inferior without your consent.

in *Catholic Digest* August 1960

Franklin D. Roosevelt 1882–1945

American Democratic statesman, 32nd President of the US
1933–45
on Roosevelt: see **Churchill** 92:5, **Holmes** 181:8,
Truman 371:1

4 These unhappy times call for the building of plans that… build from the bottom up and not from the top down, that put their faith once more in the forgotten man at the bottom of the economic pyramid.

radio address, 7 April 1932

5 The country needs and, unless I mistake its temper, the country demands bold, persistent experimentation. It is common sense to take a method and try it. If it fails, admit it frankly and try another. But above all, try something.

address at Oglethorpe University, Atlanta, Georgia, 22 May 1932

6 I pledge you, I pledge myself, to a new deal for the American people.
   accepting the presidential nomination

speech to the Democratic Convention in Chicago, 2 July 1932

7 There is no indispensable man.

campaign speech, New York, 3 November 1932

8 The only thing we have to fear is fear itself.

inaugural address, 4 March 1933

9 In the field of world policy I would dedicate this Nation to the policy of the good neighbour.

inaugural address, 4 March 1933

10 This generation of Americans has a rendezvous with destiny.

speech accepting renomination as President, 27 June 1936

1 I have seen war. I have seen war on land and sea. I have seen blood running from the wounded. I have seen men coughing out their gassed lungs. I have seen the dead in the mud. I have seen cities destroyed. I have seen 200 limping, exhausted men come out of line—the survivors of a regiment of 1,000 that went forward 48 hours before. I have seen children starving. I have seen the agony of mothers and wives. I hate war.

speech at Chautauqua, NY, 14 August 1936

2 I should like to have it said of my first Administration that in it the forces of selfishness and of lust for power met their match. I should like to have it said of my second Administration that in it these forces met their master.

speech at Madison Square Garden, 31 October 1936

3 I see one-third of a nation ill-housed, ill-clad, ill-nourished.

second inaugural address, 20 January 1937

4 War is a contagion.

speech at Chicago, 5 October 1937

5 The only sure bulwark of continuing liberty is a government strong enough to protect the interests of the people, and a people strong enough and well enough informed to maintain its sovereign control over its government.

'Fireside Chat' radio broadcast, 14 April 1938

6 When peace has been broken anywhere, the peace of all countries everywhere is in danger.

'Fireside Chat' radio broadcast, 3 September 1939

7 I am reminded of four definitions: A Radical is a man with both feet firmly planted—in the air. A Conservative is a man with two perfectly good legs who, however, has never learned to walk forward. A Reactionary is a somnambulist walking backwards. A Liberal is a man who uses his legs and his hands at the behest—at the command—of his head.

radio address to *New York Herald Tribune* Forum, 26 October 1939

8 On this tenth day of June 1940 the hand that held the dagger has struck it into the back of its neighbour.
   on hearing that Italy had declared war on France

address at the University of Virginia, Charlottesville, 10 June 1940

9 I have said this before, but I shall say it again and again and again: Your boys are not going to be sent into any foreign wars.

speech in Boston, 30 October 1940

10 We have the men—the skill—the wealth—and above all, the will…We must be the great arsenal of democracy.

'Fireside Chat' radio broadcast, 29 December 1940

11 We look forward to a world founded upon four essential human freedoms. The first is freedom of speech and expression—everywhere in the world. The second is freedom of every person to worship God in his own way—everywhere in the world. The third is freedom from want…everywhere in the world. The fourth is freedom from fear…anywhere in the world.

message to Congress, 6 January 1941

12 We, too, born to freedom, and believing in freedom, are willing to fight to maintain freedom. We, and all others who believe as deeply as we do, would rather die on our feet than live on our knees.
   on receiving the degree of Doctor of Civil Law from Oxford

on 19 June 1941; cf. **Ibarruri** 186:6

1 Yesterday, December 7, 1941—a date which will live in infamy—the United States of America was suddenly and deliberately attacked by naval and air forces of the Empire of Japan.

address to Congress, 8 December 1941

2 Books can not be killed by fire. People die, but books never die. No man and no force can abolish memory... In this war, we know, books are weapons. And it is a part of your dedication always to make them weapons for man's freedom.

'Message to the Booksellers of America' 6 May 1942

3 It is fun to be in the same decade with you.
   cabled reply to Winston Churchill, acknowledging congratulations on his 60th birthday

W. S. Churchill *The Hinge of Fate* (1950)

4 All of our people all over the country—except the pure-blooded Indians—are immigrants or descendants of immigrants, including even those who came over here on the Mayflower.

campaign speech in Boston, 4 November 1944

5 The American people are quite competent to judge a political party that works both sides of the street.

campaign speech in Boston, 4 November 1944

6 We have learned that we cannot live alone, at peace; that our own well-being is dependent on the well-being of other nations, far away. We have learned that we must live as men, and not as ostriches, no as dogs in the manger. We have learned to be citizens of the world, members of the human community.

fourth inaugural address, 20 January 1945

7 You've convinced me. Now go out and put pressure on me.

attributed; Peter Hennessy *Whitehall* (1990)

8 The work, my friend, is peace. More than an end of this war—an end to the beginnings of all wars.
   undelivered address for Jefferson Day, 13 April 1945, the day after Roosevelt died

Public Papers (1950) vol. 13

9 The only limit to our realization of tomorrow will be our doubts of today. Let us move forward with strong and active faith.
   undelivered address for Jefferson Day, 13 April 1945, final lines

Public Papers (1950) vol. 13

Theodore Roosevelt 1858–1919

American Republican statesman, 26th President of the US 1901–9
on Roosevelt: see **Hanna** 168:1, **Knox** 215:2

10 I wish to preach, not the doctrine of ignoble ease, but the doctrine of the strenuous life.

speech to the Hamilton Club, Chicago, 10 April 1899

11 Far better it is to dare mighty things, to win glorious triumphs, even though checkered by failure, than to take rank with those poor spirits who neither enjoy much nor suffer much, because they live in the grey twilight that knows not victory nor defeat.

speech to the Hamilton Club, Chicago, 10 April 1899

12 I am as strong as a bull moose and you can use me to the limit.

letter to Mark **Hanna**, 27 June 1900

'Bull Moose' subsequently became the popular name of the
Progressive Party

1 In life, as in a football game, the principle to follow is: *The Strenuous Life* (1900)
   Hit the line hard.

2 McKinley has no more backbone than a chocolate éclair!   H. T. Peck *Twenty Years of the*
   of William McKinley (1843–1901), Republican statesman and   *Republic* (1906)
   25th President of the US, whose assassination brought about
   the accession of Roosevelt

3 The first requisite of a good citizen in this Republic of   speech in New York, 11 November
   ours is that he shall be able and willing to pull his   1902
   weight.

4 There is a homely old adage which runs: 'Speak softly   speech in Chicago, 3 April 1903
   and carry a big stick; you will go far.' If the American
   nation will speak softly, and yet build and keep at a pitch
   of the highest training a thoroughly efficient navy, the
   Monroe Doctrine will go far.

5 A man who is good enough to shed his blood for the   speech at the Lincoln Monument,
   country is good enough to be given a square deal   Springfield, Illinois, 4 June 1903
   afterwards. More than that no man is entitled to, and
   less than that no man shall have.

6 Far and away the best prize that life offers is the chance   address at the State Fair,
   to work hard at work worth doing.   Syracuse, New York Labour Day, 7
                                                                    September 1903

7 No man is above the law and no man is below it; nor do   third annual message to Congress,
   we ask any man's permission when we require him to   7 December 1903
   obey it. Obedience to the law is demanded as a right; not
   asked as a favour.

8 The men with the muckrakes are often indispensable to   speech in Washington, 14 April,
   the well-being of society; but only if they know when to   1906
   stop raking the muck.

9 Malefactors of great wealth.   speech at Provincetown,
                                                                    Massachusetts, 20 August 1907

10 It is not the critic who counts; not the man who points   'Citizenship in a Republic', speech
    out how the strong man stumbles, or where the doer of   at the Sorbonne, Paris, 23 April
    deeds could have done better. The credit belongs to the   1910
    man who is actually in the arena.

11 Every man holds his property subject to the general right   speech at Osawatomie, 31 August
    of the community to regulate its use to whatever degree   1910
    the public welfare may require it.

12 We stand at Armageddon and we battle for the Lord.   speech at Progressive Party
                                                                    Convention, Chicago, 17 June 1912

13 Foolish fanatics...the men who form the lunatic fringe in   *Autobiography* (1913)
    all reform movements.

14 There is no room in this country for hyphenated   speech in New York, 12 October
    Americanism...The one absolutely certain way of   1915
    bringing this nation to ruin, of preventing all possibility
    of its continuing to be a nation at all, would be to permit
    it to become a tangle of squabbling nationalities.

1 One of our defects as a nation is a tendency to use what have been called 'weasel words'. When a weasel sucks eggs the meat is sucked out of the egg. If you use a 'weasel word' after another, there is nothing left of the other.

speech in St Louis, 31 May 1916

2 There can be no fifty-fifty Americanism in this country. There is room here for only 100 per cent Americanism, only for those who are Americans and nothing else.

speech in Saratoga, 19 July 1918

3 No man is justified in doing evil on the ground of expediency.

Works (1925) vol. 15 'Latitude and Longitude among Reformers'

4 Put out the light.
   last words

on 6 January 1919

Lord Rosebery 1847–1929

British Liberal statesman, Prime Minister 1894–5

5 There is no need for any nation, however great, leaving the Empire, because the Empire is a commonwealth of nations.

speech in Adelaide, Australia, 18 January 1884

6 There was no retirement, no concealment. He died by inches in public, sole mourner at his own protracted funeral.
   of Lord Randolph **Churchill**

attributed

7 I have never known the sweets of place with power, but of place without power, of place with the minimum of power—that is a purgatory, and if not a purgatory it is a hell.

in *The Spectator* 6 July 1895

8 Imperialism, sane Imperialism, as distinguished from what I may call wild-cat Imperialism, is nothing but this—a larger patriotism.

speech, City of London Liberal Club, 5 May 1899

9 There are two supreme pleasures in life. One is ideal, the other real. The ideal is when a man receives the seals of office from his Sovereign. The real pleasure comes when he hands them back.

Sir Robert Peel (1899)

10 It is beginning to be hinted that we are a nation of amateurs.

Rectorial address at Glasgow University, 16 November 1900

11 No one outside an asylum wishes to be rid of it.
    of the British Empire

Rectorial address at Glasgow University, 16 November 1900

12 I must plough my furrow alone.
    speech on remaining outside the Liberal Party leadership, 19 July 1901

in *The Times* 20 July 1901

13 Men who sit still with the fly-blown phylacteries bound round their obsolete policy.
    on certain members of the Liberal Party

speech at Chesterfield, 16 December 1901

Ethel Rosenberg 1916–53 and Julius Rosenberg 1918–53

American husband and wife; convicted of spying for the Russians and executed

1 We are innocent…To forsake this truth is to pay too high a price even for the priceless gift of life.
   petition for executive clemency, filed 9 January 1953

Ethel Rosenberg *Death House Letters* (1953)

2 We are the first victims of American Fascism.
   letter from Julius to Emanuel Bloch before the Rosenbergs' execution, 19 June 1953

Testament of Ethel and Julius Rosenberg (1954)

A. C. Ross fl. 1840

3 Tippecanoe and Tyler, too.
   presidential campaign song for William Henry Harrison, 1840

attributed; cf. **Morris** 266:4

Dick Ross

British economist, former Deputy Director of the Central Policy Review Staff

4 You must think the unthinkable, but always wear a dark suit when presenting the results.

in the early 1970s; Peter Hennessy *Whitehall* (1990)

Christina Rossetti 1830–94

English poet; sister of D. G. Rossetti

5 Our Indian Crown is in great measure the trapping of a splendid misery.
   on the siege of Kandahar

letter to Amelia Heimann, 29 July 1880

Jean Rostand 1894–1977

French biologist

6 Stupidity, outrage, vanity, cruelty, iniquity, bad faith, falsehood—we fail to see the whole array when it is facing in the same direction as we.

Pensées d'un biologiste (1939)

Lord Rothschild 1910–90

British administrator and scientist, first Director of the Central Policy Review Staff
*on Rothschild: see **Hurd** 185:8*

*on being appointed to the Government think-tank in 1970 where he met Burke **Trend**, the Cabinet Secretary, and William **Armstrong**, Secretary to the Treasury:*
7 Until this week I never realized that the country was run by two men I'd never heard of.

Peter Hennessy *Whitehall* (1990)

1 Politicians often believe that their world is the real one. Officials sometimes take a different view.
  on resigning as Director of the Central Policy Review Staff

in The Times 13 October 1974

2 The promises and panaceas that gleam like false teeth in the party manifestoes.

Meditations of a Broomstick (1977)

Claude-Joseph Rouget de Lisle
1760–1836

French soldier

3 *Allons, enfants de la patrie,*
  Le jour de gloire est arrivé...
  Aux armes, citoyens!
  Formez vos battaillons!
  Come, children of our country, the day of glory has
  arrived...To arms, citizens! Form your battalions!

'La Marseillaise' (25 April 1792)

Jean-Jacques Rousseau 1712–78
French philosopher and novelist

4 The social contract

title of book, 1762

5 Man was born free, and everywhere he is in chains.

The Social Contract (1762)

6 Slaves become so debased by their chains as to lose even the desire of breaking from them.

The Social Contract 1762

Maude Royden 1876–1956
English religious writer, social reformer, and preacher

7 The Church should go forward along the path of progress and be no longer satisfied only to represent the Conservative Party at prayer.

address at Queen's Hall, London, 16 July 1917

Paul Alfred Rubens 1875–1917
English songwriter

8 Oh! we don't want to lose you but we think you ought to go
  For your King and your Country both need you so;
  We shall want you and miss you but with all our might and main
  We shall cheer you, thank you, kiss you
  When you come back again.

'Your King and Country Want You' (1914 song)

Richard Rumbold c.1622–85
English republican conspirator

9 I never could believe that Providence had sent a few men into the world, ready booted and spurred to ride, and millions ready saddled and bridled to be ridden.
  on the scaffold

T. B. Macaulay *History of England* vol. 1 (1849)

Dean Rusk 1909–94

US politician; Secretary of State, 1961–9

1 We're eyeball to eyeball, and I think the other fellow just
blinked.
   on the Cuban missile crisis, 24 October 1962

in Saturday Evening Post 8
December 1962

2 Only one-third of human beings are asleep at one time,
and the other two-thirds are awake and up to some
mischief somewhere.

attributed, 1966

3 Scratch any American and underneath you'll find an
isolationist.

to the British Foreign Secretary,
George Brown; Tony Benn diary 12
January 1968

4 It has been said that power tends to corrupt, but that
loss of power tends to corrupt absolutely.

attributed, 1968

John Ruskin 1819–1900

English art and social critic

5 It ought to be quite as natural and straightforward
a matter for a labourer to take his pension from his
parish, because he has deserved well of his parish, as for
a man in higher rank to take his pension from his
country, because he has deserved well of his country.

Unto this Last (1862) preface

6 The force of the guinea you have in your pocket depends
wholly on the default of a guinea in your neighbour's
pocket. If he did not want it, it would be of no use to
you.

Unto this Last (1862)

7 Government and co-operation are in all things the laws
of life; anarchy and competition the laws of death.

Unto this Last (1862)

8 Whereas it has long been known and declared that the
poor have no right to the property of the rich, I wish it
also to be known and declared that the rich have no
right to the property of the poor.

Unto this Last (1862)

9 The first duty of a State is to see that every child born
therein shall be well housed, clothed, fed and educated,
till it attain years of discretion.

Time and Tide (1867)

10 All mastership is not alike in principle; there are just and
unjust masterships.

Time and Tide (1867)

11 You want to have voices in Parliament! Your voices are
not worth a rat's squeak, either in Parliament or out of
it, till you have some ideas to utter with them.

Time and Tide (1867)

12 Consider, for instance, the ridiculousness of the division
of parties into 'Liberal' and 'Conservative'. There is no
opposition whatever between those two kinds of men.
There is opposition between Liberals and Illiberals; that is
to say, between people who desire liberty, and who
dislike it. I am a violent Illiberal; but it does not follow
that I must be a Conservative. A Conservative is a person
who wishes to keep things as they are; and he is opposed

Fors Clavigera (1871)

to a Destructive, who wishes to destroy them, or to an Innovator, who wishes to alter them. Now, though I am an Illiberal, there are many things I should like to destroy.

1   We Communists of the old school think that our property   *Fors Clavigera* (1871)
    belongs to everybody, and everybody's property to us; so
    of course I thought the Louvre belonged to me as much
    as to the Parisians, and expected they would have sent
    word over to me, being an Art Professor, to ask whether
    I wanted it burnt down. But no message or intimation to
    that effect ever reached me.

2   You have founded an entire Science of Political Economy,   *Fors Clavigera* (1871)
    on what you have stated to be the constant instinct of
    man—the desire to defraud his neighbour.

3   Visible governments are the toys of some nations, the   *Fors Clavigera* (1871)
    diseases of others, the harness of some, the burdens of
    more, the necessity of all.

4   I am, and my father was before me, a violent Tory of the   *Praeterita* (1885)
    old school; Walter Scott's school, that is to say, and
    Homer's.

Bertrand Russell 1872–1970

British philosopher and mathematician

5   Next to enjoying ourselves, the next greatest pleasure   *Sceptical Essays* (1928)
    consists in preventing others from enjoying themselves,
    or, more generally, in the acquisition of power.

6   The opinions that are held with passion are always those   *Sceptical Essays* (1928)
    for which no good ground exists; indeed the passion is
    the measure of the holder's lack of rational conviction.

7   Envy is the basis of democracy.   *The Conquest of Happiness* (1930)

8   One should as a rule respect public opinion in so far as is   *The Conquest of Happiness* (1930)
    necessary to avoid starvation and to keep out of prison,
    but anything that goes beyond this is voluntary
    submission to an unnecessary tyranny.

9   If the Communists conquered the world it would be very   attributed, 1958
    unpleasant for a while, but not for ever.

10 Few people can be happy unless they hate some other   attributed
    person, nation, or creed.

11 Religion may in most of its forms be defined as the belief   attributed
    that the gods are on the side of the Government.

12 The trouble with the world is that the stupid are   attributed
    cocksure and the intelligent are full of doubt.

Lord John Russell 1792–1878

British Whig statesman, Prime Minister 1846–52 and
1865–6
on Russell: see **Derby** 114:2

1   It is impossible that the whisper of a faction should
prevail against the voice of a nation.
*reply to an Address from a meeting of 150,000 persons at
Birmingham on the defeat of the second Reform Bill, October
1831*

S. Walpole *Life of Lord John Russell*
(1889)

2   If peace cannot be maintained with honour, it is no
longer peace.

speech at Greenock, 19 September
1853

3   Among the defects of the Bill, which were numerous, one
provision was conspicuous by its presence and another
by its absence.

speech to the electors of the City
of London, April 1859

Anwar al-Sadat 1918–81

Egyptian statesman, President 1970–81

4   Peace is much more precious than a piece of land.

speech in Cairo, 8 March 1978

Lord St John of Fawsley 1929–

British Conservative politician and author

5   The monarchy has become our only truly popular
institution at a time when the House of Commons has
declined in public esteem and the Lords is a matter of
controversy. The monarchy is, in a real sense,
underpinning the other two estates of the realm.

in *The Times* 1 February 1982

Saki 1870–1916

Scottish writer

6   We all know that Prime Ministers are wedded to the
truth, but like other married couples they sometimes live
apart.

The Unbearable Bassington (1912)

Lord Salisbury 1830–1903

British Conservative statesman, Prime Minister 1885–6,
1886–92, and 1895–1902
on Salisbury: see **Bismarck** 47:2, **Disraeli** 120:5, **Goschen**
158:4, **Hennessy** 175:2

7   English policy is to float lazily downstream, occasionally
putting out a diplomatic boathook to avoid collisions.

letter to Lord Lytton, 9 March 1877

8   A great deal of misapprehension arises from the popular
use of maps on a small scale. As with such maps you are
able to put a thumb on India and a finger on Russia,
some persons at once think that the political situation is
alarming and that India must be looked to. If the noble

in the House of Lords, 11 June 1877

Lord would use a larger map—say one on the scale of the Ordnance Map of England—he would find that the distance between Russia and British India is not to be measured by the finger and thumb, but by a rule.

1 No lesson seems to be so deeply inculcated by the experience of life as that you never should trust experts. If you believe the doctors, nothing is wholesome: if you believe the theologians, nothing is innocent: if you believe the soldiers, nothing is safe. They all require to have their strong wine diluted by a very large admixture of insipid common sense.

letter to Lord Lytton, 15 June 1877

2 The agonies of a man who has to finish a difficult negotiation, and at the same time to entertain four royalties at a country house can be better imagined than described.

letter to Lord Lyons, 5 June 1878

3 What with deafness, ignorance of French, and Bismarck's extraordinary mode of speech, Beaconsfield has the dimmest idea of what is going on—understands everything crossways—and imagines a perpetual conspiracy.
   letter to Lady Salisbury from the Congress of Berlin, 23 June 1878

Lady Gwendolen Cecil *Life of Robert, Marquis of Salisbury* (1921–32)

4 A party whose mission it is to live entirely upon the discovery of grievances are apt to manufacture the element upon which they subsist.

speech at Edinburgh, 24 November 1882

5 They who have the absolute power of preventing lamentable events, and knowing what is taking place, refuse to exercise that power, are responsible for what happens.

in the House of Lords, 12 February 1884

6 We are part of the community of Europe and we must do our duty as such.

speech at Caernarvon, 10 April 1888

7 Where property is in question I am guilty...of erecting individual liberty as an idol, and of resenting all attempts to destroy or fetter it; but when you pass from liberty to life, in no well-governed State, in no State governed according to the principles of common humanity, are the claims of mere liberty allowed to endanger the lives of the citizens.

in the House of Lords, 29 July 1897

8 Horny-handed sons of toil.

in *Quarterly Review* October 1873; later popularized in the US by Denis Kearney, 1847–1907

9 I rank myself no higher in the scheme of things than a policeman—whose utility would disappear if there were no criminals.
   comparing his role in the Conservative Party with that of **Gladstone**

Lady Gwendolen Cecil *Biographical Studies... of Robert, Third Marquess of Salisbury* (1962)

10 By office boys for office boys.
   of the Daily Mail

H. Hamilton Fyfe *Northcliffe, an Intimate Biography* (1930)

11 To defend a bad policy as an 'error of judgement' does not excuse it—the right functioning of a man's judgement is his most fundamental responsibility.

Gwendolen Cecil *Life of Robert, Marquis of Salisbury* (1921–32) vol. 3

1 If these gentlemen had their way, they would soon be   Robert Taylor *Lord Salisbury* (1975)
   asking me to defend the moon against a possible attack
   from Mars.
      of his senior military advisers, and their tendency to see threats
      which did not exist

2 Too much poring over maps drives men mad.   Peter Hennessy *Never Again* (1992)

Lord Salisbury 1893–1972

British Conservative politician

3 Too clever by half.   in the House of Lords, 7 March
      of Iain **Macleod**, *Colonial Secretary, 'in his relationship to the*   1961
      white communities of Africa'

Sallust 86–35 BC

Roman historian

4 Greedy for the property of others, extravagant with his   *Catiline*
   own.

5 To stir up undisputed matters seemed a great reward in   *Catiline*
   itself.

6 He preferred to be rather than to seem good.   *Catiline*
      of Cato

7 A venal city ripe to perish, if a buyer can be found.   *Jugurtha*
      of Rome

8 *Punica fide.*   *Jugurtha*
   With Carthaginian trustworthiness.
      meaning treachery

Anthony Sampson 1926–

British author and journalist

9 Members [of the Order of St Michael and St George] rise   *Anatomy of Britain* (1962)
   from CMG (known sometimes in Whitehall as 'Call Me
   God') to the KCMG ('Kindly Call Me God') to—for a select
   few governors and super-ambassadors—the GCMG ('God
   Calls Me God').

10 A secret tome of *The Great and the Good* is kept, listing   *Anatomy of Britain Today* (1965)
    everyone who has the right, safe qualifications of
    worthiness, soundness and discretion; and from this tome
    came the stage army of committee people.

11 Of all the legacies of empire, the most dangerous is surely   *The Changing Anatomy of Britain*
    an immobile bureaucracy which can perpetuate its own   (1982)
    interests and values, like those ancient hierarchies which
    presided over declining civilizations...As the British
    mandarins reinforce their defences, awarding each other
    old imperial honours, do they hear any echoes from
    Castile or Byzantium?

Paul A. Samuelson 1915–

American economist

1　The consumer, so it is said, is the king...each is a voter　　*Economics* (8th ed., 1970)
who uses his money as votes to get the things done that
he wants done.

Lord Sandwich 1718–92

British politician and diplomat; First Lord of the Admiralty

2　If any man will draw up his case, and put his name at　　N. W. Wraxall *Memoirs* (1884) vol. 1
the foot of the first page, I will give him an immediate
reply. Where he compels me to turn over the sheet, he
must wait my leisure.
on appeals made by officers to the Navy Board

George Santayana 1863–1962

Spanish-born philosopher and critic

3　Fanaticism consists in redoubling your effort when you　　*The Life of Reason* (1905);
have forgotten your aim.　　introduction

4　Those who cannot remember the past are condemned to　　*The Life of Reason* (1905)
repeat it.

Jean-Paul Sartre 1905–80

French philosopher, novelist, playwright, and critic

5　When the rich wage war it's the poor who die.　　*Le Diable et le bon Dieu* (1951)

Hugh Scanlon 1913–

British trade union leader

6　Of course liberty is not licence. Liberty in my view is　　television interview, 9 August 1977
conforming to majority opinion.

Arthur Scargill 1938–

British trade union leader

7　Parliament itself would not exist in its present form had　　evidence to House of Commons
people not defied the law.　　Select Committee on Employment,
　　2 April 1980

Lord Scarman 1911–

British judge

on the need for a written constitution:
8　No bevy of men, not even parliament, could always be　　in conversation, 1982; Anthony
trusted to safeguard human rights.　　Sampson *The Essential Anatomy of
　　Britain* (1992)

1 The people as a source of sovereign power are in truth   *The Shape of Things to Come*
   only occasional partners in the constitutional minuet   (1989)
   danced for most of the time by Parliament and the
   political party in power.

2 Time and the development of our society have rendered   *The Shape of Things to Come*
   the checks and balances, such as they now are, of the   (1989)
   constitution of no avail...to restrain an oppressively
   minded executive if it should win control of a majority of
   the House of Commons...The path to an 'elected
   dictatorship' is open and must be blocked now before the
   bad boys realize their opportunity and organize
   a takeover of the British Constitution.

3 A government above the law is a menace to be defeated.   *Why Britain Needs a Written
                                                             Constitution* 1992

4 Men still feel the need to keep the government in order.   *Why Britain Needs a Written
   The feeling is deep, and as old as man.   Constitution* 1992

5 When times are abnormally alive with fear and prejudice,   in conversation, 20 July 1992;
   the common law is at a disadvantage: it cannot resist the Anthony Sampson *The Essential
   will, however frightened and prejudiced it may be, of   Anatomy of Britain* (1992)
   parliament.
   *after delivering a lecture advocating the establishment of a Bill
   of Rights*

Arthur M. Schlesinger Jr. 1917–

American historian

6 The answer to the runaway Presidency is not the   *The Imperial Presidency* (1973);
   messenger-boy Presidency. The American democracy   preface
   must discover a middle way between making the
   President a czar and making him a puppet.

7 Suppose...that Lenin had died of typhus in Siberia in   *The Cycles of American History*
   1895 and Hitler had been killed on the western front in   (1986)
   1916. What would the twentieth century have looked
   like now?

Patricia Schroeder 1940–

American Democratic politician; Congresswoman

8 Ronald Reagan...is attempting a great breakthrough in   speech in the US House of
   political technology—he has been perfecting the Teflon-   Representatives, 2 August 1983
   coated Presidency. He sees to it that nothing sticks to
   him.

9 We've got the kind of President who thinks arms control   in *Observer* 9 August 1987 'Sayings
   means some kind of deodorant.   of the Week'

E. F. Schumacher 1911–77

German-born economist

10 Small is beautiful. A study of economics as if people   title of book, 1973
   mattered.

1 Call a thing immoral or ugly, soul-destroying or   *Small is Beautiful* (1973)
   a degradation of man, a peril to the peace of the world or
   to the well-being of future generations: as long as you
   have not shown it to be 'uneconomic' you have not
   really questioned its right to exist, grow, and prosper.

Carl Schurz 1829–1906

American soldier and politician

2 My country, right or wrong; if right, to be kept right;   speech, US Senate, 29 February
   and if wrong, to be set right!   1872

Claud Schuster 1869–1956

British civil servant

*of the relationship between the Prime Minister and the
Cabinet:*
3 Like the procreation of eels, [it] is slippery and   G. H. L. Le May *The Victorian
   mysterious.   Constitution* (1979)

C. P. Scott 1846–1932

British journalist; editor of the Manchester Guardian,
1872–1929

4 A newspaper is of necessity something of a monopoly,   in *Manchester Guardian* 5 May
   and its first duty is to shun the temptations of monopoly.   1921
   Its primary office is the gathering of news. At the peril of
   its soul it must see that the supply is not tainted. Neither
   in what it gives, nor in what it does not give, nor in the
   mode of presentation must the unclouded face of truth
   suffer wrong. Comment is free, but facts are sacred.

Sir Walter Scott 1771–1832

Scottish novelist and poet

5 Breathes there the man, with soul so dead,   *The Lay of the Last Minstrel* (1805)
   Who never to himself hath said,
   This is my own, my native land!
   Whose heart hath ne'er within him burned,
   As home his footsteps he hath turned
   From wandering on a foreign strand!

John Seeley 1834–95

English historian

6 We [the English] seem, as it were, to have conquered and   *The Expansion of England* (1883);
   peopled half the world in a fit of absence of mind.   cf. **Hailsham** 163:12

John Selden 1584–1654

English historian and antiquary

1   Ignorance of the law excuses no man; not that all men   *Table Talk* (1689) 'Law'
know the law, but because 'tis an excuse every man will
plead, and no man can tell how to confute him.

2   A king is a thing men have made for their own sakes, for   *Table Talk* (1689) 'Of a King'
quietness' sake. Just as in a family one man is appointed
to buy the meat.

3   There is not anything in the world so much abused as   *Table Talk* (1689) 'People'; cf.
this sentence, *Salus populi suprema lex esto*.   **Cicero** 95:6

Arthur Seldon 1916–

British economist

4   Government of the busy by the bossy for the bully.   *Capitalism* (1990)
subheading on over-government

W. C. Sellar 1898–1951 and R. J. Yeatman
1898–1968

British writers

5   The Cavaliers (Wrong but Wromantic) and the   *1066 and All That* (1930)
Roundheads (Right but Repulsive).

6   The Rump Parliament—so called because it had been   *1066 and All That* (1930)
sitting for such a long time.

7   Charles II was always very merry and was therefore not   *1066 and All That* (1930)
so much a king as a Monarch.

8   The National Debt is a very Good Thing and it would be   *1066 and All That* (1930)
dangerous to pay it off, for fear of Political Economy.

9   Most memorable...was the discovery (made by all the   *1066 and All That* (1930)
rich men in England at once) that women and children
could work twenty-five hours a day in factories without
many of them dying or becoming excessively deformed.
This was known as the Industrial Revelation.

10 Gladstone...spent his declining years trying to guess the   *1066 and All That* (1930)
answer to the Irish Question; unfortunately whenever he
was getting warm, the Irish secretly changed the
Question.

11 AMERICA was thus clearly top nation, and History came   *1066 and All That* (1930)
to a .

Nassau William Senior 1790–1864

British economist

12 Though it is in the power of human institutions to make   diary 1849
everybody poor, they cannot make everybody rich.

William Seward 1801–72

American politician

1   I know, and all the world knows, that revolutions never   speech at Rochester, 25 October
    go backward.   1858

Edward Sexby d. 1658

English conspirator

2   Killing no murder briefly discourst in three questions.   title of pamphlet (an apology for
                                                                     tyrannicide, 1657)

Anthony Ashley Cooper, Lord Shaftesbury 1621–83

in the English Civil War, adherent first of the royalist and then
(from 1644) of the Parliamentary cause; in the reign of **Charles
II**, supporter of **Monmouth**'s claim to the succession
on Shaftesbury: see **Cromwell** 106:2, **Dryden** 125:4

refusing the claims of Cromwell's House of Lords:

3   Admit lords, and you admit all.   in *Dictionary of National Biography*

William Shakespeare 1564–1616

English playwright

4   What's the matter, you dissentious rogues,   *Coriolanus* (1608)
    That, rubbing the poor itch of your opinion,
    Make yourselves scabs?

5   He that depends   *Coriolanus* (1608)
    Upon your favours swims with fins of lead,
    And hews down oaks with rushes.

6   Hear you this Triton of the minnows? mark you   *Coriolanus* (1608)
    His absolute 'shall'?

7   What is the city but the people?   *Coriolanus* (1608)

8   You common cry of curs! whose breath I hate   *Coriolanus* (1608)
    As reek o' the rotten fens, whose loves I prize
    As the dead carcases of unburied men
    That do corrupt my air,—I banish you.

9   Despising,   *Coriolanus* (1608)
    For you, the city, thus I turn my back:
    There is a world elsewhere.

10   The beast   *Coriolanus* (1608)
    With many heads butts me away.

11 Let me have war, say I; it exceeds peace as far as day   *Coriolanus* (1608)
    does night; it's spritely, waking, audible, and full of vent.
    Peace is a very apoplexy, lethargy: mulled, deaf, sleepy,
    insensible; a getter of more bastard children than war's
    a destroyer of men.

1   I think he'll be to Rome   *Coriolanus* (1608)
As is the osprey to the fish, who takes it
By sovereignty of nature.

2   Why should we pay tribute? If Caesar can hide the sun   *Cymbeline* (1609–10)
from us with a blanket, or put the moon in his pocket,
we will pay him tribute for light; else, sir, no more
tribute.

3   The art o'th' court,   *Cymbeline* (1609–10)
As hard to leave as keep, whose top to climb
Is certain falling, or so slipp'ry that
The fear's as bad as falling.

4   But in the gross and scope of my opinion,   *Hamlet* (1601)
This bodes some strange eruption to our state.

5   His greatness weighed, his will is not his own,   *Hamlet* (1601)
For he himself is subject to his birth.
He may not, as unvalued persons do,
Carve for himself, for on his choice depends
The sanity and health of the whole state;
And therefore must his choice be circumscribed
Unto the voice and yielding of that body
Whereof he is the head.

6   Something is rotten in the state of Denmark.   *Hamlet* (1601)

7   The time is out of joint; O cursèd spite,   *Hamlet* (1601)
That ever I was born to set it right!

8   For who would bear the whips and scorns of time,   *Hamlet* (1601)
The oppressor's wrong, the proud man's contumely,
The pangs of disprized love, the law's delay,
The insolence of office, and the spurns
That patient merit of the unworthy takes,
When he himself might his quietus make
With a bare bodkin?...
Thus conscience doth make cowards of us all.

9   Madness in great ones must not unwatched go.   *Hamlet* (1601)

10   Indeed this counsellor   *Hamlet* (1601)
Is now most still, most secret, and most grave,
Who was in life a foolish prating knave.

11 And where the offence is let the great axe fall.   *Hamlet* (1601)

12 The great man down, you mark his favourite flies;   *Hamlet* (1601)
The poor advanced makes friends of enemies.

13   The cease of majesty   *Hamlet* (1601)
Dies not alone, but like a gulf doth draw
What's near with it. It is a massy wheel,
Fixed on the summit of the highest mount,
To whose huge spokes ten thousand lesser things
Are mortised and adjoined; which when it falls,
Each small annexment, petty consequence,
Attends the boist'rous ruin. Never alone
Did the King sigh, but with a general groan.

1   Diseases desperate grown,   *Hamlet* (1601)
   By desperate appliances are relieved,
   Or not at all.

2 We go to gain a little patch of ground,   *Hamlet* (1601)
   That hath in it no profit but the name.

3   Rightly to be great   *Hamlet* (1601)
   Is not to stir without great argument,
   But greatly to find quarrel in a straw
   When honour's at the stake.

4 There's such divinity doth hedge a king,   *Hamlet* (1601)
   That treason can but peep to what it would.

5 Rebellion lay in his way, and he found it.   *Henry IV, Part 1* (1597)

6 It was always yet the trick of our English nation, if they   *Henry IV, Part 2* (1597)
   have a good thing, to make it too common.

7 Uneasy lies the head that wears a crown.   *Henry IV, Part 2* (1597)

8 This is the English, not the Turkish court;   *Henry IV, Part 2* (1597)
   Not Amurath an Amurath succeeds,
   But Harry, Harry.

9 O England! model to thy inward greatness,   *Henry V* (1599)
   Like little body with a mighty heart,
   What might'st thou do, that honour would thee do,
   Were all thy children kind and natural!
   But see thy fault!

10 A little touch of Harry in the night.   *Henry V* (1599)

11 Discuss unto me; art thou officer?   *Henry V* (1599)
   Or art thou base, common and popular?

12 I think the king is but a man, as I am: the violet smells   *Henry V* (1599)
   to him as it doth to me.

13 I am afeard there are few die well that die in a battle; for   *Henry V* (1599)
   how can they charitably dispose of any thing when blood
   is their argument?

14 Every subject's duty is the king's; but every subject's soul   *Henry V* (1599)
   is his own.

15 Upon the king! let us our lives, our souls,   *Henry V* (1599)
   Our debts, our careful wives,
   Our children, and our sins lay on the king!
   We must bear all. O hard condition!

16   What infinite heart's ease   *Henry V* (1599)
   Must kings neglect, that private men enjoy!
   And what have kings that privates have not too,
   Save ceremony, save general ceremony?

17 Put forth thy hand, reach at the glorious gold.   *Henry VI, Part 2* (1592)

18 Is this the fashion of the court of England?   *Henry VI, Part 2* (1592)
   Is this the government of Britain's isle,
   And this the royalty of Albion's king?

19 I say it was never merry world in England since   *Henry VI, Part 2* (1592)
   gentlemen came up.

1 CADE: There shall be in England seven halfpenny loaves   *Henry VI, Part 2* (1592)
      sold for a penny; the three-hooped pot shall have ten
      hoops; and I will make it felony to drink small beer.
      All the realm shall be in common, and in Cheapside
      shall my palfrey go to grass. And when I am king,—as
      king I will be,—...there shall be no money; all shall
      eat and drink on my score; and I will apparel them all
      in one livery, that they may agree like brothers, and
      worship me their lord.
   DICK: The first thing we do, let's kill all the lawyers.

2 Is not this a lamentable thing, that of the skin of an   *Henry VI, Part 2* (1592)
   innocent lamb should be made parchment? that
   parchment, being scribbled o'er, should undo a man?

3 Thou hast most traitorously corrupted the youth of the   *Henry VI, Part 2* (1592)
   realm in erecting a grammar school: and whereas,
   before, our forefathers had no other books but the score
   and the tally, thou hast caused printing to be used; and,
   contrary to the king, his crown and dignity, thou hast
   built a paper-mill.

4 Peace! impudent and shameless Warwick, peace;   *Henry VI, Part 3* (1592)
   Proud setter up and puller down of kings.

5 Farewell! a long farewell, to all my greatness!   *Henry VIII* (1613)

6   I have ventured,   *Henry VIII* (1613)
   Like little wanton boys that swim on bladders,
   This many summers in a sea of glory,
   But far beyond my depth...
   Vain pomp and glory of this world, I hate ye:
   I feel my heart new opened. O how wretched
   Is that poor man that hangs on princes' favours!
   There is, betwixt that smile we would aspire to,
   That sweet aspect of princes, and their ruin,
   More pangs and fears than wars or women have;
   And when he falls, he falls like Lucifer,
   Never to hope again.

7 Cromwell, I charge thee, fling away ambition: *Henry VIII* (1613)
   By that sin fell the angels; how can man then,
   The image of his Maker, hope to win by't?
   Love thyself last: cherish those hearts that hate thee;
   Corruption wins not more than honesty.
   Still in thy right hand carry gentle peace,
   To silence envious tongues: be just, and fear not.
   Let all the ends thou aim'st at be thy country's,
   Thy God's, and truth's: then if thou fall'st, O Cromwell!
   Thou fall'st a blessed martyr.

8 Had I but served my God with half the zeal   *Henry VIII* (1613)
   I served my king, he would not in mine age
   Have left me naked to mine enemies.

9 In her days every man shall eat in safety   *Henry VIII* (1613)
   Under his own vine what he plants; and sing
   The merry songs of peace to all his neighbours.

1 You blocks, you stones, you worse than senseless things! *Julius Caesar* (1599)
   O you hard hearts, you cruel men of Rome,
   Knew you not Pompey?

2 CAESAR: Who is it in the press that calls on me? *Julius Caesar* (1599)
   I hear a tongue, shriller than all the music,
   Cry 'Caesar'. Speak; Caesar is turned to hear.
   SOOTHSAYER: Beware the ides of March.

3   Ye gods, it doth amaze me, *Julius Caesar* (1599)
   A man of such a feeble temper should
   So get the start of the majestic world,
   And bear the palm alone.

4 Why, man, he doth bestride the narrow world *Julius Caesar* (1599)
   Like a Colossus; and we petty men
   Walk under his huge legs, and peep about
   To find ourselves dishonourable graves.
   Men at some time are masters of their fates:
   The fault, dear Brutus, is not in our stars,
   But in ourselves, that we are underlings.

5 'Brutus' will start a spirit as soon as 'Caesar'. *Julius Caesar* (1599)
   Now in the names of all the gods at once,
   Upon what meat doth this our Caesar feed,
   That he is grown so great?

6 When could they say, till now, that talked of Rome, *Julius Caesar* (1599)
   That her wide walls encompassed but one man?
   Now is it Rome indeed and room enough,
   When there is in it but one only man.

7 Let me have men about me that are fat; *Julius Caesar* (1599)
   Sleek-headed men and such as sleep o' nights;
   Yond' Cassius has a lean and hungry look;
   He thinks too much: such men are dangerous.

8 Such men as he be never at heart's ease, *Julius Caesar* (1599)
   Whiles they behold a greater than themselves,
   And therefore are they very dangerous.

9 Th' abuse of greatness is, when it disjoins *Julius Caesar* (1599)
   Remorse from power.

10   'Tis a common proof, *Julius Caesar* (1599)
   That lowliness is young ambition's ladder,
   Whereto the climber-upward turns his face;
   But when he once attains the upmost round,
   He then unto the ladder turns his back,
   Looks in the clouds, scorning the base degrees
   By which he did ascend.

11   O conspiracy! *Julius Caesar* (1599)
   Sham'st thou to show thy dangerous brow by night,
   When evils are most free?

12 Let us be sacrificers, but not butchers, Caius. *Julius Caesar* (1599)

13 Let's carve him as a dish fit for the gods, *Julius Caesar* (1599)
   Not hew him as a carcass fit for hounds.

1   But when I tell him he hates flatterers,   *Julius Caesar* (1599)
    He says he does, being then most flattered.

2   CAESAR: The ides of March are come.   *Julius Caesar* (1599)
    SOOTHSAYER: Ay, Caesar; but not gone.

3   If I could pray to move, prayers would move me;   *Julius Caesar* (1599)
    But I am constant as the northern star,
    Of whose true-fixed and resting
    There is no fellow in the firmament.
    The skies are painted with unnumbered sparks,
    They are all fire and every one doth shine,
    But there's but one in all doth hold his place:
    So, in the world; 'tis furnished well with men,
    And men are flesh and blood, and apprehensive;
    Yet in the number I do know but one
    That unassailable holds on his rank,
    Unshaked of motion: and that I am he.

4   *Et tu, Brute?* Then fall, Caesar!   *Julius Caesar* (1599)

5   Ambition's debt is paid.   *Julius Caesar* (1599)

6   CASSIUS: How many ages hence   *Julius Caesar* (1599)
    Shall this our lofty scene be acted o'er,
    In states unborn, and accents yet unknown!
    BRUTUS: How many times shall Caesar bleed in sport.

7   Waving our red weapons o'er our heads   *Julius Caesar* (1599)
    Let's all cry 'Peace, freedom, and liberty!'

8   O mighty Caesar! dost thou lie so low?   *Julius Caesar* (1599)
    Are all thy conquests, glories, triumphs, spoils,
    Shrunk to this little measure?

9   Caesar's spirit, ranging for revenge,   *Julius Caesar* (1599)
    With Ate by his side, come hot from hell,
    Shall in these confines, with a monarch's voice
    Cry, 'Havoc!' and let slip the dogs of war;
    That this foul deed shall smell above the earth
    With carrion men, groaning for burial.

10 Not that I loved Caesar less, but that I loved Rome more.   *Julius Caesar* (1599)

11 As he was valiant, I honour him: but, as he was   *Julius Caesar* (1599)
    ambitious, I slew him.

12 Who is here so base that would be a bondman? If any,   *Julius Caesar* (1599)
    speak; for him have I offended. Who is here so rude that
    would not be a Roman? If any, speak; for him have
    I offended. Who is here so vile that will not love his
    country? If any, speak; for him have I offended. I pause
    for a reply.

13 Friends, Romans, countrymen, lend me your ears;   *Julius Caesar* (1599)
    I come to bury Caesar, not to praise him.
    The evil that men do lives after them,
    The good is oft interrèd with their bones;
    So let it be with Caesar. The noble Brutus
    Hath told you Caesar was ambitious;

If it were so, it was a grievous fault;
And grievously hath Caesar answered it.

1 He was my friend, faithful and just to me: *Julius Caesar* (1599)
   But Brutus says he was ambitious;
   And Brutus is an honourable man.

2 When that the poor have cried, Caesar hath wept;   *Julius Caesar* (1599)
   Ambition should be made of sterner stuff.

3   On the Lupercal   *Julius Caesar* (1599)
   I thrice presented him a kingly crown
   Which he did thrice refuse: was this ambition?

4 You all did love him once, not without cause.   *Julius Caesar* (1599)

5 But yesterday the word of Caesar might   *Julius Caesar* (1599)
   Have stood against the world; now lies he there,
   And none so poor to do him reverence.

6 This was the most unkindest cut of all.   *Julius Caesar* (1599)

7 O! what a fall was there, my countrymen;   *Julius Caesar* (1599)
   Then I, and you, and all of us fell down,
   Whilst bloody treason flourished over us.

8 I come not, friends, to steal away your hearts: *Julius Caesar* (1599)
   I am no orator, as Brutus is;
   But, as you know me all, a plain, blunt man,
   That love my friend.

9 For I have neither wit, nor words, nor worth,   *Julius Caesar* (1599)
   Action, nor utterance, nor power of speech,
   To stir men's blood; I only speak right on;
   I tell you that which you yourselves do know.

10   But were I Brutus,   *Julius Caesar* (1599)
   And Brutus Antony, there were an Antony
   Would ruffle up your spirits, and put a tongue
   In every wound of Caesar, that should move
   The stones of Rome to rise and mutiny.

11 Now let it work; mischief, thou art afoot,   *Julius Caesar* (1599)
   Take thou what course thou wilt!

12 He shall not live; look, with a spot I damn him.   *Julius Caesar* (1599)

13 This is a slight unmeritable man,   *Julius Caesar* (1599)
   Meet to be sent on errands.

14 There is a tide in the affairs of men,   *Julius Caesar* (1599)
   Which, taken at the flood, leads on to fortune;
   Omitted, all the voyage of their life
   Is bound in shallows and in miseries.
   On such a full sea are we now afloat,
   And we must take the current when it serves,
   Or lose our ventures.

15 O Julius Caesar! thou art mighty yet!   *Julius Caesar* (1599)
   Thy spirit walks abroad, and turns our swords
   In our own proper entrails.

16 This was the noblest Roman of them all;   *Julius Caesar* (1599)
   All the conspirators save only he

Did that they did in envy of great Caesar;
He only in a general honest thought
And common good to all, made one of them.
His life was gentle, and the elements
So mixed in him that Nature might stand up
And say to all the world, 'This was a man!'

1 This England never did, nor never shall,   *King John* (1591–8)
Lie at the proud foot of a conqueror,
But when it first did help to wound itself.
Now these her princes are come home again,
Come the three corners of the world in arms,
And we shall shock them: nought shall make us rue,
If England to itself do rest but true.

2 Think'st thou that duty shall have dread to speak   *King Lear* (1605–6)
When power to flattery bows? To plainness honour's
     bound
When majesty falls to folly.

3 Let go thy hold when a great wheel runs down a hill,   *King Lear* (1605–6)
lest it break thy neck with following; but the great one
that goes upward, let him draw thee after.

4 A dog's obeyed in office.   *King Lear* (1605–6)

5   Get thee glass eyes;   *King Lear* (1605–6)
And, like a scurvy politician, seem
To see the things thou dost not.

6 MALCOLM: Nothing in his life   *Macbeth* (1606)
Became him like the leaving it: he died
As one that had been studied in his death
To throw away the dearest thing he owed
As 'twere a careless trifle.
DUNCAN: There's no art
To find the mind's construction in the face;
He was a gentleman on whom I built
An absolute trust.

7   Besides, this Duncan   *Macbeth* (1606)
Hath borne his faculties so meek, hath been
So clear in his great office, that his virtues
Will plead like angels trumpet-tongued, against
The deep damnation of his taking-off.

8   I have no spur   *Macbeth* (1606)
To prick the sides of my intent, but only
Vaulting ambition, which o'erleaps itself,
And falls on the other.

9 Confusion now hath made his masterpiece!   *Macbeth* (1606)
Most sacrilegious murder hath broke ope
The Lord's anointed temple, and stole thence
The life o' the building!

10 Thou hast it now: King, Cawdor, Glamis, all,   *Macbeth* (1606)
As the weird women promised; and, I fear,
Thou play'dst most foully for't.

1 LADY MACBETH: Things without all remedy   *Macbeth* (1606)
Should be without regard: what's done is done.
MACBETH: We have scotched the snake, not killed it:
She'll close and be herself.

2   Duncan is in his grave;   *Macbeth* (1606)
After life's fitful fever he sleeps well;
Treason has done his worst: nor steel, nor poison,
Malice domestic, foreign levy, nothing,
Can touch him further.

3 Stands Scotland where it did?   *Macbeth* (1606)

4   Now, as fond fathers,   *Measure for Measure* (1604)
Having bound up the threat'ning twigs of birch,
Only to stick it in their children's sight
For terror, not to use, in time the rod
Becomes more mocked than feared; so our decrees,
Dead to infliction, to themselves are dead,
And liberty plucks justice by the nose;
The baby beats the nurse, and quite athwart
Goes all decorum.

5 We must not make a scarecrow of the law,   *Measure for Measure* (1604)
Setting it up to fear the birds of prey,
And let it keep one shape, till custom make it
Their perch and not their terror.

6 'Tis one thing to be tempted, Escalus,   *Measure for Measure* (1604)
Another thing to fall. I not deny,
The jury, passing on the prisoner's life,
May in the sworn twelve have a thief or two
Guiltier than him they try.

7 No ceremony that to great ones 'longs,   *Measure for Measure* (1604)
Not the king's crown, nor the deputed sword,
The marshal's truncheon, nor the judge's robe,
Become them with one half so good a grace
As mercy does.

8   O! it is excellent   *Measure for Measure* (1604)
To have a giant's strength, but it is tyrannous
To use it like a giant.

9   Man, proud man,   *Measure for Measure* (1604)
Drest in a little brief authority,
Most ignorant of what he's most assured,
His glassy essence, like an angry ape,
Plays such fantastic tricks before high heaven,
As make the angels weep.

10 The quality of mercy is not strained,   *The Merchant of Venice* (1596–8)
It droppeth as the gentle rain from heaven
Upon the place beneath.

11 A substitute shines brightly as a king   *The Merchant of Venice* (1596–8)
Until a king be by, and then his state
Empties itself, as doth an inland brook
Into the main of waters.

1 The purest treasure mortal times afford   *Richard II* (1595)
Is spotless reputation; that away,
Men are but gilded loam or painted clay.
A jewel in a ten-times-barred-up chest
Is a bold spirit in a loyal breast.
Mine honour is my life; both grow in one;
Take honour from me, and my life is done.

2 We were not born to sue, but to command.   *Richard II* (1595)

3 How long a time lies in one little word!   *Richard II* (1595)
Four lagging winters and four wanton springs
End in a word; such is the breath of kings.

4 This royal throne of kings, this sceptered isle,   *Richard II* (1595)
This earth of majesty, this seat of Mars,
This other Eden, demi-paradise,
This fortress built by Nature for herself
Against infection and the hand of war,
This happy breed of men, this little world,
This precious stone set in the silver sea,
Which serves it in the office of a wall,
Or as a moat defensive to a house,
Against the envy of less happier lands,
This blessèd plot, this earth, this realm, this England,
This nurse, this teeming womb of royal kings,
Feared by their breed and famous by their birth,
Renownèd for their deeds as far from home,—
For Christian service and true chivalry,—
As is the sepulchre in stubborn Jewry
Of the world's ransom, blessèd Mary's Son:
This land of such dear souls, this dear, dear land,
Dear for her reputation through the world,
Is now leased out,—I die pronouncing it,—
Like to a tenement or pelting farm:
England, bound in with the triumphant sea,
Whose rocky shore beats back the envious siege
Of watery Neptune, is now bound in with shame,
With inky blots, and rotten parchment bonds:
That England, that was wont to conquer others,
Hath made a shameful conquest of itself.

5 The caterpillars of the commonwealth.   *Richard II* (1595)

6 Not all the water in the rough rude sea   *Richard II* (1595)
Can wash the balm from an anointed king;
The breath of worldly men cannot depose
The deputy elected by the Lord.

7 Is not the king's name twenty thousand names?   *Richard II* (1595)
Arm, arm, my name! A puny subject strikes
At thy great glory.

8 For God's sake, let us sit upon the ground   *Richard II* (1595)
And tell sad stories of the death of kings:
How some have been deposed, some slain in war,
Some haunted by the ghosts they have deposed,
Some poisoned by their wives, some sleeping killed;

All murdered: for within the hollow crown
That rounds the mortal temples of a king
Keeps Death his court, and there the antick sits,
Scoffing his state and grinning at his pomp;
Allowing him a breath, a little scene,
To monarchize, be feared, and kill with looks,
Infusing him with self and vain conceit
As if this flesh which walls about our life
Were brass impregnable; and humoured thus
Comes at the last, and with a little pin
Bores through his castle wall, and farewell king!

1 See, see, King Richard doth himself appear,   *Richard II* (1595)
   As doth the blushing discontented sun
   From out the fiery portal of the east.

2 What must the king do now? Must he submit?   *Richard II* (1595)
   The king shall do it: must he be deposed?
   The king shall be contented: must he lose
   The name of king? o' God's name, let it go.

3 Give me the crown. Here, cousin, seize the crown;   *Richard II* (1595)
   Here cousin,
   On this side my hand and on that side thine.
   Now is this golden crown like a deep well
   That owes two buckets filling one another;
   The emptier ever dancing in the air,
   The other down, unseen, and full of water:
   That bucket down and full of tears am I,
   Drinking my griefs, whilst you mount up on high.

4 You may my glories and my state depose,   *Richard II* (1595)
   But not my griefs; still am I king of those.

5 Now mark me how I will undo myself.   *Richard II* (1595)

6 With mine own tears I wash away my balm,   *Richard II* (1595)
   With mine own hands I give away my crown.

7 Mine eyes are full of tears, I cannot see: *Richard II* (1595)
   And yet salt water blinds them not so much
   But they can see a sort of traitors here.
   Nay, if I turn my eyes upon myself,
   I find myself a traitor with the rest.

8 Now is the winter of our discontent   *Richard III* (1591)
   Made glorious summer by this sun of York.

9 Grim-visaged war hath smoothed his wrinkled front;   *Richard III* (1591)
   And now, instead of mounting barbèd steeds,
   To fright the souls of fearful adversaries,—
   He capers nimbly in a lady's chamber
   To the lascivious pleasing of a lute.

10 Since every Jack became a gentleman   *Richard III* (1591)
   There's many a gentle person made a Jack.

11 And thus I clothe my naked villainy   *Richard III* (1591)
   With odd old ends stol'n forth of holy writ,
   And seem a saint when most I play the devil.

1   Woe to the land that's governed by a child!   *Richard III* (1591)

2   Talk'st thou to me of 'ifs'? Thou art a traitor: *Richard III* (1591)
Off with his head!

3   I am not in the giving vein to-day.   *Richard III* (1591)

4   Men shut their doors against a setting sun.   *Timon of Athens* (c.1607)

5   A stone is soft as wax, tribunes more hard than stones.   *Titus Andronicus* (1590)
A stone is silent and offendeth not,
And tribunes with their tongues doom men to death.

6   Rome is but a wilderness of tigers.   *Titus Andronicus* (1590)

7   The heavens themselves, the planets, and this centre   *Troilus and Cressida* (1602)
Observe degree, priority, and place,
Insisture, course, proportion, season, form,
Office, and custom, in all line of order.

8   O! when degree is shaked,   *Troilus and Cressida* (1602)
Which is the ladder to all high designs,
The enterprise is sick.

9   Take but degree away, untune that string,   *Troilus and Cressida* (1602)
And, hark! what discord follows; each thing meets
In mere oppugnancy. The bounded waters
Should lift their bosoms higher than the shores
And make a sop of all this sordid globe;
Strength should be lord of imbecility
And the rude son should strike his father dead.

10   A plague of opinion! a man may wear it on both sides,   *Troilus and Cressida* (1602)
like a leather jerkin.

11   How my achievements mock me!   *Troilus and Cressida* (1602)

Robert Shapiro 1942–

American lawyer; originally leader of the defence team at the
trial of O. J. Simpson

*of the change of strategy embraced after Johnnie Cochran took
over from him the leadership of the defence team:*

12   Not only did we play the race card, we played it from the   in *The Times* 5 October 1995; cf.
bottom of the deck.   **Churchill** 86:8

    *to which Cochran responded, 'We didn't play the race card, we
played the credibility card'*

George Bernard Shaw 1856–1950

Irish playwright

13   There is nothing so bad or so good that you will not find   *The Man of Destiny* (1898)
Englishmen doing it; but you will never find an
Englishman in the wrong. He does everything on
principle. He fights you on patriotic principles; he robs
you on business principles; he enslaves you on imperial
principles; he bullies you on manly principles; he
supports his king on loyal principles and cuts off his
king's head on republican principles.

1 SWINDON: What will history say? BURGOYNE: History, sir, will tell lies as usual.

The Devil's Disciple (1901)

2 He [the Britón] is a barbarian, and thinks that the customs of his tribe and island are the laws of nature.

Caesar and Cleopatra (1901)

3 Your friend the British soldier can stand up to anything except the British War Office.

The Devil's Disciple (1901)

4 Englishmen never will be slaves: they are free to do whatever the Government and public opinion allow them to do.

Man and Superman (1903)

5 In the arts of peace Man is a bungler.

Man and Superman (1903)

6 Revolutions have never lightened the burden of tyranny: they have only shifted it to another shoulder.

Man and Superman (1903) 'The Revolutionist's Handbook' foreword

7 Democracy substitutes election by the incompetent many for appointment by the corrupt few.

Man and Superman (1903) 'Maxims: Democracy'

8 Liberty means responsibility. That is why most men dread it.

Man and Superman (1903) 'Maxims: Liberty and Equality'

9 The art of government is the organization of idolatry.

Man and Superman (1903) 'Maxims: Idolatry'

10 Titles distinguish the mediocre, embarrass the superior, and are disgraced by the inferior.

Man and Superman (1903) 'Maxims for Revolutionists: Titles'

11 Money is indeed the most important thing in the world; and all sound and successful personal and national morality should have this fact for its basis.

The Irrational Knot (1905) preface

12 An Irishman's heart is nothing but his imagination.

John Bull's Other Island (1907)

13 He knows nothing; and he thinks he knows everything. That points clearly to a political career.

Major Barbara (1907)

14 Nothing is ever done in this world until men are prepared to kill one another if it is not done.

Major Barbara (1907)

15 Assassination is the extreme form of censorship.

The Showing-Up of Blanco Posnet (1911) 'Limits to Toleration'

16 Anarchism is a game at which the police can beat you.

Misalliance (1914)

17 Go anywhere in England where there are natural, wholesome, contented, and really nice English people; and what do you always find? That the stables are the real centre of the household.

Heartbreak House (1919)

18 The captain is in his bunk, drinking bottled ditch-water; and the crew is gambling in the forecastle. She will strike and sink and split. Do you think the laws of God will be suspended in favour of England because you were born in it?

Heartbreak House (1919)

19 You'll never have a quiet world till you knock the patriotism out of the human race.

O'Flaherty V.C. (1919)

20 All great truths begin as blasphemies.

Annajanska (1919)

21 It is evident that if the incomes of the rich were taken from them and divided among the poor as we stand at

The Intelligent Woman's Guide to Socialism and Capitalism (1928)

present, the poor would be very little less poor; the
supply of capital would cease because nobody could
afford to save; the country houses would fall into ruins;
and learning and science and art and literature and all
the rest of what we call culture would perish.

1 What Englishman will give his mind to politics as long as   *The Apple Cart* (1930)
he can afford to keep a motor car?

2 A government which robs Peter to pay Paul can always   *Everybody's Political What's What?*
depend on the support of Paul.   (1944)

3 England and America are two countries divided by   attributed in this and other forms,
a common language.   but not found in Shaw's published
    writings; cf. **Wilde** 388:7

Hartley Shawcross 1902–

British Labour politician and barrister

4 'But,' said Alice, 'the question is whether you can make   in the House of Commons, 2 April
a word mean different things.' 'Not so,' said Humpty-   1946; cf. **Carroll** 77:1
Dumpty, 'the question is which is to be the master.
That's all.' We are the masters at the moment, and not
only at the moment, but for a very long time to come.
often quoted as 'We are the masters now'

Charles Shaw-Lefevre 1794–1888

5 What is that fat gentleman in such a passion about?   G. W. E. Russell *Collections and*
as a child, on hearing Charles James **Fox** *speak in Parliament*   *Recollections* (1898)

Lord Shelburne 1737–1805

British Whig politician; Prime Minister

6 The country will neither be united at home nor respected   in the House of Lords, 22
abroad, till the reins of government are lodged with men   November 1770
who have some little pretensions to common sense and
common honesty.

*of the defence of the king's speech at the opening of the
parliamentary session:*
7 Nothing more than a string of sophisms, no less   in the House of Lords, 31 October
wretched in their texture than insolent in their tenor.   1776

8 The sun of Great Britain will set whenever she   in the House of Lords, October
acknowledges the independence of America...the   1782
independence of America would end in the ruin of
England.

Percy Bysshe Shelley 1792–1822

English poet

9 'My name is Ozymandias, king of kings: 'Ozymandias' (1819)
Look on my works, ye Mighty, and despair!'

1   An old, mad, blind, despised, and dying king.   'Sonnet: England in 1819' (written 1819)

2   I met Murder on the way—   'The Mask of Anarchy' (1819)
    He had a mask like Castlereagh.

3   Men of England, wherefore plough   'Song to the Men of England'
    For the lords who lay ye low?   (written 1819)

4   The seed ye sow, another reaps;   'Song to the Men of England'
    The wealth ye find, another keeps;   (written 1819)
    The robes ye weave, another wears;
    The arms ye forge, another bears.

5   Kingly conclaves stern and cold   *Prometheus Unbound* (1820)
    Where blood with guilt is bought and sold.

6   Tyranny entrenches itself within the existing interests of   *A Philosophical View of Reform*
    the most refined citizens of a nation and says 'If you dare   (written 1819–20)
    trample upon these, be free.'

7   Monarchy is only the string that ties the robber's bundle.   *A Philosophical View of Reform*
                                                                  (written 1819–20)

8   Let there be light! said Liberty,   *Hellas* (1822)
    And like sunrise from the sea,
    Athens arose!

William Shenstone 1714–63

English poet and essayist

9   Laws are generally found to be nets of such a texture, as   *Works in Verse and Prose* (1764)
    the little creep through, the great break through, and the   vol. 2 'On Politics'; cf. **Anarcharsis**
    middle-sized are alone entangled in.   8:3, **Swift** 353:4

Philip Henry Sheridan 1831–88

American Union cavalry commander in the Civil War

10 The only good Indian is a dead Indian.   attributed; perhaps already
    at Fort Cobb, January 1869   proverbial

Richard Brinsley Sheridan 1751–1816

Anglo-Irish playwright and Whig politician

11 The newspapers! Sir, they are the most villainous—   *The Critic* (1779)
    licentious—abominable—infernal—Not that I ever read
    them—No—I make it a rule never to look into
    a newspaper.

12 The throne *we* honour is the *people's* choice.   *Pizarro* (1799)

13 The Right Honourable gentleman is indebted to his   in the House of Commons; T.
    memory for his jests, and to his imagination for his facts. Moore *Life of Sheridan* (1825)
    in reply to Mr Dundas   vol. 2

William Tecumseh Sherman 1820–91

American general; from 1864 chief Union commander in the
west in succession to Ulysses S. **Grant**

1 War is the remedy our *enemies* have chosen, and I say let
us give them all they want.

in 1864; Geoffrey C. Ward The Civil War (1991)

2 [Grant] stood by me when I was crazy, and I stood by
him when he was drunk; and now we stand by each
other always.
  of his relationship with his fellow Union commander, Ulysses S.
  Grant

in 1864; Geoffrey C. Ward The Civil War (1991)

3 I think we understand what military fame is. To be killed
on the field of battle and have our name spelled wrong in
the newspapers.

Ken Burns The Civil War (documentary, 1989) episode 9

4 I will not accept if nominated, and will not serve if
elected.
  *on being urged to stand as Republican candidate in the 1884
  presidential election*

telegram to General Henderson; Memoirs (4th ed., 1891)

Emanuel Shinwell 1884–1986

British Labour politician

5 We know that the organised workers of the country are
our friends. As for the rest, they don't matter a tinker's
cuss.

speech to the Electrical Trades Union conference at Margate, 7 May 1947

Jonathan Shipley 1714–88

English clergyman, Bishop of St Asaph

6 I look upon North America as the only great nursery of
freemen left on the face of the earth.
  *in 1774, after voting against the alteration of the constitution of
  Massachusetts, proposed as a punishment for the tea-ship riots
  at Boston*

in Dictionary of National Biography

William Shippen 1673–1743

English Jacobite politician

7 Robin and I are two honest men: he is for King George
and I for King James, but those men in long cravats
[Sandys, Rushout, Pulteney, and their following] only
desire places under one or the other.
  view of his relationship with his political opponent Robert
  Walpole

in Dictionary of National Biography

Algernon Sidney 1622–83

English conspirator, executed for his alleged part in the Rye House Plot, 1683

1 Liars ought to have good memories.   *Discourses concerning*
                                                          Government (1698)

2 Men lived like fishes; the great ones devoured the small.   *Discourses concerning*
                                                          Government (1698)

3 'Tis not necessary to light a candle to the sun.   *Discourses concerning*
                                                          Government (1698)

Emmanuel Joseph Sieyès 1748–1836

French abbot and statesman

4 Death, without rhetoric.   attributed to Sieyès, but
    on voting in the French Convention for the death of **Louis XVI**, *16*   afterwards repudiated by him (*Le*
    January 1793   *Moniteur* 20 January 1793 records
                                                          his vote as 'La mort')

    when asked what he had done during the French Revolution:
5 I survived.   F. A. M. Mignet *Notice historique*
                                                          sur la vie et les travaux de M. le
                                                          Comte de Sieyès (1836)

Simonides *c.*556–468 BC

Greek poet

6 Go, tell the Spartans, thou who passest by,   Herodotus *Histories*; attributed
    That here obedient to their laws we lie.
    epitaph on the Spartans who died heroically defending the pass
    of Thermopylae against the Persians

Kirke Simpson

American journalist

7 [Warren] Harding of Ohio was chosen by a group of men   news report, 12 June 1920; cf.
    in a smoke-filled room early today as Republican   **Daugherty** 109:9
    candidate for President.

C. H. Sisson 1914–

English poet

8 Here lies a civil servant. He was civil   *The London Zoo* (1961)
    To everyone, and servant to the devil.

Noel Skelton 1880–1935

British Conservative politician

9 To state as clearly as may be what means lie ready to   in *The Spectator* 19 May 1923
    develop a property-owning democracy, to bring the
    industrial and economic status of the wage-earner

abreast of his political and educational, to make
democracy stable and four-square.

Adam Smith 1723–90

Scottish philosopher and economist

1 Little else is requisite to carry a state to the highest
degree of opulence from the lowest barbarism, but peace,
easy taxes, and a tolerable administration of justice; all
the rest being brought about by the natural course of
things.

*in 1755; Essays on Philosophical
Subjects (1795)*

2 And thus, *Place*, that great object which divides the wives
of aldermen, is the end of half the labours of human life;
and is the cause of all the tumult and bustle, all the
rapine and injustice, which avarice and ambition have
introduced into this world.

Theory of Moral Sentiments (1759)

3 [The man of system] seems to imagine that he can
arrange the different members of a great society with as
much ease as the hand arranges the different pieces upon
a chessboard; he does not consider that the pieces upon
the chessboard have no other principle of motion besides
that which the hand impresses upon them; but that, in
the great chessboard of human society, every single piece
has a principle of motion of its own, altogether different
from that which the legislator might choose to impress
upon it.

Theory of Moral Sentiments (1759)

4 It is not from the benevolence of the butcher, the brewer,
or the baker, that we expect our dinner, but from their
regard to their own interest. We address ourselves not to
their humanity but their self love, and never talk to them
of our necessities but of their advantages.

Wealth of Nations (1776)

5 People of the same trade seldom meet together, even for
merriment and diversion, but the conversation ends in
a conspiracy against the public, or in some contrivance
to raise prices.

Wealth of Nations (1776)

6 To found a great empire for the sole purpose of raising up
a people of customers, may at first sight appear a project
fit only for a nation of shopkeepers. It is, however,
a project altogether unfit for a nation of shopkeepers; but
extremely fit for a nation whose government is influenced
by shopkeepers.

Wealth of Nations (1776); cf.
Adams 5:4, **Napoleon** 270:1

7 It is the highest impertinence and presumption, therefore,
in kings and ministers, to pretend to watch over the
economy of private people, and to restrain their
expense…They are themselves always, and without any
exception, the greatest spendthrifts in society. Let them
look well after their own expense, and they may safely
trust private people with theirs. If their own
extravagance does not ruin the state, that of their
subjects never will.

Wealth of Nations (1776)

1 Consumption is the sole end and purpose of production; and the interest of the producer ought to be attended to only so far as it may be necessary for promoting that of the consumer.

Wealth of Nations (1776)

2 There is no art which one government sooner learns of another than that of draining money from the pockets of the people.

Wealth of Nations (1776)

3 If any of the provinces of the British empire cannot be made to contribute towards the support of the whole empire, it is surely time that Great Britain should free herself from the expense of defending those provinces in time of war, and of supporting any part of their civil or military establishments in time of peace, and endeavour to accommodate her future views and designs to the real mediocrity of her circumstances.

Wealth of Nations (1776)

4 Every individual necessarily labours to render the annual revenue of society as great as he can. He generally neither intends to promote the public interest, nor knows how much he is promoting it. He intends only his own gain, and he is, in this, as in many other cases, led by an invisible hand to promote an end which was no part of his intention.

Wealth of Nations (1776)

5 Great nations are never impoverished by private, though they sometimes are by public prodigality and misconduct. The whole, or almost the whole public revenue, is in most countries employed in maintaining unproductive hands.

Wealth of Nations (1776)

6 What is prudence in the conduct of every private family, can scarce be folly in that of a great kingdom. If a foreign country can supply us with a commodity cheaper than we ourselves can make it, better buy it of them with some part of the produce of our own industry, employed in a way in which we have some advantage.

Wealth of Nations (1776)

7 The natural advantages which one country has over another in producing particular commodities are sometimes so great, that it is acknowledged by all the world to be in vain to struggle with them. By means of glasses, hotbeds, and hotwalls, very good grapes can be raised in Scotland, and very good wine too can be made of them at about thirty times the expense for which at least equally good can be bought from foreign countries. Would it be a reasonable law to prohibit the importation of all foreign wines, merely to encourage the making of claret and burgundy in Scotland? But if there would be manifest absurdity in turning towards any employment, thirty times more of the capital and industry of the country, than would be necessary to purchase from foreign countries an equal quantity of the commodities wanted, there must be an absurdity, though not altogether so glaring, yet exactly of the same kind, in turning towards any such employment a thirtieth, or even a three hundredth part more of either.

Wealth of Nations (1776)

1 Those parts of education, it is to be observed, for the   *Wealth of Nations* (1776)
   teaching of which there are no public institutions, are
   generally the best taught.

2 Princes...have frequently engaged in many...mercantile   *Wealth of Nations* (1776)
   projects, and have been willing, like private persons, to
   mend their fortunes by becoming adventurers in the
   common branches of trade. They have scarcely ever
   succeeded. The profusion with which the affairs of
   princes are always managed, renders it almost impossible
   that they should. The agents of a prince regard the
   wealth of their master as inexhaustible; are careless at
   which price they buy; are careless at which price they
   sell; are careless at what expense they transport his
   goods from one place to another.

3 The natural effort of every individual to better his own   *Wealth of Nations* (1776)
   condition...is so powerful, that it is alone, and without
   any assistance, not only capable of carrying on the
   society to wealth and prosperity, but of surmounting
   a hundred impertinent obstructions with which the folly
   of human laws too often encumbers its operations.

Alfred Emanuel Smith 1873–1944

American politician; presidential candidate in 1928

4 The crowning climax to the whole situation is the   in *New York Times* 25 October
   undisputed fact that William Randolph Hearst gave him   1926
   the kiss of death.
     *on **Hearst**'s support for Ogden Mills, Smith's unsuccessful*
     opponent for the governorship of New York State

5 All the ills of democracy can be cured by more   speech in Albany, 27 June 1933
   democracy.

6 No sane local official who has hung up an empty   in *New Outlook* December 1933
   stocking over the municipal fireplace, is going to shoot
   Santa Claus just before a hard Christmas.
     comment on the New Deal

Cyril Smith 1928–

British Liberal politician

of the House of Commons:
7 The longest running farce in the West End.   *Big Cyril* (1977)

F. E. Smith, Lord Birkenhead 1872–1930

British Conservative politician and lawyer
on Smith: see **Asquith** 19:1

8 The world continues to offer glittering prizes to those   Rectorial address, Glasgow
   who have stout hearts and sharp swords.   University, 7 November 1923

9 We have the highest authority for believing that the   *Contemporary Personalities* (1924)
   meek shall inherit the earth; though I have never found   'Marquess Curzon'

any particular corroboration of this aphorism in the
records of Somerset House.

1 Nature has no cure for this sort of madness [Bolshevism],
though I have known a legacy from a rich relative work
wonders.

Law, Life and Letters (1927)

2 Austen [Chamberlain] always played the game, and he
always lost it.

Lord Beaverbrook *Men and Power*
(1956)

Howard Smith 1919–

British diplomat; former Ambassador to Moscow

3 I have not had major experience of talking with people
once pronounced brain-dead, but I think we could be safe
in saying he did not have great zip.
   of Leonid Brezhnev

in *Times* 8 September 1988

Ian Smith 1919–

Rhodesian politician; Prime Minister, 1964–79

4 I don't believe in black majority rule in Rhodesia—not in
a thousand years.

broadcast speech, 20 March 1976

Samuel Francis Smith 1808–95

American poet and divine

5 My country, 'tis of thee,
Sweet land of liberty,
Of thee I sing:
Land where my fathers died,
Land of the pilgrims' pride,
From every mountain-side
Let freedom ring.

'America' (1831)

Sydney Smith 1771–1845

English clergyman and essayist

6 The moment the very name of Ireland is mentioned, the
English seem to bid adieu to common feeling, common
prudence, and common sense, and to act with the
barbarity of tyrants, and the fatuity of idiots.

Letters of Peter Plymley (1807)

7 Tory and Whig in turns shall be my host,
I taste no politics in boiled and roast.

letter to John Murray, November
1834

8 Daniel Webster struck me much like a steam-engine in
trousers.

Lady Holland *Memoir* (1855)

9 He [Macaulay] has occasional flashes of silence, that
make his conversation perfectly delightful.

Lady Holland *Memoir* (1855)

10 Minorities...are almost always in the right.

H. Pearson *The Smith of Smiths*
(1934)

1 My brother [Bobus] and I have inverted the laws of   Alan Bell (ed.) *The Sayings of*
   nature. He rose by his gravity; I sank by my levity.   *Sydney Smith* (1993); attributed

Tobias Smollett 1721–71

Scottish novelist

2 I think for my part one half of the nation is mad—and   *The Adventures of Sir Launcelot*
   the other not very sound.   *Greaves* (1762)

3 Mourn, hapless Caledonia, mourn   'The Tears of Scotland' (1746)
   Thy banished peace, thy laurels torn.

C. P. Snow 1905–80

English novelist and scientist

4 The official world, the corridors of power.   *Homecomings* (1956)

Philip Snowden 1864–1937

British Labour politician

5 It would be desirable if every Government, when it comes   C. E. Bechofer Roberts ('Ephesian')
   to power, should have its old speeches burnt.   *Philip Snowden* (1929)

6 This is not Socialism. It is Bolshevism run mad.   radio broadcast, 17 October 1931
   on the Labour Party's 1931 election programme

Socrates 469–399 BC

Greek philosopher

7 Most excellent man, are you who are a citizen of Athens,   Plato *Apology*
   the greatest of cities and the most famous for wisdom
   and power, not ashamed to care for the acquisition of
   wealth and for reputation and honour, when you neither
   care nor take thought for wisdom and truth and the
   perfection of your soul?

8 And I tell you that virtue does not come from money,   Plato *Apology*
   but from virtue comes money and all other good things
   to man, both to the individual and to the state.

Alexander Solzhenitsyn 1918–

Russian novelist

9 The thoughts of a prisoner—they're not free either. They   *One Day in the Life of Ivan*
   keep returning to the same things.   *Denisovich* (1962)

10 You only have power over people as long as you don't   *The First Circle* (1968)
   take *everything* away from them. But when you've robbed
   a man of *everything* he's no longer in your power—he's
   free again.

11 Mankind's salvation lies exclusively in everyone's making   Nobel Prize Lecture, 1970
   everything his business, in the people of the East being
   anything but indifferent to what is thought in the West,

and in the people of the West being anything but indifferent to what happens in the East.

1 In our country the lie has become not just a moral category but a pillar of the State.

interview in 1974; in appendix to *The Oak and the Calf* (1975)

2 The Gulag Archipelago.
referring to the political prison camps dotted around the Soviet Union

title of book (1973–5)

3 Yes, we are still the prisoners of communism, and yet, for us in Russia, Communism is a dead dog, while for many people in the West it is still a living lion.

broadcast on BBC Russian Service, in *Listener* 15 February 1979

4 In the United States the difficulties are not a Minotaur or a dragon—not imprisonment, hard labour, death, government harassment, and censorship—but cupidity, boredom, sloppiness, and indifference. Not the acts of a mighty all-pervading repressive government but the failure of a listless public to make use of the freedom that is its birthright.

in *Policy Review* Winter 1994

Anastasio Somoza 1925–80

elected President of Nicaragua in 1967, he was overthrown by the Sandinistas in 1979, and assassinated while in exile in Paraguay

replying to an accusation of ballot-rigging:
5 You won the elections, but I won the count.

in *Guardian* 17 June 1977

Susan Sontag 1933–

American writer

6 The white race *is* the cancer of human history, it is the white race, and it alone—its ideologies and inventions—which eradicates autonomous civilizations wherever it spreads, which has upset the ecological balance of the planet, which now threatens the very existence of life itself.

in *Partisan Review* Winter 1967

Lord Soper 1903–

British Methodist minister

of the quality of debate in the House of Lords:
7 It is, I think, good evidence of life after death.

in *Listener* 17 August 1978

John L. B. Soule 1815–91

American journalist

8 Go West, young man, go West!

in *Terre Haute* [Indiana] *Express* (1851) editorial

Robert Southey 1774–1843

English poet and writer

1 Now tell us all about the war,   'The Battle of Blenheim' (1800)
   And what they fought each other for.

2 'And everybody praised the Duke,   'The Battle of Blenheim' (1800)
   Who this great fight did win.'
   'But what good came of it at last?'
   Quoth little Peterkin.
   'Why that I cannot tell,' said he,
   'But 'twas a famous victory.'

3 The death of Nelson was felt in England as something   *The Life of Nelson* (1813)
   more than a public calamity; men started at the
   intelligence, and turned pale, as if they had heard of the
   loss of a dear friend.

Henry D. Spalding d. 1990

4 I like Ike.   in *New Republic* 27 October 1947
   US button badge first used in 1947 when General **Eisenhower**
   was seen as a potential presidential nominee

Herbert Spencer 1820–1903

Engish philosopher

5 The Republican form of Government is the highest form   *Essays* (1891) vol. 3 'The
   of government; but because of this it requires the highest Americans'
   type of human nature—a type nowhere at present
   existing.

6 The ultimate result of shielding men from the effects of   *Essays* (1891) vol. 3 'State
   folly, is to fill the world with fools.   Tamperings with Money and
                                                              Banks'

Oswald Spengler 1880–1936

German historian

7 Socialism is nothing but the capitalism of the working   *The Hour of Decision* (1933)
   class.

Edmund Spenser c.1552–99

English poet

8 Ill can he rule the great that cannot reach the small.   *The Faerie Queen* (1596)

Benjamin Spock 1903–

American paediatrician

9 To win in Vietnam, we will have to exterminate   *Dr Spock on Vietnam* (1968)
   a nation.

Cecil Spring-Rice 1859–1918

British diplomat; Ambassador to Washington from 1912

1 I vow to thee, my country—all earthly things above—
Entire and whole and perfect, the service of my love,
The love that asks no question: the love that stands the
test,
That lays upon the altar the dearest and the best:
The love that never falters, the love that pays the price,
The love that makes undaunted the final sacrifice.

'I Vow to Thee, My Country'
(written on the eve of his
departure from Washington, 12
January 1918)

2 Wilson is the nation's shepherd and McAdoo his crook.
*of President Woodrow **Wilson** and his secretary of the treasury,
a remark considered unfortunate in the light of British attempts
to draw the US into the First World War*

Robert Skidelsky *John Maynard
Keynes* vol. 1 (1983)

Joseph Stalin 1879–1953

Soviet dictator

3 The State is an instrument in the hands of the ruling
class, used to break the resistance of the adversaries of
that class.

Foundations of Leninism (1924)

4 There is the question: Can Socialism *possibly* be
established in one country alone by that country's
unaided strength? The question must be answered in the
affirmative.

Problems of Leninism (1926)

5 The Pope! How many divisions has *he* got?
*on being asked to encourage Catholicism in Russia by way of
conciliating the Pope*

on 13 May 1935; W. S. Churchill
The Gathering Storm (1948)

6 There is one eternally true legend—that of Judas.
at the trial of Radek in 1937

Robert Payne *The Rise and Fall of
Stalin* (1966)

7 One death is a tragedy, one million is a statistic.

attributed

Charles E. Stanton 1859–1933

American soldier

8 Lafayette, we are here.
at the tomb of Lafayette in Paris, 4 July 1917

in *New York Tribune* 6 September
1917

Edwin McMasters Stanton 1814–69

American lawyer

9 Now he belongs to the ages.
*of Abraham **Lincoln**, following his assassination, 15 April 1865*

I. M. Tarbell *Life of Abraham
Lincoln* (1900)

David Steel 1938–

British Liberal politician; Leader of the Liberal Party 1976–88
on Steel: see **Foot** 138:8

10 I have the good fortune to be the first Liberal leader for
over half a century who is able to say to you at the end

speech to the Liberal Party
Assembly, 18 September 1981

of our annual assembly: go back to your constituencies
and prepare for government.

Lincoln Steffens 1866–1936

American journalist

1 I have seen the future; and it works.
   following a visit to the Soviet Union in 1919

Letters (1938) vol. 1; see J. M.
Thompson *Russia, Bolshevism and
the Versailles Treaty* (1954), where
it is recalled that Steffens had
composed the expression before
he had even arrived in Russia

Gertrude Stein 1874–1946

American writer

2 In the United States there is more space where nobody is
   than where anybody is. That is what makes America
   what it is.

*The Geographical History of
America* (1936)

James Fitzjames Stephen 1829–94

English lawyer

3 The way in which the man of genius rules is by
   persuading an efficient minority to coerce an indifferent
   and self-indulgent majority.

Liberty, Equality and Fraternity
(1873)

Thaddeus Stevens 1792–1868

American politician

4 Though the President is Commander-in-Chief, Congress is
   his commander; and, God willing, he shall obey. He and
   his minions shall learn that this is not a Government of
   kings and satraps, but a Government of the people, and
   that Congress is the people.

speech in House of
Representatives, 3 January 1867

Adlai Stevenson 1900–65

American Democratic politician

5 I am not a politician, I am a citizen.
   speech during the 1948 election campaign

Bert Cochran *Adlai Stevenson*
(1969)

6 We must be patient—making peace is harder than
   making war.

speech to Chicago Council on
Foreign Relations, 21 March 1946

7 I suppose flattery hurts no one, that is, if he doesn't
   inhale.

television broadcast, 30 March
1952

8 Better we lose the election than mislead the people.
   on accepting the Democratic nomination in 1952

Herbert Muller *Adlai Stevenson*
(1968)

9 Let's talk sense to the American people. Let's tell them
   the truth, that there are no gains without pains.
   accepting the Democratic nomination

speech at the Democratic National
Convention, Chicago, Illinois, 26
July 1952

1 If they [the Republicans] will stop telling lies about the Democrats, we will stop telling the truth about them.

speech during 1952 Presidential campaign; J. B. Martin *Adlai Stevenson and Illinois* (1976)

2 When an American says that he loves his country, he... means that he loves an inner air, an inner light in which freedom lives and in which a man can draw the breath of self-respect.

speech in New York City, 27 August 1952

3 A hungry man is not a free man.

speech at Kasson, Minnesota, 6 September 1952

4 The time to stop a revolution is at the beginning, not the end.

speech in San Francisco, 9 September 1952

5 There is no evil in the atom; only in men's souls.

speech at Hartford, Connecticut, 18 September 1952

6 In America any boy may become President and I suppose it's just one of the risks he takes!

speech in Indianapolis, 26 September 1952

7 A free society is a society where it is safe to be unpopular.

speech in Detroit, 7 October 1952

8 The Republican party did not have to...encourage the excesses of its Vice-Presidential nominee [Richard Nixon]—the young man who asks you to set him one heart-beat from the Presidency of the United States.
commonly quoted as 'just a heart-beat away...'

speech at Cleveland, Ohio, 23 October 1952

9 A funny thing happened to me on the way to the White House.
speech in Washington, 13 December 1952, following his defeat in the Presidential election

Alden Whitman *Portrait: Adlai E. Stevenson* (1965)

10 We hear the Secretary of State [John Foster Dulles] boasting of his brinkmanship—the art of bringing us to the edge of the abyss.

speech in Hartford, Connecticut, 25 February 1956; cf. **Dulles** 126:9

11 The idea that you can merchandize candidates for high office like breakfast cereal—that you can gather votes like box tops—is, I think, the ultimate indignity to the democratic process.

speech at the Democratic National Convention, 18 August 1956

12 You have taught me a lesson I should have learned long ago—to take counsel always of your courage and never of your fears.
on losing the Presidential nomination in 1960

Herbert J. Muller *Adlai Stevenson* (1968)

13 Do you remember that in classical times when Cicero had finished speaking, the people said, 'How well he spoke', but when Demosthenes had finished speaking, they said, 'Let us march.'
*introducing John Fitzgerald **Kennedy** in 1960*

Bert Cochran *Adlai Stevenson* (1969)

14 She would rather light a candle than curse the darkness, and her glow has warmed the world.
*on learning of Eleanor **Roosevelt**'s death*

in *New York Times* 8 November 1962

15 Eggheads of the world unite; you have nothing to lose but your yolks.
perhaps a reworking of 'Eggheads of the world, arise — I was

attributed

even going to add that you have nothing to lose but your yolks',
speech at Oakland, 1 February 1956

1 If I had any epitaph that I would rather have more than
another, it would be to say that I had disturbed the sleep
of my generation.

epigraph to Jack W. Germand and
Jules Witcover *Wake Us When It's
Over* (1985)

2 A politician is a person who approaches every subject
with an open mouth.

attributed

3 The sound of tireless voices is the price we pay for the
right to hear the music of our own opinions.

in *The Guide to American Law*
(1984)

Robert Louis Stevenson 1850–94

Scottish writer

4 Politics is perhaps the only profession for which no
preparation is thought necessary.

Familiar Studies of Men and Books
(1882)

Caskie Stinnett 1911–

5 A diplomat...is a person who can tell you to go to hell
in such a way that you actually look forward to the trip.

Out of the Red (1960)

Baroness Stocks 1891–1975

British educationist

6 The House of Lords is a perfect eventide home.

My Commonplace Book (1970)

Tom Stoppard 1937–

British playwright

7 The House of Lords, an illusion to which I have never
been able to subscribe—responsibility without power, the
prerogative of the eunuch throughout the ages.

Lord Malquist and Mr Moon (1966)

8 It's not the voting that's democracy, it's the counting.

Jumpers (1972)

9 War is capitalism with the gloves off and many who go
to war know it but they go to war because they don't
want to be a hero.

Travesties (1975)

10 Comment is free but facts are on expenses.

Night and Day (1978); cf.
Scott 322:4

11 I'm with you on the free press. It's the newspapers
I can't stand.

Night and Day (1978)

William Stoughton 1631–1701

12 God hath sifted a nation that he might send choice grain
into this wilderness.

election sermon in Boston, 29 April
1669

Lord Stowell 1745–1836

English jurist

1 A precedent embalms a principle.
   an opinion, while Advocate-General, 1788

quoted by Disraeli in the House of
Commons, 22 February 1848

2 The elegant simplicity of the three per cents.

Lord Campbell *Lives of the Lord
Chancellors* (1857);
cf. **Disraeli** 120:19

Thomas Wentworth, Lord Strafford
1593–1641

English statesman

3 The authority of a King is the keystone which closeth up
   the arch of order and government which, once shaken,
   all the frame falls together in a confused heap of
   foundation and battlement.

Hugh Trevor-Roper *Historical
Essays* (1952)

Simeon Strunsky 1879–1948

4 People who want to understand democracy should spend
   less time in the library with Aristotle and more time on
   buses and in the subway.

No Mean City (1944)

Louis Sullivan 1933–

American Secretary of Health and Human Services

on the probable nature of a nationalized health service:
5 What we would have is a combination of the compassion
   of the Internal Revenue Service and the efficiency of the
   post office.

in *Newsweek* February 1992

Maximilien de Béthune, Duc de Sully
1559–1641

French statesman

6 Tilling and grazing are the two breasts by which France
   is fed.

Mémoires (1638)

7 The English take their pleasures sadly after the fashion of
   their country.

attributed

Arthur Hays Sulzberger 1891–1968

American newspaper proprietor

8 We tell the public which way the cat is jumping. The
   public will take care of the cat.
   on journalism

in *Time* 8 May 1950

Charles Sumner 1811–74

American politician and orator
on Sumner: see **Adams** 2:9

1 Where Slavery is, there Liberty cannot be; and where
   Liberty is, there Slavery cannot be.

   'Slavery and the Rebellion'; speech
   at Cooper Institute 5 November
   1864

2 There is the National flag. He must be cold, indeed, who
   can look upon its folds rippling in the breeze without
   pride of country. If in a foreign land, the flag is
   companionship, and country itself, with all its
   endearments.

   Are We a Nation? 19 November
   1867

Hannen Swaffer 1879–1962

British journalist

3 Freedom of the press in Britain means freedom to print
   such of the proprietor's prejudices as the advertisers don't
   object to.

   said to Tom Driberg *c.*1928; Tom
   Driberg *Swaff* (1974)

Jonathan Swift 1667–1745

Anglo-Irish poet and satirist

4 Laws are like cobwebs, which may catch small flies, but
   let wasps and hornets break through.

   *A Critical Essay upon the Faculties
   of the Mind* (1709); cf. **Anarcharsis**
   8:3, **Shenstone** 338:9

5 It is the folly of too many, to mistake the echo of
   a London coffee-house for the voice of the kingdom.

   The Conduct of the Allies (1711)

6 I cannot but conclude the bulk of your natives to be the
   most pernicious race of little odious vermin that nature
   ever suffered to crawl upon the surface of the earth.

   Gulliver's Travels (1726) 'A Voyage
   to Brobdingnag'

7 And he gave it for his opinion, that whoever could make
   two ears of corn or two blades of grass to grow upon
   a spot of ground where only one grew before, would
   deserve better of mankind, and do more essential service
   to his country than the whole race of politicians put
   together.

   Gulliver's Travels (1726) 'A Voyage
   to Brobdingnag'

8 These unhappy people were proposing schemes for
   persuading monarchs to choose favourites upon the score
   of their wisdom, capacity and virtue; of teaching
   ministers to consult the public good; of rewarding merit,
   great abilities and eminent services; of instructing princes
   to know their true interest by placing it on the same
   foundation with that of their people: of choosing for
   employment persons qualified to exercise them; with
   many other wild impossible chimeras, that never entered
   before into the heart of man to conceive, and confirmed
   in me the old observation, that there is nothing so
   extravagant and irrational which some philosophers have
   not maintained for truth.

   Gulliver's Travels (1726) 'A Voyage
   to Laputa, etc.'

1 I have been assured by a very knowing American of my   *A Modest Proposal for Preventing*
   acquaintance in London, that a young healthy child well   *the Children of Ireland from being*
   nursed is at a year old a most delicious, nourishing, and   *a Burden to their Parents or*
   wholesome food, whether stewed, roasted, baked, or   *Country* (1729)
   boiled, and I make no doubt that it will equally serve in
   a fricassee, or a ragout.

Tacitus AD *c.*56–AFTER 117

Roman senator and historian

2 Now the boundary of Britain is revealed, and everything   *Agricola*
   unknown is held to be glorious.
     reporting the speech of a British leader, Calgacus

3 They make a wilderness and call it peace.   *Agricola*

4 You were indeed fortunate, Agricola, not only in the   *Agricola*
   distinction of your life, but also in the lucky timing of
   your death.

5 With neither anger nor partiality.   *Annals*

6 The more corrupt the republic, the more numerous the   *Annals*
   laws.

7 These times having the rare good fortune that you may   *Histories*
   think what you like and say what you think.

8 He seemed much greater than a private citizen while he   *Histories*
   still was a private citizen, and by everyone's consent
   capable of reigning if only he had not reigned.
     of the Emperor Galba

9 The gods are on the side of the stronger.   *Histories*; cf. **Voltaire** 375:8

William Howard Taft 1857–1930

American Republican statesman, 27th President of the US
1909–13

10 Next to the right of liberty, the right of property is the *Popular Government* (1913)
   most important individual right guaranteed by the
   Constitution and the one which, united with that of
   personal liberty, has contributed more to the growth of
   civilization than any other institution established by the
   human race.

Charles-Maurice de Talleyrand
1754–1838

French statesman
on Talleyrand: see **Napoleon** 270:4

of the Bourbons in exile:
11 They have learnt nothing, and forgotten nothing.   oral tradition, attributed to
     a similar comment on the courtiers of **Louis XVIII**, *attributed to*   Talleyrand by the Chevalier de
     the French general Dumouriez, was quoted by **Napoleon** *in his*   Panat, January 1796
     Declaration to the French on his return from Elba

on hearing of **Napoleon**'s *costly victory at Borodino, 1812:*

1 This is the beginning of the end.

Sainte-Beuve *M. de Talleyrand* (1870); attributed

2 It is not an event, it is an item of news.
 on hearing of the death of **Napoleon** *in 1821*

Philip Henry Stanhope *Notes of Conversations with the Duke of Wellington* (1888) 1 November 1831

3 Above all, gentlemen, not the slightest zeal.

P. Chasles *Voyages d'un critique à travers la vie et les livres* (1868) vol. 2

4 He who has not lived during the years around 1789 can not know what is meant by the pleasure of life.

M. Guizot *Mémoires pour servir à l'histoire de mon temps* (1858) vol. 1

5 [Treason] is a question of dates.

Duff Cooper *Talleyrand* (1932)

R. H. Tawney 1880–1962

British economic historian

6 By making the most fundamental of all industries a public service carried on in partnership between the state and the workers, it will call into operation motives of public spirit and professional zeal which are at present stifled by subordination of the industry to the pursuit of private gain, and will raise the whole tone and quality of our industrial civilization.
 on the nationalization of the coal industry in 1919

Anthony Sampson *The Changing Anatomy of Britain* (1982)

7 The characteristic virtue of Englishmen is power of sustained practical activity and their characteristic vice a reluctance to test the quality of that activity by reference to principles.

The Acquisitive Society (1921)

8 Militarism... is fetish worship. It is the prostration of men's souls and the laceration of their bodies to appease an idol.

The Acquisitive Society (1921)

9 Those who dread a dead-level of income or wealth... do not dread, it seems, a dead-level of law and order, and of security for life and property.

Equality (1931 ed.)

10 Private property is a necessary institution, at least in a fallen world; men work more and dispute less when goods are private than when they are common. But it is to be tolerated as a concession to human frailty, not applauded as desirable in itself.

Religion and the Rise of Capitalism (1926)

11 To take usury is contrary to Scripture; it is contrary to Aristotle; it is contrary to nature, for it is to live without labour; it is to sell time, which belongs to God, for the advantage of wicked men; it is to rob those who use the money lent, and to whom, since they make it profitable, the profits should belong.

Religion and the Rise of Capitalism (1926)

12 Both the existing economic order, and too many of the projects advanced for reconstructing it, break down

Religion and the Rise of Capitalism (1926) conclusion

through their neglect of the truism that, since even quite
common men have souls, no increase in material wealth
will compensate them for arrangements which insult
their self-respect and impair their freedom. A reasonable
estimate of economic organisation must allow for the fact
that, unless industry is to be paralysed by recurrent
revolts on the part of outraged human nature, it must
satisfy criteria which are not purely economic.

1 Freedom for the pike is death for the minnows.   *Equality* (1938 ed.)

2 Democracy a society where ordinary men exercise   unpublished fragment of Chicago
initiative. Dreadful respect for superiors. Mental   lecture (1939), read at Tawney's
enlargement...Real foe to be overcome...fact that large   funeral
section of the public *like* plutocratic government, and are
easily gullible. How shake them!

3 That seductive border region where politics grease the   *Business and Politics under James*
wheels of business and polite society smiles hopefully on   *I* (1958)
both.

declining the offer of a peerage:
4 What harm have I ever done to the Labour Party?   in *Evening Standard* 18 January
1962

A. J. P. Taylor 1906–90

British historian

5 Without democracy socialism would be worth nothing,   in *Manchester Guardian* 7 March
but democracy is worth a great deal even when it is not   1941
socialist.

6 What is wrong with Germany is there is too much of it.   in *Manchester Guardian* 29 March
There are too many Germans, and Germany is too   1944
strong, too well organized, too well equipped with
industrial resources.

7 The British political system has no room for the rogue   in *History Today* July 1951 'Lord
elephant.   Palmerston'

8 Crimea: The War That Would Not Boil.   *Rumours of Wars* (1952); originally
the title of an essay in *History
Today* 2 February 1951

9 Bismarck was a political genius of the highest rank, but   in *Encyclopedia Britannica* (1954)
he lacked one essential quality of the constructive
statesman: he had no faith in the future.

10 The politician performs upon the stage; the historian   *Englishmen and Others* (1956)
looks behind the scenery.

11 We may remind ourselves over and over again, that the   *The Troublemakers* (1957)
foreign policy of a country is made by a few experts and
a few rather less expert politicians...We write 'the
British' when we mean 'the few members of the Foreign
Office who happened to concern themselves with this
question'.

12 Conformity may give you a quiet life; it may even bring   *The Troublemakers* (1957)
you a University Chair. But all change in history, all

advance, comes from the nonconformist. If there had
been no trouble makers, no Dissenters, we should still be
living in caves.

1 Appeasement was a sensible course, even though it was
tried with the wrong man; and it remains the noblest
word in the diplomatist's vocabulary.

*in Manchester Guardian 30
September 1958*

2 A racing tipster who only reached Hitler's level of
accuracy would not do well for his clients.

*The Origins of the Second World
War (1961)*

3 Communism continued to haunt Europe as a spectre—a
name men gave to their own fears and blunders. But the
crusade against Communism was even more imaginary
than the spectre of Communism.

*The Origins of the Second World
War (1961)*

4 Human blunders, however, usually do more to shape
history than human wickedness.

*The Origins of the Second World
War (1961)*

5 With Hitler guilty, every other German could claim
innocence.

*The Origins of the Second World
War (1961)*

6 'Democratic, federal Yugoslavia' translated into practice
the great might-have-been of Habsburg history.

*The Habsburg Monarchy,
1809–1918 (2nd ed. 1961)*

7 Like most of those who study history, he [Napoleon III]
learned from the mistakes of the past how to make new
ones.

in *Listener* 6 June 1963 'Mistaken
Lessons from the Past'

8 The First World War had begun—imposed on the
statesmen of Europe by railway timetables. It was an
unexpected climax to the railway age.

The First World War (1963)

9 He aspired to power instead of influence, and as a result
forfeited both.
    of Lord **Northcliffe**

English History 1914–45 (1965)

10 History gets thicker as it approaches recent times.

English History 1914–45 (1965)
Bibliography

11 In the Second World War the British people came of age.
This was a people's war...Few now sang *Land of Hope
and Glory*. Few even sang *England Arise*. England had
risen all the same.

*English History, 1914–1945
(1965)*

12 He aroused every feeling except trust.
    of **Lloyd George**

English History 1914–1945 (1965)

of the period after the First World War:
13 Civilization was held together by the civilized behaviour
of ordinary people...In reality the masses were calmer
and more sensible than those who ruled over them.

From Sarajevo to Potsdam (1966)

14 Like Johnson's friend Edwards, I, too have tried to be
a Marxist but common sense kept breaking in.

'Accident Prone' in *Journal of
Modern History* 1977

15 If men are to respect each other for what they are, they
must cease to respect each other for what they own.

*Politicians, Socialism and
Historians (1980)*

Henry Taylor 1800–86

British writer and civil servant

1 It is of far greater importance to a statesman to make one friend who will hold out with him for twenty years, than to find twenty followers in each year, losing as many.

The Statesman (1836)

2 No statesman, be he as discreet as he may, will escape having ascribed to him, as the result of interviews, promises and understandings which it was not his purpose to convey; and yet in a short time he will be unable to recollect what was said with sufficient distinctness to enable him to give a confident contradiction.

The Statesman (1836)

3 The conscience of a statesman should be rather a strong conscience than a tender conscience.

The Statesman (1836)

4 It is very certain that there may be met with, in public life, a species of conscience which is all bridle and no spurs.

The Statesman (1836)

5 The hand which executes a measure should belong to the head which propounds it.

The Statesman (1836)

6 One who would thrive by seeking favours from the great, should never trouble them for small ones.

The Statesman (1836)

7 [A statesman] should steer by the compass, but he must lie with the wind.

The Statesman (1836)

8 A secret may be sometimes best kept by keeping the secret of its being a secret.

The Statesman (1836)

9 Indecisiveness will be *caeteris paribus* most pernicious in affairs which require secrecy;—1st. Because the greatest aid to secrecy is celerity; 2nd. Because the undecided man, seeking after various counsels, necessarily multiplies confidences.

The Statesman (1836)

10 To choose that which will bring him the most credit with the least trouble, has hitherto been the sole care of the statesman in office.

The Statesman (1836)

11 Good nature and kindness towards those with whom they come in personal contact, at the expense of public interests, that is of those whom they never see, is the besetting sin of public men.

The Statesman (1836)

12 He who has once advanced by a stride will not be content to advance afterwards by steps. Public servants, therefore, like racehorses, should be well fed with reward, but not to fatness.

The Statesman (1836)

13 Men in high places, from having less personal interest in the characters of others—being safe from them—are commonly less acute observers, and with their progressive elevation in life become, as more and more indifferent to what other men are, so more and more ignorant of them.

The Statesman (1836)

Norman Tebbit 1931–

British Conservative politician
on Tebbit: see **Foot** 138:7

1 I grew up in the Thirties with our unemployed father. He did not riot, he got on his bike and looked for work.

speech at Conservative Party Conference, 15 October 1981

2 The trigger of today's outburst of crime and violence... lies in the era and attitudes of postwar funk which gave birth to the 'permissive society'.

in *Guardian* 4 November 1985

3 The word 'conservative' is used by the BBC as a portmanteau word of abuse for anyone whose views differ from the insufferable, smug, sanctimonious, naive, guilt-ridden, wet, pink orthodoxy of that sunset home of the third-rate minds of that third-rate decade, the nineteen-sixties.

in *Independent* 24 February 1990

4 The cricket test—which side do they cheer for?...Are you still looking back to where you came from or where you are?
    on the loyalties of Britain's immigrant population

interview in *Los Angeles Times*, reported in *Daily Telegraph* 20 April 1990

William Temple 1881–1944

English theologian; Archbishop of Canterbury from 1942

5 In place of the conception of the power-state we are led to that of the welfare-state.

Citizen and Churchman (1941)

John Tenniel 1820–1914

English draughtsman

6 Dropping the pilot.
    cartoon caption, and title of poem, on **Bismarck**'s *dismissal from office by Kaiser* **Wilhelm II**

in *Punch* 29 March 1890

Lord Tennyson 1809–92

English poet

7   Forward, forward let us range,
   Let the great world spin for ever down the ringing
      grooves of change.

'Locksley Hall' (1842)

8 A land of settled government,
   A land of just and old renown,
   Where Freedom slowly broadens down
   From precedent to precedent.

'You ask me, why, though ill at ease' (1842)

9 The last great Englishman is low.

'Ode on the Death of the Duke of Wellington' (1852)

10 O good grey head which all men knew!

'Ode on the Death of the Duke of Wellington' (1852)

11 O fall'n at length that tower of strength
    Which stood four-square to all the winds that blew!

'Ode on the Death of the Duke of Wellington' (1852)

1 That world-earthquake, Waterloo!

'Ode on the Death of the Duke of Wellington' (1852)

2 Who never sold the truth to serve the hour,
Nor paltered with Eternal God for power.

'Ode on the Death of the Duke of Wellington' (1852)

3 Not once or twice in our rough island-story,
The path of duty was the way to glory.

'Ode on the Death of the Duke of Wellington' (1852)

4 Authority forgets a dying king.

'The Passing of Arthur' (1869)

5 The old order changeth, yielding place to new,
And God fulfils himself in many ways,
Lest one good custom should corrupt the world.

'The Passing of Arthur' 1869

Terence 190–159 BC

Roman comic playwright

6 *Quot homines tot sententiae: suus cuique mos.*
There are as many opinions as there are people: each has
his own correct way.

Phormio

Margaret Thatcher 1925–

British Conservative stateswoman, Prime Minister 1979–90
on Thatcher: see **Anonymous** 11:2, **Biffen** 45:1, **Callaghan**
73:2, **Critchley** 104:5, 104:8, **Healey** 173:1, 173:2, 173:4,
Hennessy 175:2, **Kinnock** 211:9, **Mitterrand** 261:8, **Parris**
286:10, **West** 385:8

7 No woman in my time will be Prime Minister or
Chancellor or Foreign Secretary—not the top jobs.
Anyway I wouldn't want to be Prime Minister. You have
to give yourself 100%.
on her appointment as Shadow Education Spokesman

in *Sunday Telegraph* 26 October
1969

8 In politics if you want anything said, ask a man. If you
want anything done, ask a woman.

in *People* (New York) 15
September 1975

9 I'll always be fond of dear Ted, but there's no sympathy
in politics.
of her predecessor, Edward **Heath**

attributed, 1975

10 I stand before you tonight in my red chiffon evening
gown, my face softly made up, my fair hair gently
waved...the Iron Lady of the Western World! Me? A
cold war warrior? Well, yes—if that is how they wish to
interpret my defence of values and freedoms fundamental
to our way of life.

speech at Finchley, 31 January 1976

11 I've got no hang-ups about my background, like you
intellectual commentators in the south-east. When you're
actually *doing* things you don't have time for hang-ups.

in conversation with Anthony
Sampson in 1977; Anthony
Sampson *The Changing Anatomy
of Britain* (1982)

12 Pennies don't fall from heaven. They have to be earned
on earth.

in *Observer* 18 November 1979
'Sayings of the Week'

13 I don't mind how much my Ministers talk, as long as
they do what I say.

in *Observer* 27 January 1980

1 We have to get our production and our earnings in balance. There's no easy popularity in what we are proposing, but it is fundamentally sound. Yet I believe people accept there is no real alternative.
popularly encapsulated in the acronym TINA

speech at Conservative Women's Conference, 21 May 1980

2 To those waiting with bated breath for that favourite media catch-phrase, the U-turn, I have only this to say. 'You turn if you want; the lady's not for turning.'

speech at Conservative Party Conference in Brighton, 10 October 1980

3 Economics are the method; the object is to change the soul.

in *Sunday Times* 3 May 1981

4 My politics are based...on things I and millions like me were brought up with. An honest day's work for an honest day's pay; live within your means; put by a nest egg for a rainy day; pay your bills on time; support the police.

in *News of the World* 20 September 1981

5 Let me make one thing absolutely clear. The National Health Service is safe with us.

speech at Conservative Party Conference, 8 October 1982

6 Just rejoice at that news and congratulate our armed forces and the Marines. Rejoice!
on the recapture of South Georgia, usually quoted as, 'Rejoice, rejoice!'

to newsmen outside 10 Downing Street, 25 April 1982

7 It is exciting to have a real crisis on your hands, when you have spent half your political life dealing with humdrum issues like the environment.
on the Falklands campaign, 1982

speech to Scottish Conservative Party conference, 14 May 1982

8 I was asked whether I was trying to restore Victorian values. I said straight out I was. And I am.

speech to the British Jewish Community, 21 July 1983, referring to an interview with Brian Walden on 17 January 1983

9 Now it must be business as usual.
on the steps of Brighton police station a few hours after the bombing of the Grand Hotel, Brighton; often quoted as 'We shall carry on as usual'

in *The Times* 13 October 1984

10 In church on Sunday morning—it was a lovely morning and we haven't had many lovely days—the sun was coming through a stained glass window and falling on some flowers, falling right across the church. It just occurred to me that this was the day I was meant not to see. Then all of a sudden I thought, 'there are some of my dearest friends who are not seeing this day.'
after the Brighton bombing

television interview, 15 October 1984

*of Mikhail **Gorbachev***:

11 We can do business together.

in *The Times* 18 December 1984

12 We got a really good consensus during the last election. Consensus behind my convictions.

attributed, 1984

13 We must try to find ways to starve the terrorist and the hijacker of the oxygen of publicity on which they depend.

speech to American Bar Association in London, 15 July 1985

14 I don't spend a lifetime watching which way the cat jumps. I know really which way I want the cats to go.

interview with Michael Charlton on BBC radio, 17 December 1985

1 No one would remember the Good Samaritan if he'd only   television interview, 6 January
   had good intentions. He had money as well.   1986

2 There is no such thing as Society. There are individual   in *Woman's Own* 31 October 1987
   men and women, and there are families.

3 We have become a grandmother.   in *The Times* 4 March 1989

4 I am extraordinarily patient, provided I get my own way   in *Observer* 4 April 1989
   in the end.

5 Advisers advise and ministers decide.   in the House of Commons, 26
   on the respective roles of the her personal economic adviser,   October 1989
   Alan Walters, and her Chancellor, Nigel **Lawson** *(who resigned*
   the following day)

   of Nigel **Lawson**, *who had resigned two days before:*
6 To me, the Chancellor's position was unassailable.   in an interview with Brian Walden,
                                                             29 October 1989

7 You don't reach Downing Street by pretending you've   in *Independent* 14 October 1989
   travelled the road to Damascus when you haven't even
   left home.
   of Neil **Kinnock**

8 I am naturally very sorry to see you go, but   in *Guardian* 4 January 1990; cf.
   understand...your wish to be able to spend more time   **Fowler** 140:3
   with your family.
   reply to Norman **Fowler**'s *resignation letter*

9 Others bring me problems, David brings me solutions.   in *Observer* 1 July 1990
   of Lord Young

10 No! No! No!   in the House of Commons, 30
   making clear her opposition to a single European currency, and   October 1990
   more centralized controls from Brussels

11 I shan't be pulling the levers there but I shall be a very in *Independent* 27 November 1990
   good back-seat driver.
   on the appointment of John **Major** *as the next Prime Minister*

12 Every Prime Minister needs a Willie.   in *Guardian* 7 August 1991
   at the farewell dinner to Lord **Whitelaw**

   of being told by a majority of her Cabinet that she could not
   continue as Prime Minister:
13 Treachery with a smile on its face.   on 'The Thatcher Years' (BBC 1), 20
                                                             October 1993

14 I think sometimes the Prime Minister should be   on 'The Thatcher Years' (BBC 1), 21
   intimidating. There's not much point being a weak,   October 1993
   floppy thing in the chair, is there?

   of the poll tax:
15 Given time, it would have been seen as one of the most   *The Downing Street Years* (1993)
   far-reaching and beneficial reforms ever made in the
   working of local government.

William Roscoe Thayer 1859–1923

American biographer and historian

1   From log-cabin to White House.   title of biography (1910) of James **Garfield**

Louis Adolphe Thiers 1797–1877

French statesman and historian

2   The king reigns, and the people govern themselves.   unsigned article in *Le National*, 20 January 1830; a signed article, 4 February 1830, reads: 'The king neither administers nor governs, he reigns'

Dylan Thomas 1914–53

Welsh poet

3   The hand that signed the paper felled a city;   'The Hand That Signed the Paper Felled a City'
Five sovereign fingers taxed the breath,
Doubled the globe of death and halved a country;
These five kings did a king to death.

4   The hand that signed the treaty bred a fever,   'The Hand That Signed the Paper Felled a City'
And famine grew, and locusts came;
Great is the hand that holds dominion over
Man by a scribbled name.

J. H. Thomas 1874–1949

British Socialist politician

5   And now 'ere we 'ave this obstinate little man with 'is   Harold Nicolson letter 26 February 1936
Mrs Simpson. Hit won't do, 'arold, I tell you that
straight.
    to Harold **Nicolson** *on* **Edward VIII** *and the Abdication crisis*

6   They 'ate 'aving no family life at Court.   Harold Nicolson letter 26 February 1936
    of the British people and the Abdication crisis

Norman Thomas 1884–1968

American Presbyterian minister and writer

7   I'd rather see America save her soul than her face.   speech in Washington, DC, 27 November 1965
    protesting against the Vietnam War

Lord Thomson of Fleet 1894–1976

Canadian-born British newspaper and television proprietor

on owning a commercial television station:
8   Like having your own licence to print money.   R. Braddon *Roy Thomson* (1965)

Henry David Thoreau 1817–62

American writer

1 I heartily accept the motto, 'That government is best   *Civil Disobedience* (1849)
which governs least'...Carried out, it finally amounts to
this, which I also believe,—'That government is best
which governs not at all.'

2 Under a government which imprisons any unjustly, the   *Civil Disobedience* (1849)
true place for a just man is also a prison.

3 It takes two to speak the truth,—one to speak, and   *A Week on the Concord and*
another to hear.   *Merrimack Rivers* (1849)
                                                               'Wednesday'

4 The oldest, wisest politician grows not more human so,   *Journal* 1853
but is merely a grey wharf-rat at last.

5 The government of the world I live in was not framed,   *Walden* (1854) 'Conclusion'
like that of Britain, in after-dinner conversations over the
wine.

Julian Thompson 1934–

British soldier, second-in-command of the land forces during
the Falklands campaign.

6 You don't mind dying for Queen and country, but you   'The Falklands War — the Untold
certainly don't want to die for politicians.   Story' (Yorkshire Television) 1 April
                                                               1987

Jeremy Thorpe 1929–

British Liberal politician; Liberal Party leader 1967–76

of Harold **Macmillan**'s *sacking seven of his Cabinet on 13 July
1962*

7 Greater love hath no man than this, that he lay down   D. E. Butler and Anthony King *The*
his friends for his life.   *General Election of 1964* (1965)

James Thurber 1894–1961

American humorist

8 You can fool too many of the people too much of the   *Fables for our Time* (1940); cf.
time.   **Lincoln** 227:8

Lord Thurlow 1731–1806

English jurist; Lord Chancellor, 1778–83, 1783–92

9 Corporations have neither bodies to be punished, nor   John Poynder *Literary Extracts*
souls to be condemned, they therefore do as they like.   (1844) vol. 1
   *usually quoted as 'Did you ever expect a corporation to have
   a conscience, when it has no soul to be damned, and no body to
   be kicked?'*

Alexis de Tocqueville 1805–59

French historian and politician

1 The French want no-one to be their *superior*. The English want *inferiors*. The Frenchman constantly raises his eyes above him with anxiety. The Englishman lowers his beneath him with satisfaction. On either side it is pride, but understood in a different way.

Voyage en Angleterre et en Irlande de 1835 (1958) 8 May 1835

2 It is from the midst of this putrid sewer that the greatest river of human industry springs up and carries fertility to the whole world. From this foul drain pure gold flows forth. Here it is that humanity achieves for itself both perfection and brutalization, that civilization produces its wonders, and that civilized man becomes again almost a savage.
    of Manchester

Voyage en Angleterre et en Irlande de 1835 (1958) 2 July 1835

3 The surface of American society is covered with a layer of democratic paint, but from time to time one can see the old aristocratic colours breaking through.

Democracy in America (1835–40) vol.1

4 Americans rightly think their patriotism is a sort of religion strengthened by practical service.

Democracy in America (1835–40) vol.1

5 The President may slip without the state suffering, for his duties are limited. Congress may slip without the Union perishing, for above Congress there is the electoral body which can change its spirit by changing its membership. But if ever the Supreme Court came to be composed of rash or corrupt men, the confederation would be threatened by anarchy or civil war.

Democracy in America (1835–40) vol.1

6 Providence has not created mankind entirely independent or entirely free. It is true that around every man a fatal circle is traced, beyond which he cannot pass; but within the wide verge of that circle he is powerful and free.

Democracy in America (1835–40) vol. 1

7 Of all nations, those submit to civilization with the most difficulty which habitually live by the chase.

Democracy in America (1835–40) vol. 1

8 What is understood by republican government in the United States is the slow and quiet action of society upon itself.

Democracy in America (1835–40) vol. 1

9 There are, at the present time, two great nations in the world, which seem to tend towards the same end, although they started from different points; I allude to the Russians and the Americans...Their starting point is different, and their courses are not the same; yet each of them seems to be marked out by the will of Heaven to sway the destinies of half the globe.

Democracy in America (1835–40) vol. 1

10 Unable to judge at once of the social position of those he meets, an Englishman prudently avoids all contact with them. Men are afraid less some slight service rendered should draw them into an unsuitable acquaintance; they dread civilities, and they avoid the obtrusive gratitude of a stranger quite as much as his hatred.

Democracy in America (1835–40) vol. 2

1   On my arrival in the United States I was struck by the   *Democracy in America* (1835–40)
    degree of ability among the governed and the lack of it   vol. 2
    among the governing.

2   Freedom alone...substitutes from time to time for the   *The Ancien Régime* (1856)
    love of material comfort more powerful and more lofty
    passions; it alone supplies ambition with greater
    objectives than the acquisition of riches, and creates the
    light that makes it possible to see and to judge the vices
    and virtues of mankind.

3   Where is the man of soul so base that he would prefer to   *The Ancien Régime* (1856)
    depend on the caprices of one of his fellow men rather
    than obey the laws which he has himself contributed to
    establish?

4   Despots themselves do not deny that freedom is excellent;   *The Ancien Régime* (1856)
    only they desire it for themselves alone, and they
    maintain that everyone else is altogether unworthy of it.

5   The French Revolution operated in reference to this   *The Ancien Régime* (1856)
    world in exactly the same manner as religious
    revolutions acted in view of the other world. It
    considered the citizen as an abstract proposition apart
    from any particular society, in the same way as religions
    considered man as man, independent of country and
    time.

6   History is a gallery of pictures in which there are few   *The Ancien Régime* (1856)
    originals and many copies.

7   When a nation abolishes aristocracy, centralization   *The Ancien Régime* (1856)
    follows as a matter of course.

8   The only substantial difference between the custom of   *The Ancien Régime* (1856)
    those days and our own resides in the price paid for
    office. Then they were sold by government, now they are
    bestowed; it is no longer necessary to pay money; the
    object can be attained by selling one's soul.

9   The student of our revolution soon discovers that it was   *The Ancien Régime* (1856)
    led and managed by the same spirit which gave birth to
    so many abstract treatises on government. In both he
    finds the same love for general theories, sweeping
    legislative systems, and symmetrical laws; the same
    confidence in theory; the same desire for new and
    original institutions; the same wish to reconstruct the
    whole Constitution according to the rules of logic, and in
    conformity with a set plan, instead of attempting partial
    amendments. A terrible sight! for what is merit in an
    author is often a defect in a statesman, and
    characteristics which improve a book may be fatal to
    a revolution.

10 Centralization and socialism are native of the same soil: *The Ancien Régime* (1856)
    one is the wild herb, the other the garden plant.

11 What do men need in order to remain free? A taste for   *The Ancien Régime* (1856)
    freedom. Do not ask me to analyze that sublime taste; it
    can only be felt. It has a place in every great heart which

God has prepared to receive it; it fills and inflames it. To
try to explain it to those inferior minds who have never
felt it is to waste time.

1 No example is so dangerous as that of violence employed   *The Ancien Régime* (1856)
   by well-meaning people for beneficial objects.

2 He who desires in liberty anything other than itself is   *The Ancien Régime* (1856)
   born to be a servant.

3 It is not always by going from bad to worse that   *The Ancien Régime* (1856)
   a society falls into revolution ... The social order destroyed
   by a revolution is almost always better than that which
   immediately preceded it, and experience shows that the
   most dangerous moment for a bad government is
   generally that in which it sets about reform.

Robert Torrens 1780–1864

British economist

4 In the first stone which he [the savage] flings at the wild   *An Essay on the Production of*
   animals he pursues, in the first stick that he seizes to   *Wealth* (1821) ch. 2
   strike down the fruit which hangs above his reach, we
   see the appropriation of one article for the purpose of
   aiding in the acquisition of another, and thus discover
   the origin of capital.

Arnold Toynbee 1889–1975

English historian

5 America is a large, friendly dog in a very small room.   attributed
   Every time it wags its tail it knocks over a chair.

Joseph Trapp 1679–1747

English poet and pamphleteer

6 The King, observing with judicious eyes   John Nichols *Literary Anecdotes*
   The state of both his universities,   (1812–16) vol. 3; cf.
   To Oxford sent a troop of horse, and why?   **Browne** 59:6
   That learned body wanted loyalty;
   To Cambridge books, as very well discerning
   How much that loyal body wanted learning.
     lines written on **George I**'s *donation of the Bishop of Ely's*
     Library to Cambridge University

Lord Trend 1914–87

British civil servant; Cabinet Secretary 1963–73
on Trend: see **Rothschild** 313:7

7 The acid test of any political decision is, 'What is the   attributed, 1975
   alternative?'

Charles Trevelyan 1807–86

British civil servant

on the organization of a new system of admission into the civil service:

1 It is proposed to invite the flower of our youth to the aid of public service.

to John Thadeus Delane, Editor of The Times, in 1853; Asa Briggs Victorian People (1965)

G. M. Trevelyan 1876–1962

English historian

2 If the French noblesse had been capable of playing cricket with their peasants, their chateaux would never have been burnt.

English Social History (1942)

3 In a world of voluble hates, he plotted to make men like, or at least tolerate one another.
   of Stanley Baldwin

in Dictionary of National Biography 1941–50 (1959)

William Trevor 1928–

Anglo-Irish novelist and short story writer

of the troubles in Northern Ireland:

4 A disease in the family that is never mentioned.

in Observer 18 November 1990

Hugh Trevor-Roper 1914–

British historian

5 Aristocracies...may preserve themselves longest, but only democracies, which refresh their ruling class, can expand.

Historical Essays (1952)

6 Any reaction which is to be successful over a long period must have radical origins...A reaction which is to last, which is to be accepted as orthodoxy over several generations, must spring out of the same social circumstances as the progress which it resists.

The Rise of Christian Europe (1965)

7 Historians in general are great toadies of power.

History and Imagination (1981)

8 Those who exercise power and determine policy are generally men whose minds have been formed by events twenty or thirty years before.

From Counter-Reformation to Glorious Revolution (1992); introduction

9 How are we to disentangle religion from politics in a revolution? Religion may form the outlook of an individual. It may serve as an ideological intoxicant for a crowd. But in high politics it is a variable.

From Counter-Reformation to Glorious Revolution (1992)

Tommy Trinder 1909–89

British comedian

of American troops in Britain during the Second World War:
1 Overpaid, overfed, oversexed, and over here.

associated with Trinder, but
probably not his invention

Anthony Trollope 1815–82

English novelist

2 No reform, no innovation…stinks so foully in the
nostrils of an English Tory politician as to be absolutely
irreconcilable to him. When taken in the refreshing
waters of office any such pill can be swallowed.

The Bertrams (1859)

3 To me it seems that no form of existing government—no
form of government that ever did exist, gives or has
given so large a measure of individual freedom to all who
live under it as a constitutional monarchy.

North America (1862)

4 There is nothing more tyrannical than a strong popular
feeling among a democratic people.

North America (1862)

5 I have sometimes thought that there is no being so
venomous, so bloodthirsty as a professed philanthropist.

North America (1862)

6 [Equality] is a doctrine to be forgiven when he who
preaches it is…striving to raise others to his own level.

North America (1862)

7 Mr Palliser was one of those politicians in possessing
whom England has perhaps more reason to be proud
than of any other of her resources, and who, as a body,
give to her that requisite combination of conservatism
and progress which is her present strength and best
security for the future.

Can You Forgive Her? (1864)

8 A fainéant government is not the worst government that
England can have. It has been the great fault of our
politicians that they have all wanted to do something.

Phineas Finn (1869)

of the radical politician:
9 Having nothing to construct, he could always deal with
generalities. Being free from responsibility, he was not
called upon either to study details or to master even
great facts. It was his business to inveigh against existing
evils, and perhaps there is no easier business when once
the privilege of an audience has been attained. It was his
work to cut down forest-trees, and he had nothing to do
with the subsequent cultivation of the land.

Phineas Finn (1869)

10 The first necessity for good speaking is a large audience.

Phineas Finn (1869)

11 It is the necessary nature of a political party in this
country to avoid, as long as it can be avoided, the
consideration of any question which involves a great
change…The best carriage horses are those which can
most steadily hold back against the coach as it trundles
down the hill.

Phineas Redux (1874)

1 A man destined to sit conspicuously on our Treasury Bench, or on the seat opposite to it, should ask the Gods for a thick skin as a first gift.

Phineas Redux (1874)

2 Equality would be a heaven, if we could attain it.

The Prime Minister (1876)

3 I have hardly as yet met two Englishmen who were agreed as to the political power of the sovereign.

The American Senator (1877)

4 What Good Government ever was not stingy?

South Africa (1878)

5 How seldom is it that theories stand the wear and tear of practice!

Thackeray (1879)

6 Let the Toryism of the Tory be ever so strong, it is his destiny to carry out the purposes of his opponents.

Why Frau Frohmann Raised Her Prices (1882)

7 A man who entertains in his mind any political doctrine, except as a means of improving the condition of his fellows, I regard as a political intriguer, a charlatan, and a conjuror.

Autobiography (1883)

of political life:

8 The hatreds which sound so real when you read the mere words, which look so true when you see their scornful attitudes, on which for the time you are inclined to pin your faith so implicitly, amount to nothing.

The Landleaguers (1883)

9 But in truth the capacity of a man...[to be Prime Minister] does not depend on any power of intellect, or indomitable courage, or far-seeing cunning. The man is competent simply because he is believed to be so.

Lord Palmerston (1882)

Leon Trotsky 1879–1940

Russian revolutionary

10 Where force is necessary, there it must be applied boldly, decisively and completely. But one must know the limitations of force; one must know when to blend force with a manoeuvre, a blow with an agreement.

What Next? (1932)

11 Civilization has made the peasantry its pack animal. The bourgeoisie in the long run only changed the form of the pack.

History of the Russian Revolution (1933) vol. 3

12 You [the Mensheviks] are pitiful isolated individuals; you are bankrupts; your role is played out. Go where you belong from now on—into the dustbin of history!

History of the Russian Revolution (1933) vol. 3

13 Old age is the most unexpected of all things that happen to a man.

Diary in Exile (1959) 8 May 1935

14 In a country where the sole employer is the State, opposition means death by slow starvation. The old principle: who does not work shall not eat, has been replaced by a new one: who does not obey shall not eat.

attributed

15 Not believing in force is the same thing as not believing in gravitation.

G. Maximov *The Guillotine at Work* (1940)

Harry S Truman 1884–1972

American Democratic statesman, 33rd President of the US
1945–53
on Truman: see **Mencken** 256:14; cf. **Vaughan** 373:4

*to reporters the day after his accession to the Presidency on
the death of Franklin* **Roosevelt**:

1 When they told me yesterday what had happened, I felt   on 13 April 1945
like the moon, the stars and all the planets had fallen on
me.

2 Sixteen hours ago an American airplane dropped one   on 6 August 1945
bomb on Hiroshima...The force from which the sun
draws its power has been loosed against those who
brought war to the Far East.
first announcement of the dropping of the atomic bomb

3 The release of atomic energy constitutes a new force too   message to Congress 3 October
revolutionary to consider in the framework of old ideas.   1945

4 Effective, reciprocal, and enforceable safeguards   on 15 November 1945
acceptable to all nations.
Declaration on Atomic Energy by President Truman, Clement
Attlee, *and W. L. Mackenzie King, Prime Minister of Canada*

5 All the President is, is a glorified public relations man   letter to his sister, 14 November
who spends his time flattering, kissing and kicking people   1947; *Off the Record* (1980)
to get them to do what they are supposed to do anyway.

6 Those who want the Government to regulate matters of   address at the National Archives,
the mind and spirit are like men who are so afraid of   Washington, DC, 15 December
being murdered that they commit suicide to avoid   1952
assassination.

7 Once a decision was made, I did not worry about it   *Memoirs* (1955) vol. 2
afterward.

8 Most of the problems a President has to face have their   *Memoirs* (1955) vol. 2
roots in the past.

9 To me, party platforms are contracts with the people.   *Memoirs* (1955) vol. 2

10 A President needs political understanding to *run* the   *Memoirs* (1955) vol. 2
government, but he may be *elected* without it.

11 If there is one basic element in our Constitution, it is   *Memoirs* (1955) vol. 2
civilian control of the military.

12 I never give them [the public] hell. I just tell the truth,   in *Look* 3 April 1956
and they think it is hell.

13 A politician is a man who understands government, and   in *New York World Telegram and*
it takes a politician to run a government. A statesman is   *Sun* 12 April 1958
a politician who's been dead 10 or 15 years.

14 It's a recession when your neighbour loses his job; it's   in *Observer* 13 April 1958
a depression when you lose yours.

15 Wherever you have an efficient government you have   lecture at Columbia University, 28
a dictatorship.   April 1959

16 Always be sincere, even if you don't mean it.   Attributed

1 The buck stops here.   unattributed motto
   on Truman's desk

2 I didn't fire him [General MacArthur] because he was   Merle Miller *Plain Speaking* (1974)
   a dumb son of a bitch, although he was, but that's not
   against the law for generals. If it was, half to three-
   quarters of them would be in jail.

3 Secrecy and a free, democratic government don't mix.   Merle Miller *Plain Speaking* (1974)

Barbara W. Tuchman 1912–89

American historian and writer

4 Dead battles, like dead generals, hold the military mind   *August 1914* (1962)
   in their dead grip and Germans, no less than other
   peoples, prepare for the last war.

5 No more distressing moment can ever face a British   *August 1914* (1962)
   government than that which requires it to come to
   a hard, fast and specific decision.

6 For one August in its history Paris was French—and   *August 1914* (1962)
   silent.

A. R. J. Turgot 1727–81

French economist and statesman

7 He snatched the lightning shaft from heaven, and the   inscription
   sceptre from tyrants.
   for a bust of Benjamin **Franklin,** *inventor of the lightning
   conductor and one of those who drafted the Declaration of
   Independence*

Mark Twain 1835–1910

American writer

8 It could probably be shown by facts and figures that   *Following the Equator* (1897)
   there is no distinctly native American criminal class
   except Congress.

9 It is by the goodness of God in our country that we have   *Following the Equator* (1897)
   those three unspeakably precious things: freedom of
   speech, freedom of conscience, and the prudence never to
   practise either of them.

10 Get your facts first, and then you can distort them as   Rudyard Kipling *From Sea to Sea*
    much as you please.   (1899)

11 Suppose you were an idiot. And suppose you were   A. B. Paine *Mark Twain* (1912)
    a member of Congress. But I repeat myself.

Paul Valéry 1871–1945

French poet, critic, and man of letters

12 An attitude of permanent indignation signifies great   *Tel Quel* (1941–3)
    mental poverty. Politics compels its votaries to take that

line and you can see their minds growing more and more
impoverished every day, from one burst of righteous
anger to the next.

1 Politics is the art of preventing people from taking part in   *Tel Quel* (1941–3)
affairs which properly concern them.

William Henry Vanderbilt 1821–85

American railway magnate

2 The public be damned!   A. W. Cole letter to *New York Times*
on whether the public should be consulted about luxury trains   25 August 1918

Laurens van der Post 1906–96

South African explorer and writer

3 Human beings are perhaps never more frightening than   *The Lost World of the Kalahari*
when they are convinced beyond doubt that they are   (1958)
right.

Harry Vaughan

4 If you can't stand the heat, get out of the kitchen.   in *Time* 28 April 1952; associated
with Harry S **Truman**, but
attributed by him to Vaughan, his
'military jester'

Thorstein Veblen 1857–1929

American economist and social scientist

5 Conspicuous consumption of valuable goods is a means   *Theory of the Leisure Class* (1899)
of reputability to the gentleman of leisure.

6 From the foregoing survey of conspicuous leisure and   *Theory of the Leisure Class* (1899)
consumption, it appears that the utility of both alike for
the purposes of reputability lies in the element of waste
that is common to both. In the one case it is a waste of
time and effort, in the other it is a waste of goods.

Vegetius AD 379–95

Roman military writer

7 Let him who desires peace, prepare for war.   *Epitoma Rei Militaris*
usually quoted as 'If you want peace, prepare for war'

Pierre Vergniaud 1753–93

French revolutionary; executed with other Girondists

8 There was reason to fear that the Revolution, like   Alphonse de Lamartine *Histoire*
Saturn, might devour in turn each one of her children.   *des Girondins* (1847)

Hendrik Frensch Verwoerd 1901–66

South African statesman, Prime Minister 1958–66

1 Up till now he [the Bantu] has been subjected to a school system which drew him away from his own community and practically misled him by showing him the green pastures of the European but still did not allow him to graze there...It is abundantly clear that unplanned education creates many problems, disrupts the communal life of the Bantu and endangers the communal life of the European.

speech in South African Senate, 7 June 1954

Vespasian AD 9–79

Roman emperor from AD 69

2 *Pecunia non olet.*
Money has no smell.
replying to Titus's objection to his tax on public lavatories; holding a coin to Titus's nose and being told it didn't smell, he replied, 'Atque e lotio est [Yes, that's made from urine]'

traditional summary of Suetonius *Lives of the Caesars* 'Vespasian'

3 Woe is me, I think I am becoming a god.
when fatally ill

Suetonius *Lives of the Caesars* 'Vespasian'

Queen Victoria 1819–1901

Queen of the United Kingdom from 1837
on Victoria: see **Gladstone** 155:10

4 I will be good.
on being shown a chart of the line of succession, 11 March 1830

Theodore Martin *The Prince Consort* (1875)

5 The Queen is most anxious to enlist every one who can speak or write to join in checking this mad, wicked folly of 'Woman's Rights', with all its attendant horrors, on which her poor feeble sex is bent, forgetting every sense of womanly feeling and propriety.

letter to Theodore Martin, 29 May 1870

on **Gladstone**'s *last appointment as Prime Minister:*
6 The danger to the country, to Europe, to her vast Empire, which is involved in having all these great interests entrusted to the shaking hand of an old, wild, and incomprehensible man of 82, is very great!

letter to Lord Lansdowne, 12 August 1892

7 The future Viceroy must...not be guided by the *snobbish* and vulgar, over-bearing and offensive behaviour of our Civil and Political Agents, if we are to go on peaceably and happily in India...not trying to trample on the people and continuously reminding them and making them feel they are a conquered people.

letter to Lord **Salisbury**, 27 May 1898

8 He speaks to Me as if I was a public meeting.
of **Gladstone**

G. W. E. Russell *Collections and Recollections* (1898)

9 We are not interested in the possibilities of defeat; they do not exist.
on the Boer War during 'Black Week', December 1899

Lady Gwendolen Cecil *Life of Robert, Marquis of Salisbury* (1931)

1 We are not amused.   attributed; Caroline Holland
                                                  Notebooks of a Spinster Lady
                                                  (1919), 2 January 1900

Gore Vidal 1925–
American novelist and critic

of Ronald **Reagan**:
2 A triumph of the embalmer's art.   in *Observer* 26 April 1981

José Antonio Viera Gallo 1943–
Chilean politician

3 Socialism can only arrive by bicycle.   Ivan Illich *Energy and Equity* (1974)
                                                  epigraph

Virgil 70–19 BC
Roman poet

4 So massive was the effort to found the Roman nation.   *Aeneid*

5 Do not trust the horse, Trojans. Whatever it is, I fear the   *Aeneid*
   Greeks even when they bring gifts.

6 I see wars, horrible wars, and the Tiber foaming with   *Aeneid*; cf. **Powell** 297:1
   much blood.

Voltaire 1694–1778
French writer and philosopher

7 Governments need both shepherds and butchers.   'The Piccini Notebooks'
                                                    (*c.*1735–50)

8 God is on the side not of the heavy battalions, but of the   'The Piccini Notebooks'
   best shots.   (*c.*1735–50)

9 This agglomeration which was called and which still calls   *Essai sur l'histoire générale et sur*
   itself the Holy Roman Empire was neither holy, nor   *les moeurs et l'esprit des nations*
   Roman, nor an empire.   (1756)

10 *Dans ce pays-ci il est bon de tuer de temps en temps un*   *Candide* (1759)
    amiral pour encourager les autres.
    In this country [England] it is thought well to kill an
    admiral from time to time to encourage the others.

11 I disapprove of what you say, but I will defend to the   in *The Friends of Voltaire* (1907)
    death your right to say it.
       attributed; the words are in fact S. G. Tallentyre's summary of
       Voltaire's attitude towards Helvétius following the burning of
       the latter's De l'esprit *in 1759*

    what Voltaire apparently said on the burning of De l'esprit:
12 What a fuss about an omelette!   James Parton *Life of Voltaire* (1881)
                                                  vol. 2

13 Whatever you do, stamp out abuses, and love those who   letter to M. d'Alembert, 28
    love you.   November 1762

1 The art of government consists in taking as much money as possible from one class of citizens to give to the other.

Dictionnaire philosophique (1764) 'Money'

2 Superstition sets the whole world in flames; philosophy quenches them.

Dictionnaire philosophique (1764) 'Superstition'

3 Indeed, history is nothing more than a tableau of crimes and misfortunes.

L'Ingénu (1767)

4 If one must serve, I hold it better to serve a well-bred lion, who is naturally stronger than I am, than two hundred rats of my own breed.

letter to a friend; Alexis de Tocqueville *The Ancien Régime* (1856)

5 To succeed in chaining the crowd you just seem to wear the same fetters.

attributed

William Waldegrave 1946–

British Conservative politician

6 In exceptional circumstances it is necessary to say something that is untrue in the House of Commons.

to a House of Commons select committee, in *Guardian* 9 March 1994

George Walden 1939–

British Conservative politician and columnist

7 Our politics seem to be increasingly about the management of illusions.
    announcing that he would not seek re-election to Parliament

on 23 July 1995

Felix Walker fl. 1820

American politician

excusing a long, dull, irrelevant speech in the House of Representatives, c.1820 (Buncombe being his constituency):
8 I'm talking to Buncombe ['bunkum'].

W. Safire *New Language of Politics* (2nd ed., 1972); cf. **Carlyle** 76:7

George Wallace 1919–

American Democratic politician; Governor of Alabama

9 Segregation now, segregation tomorrow and segregation forever!

inaugural speech as Governor of Alabama, January 1963

Henry Wallace 1888–1965

American Democratic politician

10 The century on which we are entering—the century which will come out of this war—can be and must be the century of the common man.

speech, 8 May 1942

Edmund Waller 1606–87

English poet

1 Rome, though her eagle through the world had flown,   'Panegyric to My Lord Protector'
   Could never make this island all her own.   (1655)

2 Others may use the ocean as their road,   'Of a War with Spain' (1658)
   Only the English make it their abode.

3 Under the tropic is our language spoke,   'Upon the Late Storm, and of the
   And part of Flanders hath received our yoke.   Death of His Highness Ensuing the
   Same' (1659)

Horace Walpole 1717–97

English writer and connoisseur, son of Robert **Walpole**

4 Our supreme governors, the mob.   letter to Horace Mann, 7
   September 1743

5 Everybody talks of the constitution, but all sides forget   letter to Horace Mann, 18–19
   that the constitution is extremely well, and would do   January 1770
   very well, if they would but let it alone.

6 His speeches were fine, but as much laboured as his   *Memoirs of the Reign of King*
   extempore sayings.   *George II* (1846) vol. 1
   of Lord **Chesterfield**, *1751*

7 Whoever knows the interior of affairs, must be sensible to   in 1754; *Memoirs of the Reign of*
   how many more events the faults of statesmen give birth,   *King George II* (1846) vol. 1
   than are produced by their good intentions.

8 The keenness of his sabre was blunted by the difficulty   *Memoirs of the Reign of King*
   with which he drew it from the scabbard; I mean, the   *George II* (1846) vol. 2
   hesitation and ungracefulness of his delivery took off
   from the force of his arguments.
   of Henry Fox, Lord **Holland**, *1755*

9 While he felt like a victim, he acted like a hero.   *Memoirs of the Reign of King*
   of Admiral Byng, on the day of his execution, 1757   *George II* (1846) vol. 2

10 Perhaps those, who, trembling most, maintain a dignity   in 1757; *Memoirs of the Reign of*
   in their fate, are the bravest: resolution on reflection is   *King George II* (1846) vol. 2
   real courage.

11 They seem to know no medium between a mitre and   in 1758; *Memoirs of the Reign of*
   a crown of martyrdom. If the clergy are not called to the   *King George II* (1846) vol. 3
   latter, they never deviate from the pursuit of the former.
   One would think their motto was, *Canterbury or*
   Smithfield.

12 All his passions were expressed by one livid smile.   *Memoirs of the Reign of King*
   of George **Grenville**, *1763*   *George III* (1845) vol. 1

13 He lost his dominions in America, his authority over   *Memoirs of the Reign of King*
   Ireland, and all influence in Europe, by aiming at   *George III* (1845) vol. 4
   despotism in England; and exposed himself to more
   mortifications and humiliations than can happen to
   a quiet Doge of Venice.
   of **George III**, *1770*

1 It was easier to conquer it [the East] than to know what to do with it.

letter to Horace Mann, 27 March 1772

2 By the waters of Babylon we sit down and weep, when we think of thee, O America!

letter to Revd William Mason, 12 June 1775

Robert Walpole 1676–1745

English Whig statesman; first British Prime Minister, 1721–42; father of Horace **Walpole**
on Walpole: see **Peel** 288:12, **Shippen** 339:7

3 Madam, there are fifty thousand men slain this year in Europe, and not one Englishman.
    to Queen Caroline, 1734, on the war of the Polish succession, in which the English had refused to participate

John Hervey *Memoirs* (written 1734–43, published 1848) vol. 1

4 We must muzzle this terrible young cornet of horse.
    of the elder William **Pitt**, *who had held a cornetcy before his election to Parliament, but whose speech in support of the congratulatory address on the Prince of Wales's marriage in 1736 was regarded as so offensive through its covert satire that he was shortly afterwards dismissed from the army*

in *Dictionary of National Biography*

5 They now *ring* the bells, but they will soon *wring* their hands.
    on the declaration of war with Spain, 1739

W. Coxe *Memoirs of Sir Robert Walpole* (1798) vol. 1

6 All those men have their price.
    of fellow parliamentarians

W. Coxe *Memoirs of Sir Robert Walpole* (1798) vol. 1

7 [Gratitude of place-expectants] is a lively sense of future favours.

W. Hazlitt *Lectures on the English Comic Writers* (1819) 'On Wit and Humour'

the normally imperturbable Walpole, having lost his temper at a Council, broke up the meeting:
8 No man is fit for business with a ruffled temper.

Edmund Fitzmaurice *Life of Shelburne* (1875)

9 There is enough pasture for all the sheep.
    on his ability to spread round patronage satisfactorily

attributed

on seeing Henry Fox (Lord **Holland**) *reading in the library at Houghton:*
10 You can read. It is a great happiness. I totally neglected it while I was in business, which has been the whole of my life, and to such a degree that I cannot now read a page—a warning to all Ministers.

Edmund Fitzmaurice *Life of Shelburne* (1875) vol. 1

Charles Dudley Warner 1829–1900

US author and editor

11 Politics makes strange bedfellows.

My Summer in a Garden (1871)

Earl Warren 1891–1974

American Chief Justice

1 In civilized life, law floats in a sea of ethics.

in *New York Times* 12 November 1962

Booker T. Washington 1856–1915

American educationist and emancipated slave

2 In all things that are purely social we can be as separate as the fingers, yet one as the hand in all things essential to mutual progress.

speech at the Cotton States and International Exposition, Atlanta, 18 September 1895

3 No race can prosper till it learns that there is as much dignity in tilling a field as in writing a poem.

Up from Slavery (1901)

4 You can't hold a man down without staying down with him.

attributed

George Washington 1732–99

American soldier and statesman, 1st President of the US 1789–97
on Washington: see **Byron** 71:2, **Franklin** 142:3, 142:5, **Lee** 220:2

5 I can't tell a lie, Pa; you know I can't tell a lie. I did cut it with my hatchet.

M. L. Weems *Life of George Washington* (10th ed., 1810)

6 The time is now near at hand which must probably determine whether Americans are to be freemen or slaves; whether they are to have any property they can call their own...The fate of unborn millions will now depend, under God, on the courage and conduct of this army. Our cruel and unrelenting enemy leaves us only the choice of brave resistance, or the most abject submission. We have, therefore, to resolve to conquer or die.

general orders, 2 July 1776

7 Few men have virtue to withstand the highest bidder.

letter 17 August 1779

8 Without a decisive naval force we can do nothing definitive. And with it, everything honorable and glorious.

to Lafayette, 15 November 1781

9 There can be no greater error than to expect or calculate upon real favours from nation to nation.

President's Address...retiring from Public Life (17 September 1796)

10 'Tis our true policy to steer clear of permanent alliances, with any portion of the foreign world.

President's Address... (17 September 1796)

11 Let me...warn you in the most solemn manner against the baneful effects of the spirit of party.

President's Address... (17 September 1796)

12 The nation which indulges toward another an habitual hatred or an habitual fondness is in some degree a slave. It is a slave to its animosity or to its affection, either of

President's Address... (17 September 1796)

which is sufficient to lead it astray from its duty and its interest.

1 Liberty, when it begins to take root, is a plant of rapid growth.

attributed

2 It is well, I die hard, but I am not afraid to go.
   last words

on 14 December 1799

William Watson *c.*1559–1603

English Roman Catholic conspirator

3 *Fiat justitia et ruant coeli.*
   Let justice be done even though the heavens fall.

A Decacordon of Ten Quodlibeticall Questions Concerning Religion and State (1602), being the first citation in an English work of a famous maxim; cf. **Adams** 4:6

Evelyn Waugh 1903–66

English novelist

4 *The Beast* stands for strong mutually antagonistic governments everywhere…Self-sufficiency at home, self-assertion abroad.

Scoop (1938)

5 Remember that the Patriots are in the right and are going to win…But they must win quickly. The British public has no interest in a war that drags on indecisively. A few sharp victories, some conspicuous acts of personal bravery on the Patriot side and a colourful entry into the capital. That is *The Beast* Policy for the war.

Scoop (1938)

6 Other nations use 'force'; we Britons alone use 'Might'.

Scoop (1938)

7 'In a democracy,' said Mr Pinfold, with more weight than originality, 'Men do not seek authority so that they may impose a policy. They seek a policy so that they may achieve authority.'

The Ordeal of Gilbert Pinfold (1957)

8 Is there any place that is free from evil? It is too simple to say that only the Nazis wanted war…Even good men thought that their private honour would be satisfied by war. They could assert their manhood by killing and being killed. They would accept hardship in recompense for having been selfish and lazy. Danger justified privilege.

Unconditional Surrender (1961)

9 Randolph Churchill went into hospital…to have a lung removed. It was announced that the trouble was not 'malignant'…it was a typical triumph of modern science to find the only part of Randolph that was not malignant and remove it.

Michael Davie (ed.) *Diaries of Evelyn Waugh* (1976) 'Irregular Notes 1960–65', March 1964

10 George VI's reign will go down in history as the most disastrous my country has known since Matilda and Stephen.

Andrew Roberts *Eminent Churchillians* (1994)

1 The trouble with the Conservative Party is that it has not   attributed
   turned the clock back a single second.

Beatrice Webb 1858–1943

English socialist, wife of Sidney **Webb**

2 Restless, almost intolerably so, without capacity for   Martin Gilbert *In Search of*
   sustained and unexcited labour, egotistical, bumptious,   *Churchill* (1994)
   shallow-minded and reactionary, but with a certain
   personal magnetism, great pluck and some originality,
   not of intellect but of character.
   in 1903, of Winston **Churchill**

3 I never visualised labour as separate men and women of   *My Apprenticeship* (1926)
   different sorts and kinds…labour was an abstraction,
   which seemed to denote an arithmetically calculable
   mass of human beings, each individual a repetition of the
   other.

Sidney Webb 1859–1947

English socialist, husband of Beatrice **Webb**

4 Once we face the necessity of putting our principles first   presidential address to the annual
   into Bills, to be fought through committee clause by   conference of the Labour Party, 26
   clause; and then into the appropriate machinery for   June 1923
   carrying them into execution from one end of the
   kingdom to the other…the inevitability of gradualness
   cannot fail to be appreciated.

5 Nobody told us we could do this.   Nigel Rees *Brewer's Quotations*
   when the new National Government came off the Gold Standard   (1994)
   in 1931, the outgoing Labour Government not having resorted to
   this tactic

6 Marriage is the waste-paper basket of the emotions.   Bertrand Russell *Autobiography*
                                                                       (1967) vol. 1

Max Weber 1864–1920

German economist

7 The Protestant ethic and the spirit of capitalism.   *Archiv für Sozialwissenschaft*
                                                                       Sozialpolitik vol. 20 (1904–5)
                                                                       (title of article)

8 The State is a relation of men dominating men, a relation   'Politik als Beruf' (1919)
   supported by means of legitimate (i.e. considered to be
   legitimate) violence.

9 The authority of the 'eternal yesterday'.   'Politik als Beruf' (1919)

10 The experience of the irrationality of the world has been   'Politik als Beruf' (1919)
   the driving force of all religious revolution.

11 The concept of the 'official secret' is its [bureaucracy's]   'Politik als Beruf' (1919)
   specific invention.

1 In Baxter's view the care for external goods should only lie on the shoulders of the saint like 'a light cloak, which can be thrown aside at any moment.' But fate decreed that the cloak should become an iron cage.

Gesammelte Aufsätze zur Religionssoziologie (1920) vol. 1

Daniel Webster 1782–1852

American politician
on Webster: see **Smith** 344:8

2 The people's government, made for the people, made by the people, and answerable to the people.

second speech in the Senate on Foote's Resolution, 26 January 1830; cf. **Lincoln** 226:3

3 Liberty *and* Union, now and forever, one and inseparable!

second speech in the Senate on Foote's Resolution, 26 January 1830

4 When my eyes shall be turned to behold for the last time the sun in heaven, may I not see him shining on the broken and dishonored fragments of a once glorious Union; on States dissevered, discordant, belligerent; on a land rent with civil feuds, or drenched, it may be, in fraternal blood.

second speech in the Senate on Foote's Resolution, 26 January 1830

5 Fearful concatenation of circumstances.
    argument on the murder of Captain Joseph White

speech on 6 April 1830

6 He smote the rock of the national resources, and abundant streams of revenue gushed forth. He touched the dead corpse of the Public Credit, and it sprung upon its feet.
    of Alexander **Hamilton**

speech 10 March 1831

7 On this question of principle, while actual suffering was yet afar off, they [the Colonies] raised their flag against a power, to which, for purposes of foreign conquest and subjugation, Rome, in the height of her glory, is not to be compared; a power which has dotted over the surface of the whole globe with her possessions and military posts, whose morning drum-beat, following the sun, and keeping company with the hours, circles the earth with one continuous and unbroken strain of the martial airs of England.

speech in the Senate on the President's Protest, 7 May 1834

8 Whatever government is not a government of laws, is a despotism, let it be called what it may.

at a reception in Bangor, Maine, 25 August 1835

9 One country, one constitution, one destiny.

speech 15 March 1837

10 Thank God, I—I also—am an American!
    speech on the completion of Bunker Hill Monument, 17 June 1843

Writings and Speeches vol. 1 (1903)

11 The Law: It has honoured us, may we honour it.

speech at the Charleston Bar Dinner, 10 May 1847

12 I was born an American; I will live an American; I shall die an American.

speech in the Senate on 'The Compromise Bill', 17 July 1850

1 There is always room at the top.

   *on being advised against joining the overcrowded legal
profession*

                                                      attributed

Josiah Wedgwood 1730–95

English potter

2 Am I not a man and a brother.

   *legend on Wedgwood cameo, depicting a kneeling Negro slave
in chains*

                reproduced in facsimile in E.
Darwin *The Botanic Garden* pt. 1
(1791)

Simone Weil 1909–43

French essayist and philosopher

3 I would suggest that barbarism be considered as
a permanent and universal human characteristic which
becomes more or less pronounced according to the play
of circumstances.

      Écrits Historiques et politiques
(1960) 'Réflexions sur la barbarie'
(written *c.*1939)

4 A right is not effectual by itself, but only in relation to
the obligation to which it corresponds…An obligation
which goes unrecognized by anybody loses none of the
full force of its existence. A right which goes
unrecognized by anybody is not worth very much.

      L'Enracinement (1949) 'Les
Besoins de l'âme'

5 What a country calls its vital economic interests are not
the things which enable its citizens to live, but the things
which enable it to make war.

      W. H. Auden *A Certain World* (1971)

Stanley Weiser and Oliver Stone 1946–

6 Greed—for lack of a better word—is good. Greed is right.
Greed works.

      Wall Street (1987 film); cf.
Boesky 50:4

Orson Welles 1915–85

American actor and film director

7 In Italy for thirty years under the Borgias they had
warfare, terror, murder, bloodshed—they produced
Michelangelo, Leonardo da Vinci and the Renaissance. In
Switzerland they had brotherly love, five hundred years
of democracy and peace and what did that produce…?
The cuckoo clock.

      The Third Man (1949 film); words
added by Welles to Graham
Greene's script

Duke of Wellington 1769–1852

British general and statesman; Prime Minister 1828–30
on Wellington: see **Tennyson** 359:9, 359:10, 360:2

8 As Lord Chesterfield said of the generals of his day, 'I
only hope that when the enemy reads the list of their
names, he trembles as I do.'

   *usually quoted as 'I don't know what effect these men will have
upon the enemy, but, by God, they frighten me'*

      letter, 29 August 1810

1 Trust nothing to the enthusiasm of the people. Give them a strong and a just, and, if possible, a good, government; but, above all, a strong one.

letter to Lord William Bentinck, 24 December 1811

2 Up Guards and at them!

letter from an officer in the Guards, 22 June 1815, in The Battle of Waterloo by a Near Observer [J. Booth] (1815); later denied by Wellington

3 Hard pounding this, gentlemen; let's see who will pound longest.
   at the Battle of Waterloo

Sir Walter Scott Paul's Letters (1816)

4 Publish and be damned.
   replying to Harriette Wilson's blackmail threat, c.1825

attributed; Elizabeth Longford Wellington: The Years of the Sword (1969)

of his first Cabinet meeting as Prime Minister:
5 An extraordinary affair. I gave them their orders and they wanted to stay and discuss them.

Peter Hennessy Whitehall (1990)

6 I used to say of him [Napoleon] that his presence on the field made the difference of forty thousand men.

Philip Henry Stanhope Notes of Conversations with the Duke of Wellington (1888) 2 November 1831

7 Ours [our army] is composed of the scum of the earth— the mere scum of the earth.

Philip Henry Stanhope Notes of Conversations with the Duke of Wellington (1888) 4 November 1831

8 I never saw so many shocking bad hats in my life.
   on seeing the first Reformed Parliament

William Fraser Words on Wellington (1889)

9 Nothing the people of this country like so much as to see their great men take part in their amusements. The aristocracy will commit a great error if they ever fail to mix freely with their neighbours.
   on foxhunting

in 1836; Philip Henry Stanhope Notes of Conversations with the Duke of Wellington (1888)

10 All the business of war, and indeed all the business of life, is to endeavour to find out what you don't know by what you do; that's what I called 'guessing what was at the other side of the hill'.

in The Croker Papers (1885) vol. 3

11 The battle of Waterloo was won on the playing fields of Eton.

oral tradition, but not found in this form of words; C. F. R. Montalembert De l'avenir politique de l'Angleterre (1856); cf. Orwell 278:6

to a gentleman who had accosted him in the street saying, 'Mr Jones, I believe?
12 If you believe that, you'll believe anything.
   George Jones RA (1786–1869), painter of military subjects, bore a striking resemblance to Wellington

Elizabeth Longford Pillar of State (1972)

13 I have no small talk and Peel has no manners.

G. W. E. Russell Collections and Recollections (1898)

1 Next to a battle lost, the greatest misery is a battle
   gained.

in *Diary of Frances, Lady Shelley
1787–1817* (ed. R. Edgcumbe);
see S. Rogers *Recollections* (1859)
for variations on the theme

2 You must build your House of Parliament upon the
   river…the populace cannot exact their demands by
   sitting down round you.

William Fraser *Words on
Wellington* (1889)

H. G. Wells 1866–1946

English novelist

3 The Social Contract is nothing more or less than a vast
   conspiracy of human beings to lie to and humbug
   themselves and one another for the general Good. Lies
   are the mortar that bind the savage individual man into
   the social masonry.

Love and Mr Lewisham (1900)

4 The war that will end war.

title of book (1914)

5 In England we have come to rely upon a comfortable
   time-lag of fifty years or a century intervening between
   the perception that something ought to be done and
   a serious attempt to do it.

*The Work, Wealth and Happiness
of Mankind* (1931)

of Lord **Beaverbrook**:

6 If Max gets to Heaven he won't last long. He will be
   chucked out for trying to pull off a merger between
   Heaven and Hell…after having secured a controlling
   interest in key subsidiary companies in both places, of
   course.

A. J. P. Taylor *Beaverbrook* (1972)

Rebecca West 1892–1983

writer, journalist, and literary critic

7 It was in dealing with the early feminist that the
   Government acquired the tact and skilfulness with which
   it is now handling Ireland.

in 1916; *The Young Rebecca* (1982)

8 Whatever happens, never forget that people would rather
   be led to *perdition* by a man, than to *victory* by
   a woman.
   in conversation in 1979, just before Margaret **Thatcher**'s first
   election victory

in *Sunday Telegraph* 17 January
1988

9 Having watched the form of our traitors for a number of
   years, I cannot think that espionage can be
   recommended as a technique for building an impressive
   civilization. It's a lout's game.

The Meaning of Treason (1982 ed.)

John Fane, Lord Westmorland 1759–1841

English nobleman

10 *Merit*, indeed!…We are come to a pretty pass if they talk
    of *merit* for a bishopric.

noted in Lady Salisbury's diary, 9
December 1835

Charles Wetherell 1770–1846

English lawyer and politician

1 Then there is my noble and biographical friend who has added a new terror to death.
  of Lord Campbell

Lord St Leonards
Misrepresentations in Campbell's Lives of Lyndhurst and Brougham (1869); also attributed to Lord Lyndhurst

Grover A. Whalen 1886–1962

2 There's a lot of law at the end of a nightstick.

Quentin Reynolds *Courtroom* (1950)

Thomas, Lord Wharton 1648–1715

English Whig politician

3 Ara! but why does King James stay behind?
  Lilli burlero bullen a la
  Ho! by my shoul 'tis a Protestant wind
  Lilli burlero bullen a la.
  a Williamite song in mockery of Richard Talbot, newly created Earl of Tyrconnell by the Catholic James II in Dublin in 1688; the refrain parodies the Irish language

'A New Song' (written 1687); Thomas Kinsella *The New Oxford Book of Irish Verse* (1986); attribution to Wharton has been disputed

4 I sang a king out of three kingdoms.
  said to have been Wharton's boast after 'A New Song' became a propaganda weapon against James II

in *Dictionary of National Biography*

Robert Whinney

Captain in the British Navy

5 As a captain in command he was consistently unfortunate, with one glorious defeat after another.
  on **Mountbatten**'s *wartime naval career*

Andrew Roberts *Eminent Churchillians* (1994)

E. B. White 1899–1985

American humorist

6 Democracy is the recurrent suspicion that more than half of the people are right more than half of the time.

in *New Yorker* 3 July 1944

7 The so-called science of poll-taking is not a science at all but a mere necromancy. People are unpredictable by nature, and although you can take a nation's pulse, you can't be sure that the nation hasn't just run up a flight of stairs.

in *New Yorker* 13 November 1948

Theodore H. White

American author and journalist

1 Johnson's instinct for power is as primordial as *The Making of the President* (1964)
a salmon's going upstream to spawn.
   of Lyndon **Johnson**

2 The flood of money that gushes into politics today is in *Time* 19 November 1984
a pollution of democracy.

William Allen White 1868–1944

American journalist and editor

3 Tinhorn politicians. in *Emporia Gazette* 25 October
1901

4 Liberty is the only thing you cannot have unless you are attributed
willing to give it to others.

William Whitelaw 1918–

British Conservative politician
on Whitelaw: see **Thatcher** 362:12

5 It is never wise to appear to be more clever than you are. attributed, 1975
It is sometimes wise to appear slightly less so.

6 The Labour Party is going around stirring up apathy. in *Observer* 1 May 1983
   recalled by Alan Watkins as a characteristic 'Willieism'

Gough Whitlam 1916–

Australian Labor politician, Prime Minister 1972–5

the Governor-General, Sir John Kerr, had dismissed the Labor
government headed by Gough Whitlam in November 1975:
7 Well may he say 'God Save the Queen'. But after this speech in Canberra, 11 November
nothing will save the Governor-General…Maintain your 1975
rage and your enthusiasm through the campaign for the
election now to be held and until polling day.

Walt Whitman 1819–92

American poet

8 The United States themselves are essentially the greatest *Leaves of Grass* (1855) preface
poem.

9 O Captain! my Captain! our fearful trip is done, 'O Captain! My Captain!' (1871)
The ship has weathered every rack, the prize we sought
   is won,
The port is near, the bells I hear, the people all exulting.
   allegorical poem on the death of Abraham **Lincoln**

10 The ship is anchored safe and sound, its voyage closed 'O Captain! My Captain!' (1871)
   and done.
From fearful trip the victor ship comes in with object
   won;

Exult O shores, and ring O bells! But I with mournful
   tread
Walk the deck my Captain lies, Fallen cold and dead.

1 This dust was once the man,   'This dust was once the man'
   Gentle, plain, just and resolute, under whose cautious   (1881)
      hand,
   Against the foulest crime in history known in any land
      or age,
   Was saved the Union of these States.

2 Where the populace rise at once against the never-ending   'Song of the Broad Axe' (1881)
      audacity of elected persons.

3 Where the city of the healthiest fathers stands,   'Song of the Broad Axe' (1881)
   Where the city of the best-bodied mothers stands,
   There the great city stands.

4 Strange, (is it not?) that battles, martyrs, blood, even   Geoffrey C. Ward *The Civil War*
   assassination, should so condense—perhaps only really,   (1991)
   lastingly condense—a Nationality.
      of the American Civil War

John Greenleaf Whittier 1807–92

American poet

5 'Shoot, if you must, this old grey head,   'Barbara Frietchie' (1863)
   But spare your country's flag,' she said.
   A shade of sadness, a blush of shame,
   Over the face of the leader came.

Robert Whittington

6 As time requireth, a man of marvellous mirth and   in *Vulgaria* (1521) pt. 2; Erasmus
   pastimes, and sometime of as sad gravity, as who say: famously applied the idea to More,
   a man for all seasons.   writing in his prefatory letter to *In*
      of Thomas **More**   *Praise of Folly* (1509) that he
                                                                  played *'omnium horarum hominem*
                                                                  [a man of all hours]'

Oscar Wilde 1854–1900

Anglo-Irish playwright and poet

7 We have really everything in common with America   *The Canterville Ghost* (1887); cf.
   nowadays except, of course, language.   **Shaw** 337:3

8 If the country doesn't go to the dogs or the Radicals, we   *An Ideal Husband* (1895)
   shall have you Prime Minister, some day.

Wilhelm II 1859–1941

German Emperor and King of Prussia, 1888–1918

9 We have...fought for our place in the sun and have won   speech in Hamburg, 18 June 1901;
   it. It will be my business to see that we retain this place   cf. **Bülow** 61:7
   in the sun unchallenged, so that the rays of that sun

may exert a fructifying influence upon our foreign trade
and traffic.

John Wilkes 1727–97

English parliamentary reformer

1 EARL OF SANDWICH: 'Pon my soul, Wilkes, I don't know
      whether you'll die upon the gallows or of the pox.
   WILKES: That depends, my Lord, whether I first embrace
      your Lordship's principles, or your Lordship's
      mistresses.

Charles Petrie The Four Georges
(1935); probably apocryphal

2 Give me a grain of truth and I will mix it up with a great
   mass of falsehood so that no chemist will ever be able to
   separate them.

Adrian Hamilton *The Infamous
Essay on Women, or John Wilkes
seated between Vice and Virtue*
(1972)

William III 1650–1702

Stadtholder of the Netherlands from 1672; King of Great Britain
and Ireland from 1688

3 'Do you not see your country is lost?' asked the Duke of
   Buckingham. 'There is one way never to see it lost'
   replied William, 'and that is to die in the last ditch.'

Bishop Gilbert Burnet *History of
My Own Time* (1838 ed.)

4 Every bullet has its billet.

John Wesley *Journal* (1827) 6 June
1765

Wendell Willkie 1892–1944

American lawyer and politician

5 Freedom is an indivisible word. If we want to enjoy it,
   and fight for it, we must be prepared to extend it to
   everyone, whether they are rich or poor, whether they
   agree with us or not, no matter what their race or the
   colour of their skin.

One World (1943)

6 The constitution does not provide for first and second
   class citizens.

An American Programme (1944)

Charles E. Wilson 1890–1961

American industrialist
see also **Anonymous** 9:2

7 For years I thought what was good for our country was
   good for General Motors and vice versa. The difference
   did not exist. Our company is too big. It goes with the
   welfare of the country.

testimony to the Senate Armed
Services Committee on his
proposed nomination to be
Secretary of Defence, 15 January
1953

Harold Wilson 1916–95

British Labour statesman, Prime Minister 1964–70 and
1974–6
on Wilson: see **Benn** 36:6, **Birch** 46:1, **Bulmer-Thomas**
61:6, **Home** 182:3, **Junor** 201:4

1 All these financiers, all the little gnomes in Zurich and
the other financial centres about whom we keep on
hearing.

in the House of Commons, 12
November 1956

2 I myself have always deprecated...in crisis after crisis,
appeals to the Dunkirk spirit as an answer to our
problems.

in the House of Commons, 26 July
1961; cf. **Wilson** 390:9

3 This party is a moral crusade or it is nothing.

speech at the Labour Party
Conference, 1 October 1962

4 If I had the choice between smoked salmon and tinned
salmon I'd have it tinned. With vinegar.

in *Observer* 11 November 1962

5 We are restating our socialism in terms of the scientific
revolution...the Britain that is going to be forged in the
white heat of this revolution will be no place for
restrictive practices or outdated methods on either side of
industry.
   *usually quoted as, 'the white heat of the technological
   revolution'*

speech at the Labour Party
Conference, 1 October 1963

6 What I think we are going to need is something like
what President Kennedy had when he came in after
years of stagnation in the United States. He had
a programme of a hundred days—a hundred days of
dynamic action.

in a party political broadcast, 15
July 1964

7 The Smethwick Conservatives can have the satisfaction of
having topped the poll, and of having sent here as their
Member one who, until a further General Election
restores him to oblivion, will serve his term here as
a Parliamentary leper.
   on the outcome of a by-election with racist overtones

in the House of Commons, 3
November 1964

8 A week is a long time in politics.
   *probably first said at a lobby briefing at the time of the 1964
   sterling crisis*

Nigel Rees *Sayings of the Century*
(1984); cf. **Chamberlain** 80:1

9 I believe that the spirit of Dunkirk will carry us
through...to success.

speech to the Labour Party
Conference, 12 December 1964; cf.
Wilson 390:2

10 [Labour is] the natural party of government.

in 1965; Anthony Sampson *The
Changing Anatomy of Britain*

11 On the expert advice available to me the cumulative
effects of the economic and financial sanctions might well
bring the rebellion to an end within a matter of weeks
rather than months.
   on Rhodesia's Unilateral Declaration of Independence

at the Lagos Conference, final
communiqué, 12 January 1966

12 From now the pound abroad is worth 14 per cent or so
less in terms of other currencies. It does not mean, of

ministerial broadcast, 19
November 1967

course, that the pound here in Britain, in your pocket or purse or in your bank, has been devalued.

1 Get your tanks off my lawn, Hughie.
   to the trade union leader Hugh Scanlon, at Chequers in June 1969

Peter Jenkins *The Battle of Downing Street* (1970)

2 I know what is going on. I am going on.
   at the Labour Party Conference, commenting on rumours of conspiracies against his leadership

attributed, 1969

3 One man's wage increase is another man's price increase.

speech at Blackburn, 8 January 1970

4 If one buys land on which there is a slag heap 120 ft. high and it costs £100,000 to remove that slag, that is not land speculation in the sense that we condemn it. It is land reclamation.

in the House of Commons, 4 April 1974

5 This party is a bit like an old stagecoach. If you drive along at a rapid rate, everyone aboard is either so exhilarated or so seasick that you don't have a lot of difficulty.
   of the Labour Party

Anthony Sampson *The Changing Anatomy of Britain* (1982)

6 Whichever party is in office, the Treasury is in power.
   while in opposition

Anthony Sampson *The Changing Anatomy of Britain* (1982)

7 The Monarchy is a labour-intensive industry.

in *Observer* 13 February 1977

*of Tony **Benn**:*
8 He immatures with age.

in 1981; Anthony Sampson *The Changing Anatomy of Britain* (1982)

9 The one thing we need to nationalize in this country is the Treasury, but no one has ever succeeded.

in 1984; Peter Hennessy *Whitehall* (1990)

Henry Wilson 1864–1922

British soldier, Churchill's principal military adviser 1919–21

10 He has many good qualities, some of which lie hidden, and he has many bad ones, all of which are in the shop window.
   *of Winston **Churchill**, in a letter to a senior military colleague*

Martin Gilbert *In Search of Churchill* (1994)

Woodrow Wilson 1856–1924

American Democratic statesman, 28th President of the US 1913–21
*on Wilson: see **Clemenceau** 98:5, **Keynes** 207:4, **Kissinger** 214:12*

11 Liberty has never come from the government. Liberty has always come from the subjects of government. The history of liberty is the history of resistance. The history of liberty is a history of the limitation of governmental power, not the increase of it.

speech to the New York Press Club, 9 September 1912

1 The United States must be neutral in fact as well as in name.
   at the outbreak of the First World War

   message to the Senate, 19 August 1914

2 It is like writing history with lightning. And my only regret is that it is all so terribly true.
   on seeing D. W. Griffith's film The Birth of a Nation

   at the White House, 18 February 1915

3 No nation is fit to sit in judgement upon any other nation.

   speech in New York, 20 April 1915

4 There is such a thing as a man being too proud to fight; there is such a thing as a nation being so right that it does not need to convince others by force that it is right.

   speech in Philadelphia, 10 May 1915

5 We have stood apart, studiously neutral.

   speech to Congress, 7 December 1915

6 [It] created in this country what had never existed before—a national consciousness. It was not the salvation of the Union; it was the rebirth of the Union.
   of the Civil War

   Memorial Day address 1915

7 America can not be an ostrich with its head in the sand.

   speech at Des Moines, 1 February 1916

8 It must be a peace without victory...Only a peace between equals can last.

   speech to US Senate, 22 January 1917

9 A little group of wilful men representing no opinion but their own, have rendered the Great Government of the United States helpless and contemptible.
   statement, 4 March 1917, after a successful filibuster against his bill to arm American merchant ships

   in *New York Times* 5 March 1917

10 Armed neutrality is ineffectual enough at best.

   speech to Congress, 2 April 1917

11 The day has come when America is privileged to spend her blood and her might for the principles that gave her birth and happiness and the peace which she has treasured.

   speech to Congress, 2 April 1917

12 The world must be made safe for democracy.

   speech to Congress, 2 April 1917

13 The right is more precious than peace.

   speech to Congress, 2 April 1917

14 Once lead this people into war and they will forget there ever was such a thing as tolerance.

   John Dos Passos *Mr Wilson's War* (1917)

15 The programme of the world's peace...is this:
   I. Open covenants of peace, openly arrived at.

   speech to Congress, 8 January 1918

16 A general association of nations must be formed...for the purpose of affording mutual guarantees of political independence and territorial integrity to great and small states alike.

   speech to Congress, 8 January 1918

17 America is the only idealistic nation in the world.

   speech at Sioux Falls, South Dakota, 8 September 1919

18 If I am to speak for ten minutes, I need a week for preparation; if fifteen minutes, three days; if half an hour, two days; if an hour, I am ready now.

   Josephus Daniels *The Wilson Era* (1946)

William Windham 1750–1810

English politician

1 Those entrusted with arms...should be persons of some substance and stake in the country.

in the House of Commons, 22 July 1807

John Winthrop 1588–1649

American settler

2 We must consider that we shall be a city upon a hill, the eyes of all people are on us; so that if we shall deal falsely with our God in this work we have undertaken, and so cause Him to withdraw His present help from us, we shall be made a story and a byword through the world.

Christian Charity, A Model Hereof (sermon, 1630)

Robert Charles Winthrop 1809–94

3 A Star for every State, and a State for every Star.

speech on Boston Common, 27 August 1862

Humbert Wolfe 1886–1940

British poet

4 You cannot hope
to bribe or twist,
thank God! the
British journalist.
But, seeing what
the man will do
unbribed, there's
no occasion to.

'Over the Fire' (1930)

James Wolfe 1727–59

British general; captor of Quebec

5 The General...repeated nearly the whole of Gray's Elegy...adding, as he concluded, that he would prefer being the author of that poem to the glory of beating the French to-morrow.

J. Playfair *Biographical Account of J. Robinson* in *Transactions of the Royal Society of Edinburgh* vol. 7 (1815)

Thomas Wolfe 1900–38

American novelist

6 'Where they got you stationed now, Luke?' said Harry Tugman peering up snoutily from a mug of coffee. 'At the p-p-p-present time in Norfolk at the Navy base,' Luke answered, 'm-m-making the world safe for hypocrisy.'

Look Homeward, Angel (1929); cf. **Wilson** 392:12

Tom Wolfe 1931–

American writer

1 A cult is a religion with no political power.

In Our Time (1980)

Thomas Wolsey c.1475–1530

English cardinal; Lord Chancellor, 1515–29

2 Father Abbot, I am come to lay my bones amongst you.

George Cavendish *Negotiations of Thomas Wolsey* (1641)

3 Had I but served God as diligently as I have served the King, he would not have given me over in my grey hairs.

George Cavendish *Negotiations of Thomas Wolsey* (1641)

Alexander Woollcott 1887–1943

American writer

4 I think your slogan 'Liberty or Death' is splendid, and whichever one you decide on will be all right with me.

attributed

William Wordsworth 1770–1850

English poet

5   In our halls is hung
Armoury of the invincible Knights of old:
We must be free or die, who speak the tongue
That Shakespeare spake; the faith and morals hold
Which Milton held. In every thing we are sprung
Of Earth's first blood, have titles manifold.

'It is not to be thought of that the Flood' (1807)

6 Once did she hold the gorgeous East in fee,
And was the safeguard of the West.

'On the Extinction of the Venetian Republic' (1807)

7 Bliss was it in that dawn to be alive,
But to be young was very heaven!

'The French Revolution, as it Appeared to Enthusiasts' (1809); also *The Prelude* (1850)

Henry Wotton 1568–1639

English poet and diplomat

8 Dazzled thus with height of place,
Whilst our hopes our wits beguile,
No man marks the narrow space
'Twixt a prison and a smile.

'Upon the sudden restraint of the Earl of Somerset' (1651)

9 An ambassador is an honest man sent to lie abroad for the good of his country.

written in the album of Christopher Fleckmore in 1604

Neville Wran 1926–

Australian politician

10 The average footslogger in the New South Wales Right… generally speaking carries a dagger in one hand and

in 1973; Michael Gordon *A Question of Leadership* (1993)

a Bible in the other and doesn't put either to really
elegant use.

John Wycliff *c.* 1330–82

English religious reformer

1 The Bible is for the government of the people, by the
people, and for the people.

general prologue to the Wycliff
translation of the Bible, 1384

Augustin, Marquis de Ximénèz

1726–1817

French poet

2 Let us attack in her own waters perfidious Albion!

'L'Ère des Français' (October 1793)

William Yancey 1814–63

American Confederate politician

of Jefferson **Davis,** *President-elect of the Confederacy, in 1861:*
3 The man and the hour have met.

Shelby Foote *The Civil War: Fort
Sumter to Perryville* (1991)

W. B. Yeats 1865–1939

Irish poet; senator of the Irish Free State 1922–8

4 Romantic Ireland's dead and gone,
It's with O'Leary in the grave.

'September, 1913' (1914)

5 I think it better that at times like these
We poets keep our mouths shut, for in truth
We have no gift to set a statesman right.

'A Reason for Keeping Silent'
(1916)

6 Turning and turning in the widening gyre
The falcon cannot hear the falconer;
Things fall apart; the centre cannot hold;
Mere anarchy is loosed upon the world,
The blood-dimmed tide is loosed, and everywhere
The ceremony of innocence is drowned;
The best lack all conviction, while the worst
Are full of passionate intensity.

'The Second Coming' (1920)

7 Too long a sacrifice
Can make a stone of the heart.
O when may it suffice?

'Easter, 1916' (1921)

8 I write it out in a verse—
MacDonagh and MacBride
And Connolly and Pearse
Now and in time to be,
Wherever green is worn,
Are changed, changed utterly:
A terrible beauty is born.

'Easter, 1916' (1921)

of the Anglo-Irish:

1 We...are no petty people. We are one of the great stocks of Europe. We are the people of Burke; we are the people of Swift, the people of Emmet, the people of Parnell. We have created most of the modern literature of this country. We have created the best of its political intelligence.

speech in the Irish Senate, 11 June 1925, in the debate on divorce

2 Out of Ireland have we come.
Great hatred, little room,
Maimed us at the start.
I carry from my mother's womb
A fanatic heart.

'Remorse for Intemperate Speech' (1933)

3 Cast your mind on other days
That we in coming days may be
Still the indomitable Irishry.

'Under Ben Bulben' (1939)

Boris Yeltsin 1931–

Russian statesman, President of the Russian Federation from 1990

4 Today is the last day of an era past.
at a Berlin ceremony to end the Soviet military presence in Germany

in *Guardian* 1 September 1994

5 Europe is in danger of plunging into a cold peace.
at the summit meeting of the Conference on Security and Co-operation in Europe, December 1994

in *Newsweek* 19 December 1994

Andrew Young 1932–

American Democratic politician and minister

6 Nothing is illegal if one hundred well-placed business men decide to do it.

Morris K. Udall *Too Funny to be President* (1988)

Michael Young 1915–

British writer

7 Today we frankly recognize that democracy can be no more than aspiration, and have rule not so much by the people as by the cleverest people; not an aristocracy of birth, not a plutocracy of wealth, but a true meritocracy of talent.

The Rise of the Meritocracy (1958)

Israel Zangwill 1864–1926

British author and philanthropist, son of a Russian refugee

8 America is God's Crucible, the great Melting-Pot where all the races of Europe are melting and re-forming!

The Melting Pot (1908)

Emiliano Zapata 1879–1919

Mexican revolutionary

1 Many of them, so as to curry favour with tyrants, for
a fistful of coins, or through bribery or corruption, are
shedding the blood of their brothers.
on the maderistas *who, in Zapata's view, had betrayed the
revolutionary cause*

Plan de Ayala 28 November 1911

Philip Ziegler 1929–

British historian

2 Remember. In Spite of Everything, He Was A Great Man.
notice kept on his desk while working on his biography of
Mountbatten *(published 1985)*

Andrew Roberts *Eminent
Churchillians* (1994)

Ronald L. Ziegler 1939–

American government spokesman

*reminded of the President's previous statements that the
White House was not involved in the Watergate affair:*
3 [Mr Nixon's latest statement] is the Operative White
House Position…and all previous statements are
inoperative.

in *Boston Globe* 18 April 1973

Grigori Zinoviev 1883–1936

Soviet politician

4 Armed warfare must be preceded by a struggle against
the inclinations to compromise which are embedded
among the majority of British workmen, against the ideas
of evolution and peaceful extermination of capitalism.
Only then will it be possible to count upon complete
success of an armed insurrection.

letter to the British Communist
Party, 15 September 1924, in *The
Times* 25 October 1924 (the
'Zinoviev Letter', said by some to
be a forgery)

Émile Zola 1840–1902

French novelist

5 *J'accuse.*
I accuse.
*title of an open letter to the President of the French Republic, in
connection with the Dreyfus affair*

in *L'Aurore* 13 January 1898

Keyword Index

adultery committed a. in my heart — CART 77:7
advance retrograde if it does not a. — GIBB 151:13
advancement a. in this man's party — HILL 178:7
  quality useful for political a. — LEVIN 222:10
advantage undertaking of Great a. — ANON 9:8
adventurer a. pure and simple — FOOT 138:6
  greatest a. of modern political — BUTL 70:2
adversary No, sir! I am his a. — GLAS 156:4
adverse a. to the rights — MAD 246:3
advertise a. food to hungry — GALB 145:4
advertisement no a. for a prosperous — HES 178:2
advertiser professional a. — POW 296:8
advertisers a. don't object to — SWAF 353:3
advice Get the a. of everybody — PARN 286:9
  given my a. to my countrymen — O'CON 276:6
advise Advisers a. — THAT 362:5
advisers A. advise — THAT 362:5
advocate with the intellect of an a. — BAG 24:5
advocates potent a. of peace — GEOR 149:6
affairs beginning in human a. — PRICE 298:3
  phrase 'foreign a.' — DISR 120:1
  tide in the a. of men — SHAK 330:14
  Whoever knows the interior of a. — WALP 377:7
affections a. must be confined — GALB 146:3
affluent a. society — GALB 145:6
afraid I am not a. to go — WASH 380:2
afresh begins the world a. — MONN 262:10
Africa something new out of A. — PLINY 294:5
  white man in A. — LESS 222:1
African A. is conditioned — KENY 206:6
  [A.] national consciousness — MACM 245:1
again to begin the world over a. — PAINE 281:8
against everything all the time — KENN 206:3
  He was a. it — COOL 103:5
  met anyone who wasn't a. war — LOW 233:5
  most people vote a. me — ADAMS 2:6
  not with me is a. me — BIBLE 44:6
age a. fatal to Revolutionists — DESM 114:4
  a. going to the workhouse — PAINE 283:1
  a. of chivalry is gone — BURKE 66:16
  complain of the a. we live in — BURKE 62:10
  every a. had consisted of crises — ATK 19:5
  He immatures with a. — WILS 391:8
  not the a. of pamphleteers — HOGB 181:1
  old a. is the most unexpected — TROT 370:13
agenda on any item of the a. — PARK 285:10
agents a. of a prince regard — SMITH 343:2
  our Civil and Political a. — VICT 374:7
ages nations, and the next a. — BACON 23:10
  Now he belongs to the a. — STAN 348:9
aggression a. abroad — CHUR 87:3
  It is naked a. — POW 297:13
aggressions Whensoever hostile a. — JEFF 192:11
aggressors defeat the US a. — MAO 250:7
agitation rather than to excite a. — PALM 284:5
agonizing a. reappraisal — DULL 126:8

agony a. is abated — MAC 236:1
  That a. is over — CHES 83:9
agree a., he was a statesman — LLOY 230:6
  a. in the dark — BACON 23:6
  appear to a. — PAINE 283:3
agreeable a. to their temper — BURKE 62:6
agreement a. between two men — CECIL 79:5
  a. with hell — GARR 148:4
  blow with an a. — TROT 370:10
ahead a. of your time — MCG 240:9
aid foreign a. — NIXON 274:15
Aids stop them catching A. — CURR 107:7
aim forgotten your a. — SANT 320:3
air out in healthy fresh a. — GALB 146:8
  to the Germans that of—the a. — RICH 305:3
Alamein Before A. we never had — CHUR 93:10
Albert to take a message to A. — DISR 122:2
alcohol A. didn't cause — BOAZ 50:1
  a. has taken out of me — CHUR 94:12
alderman little less like an a. — LAW 219:1
aldermen divides the wives of a. — SMITH 341:2
alien quick to blame the a. — AESC 6:3
aliens a. to this kingdom — GEOR 149:4
alimentary a. canal — REAG 301:5
alive if I am a. I shall be — HOLL 181:5
  in that dawn to be a. — WORD 394:7
  Not while I'm a. 'e ain't — BEVIN 43:3
all A. the way with LBJ — ANON 8:6
  fair shares for a., is Labour's call — JAY 190:5
  man for a. seasons — WHIT 388:6
  presuppose that a. men are evil — MACH 241:10
allegiance I pledge a. to the flag — BELL 34:11
  mystic reverence, the religious a. — BAG 24:9
  pledged a. to you — BALD 28:6
alliance how little the word 'a.' — MONN 262:8
  rumours of a morganatic a. — HARD 168:4
alliances entangling a. with none — JEFF 192:7
  steer clear of permanent a. — WASH 379:10
allies no a. to be polite to — GEOR 150:4
  no eternal a. — PALM 284:1
allons a., enfants de la patrie — ROUG 314:3
almighty A. has placed it there — LAB 216:1
  Even the a. took seven — CHUR 92:4
alone And bear the palm a. — SHAK 328:3
  plough my furrow a. — ROS 312:12
  right to be let a. — BRAN 55:2
  they would but let it a. — WALP 377:5
  we cannot live a. — ROOS 310:6
  When he is a. in the room — KEYN 208:8
along If you want to get a. — RAYB 301:4
altar lays upon the a. — SPR 348:1
altars threw our a. to the ground — JORD 199:5
alteration A. though it be from — HOOK 182:6
alterations a. on the map of Europe — CHUR 87:6
alternative there is no real a. — THAT 361:1
  What is the a. — TREND 367:7

alternatives exhausted all other a.   EBAN 127:5
amateurs we are a nation of a.   ROS 312:10
   we prefer rule by a.   ATTL 20:12
ambassador a. is an honest man   WOTT 394:9
   Russian a. would ever cross   CHAN 81:9
ambition alone supplies a.   TOCQ 366:2
   a. can creep   BURKE 68:5
   a., in a private man   MASS 254:1
   a.'s debt is paid   SHAK 329:5
   a. should be made of sterner   SHAK 330:2
   avarice and a. have introduced   SMITH 341:2
   did thrice refuse: was this a.   SHAK 330:3
   fling away a.   SHAK 327:7
   vaulting a.   SHAK 331:8
   young a.'s ladder   SHAK 328:10
ambitious as he was a., I slew him   SHAK 329:11
   Brutus says he was a.   SHAK 330:1
   Hath told you Caesar was a.   SHAK 329:13
   lasting satisfaction to an a. mind   GIBB 151:5
amendment fifth a. is an old friend   DOUG 123:3
   first a. has erected a wall   BLACK 48:2
   guarantee of the first a.   BLACK 48:4
America A. can not be an ostrich   WILS 392:7
   A. in which people can still   REAG 301:11
   A. is a large, friendly dog   TOYN 367:5
   A. is God's Crucible   ZANG 396:8
   A. is just ourselves   ARN 17:2
   A. is like a bar-room drunk   ALLEN 7:2
   A. is privileged to spend   WILS 392:11
   A. is the only idealistic nation   WILS 392:16
   A. our nation has been beaten   DOS 123:2
   A.'s international role   KISS 214:12
   A.'s present need is not heroics   HARD 168:6
   A., the land of unlimited   GOLD 157:1
   A. was thus clearly top nation   SELL 323:11
   A. well knows that by once enlisting
                             ADAMS 4:8
   A., with the same voice which   ADAMS 4:7
   and what is left of A.   HUGO 184:6
   ask not what A. will do for you   KENN 204:7
   born in A. with a black skin   MALC 248:7
   England and A. are two countries   SHAW 337:3
   Everybody in A. is soft   CHAP 82:1
   everything in common with A.   WILDE 388:7
   flag of the United States of A.   BELL 34:11
   God bless A.   BERL 38:6
   I'd rather see A. save her soul   THOM 363:7
   In A. any boy may become President
                             STEV 350:6
   in the living rooms of A.   MCL 243:9
   It's morning again in A.   RINEY 306:1
   loss of A. what can repay   FRE 143:6
   North A. as the only great nursery   SHIP 339:6
   politics ought to be in A.   HUMP 185:5
   settlement of A.   ADAMS 3:2
   war on poverty in A.   JOHN 195:10
   we think of thee, O A.   WALP 378:2

What a glorious morning for A.   ADAMS 5:3
what makes A. what it is   STEIN 349:2
whole A.   BURKE 64:8
You cannot conquer A.   PITT 293:2
American A. continents   MONR 263:4
   A. nation has very much   BAG 24:7
   A. Negro problem   BALD 28:8
   A. says that he loves   STEV 350:2
   A., this new man   CRÈV 104:1
   as A. as cherry pie   BROWN 58:7
   business of the A. people   COOL 103:3
   commander of the A. Armies   FRAN 142:5
   crisis in A. leadership   BALT 31:9
   free man, an A.   JOHN 195:5
   French government, A. culture   PEAR 287:7
   going to be an A. at all   LODGE 231:10
   Greeks in this A. empire   MACM 244:2
   I am A. bred   MILL 260:1
   I—I also—am an A.   WEBS 382:10
   intend to offer the A. people   KENN 203:9
   I shall die an A.   WEBS 382:12
   knocking the A. system   CAP 75:6
   native A. criminal class   TWAIN 372:8
   not about to send A. boys   JOHN 196:4
   not a Virginian, but an A.   HENRY 176:4
   policy of the A. government   JEFF 193:5
   political country is like an A. forest   BAG 27:5
   Scratch any A.   RUSK 315:3
   security around the A. President   MAIL 247:7
   surface of A. society   TOCQ 365:3
Americanism A. with its sleeves rolled
                             MCC 239:7
   hyphenated A.   ROOS 311:14
   no fifty-fifty A.   ROOS 312:2
Americans A. and nothing else   ROOS 312:2
   A. do not often explain   BRYCE 61:1
   A. rightly think their patriotism   TOCQ 365:4
   for A. it is just beyond   KISS 214:11
   in most A. some spark of idealism   BRAN 55:4
   keep the Russians out, the A. in   ISMAY 188:4
   Let A. disdain   HAM 167:5
   new generation of A.   KENN 204:2
   sensible A. would prefer   O'RO 277:7
   to the Russians and the A.   TOCQ 365:9
   wage war on 23 million A.   BOAZ 50:2
   whether A. are to be freemen   WASH 379:6
   working, tax-paying A.   GING 153:3
amicably a. if they can   QUIN 299:3
ammunition pass the a.   FORGY 139:3
   who has run out of a.   KISS 214:9
amphibious a. ill-born mob   DEFOE 111:6
Amurath Not A. an A. succeeds   SHAK 326:8
amused We are not a.   VICT 375:1
amusements take part in their a.   WELL 384:9
anarchism A. is a game at which   SHAW 336:16
   A., then, really, stands for   GOLD 157:2

anarchist trace of the a.   CROS 106:7
anarchy a. and competition   RUSK 315:7
   Mere a. is loosed   YEATS 395:6
   servitude is the cure of a.   BURKE 64:1
   under a *democracy*, call it a.   HOBB 180:8
ancestors a. have turned a savage wilderness
                                  BURKE 63:11
   for which your a. fought   MURR 268:4
   My a. were Puritans   KEIL 203:4
   never look backward to their a.   BURKE 66:10
ancestry without pride of a.   DONN 122:7
   without pride of a.   POWER 298:1
anchor firm a. in nonsense   GALB 145:9
anchored ship is a. safe and sound   WHIT 387:10
angel man an ape or an a.   DISR 119:10
angel of death a. has been abroad   BRIG 56:4
angels As make the a. weep   SHAK 332:9
   By that sin fell the a.   SHAK 327:7
   by the better a. of our nature   LINC 225:8
anger A. never without an argument   HAL 165:7
   a. of the sovereign is death   MORE 265:7
   With neither a. nor partiality   TAC 354:5
Anglo-Irishman He was an A.   BEHAN 34:9
Anglo-Saxon natural idol of the A.   BAG 26:3
angry I am right, I get a.   DE G 112:5
anguish howls of a.   HEAL 172:7
animal a. which devours its own   JEFF 191:5
   by nature a political a.   ARIS 16:5
animals All a. are equal   ORW 278:11
ankle put a chain about the a.   DOUG 124:3
Anne King found her [A. of Cleves]   HENR 176:1
annihilating a. peoples   MONT 263:10
annual a. income twenty pounds   DICK 115:3
annus a. horribilis   ELIZ 132:6
anointed balm from an a. king   SHAK 333:6
anonymity passion for a.   BROW 60:3
answer winds of the World, give a.   KIPL 212:7
   would not stay for an a.   BACON 23:5
answered hath Caesar a. it   SHAK 329:13
antagonistic mutually a.   WAUGH 380:4
antiblack a. laws   FRI 143:11
anti-Christ a. of Communism   BUCH 61:4
anticipate a. seldom occurs   DISR 116:11
anti-Semitic so stupid as the a.   LLOY 230:4
anti-Semitism a. may be a good   CHUR 89:4
antithesis looked for a.   LASKI 218:5
Antony there were an A.   SHAK 330:10
apart stood a., studiously neutral   WILS 392:5
apathy stirring up a.   WHIT 387:6
ape Is man an a. or an angel   DISR 119:10
aphrodisiac power is the great a.   KISS 214:3
apologize Never a.   FISH 137:4
apology make a defence or a.   CHAR 82:2
apoplexy peace is a very a.   SHAK 324:11
apostles true a. of equality   ARN 17:3
appeals a. to the Dunkirk spirit   WILS 390:2

appear a. to be more clever   WHIT 387:5
appears as bad as it first a.   BOYLE 54:2
appeasement A. was a sensible   TAYL 357:1
appeaser a. is one who feeds   CHUR 90:3
appeasers A. believe   BROUN 58:4
appendix without an a.   CHUR 89:3
appetite a. for oratory   GALB 146:9
   no a. for truth in Ireland   PEEL 288:1
apples How many a. short   MAJOR 248:4
appointment a. by the corrupt few   SHAW 336:7
   Every time I create an a.   LOU 232:11
apprenticeship a. for freedom   BAR 32:2
approbation a. of all their actions   HOBB 180:7
appropriation a. of one article   TORR 367:4
approves a. of something   BISM 48:1
Arbeit A. macht frei   ANON 8:7
arbiter a. of others' fate   BYRON 71:3
arbitrary never use a. government   CHAR 83:5
   supreme power must be a.   HAL 165:10
archbishop My Lord a.   BULL 61:5
archipelago Gulag a.   SOLZ 346:2
architecture happened to a.   LEVIN 222:9
arena who is actually in the a.   ROOS 311:10
Argentina Don't cry for me, A.   RICE 304:7
argument a. of conservatism   EMER 133:3
   a. of the broken window pane   PANK 285:2
   a. of tyrants   PITT 293:7
   in the use of an a.   BENN 37:5
   never without an a.   HAL 165:7
   not to stir without great a.   SHAK 326:3
   This is a rotten a.   ANON 13:11
   Whigs admit no force but a.   BROW 59:6
arguments from the force of his a.   WALP 377:8
   no a. for having a mean Court   BAG 25:11
arise Napoleons will duly a.   HUXL 186:3
aristocracies A....may preserve   TREV 368:5
aristocracy a. is rather apt   DISR 118:18
   a. means government by   CHES 85:1
   a. of birth   YOUNG 396:7
   a. of the Moneybag   CARL 75:10
   a. will commit a great error   WELL 384:9
   displeased with a.   HOBB 180:8
   in some countries is called a.   PAINE 282:6
   love of a.   GLAD 154:11
   natural a. among men   JEFF 193:4
   our a. the most democratic   MAC 238:12
   outdoor relief for the a.   BRIG 57:2
   When a nation abolishes a.   TOCQ 366:7
aristocrat a. who banks with Coutts   GILB 152:11
aristocratic a. class from the Philistines
                                  ARN 17:4
Aristotle contrary to A.   TAWN 355:11
   time in the library with A.   STR 352:4
arithmetical increases in an a. ratio   MALT 248:9
Armageddon We stand at A.   ROOS 311:12
armaments these bloated a.   DISR 119:5

armed A. neutrality   WILS 392:10
  A. warfare must be preceded by   ZIN 397:4
armes *Aux a., citoyens*   ROUG 314:3
armies commander of the American a.
                           FRAN 142:5
  greatly interested in a.   AUDEN 21:5
  standing a. of power   RADC 299:5
  stronger than all the a.   ANON 13:8
Arminian A. clergy   PITT 293:1
armistice a. for twenty years   FOCH 138:2
armour a. of a righteous cause   BRYAN 60:4
armoury a. of the invincible   WORD 394:5
arms a. control means some kind   SCHR 321:9
  a. ye forge, another bears   SHEL 338:4
  but it hath very long a.   HAL 166:2
  corners of the world in a.   SHAK 331:1
  Those entrusted with a.   WIND 393:1
  to keep and bear a.   ANON 14:11
  took up a. with more right   LUCAN 234:3
  youth of a state a. do flourish   BACON 23:7
army a. marches on its stomach   NAP 269:11
  a. would be a base rabble   BURKE 64:6
  contemptible little a.   ANON 10:1
  Grand a. never looked   MAHAN 247:6
  made against invasion by an a.   HUGO 184:5
  [our a.] is composed of the scum   WELL 384:7
  Your poor a.   CROM 105:12
arrest police are those who a. you   HARR 169:6
arse politician is an a. upon   CUMM 107:2
arsenal great a. of democracy   ROOS 309:10
art a. establishes the basic   KENN 205:8
  a. of government consists   VOLT 376:1
  a. of leadership is saying no   BLAIR 48:12
  a. o'th' court   SHAK 325:3
  great a. of government is to work   PEEL 289:4
  Here the great a. lies   MILT 260:7
  In free society a. is not a weapon   KENN 205:9
  minister that meddles with a.   MELB 255:9
  no a. which one government   SMITH 342:2
  politics is the a. of acquiring   GAND 147:2
  politics is the a. of preventing   VAL 373:1
  politics is the a. of the possible   BISM 46:6
  politics not the a. of the possible   GALB 145:12
  triumph of the embalmer's a.   VIDAL 375:2
article non-violence is the first a.   GAND 147:3
artificial a. man   HOBB 179:9
artists a. are not engineers   KENN 205:9
arts France, mother of a.   DU B 126:4
  No a.; no letters   HOBB 180:2
  Of all vulgar a. of government   PEEL 288:14
ascendancy a. of the Whig party   MAC 238:4
ascent a. to greatness   GIBB 151:5
ascertainable a. facts   PEEL 289:9
ashes Scatter my a.   GRAH 159:2
Asian A. boys ought to be doing   JOHN 196:4
ask a. not what your country   KENN 204:7
  but what I intend to a. of them   KENN 203:9

  could he see you now, a. why   AUDEN 21:6
  They will a., what is the road   BURKE 65:8
askance looking a.   GOGOL 156:8
asleep human beings are a.   RUSK 315:2
aspirant political a.   MENC 256:12
aspiration no more than a.   YOUNG 396:7
ass kiss my a.   JOHN 196:8
assassination absolutism moderated by a.
                           ANON 9:12
  A. has never changed   DISR 119:11
  A. is the extreme form   SHAW 336:15
  battles, martyrs, blood, even a.   WHIT 388:4
  commit suicide to avoid a.   TRUM 371:6
assent rash and precipitate a.   PEEL 288:4
asserted whatever is boldly a.   BURR 69:1
associate good must a.   BURKE 63:4
association general a. of nations   WILS 392:17
assurance a. of a sleepwalker   HITL 179:5
astonished a. at my own moderation   CLIVE 99:9
asylum lunatic a. run by lunatics   LLOY 230:5
  No one outside an a. wishes   ROS 312:11
  statesman was in an a.   PALM 284:7
ate Jefferson a. alone   KENN 205:1
  With A. by his side   SHAK 329:9
atheist town drunkard, a town a.   BROG 57:6
Athenians A. will kill thee   PHOC 292:5
Athens A. arose   SHEL 338:8
  what Pericles felt of A.   KEYN 207:3
  who are a citizen of A.   SOCR 345:7
Atlanta A. is gone   CHES 83:9
atom a. bomb is a paper tiger   MAO 250:5
  best defence against the a. bomb   ANON 8:11
  grasped the mystery of the a.   BRAD 54:4
  no evil in the a.   STEV 350:5
atomic black portent of a new a. age   BAR 32:4
  release of a. energy constitutes   TRUM 371:3
  way to win an a. war   BRAD 54:3
atoms concurrence of a.   PALM 284:3
atrocities No number of a.   NAM 269:1
atrophied a. Englishmen   JOHN 196:13
attainable We look at the a.   GLAD 155:3
attempt a. a measure of authority   BURKE 62:9
attention a. of the nation   BAG 25:9
attentive a. and favourable hearers   HOOK 182:5
Attlee A. reminds me of   ORW 278:8
  door was opened A. got out   CHUR 94:9
attribution a. of false motive   BALD 29:11
audace *toujours de l'a.*   DANT 109:6
audacity a. of elected persons   WHIT 388:2
audible spritely, waking, a.   SHAK 324:11
audience large a.   TROL 369:10
August For one A. in its history   TUCH 372:6
Austen have to resort to Jane A.   MACM 245:10
Australia take A. right back   KEAT 202:7
author a. who speaks about   DISR 120:3
authority attempt a measure of a.   BURKE 62:9
  A. doesn't work without   DE G 112:1

authority (*cont.*):

A. forgets a dying king	TENN 360:4
a. of a King is	STR 352:3
a. of the 'eternal yesterday'	WEBER 381:9
drest in a little brief a.	SHAK 332:9
English people is to resist a.	BAG 27:3
independence of his a.	MILL 259:10
no a. from God to do mischief	MAYH 254:7
royal a. is a great spring	MONT 264:14
so that they may achieve a.	WAUGH 380:7
terror instituted by 'lawful a.'	MACD 240:4

authors We a., Ma'am	DISR 119:15
autocracy Russian a. turned	HERZ 177:7
autocrat a.: that's my trade	CATH 78:4
autres *pour encourager les a.*	VOLT 375:10
autumn mists of the a. mornings	ORW 278:7
avalanche mighty a.	HOUS 183:8
avarice a. and ambition	SMITH 341:2
avoided a. simply by postponing	CHUR 94:16
awake other two-thirds are a.	RUSK 315:2
awareness positive signs of his a.	BLUNT 49:7
axe a.'s edge did try	MARV 251:7
Lay then the a. to the root	PAINE 282:5
let the great a. fall	SHAK 325:11
Axis sword is the a. of the world	DE G 112:2
under-belly of the A.	CHUR 91:11

babble coffee house b.	DISR 120:7
babies putting milk into b.	CHUR 92:1
baby b. beats the nurse	SHAK 332:4
Burn, b., burn	ANON 9:5
government is like a big b.	REAG 301:5
Babylon By the waters of B.	WALP 378:2
London is a modern B.	DISR 118:10
back b. to basics	MAJOR 248:3
boys in the b. rooms	BEAV 33:8
going into their own b. garden	KERR 206:7
stabbing himself in the b.	LEWIS 223:3
very good b.-seat driver	THAT 362:11
Winston is b.	ANON 15:4
backbone no more b.	ROOS 311:2
backed never so perfectly b.	HAL 165:11
backing b. a quitter	KERR 206:8
I'm b. Britain	ANON 10:10
backstairs prefers the b.	CAMP 74:4
backward look b. to their ancestors	BURKE 66:10
revolutions never go b.	SEW 324:1
Bacon think how B. shined	POPE 295:5
When their lordships asked B.	BENT 38:1
bad almost always b. men	ACTON 1:10
as b. as we'd been saying	KENN 204:9
B. laws are the worst sort	BURKE 65:4
B. money drives out good	ANON 8:8
brave b. man	CLAR 96:5
so many shocking b. hats	WELL 384:8
To defend a b. policy	SAL 318:11

told how b. things are	CHUR 91:4
trample b. laws	PHIL 291:9
When b. men combine	BURKE 63:4
bag b. and baggage	GLAD 154:12
like an old b. lady	HEAL 173:4
baggage bag and b.	GLAD 154:12
bagman Cobden is an inspired b.	CARL 76:13
bakeres *As b. and breweres*	LANG 217:7
balance b. of our population	JOS 200:3
b. of power	NIC 271:7
government is nothing but the b.	MART 251:6
management of a b. of power	KISS 214:8
redress the b. of the Old	CANN 75:4
tongue in the b.	BISM 47:13
tyrannize over his bank b.	KEYN 208:2
balances checks and b.	SCAR 321:2
balancing B. the budget	GRAMM 159:3
bald b. eagle	FRAN 142:7
fight between two b. men	BORG 52:7
Balkans silly thing in the B.	BISM 47:8
ballads permitted to make all the b.	FLET 137:8
ballot b.-boxing, Nigger-emancipating	CARL 76:11
b. is stronger than the bullet	LINC 224:7
rap at the b. box	CHILD 85:3
right of all to the b.	ANTH 15:7
vote by b. is the dyspepsia of	CARL 76:15
ballots peaceful b. only	LINC 224:7
balm Can wash the b.	SHAK 333:6
ban B. the bomb	ANON 8:9
baneful b. effects of the spirit	WASH 379:10
bang bigger b. for a buck	ANON 9:2
Not with a b. but a whimper	ELIOT 130:2
banish I b. you	SHAK 324:8
bank tyrannize over his b. balance	KEYN 208:2
banknotes to fill old bottles with b.	KEYN 208:4
bankrupts more b.	JOS 200:4
you are b.	TROT 370:12
banner Freedom's b. streaming	DRAKE 124:8
star-spangled b.	KEY 207:1
banners enlisting under other b.	ADAMS 4:8
Bantu [B.] has been subjected	VERW 374:1
banyan like the great b. tree	PATIL 287:2
bar member of the b.	BOK 50:5
barbarian He [the Briton] is a b.	SHAW 336:2
barbarians b. are to arrive today	CAV 79:2
b., Philistines, and Populace	ARN 17:2
become of us without the b.	CAV 79:3
in my own mind *the b.*	ARN 17:4
barbarism b. be considered	WEIL 383:3
methods of b. in South Africa	CAMP 74:2
bard this goat-footed b.	KEYN 207:11
barefoot I was born b.	LONG 232:4
bark don't b. yourself	ATTL 20:3
barrel out of the b. of a gun	MAO 250:4
barren I am but a b. stock	ELIZ 130:5
It seems to me a b. thing	DISR 117:9

bar-room America is like a b. drunk   ALLEN 7:2
base b., common and popular   SHAK 326:11
  man of soul so b.   TOCQ 366:3
  scorning the b. degrees   SHAK 328:10
basest swayed by the b. men   CLAY 97:6
basics back to b.   MAJOR 248:3
basis b. of popular government   ROB 306:11
bastard b. who gets the mail   KEAT 203:1
  getter of more b. children   SHAK 324:11
bathing caught the Whigs b.   DISR 117:15
bathroom revolutionary in a b.   LINK 227:9
baton marshal's b.   LOU 233:3
bats like b. amongst birds   BACON 23:2
batsmen sending your opening b.   HOWE 184:1
battalions side not of the heavy b.   VOLT 375:8
battle B., *n.* A method   BIER 44:15
  b., sir, is not to the strong   HENRY 176:7
  b. to the strong   BIBLE 43:16
  defeated in a great b.   LIVY 228:9
  die well that die in a b.   SHAK 326:13
  France has lost a b.   DE G 112:3
  glad of them in the b. of Britain   BEVIN 42:9
  lost the b. of Jena   ANON 10:3
  Next to a b. lost   WELL 385:1
  who shall have borne the b.   LINC 227:1
battles b., martyrs, blood   WHIT 388:4
  dead b., like dead generals   TUCH 372:4
  forced marches, b. and death   GAR 148:1
  mother of b.   HUSS 186:1
  opening b. of all subsequent   ORW 278:6
bauble fool's b., the mace   CROM 105:9
baubles *take away these b.*   CROM 105:9
bayonet b. is a weapon   ANON 8:10
bayonets throne of b.   INGE 187:7
beaches We shall fight on the b.   CHUR 90:7
bear b. the palm alone   SHAK 328:3
  not to embrace the Russian b.   CHAN 81:8
  so b. ourselves   CHUR 90:8
  to keep and b. arms   ANON 14:11
  We must b. all   SHAK 326:15
bear-baiting Puritan hated b.   MAC 239:2
beard King of Spain's b.   DRAKE 124:6
beareth b. up things light   BACON 22:15
beast B. stands for strong   WAUGH 380:4
  b. With many heads   SHAK 324:10
  dying b. lying across a railway   JENK 194:5
  either a b. or a god   ARIS 16:6
  splendorous *blond b.*   NIET 273:5
beat b. their swords into plowshares   BIBLE 43:18
  b. the King ninety-nine times   MANC 249:1
beating glory of b. the French   WOLFE 393:5
beaut make a mistake, it's a b.   LA G 216:3
beautiful black is b.   ANON 9:3
  This *is* a b. country   BROWN 59:4
beauty b. of the mountain rose   BEAV 34:2
  terrible b. is born   YEATS 395:8

Beaverbrook that of Lord B.   ATTL 20:1
become b. President   DARR 109:8
bed Down as upon a b.   MARV 251:7
bedfellows strange b.   WARN 378:11
beef roast b. of old England   BURKE 63:3
  Where's the b.   MOND 262:1
beer to drink small b.   SHAK 327:1
  torrent of gin and b.   GLAD 154:9
beg to b. in the streets   FRAN 141:2
begin But let us b.   KENN 204:5
  to b. the world over again   PAINE 281:8
  wars b. when you will   MACH 242:2
beginning b. of the end   TALL 355:1
  In my end is my b.   MARY 253:8
  not even the b. of the end   CHUR 91:10
  revolution is at the b.   STEV 350:4
beginnings All b. are small   JOUB 200:6
  time the b. and endings   BACON 22:7
begun I have not yet b. to fight   JONES 199:1
behind something b. the throne   PITT 292:12
being their social b.   MARX 252:7
Belgium until B. recovers   ASQ 18:3
belief attacks my b.   JOHN 198:5
believe B. nothing until it has been   COCK 100:6
  If you b. that, you'll b. anything   WELL 384:12
  professing to b.   PAINE 283:5
  willing to b. what they wish   CAES 71:8
believed b. during three days   MED 255:2
  b. to be so   TROL 370:9
believing b. their own lies   ARB 15:8
  Not b. in force   TROT 370:15
Bellamy *one of B.'s veal pies*   PITT 293:12
bells b. I hear   WHIT 387:9
  They now *ring* the b.   WALP 378:5
belong To betray, you must first b.   PHIL 291:4
below b. the dignity of history   MAC 238:11
belt see a b. without hitting   ASQ 19:2
bench hut, with only a simple b.   GARF 147:9
  on our Treasury b.   TROL 370:1
beneficent purposes are b.   BRAN 55:3
beneficial b. objects   TOCQ 367:1
benevolence b. of the butcher   SMITH 341:4
  enticed by b.   BAG 28:2
Benn B. flung himself   LEVIN 222:4
Berliner *Ich bin ein B.*   KENN 205:6
best b. administered is best   POPE 295:4
  b. is like the worst   KIPL 212:8
  b. lack all conviction   YEATS 395:6
  It was the b. of times   DICK 115:4
  Send forth the b. ye breed   KIPL 213:2
  we will do our b.   CHUR 91:5
bestow b. on every airth a limb   GRAH 159:2
bestride b. the narrow world   SHAK 328:4
betray guts to b. my country   FORS 139:4
  To b., you must first belong   PHIL 291:4
betrayal b. of Ulster   CAIR 72:1

betrayed one of them b. me | BEAV 34:7
better b. his own condition | SMITH 343:3
  b. if he had never lived | CHUR 92:13
  b. off than they are | DISR 118:4
  B. red than dead | ANON 9:1
  B. than a play | CHAR 83:2
  b. than light and safer than | HASK 170:2
  b. to be in chains | KAFKA 201:9
  from worse to b. | HOOK 182:6
  see the b. things, and approve | OVID 280:3
  times that were are b. | GRE 161:1
bettering prospect of b. | MILL 259:14
Bevan [B.] enjoys prophesying | MACM 244:11
Bevin speech from Ernest B. | FOOT 138:4
beware B. the ides of March | SHAK 328:2
bible b. in the other | WRAN 394:10
  B. is for the government of | WYCL 395:1
  Written by b. readers | BAIN 28:3
bicker safely afford to b. | BALF 31:2
bicycle only arrive by b. | VIER 375:3
bidder withstand the highest b. | WASH 379:7
big B. BROTHER IS WATCHING YOU | ORW 278:14
  b. enough to take away | FORD 138:10
  carry a b. stick | ROOS 311:4
  too b. for them | BULM 61:6
bigger b. bang for a buck | ANON 9:2
bigot mind of a b. | HOLM 182:1
bigotries b. that savage | LLOY 230:4
bike got on his b. | TEBB 359:1
bill absolutes in our b. of Rights | BLACK 48:3
  b. of indemnity | KRUG 215:6
  b. of Rights was not ordained | JORD 199:4
  called upon to pay the b. | HARD 168:4
billet Every bullet has its b. | WILL 389:4
billion b. dollar country | FOST 139:7
bind Go, b. your sons to exile | KIPL 213:2
  Obadiah b.-their-kings-in-chains | MAC 236:2
biographical noble and b. friend | WETH 386:1
biography B. should be written by | BALF 31:1
  Read no history: nothing but b. | DISR 116:7
bird b. of bad moral character | FRAN 142:7
  catch the b. of paradise | KHR 209:4
  forgets the dying b. | PAINE 282:4
birds b., wild flowers | BALD 29:3
  I see all the b. are flown | CHAR 82:3
  like bats amongst b. | BACON 23:2
  one's eye for the high b. | HAL 166:13
Birkenhead Lord B. is very clever | ASQ 19:1
birth accident of b. | CHES 84:3
  b. as a mark of distinction | BUR 69:2
bishop Another b. dead | MELB 255:8
  B. of Rome hath no jurisdiction | BOOK 51:7
  hitting the niece of a b. | ORW 277:10
  Make him a b. | CLARE 95:14
  No b., no King | JAM 189:9
  now he makes me a b. | KING 210:1

bishopric talk of merit for a b. | WEST 385:10
Bismarck B. was a political genius | TAYL 356:9
  his theory of politics was B.'s | KEYN 207:3
bitches businessmen were sons of b. | KENN 205:2
bite b. the hand that fed | BURKE 68:6
bites dead woman b. not | GRAY 160:7
black B. dog is back again | CHUR 94:8
  B. is beautiful | ANON 9:3
  b. majority rule in Rhodesia | SMITH 344:4
  b. men fought on the coast | MAC 239:4
  B. Panther Party | NEWT 271:3
  B. power | CARM 76:16
  Black's not so b. | CANN 75:2
  born in America with a b. skin | MALC 248:7
  equality between the white and b. | LINC 225:2
  man has a b. face | EDW 128:2
blacks running from b. | JACK 189:8
bladders boys that swim on b. | SHAK 327:6
blame b. the alien | AESC 6:3
bland b. lead the bland | GALB 145:8
blank political b. cheque | GOSC 158:4
blasphemies truths begin as b. | SHAW 336:20
blazing eyes b. with insincerity | ANON 13:10
bleed Caesar b. in sport | SHAK 329:6
Blenheim fighting B. | BEVAN 40:10
bless God b. the Prince of Wales | LINL 227:10
blessed b. mother of us all | JEFF 193:12
  This b. plot | SHAK 333:4
  Thou fall'st a b. martyr | SHAK 327:7
blessing be to us a national b. | HAM 167:1
blind b., despised, and dying king | SHEL 338:1
  In the country of the b. | ERAS 133:10
blinked other fellow just b. | RUSK 315:1
bliss b. was it in that dawn | WORD 394:7
block old b. itself | BURKE 65:6
blocks b. to cut | PEEL 288:12
  You b., you stones | SHAK 328:1
blond splendorous b. beast | NIET 273:5
blood And men are flesh and b. | SHAK 329:3
  b. and iron | BISM 47:4
  b. and the sweat of | JACK 189:6
  b. drawn with the lash | LINC 226:9
  b. of patriots and tyrants | JEFF 191:7
  B. sport is brought to its | INGH 187:10
  b., toil, tears and sweat | CHUR 90:5
  drains all the b. from the head | BEVAN 40:4
  enough of b. and tears | RABIN 299:4
  guiltless of his country's b. | GRAY 160:8
  If b. be the price of admiralty | KIPL 212:10
  In the b. of the socialist | CROS 106:7
  left this tincture in the b. | DEFOE 111:12
  Of earth's first b. | WORD 394:5
  privileged to spend her b. | WILS 392:11
  rivers of b. | JEFF 193:11
  shedding the b. of their brothers | ZAP 397:1
  stream of b. coming from beneath | ANON 12:1
  Tiber foaming with much b. | POW 297:1

Tiber foaming with much b.　　　　VIRG 375:6
when b. is their argument　　　　SHAK 326:13
Where b. with guilt is bought　　SHEL 338:5
blood-dimmed b. tide is loosed　　YEATS 395:6
bloodshed war without b.　　　　MAO 250:3
bloodthirsty so b.　　　　　　　TROL 369:5
bloody b. curtain　　　　　　　ELIS 130:3
no right in the b. circus　　　MAXT 254:5
blossom hundred flowers b.　　MAO 250:6
blot b. on the escutcheon　　　GRAY 160:6
blow b. with an agreement　　　TROT 370:10
blubbering b. Cabinet　　　　GLAD 155:9
Blücher Napoleon forgot B.　　CHUR 86:9
blunder crime, it is a b.　　　BOUL 53:5
blunders human b., however　　TAYL 357:4
blunt plain, b. man　　　　　　SHAK 330:8
blushing b. discontented sun　SHAK 334:1
board on b. while asleep　　　HUME 184:9
There wasn't any b.　　　　　　HERB 176:9
boast b. of its constitution　PAINE 283:12
Such is the patriot's b.　　　GOLD 157:3
boat They sank my b.　　　　　KENN 205:11
boathook diplomatic b.　　　　SAL 317:7
bodes b. some strange eruption　SHAK 325:4
bodies B. tied together　　　BURKE 64:16
three b. no sensible man　　　MACM 245:9
bodkin With a bare b.　　　　SHAK 325:8
body b. of a weak and feeble woman　ELIZ 130:9
liberation of the human b.　GOLD 157:2
no b. to be kicked　　　　　THUR 364:9
yielding of that b.　　　　　SHAK 325:5
Bognor Bugger B.　　　　　　GEOR 149:11
bogy b. man　　　　　　　　　BEVAN 40:9
boil War That Would Not B.　　TAYL 356:8
boiled bag of b. sweets　　　CRIT 104:4
no politics in b. and roast　SMITH 344:7
bold b. spirit in a loyal breast　SHAK 333:1
boldness b., and again boldness　DANT 109:6
b. is a child of ignorance　BACON 22:4
Bolshevism B. run mad　　　　SNOW 345:6
this sort of madness [B.]　　SMITH 344:1
bomb Ban the b.　　　　　　　ANON 8:9
best defence against the atom b.　ANON 8:11
b. them back into the Stone　LEMAY 220:8
bombed glad we've been b.　　ELIZ 132:8
protect him from being b.　　BALD 29:6
bomber b. will always get through　BALD 29:6
bombing b. begins in five minutes　REAG 301:13
bondman base that would be a b.　SHAK 329:12
b.'s two hundred and fifty years　LINC 226:9
bonds b. of civil society　　　LOCKE 231:8
boneless b. wonder　　　　　　CHUR 89:1
bones lay my b. amongst you　　WOLS 394:2
Not worth the healthy b.　　　BISM 47:10
bonkers stark, raving b.　　　HAIL 163:6
bonny rich man makes a b. traitor　PAINE 282:2

book improve a b.　　　　　　TOCQ 366:9
little woman who wrote the b.　LINC 227:4
when he can read the b.　　　BEVAN 40:8
bookie b. or of a clergyman　MUGG 268:2
books b. are weapons　　　　ROOS 310:2
to Cambridge b. he sent　　BROW 59:6
Wherever b. will be burned　HEINE 174:1
write it in the b. of law　JOHN 195:8
boomerangs they pick b.　　　MACL 243:7
boot b. stamping on a human face　ORW 279:8
order of the b.　　　　　　CHUR 92:7
booted b. and spurred to ride　RUMB 314:9
boots without any b.　　　　BULM 61:6
bore b. people at dinner parties　KISS 214:14
not only a b.; he bored　MUGG 268:1
bored I am b.　　　　　　　　BISM 47:5
boredom b. on a large scale　INGE 187:9
born all men naturally were b. free　MILT 261:1
because you were b. in it　SHAW 336:18
b. free and equal in dignity　ANON 8:4
for abortion has already been b.　REAG 301:9
If I had not been b. Perón　PERÓN 290:6
I was b. barefoot　　　　　LONG 232:4
Man was b. free　　　　　ROUS 314:5
not b. to sue, but to command　SHAK 333:2
That ever I was b. to set it right　SHAK 325:7
That's b. into the world alive　GILB 152:6
those who are to be b.　　BURKE 67:5
borough b.-mongering　　　　DISR 117:5
bossing end to b.　　　　　LENIN 221:10
nobody b. you about　　　ORW 278:1
Bossuet excite the horror of B.　MAC 237:10
bossy of the busy by the b.　SELD 323:4
Boston long way from East B.　KENN 205:13
Botany Bay colonies seek for at B.　FRE 143:6
both man may wear it on b. sides　SHAK 335:10
bottles fill old b. with banknotes　KEYN 208:4
new wine into old b.　　　ATTL 20:5
bottom b. of the economic pyramid　ROOS 308:4
sit only on our own b.　　MONT 263:9
bought blood with guilt is b.　SHEL 338:5
when he's b. stays bought　CAM 73:6
bounded b. on the north by　FISKE 137:5
bounds shall thy b. be set　BENS 37:6
bourgeois old b. society　　MARX 253:3
person of b. origin　　　ORW 277:9
Too old, too b.　　　　　GISC 153:6
bourgeoisie b. in the long run only　TROT 370:11
bowels in the b. of Christ　CROM 105:6
boy b. may become President　STEV 350:6
b. will ruin himself　　　GEOR 149:10
boys b. in the back rooms　　BEAV 33:8
By office b. for office boys　SAL 318:10
little wanton b. that swim　SHAK 327:6
not about to send American b.　JOHN 196:4
Your b. are not going　　ROOS 309:9

brag that vapour and fume and b.   KIPL 212:7
brain leave that b. outside   GILB 152:8
   once pronounced b.-dead   SMITH 344:3
   workers by hand or by b.   ANON 14:3
brains b. go to his head   ASQ 19:1
brave b. bad man   CLAR 96:5
   b. man inattentive to his duty   JACK 188:7
   home of the b.   KEY 207:1
bravery acts of personal b.   WAUGH 380:5
Bray vicar of B.   ANON 10:12
bread He took the b. and brake it   ELIZ 131:4
   looked to government for b.   BURKE 68:6
   reap, we should soon want b.   JEFF 193:16
break to b. his spirit   HOLL 181:4
breast dauntless b.   GRAY 160:8
breasts b. by which France is fed   SULLY 352:6
breath b. of worldly men   SHAK 333:6
breathes b. there the man   SCOTT 322:5
breed Feared by their b.   SHAK 333:4
   this happy b. of men   SHAK 333:4
breweres As bakeres and b.   LANG 217:7
bribe taking of a b. or gratuity   PENN 289:14
   to b. or twist   WOLFE 393:4
bribes How many b. he had taken   BENT 38:1
brick inherited it b.   AUG 21:8
   throw a b. without hitting   ORW 277:10
bride b. at a wedding   HEAD 172:1
bridge b. scores in his head   BUTL 70:6
   b. too far   BROW 59:7
   promise to build a b.   KHR 209:6
bridle all b. and no spurs   TAYL 358:4
brief drest in a little b. authority   SHAK 332:9
briefing b. is what I do   CALL 72:6
briefings I give confidential b.   LYNN 235:10
Brigade B. of Guards   MACM 245:9
brink We walked to the b.   DULL 126:9
brinkmanship boasting of his b.   STEV 350:10
Britain boundary of B. is revealed   TAC 354:2
   B. will still be   MAJOR 248:2
   dependence on, Great B.   PAINE 281:6
   further you got from B.   CALL 73:2
   Great B. has a series of capitals   CURZ 108:1
   I'm backing B.   ANON 10:10
   make B. a fit country for heroes   LLOY 229:9
   You speak for B.   BOOT 52:4
British allegiance to the B. crown   LEE 220:3
   American culture, and B. know-how   PEAR 287:7
   better rating in B. mythology   GRIGG 161:8
   B. are no longer important   MCC 240:1
   B. Constitution has always been   ELIZ 132:7
   [B. Constitution] presumes more   GLAD 154:13
   B. electors will not vote for   BEAV 34:6
   B. Empire   ROS 312:11
   B. government forms the best   HAM 167:2
   B. have the distinction   ATTL 20:5
   B. institutions   MAND 249:3

B. nation is unique in this   CHUR 91:4
B. people came of age   TAYL 357:11
B. political system has no room   TAYL 356:7
B. Prime Minister sneezes   LEVIN 222:8
B. subject, in whatever land   PALM 284:2
   destinies of the B. Empire   DISR 119:7
If the B. public falls for this   HAIL 163:6
   liquidation of the B. Empire   CHUR 91:9
   myths of the B. Parliament   MAYB 254:6
   provinces of the B. empire   SMITH 342:3
   ridiculous as the B. public   MAC 237:8
   shadow of the B. oak   BURKE 67:3
   tugged the forelock to the B.   KEAT 202:8
Briton glory in the name of B.   GEOR 149:1
   He [the B.] is a barbarian   SHAW 336:2
   procedure is all the poor B. has   PICK 292:6
Britons B. alone use 'Might'   WAUGH 380:6
broadcasters to be left to the b.   BENN 36:2
broadcasting B. is too important   BENN 36:2
broadened b. into a brotherhood   JOHN 195:9
broke If it ain't b., don't fix it   LANCE 217:3
broken bats have been b.   HOWE 184:1
   Can it be b.   JENK 194:4
   Don't tell me peace has b. out   BREC 55:10
   laws were made to be b.   NORTH 275:4
   taken up the b. blade   DEG 112:4
   When peace has been b.   ROOS 309:6
broker honest b.   BISM 47:1
bronze noontide was b.   CHUR 89:9
brook as doth an inland b.   SHAK 332:11
broomstick who can tether a b.   KEYN 208:1
brother BIG B. IS WATCHING YOU   ORW 278:14
   not a man and a b.   WEDG 383:2
   to be the white man's b.   KING 210:2
brotherhood broadened into a b.   JOHN 195:9
   together at the table of b.   KING 210:10
brother-in-law brother, not his b.   KING 210:2
brothers learn to live together as b.   KING 211:2
   that they may agree like b.   SHAK 327:1
brought b. down by the action   MACM 245:6
brow upon the b. of labour   BRYAN 60:6
Browning safety-catch of my B.   JOHST 198:14
bruiser piratical old b.   HAIL 163:10
brute Et tu, B.   CAES 71:13
   Et tu, B.   SHAK 329:4
   finest b. votes in Europe   BAG 26:6
   should be treated as a b.   EDW 128:2
brutish nasty, b., and short   HOBB 180:2
Brutus 'B.' will start a spirit as   SHAK 328:5
   You too, B.   CAES 71:13
buccaneers fallen among b.   LLOY 230:10
buck bigger bang for a b.   ANON 9:2
   b. stops here   TRUM 372:1
bucket That b. down   SHAK 334:3
buckle b. which fastens   BAG 24:13
bud I'll nip him in the b.   ROCHE 307:4

budget balancing the b.   GRAMM 159:3
buffers terminal b.   MACL 243:3
bugger B. Bognor   GEOR 149:11
builds b. up a man only if   BENN 36:6
bull strong as a b. moose   ROOS 310:12
bullet *ballot is stronger than the b.*   LINC 224:7
  Every b. has its billet   WILL 389:4
bullets not bloody b.   LINC 224:7
bully by the bossy for the b.   SELD 323:4
bulwark floating b. of the island   BLAC 48:7
  only sure b. of continuing liberty   ROOS 309:5
Buncombe I'm talking to B.   WALK 376:8
  speaking through reporters to B.   CARL 76:7
bungler good nature is a b. in it   HAL 166:12
  of peace Man is a b.   SHAW 336:5
burden heavy b. of responsibility   EDW 128:5
  pay any price, bear any b.   KENN 204:2
  public b. of the nation's care   PRIOR 298:4
  white Man's b.   KIPL 213:2
bureaucracy b. is sure to think that   BAG 26:10
  b. of the corporation state   DOUG 123:4
  [b.'s] specific invention   WEBER 381:11
  B., the rule of no one   MCC 239:8
  immobile b.   SAMP 319:11
bureaucrats b. will care more for   BAG 26:9
  Guidelines for b.   BOREN 52:6
burglar b. of others' intellect   DISR 118:13
  honest b.   MENC 256:10
burial groaning for b.   SHAK 329:9
  part, any part, in its b.   MACM 244:11
Burke [Edmund B.] is not affected   PAINE 282:4
  with B. under a shed   JOHN 198:11
burn B., baby, burn   ANON 9:5
  b. your fingers in public life   BEAV 33:4
  to b. its children to save its   MEYER 256:8
burned also, in the end, are b.   HEINE 174:1
burnt b., tortured, fined   JEFF 191:2
  chateaux would never have been b.
                                                  TREV 368:2
bury I come to b. Caesar   SHAK 329:13
  We will b. you   KHR 209:3
bus he missed the b.   CHAM 81:4
  under Sulla was like a b.   ADC 5:7
business b. carried on as usual   CHUR 87:6
  b. of government   LAWS 219:3
  b. of nobody   MAC 237:2
  difficulties in princes' b.   BACON 22:8
  fit for b. with a ruffled temper   WALP 378:8
  hundred well-placed b. men   YOUNG 396:6
  liberty is always unfinished b.   ANON 11:14
  making everything his b.   SOLZ 345:11
  Men in b. are in as much danger   HAL 165:4
  Now it must be b. as usual   THAT 361:9
  of the American people is b.   COOL 103:3
  politics grease the wheels of b.   TAWN 356:3
  totter on in b. to the last   POPE 295:6
  Treasury is the spring of b.   BAG 24:12

We can do b. together   THAT 361:11
businessman British b. has trampled   NIC 272:6
businessmen all b. were sons of bitches
                                                  KENN 205:2
  message to the b. of this country   CURR 107:7
busy of the b. by the bossy   SELD 323:4
butcher benevolence of the b.   SMITH 341:4
  on the way to the b.   CHUR 89:6
  Prime Minister has to be a b.   BUTL 70:5
butchers sacrificers, but not b.   SHAK 328:12
  shepherds and b.   VOLT 375:7
butter b. or guns   GOER 156:6
  manage without b.   GOEB 156:5
butts With many heads b. me   SHAK 324:10
buy b. it like an honest man   NORT 275:6
  Don't b. a single vote more   KENN 203:8
buyer if a b. can be found   SALL 319:7
byword made a story and a b.   WINT 393:2

cabinet blubbering c.   GLAD 155:9
  c. consists of reporting   HOGG 181:3
  c. does not propose, it decides   ATTL 20:6
  c. government 'a shambles'   HUNT 185:7
  c. is a combining committee   BAG 24:13
  c. ministers are educated   BENN 37:4
  C. minutes are studied   KAUF 202:3
  c.'s gone to its dinner   ANON 12:12
  consequence of c. government   BAG 24:14
  group of c. Ministers   CURZ 108:3
  head of the c. is *primus inter*   MORL 266:1
  looked forward to the c. meeting   LAWS 219:6
  mislead the c.   ASQ 18:6
  of his first c. meeting   WELL 384:5
  Prime Minister and the c.   SCH 322:3
  sandhills of the Baldwin c.   ASQ 18:8
  say one of two things in c.   ANON 12:6
  ways of getting into the c.   BEVAN 41:11
Caesar appealed unto C.   BIBLE 44:12
  Aut C., aut nihil   BORG 53:1
  But yesterday the word of C.   SHAK 330:5
  C. bleed in sport   SHAK 329:6
  C. hath wept   SHAK 330:2
  C.'s wife must be above suspicion   CAES 71:9
  Came from C.'s laurel crown   BLAKE 49:3
  died—that c. might be great   CAMP 73:8
  envy of great C.   SHAK 330:16
  Et tu, Brute? Then fall, C.   SHAK 329:4
  Fox divided the kingdom with C.   JOHN 198:12
  If C. can hide the sun   SHAK 325:2
  Not that I loved C. less   SHAK 329:10
  O mighty C.! dost thou lie so low   SHAK 329:8
  render therefore unto C.   BIBLE 44:7
  Speak; C. is turned to hear   SHAK 328:2
  surface of C.'s public policy   PLUT 294:9
  what meat doth this our C. feed   SHAK 328:5

Caesars C. and Napoleons　　　HUXL 186:3
cage anybody outside the c.　　　DALT 108:9
　　cloak should become an iron c.　WEBER 382:1
cake Let them eat c.　　　　　　MAR 250:9
Calais 'C.' lying in my heart　　MARY 253:9
calamity more than a public c.　SOUT 347:3
calculate c. upon real favours　WASH 379:9
calculating desiccated c. machine　BEVAN 41:5
Caledonia mourn, hapless C.　　SMOL 345:3
calico c. millenium　　　　　　CARL 76:13
Caligula C.'s horse　　　　　　RAND 300:10
　　eyes of C.　　　　　　　　　　MITT 261:8
call c. Me God　　　　　　　　SAMP 319:9
　　c. to account those who do　　GLAD 154:4
　　Fair shares for all, is Labour's c.　JAY 190:5
　　Work is the c.　　　　　　　　MORR 266:6
calling Germany c.　　　　　　JOYCE 200:8
calls in the press that c. on me　SHAK 328:2
calm pilot of the c.　　　　　　BAG 25:3
　　to c., rather than to excite　　PALM 284:5
Calvinistic We have a C. creed　PITT 293:1
Cambridge To C. books　　　　TRAPP 367:6
　　to C. books　　　　　　　　　BROW 59:6
came I c., I saw, I conquered　CAES 71:12
　　I c. through and I shall return　MAC 235:12
campaign You c. in poetry　　　CUOMO 107:3
campaigns political c.　　　　　ROB 306:12
Campbell-Bannerman C. is a mere　BALF 30:5
can label on the c. of worms　　CRIT 104:8
Canada C. was supposed to get　PEAR 287:7
Canalettos Then the C. go　　　MACM 245:11
cancer We have a c. within　　　DEAN 110:6
　　white race *is* the c.　　　　　SONT 346:6
candidate Democratic Party's c.　KENN 204:1
candidates c. were not men　　PAINE 282:10
　　merchandize c. for high office　STEV 350:11
　　when c. appeal to 'Every'　　　ADAMS 2:4
candle c. in that great turnip　　CHUR 93:3
　　light a c. to the sun　　　　　SIDN 340:3
　　light such a c. by God's grace　LAT 218:6
　　rather light a c. than curse　　STEV 350:14
candles to carry c.　　　　　　HERV 177:6
cannibals formidable body of c.　MENC 256:14
cant c. of 'Measures not men'　CANN 74:9
Canterbury C. *or* Smithfield　WALP 377:11
Cantuar O Lord, how full of C.　BULL 61:5
canvasses good in c.　　　　　BACON 22:5
capable c. of reigning if only　TAC 354:8
capers He c. nimbly　　　　　　SHAK 334:9
capital c. must be propelled by　BAG 28:2
　　colourful entry into the c.　　WAUGH 380:5
　　interests of c. and labour　　ATK 19:6
　　not been able to destroy c.　　MAC 239:3
　　thus discover the origin of c.　TORR 367:4
capitalism C., as an institutional　BERG 38:5
　　c. of the working class　　　　SPEN 347:7
　　C., wisely managed　　　　　KEYN 207:7

　　kindly c.　　　　　　　　　　KINN 211:8
　　monopoly stage of c.　　　　LENIN 221:3
　　peaceful extermination of c.　ZIN 397:4
　　spirit of c.　　　　　　　　　WEBER 381:7
　　stage beyond c. but a substitute　ROB 307:2
　　unacceptable face of c.　　　HEATH 173:8
　　Under c. man exploits man　ANON 14:5
　　war is c. with the gloves off　STOP 351:9
capitalist forces of a c. society　NEHRU 270:11
　　worker is the slave of c. society　CONN 102:2
capitals Britain has a series of c.　CURZ 108:1
Capri letter came from C.　　　JUV 201:7
caprices depend on the c.　　　TOCQ 366:3
captain c. is in his bunk, drinking　SHAW 336:18
　　game by the team c.　　　　　HOWE 184:1
　　like a ship's c. complaining　POW 297:9
　　O c.! my Captain　　　　　　WHIT 387:9
　　Walk the deck my c. lies　　　WHIT 387:10
captains c. and the kings depart　KIPL 212:11
car afford to keep a motor c.　　SHAW 337:1
　　c. in every garage and　　　　HOOV 182:9
carcases dead c. of unburied men　SHAK 324:8
carcass c. fit for hounds　　　　SHAK 328:13
card c. up his sleeve　　　　　LAB 216:1
　　Orange c.　　　　　　　　　CHUR 86:8
　　play the race c.　　　　　　　SHAP 335:12
cards pack the c.　　　　　　　BACON 22:5
care c. fifty times more　　　　BAG 25:8
　　c. of human life and happiness　JEFF 193:1
career I now close my military c.　MAC 235:14
　　loyal to his own c.　　　　　DALT 109:2
　　points clearly to a political c.　SHAW 336:13
careless As 'twere a c. trifle　　SHAK 331:6
　　C. talk costs lives　　　　　　ANON 9:7
cares c. and pleasures of domestic　GIBB 151:7
caring prosperous or c. society　HES 178:2
carnivorous sheep are born c.　FAG 135:1
carpenter walrus and c.　　　　LEVIN 222:5
carrion With c. men　　　　　　SHAK 329:9
carry c. a big stick　　　　　　ROOS 311:4
　　We shall c. on as usual　　　THAT 361:10
Carthage C. must be destroyed　CATO 79:1
Carthaginian C. trustworthiness　SALL 319:8
cartoonist life as a c.　　　　　PET 291:1
carve Let's c. him as a dish fit　SHAK 328:13
case civil servant a good c.　　CLARK 96:7
cash In epochs when c. payment　CARL 76:2
　　pay you c. to go away　　　　KIPL 213:4
cast c. your mind on other days　YEATS 396:3
　　die is c.　　　　　　　　　　CAES 71:11
castle rich man in his c.　　　　ALEX 7:1
Castlereagh He had a mask like C.　SHEL 338:2
casualty truth is the first c.　　JOHN 197:4
cat big c. detained briefly　　　PARR 286:10
　　colour of the c. doesn't matter　DENG 113:4
　　Like a powerful graceful c.　　CHUR 88:3
　　take care of the c.　　　　　SULZ 352:8

catalogue c. of human crime — CHUR 90:6
catched more wise, and not be c. — PEPYS 290:3
categorical c. imperative — KANT 202:2
caterpillars c. of the commonwealth — SHAK 333:5
Catherine Marx and C. the Great — ATTL 20:8
Catholic C. and the Communist — ORW 278:12
  C. candidate for President — KENN 204:1
  Gentlemen, I am a C. — BELL 35:2
  I cannot be a good C. — NORF 275:2
  Roman C. Church — MACM 245:9
Catholics Hitler attacked the C. — NIEM 273:1
Cato losing one pleased C. — LUCAN 234:3
  Voice of C. is the voice of Rome — JONS 199:3
cats which way I want the c. to go — THAT 361:14
cat's-paws really mere c. — COCK 100:7
cattle thousands of great c. — BURKE 67:3
cause *good old c.* — MILT 261:4
  his c. being good — MORE 265:6
  just c. reaches its flood-tide — CATT 78:7
  Our c. is just — DICK 115:9
  winning c. pleased the gods — LUCAN 234:3
causes declare the c. — JEFF 190:7
  tough on the c. of crime — BLAIR 48:11
caution Speaking with that c. — PEEL 289:2
Cavaliers C. (Wrong) — SELL 323:5
  will not do with the c. — LAMB 216:6
Cave of Adullam political C. — BRIG 56:8
cease c. of majesty — SHAK 325:13
  war will c. when men refuse — ANON 14:6
celerity aid to secrecy is c. — TAYL 358:9
cement like mixing c. — MOND 262:2
censors without c. — JEFF 191:12
censorship extreme form of c. — SHAW 336:15
centralization c. and socialism — TOCQ 366:10
  c. follows — TOCQ 366:7
centre c. cannot hold — YEATS 395:6
  My c. is giving way — FOCH 138:1
  now in the c. of politics — MOSL 267:2
  soft c. has always melted — HAIL 163:9
  stables are the real c. — SHAW 336:17
centuries All c. but this — GILB 152:10
  forty c. look down upon you — NAP 269:3
century c. of the common man — WALL 376:10
  twentieth c. have looked like — SCHL 321:7
ceremonial All c. is ridiculous — COBB 100:5
ceremony c. of innocence — YEATS 395:6
  No c. that to great ones 'longs — SHAK 332:7
  Save ceremony, save general c. — SHAK 326:16
Cervantes C. is never petulant — MAC 237:10
chain c. about the ankle — DOUG 124:3
chaining c. the crowd — VOLT 376:5
chains everywhere he is in c. — ROUS 314:5
  freedom from c. — BERL 39:3
  nothing to lose but their c. — MARX 253:4
  often better to be in c. — KAFKA 201:9
  so debased by their c. — ROUS 314:6
  Whether in c. or in laurels — PHIL 292:3

chairs carry candles and set c. — HERV 177:6
challenge times of c. — KING 210:6
chamber naked into the conference c. — BEVAN 41:3
  second c. selected by the Whips — FOOT 138:5
Chamberlain [C.] has been able — CHUR 89:11
  speech by C. — BEVAN 40:3
chambers enchanted c. of Power — LAND 217:4
chameleon Who shall paint the c. — KEYN 208:1
chance taking a c. on peace — BUSH 69:8
Chancellor C. of the Exchequer is — LOWE 233:7
  C.'s position was unassailable — THAT 362:6
  rid of a C. of the Exchequer — BIRCH 45:8
  talk with the German C. — CHAM 80:10
chances take c. for peace — DULL 126:9
change all c. in history — TAYL 356:12
  c. is constant — DISR 119:13
  commends a radical c. — FISH 137:2
  continent of revolutionary c. — BUSH 69:9
  down the ringing grooves of c. — TENN 359:7
  involves a great c. — TROL 369:11
  little more than a c. of persons — PAINE 282:11
  make c. our friend — CLIN 99:7
  necessary not to c. — FALK 135:3
  occasion for fundamental c. — BENN 36:4
  point is to c. it — MARX 252:3
  times c., and we c. with them — ANON 13:7
  torrent of c. — CHES 84:4
  why it's time for a c. — DEWEY 114:5
  wind of c. is blowing — MACM 245:1
  without the means of some c. — BURKE 66:8
changed changed, c. utterly — YEATS 395:8
  that it be not c. — BIBLE 43:20
changes c. we fear — JOHN 197:2
channel [c.] is a mere ditch — NAP 269:4
  c. through which — KENN 203:7
chaos desperation and c. — MARS 251:2
  thy dread empire, c. — POPE 295:3
chapter now to write the next c. — JOHN 195:8
character by the content of their c. — KING 210:10
  change the c. of the nation — CECIL 79:8
  fellow's c. by his way of eating — REAG 301:10
  men of the highest c. — CIC 95:8
  not of intellect but of c. — WEBB 381:2
  simplicity of c. is no hindrance — MORL 266:2
  turns on personal c. — NAP 269:7
charge trumpet for the c. — CHAM 80:3
  When in c., ponder — BOREN 52:6
charitably how can they c. dispose — SHAK 326:13
charity with c. for all — LINC 227:1
Charles C. II was always — SELL 323:7
  C. I lost his head for — CRO 107:1
  In good King C.'s golden days — ANON 10:12
cheap have things done as c. — PEPYS 290:2
  What we obtain too c. — PAINE 281:11
Cheapside in C. shall my palfrey — SHAK 327:1

cheating period of c.   BIER 44:17
check c. upon both   ADAMS 3:12
    mutual c. upon each other   BLAC 48:10
checked c. by the slightest   MONT 264:1
checks c. and balances   SCAR 321:2
cheerful c. as any man could   PEPYS 289:15
cheers Two c. for Democracy   FORS 139:5
cheese 246 varieties of c.   DE G 112:11
cheque political blank c.   GOSC 158:4
cherry American as c. pie   BROWN 58:7
chess playing their high c.-game   CARL 76:10
chessboard c. of human society   SMITH 341:3
chicken c. in every pot   HOOV 182:9
    c. in his pot every Sunday   HENR 175:5
    overnight c. shit can turn   JOHN 195:4
    some c.! Some neck   CHUR 91:7
chief c. executive of this country   ACH 1:8
    Cromwell, our c. of men   MILT 261:2
Chief Justice C. was rich, quiet   MAC 238:7
    not a C.   CLARE 95:14
child every c. born therein   RUSK 315:9
    illegitimate c. of Karl Marx   ATTL 20:8
    land that's governed by a c.   SHAK 335:1
    Right...is the c. of law   BENT 37:7
    when thy king is a c.   BIBLE 43:17
    young healthy c. well nursed   SWIFT 354:1
children burn its c. to save its pride

    MEYER 258:3
    c. could work twenty-five hours   SELL 323:9
    c. of a larger growth   CHES 83:10
    faults which 'only c.' are said   BAG 24:7
    In peace, c. inter their parents   HER 177:3
    in turn each one of her c.   VERG 373:8
    labouring c. can look out   CLEG 98:3
    no illegitimate c.   JOS 200:5
    Were all thy c. kind and natural   SHAK 326:9
    when he cried the little c. died   AUDEN 21:5
    when he died the little c. cried   MOTL 267:3
    who talks about her own c.   DISR 120:3
Chimborazo He is a C. or Everest   ASQ 18:8
chimeras wild impossible c.   SWIFT 353:8
China with your land armies in C.   MONT 265:3
Chinese C. are a great and vital   NIXON 274:7
chip c. of the old 'block'   BURKE 65:6
chips given them nothing but c.   CHUR 86:5
chivalry age of c. is gone   BURKE 66:16
    I adore his c.   GIBB 151:14
choice c. of working or starving   JOHN 197:6
    hunger allows no c.   AUDEN 21:2
    state of perpetual potential c.   BAG 26:7
    we honour is the people's c.   SHER 338:12
choose to be free to c.   BERL 39:5
    To govern is to c.   LÉVIS 223:1
choosing c. between the disastrous   GALB 145:12
    c. each stone   MARV 252:1
chosen not be c. for   BERL 39:5

Christ as though C. were coming   CART 77:5
    C. and His saints slept   ANON 12:5
    C. crucified Pontius Pilate   HOUS 183:7
Christian C. that it is better   CECIL 79:7
    I die a C.   CHAR 82:7
Christianity C. is part of the laws   HALE 164:5
    C., of course   BALF 30:9
Christians forty generations of C.   MAC 239:1
    like Gibbon on the C.   BUTL 70:7
Christmas just before a hard C.   SMITH 343:6
    vote for an early C.   CALL 73:1
chuck C. it, Smith   CHES 84:6
church c. and state forever   GRANT 160:3
    c. speaks of the legitimate right   ROM 308:2
    English c. shall be free   MAGN 247:2
    free c. in a free state   CAV 79:4
    Say to the c., it shows   RAL 300:4
    wall between c. and state   BLACK 48:2
    when c. and state hold hands   MITC 261:7
Churchill C. being a perfect   MUGG 268:2
    C. was fundamentally   MACM 245:8
    heard was that of Mr C.   ATTL 20:1
    never was a C. from John   GLAD 155:2
    Randolph C. went into hospital   WAUGH 380:9
Church of England profession of the C.

    CHAR 82:7
Cicero opinion can alienate C.   MAC 237:10
    when C. had finished speaking   STEV 350:13
cigar really good 5-cent c.   MARS 251:5
Cincinnatus C. of the West   BYRON 71:2
circle c. of our felicities   JEFF 192:3
    fatal c. is traced   TOCQ 365:6
    tightness of the magic c.   MACL 242:8
circles c. the earth   WEBS 382:7
circumstances concatenation of c.   WEBS 382:5
    play of c.   WEIL 383:3
circus no right in the c.   MAXT 254:5
    turns their proceedings into a c.   MURR 268:6
circuses bread and c.   JUV 201:8
cities government of c.   BRYCE 61:2
    streets of a hundred c.   HOOV 182:10
citizen c. as an abstract   TOCQ 366:5
    c., first in war   LEE 220:2
    c. in this world city   AUR 21:9
    c. is influenced by   RAK 300:2
    c. of no mean city   BIBLE 44:11
    first requisite of a good c.   ROOS 311:3
    greater than a private c.   TAC 354:8
    humblest c. of all the land   BRYAN 60:4
    I am a c.   STEV 349:5
    I am a Roman c.   CIC 95:10
    No cold relation is a zealous c.   BURKE 67:9
    political liberty in a c.   MONT 264:10
citizens c. of the world   ROOS 310:6
    first and second class c.   WILL 389:6
    most refined c.   SHEL 338:6
    rights of c.   HAM 167:8

coach (*cont.*):
football c. — MCC 239:5
coal island is made mainly of c. — BEVAN 40:5
miners' c. dust — BOOT 52:5
coalition rainbow c. — JACK 189:7
coalitions England does not love c. — DISR 118:17
coals c. to Newcastle — GEOR 149:9
coat republican cloth c. — NIXON 273:6
riband to stick in his c. — BROW 60:1
cobwebs laws are like c. — SWIFT 353:4
cock c. crowing on its own dunghill — ALD 6:9
Our c. won't fight — BEAV 33:6
There you are, fixed, old c. — CHUR 91:8
cocksure I wish I was as c. — MELB 255:10
stupid are c. — RUSS 316:12
coercion effect of c. — JEFF 191:2
co-exist peacefully c. — KHR 209:3
coexistence peaceful c. — FULB 144:4
coffee c. house babble — DISR 120:7
London c.-house — SWIFT 353:5
poison in your c. — ASTOR 19:3
coffin silver plate on a c. — CURR 107:5
coins fistful of c. — ZAP 397:1
cold captain lies, fallen c. — WHIT 387:10
c. and are not clothed — EIS 129:4
c. peace — YELT 396:5
c. war — BAR 32:5
c. war warrior — THAT 360:10
c. war which is getting warmer — BAR 32:6
hotbed of c. feet — EBAN 127:6
No c. relation is a zealous citizen — BURKE 67:9
offspring of c. hearts — BURKE 66:17
Our sympathy is c. — GIBB 151:11
colleague c.-free day — DALT 109:3
execution of a senior c. — CLARK 96:9
colleagues fidelity to c. — LASKI 218:4
collective C. responsibility — LYNN 235:9
sense of c. responsibility — ALD 6:9
collects one of those beautiful c. — MAC 239:1
collision avoid foreign c. — CLAY 97:2
colonies c. do not cease to be — DISR 119:6
c. seek for at Botany Bay — FRE 143:6
commerce with our c. — BURKE 64:13
existing c. or dependencies — MONR 263:6
united c. — LEE 220:3
wretched c. — DISR 119:2
colonization subjects for future c. — MONR 263:4
colony fuzzy wuzzy c. — CAIR 72:1
Colossus Like a C. — SHAK 328:4
colour c. of the cat doesn't matter — DENG 113:4
c. of their skin — KING 210:10
met by the c. line — DOUG 124:2
Our constitution is c.-blind — HARL 169:2
problem of the c. line — DU B 126:5
coloured c. man — DOUG 124:1
'white' or 'c.' signs — KENN 205:5

colourless c., odourless — PEYR 291:2
colours c. will agree in the dark — BACON 23:6
columnists political c. — ADAMS 2:4
comb two bald men over a c. — BORG 52:7
combination You may call it c. — PALM 284:3
combine bad men c. — BURKE 63:4
combining cabinet is a c. committee — BAG 24:13
come Out of Ireland have we c. — YEATS 396:2
We are c. for your good — GEOR 148:8
When you c. back again — RUB 314:8
comeback c. kid — CLIN 99:6
comfort And a' the c. we're to get — BURNS 68:13
Be of good c. Master Ridley — LAT 218:5
for the love of material c. — TOCQ 366:2
My c. hath been in my people's — ELIZ 131:2
comfortable c. and the accepted — GALB 145:8
comical I often think it's c. — GILB 152:6
coming as though Christ were c. — CART 77:5
my c. down — MORE 265:9
that c. storm — GLAD 154:1
they will be c. for us — BALD 28:9
command able to c. the rain — PEPYS 290:1
not born to sue, but to c. — SHAK 333:2
commander c. of the American — FRAN 142:5
Congress is his c. — STEV 349:4
commanding c. heights — BEVAN 41:6
commandments ten c. — BIGG 45:3
comment c. is free, but facts — SCOTT 322:4
c. is free but facts — STOP 351:10
I couldn't possibly c. — DOBBS 122:4
commerce c. with our colonies — BURKE 64:13
matters of c. — CANN 75:3
peace, c., and honest friendship — JEFF 192:7
commercial c. world — BURKE 68:8
commissions *royal* c. — FRAN 142:12
committed [Earl Haig] c. suicide — BEAV 34:4
committee cabinet is a combining c. — BAG 24:13
c. is organic — PARK 285:9
committing c. another evil — HAVEL 170:6
c. ourselves to the truth — NIXON 274:3
commodities particular c. — SMITH 342:7
commodity supply us with a c. — SMITH 342:6
common according to the c. weal — JAM 190:2
carrying on the c. cause — HAL 166:6
century of the c. man — WALL 376:10
c. interest — PAINE 282:14
c. interests of capital and labour — ATK 19:6
c. law — JEFF 192:2
c. law is at a disadvantage — SCAR 321:5
C. Law of England — HERB 177:1
c. man, I think — BEVIN 42:10
c. market is a process — MONN 262:6
c. opinion and uncommon abilities — BAG 23:14
c. sense and c. honesty — SHEL 337:6
c. sense kept breaking in — TAYL 357:14
He nothing c. did or mean — MARV 251:7
Lord prefers c.-looking people — LINC 227:5

make it too c.	SHAK 326:6
Or art thou base, c. and popular	SHAK 326:11
Who steals the c. from the goose	ANON 14:2
commoner persistent c.	BENN 36:1
commonplace some c. mind	HARDY 168:7
Common Prayer they hated C.	JORD 199:5
Commons C. as a mere vestry	DISR 120:16
C., faithful to their	MACK 242:4
C. has declined in public esteem	STJ 317:5
C. is absolute	DISR 117:2
C. is the greatest closed shop	HOSK 183:5
C. lives in a state of	BAG 26:7
C. resembles a private company	REYN 303:8
institutions than the House of C.	ASQ 18:4
libraries of the House of C.	CHAN 81:6
majority of the House of C.	SCAR 321:2
member of the House of C.	POW 297:14
proceedings in the House of C.	MURR 268:4
seat in the House of C.	DISR 120:18
untrue in the house of C.	WALD 376:6
common sense insipid c.	SAL 318:1
commonwealth caterpillars of the c.	SHAK 333:5
empire is a c. of nations	ROS 312:5
service and conduct of the c.	BURKE 63:6
that great leviathan, called a c.	HOBB 179:9
Whether a c. be monarchical	HOBB 180:4
commonwealths To raise up c.	DRYD 125:3
uniting into c.	LOCKE 231:7
communication first c.	PAINE 283:6
communion hunting and Holy C.	ATTL 20:15
They plucked c. tables down	JORD 199:5
Communism anti-Christ of C.	BUCH 61:4
C. continued to haunt Europe	TAYL 357:3
C. equals Soviet power plus	LENIN 221:8
C. is a Russian autocracy	HERZ 177:7
C. is like prohibition	ROG 307:8
in Russia, C. is a dead dog	SOLZ 346:3
[Russian C. is] the illegitimate	ATTL 20:8
spectre of C.	MARX 253:1
under C. it is just the reverse	ANON 14:5
Communist Catholic and the C.	ORW 278:12
members of the C. Party	MCC 239:6
What is a c.	ELL 133:1
Communists If the C. conquered	RUSS 316:9
phrase 'C.' to include Fascists	ANON 10:2
We C. of the old school	RUSK 316:1
communities nation of c.	BUSH 69:6
community c. uniting peoples	MONN 262:4
most perfect political c.	ARIS 16:10
not aware that any c.	MILL 259:3
part of the c. of Europe	SAL 318:6
rest of the c.	KALD 201:10
right of the c. to regulate	ROOS 311:10
unite into a c.	LOCKE 231:8
compact c. which exists	GARR 148:4
companies help British c.	HES 178:4

company c. for carrying on	ANON 9:8
private c.	REYN 303:8
compass steer by the c.	TAYL 358:7
compassion c. is not weakness	HUMP 185:6
c. of the Internal Revenue Service	SULL 352:5
competence c. and good sense	BIRCH 45:10
high c.	BROW 60:3
competent man is c.	TROL 370:9
competition anarchy and c.	RUSK 315:7
complain Never c. and never	BALD 29:11
Never c. and never explain	DISR 121:8
complainers loudest c.	BURKE 62:7
complaints c. of ill-usage	MELB 255:5
complexion c. of my pony	CHUR 90:13
compliance c. with my wishes	CHUR 93:11
comprehensive most c. of rights	BRAN 55:2
compromise *definition of a c.*	CECIL 79:5
inclinations to c.	ZIN 397:4
concatenation Fearful c.	WEBS 382:5
conceal c. a fact with words	MACH 242:1
c. your own mind	DISR 118:5
conceit self and vain c.	SHAK 333:8
concentrate I am unable to c.	GEOR 150:2
concept geographical c.	BISM 46:9
concessions c. of the weak	BURKE 64:11
knowing what c. to make	METT 258:1
conciliate c. with dignity	GREN 161:4
conciliation policy of c.	PARN 286:6
conciseness sacrificed to c.	JOHN 197:5
conclaves Kingly c. stern and cold	SHEL 338:5
condemn c. a little more	MAJOR 248:1
condense lastingly c.	WHIT 388:4
condition as any man could do in that c.	
	PEPYS 289:15
c. upon which God	CURR 107:4
O hard c.	SHAK 326:15
primordial c. of liberty	BAK 28:5
conditions c. for its solution	MARX 252:6
condottiere roamed like a c.	HURD 185:8
conduct adapting my c.	PEEL 288:2
c. of a losing party	BURKE ,67:13
rottenness begins in his c.	JEFF 191:14
confederacy c. done to death	CHES 83:8
If the c. fails	DAVIS 110:3
conference into the c. chamber	BEVAN 41:3
confidence c. is a plant	PITT 292:10
diminishes my c. in it	JOHN 198:5
perspiration of firm c. exudes	FOOT 138:3
confidences multiplies c.	TAYL 358:9
confident begin to feel c.	ARIS 16:11
glad c. morning	BROW 60:2
confidential c. means it won't be	LYNN 235:7
confiscation We have legalized c.	DISR 119:16
conflict America is soft, and hates c.	CHAP 82:1
armed c.	EDEN 127:7
in the field of human c.	CHUR 90:10
irregular and lawless c.	MILL 259:9

conflict (cont.):

risks of spreading c.	JOHN 196:3
tragic c. of loyalties	HOWE 184:2

conflicts disputes or c. — BRI 56:2

conform either c., or be more wise — PEPYS 290:3

conforming c. to the times — MACH 241:11

confound c. their politics — ANON 9:9

confrontation c. with the politics — HAIL 163:9

confused Anyone who isn't c. — MURR 268:7

confusion c. now hath made — SHAK 331:9

confute man can tell how to c. him — SELD 323:1

Congress C. is his commander — STEV 349:4

C. makes no progress	LIGNE 224:1
C. may slip without the Union	TOCQ 365:5
criminal class except C.	TWAIN 372:8
you were a member of C.	TWAIN 372:11

conjuror superlative Hebrew c. — CARL 76:12

conquer it is possible to c. poverty — JOHN 196:1

It was easier to c. it	WALP 378:1
resolve to c. or die	WASH 379:6
wont to c. others	SHAK 333:4

conquered feel they are a c. people — VICT 374:7

I came, I saw, I c.	CAES 71:12
If the Communists c. the world	RUSS 316:9
perpetually to be c.	BURKE 64:12
to have c. and peopled	SEEL 322:6

conqueror Every other c. — BURKE 65:9

proud foot of a c. — SHAK 331:1

conquest for purposes of foreign c. — WEBS 382:7

shameful c. of itself — SHAK 333:4

conquests Are all thy c., glories — SHAK 329:8

conscience c. is a still small voice — ATTL 20:7

c. of a statesman	TAYL 358:3
dominion of reason and c.	PRICE 298:3
England was the 'courage of c.'	CHO 85:6
freedom of speech, freedom of c.	TWAIN 372:9
have a c., when it has no soul	THUR 364:9
human happiness or a quiet c.	BERL 39:1
keep your c. well under control	LLOY 229:12
meddle not with any man's c.	CROM 105:5
power without c.	BRAD 54:5
public life, a species of c.	TAYL 358:4
Sufficient c. to bother him	LLOY 231:2
taking your c. round	BEVIN 42:7
will not cut my c.	HELL 174:3

consciences binding on the c. — JOHN 195:1

conscientious c. stupidity — KING 210:5

consciousness determines their c. — MARX 252:2

consecrated c. by the experience — GIBB 152:2

c. obstruction — BAG 25:10

consensus c. behind my convictions — THAT 361:12

c. breaking up — CROS 106:11

consent c. of the governed — PAGE 280:7

feel inferior without your c.	ROOS 308:3
voice of Rome is the c. of heaven	JONS 199:3
without his c.	CAMD 73:5

consequence c. of cabinet government — BAG 24:14

consequences damn the c. — MILN 260:3

I renounce war for its c.	FOSD 139:6
political c.	GALB 146:12
We must not regard political c.	MANS 249:6

conservation means of its c. — BURKE 66:8

conservatism c. and progress — TROL 369:7

C.—an unhappy cross-breed	DISR 117:9
C. discards Prescription	DISR 117:6
c. is based upon the idea	CHES 84:4
harder shores of modern C.	HENN 175:1
meanness in the argument of c.	EMER 133:3
party of C. and that of Innovation	EMER 133:2
What is c.	LINC 225:3

conservative belief that it is really c. — FISH 137:2

C. Government	DISR 117:17
C. is a man	ROOS 309:7
c., n. A statesman	BIER 44:16
c. on the day after the revolution	AREN 15:10
C. Party always in time forgives	MACL 243:1
C. Party at prayer	ROYD 314:7
C. party must rule	BAG 27:7
C. party takes office	BISM 47:7
fear it would make me c.	FROST 144:3
I must be a C.	RUSK 315:12
most c. man in this world	BEVIN 42:6
Or else a little C.	GILB 152:6
password of C. government	POW 297:6
sound C. government	DISR 117:7
trouble with the C. Party	WAUGH 381:1
We [the C. Party] found it hard	JOS 199:7
which makes a man more c.	KEYN 207:9
word 'c.' is used by the BBC	TEBB 359:3

conservatives C. being by the law — MILL 259:7

C. do not believe	HAIL 163:9
C. were to set the people free	HEATH 173:7
liberals and c. clashed	MOYN 267:5
more formalistic than c.	CALV 73:4
trouble with c.	CARV 78:1

consideration Under active c. — LYNN 235:2

consistency no c., except — BYRON 71:1

conspicuous c. by its presence — RUSS 317:3

c. consumption — VEBL 373:5

conspiracy c. against the public — SMITH 341:5

imagines a perpetual c.	SAL 318:3
kind of c. against the rest	HAL 166:4
O c.	SHAK 328:11
society is in an organized c.	DOUG 124:4

conspirators All the c. save only — SHAK 330:16

constant c. as the northern star — SHAK 329:3

His inconstancy is his great c. — DUPIN 127:2

constellation bright c. — JEFF 192:8

constituencies go back to your c. — STEEL 348:10

constituents mob of their c. — BURKE 66:3

constitution act against the C. — OTIS 280:1

boast of its c. — PAINE 283:12

British C.	ELIZ 132:7
[British C.] presumes	GLAD 154:13
c. does not provide	WILL 389:6
C., in all its provisions	CHASE 83:7
C. is an equally forthright piece	O'RO 277:4
c. is extremely well	WALP 377:5
C. is what happens	GRIF 161:6
C. of the United States is	DAVIS 110:2
C. of the United States was	CLAY 98:1
[C.] was framed upon	CARD 75:7
construe the C. or laws	LINC 225:6
English c.	BLAC 48:8
Every country has its own c.	ANON 9:12
invoke the genius of the C.	PITT 293:3
need for a written c.	SCAR 320:8
oath to support the c.	JACK 188:9
one basic element in our C.	TRUM 371:11
One country, one c., one destiny	WEBS 382:9
Our c. is colour-blind	HARL 169:2
Our C. works	FORD 138:12
people made the C.	MARS 251:4
principles of a free c.	GIBB 151:4
reconstruct the whole C.	TOCQ 366:9
set down in writing a C.	DANG 109:4
support its C., to obey its laws	PAGE 280:7
takeover of the British C.	SCAR 321:2
very essence of the c.	JUN 200:9
What's the C. between friends?	CAMP 74:1
When the C. was framed	BEARD 33:3
written c.	CALL 73:3
constitutional c. right	LINC 225:7
I have no eyes but c. eyes	LINC 227:2
live under it as a c. monarchy	TROL 369:3
most influential of c. statesmen	BAG 23:15
only fit material for a c. king	BAG 26:2
partners in the c. minuet	SCAR 321:1
constitutions c. of later Greece	BAG 25:7
constrained by violence c.	ELIZ 130:4
construct Having nothing to c.	TROL 369:9
construction mind's c. in the face	SHAK 331:6
consul horse was made C.	RAND 300:10
consult here to c. the interests	PEEL 288:6
consulted right to be c.	BAG 26:1
consume c. more than	HAYEK 171:10
consumer c., is the king	SAM 320:1
c. society	ILL 187:4
consumes c. without producing	ORW 278:9
consumption conspicuous c.	VEBL 373:5
c. is the sole end	SMITH 342:1
not increase its c.	KEYN 208:3
contagion War is a c.	ROOS 309:4
contemptible c. little army	ANON 10:1
ill-usage c.	MELB 255:5
those poor c. men	CROM 105:12
contending fierce c. nations	ADD 5:9
content I am c.	ADAMS 5:1
Nothing less will c. me	BURKE 64:8

contented king shall be c.	SHAK 334:2
continent c. allotted by Providence	O'SUL 279:13
c., frozen in hostility	BUSH 69:9
c. will [not] suffer England	DISR 117:1
involve this c.	PAINE 281:6
striving to grasp a c.	PARK 286:3
upon this c. a new nation	LINC 226:3
continental c. union	PAINE 281:5
continentally Learn to think c.	HAM 167:7
continents American c.	MONR 263:4
contingent play of the c.	FISH 136:8
continuation *war is the c. of politics*	CLA 96:11
continue c. for five years too long	BIFF 45:2
continuous c. tolerance	BAG 27:6
contract labour c.	CHUR 87:4
new social c.	CALL 72:7
social c.	ROUS 314:4
social c. is left-wing	DEBR 111:1
social c. is nothing more or less	WELLS 385:3
society is indeed a c.	BURKE 67:5
contracting high c. powers	BRI 56:2
contracts party platforms are c.	TRUM 371:9
preserve c.	MELB 256:6
contradict I never deny; I never c.	DISR 121:7
Never c.	FISH 137:4
contrary Every law is c. to liberty	BENT 37:10
To take usury is c. to Scripture	TAWN 355:11
contrive How nature always does c.	GILB 152:6
control c. the governed	MAD 246:7
controlling no longer c. events	HATT 170:3
controls Who c. the past	ORW 279:2
controversy man of c.	GALB 145:8
times of challenge and c.	KING 210:6
contumely proud man's c.	SHAK 325:8
conventional c. wisdom	GALB 145:7
Too c. a thinker	MONC 261:11
conversation c. perfectly delightful	SMITH 344:9
His c. turned on	BEAV 34:2
conversations after-dinner c.	THOR 364:5
taping of c.	NIXON 274:12
converted You have not c. a man	MORL 265:10
conviction best lack all c.	YEATS 395:6
c. politicians	BANC 32:1
convictions behind my c.	THAT 361:12
convince we c. ourselves	JUN 200:11
convinced c. beyond doubt	VAN 373:3
You've c. me	ROOS 310:7
cool In any case, keep c.	LIDD 223:5
Coolidge admiration for Mr C.	ANON 13:12
Mr C.'s genius for inactivity	LIPP 228:1
Nero fiddled, but C. only snored	MENC 256:13
Cooper Gary C. killing off	BALD 28:6
co-operation government and c.	RUSK 315:7
copies few originals and many c.	TOCQ 366:6
cord triple c.	BURKE 68:3
cordial c. with everyone	MAUG 254:4

Corinthian C. capital	BURKE 67:6
corn lower the price of c.	MELB 256:2
raise the price of c.	BYRON 71:5
two ears of c.	SWIFT 353:7
corner Never c. an opponent	LIDD 223:5
corners three c. of the world	SHAK 331:1
turn square c.	HOLM 181:6
cornet muzzle this terrible young c.	WALP 378:4
Cornish twenty thousand C. men	HAWK 170:7
coronation king's c.	BLUNT 49:7
corporate c. officials	FRI 143:7
corporation c. state	DOUG 123:4
expect a c.	THUR 364:9
corps effete c. of impudent snobs	AGNEW 6:6
strike at the whole c.	BURKE 66:1
Corps d'Armée Tory C.	GLAD 154:14
corpse c. at the funeral	HEAD 172:1
politician's c. was laid away	BELL 35:5
corridors c. of power	SNOW 345:4
corrupt equally wicked and c.	BURKE 63:2
good custom should c. the world	TENN 360:5
legislative power is more c.	MONT 264:12
more c. the republic	TAC 354:6
most c. government on the earth	JEFF 192:2
people generally c.	BURKE 64:18
power tends to c.	RUSK 315:4
That do c. my air,—I banish you	SHAK 324:8
Unlimited power is apt to c.	PITT 292:11
corrupted c. governments	HAL 165:12
c. the youth of the realm	SHAK 327:3
principle of democracy is c.	MONT 264:5
corruption c. at home	CHUR 87:3
c. of each government	MONT 264:4
c., the most infallible symptom	GIBB 151:9
c. wins not more than honesty	SHAK 327:5
corrupts absolute power c.	ACTON 1:9
cosmopolitan c. critics	DISR 120:8
cost c. of liberty	DU B 126:7
c. of setting him up	NAIDU 268:9
costs duke c. as much to keep up	LLOY 229:3
obedience generally c. more	MAC 238:5
cottage poorest man may in his c.	PITT 292:9
the c. is not happy	DISR 121:13
cotton C. is King	CHR 86:1
council In c. rooms apart	RICE 304:5
labour c. hiring taxis	KINN 211:11
councillor c. is like a mushroom	MAG 247:5
councillors c. of state	CARL 76:10
counsel Dost sometimes c. take	POPE 295:2
intention to keep my c.	GLAD 155:6
religion, justice, c., and treasure	BACON 22:16
take c. always of your courage	STEV 350:12
counsellor Indeed this c.	SHAK 325:10
counsels crooked c. fit	DRYD 125:4
seeking after various c.	TAYL 358:9
count I won the c.	SOM 346:5

counted the faster we c.	EMER 133:4
counting it's the c.	STOP 351:8
countries bowels of whole c.	PAINE 281:12
country Anyone who loves his c.	GAR 148:1
Britain a fit c. for heroes	LLOY 229:9
choose between betraying my c.	FORS 139:4
c. which has 246 varieties	DE G 112:11
c. will be called upon	HARD 168:4
dying for Queen and c.	THOM 364:6
ends thou aim'st at be thy c.'s	SHAK 327:7
established in one c. alone	STAL 348:4
ever exist in a free c.	BURKE 64:9
every c. but his own	GILB 152:10
Every c. has its own constitution	ANON 9:12
Every c. has the government	MAIS 248:5
fate of this c. depends	DISR 120:6
fight for its king and c.	GRAH 158:6
for the good of his c.	WOTT 394:9
friend of every c. but his own	CANN 75:1
friends of every c.	DISR 120:8
His first, best c.	GOLD 157:3
how I leave my c.	PITT 293:12
insular c., subject to fogs	DISR 120:15
In the c. of the blind	ERAS 133:10
I pray for the c.	HALE 164:4
Isn't this a billion dollar c.	FOST 139:7
leave his c. as good	COBB 100:4
Liberty is not, there is my c.	PAINE 283:11
life to lose for my c.	HALE 164:6
Love thy c.	DOD 122:5
may our c. be always successful	ADAMS 4:6
merchants have no c.	JEFF 193:5
My c. is the world	PAINE 283:2
My c., right or wrong	CHES 84:1
My c., right or wrong; if right	SCH 322:2
My c., 'tis of thee	SMITH 344:5
never let my c. die for me	KINN 212:1
No man attached to his c.	PEEL 288:7
not see much of the c.	GLAD 154:8
old c. must wake up	GEOR 149:5
One c., one constitution	WEBS 382:9
our c., right or wrong	DEC 111:4
party before c.	CREWE 104:2
prepare the mind of the c.	DISR 119:12
quarrel in a far away c.	CHAM 80:9
right to leave any c.	ANON 9:13
says that he loves his c.	STEV 350:2
serve my c. as a faithful servant	GIBR 152:3
serve our c.	ADD 5:8
service of their c.	PAINE 281:10
take a c. into a war	CHAM 81:2
that will not love his c.	SHAK 329:10
these c. patriots	BYRON 71:5
The union, sir, is my c.	CLAY 97:12
They died to save their c.	CHES 84:10
This c. needs good farmers	NIXON 274:11
This c. was a lot better off	DEL 113:1

This *is* a beautiful c.   BROWN 59:4
tremble for my c.   JEFF 191:3
understand the c.   LESS 221:13
wants of the c.   PEEL 288:2
what was good for our c.   WILS 389:7
Where liberty is, there is my c.   OTIS 280:2
with women, to a single c.   GALB 146:3
you can do for your c.   KENN 204:7
your c. is lost   WILL 389:3
Your king and c. need you   FIELD 136:5
your king and your c.   RUB 314:8
countrymen Friends, Romans, c.   SHAK 329:13
given my advice to my c.   O'CON 276:6
hearts of his c.   LEE 220:2
rebels are our c. again   GRANT 159:8
counts not the critic who c.   ROOS 311:10
courage accuse himself of c.   BIRCH 34:1
c. is the rarest of all   DISR 121:19
c. of conscience   CHO 85:6
c. to be the secret of liberty   BRAN 54:10
One man with c.   JACK 189:4
resolution on reflection is real c.   WALP 377:10
take counsel always of your c.   STEV 350:12
two o'clock in the morning c.   NAP 269:10
vain faith, and c. vain   MAC 238:9
courageous describe it as *c.*   LYNN 235:5
course c. by course   CHUR 89:11
c. of human events   JEFF 190:7
Take thou what c. thou wilt   SHAK 330:11
court art o'th' c.   SHAK 325:3
'aving no family life at c.   THOM 363:6
bright lustre of a c.   CECIL 79:9
mean c.   BAG 25:11
Say to the c., it glows   RAL 300:4
courtesan pampered c. of Europe   MACM 244:3
courtmartialled I was c.   BEHAN 34:10
Coutts banks with C.   GILB 152:11
covenant c. with death   GARR 148:4
covenants open c. of peace   WILS 392:15
cow Three acres and a c.   ANON 14:1
cowboy that damned c.   HANNA 168:1
cracking c. sound   CROS 106:11
cradle from the c. to the grave   CHUR 91:12
rocking the c.   ROB 307:3
crash c. will come   BISM 47:6
cravats men in long c.   SHIP 339:7
crawl c. up the staircase   BEVAN 41:11
crazy should they go c.   PHOC 292:5
when I was c.   SHER 339:2
create c. the current of events   BISM 47:9
One must genuinely c. Europe   MONN 262:5
qualities which c. publicity   ATTL 20:4
created all men are c. equal   JEFF 191:1
creates not only in what it c.   BAG 26:3
creation since the c.   NIXON 274:5
creative destruction is also a c. urge   BAK 28:4

creator go up to his c. and say   LLOY 230:9
credibility *we played the c. card*   SHAP 335:12
credit most c.   TAYL 358:10
credulity present age is craving c.   DISR 119:8
soften into a c.   BURKE 63:2
youth is the season of c.   PITT 292:10
creed c. of slaves   PITT 293:7
c. of the moment   BAG 23:15
last article of my c.   GAND 147:3
political c.   ADAMS 4:3
creep ambition can c.   BURKE 68:5
cricket c.—a game   MANC 249:2
c. civilizes people   MUG 267:6
c. test   TEBB 359:4
playing c. with their peasants   TREV 368:2
cried he died the little children c.   MOTL 267:3
poor have c., Caesar hath wept   SHAK 330:2
when he c. the little children died   AUDEN 21:5
Crillon brave C.   HENR 175:3
crime catalogue of human c.   CHUR 90:6
c. of being a young man   PITT 292:7
foulest c. in history   WHIT 388:1
high c. rates   BOAZ 50:1
parent of revolution and c.   ARIS 16:8
prevent c.   MELB 256:6
tough on c. and tough on   BLAIR 48:11
worse than a c.   BOUL 53:5
crimes register of the c.   GIBB 151:6
Successful c. alone   DRYD 125:13
criminal c. element   DEBS 111:3
ends I think c.   KEYN 207:2
native American c. class   TWAIN 372:8
severity of the c. law   PEEL 287:9
criminals if there were no c.   SAL 318:9
squalid c.   REAG 302:1
cringe cultural c.   KEAT 202:7
crises c. that seemed intolerable   ATK 19:5
crisis c. in American leadership   BALT 31:9
c. that we inherit   BENN 36:4
C.? What Crisis?   ANON 9:10
fit for a great c.   BAG 25:2
never panics, except in a c.   HOSK 183:6
real c. on your hands   THAT 361:7
There cannot be a c.   KISS 214:2
criterion infallible c. of wisdom   BURKE 67:13
critic not the c. who counts   ROOS 311:10
criticism c. as a good dutiful boy   MAC 236:9
c. of administration   BAG 24:14
permits c.   FORS 139:5
criticize never to c. or attack   CHUR 93:2
critics cosmopolitan c.   DISR 120:8
crocodile one who feeds a c.   CHUR 90:3
Cromwell C., damned to everlasting fame   POPE 295:5
C. guiltless   GRAY 160:8
C., I charge thee   SHAK 327:7
C., our chief of men   MILT 261:2

Cromwell (*cont.*):
They set up C. and his heir — JORD 199:5
crony against government by c. — ICKES 187:3
crook McAdoo his c. — SPR 348:2
their President is a c. — NIXON 274:10
crooked c. timber of humanity — KANT 202:1
crops all the c. I raise — PAINE 282:1
cross c. of gold — BRYAN 60:6
crosses And tumbled down the c. — JORD 199:5
Are they clinging to their c. — CHES 84:5
crossroads midnight at a c. — O'BR 276:4
crossways understands everything c. — SAL 318:3
crowd chaining the c. — VOLT 376:5
crown allegiance to the British c. — LEE 220:3
As minister of the C. — PEEL 288:2
can't have the c. of thorns — BEVAN 41:1
C. is, according to the saying — BAG 24:12
Give me the c. — SHAK 334:3
glory of my c. — ELIZ 132:1
head that wears a c. — SHAK 326:7
I give away my c. — SHAK 334:6
influence of the C. — DUNN 127:1
never wears the c. — HES 177:9
Not the king's c. — SHAK 332:7
Our Indian C. — ROSS 313:5
power of the c. — BURKE 63:1
put the c. in possession — PAINE 280:8
restore the C. — JOHN 198:2
this c. of thorns — BRYAN 60:6
thrice presented him a kingly c. — SHAK 330:3
understand the power of the C. — BENN 36:12
within the hollow c. — SHAK 333:8
crowned all the c. ruffians — PAINE 281:4
Roman Empire, sitting c. — HOBB 180:9
crowning c. mercy — CROM 105:7
crowns c. are empty things — DEFOE 111:11
crucible America is God's c. — ZANG 396:8
crucify you shall not c. mankind — BRYAN 60:6
cruel c. men of Rome — SHAK 328:1
c. necessity — CROM 105:4
state business is a c. trade — HAL 166:12
crusade party is a moral c. — WILS 390:3
crush c. people to the earth — CHILD 85:2
cry Don't c. for me, Argentina — RICE 304:7
he was too big to c. — LINC 225:10
crystal Why read the c. — BEVAN 40:8
cuckoo The c. clock — WELL 383:7
cult c. is a religion — WOLFE 394:1
c. of the individual — KHR 209:2
cultural c. cringe — KEAT 202:7
culture men of c. — ARN 17:3
Whenever I hear the word c. — JOHST 198:14
cunning c. men pass for wise — BACON 22:6
cure c. for admiring the House — BAG 26:4
we palliate what we cannot c. — JOHN 197:2
currency debauch the c. — KEYN 207:5

current create the c. of events — BISM 47:9
we must take the c. — SHAK 330:14
curs You common cry of c. — SHAK 324:8
curst to all succeeding ages c. — DRYD 125:4
curtain bloody c. — ELIS 130:3
iron c. has descended — CHUR 92:10
lets the c. fall — POPE 295:8
Lift the c. — POW 297:16
something kept behind a c. — PAINE 282:15
Curzon C. will be remembered — NEHRU 270:12
cuss don't matter a tinker's c. — SHIN 339:5
custodes *ipsos* C. — JUV 201:6
custodiet Sed quis c. ipsos — JUV 201:6
custom c., that unwritten law — D'AV 110:1
Lest one good c. should corrupt — TENN 360:5
unwritten c. — CATT 78:6
customary action, which is not c. — CORN 103:8
customers people of c. — SMITH 341:6
customs survives by its ancient c. — ENN 133:8
cut he had blocks to c. — PEEL 288:12
most unkindest c. of all — SHAK 330:6
So he has c. his throat at last — BYRON 71:4
they will c. off my head — CHAR 82:5
will not c. my conscience — HELL 174:3
cuttlefish idioms, like a c. — ORW 279:10
cycle c. of deprivation — JOS 199:6
cyclops state policy, a c. — COL 101:3
czar making the President a c. — SCHL 321:6
Czechoslovakia gain for C. — CHUR 89:11

dabbling d. their fingers — MCGR 241:1
daddy Look, d., no hands — ANON 12:6
dagger d. in one hand — WRAN 394:10
hand that held the d. — ROOS 309:8
daggers few, but they shall be d. — PITT 292:8
damage moral or intellectual d. — KRUG 215:6
Damascus road to D. — THAT 362:7
damn d. the consequences — MILN 260:3
look, with a spot I d. him — SHAK 330:12
damnation deep d. of his taking-off — SHAK 331:7
damned d. to everlasting fame — POPE 295:5
lies, d. lies and statistics — DISR 121:15
public be d. — VAND 373:2
publish and be d. — WELL 384:4
dances makes no progress; it d. — LIGNE 224:1
dancing d. on a torrent — BALF 30:5
Dane never get rid of the D. — KIPL 213:4
Dane-geld paying the D. — KIPL 213:4
danger d. justified privilege — WAUGH 380:8
d. of great nations — BAG 27:12
d. to the country, to Europe — VICT 374:6
in as much d. — HAL 165:4
Pleased with the d. — DRYD 125:5
dangerous he would be d. — MELB 255:6
most d. moment — TOCQ 367:3
such men are d. — SHAK 328:7

when they are no longer d.   BOUL 53:6
Dante D. never stays too long   MAC 237:10
dare none d. call it treason   HAR 169:1
Take me if you d.   PANK 285:1
dark always wear a d. suit   ROSS 313:4
colours will agree in the d.   BACON 23:6
things go around in the d.   HOOV 182:11
darkness curse the d.   STEV 350:14
Go out into the d.   HASK 170:2
light cut into the d.   KENN 205:7
there is d. everywhere   NEHRU 270:8
universal d. buries all   POPE 295:8
darning d. needle is broader   NIC 272:2
Darwin evidence to upset D.   ADAMS 2:10
date d. which will live   ROOS 310:1
dates question of d.   TALL 355:5
daughter d. am I in my mother's   KIPL 213:1
d. of debate, that eke discord   ELIZ 130:8
dauntless with d. breast   GRAY 160:8
dawn bliss was it in that d.   WORD 394:7
catch and to reflect the d.   MAC 238:2
day close the drama with the d.   BERK 38:4
d. I was meant not to   THAT 361:10
d. of small nations   CHAM 80:6
not a second on the d.   COOK 102:5
daylight not let in d. upon magic   BAG 25:13
days cast your mind on other d.   YEATS 396:3
finished in the first 1,000 d.   KENN 204:5
hundred d. of dynamic action   WILS 390:6
In the brave d. of old   MAC 237:1
dazzled d. thus with height   WOTT 394:8
dead better red than d.   ANON 9:1
d. battles, like dead generals   TUCH 372:4
d., but in the Elysian fields   DISR 121:6
d. or dying beast   JENK 194:5
d. shall not have died in vain   LINC 226:3
d. woman bites not   GRAY 160:7
democracy of the d.   CHES 84:2
if I am d. he would like to see   HOLL 181:5
protection is not only d.   DISR 121:11
those who are d.   BURKE 67:5
we are all d.   KEYN 207:6
With the d. there is no rivalry   MAC 237:10
dead-level d. of income or wealth   TAWN 355:9
deadliness d. to fight Germany   CHUR 86:2
Dead Sea like a D. fruit   MACM 245:7
whole thing was D. Fruit   LEVIN 222:11
deal I want to d. closely   MACL 242:6
new d.   ROOS 308:6
square d.   ROOS 311:5
dean no dogma, no D.   DISR 121:10
dear fault, d. Brutus   SHAK 328:4
this d., dear land   SHAK 333:4
dearest throw away the d. thing   SHAK 331:6
death added a new terror to d.   WETH 386:1
anger of the sovereign is d.   MORE 265:3
certain, except d. and taxes   FRAN 142:9

covenant with d.   GARR 148:4
d. and sorrow   CHUR 90:11
d. for the minnows   TAWN 356:1
D. is the most convenient time   LLOY 229:13
d. of any state   HOBB 180:7
d. of democracy is not likely   HUTC 186:2
d., without rhetoric   SIEY 340:4
disqualified by the accident of d.   CHES 84:3
forced marches, battles and d.   GAR 148:1
give me d.   HENRY 176:5
kiss of d.   SMITH 343:4
laws of d.   RUSK 315:7
loving ourselves to d.   PRES 298:2
lucky timing of your d.   TAC 354:4
nearest thing to d. in life   ANON 12:8
One d. is a tragedy, one million   STAL 348:7
signed my d. warrant   COLL 101:4
sign her own d.-warrant   BAG 25:12
sorry for the d.   BAG 24:4
studied in his d.   SHAK 331:6
suicide 25 years after his d.   BEAV 34:4
tell sad stories of the d. of kings   SHAK 333:8
their tongues doom men to d.   SHAK 335:5
Those by d. are few   JEFF 192:9
While there is d. there is hope   CROS 106:9
your slogan 'liberty or d.'   WOOL 394:4
debatable d. line   MAC 236:6
debate better to d. a question   JOUB 200:7
daughter of d.   ELIZ 130:8
d. on public issues   BREN 55:11
Rupert of d.   BULW 62:1
talk fluently, d. forcefully   HOGB 181:1
debating reporting, rather than d.   HOGG 181:3
debt ambition's d. is paid   SHAK 329:5
national d.   HAM 167:1
national up is a very Good Thing   SELL 323:8
running up a $4 trillion d.   PEROT 290:9
We've a war, an' a d.   LOW 233:8
debts so we can pay our d.   NYER 276:1
decade in the same d. with you   ROOS 310:3
decades underestimated for d.   KOHL 215:3
deceiving nearly d. your friends   CORN 103:9
decide ministers d.   THAT 362:5
moment to d.   LOW 234:1
power elite are those who d.   MILLS 260:2
decides does not propose, it d.   ATTL 20:6
decision hard, fast and specific d.   TUCH 372:5
life is to act with d.   PEEL 288:16
monologue is not a d.   ATTL 19:10
offhand d.   HARDY 168:7
Once a d. was made   TRUM 371:7
political d.   TREND 367:7
that is a power of d.   HEAD 172:5
decisions d. of importance   PARK 286:1
important d.   ATTL 20:14
decisive short d. war   LYND 234:9

deck to shoulder on a burning d.   MACL 243:6
   Walk the d.   WHIT 387:10
declaration D. of Independence   CHO 85:8
   There has been no d. of war   EDEN 127:7
decline neighbouring state is in d.   MONT 264:7
   orderly management of d.   ARMS 17:1
decorated d., and got rid of   CIC 95:13
decorum Goes all d.   SHAK 332:4
decree establish the d.   BIBLE 43:20
decry not one of those who d. Eton   BEVIN 42:9
defeat d. is an orphan   CIANO 95:4
   In d.: defiance   CHUR 93:5
   In d., Malice   LYNN 235:4
   In d. unbeatable   CHUR 94:5
   knows not victory nor d.   ROOS 310:11
   one glorious d. after another   WHIN 386:5
   possibilities of d.; they do not exist   VICT 374:9
   price of ultimate d.   NIC 272:1
   we know we should d. you   KIPL 213:4
   we never had a d.   CHUR 93:10
defeated d. in a great battle   LIVY 228:9
   Down with the d.   LIVY 228:8
defence best d. against the atom   ANON 8:11
   d. of the indefensible   ORW 279:9
   extremism in the d. of liberty   GOLD 157:8
   millions for d., but not one cent   HARP 169:5
   Never make a d. or apology   CHAR 82:2
   only d. is in offence, which means   BALD 29:6
   think of the d. of England   BALD 29:7
defend d. to the death your right   VOLT 375:11
   refuses to d. his rights   JACK 188:6
defiance In defeat: d.   CHUR 93:5
definitive we can do nothing d.   WASH 379:8
defrauding d. of the State   PENN 289:14
degree Observe d.   SHAK 335:7
   O! when d. is shaked   SHAK 335:8
dehumanizing d. the Negro   LINC 224:9
Dei *vox D.*   ALC 6:8
delay d., right or justice   MAGN 247:4
delaying by d. put the state to rights   ENN 133:9
delenda D. *est Carthago*   CATO 79:1
deleted expletive d.   ANON 9:14
delighteth king d. to honour   BIBLE 43:13
delivered d. him into mine hand   BIBLE 43:11
delivery ungracefulness of his d.   WALP 377:8
deluge as the d. subsides   CHUR 88:4
demand inordinate d. for peace   PEEL 288:10
demands cannot exact their d.   WELL 385:2
demi-paradise This other Eden, d.   SHAK 333:4
demise its own d.   BLAIR 49:1
democracies d. against despots   DEM 113:2
   d., which refresh their ruling class   TREV 368:5
   sacred thing; in d.   FRAN 141:3
democracy be an empire or a d.   BRZ 61:3
   before D. go through its due   CARL 75:8
   cured by more d.   SMITH 343:5
   death of d.   HUTC 186:2

D. and proper drains   BETJ 40:1
D. and socialism   NEHRU 270:10
D. a society where ordinary men   TAWN 356:2
d. can be no more than   YOUNG 396:7
d., for the starvation   FOSD 139:6
d. in a republic   PAGE 280:7
D. is a *State* which recognizes   LENIN 221:6
D. is clearly most appropriate   POTT 296:3
d. is that it has tolerated   BEVAN 40:2
D. is the name we give   FLERS 137:7
D. is the recurrent suspicion   WHITE 386:6
D. is the theory   MENC 256:8
D. means government   ATTL 20:11
D. means government   CHES 85:1
D. never lasts long   ADAMS 4:2
D. no longer works   FIELD 136:6
d. of the dead   CHES 84:2
D. substitutes election   SHAW 336:7
d.—that is a government   PARK 285:6
d. the worst form of Government   CHUR 93:1
D., which means despair   CARL 76:14
D. will not be salvaged   HOGB 181:1
envy is the basis of d.   RUSS 316:7
extreme d. or absolute oligarchy   ARIS 16:9
great arsenal of d.   ROOS 309:10
grieved under a *d.*   HOBB 180:8
holy name of liberty or d.   GAND 147:5
'In a d.,' said Mr Pinfold   WAUGH 380:7
in a d. the whores are us   O'RO 277:8
justice makes d. possible   NIEB 272:10
leaving d. more unsafe   ROB 307:1
made safe for d.   WILS 392:12
myth of d.   CROS 106:12
no d. can afford   BEV 42:4
not the voting that's d.   STOP 351:8
our d. was, from an early period   MAC 238:12
People who want to understand d.   STR 352:4
perfect d.   BURKE 67:4
political aspirant under d.   MENC 256:12
pollution of d.   WHITE 387:2
principle of d.   MONT 264:5
property-owning d.   SKEL 340:9
there is a little less d. to save   ATK 19:4
This expresses my idea of d.   LINC 224:8
Two cheers for D.   FORS 139:5
Under d. one party always   MENC 257:4
what Tory D. is   CHUR 86:3
Wisconsin was a triumph for d.   HOPE 183:2
Without d. socialism would   TAYL 356:5
democrat called himself or herself a d.   BEARD 33:3
Santa Claus is a D.   O'RO 277:3
United States senator, and a D.   JOHN 195:5
democratic among a d. people   TROL 369:4
d. and accountable   HUNT 185:7
D. Party is like a mule   DONN 122:7
d. socialism   FOOT 138:9

dwelling in a state of d. freedom CHUR 88:14
free, d. government TRUM 372:3
indignity to the d. process STEV 350:11
layer of d. paint TOCQ 365:5
no D. or Republican LA G 216:5
democratically d. governed HAIL 164:1
democratization d. of civil society KEANE 202:5
democrats all D. were saloon keepers GRE 161:2
D. object CHES 84:3
stop telling lies about the D. STEV 350:1
town atheist, and a few D. BROG 57:6
Demosthenes D. had finished STEV 350:13
D. never comes MAC 237:10
denied until it has been officially d. COCK 100:6
Denmark rotten in the state of D. SHAK 325:6
deny d. them this participation BURKE 63:12
I never d.; I never contradict DISR 121:7
will we sell, or d., or delay MAGN 247:4
deodorant some kind of d. SCHR 321:9
depart D., I say AMERY 8:1
departed glory is d. BIBLE 43:10
departments other d. MELB 255:7
departure point of d. METT 258:2
twenty years after my d. BISM 47:6
depose my glories and my state d. SHAK 334:4
depositary d. of power DISR 117:10
depression d. when you lose TRUM 371:14
deprivation cycle of d. JOS 199:6
depths d. of insincerity ANON 13:10
deputy d. elected by the Lord SHAK 333:6
deserve d. to get it MENC 256:8
desiccated d. calculating machine BEVAN 41:5
designs ladder to all high d. SHAK 335:8
desire d. for honour CIC 95:8
d. of power HOBB 179:10
desires doing what one d. MILL 259:4
desk subservience to the d. FRAN 142:10
desolated province they have d. GLAD 154:12
desolation d. of war GEOR 149:6
years of d. pass over JEFF 193:11
despair ye Mighty, and d. SHEL 337:9
desperate Diseases d. grown SHAK 326:1
desperation hunger, poverty, d. MARS 251:2
despised old, mad, blind, d. SHEL 338:1
despot wise d. HERB 177:2
despotic create a d. government HERB 177:2
d. states MONT 264:15
There you have d. government MONT 264:2
despotism D. accomplishes great things BALZ 31:10
d. in England WALP 377:13
D. is essential in most enterprises CARL 76:6
d. of liberty against tyranny ROB 306:8
d., or unlimited sovereignty ADAMS 4:3
d. tempered by epigrams CARL 75:11
d. will come ARIS 16:9
government of laws, is a d. WEBS 382:8

modern form of d. MCC 239:8
translated from d. to liberty JEFF 191:11
wickedness is the root of d. ROB 306:9
despots democracies against d. DEM 113:2
D. themselves do not deny TOCQ 366:4
destinies d. of half the globe TOCQ 365:9
d. of the British Empire DISR 119:7
development of human d. FISH 136:8
destiny one constitution, one d. WEBS 382:9
our manifest d. O'SUL 279:13
rendezvous with d. ROOS 308:10
walking with d. CHUR 90:4
destroy d. all respect CHUR 94:14
d. the juridical safeguards HAYEK 171:9
d. the town to save it ANON 11:3
tax involves the power to d. MARS 251:3
Whom the mad would d. LEVIN 222:3
destroyed Carthage must be d. CATO 79:1
treated generously or d. MACH 241:2
destruction happiness, and not their d. JEFF 193:1
law on the side of d. KEYN 207:5
mad d. GAND 147:5
rush and rumble of d. NIC 271:7
urge for d. is also a creative urge BAK 28:4
world peace or world d. BAR 32:4
destructive he would be simply d. MELB 255:6
detected he was d. only once BENN 37:5
detest I d. him more than cold MAC 236:10
detestation d. of the high DICK 115:6
Deutschland D. über alles HOFF 180:11
de Valera negotiating with d. LLOY 230:3
developed have a d. society NYER 276:2
devil first Whig was the d. JOHN 198:8
go to the d., he may as well go NORF 275:2
his cause being good, the d. MORE 265:6
name a synonym for the d. MAC 237:5
when most I play the d. SHAK 334:11
devils always d. would set on me LUTH 234:7
devour always opened to d. ADAMS 3:3
devourers become so great d. MORE 265:5
diaper Dewey threw his d. ICKES 187:2
dictator begin a career as a d. DE G 112:7
German d., instead of snatching CHUR 89:11
dictators d. ride to and fro upon CHUR 89:8
evil weed, which d. may cultivate BEV 42:4
gain success can set up d. LINC 226:4
dictatorship d. of the proletariat MARX 252:5
d. seriously violates human ROM 308:2
elective d. HAIL 163:8
government you have a d. TRUM 371:15
inherent inefficiencies of d. GALB 145:3
One does not establish a d. ORW 279:7
path to an 'elected d.' SCAR 321:2
dictatorships d. it puts in FOSD 139:6
die afeard there are few d. well SHAK 326:13
And shall Trelawny d. HAWK 170:7

die (*cont.*):

better to d. on your feet than to	IBAR 186:6
d. in the last ditch	WILL 389:3
d. is cast	CAES 71:11
D., my dear Doctor, that's	PALM 284:9
d. to-day, and you to-morrow	MORE 265:7
don't want to d. for politicians	THOM 364:6
faith is something you d. for	BENN 36:10
He will, he must d.	NICH 271:4
I believe they d. to vex me	MELB 255:8
I d. a Christian, according to	CHAR 82:7
I d. happy	FOX 141:1
in the sky when you d.	HILL 178:8
It is well, I d. hard	WASH 380:2
I will d. like a true-blue rebel	HILL 178:9
leased out,—I d. pronouncing it	SHAK 333:4
Let us do—or d.	BURNS 68:12
never let my country d. for me	KINN 212:1
People d., but books never die	ROOS 310:2
something he will d. for	KING 210:9
That we can d. but once to serve	ADD 5:8
to resolve to conquer or d.	WASH 379:6
you asked this man to d.	AUDEN 21:6
youth who must fight and d.	HOOV 183:1
died As He d. to make men holy	HOWE 184:4
He d. by inches in public	ROS 312:6
on its tombstone: *d. of a Theory*	DAVIS 110:3
They d. to save their country	CHES 84:10
difference d. of forty thousand men	WELL 384:6
no more d. between your grace	MORE 265:7
tough-minded…respect d.	BEN 35:7
What d. does it make	GAND 147:5
differences of course a nation of d.	CART 77:6
differently for the one who thinks d.	LUX 234:8
difficult d. to speak	BURKE 66:4
difficulties d. in princes' business	BACON 22:8
source of d. for several	NAP 270:2
these little local d.	MACM 244:8
dig D. for Victory	DORM 123:1
digging you're in a hole, stop d.	HEAL 173:3
dignified d. parts	BAG 24:10
dignities men come to d.	BACON 22:11
dignity added to his d.	CHUR 94:13
as much d. in tilling a field	WASH 379:3
below the d. of history	MAC 238:11
d. of a person is acknowledged	JOHN 195:3
free and equal in d. and rights	ANON 8:4
I see no d. in persevering in error	PEEL 288:11
kept up the d. of the office	GEOR 149:7
maintain a d. in their fate	WALP 377:10
diminished ought to be d.	DUNN 127:1
dimming gradual d. of the lights	NIC 272:4
dinner inviting people to d.	MAO 250:2
to their talking politics after d.	DISR 120:4
we expect our d.	SMITH 341:4
dinners consists in giving d.	ADAMS 4:10

diplomacy d. is about surviving till	LYNN 235:8
d. is saying 'Nice doggie'	CATL 78:5
d. is to do and say	GOLD 156:9
science of d. consists	ADAMS 4:10
diplomat chief distinction of a d.	PEAR 287:6
d.…is a person who can tell	STIN 351:5
diplomatic d. boathook	SAL 317:7
diplomatist d.'s vocabulary	TAYL 357:1
directed d. from Washington	JEFF 193:16
direction facing in the same d.	ROST 313:6
dirt D. is only matter out of	GRAY 160:6
thicker will be the d.	GALB 145:11
disappearance d. from the human	CLAY 97:5
disappointing be the least d.	BAR 32:7
disapprove I d. of what you say	VOLT 375:11
disaster meet with triumph and d.	KIPL 213:3
press lives on d.	ATTL 20:10
disastrous between the d.	GALB 145:12
discipline d., unless operated	COCK 100:8
discontent D. arises from	BEVAN 40:11
permanent fund of d.	PEEL 288:9
winter of our d.	SHAK 334:8
discontented blushing d. sun	SHAK 334:1
discord And, hark! what d. follows	SHAK 335:9
debate, that eke d. doth sow	ELIZ 130:8
What dire effects from civil d. flow	ADD 5:9
discoveries consequence of d.	BACON 22:2
discovery d. of grievances	SAL 318:4
discretion inform their d.	JEFF 193:8
their happiness in thy d.	ELIZ 131:2
discrimination all life is about d.	POW 297:4
in the face of d.	BETH 39:9
discuss stay and d. them	WELL 384:5
discussion administration is by d.	GALB 146:11
after reasonable d.	CHUR 93:11
capable of enduring continuous d.	BAG 27:6
government by d.	ATTL 20:11
disease desperate d. requires	FAWK 136:1
D., Ignorance, Squalor	BEV 42:3
d. in the family that is	TREV 368:4
mortal d. by which the Socialist	CHUR 88:8
diseases D. desperate grown	SHAK 326:1
disgraces Labour d. no more	GRANT 160:4
disguised England is a d. republic	BAG 27:2
dish d. fit for the gods	SHAK 328:13
dishonesty allegation of d.	LEVER 222:2
dishonour in honour or d.	LINC 225:12
dishonourable find ourselves d. graves	
	SHAK 328:4
dishwatery silly, flat, d. utterances	ANON 13:6
disillusion one d.—mankind	KEYN 207:3
disintegration through rapine to d.	GLAD 154:16
disinter not be too ready to d.	JOUB 200:6
disloyalty D. is the secret weapon	CRIT 104:9
dismal D. Science	CARL 76:9
dismemberment disintegration and d.	
	GLAD 154:16

dismount they dare not d.   CHUR 89:8
disobliging d. the few   MAC 238:15
disorder to preserve d.   DALEY 108:8
disorderly in a d. government   HAL 165:13
disposed way she d. of an empire   HARL 169:3
dispossessed imprisoned or d.   MAGN 247:3
disputes solution of all d.   BRI 56:2
dissatisfaction discontent and d.   PEEL 288:9
dissent in the West is called 'd.'   HAVEL 170:4
dissentious you d. rogues   SHAK 324:4
dissimulation by one word—d.   DISR 116:8
dissolved union will be d.   COBB 100:1
distance d. between Russia and   SAL 317:8
  prestige without d.   DE G 112:1
distant too bourgeois, too d.   GISC 153:6
distinction birth as a mark of d.   BUR 69:2
  d. of being without an honour   PEEL 288:17
distinctions artificial d.   JACK 189:1
distort then you can d. them   TWAIN 372:10
distress when they are in obvious d.   BALF 30:8
distresses d. of humanity   JOHN 197:2
distribute d. as fairly as he can   LOWE 233:7
ditch [Channel] is a mere d.   NAP 269:4
  die in the last d.   WILL 389:3
  environed with a great d.   CROM 105:13
  with one in the last d.   MACL 242:9
diversity world safe for d.   KENN 205:4
divided d. by a common language   SHAW 337:3
  Fox d. the kingdom with Caesar   JOHN 198:12
  Gaul as a whole is d. into three   CAES 71:7
  world is d. into three classes   RIPP 306:2
dividing by d. we fall   DICK 115:8
divine no government by d. right   HARR 169:7
divinity d. doth hedge a king   SHAK 326:4
division d. of Europe into a number   GIBB 151:2
do diplomacy is to d. and say   GOLD 156:9
  government is not to d.   KEYN 207:10
  I am to d. what I please   FRED 143:4
  I can d. no other   LUTH 234:6
  Let us d.—or die   BURNS 68:12
  little done, so much to d.   RHOD 304:3
  machinery so that we can d.   CHOD 85:9
  Nobody told us we could d. this   WEBB 381:5
  Step One: We must d. something   LYNN 235:11
  supposed to d. anyway   TRUM 371:9
  what can I d. for myself?   NIXON 274:8
  what it can d. for the nation   HARD 168:5
docile more d. instruments   MILL 259:5
doctors If you believe the d.   SAL 318:1
doctrine any political d., except   TROL 370:7
  d. is something you kill for   BENN 36:10
  d. to be forgiven   TROL 369:6
  not the d. of ignoble ease   ROOS 310:10
dog America is a large, friendly d.   TOYN 367:5
  Black d. is back again   CHUR 94:8
  Communism is a dead d.   SOLZ 346:3
  d.'s obeyed in office   SHAK 331:4

drover's d. could lead   HAYD 171:3
  I must love the d.   GIBB 152:1
  kids love that d.   NIXON 273:7
  That d. won't hunt   RICH 305:1
  This mad d. of the Middle East   REAG 302:2
  very good d. in Mr Ernest Bevin   ATTL 20:13
  woman's preaching is like a d.'s   JOHN 197:9
Doge quiet D. of Venice   WALP 377:15
doggie diplomacy is saying 'Nice d.'   CATL 78:5
dogma no d., no Dean   DISR 121:10
dogs country doesn't go to the d.   WILDE 388:8
  let slip the d. of war   SHAK 329:9
  their running d.   MAO 250:7
dole 1930s d. queue   JOS 199:7
dollar billion d. country   FOST 139:7
domestic d. business   MONT 263:7
  pleasures of d. life   GIBB 151:7
dominating relation of men d. men   WEBER 381:8
domination d. and equilibrium   KISS 214:10
  Soviet d.   FORD 139:2
dominion d. of kings   PRICE 298:3
  d. of laws, and the dominion   PRICE 298:3
  d. of religion; the liberation of   GOLD 157:2
  d. of the master   HUME 184:9
  d. of the world   MAHAN 247:6
  d. over palm and pine   KIPL 212:11
  D., the blessed mother   JEFF 193:12
  inglorious period of our d.   BURKE 65:9
dominions His Majesty's d.   NORTH 275:3
domino 'falling d.' principle   EIS 129:5
done anything remained to be d.   LUCAN 234:5
  at present are not d. at all   KEYN 207:10
  d. very well out of the war   BALD 29:1
  should be d., do nothing   MELB 256:5
  something ought to be d.   WELLS 385:5
  surprised to find it d. at all   JOHN 197:9
  that which gets things d.   LLOY 229:10
  want anything d., ask a woman   THAT 360:8
  We have d. it ourselves   LAO-T 217:8
  what is to be d.   LENIN 221:1
door from beneath a closed d.   ANON 12:1
  open d.   HAY 171:2
  prejudices through the d.   FRED 143:3
  shut and lock a d.   PAINE 280:8
doors Men shut their d.   SHAK 335:4
doorstep do this on the d.   JUNOR 201:4
dots what those damned d. meant   CHUR 87:1
doublethink d. means the power   ORW 279:6
doubt intelligent are full of d.   RUSS 316:12
  When in d.   MELB 256:5
  When in d., mumble   BOREN 52:6
Dover chalk cliffs of D.   BALD 29:7
down many kicked d. stairs   HAL 165:1
  You can't hold a man d.   WASH 379:4
downhearted We are not d.   CHAM 80:7
Downing Street from Germany to D.   CHAM 81:1
  You don't reach D.   THAT 362:7

drain From this foul d. pure gold | TOCQ 365:2
drains democracy and proper d. | BETJ 40:1
drawers d. of water | BIBLE 43:8
drawing through my d. room | EDEN 128:1
drawing-room same men in the d. | HAL 165:8
dread That is why most men d. it | SHAW 336:8
Dreadnoughts to keep up as two D. | LLOY 229:3
dream I have a d. | KING 210:10
  perfectibility as a d. | MILL 258:7
  vision and the old men's d. | DRYD 125:7
dreams not make d. your master | KIPL 213:3
dredging Scott wearily d. | MASS 254:3
dregs among the d. of Romulus | CIC 95:5
  d. are often filthy-tasting | CHUR 87:2
drest d. in a little brief authority | SHAK 332:9
drift adamant for d. | CHUR 89:7
drinking d. my griefs | SHAK 334:3
drive difficult to d. | BRO 58:2
driver be a very good back-seat d. | THAT 362:11
  providing he was in the d.'s seat | BEAV 34:5
drizzle d. of Empires | CHUR 88:1
drollery That fatal d. | DISR 118:7
dropping D. the pilot | TENN 359:6
drover d.'s dog could lead | HAYD 171:3
drowns d. things weighty and solid | BACON 22:15
drum-beat morning d. | WEBS 382:7
drunk America is like a bar-room d. | ALLEN 7:2
  My mother, d. or sober | CHES 84:1
  stood by him when he was d. | SHER 339:2
duchess every d. in London | MACD 240:6
duchesses what Grand d. are doing | NAP 269:8
duck Honey, I just forgot to d. | DEMP 113:3
  If it looks like a d. | REUT 303:4
ducking see a parapet without d. | CRIT 104:7
duke everybody praised the d. | SOUT 347:2
  Had we beaten the d. | CLAY 97:11
dukes d. are just as great | LLOY 229:3
dull statesman is that he be d. | ACH 1:6
dullness in Parliamentary | BAG 23:12
duncery tyrannical d. | MILT 260:4
dunghill cock crowing on its own d. | ALD 6:9
Dunkirk D. spirit | WILS 390:2
  spirit of D. will carry us through | WILS 390:9
duplicity continuous acts of d. | COCK 100:9
dust not without d. and heat | MILT 260:6
  O'er English d. | MAC 238:10
  This d. was once the man | WHIT 388:1
dustbin d. of history | TROT 370:12
Dutch commerce the fault of the D. | CANN 75:3
duty brave man inattentive to his d. | JACK 188:7
  Do your d. bravely | KITC 214:15
  d. of an Opposition | DERBY 114:1
  every man's d. to do all | COBB 100:4
  Every subject's d. is the king's | SHAK 326:14
  first d. of a State | RUSK 315:9
  indispensable d. of government | PAINE 281:9
  path of d. was the way to glory | TENN 360:3

  right as well as our d. | PANK 284:10
  we must do our d. | SAL 318:6
dwarfs state which d. its men | MILL 259:5
dwellings our d. shape us | CHUR 92:3
dying At last d. in the last dyke | BURKE 66:5
  forgets a d. king | TENN 360:4
  Turkey is a d. man | NICH 271:4
  unconscionable time d. | CHAR 83:6
  without many of them d. | SELL 323:9
dyke last d. of prevarication | BURKE 66:5
dyspepsia d. of the society | CARL 76:15

eagle bald e. had not been chosen | FRAN 142:7
  Rome, though her e. | WALL 377:1
ear right sow by the e. | HENR 176:2
earl As far as the fourteenth e. is | HOME 182:3
  e. and a knight | ATTL 20:9
early vote for an e. Christmas | CALL 73:1
earned They have to be e. on earth | THAT 360:12
earnest I am in e. | GARR 148:3
ears countrymen, lend me your e. | SHAK 329:13
earth Everything on e. is flying past | GOGOL 156:8
  have to be earned on e. | THAT 360:12
  meek shall inherit the e. | SMITH 343:9
  Of e.'s first blood | WORD 394:5
  returning him safely to e. | KENN 204:8
  return seven years later to e. | BEAV 34:1
  This e. of majesty | SHAK 333:4
  this is the end of e. | ADAMS 5:1
  whole e. as their memorial | PER 290:5
ease he be never at heart's e. | SHAK 328:8
  not the doctrine of ignoble e. | ROOS 310:10
easier It is e. to make war | CLEM 98:6
  It will be e. for you | CHIL 85:4
east fiery portal of the e. | SHAK 334:1
  hold the gorgeous e. in fee | WORD 394:6
  Oh, E. is E., and West is West | KIPL 212:6
  politics in the e. may be defined | DISR 116:8
  ship me somewheres e. of Suez | KIPL 212:8
  what happens in the e. | SOLZ 345:11
East End I can look the E. in the face | ELIZ 132:8
Easter E. Island statue with an arse | KEAT 202:6
eastern civilizing both the e. | PAINE 281:12
  spectre is haunting e. Europe | HAVEL 170:4
easy no e. walk-over to freedom | NEHRU 270:5
eat e. one of Bellamy's veal pies | PITT 293:12
  hoping it will e. him last | CHUR 90:3
  I have often had to e. my words | CHUR 94:15
  Let them e. cake | MAR 250:9
  so wild, that they e. up | MORE 265:5
  You will e., bye and bye | HILL 178:8
ecclesiastic e. tyranny's the worst | DEFOE 111:10
éclair than a chocolate é. | ROOS 311:2

ecological upset the e. balance — SONT 346:6
economic bettering their own e. condition
— MILL 259:14
  countries which enjoy an e. surplus
— POTT 296:3
  criteria which are not purely e. — TAWN 355:12
  e. ones are incomprehensible — HOME 182:4
  great social and e. experiment — HOOV 182:7
  green shoots of e. spring — LAM 217:1
  hidden forces of e. law — KEYN 207:5
  lay bare the e. law of motion — MARX 252:8
  read e. documents — HOME 182:2
  vital e. interests — WEIL 383:5
economical e. with the truth — ARMS 16:12
economics e. are the method — THAT 361:3
  I evidently knew more about e. — KEYN 208:5
  politics of Versailles, only the e. — MONN 262:7
  speech on e. like pissing — JOHN 196:12
economist death of a political e. — BAG 24:4
  no e. should be denied it — GALB 146:5
  no need for the e. to prove — KALD 201:10
  slaves of some defunct e. — KEYN 208:6
economists e. may not know how — FRI 143:8
  ideas of e. and political — KEYN 208:6
  sophisters, e., and calculators — BURKE 66:16
economy e. of private people — SMITH 341:7
  e. of truth — BURKE 68:2
  for fear of political e. — SELL 323:8
  heights of the e. — BEVAN 41:6
  in favour of general e. — EDEN 127:8
  no e. where there is no efficiency — DISR 119:14
  not know how to run the e. — FRI 143:8
  science of political e. — RUSK 316:2
Eden This other E., demi-paradise — SHAK 333:4
edge e. of the abyss — STEV 350:10
educate e. our party — DISR 119:12
  We must e. our masters — LOWE 233:6
educated by the badly e. — CHES 85:1
  times of stress 'e.' people tend — ORW 277:9
  well housed, clothed, fed and e. — RUSK 315:9
education as in the case of e. — JAY 190:4
  E. makes a people easy to — BRO 58:2
  first part of politics? e. — MICH 258:4
  No part of the e. of a politician — CHUR 89:10
  parts of e., it is to be observed — SMITH 343:1
  unplanned e. creates problems — VERW 374:1
  Upon the e. of the people — DISR 120:6
Edward VIII this boy [the future E.] — HARD 168:4
eels e. get used to skinning — CHUR 90:9
  procreation of e. — SCH 322:3
effects What dire e. — ADD 5:9
efficiencies inherent e. of freedom — GALB 145:3
efficiency e. of the post office — SULL 352:5
  where there is no e. — DISR 119:14
efficient e. government — TRUM 371:15
  next, the e. parts — BAG 24:10

effort redoubling your e. — SANT 320:3
egg e. of a North African — GLAD 155:4
eggheads e. of the world unite — STEV 350:15
Egypt Our first site in E. — GLAD 155:4
  We do not want E. any more — PALM 284:4
eight We want e. — ANON 14:10
ein *E. Reich, ein Volk, ein Führer* — ANON 9:11
elder rising hope to e. statesman — FOOT 138:8
elect To e., and to reject — PAINE 283:7
  we must e. world peace — BAR 32:4
elected audacity of e. persons — WHIT 388:2
  e. a Labour Government — ANON 9:6
  will not serve if e. — SHER 339:4
election After the e. — PEROT 290:7
  Better we lose the e. than — STEV 349:8
  e. by the incompetent many — SHAW 336:7
  e. is coming — ELIOT 130:1
  I've won the e. — GEOR 150:5
  loss of the e. — BALD 29:10
  right of e. is the very essence — JUN 200:9
  Tories, every e., must have — BEVAN 40:9
  which a good e. can't fix — NIXON 274:4
elections e. are won — ADAMS 2:6
  fighting of e. — CHUR 89:10
  I do not like e. — CHUR 89:2
  You won the e., but I won — SOM 346:5
elective e. dictatorship — HAIL 163:8
  In e. monarchies — GIBB 151:1
electors British e. will not vote — BEAV 34:6
electricity *usefulness of e.* — FAR 135:4
electrification e. of the whole — LENIN 221:8
elegant e. simplicity of the three — STOW 352:2
elegy whole of Gray's E. — WOLFE 393:5
elements e. of modern civilization — CARL 75:12
  life was gentle, and the e. — SHAK 330:16
  natural e. of a country — MART 251:6
elephant e. pit of socialism — POW 297:2
  he was like an e. — LASKI 218:3
  no room for the rogue e. — TAYL 356:7
elite power e. — MILLS 260:2
eloquence finest e. is that which — LLOY 229:10
  I admire his e. — GIBB 151:14
  parliamentary e. — CARL 76:8
eloquent e., impressive and wrong — BLYT 49:8
  e. in a more sublime — MAC 237:7
Elysian dead, but in the E. fields — DISR 121:6
embalmer triumph of the e.'s art — VIDAL 375:2
embarrassed e. phantom — DISR 120:14
emblem e. of mortality — DISR 121:12
embrace e. your Lordship's — WILK 389:1
emergency one e. following — FISH 136:8
emotion never a dependable e. — ALSOP 7:5
emotional e. orgies — ROB 306:12
  e. spasm — BEVAN 41:4
emotions e., the music — NAM 269:2
  waste-paper basket of the e. — WEBB 381:6

emperor e. is everything — METT 257:10
  to which the e. holds the key — CUST 108:6
emperors e. can actually do nothing — BREC 55:8
empire All e. is no more than — DRYD 125:8
  British E. — ROS 312:11
  course of e. takes its way — BERK 38:4
  destinies of the British E. — DISR 119:7
  dismemberment of the E. — GLAD 154:16
  E. is a commonwealth of nations — ROS 312:5
  England is an e., Germany is — MICH 258:5
  Great Britain has lost an e. — ACH 1:5
  great e. and little minds — BURKE 64:7
  great Mother E. stands — FOST 140:1
  Greeks in this American e. — MACM 244:2
  holy, nor Roman, nor an e. — VOLT 375:9
  How's the E. — GEOR 150:1
  impulses of an evil e. — REAG 301:12
  legacies of e. — SAMP 319:11
  liquidation of the British E. — CHUR 91:9
  metropolis of the e. — COBB 100:3
  preserve the unity of the e. — BURKE 63:12
  provinces of the British e. — SMITH 342:3
  Russia can be an e. or a democracy — BRZ 61:3
  strength of the E., India — GLAD 155:1
  that is the meaning of E. Day — CHES 84:11
  This e., vast as it is — CUST 108:6
  this E. will perish — DISR 121:17
  To found a great e. — SMITH 341:6
  way she disposed of an e. — HARL 169:3
  wilderness into a glorious e. — BURKE 63:11
empires day of E. has come — CHAM 80:6
  drizzle of E. — CHUR 88:1
  e. of the mind — CHUR 92:2
employed innocently e. — JOHN 198:1
employer sole e. is the State — TROT 370:14
employers e. of past generations — BALD 29:5
employment e. of what the world — PEEL 288:3
  known as gainful e. — ACH 1:4
empty e. taxi arrived — CHUR 94:9
  flamboyant labels on e. luggage — BEVAN 41:7
  patriot on an e. stomach — BRANN 55:5
encompassed her wide walls e. — SHAK 328:6
encourage right to e. — BAG 26:1
  to e. the others — VOLT 375:10
encourager *pour e. les autres* — VOLT 375:10
encourages It only e. them — ANON 11:1
encroachment gradual and silent e. — MAD 246:6
end beginning of the e. — TALL 355:1
  but the e. is not yet — BIBLE 44:8
  came to an e. all wars — LLOY 229:8
  e. of ane old song — OGIL 276:7
  e. of a thousand years of — GAIT 145:2
  e. of the beginning — CHUR 91:10
  In my e. is my beginning — MARY 253:8
  Power is not a means, it is an e. — ORW 279:7
  reserved for some e. or other — CLIVE 99:8
  This, this is the e. of earth — ADAMS 5:1

war that will e. war — WELLS 385:4
ended Georges e. — LAND 217:5
ending quickest way of e. a war — ORW 278:13
endings beginnings and e. — BACON 22:7
endogenous e. growth theory — BROWN 58:6
ends e. I think criminal — KEYN 207:2
  in regarding the *e.* as beyond — POPP 296:2
  Let all the e. thou aim'st at — SHAK 327:7
  outdistanced the e. — KING 211:1
endure of all that human hearts e. — JOHN 197:7
enemies e. in war, in peace friends — JEFF 190:6
  e. of Freedom — INGE 187:8
  e. of man: tyranny, poverty — KENN 204:6
  for the e. he has made — BRAGG 54:9
  just friends and brave e. — JEFF 192:11
  left me naked to mine e. — SHAK 327:8
  priests have been e. of liberty — HUME 185:1
  remedy our *e.* have chosen — SHER 339:1
  they will be e. to laws — BURKE 65:3
  we have no perpetual e. — PALM 284:1
enemy ancient inveterate e. — PITT 293:4
  e., but, by God, they frighten me — WELL 383:8
  more formidable e. than Germany — BROG 57:5
  our friend and not our e. — CLIN 99:7
  spoils of the e. — MARCY 250:8
  written by an acute e. — BALF 31:1
energy atomic e. — TRUM 371:3
  problems of our country—e. — CART 77:8
enfants *allons, e. de la patrie* — ROUG 314:3
enforce how to e. with temper — GREN 161:4
enforced laws which cannot be e. — EINS 128:7
Engels Marx, E. and Lenin — KHR 209:1
engine not connected to the e. — GOOD 158:1
  stopped the e. in its tracks — JENK 194:3
engineering Piecemeal social e. — POPP 296:2
engineers artists are not e. — KENN 205:9
engines cannot be amiss for the e. — BURKE 66:7
England better that E. should be free — MAGEE 247:1

between France and E. — PEEL 289:1
bored for E. — MUGG 268:1
deep sleep of E. — ORW 278:3
defence of E. — BALD 29:7
Elizabethan E. — INGE 187:6
end in the ruin of E. — SHEL 337:8
E. and America are two — SHAW 337:3
E. does not love coalitions — DISR 118:17
E. had risen all the same — TAYL 357:11
E. has saved herself — PITT 293:10
E. is a disguised republic — BAG 27:2
E. is a nation of shopkeepers — NAP 270:1
E. is an empire, Germany is — MICH 258:5
E....resembles a family — ORW 278:5
E.'s not a bad country — DRAB 124:5
E. was too pure an Air — ANON 12:13
E. will have her neck wrung — CHUR 91:7
fashion of the court of E. — SHAK 326:18

God punish E.	FUNKE 144:7	E. prudently avoids all contact	TOCQ 365:10
Gott strafe E.	FUNKE 144:7	E.'s heaven-born privilege	ARN 17:5
history of E.	POW 297:8	in Europe, and not one E.	WALP 378:3
history of E. is emphatically	MAC 238:3	last E. to rule in India	NEHRU 271:1
In E.'s green and pleasant land	BLAKE 49:6	last great E.	TENN 359:9
jurisdiction in this Realm of E.	BOOK 51:7	never find an E. in the wrong	SHAW 335:13
keeps Ireland bound to E.	PARN 286:7	religious rights of an E.	JUN 201:3
last king of E.	EDW 128:3	vain, ill-natured thing, an E.	DEFOE 111:6
Let not E. forget her precedence	MILT 260:5	What E. will give his mind	SHAW 337:1
never have seen E. more	CROM 105:1	**Englishmen** E. never will be slaves	SHAW 336:4
no man in E.	CHAR 83:3	our very name as E.	PITT 293:9
[not] suffer E. to be the workshop	DISR 117:1	they would prefer to be E.	RHOD 304:1
not yet ordained that E.	ELIZ 131:6	Tories, in short, are atrophied E.	JOHN 196:13
O E.! model to thy inward	SHAK 326:9	virtue of E.	TAWN 355:7
people of E., that never	CHES 84:7	what Scotchmen are to E.	PEEL 288:15
roast beef of old E.	BURKE 63:3	**enigma** in a mystery inside an e.	CHUR 90:1
Speak for E.	AMERY 7:7	**enjoy** private men e.	SHAK 326:16
strong arm of E. will protect	PALM 284:2	**enjoying** e. themselves	RUSS 316:5
suspended in favour of E.	SHAW 336:18	**enmities** e. of twenty	MAC 238:8
this earth, this realm, this E.	SHAK 333:4	**enough** e. of blood and tears	RABIN 299:4
This E. never did	SHAK 331:1	**enslave** impossible to e.	BRO 58:2
This state [E.] will perish	MONT 264:12	**entangled** alone e.	SHEN 338:9
total reformation is wanted in E.	PAINE 282:3	**enter** king of England cannot e.	PITT 292:9
weave old E.'s winding sheet	BLAKE 49:4	**enterprise** e. is sick	SHAK 335:8
what is left of E.	HUGO 184:6	**enterprises** essential in most e.	CARL 76:6
Whereas in E. all is permitted	MEG 255:3	**entertain** e. four royalties	SAL 318:2
where E. is finished and dead	MILL 260:1	**enthusiasm** e. moves the world	BALF 30:4
who only E. know	KIPL 212:7	e. of the people	WELL 384:1
English But marks our E. dead	KIPL 212:10	**enthusiasts** few e. can be trusted	BALF 30:4
characteristic of the E. Monarchy	BAG 25:7	**entire** e. and whole and perfect	SPR 348:1
cricket—a game which the E.	MANC 249:2	**entitled** no man is e. to	ROOS 311:5
E. have taken their idea	MONT 264:11	**entourage** e. before the Party	GORB 158:2
E. in taste, in opinions	MAC 236:11	**entrails** In our own proper e.	SHAK 330:15
E., not the Turkish court	SHAK 326:8	**entreat** I do e. heaven daily	ELIZ 131:2
E. people never expect any one	BAG 23:13	**entrusted** Those e. with arms	WIND 393:1
E. policy is to float lazily	SAL 317:7	**envious** e. siege	SHAK 333:4
E. subject's sole prerogative	DRYD 125:14	To silence e. tongues: be just	SHAK 327:7
E. take their pleasures sadly	SULLY 352:7	**environed** e. with a great ditch	CROM 105:13
E. up with which I will not put	CHUR 93:4	**environment** issues like the e.	THAT 361:7
E. want *inferiors*	TOCQ 365:1	**envy** Against the e. of less	SHAK 333:4
excellence of the E. government	BLAC 48:10	e. is the basis of democracy	RUSS 316:7
fragments, of the E. scene	ORW 278:7	in e. of great Caesar	SHAK 330:16
if the E. people, directing	BAG 26:11	prisoners of e.	ILL 187:4
impulse of the E. people	BAG 27:3	**epigrams** despotism tempered by e.	CARL 75:11
in favour of boys learning E.	CHUR 88:12	**episode** Marxism is only an e.	POPP 296:1
Only the E. make it their abode	WALL 377:2	**epitaph** If I had any e.	STEV 351:1
principle of the E. constitution	BLAC 48:8	**equal** All shall e. be	GILB 152:11
really nice E. people	SHAW 336:17	born free and e. in dignity	ANON 8:4
Roman-Saxon-Danish-Norman E.	DEFOE 111:7	can be both free and e.	BAG 24:6
seven feet of E. ground	HAR 169:4	created e. and independent	JEFF 191:1
shed one E. tear	MAC 238:10	created e.…In a larger sense	LINC 226:3
talent of our E. nation	DRYD 125:2	created e., that they are	ANON 14:7
to the E. that of the sea	RICH 305:3	earth the separate and e. station	JEFF 190:7
yet the trick of our E. nation	SHAK 326:6	*E. Pay for Equal Work*	ANTH 15:6
Englishman Being an E. is the greatest prize		e. rights	JOHN 195:8
	RHOD 304:2	For e. division of unequal earnings	ELL 133:1
can be offered to an E.—a seat	DISR 120:18	we are all e.	JUN 200:12

equality [e.] is a doctrine — TROL 369:6
e. would be a heaven — TROL 370:2
general state of e. — JOHN 198:6
liberty is liberty, not e. — BERL 39:1
majestic e. of the law — FRAN 141:2
makes e. such a difficult — BECQ 34:8
neither e. nor freedom — FRI 143:10
political and social e. — LINC 225:2
spirit of extreme e. — MONT 264:5
this pretty state of e. — JOHN 198:13
true apostles of e. — ARN 17:3
We wish, in a word, e. — BAK 28:5
equalize attempt to level never e. — BURKE 66:11
equals peace between e. — WILS 392:8
pigs treat us as e. — CHUR 94:11
equanimity face with e. — GILB 152:9
equation e. is something for eternity — EINS 129:2
equilibrium legitimacy and e. — KISS 214:13
stability: domination and e. — KISS 214:10
equipped e. to be the chief executive — ACH 1:8
equivocate I will not e. — GARR 148:3
erecting there e. new — MARV 252:1
err e. as grossly as the few — DRYD 125:11
errands Meet to be sent on e. — SHAK 330:13
error e. has never approached — METT 257:9
no dignity in persevering in e. — PEEL 288:11
than all the hosts of e. — BRYAN 60:4
errors e. of those who think — BID 44:14
eruption strange e. to our state — SHAK 325:4
escutcheon e. of the Common Law — GRAY 160:6
espionage I cannot think that e. — WEST 385:9
essenced his long e. hair — MAC 236:4
essentials all the e. of life — CHUR 87:8
established e. Clergy — GLAD 154:14
socialism *possibly* be e. — STAL 348:4
establishment British e. — KEAT 202:8
estate And ordered their e. — ALEX 7:1
dealing with e. workers — DOUG 123:5
e.-owners, in come the e. agents — HEATH 173:11
fourth e. of the realm — MAC 237:3
esteem too cheap, we e. too lightly — PAINE 281:11
État *L'É. c'est moi* — LOU 232:9
eternal e. yesterday — WEBER 381:9
eternity some conception of e. — MANC 249:2
ethical nuclear giants and e. infants — BRAD 54:5
ethics floats in a sea of e. — WARR 379:1
Eton decry E. and Harrow — BEVIN 42:9
on the playing fields of E. — WELL 384:11
eunuch prerogative of the e. — STOP 351:7
eunuchs seraglio of e. — FOOT 138:5
Europe alterations on the map of E. — CHUR 87:6
commence the salvation of E. — PITT 293:8
Communism continued to haunt E. — TAYL 357:3
division of E. — GIBB 151:2
domination of Eastern E. — FORD 139:2

E. des patries — DE G 112:10
E. has never existed — MONN 262:5
E. is a continent of energetic — FISH 137:1
E. is in danger of plunging — YELT 396:5
glory of E. is extinguished — BURKE 66:16
great stocks of E. — YEATS 396:1
kind of United States of E. — CHUR 92:11
lamps are going out all over E. — GREY 161:5
map of E. has been changed — CHUR 88:4
pampered courtesan of E. — MACM 244:3
part of the community of E. — SAL 318:6
rest of E. is marching — HEAL 173:4
save E. by her example — PITT 293:10
should not create a nation E. — MONN 263:2
smaller nationalities of E. — ASQ 18:3
spectre is haunting eastern E. — HAVEL 170:4
take over the whole of E. — RIDL 305:6
Whoever speaks of E. is wrong — BISM 46:9
whole of E., that will decide — DE G 112:8
word E. on the lips — BISM 46:10
European any E. power — MONR 263:6
colonization by any E. powers — MONR 263:4
common E. causes and affairs — BAG 26:11
communal life of the E. — VERW 374:1
descendant of a E. — CRÈV 104:1
E. exchange rate mechanism — MAJOR 247:10
E. talks of progress — DISR 118:9
E. war might do it — REDM 302:9
E. wars and quarrels — PAINE 281:6
head of E. liberal principles — CLAY 97:4
instruments of E. greatness — HAM 167:5
not be involved in a E. war — BEAV 33:7
of the E. Community — RIDL 305:7
opposition to a single E. currency — THAT 362:10
wars of the E. powers — MONR 263:5
Europeans E. often ask — BRYCE 61:1
event greatest e. it is — FOX 140:6
It is not an e., it is an item — TALL 355:2
eventide perfect e. home — STOC 351:6
events current of e. — BISM 47:9
e. have controlled me — LINC 226:5
We cannot make e. — ADAMS 5:6
Everest He is a Chimborazo or E. — ASQ 18:8
everything for e. dear and valuable — PITT 293:9
Macaulay is of e. — MELB 255:10
robbed a man of *e.* — SOLZ 345:10
Woolworth's: e. in its place — BEVAN 40:3
evidence e. of life after death — SOPER 346:7
give e. against their own — HAL 165:9
evil all government is e. — O'SUL 279:12
but a necessary e. — PAINE 281:1
do nothing for e. to triumph — BURKE 68:7
e. that men do lives after them — SHAK 329:13
He overcame e. with good — KING 210:4
impulses of an e. empire — REAG 301:12
indistinguishable from the e. — DAWS 110:4
justified in doing e. — ROOS 312:3

no e. in the atom   STEV 350:5
place that is free from e.   WAUGH 380:8
presuppose that all men are e.   MACH 241:10
respond to e. by committing   HAVEL 170:6
evils no necessary e. in government   JACK 189:2
not live only by fighting e.   BERL 39:4
When e. are most free   SHAK 328:11
evolution against the ideas of e.   ZIN 397:4
progress of e.   ADAMS 2:10
examination e. of the acts of   HARR 170:1
examine e. but my humours   NORT 275:8
examiners economics than my e.   KEYN 208:5
example save Europe by her e.   PITT 293:10
excess poverty and e.   PENN 289:13
excited When the populace is e.   LA BR 216:2
excitement means of intellectual e.   BAG 24:3
excuse e. every man will plead   SELD 323:1
will not equivocate—I will not e.   GARR 148:3
execute people who e. them   MILL 259:11
executes hand which e. a measure   TAYL 358:5
execution fascination of a public e.   FOOT 138:4
imminent e. of a senior colleague   CLARK 96:9
so effective as their stringent e.   GRANT 160:2
executive both the legislative and e. ADAMS 3:12
more corrupt than e. power   MONT 264:12
new powers of the e.   DENN 113:8
power is nominated by the e.   GIBB 151:4
exercise greater the desire to e. it   LEVIN 222:12
exhausted enemies are not yet e.   GLAD 154:15
range of e. volcanoes   DISR 119:19
exile therefore I die in e.   GREG 161:3
exiled outlawed or e.   MAGN 247:3
exiles politicians are e.   GRIGG 161:9
existence our e. as a nation   PITT 293:9
strong enough to maintain its e.   LINC 226:7
Their e. only adds to our perils   MOUN 267:4
existing shake off the e. government   LINC 224:5
exit Such a graceful e.   JUNOR 201:4
expectation public e. be kept   GALB 146:6
expectations political e. to military POW 296:5
revolution of rising e.   CLEV 99:4
expected what we least e.   DISR 116:11
expediency on the ground of e.   ROOS 312:3
taint pure laws with mere e.   AESC 6:2
expedient not a principle, but an e.   DISR 117:16
expenditure annual e. nineteen   DICK 115:3
economy and particular e.   EDEN 127:8
e. rises to meet income   PARK 285:7
expense regardless of e.   PEEL 289:6
expenses facts are on e.   STOP 351:10
private e.   NORT 275:8
experience e. is the child of   DISR 116:4
e. of being disastrously wrong   GALB 146:5
man of no e.   CURZ 108:4
that is the lamp of e.   HENRY 176:6
experiment full tide of successful e. JEFF 192:6
great social and economic e.   HOOV 182:7

experimentation persistent e.   ROOS 308:5
experts divine right of e.   MACM 244:4
'e.' make the worst possible   ATTL 20:12
few e. and a few rather less   TAYL 356:11
you never should trust e.   SAL 318:1
explain e. why it didn't happen   CHUR 94:6
Never complain and never e.   BALD 29:11
Never complain and never e.   DISR 121:8
never e.   FISH 137:4
explained when being e.   BALF 31:4
explanation simple e. of stupidity   LEVER 222:2
expletive e. deleted   ANON 9:14
exploits capitalism man e. man   ANON 14:5
extempore his e. sayings   WALP 377:6
exterminate e. a nation   SPOCK 347:9
extol How shall we e. thee   BENS 37:6
extraordinary this is an e. man   JOHN 198:11
extravagant e. with his own   SALL 319:4
nothing so e. and irrational   SWIFT 353:8
extreme e. party is most irritated   BAG 27:11
extremism e. in the defence   GOLD 157:8
e. in the pursuit   JOHN 196:5
exult e. O shores, and ring   WHIT 387:10
exulting people all e.   WHIT 387:9
eye cast a longing e. on them   JEFF 191:14
e. to the main chance   CECIL 79:6
neither e. to see, nor tongue   LENT 221:12
spoils one's e. for the high birds   HAL 166:13
watchful e. and the strong arm   PALM 284:2
eyeball We're e. to eyeball   RUSK 315:1
eyes e. blazing with insincerity   ANON 13:10
e. of Caligula, but the mouth   MITT 261:8
Get thee glass e.   SHAK 331:5
have no e. but constitutional e.   LINC 227:2
Mine e. are full of tears   SHAK 334:7
Mine e. have seen the glory   HOWE 184:3

Fabians F....found socialism   HEAL 172:6
farmyard civilization of the F.   INGE 187:9
good man fallen among F.   LENIN 221:5
face changed the whole f.   BACON 22:2
mind's construction in the f.   SHAK 331:6
not lose its human f.   DUBC 126:3
save her soul than her f.   THOM 363:7
stamping on a human f.   ORW 279:8
unacceptable f. of capitalism   HEATH 173:8
whole f. of the world   PASC 287:1
faces private f. in public places   AUDEN 21:1
facing f. in the same direction   ROST 313:6
fact certain superiority in its f.   EMER 133:3
physical f. into a legal right   MILL 259:9
faction By a f.   MAD 246:3
it made them a f.   MAC 238:13
liberty is to f. what air is to fire   MAD 246:1
men who shine in a f.   HAL 166:5
party...is not a f.   POW 297:5

faction (*cont.*):

whisper of a f. should prevail	RUSS 317:1
factions canvasses and f.	BACON 22:5
durable source of f.	MAD 246:4
facts f. are on expenses	STOP 351:10
f. are sacred	SCOTT 322:4
few f., at least ascertainable f.	PEEL 289:9
Get your f. first	TWAIN 372:10
ignoring f.	ADAMS 3:1
report the f.	ROG 307:9
to his imagination for his f.	SHER 338:13
faculties diversity in the f. of men	MAD 246:2
From each according to his f.	BAK 28:5
Hath borne his f. so meek	SHAK 331:7
fade just f. away	MAC 235:14
fail f. from not comprehending	BAG 27:12
We shall not flag or f.	CHUR 90:7
failing from f. hands we throw	MCCR 240:2
failure end in f.	POW 297:7
f. of a listless public	SOLZ 346:4
His f. is ignominious	MENC 256:12
fain F. would I climb	RAL 300:3
fair f. shares for all	JAY 190:5
fairness liberty, not equality or f.	BERL 39:1
faith Courage and f.; vain f.	MAC 238:9
f. and morals	WORD 394:5
f. in a nation of sectaries	DISR 117:11
f. is something you die for	BENN 36:10
first article of my f.	GAND 147:3
good sense and the good f.	GLAD 154:13
If ye break f. with us who die	MCCR 240:2
Marxism is now a world f.	BENN 36:7
My f. in the people governing	DICK 115:7
faithful He was my friend, f.	SHAK 330:1
mentally f. to himself	PAINE 283:5
falcon f. cannot hear the falconer	YEATS 395:6
Falklands F. thing was a fight	BORG 52:7
fall Another thing to f.	SHAK 332:6
by dividing we f.	DICK 115:8
Et tu, Brute? Then f., Caesar	SHAK 329:4
O! what a f. was there	SHAK 330:7
things f. apart	YEATS 395:6
fallacies f. leading to inappropriate	BAL 31:7
fallen all the planets had f. on me	TRUM 371:1
captain lies, f. cold and dead	WHIT 387:10
good man f. among Fabians	LENIN 221:5
falling 'f. domino' principle	EIS 129:5
fear's as bad as f.	SHAK 325:3
false attribution of f. motive	BALD 29:11
f. report, if believed	MED 255:2
falsehood great mass of f.	WILK 389:2
strife of truth with f.	LOW 234:1
falsehoods f. which interest dictates	JOHN 197:4
falters love that never f.	SPR 348:1
fame damned to everlasting f.	POPE 295:5
F. and tranquillity	MONT 263:8
F. is like a river	BACON 22:15

understand what military f.	SHER 339:3
We came here for f.	DISR 121:16
families Great f. of yesterday	DEFOE 111:9
women, and there are f.	THAT 362:2
family f. with the wrong members	ORW 278:5
I have a young f.	FOWL 140:3
in the running of a f.	MONT 263:7
no f. life at Court	THOM 363:6
selling the f. silver	MACM 245:11
spend more time with my f.	RIDL 305:5
spend more time with your f.	THAT 362:8
famous But 'twas a f. victory	SOUT 347:2
f. by their birth	SHAK 333:4
For f. men have the whole earth	PER 290:5
Let us now praise f. men	BIBLE 44:2
main advantage of being f.	KISS 214:14
fanatic f. heart	YEATS 396:2
f. is a great leader	BROUN 58:3
fanaticism F. consists in	SANT 320:3
fanatics But when f. are on top	MENC 257:5
far bridge too f.	BROW 59:7
It is a f., far better thing	GALB 145:9
Poor Mexico, so f. from God	DIAZ 114:6
quarrel in a f. away country	CHAM 80:9
farce as tragedy, the second as f.	MARX 252:4
longest running f.	SMITH 343:7
farewell F.! a long f.	SHAK 327:5
f. king	SHAK 333:8
must bid the company f.	RAL 300:7
farmer I am a f. of thoughts	PAINE 282:1
farmers country needs good f.	NIXON 274:11
fart My Lord, I had forgot the f.	ELIZ 131:11
So dumb he can't f.	JOHN 196:10
fascination f. of a public execution	FOOT 138:4
subject myself to his f.	GLAS 156:4
Fascism first victims of American F.	ROS 313:2
Fascists to include F.	ANON 10:2
fashion f. in these things	FRAN 142:12
fashionable join the f. madmen	DID 116:2
fashions to fit this year's f.	HELL 174:3
fastidiousness Since when was f.	LEVIN 222:10
fat Butter merely makes us f.	GOER 156:6
f. and long-haired fellows	PLUT 294:8
men about me that are f.	SHAK 328:7
What is that f. gentleman	SHAW 337:5
fate arbiter of others' f.	BYRON 71:3
become the makers of our f.	POPP 295:10
decide the f. of the world	DE G 112:8
f. of this country depends	DISR 120:6
f. of unborn millions	WASH 379:6
German whom f. has raised up	BRY 60:7
grief to thy too rigid f.	GRAH 159:1
fates masters of their f.	SHAK 328:4
father Lloyd George knew my f.	ANON 12:2
my f. was before me	RUSK 316:4
polite f. of his people	JAM 189:10
rude son should strike his f. dead	SHAK 335:9

they will cut off thy f.'s head   CHAR 82:5
fatherland unity of our f.   KOHL 215:5
fathers city of the healthiest f.   WHIT 388:3
   our f. brought forth   LINC 226:3
   victory has a hundred f.   CIANO 95:4
fatuity f. of idiots   SMITH 344:6
fault But see thy f.   SHAK 326:9
   f., dear Brutus, is not   SHAK 328:4
   it was a grievous f.   SHAK 329:13
faults f. of statesmen   WALP 377:7
   f. which 'only children'   BAG 24:7
Faust this shabby F.   HEAL 173:1
favour f. of the people   BURKE 62:11
   Fools out of f.   DEFOE 111:5
favourable most f. opportunity   BISM 47:14
favourite mark his f. flies   SHAK 325:12
favourites choose f.   SWIFT 353:8
favours calculate upon real f.   WASH 379:9
   lively sense of future f.   WALP 378:7
   man that hangs on princes' f.   SHAK 327:6
   seeking f. from the great   TAYL 358:6
   Upon your f. swims   SHAK 324:5
fear acting and reasoning as f.   BURKE 62:3
   be just, and f. not   SHAK 327:7
   But let us never f. to negotiate   KENN 204:4
   concessions of f.   BURKE 64:11
   do not wholly banish f.   AESC 6:2
   F. God   KITC 214:15
   F. is the foundation   ADAMS 3:11
   f. of the political consequences   GALB 146:12
   f.'s as bad as falling   SHAK 325:3
   freedom from f.   ROOS 309:11
   hate, so long as they f.   ACC 1:3
   In politics, what begins in f.   COL 101:2
   No tyrant need f. till men   ARIS 16:11
   ocean in the eventide of f.   MORR 266:5
   prevent war is not to f. it   RAND 300:8
   thing we have to f. is f. itself   ROOS 308:8
   will try to have no f.   CHES 83:9
feared prince to be f. than loved   MACH 241:3
fearful our f. trip is done   WHIT 387:9
fears bondage of irrational f.   BRAN 55:1
   never of your f.   STEV 350:12
feast At nature's mighty f.   MALT 248:11
   LIBERTY's glorious f.   BURNS 68:11
featherbed liberty in a f.   JEFF 191:11
fed We have f. our sea   KIPL 212:10
federal Our f. Union   JACK 188:8
Federalists we are all F.   JEFF 192:4
fee hold the gorgeous east in f.   WORD 394:6
feeble f. can seldom persuade   GIBB 151:12
   man of such a f. temper   SHAK 328:3
   unjust as a f. government   BURKE 67:12
feed meat doth this our Caesar f.   SHAK 328:5
feeling appeals to diffused f.   BAG 25:9
   He aroused every f. except trust   TAYL 357:12

feelings governed more by their f.   ADAMS 5:6
feet better to die on your f.   IBAR 186:6
   careful where he put his f.   NIC 272:6
   f. are always in the water   AMES 8:2
   hotbed of cold f.   EBAN 127:6
   seven f. of English ground   HAR 169:4
   would rather die on our f.   ROOS 309:12
felicities close the circle of our f.   JEFF 192:3
fellow ankle of his f. man   DOUG 124:3
   I am a f.-traveller   MACL 243:3
felony f. to drink small beer   SHAK 327:1
female f. worker is the slave   CONN 102:5
   patriotism in the f. sex   ADAMS 2:3
feminist dealing with the early f.   WEST 385:7
fence sat on the f. so long   LLOY 230:15
Fenian left us our F. dead   PEAR 287:3
fens rotten f., whose loves   SHAK 324:8
Fermanagh dreary steeples of F.   CHUR 88:4
fertility less by reason of their f.   MONT 265:1
fetish militarism…is f. worship   TAWN 355:8
fetters his f. fall   GAND 147:7
   seem to wear the same f.   VOLT 376:5
feuds forget all f.   MAC 238:10
fever After life's fitful f.   SHAK 332:2
   bred a f.   THOM 363:4
février f. [February]   NICH 271:5
few by so many to so f.   CHUR 90:10
   f. thought he was even   ATTL 20:9
fewer there was merely one man f.   METT 257:8
fiat f. justitia et pereat mundus   FERD 136:4
   f. justitia et ruant coeli   WATS 380:3
   say 'f. justitia, ruat caelum'   MANS 249:6
fiction f. lags after truth   BURKE 64:13
   It is sometimes f.   MAC 236:6
   my one form of continuous f.   BEVAN 41:9
fiddler Like a village f.   NIC 272:5
fide Punica f.   SALL 319:8
fidelity I respect f. to colleagues   LASKI 218:3
   malignant f.   BALF 31:3
field f. of human conflict   CHUR 90:10
fiery out the f. portal of the east   SHAK 334:1
fifth F. Amendment is an old friend   DOUG 123:3
   f. of November   ANON 13:2
fifty f.-four forty, or fight   ALLEN 7:3
   no f.-fifty Americanism   ROOS 312:2
fight cease when men refuse to f.   ANON 14:6
   deadliness to f. Germany   CHUR 86:2
   fifty-four forty, or f.   ALLEN 7:3
   f. and f. and f. again   GAIT 145:1
   f. for freedom and truth   IBSEN 186:9
   f. for its King and Country   GRAH 158:6
   f. it out on this line   GRANT 159:7
   f. on to the end   HAIG 163:2
   For those who bade me f.   EWER 134:5
   have not yet begun to f.   JONES 199:1
   it is youth who must f. and die   HOOV 183:1
   man being too proud to f.   WILS 392:4

fight (*cont.*):

Ulster will f.   CHUR 86:6

We shall f. on the beaches   CHUR 90:7

You cannot f. against the future   GLAD 154:6

fighting between two periods of f.   BIER 44:17

f. the politicians   MONT 265:4

He is still f. Blenheim   BEVAN 40:10

war consisteth not in actual f.   HOBB 180:1

fights knows what he f. for   CROM 105:3

figure extraordinary f. of our time   KEYN 207:11

figures prove anything by f.   CARL 76:1

file we've lost the f.   LYNN 235:2

filtered opinion is truth f.   PHIL 292:4

finality f. is not the language   DISR 119:3

finance f. is, as it were   GLAD 154:3

financial unsordid f. act   CHUR 92:5

financiers All these f.   WILS 390:1

finest This was their f. hour   CHUR 90:8

finger measured by the f.   SAL 317:8

pointing like a rugged f.   LLOY 229:6

time we pulled our f. out   PHIL 291:5

whose f. do you want   ANON 15:1

fingers as separate as the f.   WASH 379:2

burn your f. in public life   BEAV 33:4

fifteen f. on the safety catch   MACM 245:2

journalists dabbling their f.   MCGR 241:1

finish tools and we will f. the job   CHUR 91:6

finished All this will not be f.   KENN 204:5

England is f. and dead   MILL 260:1

fins swims with f. of lead   SHAK 324:5

fire f. brigade and the fire   CHUR 88:7

I didn't f. him   TRUM 372:2

our neighbour's house is on f.   BURKE 66:7

take a walk into the f.   ENG 133:7

firebell f. in the night   JEFF 193:7

firm *smack of f. government*   MCL 242:5

first ever be done for the f. time   CORN 103:8

F. Amendment has erected a wall   BLACK 48:2

f. and second class citizens   WILL 389:6

f. article of my faith   GAND 147:3

f. in peace, and f. in the hearts   LEE 220:2

f. to catch and to reflect   MAC 238:2

guarantee of the F. Amendment   BLACK 48:4

rather be f. in a village   CAES 71:10

fish 88 poor f.   MENC 257:3

pretty kettle of f.   MARY 253:5

recently dead f.   ORW 278:8

surrounded by f.   BEVAN 40:5

fishes like f. in a saucepan   KHR 209:5

men lived like f.   SIDN 340:2

fistful for a f. of coins   ZAP 397:1

fit I am f. for nothing but to carry   HERV 177:6

fitful After life's f. fever he sleeps   SHAK 332:2

fitting It is f.   ASQ 18:7

five f. per cent is the natural   MAC 237:9

Want is one only of f. giants   BEV 42:3

fix If it ain't broke, don't f. it   LANCE 217:3

which a good election can't f.   NIXON 274:4

fixed There you are, f., old cock   CHUR 91:8

fixers We need fixed rules, not f.   HAYEK 171:8

flag debt, an' a f.   LOW 233:8

discover that the f.   BALD 28:6

f. is companionship   SUMN 353:2

I pledge allegiance to the f.   BELL 34:11

It is the f. just as much of   LODGE 232:1

raised their f. against   WEBS 382:7

respect its f.   PAGE 280:7

spare your country's f.   WHIT 388:5

that does not carry the f.   CHO 85:7

We'll keep the red f. flying here   CONN 101:7

We shall not f. or fail   CHUR 90:7

flagpole run it up the f. and see   ANON 11:12

Flanders In F. fields   MCCR 240:2

part of F. hath received   WALL 377:3

they had brought him a F. mare   HENR 176:1

flashes occasional f. of silence   SMITH 344:9

flattered being then most f.   SHAK 329:1

flatterers I tell him he hates f.   SHAK 329:1

sycophants and f.   HARD 168:4

within a week the same f.   HAL 165:8

flatteries against f.   MACH 241:7

flattering f., kissing and kicking   TRUM 371:5

flattery Everyone likes f.   DISR 121:4

f. corrupts both the receiver   BURKE 66:13

I suppose f. hurts no one   STEV 349:7

When power to f. bows   SHAK 331:2

fleas like a monkey looking for f.   LASKI 218:5

flesh f. which walls about our life   SHAK 333:8

men are f. and blood   SHAK 329:3

flies catch small f.   SWIFT 353:4

for you to keep the f. off the meat   CHUR 90:14

you mark his favourite f.   SHAK 325:12

float f. lazily downstream   SAL 317:7

floating f. bulwark of the island   BLAC 48:7

flog f. the rank and file   ARN 17:6

flood just cause reaches its f.-tide   CATT 78:7

return it as a f.   GLAD 155:11

taken at the f., leads on   SHAK 330:14

floor I could f. them all   DISR 116:9

floppy weak, f. thing in the chair   THAT 362:14

flourish princes and lords may f.   GOLD 157:6

flow rivers of blood must yet f.   JEFF 193:11

flower f. of our youth   TREV 368:1

little f., this delicate little beauty   KEAT 202:9

flowers wild f., and Prime Ministers   BALD 29:3

flowing Suez Canal was f. through   EDEN 128:5

flown all the birds are f.   CHAR 82:3

fluidity solid for f.   CHUR 89:7

fly they ever f. by twilight   BACON 23:2

fly-blown f. phylacteries   ROS 312:13

foaming Tiber f. with much blood   POW 297:1

focus f. of politics on real people   HAVEL 170:5

foe friend than as a f.   GLAD 156:1
  Where breathes the f.   DRAKE 124:8
  willing f. and sea room   ANON 15:3
foliage f. which we call the myth   CROS 106:12
follies crimes, f., and misfortunes   GIBB 151:6
follow I f. the worse   OVID 280:3
  I really had to f. them   LEDR 219:8
following to find nobody f.   CHAM 80:3
folly effects of f., is to fill the world SPEN 347:6
  He knew human f.   AUDEN 21:5
  usually ends in f.   COL 101:2
  wicked f. of 'Woman's Rights'   VICT 374:5
fond We should grow too f. of it   LEE 220:4
fondly f. do we hope   LINC 226:9
fondness habitual f.   WASH 379:12
food advertise f. to hungry   GALB 145:4
  because f. isn't available   REAG 302:3
  struggle for room and f.   MALT 248:10
  wholesome f., whether stewed   SWIFT 354:1
fool f. all of the people all   ADAMS 2:5
  f. too many of the people   THUR 364:8
  Take away that f.'s bauble   CROM 105:9
  wisest f. in Christendom   HENR 175:4
  You may f. all the people some of LINC 227:8
foolish He never said a f. thing   ROCH 307:5
  Nobody ever did anything very f.   MELB 256:1
fools did he not suffer f. gladly   PEAR 287:5
  fill the world with f.   SPEN 347:6
  f. are in a terrible   IBSEN 186:8
  f. out of favour   DEFOE 111:5
  f. said would happen has   MELB 255:4
  f., they have left us our   PEAR 287:3
  make one half the world f.   JEFF 191:2
  perish together as f.   KING 211:2
foot f. of the first page   SAND 320:2
  born with a silver f. in his mouth   RICH 305:2
football In life, as in a f. game   ROOS 311:1
  politics is like being a f. coach   MCC 239:5
footlights couldn't get in the f.   COOK 102:7
footslogger average f.   WRAN 394:10
forbearance f. ceases to be a virtue BURKE 62:8
force blend f. with a manoeuvre   TROT 370:10
  driving f. of all religious   WEBER 381:10
  f., and fraud, are in war   HOBB 180:3
  f. from which the sun   TRUM 371:2
  f. is not a remedy   BRIG 57:1
  Not believing in f.   TROT 370:15
  Other nations use 'f.'   WAUGH 380:6
  use of f. alone is but *temporary* BURKE 64:12
  use of f. by one class against   LENIN 221:6
forcibly f. if we must   CLAY 97:3
Ford I am a F., not a Lincoln   FORD 138:11
forefathers contemplate our f.   ADAMS 5:2
  think of your f.   ADAMS 4:5
foreign destroyed by a f. force   MONT 264:6
  devilish thing about f. affairs   REST 303:2
  F. aid is a system   BAU 33:1

f. aid is the most unpopular   NIXON 274:15
f. policy of a country   TAYL 356:11
I do not speak any f. language   LLOYD 228:10
If a f. country can supply us   SMITH 342:6
If in a f. land, the flag   SUMN 353:2
If you wish to avoid f. collision   CLAY 97:2
influences on our f. policy   GALB 146:12
my f. policy: I wage war   CLEM 98:4
phrase 'f. affairs'   DISR 120:1
purchase from f. countries   SMITH 342:7
This is the idea behind f. policy   O'RO 277:7
to be sent into any f. wars   ROOS 309:9
foreigners I do not like f.   LLOYD 228:10
  To admit f. indiscriminately   HAM 167:8
Foreign Secretary attacking the F.   BEVAN 41:2
  send Britain's F. naked   BEVAN 41:3
forelock tugged the f.   KEAT 202:8
forest f. laments   CHUR 86:4
  like an American f.   BAG 27:5
foretell f. what is going to happen   CHUR 94:6
forged f. in controversies   FRAN 141:8
forget do not quite f.   CHES 84:7
  f. all feuds, and shed one   MAC 238:10
  I never contradict; I sometimes f. DISR 121:7
  lest we f.   KIPL 212:11
  never forgive but I always f.   BALF 31:5
  not to f. we are gentlemen   BURKE 63:6
  they will f. there ever was   WILS 392:14
forgets authority f. a dying king   TENN 360:4
forgive f. those who were right   MACL 243:1
  good Lord will f. me   CATH 78:4
  I never f. but I always forget   BALF 31:5
  Reason to rule, but mercy to f.   DRYD 125:15
forgot Honey, I just f. to duck   DEMP 113:3
  My Lord, I had f. the fart   ELIZ 131:11
forgotten f. man at the bottom   ROOS 308:4
  learnt nothing, and f. nothing   TALL 354:11
fork pick up mercury with a f.   LLOY 230:3
formalistic revolutionaries more f.   CALV 73:4
forms For f. of government   POPE 295:4
fortnight beyond the next f.   CHAM 80:1
fortress This f. built by Nature   SHAK 333:4
fortune leads on to f.   SHAK 330:14
fortunes greater part of our f.   CHUR 93:8
forward F., forward let us range   TENN 359:7
  not look f. to posterity   BURKE 66:10
fought we f. at Arques   HENR 175:3
  what they f. each other for   SOUT 347:1
foully Thou play'dst most f. for't   SHAK 331:10
found as good as he had f. it   COBB 100:4
  effort to f. the Roman nation   VIRG 375:4
  has not yet f. a role   ACH 1:5
foundation f. of morals   BENT 37:9
  Good order is the f.   BURKE 67:10
founding f. a firm state   MARV 252:1
fountain He is the f. of honour   BACON 23:8
  saying, the 'f. of honour'   BAG 24:12

four f. essential human ROOS 309:12
f. lagging winters SHAK 333:3
F. legs good, two legs bad ORW 278:10
two plus two make f. ORW 279:4
fourteenth f. Mr Wilson HOME 182:3
fourth f. estate of the realm MAC 237:3
This is the f. JEFF 194:1
your f. of July DOUG 123:6
fox F. divided the kingdom JOHN 198:12
mentality of a f. at large LEVIN 222:6
My God! They've shot our f. BIRCH 45:6
prince must be a f. MACH 241:5
foxes f. have a sincere interest ELIOT 130:1
foxholes 'coloured' signs on the f. KENN 205:5
fox-hunting f. and writing poetry POW 297:3
simplest of them prefer f. HAIL 163:3
fracture f. the Labour party KINN 212:3
fragment geographical f. PARN 286:5
France between F. and England PEEL 289:1
F....a nation of forty millions CRILE 104:3
F. has lost a battle DE G 112:3
F., mother of arts, of warfare DU B 126:4
F. was long a despotism tempered CARL 75:11
He felt about F. what Pericles KEYN 207:3
in F. all is permitted MEG 255:3
nation, a race, F. is a person MICH 258:5
nation F. MONN 263:2
political thought, in F. ARON 17:7
Shall F. remain here PARK 286:4
two breasts by which F. is fed SULLY 352:6
until F. is adequately secured ASQ 18:3
wield the sword of F. DE G 112:4
frank f. and explicit DISR 118:5
fraud force, and f., are in war HOBB 180:3
frauds all great men are f. BON 51:6
Frederick death of F. the Great BISM 47:6
free all men everywhere could be f. LINC 226:2
all men naturally were born f. MILT 261:1
assure freedom to the f. LINC 226:1
better that England should be f. MAGEE 247:1
born f. and equal in dignity ANON 8:4
comment is f. but facts are STOP 351:10
dare trample upon these, be f. SHEL 338:6
die to make men f. HOWE 184:4
English church shall be f. MAGN 247:2
essence of a f. government CALH 72:2
expects to be ignorant and f. JEFF 193:6
forever f. LINC 225:11
f. as they want to be BALD 28:7
f. at last! Thank God Almighty KING 210:11
f. development of each MARX 253:3
f. press is not a privilege LIPP 228:4
f. society is a society where STEV 350:7
F. speech, free passes BETJ 40:1
function of speech to f. men BRAN 55:1
half slave and half f. LINC 225:1
he is powerful and f. TOCQ 365:6

he's f. again SOLZ 345:10
hungry man is not a f. man STEV 350:3
I am a f. man, an American JOHN 195:5
I'm with you on the f. press STOP 351:11
in chains than to be f. KAFKA 201:9
in prison, I am not f. DEBS 111:3
land of the f. KEY 207:1
leave their citizens f. JEFF 193:15
Long Live F. Quebec DE G 112:14
man is either f. or he is not BAR 32:2
Man was born f. ROUS 314:5
men can be both f. and equal BAG 24:6
mother of the f. BENS 37:6
must ever exist in a f. country BURKE 64:9
need in order to remain f. TOCQ 366:11
No f. man shall be taken MAGN 247:3
no such thing as a f. lunch ANON 13:9
only maxim of a f. government ADAMS 3:5
prerogative of a f. people PAINE 283:7
set the people f. HEATH 173:7
should themselves be f. BRO 57:7
so far kept us f. and firm JEFF 192:6
they are f. to do whatever SHAW 336:4
through f. trade CHOD 85:10
truth which makes men f. AGAR 6:4
want not really a f. press RADC 299:6
Was he f.? Was he happy AUDEN 21:4
We must be f. or die WORD 394:5
wholly slaves or wholly f. DRYD 125:16
will to be f. is perpetually LIPP 228:5
women, not only to be f. PANK 284:10
work makes f. ANON 8:7
yearning to breathe f. LAZ 219:7
freed not be many f. men HAL 166:9
freedom better organized than f. PÉGUY 289:11
born to f., and believing in f. ROOS 309:12
call it the idea of f. PARK 285:6
cannot be any apprenticeship for f. BAR 32:2
deny them this participation of f. BURKE 63:12
do not deny that f. is excellent TOCQ 366:4
enemies of f. do not argue INGE 187:8
fit to use their f. MAC 237:6
F. alone...substitutes TOCQ 366:2
F. and not servitude BURKE 64:1
F. and slavery are mental states GAND 147:7
f. cannot exist without METT 258:2
F. for the pike is death TAWN 356:1
F. hath been hunted round PAINE 281:7
F. is always and exclusively LUX 234:8
F. is an indivisible word WILL 389:5
F. is slavery ORW 279:1
f. is something people take BALD 28:7
F. is the freedom to say ORW 279:4
f. of the press CHUR 94:7
f. of the press, and f. of person JEFF 192:8
F. of the press in Britain SWAF 353:3
F. of the press is guaranteed LIEB 223:6

f. of thought	ADAMS 5:5
f. of thought	HAYEK 171:7
f. of which Europe has little	KENY 206:6
f. that is its birthright	SOLZ 346:4
f. which in no other land	DRYD 125:14
go out to fight for f. and truth	IBSEN 186:9
I desire their liberty and f.	CHAR 82:6
I gave my life for f.	EWER 134:5
impair their f.	TAWN 355:12
In giving f. to the slave	LINC 226:1
inherent efficiencies of f.	GALB 145:3
Let f. ring	SMITH 344:5
love not f., but licence	MILT 260:8
love of f. itself	GLAD 154:11
measure of individual f.	TROL 369:3
most important guarantee of f.	HAYEK 171:4
neither equality nor f.	FRI 143:10
no easy walk-over to f.	NEHRU 270:5
not f. from, but f. to	BERL 39:2
O f., what liberties are taken	GEOR 150:9
of the f. of the people	MAD 246:6
only f. worth the name	MILL 258:9
original source of f.	LIPP 228:2
peace, f., and liberty	SHAK 329:7
precious things: f. of speech	TWAIN 372:9
principles of f., equality, justice	PAGE 280:7
rights of f. we are all equal	JUN 200:12
right to f. of movement	ANON 9:13
safeguards of individual f.	HAYEK 171:9
sense of f. is f. from chains	BERL 39:3
taste for f.	TOCQ 366:11
we can do for the f. of man	KENN 204:7
We must plan for f.	POPP 295:11
When there is f.	LENIN 221:7
When we let f. ring	KING 210:11
Where f. slowly broadens down	TENN 359:8
With f.'s soil beneath our feet	DRAKE 124:8
freedoms four essential human f.	ROOS 309:11
freeing f. some and leaving others	LINC 226:2
freemen f. or slaves	WASH 379:6
only f.	MASS 254:2
only great nursery of f.	SHIP 339:6
To rule o'er f.	BRO 57:7
frei *Arbeit macht f.*	ANON 8:7
French beating the F.	WOLFE 393:5
F. are with equal advantage	CANN 75:3
F. government, American culture	PEAR 287:7
F. noblesse	TREV 368:2
F. Revolution operated	TOCQ 366:5
F. want no-one to be	TOCQ 365:1
in its history Paris was F.	TUCH 372:6
Providence has given to the F.	RICH 305:3
fresh healthy f. air	GALB 146:8
fricassee equally serve in a f.	SWIFT 354:1
friend betraying my f.	FORS 139:4
Fifth Amendment is an old f.	DOUG 123:3
f. in power is a f. lost	ADAMS 2:8

f. of every country but his own	CANN 75:1
lose her as a f. than as a foe	GLAD 156:1
loss of a dear f.	SOUT 347:3
make change our f.	CLIN 99:7
make one f.	TAYL 358:1
my f., faithful and just to me	SHAK 330:1
one f. left	LINC 226:8
That love my f.	SHAK 330:8
who lost no f.	POPE 295:3
friends between f.	CAMP 74:1
enemies in war, in peace f.	JEFF 190:6
f. of every country	DISR 120:8
F., Romans, countrymen	SHAK 329:13
just f. and brave enemies	JEFF 192:11
lay down his f. for his life	THOR 364:7
There are no true f. in politics	CLARK 96:10
very nearly deceiving your f.	CORN 103:9
workers of the country are our f.	SHIN 339:5
friendship honest f. with all nations	JEFF 192:7
In f. false	DRYD 125:6
There is no f. at the top	LLOY 230:13
fright f. the souls	SHAK 334:9
frighten *by God, they f. me*	WELL 383:8
frightening never more f. than	VAN 373:3
fringe lunatic f.	ROOS 311:13
frivolity irresponsible f.	DISR 120:12
frog f. in my throat	MAJOR 247:10
from not freedom f.	BERL 39:2
front I've been stabbed in the f.	INGH 188:2
frontier edge of a new f.	KENN 203:9
frontiers old f. are gone	BALD 29:7
frozen f. in an out-of-date mould	JENK 194:4
fructify f. in the pockets	GLAD 156:2
frustrate f. their knavish tricks	ANON 9:9
frying-pan frizzled in my f.	ENG 133:7
fugitive f. and cloistered virtue	MILT 260:6
Führer *Ein Reich, ein Volk, ein F.*	ANON 9:11
F. is the proper name	LLOY 230:8
full God, we ha' paid in f.	KIPL 212:10
fun It is f.	ROOS 310:3
Mr Gladstone read Homer for f.	CHUR 88:13
no reference to f.	HERB 176:11
function must f. to perfection	MUSS 268:8
fundamental f. sense of freedom	BERL 39:3
funeral corpse at the f.	HEAD 172:1
heaping up its own f. pyre	POW 296:10
funk attitudes of postwar f.	TEBB 359:2
funny f. thing happened to me	STEV 350:9
furnish f. the pictures and I'll f.	HEAR 173:5
furniture all that nice f.	MACM 245:11
not going to rearrange the f.	MORT 267:1
furrow I must plough my f. alone	ROS 312:12
further f. you got from Britain	CALL 73:2
gates of hell—but no f.	PIUS 294:1
fuss What a f. about an omelette	VOLT 375:12
future controls the f.	ORW 279:2
doubted your f.	MURR 268:3

future (*cont.*):

empires of the f.	CHUR 92:2
extravagant hopes of the f.	BURKE 62:10
have any political f.	MONC 261:9
if you want a f. in politics	HES 178:1
I have seen the f.; and it works	STEF 349:1
lively sense of f. favours	WALP 378:7
never plan the f. by the past	BURKE 67:16
no preparation for the f.	DISR 117:6
no way of judging the f.	HENRY 176:6
picture of the f., imagine a boot	ORW 279:8
promise us everything for the f.	KHR 209:8
that scaffold sways the f.	LOW 234:2
You cannot fight against the f.	GLAD 154:6

Fyfe Is David Patrick Maxwell F.   ANON 12:8

gained misery is a battle g.	WELL 385:1
gainful g. employment	ACH 1:4
gains no g. without pains	STEV 349:9
gallery history is a g. of pictures	TOCQ 366:6
Gallia G. *est omnis divisa in partes*	CAES 71:7
gallows die upon the g.	WILK 389:1
you see nothing but the g.	BURKE 67:1
gambler whore and g.	BLAKE 49:4
game always played the g.	SMITH 344:2
anarchism is a g.	SHAW 336:16
war is a very rough g.	MONT 265:2
win the g., and to thrash	DRAKE 124:7
Gandhi If only Bapu [G.] knew	NAIDU 268:9
gangsters acted like g.	KUBR 215:7
garage to the full g.	HOOV 182:9
garden their own back g.	KERR 206:7
wild herb, the other the g. plant	TOCQ 366:10
gardening g. with a staff of three	BIRCH 45:7
garland immortal g.	MILT 260:6
garlic wear a clove of g.	O'BR 276:4
garments reasons are not like g.	ESSEX 134:2
garter Order of the G.	CHUR 92:7
gate poor man at his g.	ALEX 7:1
stood at the g. of the year	HASK 170:2
gates And shut the g. of mercy	GRAY 160:8
g. are mine to open	KIPL 213:1
open the g. of opportunity	JOHN 196:7
prepared to go to the g. of Hell	PIUS 294:1
Gaul G. as a whole is divided	CAES 71:7
general feet of the great g.	OVID 280:4
hands of the g. government	JEFF 192:1
generalities g. of natural right	CHO 85:8
General Motors good for G.	WILS 389:7
generals dead battles, like dead g.	TUCH 372:4
not against the law for g.	TRUM 372:2
Only those g. who gain success	LINC 226:4
Russia has two g.	NICH 271:5
generation sleep of my g.	STEV 351:1
generations thousand g.	KINN 212:2

generously treated g. or destroyed	MACH 241:2
geniality g. of the politician	MAUG 254:4
genius Bismarck was a political g.	TAYL 356:9
g. of its scientists	EIS 129:4
g. of the Constitution	PITT 293:3
talent and g. in this house	KENN 205:1
times in which a g.	ADAMS 2:2
gent gentleman is to a g.	BALD 30:2
gentle droppeth as the g. rain	SHAK 332:10
His life was g.	SHAK 330:16
gentleman cannot make a g.	BURKE 67:17
g. in Whitehall	JAY 190:4
No real English g.	BAG 24:4
scribbling—never a g.	DISR 121:9
Since every Jack became a g.	SHAK 334:10
that which you call 'a g.'	CROM 105:3
to the intelligentsia what a g. is	BALD 30:2
gentlemen creates good g.	MUG 267:6
g. do not take soup	CURZ 108:5
not to forget we are g.	BURKE 63:6
since g. came up	SHAK 326:19
When g. cease to be returned	DISR 121:17
geographical g. concept	BISM 46:9
Ireland is not a g. fragment	PARN 286:5
Italy is a g. expression	METT 257:7
geometrical increases in a g. ratio	MALT 248:9
George Any good of G. the Third	LAND 217:5
G. III was a kind of	BAG 25:10
G. the First knew nothing	JOHN 198:2
G. the First was always reckoned	LAND 217:5
G. the Third	BENT 38:2
G. VI's reign will go down	WAUGH 380:10
Georges G. ended	LAND 217:5
Georgia on the red hills of G.	KING 210:10
Georgian G. silver goes	MACM 245:11
German G. Chancellor, Herr Hitler	CHAM 80:10
G. dictator	CHUR 89:11
great G. whom fate has raised up	BRY 60:7
This is all a G. racket	RIDL 305:6
With Hitler guilty, every other G.	TAYL 357:5
Germans G. down	ISMAY 188:4
G., if this Government	GEDD 148:7
government from the G.	MONT 264:11
much easier to fight the G.	MONT 265:4
There are too many G.	TAYL 356:6
to the G. that of—the air	RICH 305:3
We G. now have the historic	KOHL 215:5
Germany country is at war with G.	CHAM 81:3
deadliness to fight G.	CHUR 86:2
from G. to Downing Street	CHAM 81:1
G. above all	HOFF 180:11
G. calling! Germany calling	JOYCE 200:8
G. is a nation, a race	MICH 258:5
G., now cast down, despised	MACM 244:3
G. was rearming	BALD 29:10
How you, rebellious G.	OVID 280:4
in G. all is prohibited	MEG 255:3

Let us...put G. in the saddle | BISM 46:8
offering G. too little | NEV 271:2
What is wrong with G. | TAYL 356:6
get governments had better g. out | EIS 129:7
If you want to g. along | RAYB 301:4
ghost conjure a great g. | DANG 109:4
g. of a great name | LUCAN 234:4
g. of the deceased Roman | HOBB 180:9
giant To have a g.'s strength | SHAK 332:8
giants one only of five g. | BEV 42:3
prepare for war like precocious g. | PEAR 287:4
world of nuclear g. | BRAD 54:5
Gibbon like G. on the Christians | BUTL 70:7
gibes master of g. and flouts | DISR 120:5
gifts even when they bring g. | VIRG 375:5
gilded Men are but g. loam | SHAK 333:1
gin torrent of g. and beer | GLAD 154:9
Gipper win just one for the G. | GIPP 153:5
girls treaties, you see, are like g. | DE G 112:13
give me back my legions | AUG 21:7
g. us the tools | CHUR 91:6
never g. up their liberties | BURKE 65:10
not to take than to g. | POW 296:6
willing to g. it to others | WHITE 387:4
given I would have g. gladly | JOHN 195:7
not have g. me over | WOLS 394:3
giver both the receiver and the g. | BURKE 66:13
giving not in the g. vein to-day | SHAK 335:3
glad I'm g. we've been bombed | ELIZ 132:8
never g. confident morning | BROW 60:2
Gladstone G....spent his declining | SELL 323:10
in order that Mr G. may perspire | CHUR 86:4
Mr G. read Homer for fun | CHUR 88:13
voting against G. all my life | KING 210:1
glass Get thee g. eyes | SHAK 331:15
glittering g. and sounding generalities | CHO 85:8
merely the g. scum | CHUR 88:9
world continues to offer g. prizes | SMITH 343:8
glitters medal g., but it also | CHUR 93:8
globe hunted round the g. | PAINE 281:7
sop of all this sordid g. | SHAK 335:9
gloria *transit g. mundi* | ANON 13:5
glories my g. and my state depose | SHAK 334:4
glorious reach at the g. gold | SHAK 326:17
To the memory of the g. | REV 303:6
What a g. morning is this | ADAMS 5:3
glory day of g. has arrived | ROUG 314:3
duty was the way to g. | TENN 360:3
g. is departed from Israel | BIBLE 43:10
I g. in the name of Briton | GEOR 149:1
I name thee Old G. | DRIV 124:9
land of hope and g. | BENS 37:6
lost the hope of g. | BALF 30:10
Mine eyes have seen the g. | HOWE 184:3
not the g. of rulers or of races | BEV 42:2
this I count the g. of my crown | ELIZ 132:1
Vain pomp and g. of this world | SHAK 327:6

gloves capitalism with the g. off | STOP 351:9
glow her g. has warmed | STEV 350:14
glue truth is the g. | FORD 139:1
gnomes little g. in Zurich | WILS 390:1
go g. anywhere I damn well please | BEVIN 43:4
Good-night—and g. to it | MORR 266:6
In the name of God, g. | AMERY 8:1
In the name of God, g. | CROM 105:8
let my people g. | BIBLE 43:7
thus far shalt thou g. | PARN 286:8
unto Caesar shalt thou g. | BIBLE 44:12
we think you ought to g. | RUB 314:8
you want to get along, g. along | RAYB 301:4
goals They live by positive g. | BERL 39:4
work for long-term g. | MONN 262:9
God but for the grace of G. | CHUR 93:12
Caesar's; and unto G. the things | BIBLE 44:7
either a beast or a g. | ARIS 16:6
Fellow-citizens: G. reigns | GARF 147:8
GCMG ('G. Calls Me God') | SAMP 319:9
G. also is a Trinity man | BIRR 46:2
G. bless America | BERL 38:6
G. bless the Prince of Wales | LINL 227:10
G. fulfils himself | TENN 360:5
G. has given us Missouri | RAND 300:9
G. has more right | JOHN 195:1
G. help the Minister that meddles | MELB 255:9
G. is any respecter of persons | BROWN 59:2
G. is a Republican | O'RO 277:3
G. is on the side | VOLT 375:8
G. punish England | FUNKE 144:7
G. save the king | HOGG 181:2
G. who made thee mighty | BENS 37:6
Had I but served G. as diligently | WOLS 394:3
Had I but served my G. | SHAK 327:8
hand into the Hand of G. | HASK 170:2
he hears the steps of G. | BISM 47:11
In the name of G., go | AMERY 8:1
like G.'s infinite mercy | O'RO 277:2
Nor paltered with Eternal G. | TENN 360:2
of the people is the voice of G. | ALC 6:8
One on G.'s side is a majority | PHIL 292:1
Standeth G. within the shadow | LOW 234:2
thick skin is a gift from G. | ADEN 6:1
think I am becoming a g. | VESP 374:3
This is the negation of G. | GLAD 154:2
when I reflect that G. is just | JEFF 191:3
gods dish fit for the g. | SHAK 328:13
g. are on the side of | RUSS 316:11
g. are on the side of the stronger | TAC 354:9
they are called g. | JAM 189:11
would destroy, they first make g. | LEVIN 222:3
goes As Maine g., so g. Vermont | FARL 135:5
for the grace of God, g. God | CHUR 93:12
going Everything is g. nowadays | GEOR 150:8
g. gets tough, the tough get g. | KENN 206:2
I am g. on | WILS 391:2

going (cont.):
knows not whither he is g. — CROM 106:1
gold came off the G. Standard — WEBB 381:5
I stuffed their mouths with g. — BEVAN 41:10
mankind upon a cross of g. — BRYAN 60:6
pure g. flows forth — TOCQ 365:2
reach at the glorious g. — SHAK 326:17
golden g. moments of our history — GLAD 155:7
Happy the g. mean — MASS 254:2
In good King Charles's g. days — ANON 10:12
lift my lamp beside the g. door — LAZ 219:7
morning had been g. — CHUR 89:9
golf g.-links lie so near the mill — CLEG 98:3
gone what haste I can to be g. — CROM 106:3
good And common g. to all — SHAK 330:16
Any g. of George the Third — LAND 217:5
as much g. as it must — LEWIS 223:2
Asquith is g. and immoral — CHUR 88:2
discretion for the public g. — LOCKE 231:9
g. government could never be — CAMP 74:3
g. is oft interrèd — SHAK 329:13
g. must associate — BURKE 63:4
g. nature is a bungler — HAL 166:12
g. of subjects — DEFOE 111:11
g. of the people — CIC 95:6
'g. old days' were a myth — ATK 19:5
g. words will not do — LAMB 216:6
Great and the G. — SAMP 319:10
He overcame evil with g. — KING 210:4
His own g. — MILL 258:10
If he is no g. he must — CHUR 93:6
if they have a g. thing — SHAK 326:6
I will be g. — VICT 374:4
know better what is g. for people — JAY 190:4
leave his country as g. — COBB 100:4
maintain g. government — HAM 167:3
Men are never so g. or so bad — MACK 242:3
necessary only for the g. man — BURKE 68:7
never had it so g. — MACM 244:7
not called amiss *The g. old Cause* — MILT 261:4
object of g. government — JEFF 193:1
only g. Indian is a dead Indian — SHER 338:10
policy of the g. neighbour — ROOS 308:9
pursuing our own g. — MILL 258:9
rather than to seem g. — SALL 319:6
That would be a g. idea — GAND 147:4
their g. becomes indistinguishable — DAWS 110:4
Therefore, the g. of man must be — ARIS 16:2
This is the sum of g. government — JEFF 192:3
We are come for your g. — GEOR 148:8
We threw g. housekeeping — KEYN 208:7
What g. Government ever — TROL 370:4
What's g., and doth no g. — RAL 300:4
what was g. for our country was — WILS 389:7
goods care for external g. — WEBER 382:1
dispute less when g. are — TAWN 355:10
your good, for all your g. — GEOR 148:8

goodwill In peace: g. — CHUR 93:5
goose common from the g. — ANON 14:2
Goose Green on the ground at G. — KINN 211:9
Gorbachev Mr G., tear down — REAG 302:5
Goschen I forgot G. — CHUR 86:9
gossip in the g. columns — INGH 187:10
govern easy to g., but impossible — BRO 58:2
good enough to g. another man — LINC 224:6
Go out and g. New South Wales — BELL 35:3
g. according to the common weal — JAM 190:2
heroes to g. you — CARL 76:14
How can you g. a country — DE G 112:11
No man is fit to g. great societies — MAC 238:15
not to g. the country but — GLAD 154:4
people g. themselves — THI 363:2
To g. is to choose — LÉVIS 223:1
You g. in prose — CUOMO 107:3
governed ability among the g. — TOCQ 366:1
democratically g. republic — HAIL 164:1
g. by your inferiors — PLATO 294:3
government to control the g. — MAD 246:7
my faith in The People g. is — DICK 115:7
nation is not g. — BURKE 64:12
not so well g. as they ought — HOOK 182:5
People must be g. in a manner — BURKE 62:6
they are g. by the weakness — BAG 25:6
To understand how we're g. — BENN 36:12
governing lack of it among the g. — TOCQ 366:1
right of g. was not property — FOX 140:5
totally incapable of g. — CHES 83:12
government abandon a g. — JEFF 192:6
actual work of g. — O'RO 277:6
America as a g. of the people — PAGE 280:7
any established institution of g. — BURKE 65:7
any G. which commands — PICK 292:6
art of g. consists in taking — VOLT 376:1
art of g. is the organization — SHAW 336:9
asks you to form a G. you say — ATTL 19:9
attack the G. of my country — CHUR 93:2
basis of popular g. — ROB 306:11
be outlawed in a well-ordered g. — HAL 165:6
best definition of the best g. is — HAL 165:14
best g. is that which — O'SUL 279:12
Bible is for the g. of the people — WYCL 395:1
British g. forms the best model — HAM 167:2
cheerfully support their g. — CLEV 99:3
consequence of cabinet g. — BAG 24:14
corruption of each g. — MONT 264:4
dangerous moment for a bad g. — TOCQ 367:3
democracy means g. by discussion — ATTL 20:11
determined that no British g. — MACM 245:6
dullness in parliamentary g. — BAG 23:12
duty of g. is to prevent crime — MELB 256:6
efficient g. you have a dictatorship — TRUM 371:15
erected into a system of G. — GLAD 154:2
essence of a free g. — CALH 72:2

government (cont.):

revolutionary g. is the despotism	ROB 306:8
rights when called by his G.	JACK 188:6
risen up in the g. greater than	CALH 72:3
second office of g. is honourable	JEFF 191:13
secrecy and a free, democratic g.	TRUM 372:3
shackles and restraints of g.	GOLD 157:2
shake off the existing g.	LINC 224:5
signifies the want of g.	HOBB 180:8
society is the end of g.	ADAMS 3:10
springs of the g. are stretched	MONT 264:13
sum of good g.	JEFF 192:3
That g. is best which governs not	THOR 364:1
that g. of the people	LINC 226:3
Then they were sold by g.	TOCQ 366:8
There you have despotic g.	MONT 264:2
To inherit a g., is to inherit	PAINE 282:13
Under a g. which imprisons	THOR 364:2
under one form of g. rather than	JOHN 197:13
Unfortunately, it's the g.	ALLEN 7:4
unjust as a feeble g.	BURKE 67:12
virtue of paper g.	BURKE 64:3
want the G. to regulate	TRUM 371:6
Whatever g. is not a g. of laws	WEBS 382:8
Whatever it is that the g. does	O'RO 277:7
what the g. can do for it	HARD 168:5
when a g. can only secure	BLAIR 49:1
when they deal with the G.	HOLM 181:6
Why has g. been instituted	HAM 167:6
why monarchy is a strong g.	BAG 25:5
will ever maintain good g.	HAM 167:3
will never use arbitrary g.	CHAR 83:5
wise g. knows how to enforce	GREN 161:4
works for the federal g.	REAG 301:14
worst form of G. except	CHUR 93:1
worst g. is often the most moral	MENC 257:5
you will create a despotic g.	HERB 177:2

governmental unwarranted g. intrusion

	BREN 56:1

governments foundation of most g. | ADAMS 3:11 |

G. always tend to want	RADC 299:6
G. are far more stupid	EIS 129:6
g. had better get out	EIS 129:7
G. need both shepherds	VOLT 375:7
g. to gain ground	JEFF 191:8
In all tyrannical g.	BLAC 48:9
In corrupted g. the place is given	HAL 165:12
Visible g. are the toys	RUSK 316:3

governor once knew a g. | BOK 50:5 |

save the G.-General	WHIT 387:7

governors Our supreme g. | WALP 377:4 |

governs best which g. not at all | THOR 364:1 |

that which g. least	O'SUL 279:12

grab all smash and no g. | NIC 272:8 |

grace keep those of g. | MACH 241:9 |

retains the means of g.	BALF 30:10

graces ought to sacrifice to the g.	BURKE 67:11
gradualness inevitability of g.	WEBB 381:4
grain send choice g.	STO 351:12
grammar erecting a g. school	SHAK 327:3
every fucking g. school	CROS 106:5
talking bad g.	DISR 122:1
grandmother We have become a g.	THAT 362:3
Grant go and see General G.	LEE 220:5
grapes g. can be raised	SMITH 342:7
g. of the wine-press	MAC 236:3
g. of wrath are stored	HOWE 184:3
grass g. will grow in the streets	BRYAN 60:5
g. will grow in the streets	HOOV 182:10
they nibble g.	FAG 135:1
This party comes from the g. roots	BEV 42:1
two blades of g.	SWIFT 353:7
grasshopper with a g.	LLOY 229:7
grasshoppers half a dozen g.	BURKE 67:3
gratitude g. is not a normal feature	KILM 209:10
G., like love	ALSOP 7:5
obtrusive g. of a stranger	TOCQ 365:10
gratuity taking of a bribe or g.	PENN 289:14
grave crowned upon the g.	HOBB 180:9
from the cradle to the g.	CHUR 91:12
Is that ayont the g., man	BURNS 68:13
It's with O'Leary in the g.	YEATS 395:4
life beyond the g.	KHR 209:8
ought to be g., and not taunting	BACON 22:12
Gravedigger part of the First G.	MACL 242:7
graves dishonourable g.	SHAK 328:4
graveyards fills political g.	KINN 211:7
foxholes or g. of battle	KENN 205:5
gravitation not believing in g.	TROT 370:15
gravity He rose by his g.	SMITH 345:1
Gray whole of G.'s Elegy	WOLFE 393:5
graze not allow him to g. there	VERW 374:1
greasy to the top of the g. pole	DISR 121:5
great All g. men make mistakes	CHUR 86:9
g. break through	SHEN 338:9
G., Good and Just	GRAH 159:1
G. hatred, little room	YEATS 396:2
g. man down, you mark	SHAK 325:12
G. men are almost always bad	ACTON 1:10
g. men are not always wise	BIBLE 43:14
g. ones devoured the small	SIDN 340:2
g. that cannot reach the small	SPEN 347:8
He Was A G. Man	ZIEG 397:2
If I am a g. man, then all g. men	BON 51:6
madness in g. ones	SHAK 325:9
Rightly to be g.	SHAK 326:3
seeking favours from the g.	TAYL 358:6
That he is grown so g.	SHAK 328:5
Then the g. man helped the poor	MAC 237:1
tome of The G. and the Good	SAMP 319:10
upward to the G. Society	JOHN 196:3
with small men no g. thing	MILL 259:5

Great Britain G. has lost an empire   ACH 1:5
   G. is going to make war   BETH 39:8
   G. should free herself   SMITH 342:3
   G. will not be involved   BEAV 33:7
   sun of G. will set   SHEL 337:8
greater behold a g. than themselves   SHAK 328:8
   g. than a private citizen   TAC 354:8
   g. the power, the more dangerous   BURKE 63:7
greatest g. happiness of the g. number
                                                 BENT 37:9
   How much the g. event   FOX 140:6
greatness ascent to g.   GIBB 151:5
   G., with private men Esteemed   MASS 254:2
   His g. weighed   SHAK 325:5
   long farewell, to all my g.   SHAK 327:5
   nature of all g. not to be exact   BURKE 64:14
   Th' abuse of g.   SHAK 328:9
   Those who have g. within them   CAMUS 74:5
Grecian admit the G. horse   HAM 167:8
Greece constitutions of later G.   BAG 25:7
greed g. is all right...G. is healthy   BOES 50:4
   g. is right   WEIS 383:6
greedy G. for the property   SALL 319:4
Greek G. as a treat   CHUR 88:12
Greeks G. in this American empire   MACM 244:2
   I fear the G. even when   VIRG 375:5
green for the wearin' o' the g.   ANON 10:11
   g. shoots of economic spring   LAM 217:1
   In England's g. and pleasant land   BLAKE 49:6
   Wherever is worn   YEATS 395:8
greenroom hang about the g.   MACM 245:14
grenadier single Pomeranian g.   BISM 47:10
grey given me over in my g. hairs   WOLS 394:3
   this old g. head   WHIT 388:5
gridlock g. might be good   DOLE 122:6
grief My g. to thy too rigid fate   GRAH 159:1
griefs drinking my g.   SHAK 334:3
   ere England's g. began   GOLD 157:6
   g. of forty generations   MAC 239:1
   not my g.; still am I king of   SHAK 334:4
grievance prefer the g.   PEEL 289:5
   There is no g. that is a fit object   LINC 224:3
grievances discovery of g.   SAL 318:4
grieve one suffer, than a nation g.   DRYD 125:9
grind laws g. the poor   GOLD 157:4
grooves ringing of change   TENN 359:7
grotesque g. chaos of a Labour   KINN 211:11
ground every rood of g.   GOLD 157:6
   gain a little patch of g.   SHAK 326:2
   g. which a coloured man   DOUG 124:1
   let us sit upon the g.   SHAK 333:8
   seven feet of English g.   HAR 169:4
grounds g. to make war   FAIR 135:2
grouse English g. are to Scotch   PEEL 288:15
grovelling g. tyranny   DISR 118:12
groves In the g. of *their* academy   BURKE 67:1

growth endogenous g. theory   BROWN 58:6
   plant of rapid g.   WASH 380:1
guards up g. and at them   WELL 384:2
   who is to guard the g. themselves   JUV 201:6
guessing what I called 'g.'   WELL 384:10
guided g. missiles and misguided   KING 211:1
guiding g. star of my political life   CARS 77:4
guiding-star g. of a whole brave nation
                                                 MOTL 267:3
guilt blood with g. is bought   SHEL 338:5
   g. of Stalin   GORB 158:2
   not allow middle-class g.   HEAL 172:9
guiltier g. than him   SHAK 332:6
guilty With Hitler g.   TAYL 357:5
guinea g. you have in your pocket   RUSK 315:6
   rank is but the g.'s stamp   BURNS 68:10
Gulag G. Archipelago   SOLZ 346:2
gum can't fart and chew g.   JOHN 196:10
gun barrel of a g.   MAO 250:4
   Every g. that is made   EIS 129:4
   We have got the Maxim G.   BELL 35:1
gun-boat send a g.   BEVAN 40:10
gunfire towards the sound of g.   GRIM 162:1
gunpowder civilization, g., Printing   CARL 75:12
   inglorious; namely, printing, g.   BACON 22:2
   invention of g.   MONT 263:10
   no reason why g. treason   ANON 13:2
guns not, for example, without g.   GOEB 156:5
   rather have butter or g.   GOER 156:6
guts g. of the last priest   DID 116:1
   strangled with the g. of the last   MESL 257:6
gyre turning in the widening g.   YEATS 395:6

habeas corpus protection of *h.*   JEFF 192:8
habits respect the prejudices and h.   GIBB 152:2
habitual h. hatred   WASH 379:12
Habsburg H. history   TAYL 357:6
hack Do not h. me   MONM 262:3
Haig [Earl H.] committed suicide   BEAV 34:4
hair his long essenced h.   MAC 236:4
Haldane H. always prefers   CAMP 74:4
half h. slave and half free   LINC 225:1
   Too clever by h.   SAL 319:3
Halifax H. of the latter   MUGG 268:2
halitosis h. of the intellect   ICKES 187:1
hallow cannot h. this ground   LINC 226:3
halls In our h. is hung   WORD 394:5
Hamlet like putting on H. with no   MACL 242:7
hamsters tigress surrounded by h.   BIFF 45:1
hand bite the h. that fed them   BURKE 68:6
   delivered him into mine h.   BIBLE 43:11
   h. into the H. of God   HASK 170:2
   h. that held the dagger   ROOS 309:8
   h. that signed the paper   THOM 363:3
   h. to execute   GIBB 151:10
   h. to execute any mischief   CLAR 96:2

hand (*cont.*):

h. which executes a measure	TAYL 358:5
invisible h. in politics	FRI 144:1
led by an invisible h.	SMITH 342:4
never stretch out the h.	HES 177:10
one as the h.	WASH 379:2
On this side my h.	SHAK 334:3
workers by h. or by brain	ANON 14:3
handbag hitting it with her h.	CRIT 104:5
handkerchief lady's pocket h.	LLOY 230:2
hands *chained up the h. of the loyal*	ANON 13:3
h. of the oppressor	BIKO 45:4
Look, daddy, no h.	ANON 12:6
With mine own h.	SHAK 334:6
hang h. yourself, brave Crillon	HENR 175:3
We must indeed all h. together	FRAN 142:2
we ought to let him h. there	EHRL 128:6
hanged had longed to see him h.	BELL 35:5
h., drawn, and quartered	PEPYS 289:15
Men are not h. for stealing horses	HAL 166:10
hanging h.' men an' women	ANON 10:11
hangman fit for the h.	LASKI 218:4
only the arm of the h.	ANON 13:3
hangs h. on princes' favours	SHAK 327:6
hang-ups don't have time for h.	THAT 360:11
happen d—d fools said would h.	MELB 255:4
what is going to h. tomorrow	CHUR 94:6
happens constitution is what h.	GRIF 161:6
happiness greatest h. of the greatest number	BENT 37:9
h. of an individual	JOHN 197:13
h. of society is the end	ADAMS 3:10
h. of the common man	BEV 42:2
hath been in my people's h.	ELIZ 131:2
in America, the politics of h.	HUMP 185:5
justice or human h.	BERL 39:1
liberty and the pursuit of h.	ANON 14:7
liberty, and the pursuit of h.	JEFF 191:1
secret of h. and courage	BRAN 54:10
happy accounted yourselves h.	CROM 105:13
Few people can be h. unless	RUSS 316:10
h. is that city	ANON 10:4
I'm h. tonight	KING 211:4
My poor are h.	PAINE 283:12
someone, somewhere, may be h.	MENC 257:2
splendid and a h. land	GOLD 157:7
than that none should be h.	JOHN 198:6
this h. breed of men	SHAK 333:4
Was he free? Was he h.	AUDEN 21:4
hard I die h., but I am not afraid	WASH 380:2
hard-faced lot of h. men	BALD 29:1
hare-brained h. chatter	DISR 120:12
hark h. the herald angels sing	ANON 10:5
harlot prerogative of the h.	KIPL 214:1
harm government will do as much h.	LEWIS 223:2
his will, is to prevent h. to others	MILL 258:10

It does no h.	MONC 261:10
thyse men don most h.	LANG 217:7
Harrow who decry Eton and H.	BEVIN 42:9
worthy to pass into H.	CHUR 88:10
Harry But H., H.	SHAK 326:8
little touch of H. in the night	SHAK 326:10
haste make what h. I can	CROM 106:3
hat who does not wear a h.	BEAV 34:6
hatchet did cut it with my h.	WASH 379:5
hate h. some other person	RUSS 316:10
I h. war	ROOS 309:1
I have seen much to h. here	MILL 260:1
implacable in h.	DRYD 125:6
Let them h., so long as they fear	ACC 1:3
hated He rather h. the ruling few	BENT 37:11
hates In a world of voluble h.	TREV 368:3
hating By h. vices too much	BURKE 67:8
don't give way to h.	KIPL 213:3
hatred burning h. for the Tory Party	BEVAN 40:6
great h., little room	YEATS 396:2
toward another an habitual h.	WASH 379:12
undying h. it arouses	FOSD 139:6
hatreds h. which sound so real	TROL 370:8
systematic organization of h.	ADAMS 2:7
hats so many shocking bad h.	WELL 384:8
Haughey Mr H. buried at midnight	O'BR 276:4
have between the House of H.	GEOR 150:10
only thing you cannot h.	WHITE 387:4
havoc Cry, 'h.!' and let slip	SHAK 329:9
hawk Browne was like a h.	ANON 9:4
hawking h. his conscience	BEVIN 42:7
hay work and pray, live on h.	HILL 178:8
he h. would, wouldn't he?	RICE 304:8
live as the greatest h.	RAIN 300:1
head all the blood from the h.	BEVAN 40:4
bad legs, but for your good h.	ELIZ 131:3
bridge scores in his h.	BUTL 70:6
But bowed his comely h.	MARV 251:7
Charles I lost his h. for no less	CRO 107:1
h. of the Cabinet	MORL 266:1
h. that wears a crown	SHAK 326:7
h. to contrive, and a hand	GIBB 151:10
h. to contrive, a tongue	CLAR 96:2
his brains go to his h.	ASQ 19:1
If you can keep your h.	KIPL 213:3
if you strike at the h.	BURKE 66:1
laid your wretched h.	OVID 280:4
make you shorter by the h.	ELIZ 130:7
no matter which way the h. lies	RAL 300:6
not tell which was the h.	BRIG 56:9
O good grey h.	TENN 359:10
"On my h.," was the reply	DISR 116:10
parboiled h. upon a stake	GRAH 159:2
should belong to the h.	TAYL 358:5
show my h. to the people	DANT 109:7
Whereof he is the h.	SHAK 325:5

wholly admirable h. of state	HAIL 164:1
headline I don't want the last h.	HES 178:1
headmasters h. have powers	CHUR 88:11
healing not heroics, but h.	HARD 168:6
health case of nutrition and h.	JAY 190:4
National H. Service is safe	THAT 361:5
war is the h. of the state	BOUR 53:7
healthy Greed is h.	BOES 50:4
h. state of political life	MILL 259:1
hear I h. a smile	CROSS 106:8
men prefer not to h.	AGAR 6:4
one to speak, and another to h.	THOR 364:3
will come when you will h. me	DISR 116:12
heard by two men I'd never h. of	ROTH 313:7
I will be h.	GARR 148:3
right to be h.	HUMP 185:4
we should certainly have h.	AUDEN 21:4
hearers favourable h.	HOOK 182:5
Hearst William Randolph H.	SMITH 343:4
heart broken h. lies here	MAC 238:10
committed adultery in my h.	CART 77:7
fanatic h.	YEATS 396:2
find 'Calais' lying in my h.	MARY 253:9
h. and stomach of a king	ELIZ 130:9
he had a h. to resolve	GIBB 151:10
I feel my h. new opened	SHAK 327:6
If thy h. fails thee, climb not	ELIZ 131:8
Irishman's h.	SHAW 336:12
key to my h.	CLAY 97:9
largely a matter of h.	BUTL 70:8
little body with a mighty h.	SHAK 326:9
make a stone of the h.	YEATS 395:7
So the h. be right	RAL 300:6
heart-beat *just a h. away*	STEV 350:8
hearts all that human h. endure	GOLD 157:5
h. of his countrymen	LEE 220:2
offspring of cold h.	BURKE 66:17
O you hard h.	SHAK 328:1
to steal away your h.	SHAK 330:8
heat can't stand the h., get out of	VAUG 373:4
not without dust and h.	MILT 260:6
white h. of the technological revolution	
	WILS 390:5
heaven consent of h.	JONS 199:3
equality would be a h.	TROL 370:2
I cannot go to h.	NORF 275:2
If Max gets to H.	WELLS 385:6
like going to h.	GRAMM 159:3
not go to H. but with a party	JEFF 191:9
pennies don't fall from h.	THAT 360:12
Son of Saint Louis, ascend to h.	FIRM 136:7
sudden journey to h.	BEAV 34:1
to be young was very h.	WORD 394:7
[Tower of London] as nigh h.	MORE 265:8
heavens h. themselves, the planets	SHAK 335:7
Hebrew superlative H. conjuror	CARL 76:12

hedge such divinity doth h. a king	SHAK 326:4
hedgehogs start throwing h.	KHR 209:7
heights h. of the economy	BEVAN 41:6
helicopters stay up in h.	BEVIN 43:2
hell agreement with h.	GARR 148:4
come hot from h.	SHAK 329:9
go to the gates of H.	PIUS 294:1
H. of not making money	CARL 76:4
h. upon earth	MILL 259:11
tell you to go to h.	STIN 351:5
they think it is h.	TRUM 371:12
help do without the h.	EDW 128:5
God h. me	LUTH 234:6
I'm here to h.	REAG 302:4
helped We shall have h. it	DICK 115:5
helping h. industry	POW 297:2
hen better take a wet h.	KHR 209:4
h.-roost to rob	LLOY 229:2
herd-instinct Morality is the h.	NIET 273:2
here H. I am	MACM 243:10
hereditary folly of h. right in kings	PAINE 281:2
h. government	PAINE 282:13
idea of h. legislators	PAINE 282:8
in 1802 every h. monarch	BAG 27:1
heresy h. signifies no more than	HOBB 179:11
No h. can excite the horror	MAC 237:10
heretic oppressor or a h.	CAMUS 74:8
hero he acted like a h.	WALP 377:9
I may be the h. of a novel	MAC 236:8
heroes Britain a fit country for h.	LLOY 229:9
despair of finding any h.	CARL 76:14
unhappy the land that needs h.	BREC 55:6
heroics not h., but healing	HARD 168:6
Herr H....H. and there	COOK 102:6
hew Not h. him as a carcass	SHAK 328:13
hewers let them be h. of wood	BIBLE 43:8
hide nothing to h.	CHUR 92:9
hiding bloody good h.	GRANT 159:5
high Be ye never so h., the law	DENN 113:6
Be you never so h., the law	FULL 144:6
detestation of the h.	DICK 115:6
Men in h. places	TAYL 358:13
None climbs so h.	CROM 106:1
spoils one's eye for the h. birds	HAL 166:13
higher h. they climb	LLOY 231:3
hijacker terrorist and the h.	THAT 361:13
hill be a city upon a h.	WINT 393:2
other side of the h.	WELL 384:10
hills on the red h. of Georgia	KING 210:10
hip He smote them h. and thigh	BIBLE 43:9
hippopotamus tact than a h.	CAMP 74:4
hired They h. the money	COOL 103:4
hireling pay given to a state h.	JOHN 197:3
Hiroshima one bomb on H.	TRUM 371:2
historian h. can be so obsessed	POW 297:12
h. looks behind the scenery	TAYL 356:10
one safe rule for the h.	FISH 136:8

historians h. in general | TREV 368:7
historical for h. purposes | NIXON 274:12
history But all change in h. | TAYL 356:12
cancer of human h. | SONT 346:6
descended below the dignity of h. | MAC 238:11
do more to shape h. | TAYL 357:4
dustbin of h. | TROT 370:12
H. came to a | SELL 323:11
H. consists, for the greater part | BURKE 67:7
H. gets thicker | TAYL 357:10
H. is a gallery of pictures | TOCQ 366:6
H. is almost always written | NEHRU 270:6
H....is, indeed, little more | GIBB 151:5
H. is littered with the wars | POW 296:9
h. is on our side | KHR 209:3
H. is past politics | FRE 143:5
H. knows no resting places | KISS 214:7
h. of all hitherto existing society | MARX 253:2
h. of England | POW 297:8
h. of progress | MAC 238:3
h. to his patriotism | ADAMS 4:11
I admired your h. | MURR 268:3
I have discerned in h. a plot | FISH 136:8
Indeed, h. is nothing more | VOLT 376:3
in the h. of the world | NIXON 274:5
like writing h. with lightning | WILS 392:2
marked through h. | BAG 24:2
never changed the h. | DISR 119:11
never learned anything from h. | HEGEL 173:12
not learning from our h. | BLAIR 49:2
One of the uses of h. is to free us | BORK 53:2
Phrases make h. here | MAFF 246:8
political h. of the West | HAIL 163:7
Read no h. | DISR 116:7
Thames is liquid h. | BURNS 68:9
There is no h. of mankind | POPP 295:12
This province of literature [h.] | MAC 236:6
thousand years of h. | GAIT 145:2
we cannot except a h. | LINC 225:12
What is h. except a nation's | POW 297:15
What will h. say | SHAW 336:1
Hitler for a man like Adolf H. | BUCH 61:4
H. and Mussolini | LOW 233:5
H.'s level of accuracy | TAYL 357:2
H. swept out of his Berlin | ANON 11:5
H. thought he might get away | CHAM 81:4
that villain H. | GEOR 150:3
well give it to Adolf H., frankly | RIDL 305:8
When H. attacked the Jews | NIEM 273:1
With H. guilty, every other | TAYL 357:5
Hoares no more H. to Paris | GEOR 149:9
hobby as a h., a miniature | MORT 266:8
hobgoblins endless series of h. | MENC 256:9
hoi polloi multitude, the *h.* | DRYD 125:1
hold Once did she h. the gorgeous | WORD 394:6
we can neither h. him | JEFF 193:9
You can't h. a man down | WASH 379:4

holder what its h. chooses | ASQ 18:5
hole when you're in a h. | HEAL 173:3
hollow within the h. crown | SHAK 333:8
holy He died to make men h. | HOWE 184:4
neither h., nor Roman | VOLT 375:9
old ends stol'n forth of h. writ | SHAK 334:11
homage h. of the low | DICK 115:6
home her princes are come h. again | SHAK 331:1
h. his footsteps he hath | SCOTT 322:5
h. of the brave | KEY 207:1
homeless send these, the h. | LAZ 219:7
Homer Mr Gladstone read H. for fun | CHUR 88:13
Home Ruler Be H. if you must | CHAM 80:2
homines *Quot h. tot sententiae* | TER 360:6
honest buy it like an h. man | NORT 275:6
few h. men are better | CROM 105:2
He only in a general h. thought | SHAK 330:16
h. man is laughed at | HAL 166:11
h. politician | CAM 73:6
more that of an h. broker | BISM 42:1
Of more worth is one h. man | PAINE 281:4
Robin and I are two h. men | SHIP 339:7
unthinkable as an h. burglar | MENC 256:10
honesty common h. | SHEL 337:6
honour *All is lost, save h.* | FRAN 141:4
As he was valiant, I h. him | SHAK 329:11
but a peace I hope with h. | DISR 120:9
deprived of either property or h. | MACH 241:6
for reputation and h. | SOCR 345:7
fountain of h. | BAG 24:12
gained immortal h. | CLAY 97:11
great peaks of h. | LLOY 229:6
He is the fountain of h. | BACON 23:8
h. the King | KITC 214:15
In action faithful, and in h. clear | POPE 295:3
in politics there is no h. | DISR 116:5
light us down in h. | LINC 225:12
louder he talked of his h. | EMER 133:4
maintained with h. | RUSS 317:2
may we h. it | WEBS 382:11
Mine h. is my life | SHAK 333:1
national h. | MONR 263:3
office before h. | POW 297:6
peace with h. | CHAM 81:5
roll of h. | CLEV 99:2
safety, h., and welfare | CHAR 82:8
their private h. | WAUGH 380:8
throne *we* h. | SHER 338:12
When h.'s at the stake | SHAK 326:3
whom the king delighteth to h. | BIBLE 43:13
without an h. | PEEL 288:17
honourable Brutus is an h. man | SHAK 330:1
h. alike in what we give | LINC 226:1
honours Examine the H. List | BENN 37:3
Excluded from h. and from offices | ADAMS 2:3
flagrant sale of h. | DISR 117:5
good card to play for H. | BENN 37:4

neither h. nor wages	GAR 148:1
hope Land of H. and Glory	BENS 37:6
last, best h. of earth	LINC 226:1
Never to h. again	SHAK 327:6
rising h.	MAC 238:1
rising h. to elder statesman	FOOT 138:8
There is no h.	CHES 83:9
While there is death there is h.	CROS 106:9
hopes h. of its children	EIS 129:4
no h. but from power	BURKE 65:3
Whilst our h. our wits beguile	WOTT 394:8
horizon just beyond the h.	KISS 214:11
hornets let wasps and h.	SWIFT 353:4
horny h.-handed sons of toil	SAL 318:8
horribilis annus h.	ELIZ 132:6
horse admit the Grecian h.	HAM 167:8
Caligula's h.	RAND 300:10
Do not trust the h., Trojans	VIRG 375:5
this terrible young cornet of h.	WALP 378:4
horses best carriage h.	TROL 369:11
h. may not be stolen	HAL 166:10
if you cannot ride two h.	MAXT 254:5
not best to swap h.	LINC 226:6
hostility frozen in h.	BUSH 69:9
hotbed h. of cold feet	EBAN 127:6
hounds as a carcass fit for h.	SHAK 328:13
hour man and the h. have met	YANC 395:3
This was their finest h.	CHUR 90:8
truth to serve the h.	TENN 360:2
hours better wages and shorter h.	ORW 278:1
company with the h.	WEBS 382:7
in two h.	EVER 134:4
house build your H. of Parliament	WELL 385:2
commands 51 per cent of the H.	PICK 292:6
cure for admiring the H. of Lords	BAG 26:4
[duty is] to make a H.	CANN 75:5
everything before me in that H.	DISR 116:9
go thither from the H. of Lords	NORF 275:2
h. divided against itself	LINC 225:1
H. of Commons	ASQ 18:4
H. of Commons has declined	ST J 317:5
H. of Commons is absolute	DISR 117:2
H. of Commons is the greatest	HOSK 183:5
H. of Commons lives	BAG 26:7
H. of Commons resembles	REYN 303:8
H. of Lords, an illusion	STOP 351:7
H. of Lords is a perfect	STOC 351:6
H. of Peers, throughout the war	GILB 152:7
jest they call the Lower H.	DISR 117:3
libraries of the H. of Commons	CHAN 81:6
look upon the H. of Commons	DISR 120:16
majority of the H. of Commons	SCAR 321:2
member of the H. of Commons	POW 297:14
on both sides of the H.	BROWN 58:5
pleases or displeases this h.	O'CON 276:6
proceedings in the H. of Commons	
	MURR 268:4
put the h. in his pocket	GARV 148:6
reform the H. of Lords	DANG 109:4
seat in the H. of Commons	DISR 120:18
this h. [the Tower of London]	MORE 265:8
untrue in the H. of Commons	WALD 376:6
we love our H. of Peers	GILB 152:5
housed well h., clothed, fed	RUSK 315:9
household real centre of the h.	SHAW 336:17
housekeeping We threw good h.	KEYN 208:7
houses build h. and the like	KEYN 208:4
if the two H. unanimously	BAG 25:12
looking for h., Nye	ATTL 20:2
With respect to the two H.	PAINE 282:12
howls h. of anguish	HEAL 172:7
huddled Your h. masses	LAZ 219:7
human all that h. hearts endure	JOHN 197:7
calculable mass of h. beings	WEBB 381:3
care of h. life and happiness	JEFF 193:1
chessboard of h. society	SMITH 341:3
disappearance from the h. family	CLAY 97:5
expression of h. immaturity	BRIT 57:3
grows not more h.	THOR 364:4
highest type of h. nature	SPEN 347:5
H. beings are perhaps	VAN 373:3
H. blunders	TAYL 357:4
H. justice	GLAD 154:10
H. probabilities	FAIR 135:2
in the course of h. events	JEFF 190:7
measles of the h. race	EINS 129:1
never in the field of h. conflict	CHUR 90:10
Only one-third of h. beings	RUSK 315:2
opinion is so painful to h. nature	BAG 27:9
recognition as h. beings	MALC 248:8
safeguard h. rights	SCAR 320:8
sum of h. knowledge	REED 302:11
universal h. characteristic	WEIL 383:3
want of h. wisdom	BON 51:4
what makes h. beings h.	BERL 39:5
would not lose its h. face	DUBC 126:3
humanitarian h. with an eye to	CECIL 79:6
humanity h., reason, and justice	BURKE 64:5
My h. is not dependent	BOES 50:3
not to their h.	SMITH 341:4
religion of h.	PAINE 283:9
teach governments h.	PAINE 282:5
humblest h. citizen of all the land	BRYAN 60:4
humbug H.	PALM 284:8
Of H. or Humdrum	DISR 117:4
part that h. plays	CHUR 88:14
humdrum Of Humbug or H.	DISR 117:4
humiliation five years' h.	HATT 170:3
humiliations mortifications and h.	WALP 377:13
humorous Very h., all hunting	ATTL 20:15
humours examine but my h.	NORT 275:8
hundred h. days of dynamic action	WILS 390:6
h. flowers blossom	MAO 250:6
h.-horse-power mind	BALD 30:3

hunger against h., poverty | MARS 251:2
h. allows no choice | AUDEN 21:2
I offer you h., thirst | GAR 148:1
those who h. and are not fed | EIS 129:4
hungry advertise food to h. people | GALB 145:4
And the tigers are getting h. | CHUR 89:8
Cassius has a lean and h. look | SHAK 328:7
h. man is not a free man | STEV 350:3
hunt That dog won't h. | RICH 305:1
hunting Very humorous, all h. | ATTL 20:15
hurry old man in a h. | CHUR 86:7
hurt Nothing doth more h. | BACON 22:6
hurting If the policy isn't h. | MAJOR 247:9
husband words 'My h. and I' | ELIZ 132:5
hypercritical any h. rules | LINC 225:6
hyphen h. which joins | BAG 24:13
hyphenated h. Americanism | ROOS 311:14
hypocrisy organized h. | DISR 117:17
world safe for h. | WOLFE 393:6
hypocrites other half h. | JEFF 191:2
hysteria h. is heard in the land | DID 116:2

I I am a free man | JOHN 195:5
words 'My husband and I' | ELIZ 132:5
iceberg ill-concealed i. | LAWS 219:5
idea i. whose time has come | ANON 13:8
invasion by an i. | HUGO 184:5
That would be a good i. | GAND 147:4
idealism i. is the noble toga | HUXL 186:4
some spark of i. | BRAN 55:4
idealist I'm an i. without illusions | KENN 205:10
idealistic only i. nation | WILS 392:16
ideals illusionist without i. | MACL 243:4
ideas I still have the i., Walter | CHUR 94:4
it would be to have i. | FRANK 141:5
none of the sound i. | MACM 245:3
political i. | NAM 269:2
resistance of established i. | BERL 39:6
ideological i. difference | KENN 203:5
ides Beware the i. of March | SHAK 328:2
i. of March are come | SHAK 329:2
idiot i. who praises | GILB 152:10
Suppose you were an i. | TWAIN 372:11
idiots fatuity of i. | SMITH 344:6
idle vivacity of an i. man | BAG 27:8
idleness i. and pride | FRAN 142:1
idol obvious and natural i. | BAG 26:3
to appease an i. | TAWN 355:8
idolatry organization of i. | SHAW 336:9
if i. I had to choose between | FORS 139:4
ifs Talk'st thou to me of 'i.' | SHAK 335:2
ignoble not the doctrine of i. ease | ROOS 310:10
ignorance boldness is a child of i. | BACON 22:4
I. is an evil weed | BEV 42:4
I. is strength | ORW 279:1
I. of the law excuses no man | SELD 323:1

just i. | CURR 107:6
more dangerous than sincere i. | KING 210:5
ignorant expects to be i. and free | JEFF 193:6
right of the i. man | CARL 76:3
Ike I like I. | SPAL 347:4
ill i.-concealed iceberg | LAWS 219:5
I. fares the land | GOLD 157:6
warn you not to fall i. | KINN 211:10
illegal i. we do immediately | KISS 214:5
it is not i. | NIXON 274:13
Nothing is i. if | YOUNG 396:6
illegally accomplishes great things i. | BALZ 31:10
illegitimate i. child of Karl Marx | ATTL 20:8
no i. children, only i. parents | JOS 200:5
ill-housed one-third of a nation i. | ROOS 309:3
illiberal I am a violent i. | RUSK 315:12
illimitable unlimited and i. | BARK 32:3
ill-nourished ill-housed, ill-clad, i. | ROOS 309:3
ills All the i. of democracy | SMITH 343:5
illumination support rather than i. | LANG 217:6
ill-usage complaints of i. | MELB 255:5
illusion He had one i.—France | KEYN 207:3
i. that times that were | GRE 161:1
illusionist Prime Minister as an i. | MACL 243:4
illusions I'm an idealist without i. | KENN 205:10
management of i. | WALD 376:7
image political i. is like mixing | MOND 262:2
images reflects i. | ADAMS 2:9
imagination initiative and i. | GALB 145:5
nothing but his i. | SHAW 336:12
reason and the i. | MAC 236:6
to his i. for his facts | SHER 338:13
Wanting i. he lacked prescience | DISR 119:1
imaginations weakness of their i. | BAG 25:6
imagined free us of a falsely i. past | BORK 53:2
immatures He i. with age | WILS 391:8
immaturity human i. | BRIT 57:3
immigrants i. or descendants of i. | ROOS 310:4
immobility i. of British institutions | ASQ 18:4
immoral Asquith is good and i. | CHUR 88:2
Call a thing i. or ugly | SCH 322:1
impartial for its i. administration | PEEL 287:9
I decline utterly to be i. | CHUR 88:7
impeached Richard Nixon i. himself | ABZUG 1:2
imperative one categorical i. | KANT 202:2
imperfect on i. knowledge | ATTL 20:14
imperial our great i. family | ELIZ 132:4
imperialism i. is the monopoly | LENIN 221:3
what I may call wild-cat i. | ROS 312:8
imperialisms prey of rival i. | KENY 206:6
imperialist Through its i. system | MAND 249:3
imperialists make the i. dance | KHR 209:5
imperially Learn to think i. | CHAM 80:5
imperium i. et Libertas | DISR 120:13
implacable i. in hate | DRYD 125:6
important British are no longer i. | MCC 240:1
less importunate for being less i. | MONT 263:7

money is indeed the most i.   SHAW 336:11
importunate no less i.   MONT 263:7
impossible i. to be silent   BURKE 66:4
imposters And treat those two i.   KIPL 213:3
impressive eloquent, i. and wrong   BLYT 49:8
imprisoned taken or i.   MAGN 247:3
improvement schemes of political i.   JOHN 197:10
improvements No great i.   MILL 259:12
improving as a means of i.   TROL 370:7
inactivity in a wise and masterly i.   MACK 242:4
    Mr Coolidge's genius for i.   LIPP 228:1
inadvertence by chance or i.   HAIL 163:12
inattentive brave man i. to his duty   JACK 188:7
incapable i. of governing   CHES 83:12
income annual i. twenty pounds   DICK 115:3
    expenditure rises to meet i.   PARK 285:7
    moderate i.   LAMB 216:7
    source of the family i.   ORW 278:5
    when its real i. is increased   KEYN 208:3
    who dread a dead-level of i.   TAWN 355:9
incomes if the i. of the rich   SHAW 336:21
    i. policy alone   JOS 200:2
incompatible at times i.   BERL 39:4
incompetent election by the i.   SHAW 336:7
incomprehensibility When i.   LYNN 234:10
incomprehensible i. man of 82   VICT 374:6
    ones are i.   HOME 182:4
inconstancy His i. is his great   DUPIN 127:2
inconveniences i., and those weighty
                                                 HOOK 182:6
    no i. but such as are   HAL 165:14
incorruptible seagreen i.   CARL 75:9
increase i. of his government   BIBLE 43:19
    One man's wage i. is another   WILS 391:3
increasing has increased, is i.   DUNN 127:1
increment unearned i.   LLOY 229:4
    unearned i. of rent   MILL 259:13
indefensible defence of the i.   ORW 279:9
indemnity bill of i....for raid   KRUG 215:6
independence i. of America   SHEL 337:8
    i. of judges   DENN 113:7
    its right to i.   NAM 269:1
independent Ain't to be i.   LOW 233:8
    i. states connected   GIBB 151:2
    not created mankind entirely i.   TOCQ 365:6
    wretched colonies will all be i.   DISR 119:2
indestructible i. Union   CHASE 83:7
India all that was beautiful in I.   NEHRU 270:12
    driven out of I. this day   BURKE 65:9
    I. adds nothing   GLAD 155:1
    I. will awake to life   NEHRU 270:7
    key of I. is London   DISR 121:2
    last Englishman to rule in I.   NEHRU 271:1
    peaceably and happily in I.   VICT 374:7
Indian good I. is a dead I.   SHER 338:10
    I. in blood and colour   MAC 236:11
    Our I. Crown   ROSS 313:5

Indians Cooper killing off the I.   BALD 28:6
    I. are you   BALD 28:6
    pure-blooded I.   ROOS 310:4
    to be like the I.   PEEL 288:5
    when the I. were running it   DEL 113:1
indictment drawing up an i.   BURKE 64:2
indifference i. of the majority   REST 303:3
indignatio i. principis mors est   MORE 265:7
indignation permanent i.   VAL 372:12
indignities by i. men come   BACON 22:11
indignity He has spared me the i.   BELL 35:2
    no escape from the i.   HATT 170:3
indiscretion cliché and an i.   MACM 244:6
indispensable There is no i. man   ROOS 308:7
individual abolish the cult of the i.   KHR 209:2
    each i. a repetition   WEBB 381:3
    Every i. necessarily labours   SMITH 342:4
    I. liberty is individual power   ADAMS 4:9
    injustice done to an i.   JUN 201:1
    liberty of the i.   MILL 259:2
    natural effort of every i.   SMITH 343:3
    property rights of the i.   MORSE 266:7
individualism rugged i.   HOOV 182:8
individuals by the poverty of i.   HUME 184:8
indivisible freedom is an i. word   WILL 389:5
    peace is i.   LITV 228:6
indomitable Still the i. Irishry   YEATS 396:3
industrial i. strategy   BENN 36:5
    known as the I. Revelation   SELL 323:9
Industrial Revolution in the I.   ROB 307:2
industry greatest river of human i.   TOCQ 365:2
    helping i.   POW 297:2
    owes you, not his i. only   BURKE 63:8
    unless i. is to be paralysed   TAWN 355:12
    war is the national i. of Prussia   MIR 261:6
ineffectual i. liberal's problem   FRAYN 143:1
inefficiencies inherent i.   GALB 145:3
inequality happier in a state of i.   JOHN 198:13
inevitability i. of gradualness   WEBB 381:4
inevitable war regarded as i.   KENN 203:6
inexactitude terminological i.   CHUR 87:4
infamous rich, quiet, and i.   MAC 238:7
infamy date which will live in i.   ROOS 310:1
infancy like men, have their i.   BOL 50:8
infants nuclear giants and ethical i.   BRAD 54:5
infection i. and the hand of war   SHAK 333:4
inferior disgraced by the i.   SHAW 336:10
    make you feel i.   ROOS 308:3
inferiority acknowledgement of i.   CALH 72:4
inferiors English want i.   TOCQ 365:1
    governed by your i.   PLATO 294:3
infidelity i. does not consist   PAINE 283:5
inflation as a way to abate i.   JOS 200:2
    Having a little i. is like   HEND 174:7
    I. in the Sixties   LEVIN 222:7
    one place where i. is made   FRI 143:9

influence i. of the Crown   DUNN 127:1
    odium, under the name of i.   BURKE 63:1
    power instead of i.   TAYL 357:9
    public opinion is a permeating i.   BAG 24:1
inform not to i. the reader   ACH 1:7
information war-time Minister of i.   COCK 100:9
ingeminate i. the word *Peace*   CLAR 96:3
inhale I didn't i.   CLIN 99:5
    if he doesn't i.   STEV 349:7
inherent i. efficiencies of freedom   GALB 145:3
inherited Indians—they i.   PEEL 288:5
iniquity loved justice and hated i.   GREG 161:3
initiative i. and imagination   GALB 145:5
injuries against the i.   LOCKE 231:5
    take revenge for slight i.   MACH 241:2
injustice I. anywhere is a threat   KING 210:7
    i. done to an individual   JUN 201:1
    I., poverty, slavery   BERL 39:4
    I. was as common as streetcars   REUT 303:5
    man's inclination to i.   NIEB 272:10
    protect him against i.   PALM 284:2
    rapine and i.   SMITH 341:2
innocence ceremony of i.   YEATS 395:6
    other German could claim i.   TAYL 357:5
innocent Millions of i. men   JEFF 191:2
    sweat of the i.   JACK 189:6
    We are i.   ROS 313:1
innovate To i. is not to reform   BURKE 68:4
innovation In well-framed politics, i.   BAG 27:7
    totalitarian i.   O'BR 276:5
inns i. should be well kept   PALM 284:4
inoperative statements are i.   ZIEG 397:3
inquisition little less than an i.   HAL 166:6
insane hereditary monarch was i.   BAG 27:1
inseparable one and i.   WEBS 382:3
inside i. the tent pissing out   JOHN 196:9
insignificance And of the utmost i.   CURZ 108:4
insignificant most i. office   ADAMS 4:1
insincerity depths of i.   ANON 13:10
    enemy of clear language is i.   ORW 279:10
insistence i. of some liberals   HAYEK 171:5
insolence i. is not invective   DISR 118:16
insoluble political ones are i.   HOME 182:4
instability mark of i.   GALB 145:8
instantaneous i. courage   NAP 269:10
institution Any i. which does not   ROB 306:7
    cannot see an i. without hitting   CRIT 104:5
    destroy any established i.   BURKE 65:7
institutions acquiring their i.   HAIL 163:12
    British i.   MAND 249:3
    great i. which they have created   BAG 27:12
    immobility of British i.   ASQ 18:4
    I. govern relationships   MONN 263:1
    in the power of human i.   SEN 323:12
    It is the same with i.   JOUB 200:6
    nations begin by forming their i.   HAIL 163:11
    Only i. grow wiser   MONN 262:10

public i.   SMITH 343:1
    Tory is someone who thinks i.   POW 297:10
instructions operating i.   O'RO 277:4
instrument state is an i.   STAL 348:3
instruments work by such i.   PEEL 289:4
insular i. both in situation   BAG 26:11
    i. country, subject to fogs   DISR 120:15
insurance National compulsory i.   CHUR 91:12
insurrection success of an armed i.   ZIN 397:4
insurrectional right of i. violence   ROM 308:2
integration not fighting for i.   MALC 248:8
intellect burglar of others' i.   DISR 118:13
    i. of an advocate   BAG 24:5
    no hindrance to subtlety of i.   MORL 266:2
    originality, not of i.   WEBB 381:2
    second-class i.   HOLM 181:8
    suffering from halitosis of the i.   ICKES 187:1
intellects highest i.   MAC 238:2
intellectual act of i. resistance   O'BR 276:5
    i. commentators   THAT 360:11
    means of i. excitement   BAG 24:3
    moral or i. damage   KRUG 215:6
intellectuals themselves as i.   AGNEW 6:6
    treachery of the i.   BENDA 35:6
intelligence i. of the great masses   MENC 256:11
    personality with so little i.   JENK 194:2
intelligent Every i. voter   ADAMS 2:4
    i. are full of doubt   RUSS 316:12
    i. are to the intelligentsia   BALD 30:2
intelligentsia intelligent are to the i.   BALD 30:2
intelligible it is an i. government   BAG 25:5
intensity full of passionate i.   YEATS 395:6
intent prick the sides of my i.   SHAK 331:8
intention i. to keep my counsel   GLAD 155:6
intentions if he'd only had good i.   THAT 362:1
    i. of a government   GALB 145:13
    their good i.   WALP 377:7
interest common i. always will   DRYD 125:10
    common i. produces   PAINE 282:14
    from its duty and its i.   WASH 379:12
    I., not sentiment, directs them   CHES 83:11
    it's i. that keeps peace   CROM 105:10
    natural i. of money   MAC 237:9
    their regard to their own i.   SMITH 341:4
interested not i. too much   BAR 32:8
interests common i. of capital and labour
                                                      ATK 19:6
    consult the i.   PEEL 288:6
    men who have i. aside from   LINC 224:2
    Our i. are eternal and perpetual   PALM 284:1
interfered i. in behalf of the rich   BROWN 59:1
    i. too much with other   MELB 255:7
interfering i. with the liberty   MILL 258:8
internal destroyed by an i. vice   MONT 264:6
international dependable i. emotion   ALSOP 7:5
interpreted only i. the world   MARX 252:3

interpreters class who may be i.   MAC 236:11
interrèd oft i. with their bones   SHAK 329:13
intervene i. to help British   HES 178:4
intervention effect of state i.   DICEY 114:7
interviews result of i., promises   TAYL 358:2
intimacy you should avoid any i.   KITC 214:15
intimidating Minister should be i.   THAT 362:14
intoxicated once i. with power   BURKE 67:14
intrusion governmental i.   BREN 56:1
invasion i. by an idea   HUGO 184:5
invective insolence is not i.   DISR 118:16
invention [bureaucracy's] specific i.
                                             WEBER 381:11
   since the i. of gunpowder   MONT 263:10
inverse in i. proportion   HAIL 163:4
inverted i. the laws of nature   SMITH 345:1
   There they sit, like i. Micawbers   GUED 162:5
investigation duty of i.   HALD 164:2
invisible i. hand in politics   FRI 144:1
   led by an i. hand   SMITH 342:4
invitations don't accept our i.   KHR 209:3
involuntary It was i.   KENN 205:11
Iranian I. moderate is one who   KISS 214:9
Ireland How's poor ould I.   ANON 10:11
   I. is not a geographical   PARN 286:5
   I.! that cloud in the west   GLAD 154:1
   I. unfree shall never be   PEAR 287:3
   keeps I. bound to England   PARN 286:7
   many parties in I. who desire   PEEL 289:5
   My mission is to pacify I.   GLAD 154:7
   name of I. is mentioned   SMITH 344:6
   no appetite for truth in I.   PEEL 288:1
   One prayer absorbs all others: I.   GLAD 155:8
   Out of I. have we come   YEATS 396:2
   romantic I.'s dead and gone   YEATS 395:4
   We are bound to lose I.   GLAD 156:1
   with which it is now handling I.   WEST 385:7
Irish answer to the I. Question   SELL 323:10
   now the I. are ashamed   MARV 251:8
   That is the I. Question   DISR 117:13
Irishman I. has no sense of   PEEL 289:8
   I.'s heart is nothing but   SHAW 336:12
Irishry Still the indomitable I.   YEATS 396:3
iron become an i. cage   WEBER 382:1
   i. curtain at its frontier   CRILE 104:3
   i. curtain has descended   CHUR 92:10
   i. has entered into his soul   LLOY 230:15
   i. lady   ANON 11:2
   I. Lady of the Western World   THAT 360:10
   nice smile, but he's got i. teeth   GROM 162:4
   through blood and i.   BISM 47:4
   wood painted to look like i.   BISM 47:2
irrational bondage of i. fears   BRAN 55:1
   extravagant and i.   SWIFT 353:8
irrationality [House of] Lords is its i. CAMP 73:7
   i. of the world   WEBER 381:10

irregular another of those i. verbs   LYNN 235:10
irritated most i. against the party   BAG 27:11
Islam If laws are needed, I.   KHOM 208:9
island floating bulwark of the i.   BLAC 48:7
   honour the people of this i.   CHUR 89:2
   never make this i.   WALL 377:1
   This i. is made mainly of coal   BEVAN 40:5
   twice in our rough i.-story   TENN 360:3
isle this sceptered i.   SHAK 333:4
isms All the 'i. are wasms   ANON 8:5
isolationist find an i.   RUSK 315:3
Israel glory is departed from I.   BIBLE 43:10
   there is a prophet in I.   BIBLE 43:12
issue It *is* a moral i.   HALEY 164:7
   one i. at a time   MACM 244:10
Italy I. is a geographical expression   METT 257:7

Jack J. became a gentleman   SHAK 334:10
Jacksonian J. vulgarity   POTT 296:4
jail would be in j.   TRUM 372:2
jam j. we thought was   BENN 36:3
   never j. today   CARR 77:2
James why does King J. stay   WHAR 386:3
Jameson raid by Dr J.   KRUG 215:6
janvier Generals J. [January]   NICH 271:5
Japan forces of the Empire of J.   ROOS 310:1
   not necessarily to J.'s advantage   HIR 179:1
Japanese reconcile J. action   CHUR 91:3
jaw-jaw To j. is always better   CHUR 94:2
jaws j. of power are always opened   ADAMS 3:3
jeers gibes and flouts and j.   DISR 120:5
Jefferson Thomas—J.   ADAMS 4:4
   when Thomas J. ate alone   KENN 205:1
Jeffersonian J. simplicity   POTT 296:4
jellybeans his way of eating j.   REAG 301:10
Jena battle of J.   ANON 10:3
   J. came twenty years after   BISM 47:6
Jerusalem And was J. builded here   BLAKE 49:5
   Till we have built J.   BLAKE 49:6
jests to his memory for his j.   SHER 338:13
Jesus *bon Sansculotte* J.   DESM 114:4
   thinks he is J. Christ   CLEM 98:5
Jew am a J. of Tarsus   BIBLE 44:11
   especially a J.   MAL 248:6
   old J.! That is the man   BISM 47:3
jewel Common Law may be a j.   GRAY 160:6
Jewish home for the J. people   BALF 30:6
   total solution of the J. question   GOER 156:7
Jews When Hitler attacked the J.   NIEM 273:1
jingo But be a little j. if you can   CHAM 80:2
job MI5 is a j. creation scheme   HENN 174:8
   MP is the sort of j.   ABB 1:1
   politician who has lost his j.   MENC 257:1
   really get on with the j.   DALT 109:3
   we will finish the j.   CHUR 91:6

jog as a man *might j. on with* — LAMB 216:7
joint time is out of j. — SHAK 325:7
joints know the j. — BUTL 70:5
jokes civil servant doesn't make j. — ION 188:3
I don't know j. — ROG 307:9
Josephine Not tonight, J. — NAP 270:3
journalism why j. — BALF 30:9
journalist British j. — WOLFE 393:4
journalists j. dabbling their fingers — MCGR 241:1
journey companions of our j. — CHUR 90:11
I have a long j. to take — RAL 300:7
I now begin the j. — REAG 302:8
joy politics of j. — HUMP 185:5
strength through j. — LEY 223:4
Judas true legend—that of J. — STAL 348:6
judge j. is a member — BOK 50:5
J. not, that ye be not judged — BIBLE 44:4
Justly to j. — BRO 57:7
nor the j.'s robe — SHAK 332:7
judged not be j. by the colour — KING 210:10
judgement j. is a mere lottery — DRYD 125:1
j. which is needed — ATTL 20:14
lawful j. of his peers — MAGN 247:3
Nor is the people's j. — DRYD 125:11
not his industry only, but his j. — BURKE 63:8
right functioning of a man's j. — SAL 318:11
sit in j. upon any other nation — WILS 392:3
your j. — MANS 250:1
judges independence of j. — DENN 113:7
judicial j. power — ADAMS 3:12
jump what Trojan 'orses will j. out — BEVIN 43:5
jumps which way the cat j. — THAT 361:14
jungle air-conditioned j. — KINN 211:8
law of the j. — KIPL 212:9
juridical destroy the j. safeguards — HAYEK 171:9
jurisdiction Rome hath no j. — BOOK 51:7
jury j., passing on the prisoner's — SHAK 332:6
just be j., and fear not — SHAK 327:7
I reflect that God is j. — JEFF 191:3
j. and unjust masterships — RUSK 315:10
j. cause reaches its flood-tide — CATT 78:7
'j.' or 'right' means nothing — PLATO 294:2
land of j. and old renown — TENN 359:8
my friend, faithful and j. to me — SHAK 330:1
this may not be a j. peace — IZET 188:5
true place for a j. man — THOR 364:2
justice administration of j. — SMITH 341:1
And liberty plucks j. by the nose — SHAK 332:4
call for j. — MORE 265:6
deny, or delay, right or j. — MAGN 247:4
furtherance of the ends of j. — BROWN 59:3
humanity, reason, and j. — BURKE 64:5
human j. is ever lagging — GLAD 154:10
I have never obstructed j. — NIXON 274:10
J. is in one scale — JEFF 193:9
J. is truth in action — DISR 118:14
j. should not only be done — HEW 178:5

kings the sword of j. — DEFOE 111:11
let j. be done, though the world — FERD 136:4
loved j. and hated iniquity — GREG 161:3
Man's capacity for j. — NIEB 272:10
more devoted to order than to j. — KING 210:8
not equality or fairness or j. — BERL 39:1
of moral good and of j. — JOHN 195:3
threat to j. everywhere — KING 210:7
what you think j. requires — MANS 250:1
justifiable perfectly j. — BURKE 65:12
justification j. of America's — KISS 214:12
justified No man is j. in doing evil — ROOS 312:3
justitia *fiat j. et pereat mundus* — FERD 136:4

Kaiser put the kibosh on the K. — ELL 132:10
kebabbed not going to be bloody k. — KINN 212:5
keener But with his k. eye — MARV 251:7
keep If you can k. your head — KIPL 213:3
intention to k. my counsel — GLAD 155:6
keeping k. the secret — TAYL 358:8
Kennedy senator, you're no Jack K. — BENT 38:3
kettle back to the tea-k. — DISR 118:1
This is a pretty k. of fish — MARY 253:5
key emperor holds the k. — CUST 108:6
in possession of the k. — PAINE 280:8
k. of India is London — DISR 121:2
take the k. of the Union — CLAY 97:9
keyholes screaming through the k. — LLOY 229:11
keystone king is the k. — STR 352:3
kibosh put the k. on the Kaiser — ELL 132:10
kick k. 'em the next — KIPL 214:1
k. them in the teeth — BEVAN 41:11
won't have Nixon to k. around — NIXON 274:2
kicked k. up stairs — HAL 165:1
no body to be k. — THUR 364:9
kicking kissing and k. people — TRUM 371:5
kid comeback k. — CLIN 99:6
kids k. love that dog — NIXON 273:7
LBJ, LBJ, how many k. — ANON 11:11
kill But they will k. thee — PHOC 292:5
did nothing at all but k. animals — NIC 272:7
doctrine is something you k. for — BENN 36:10
let's k. all the lawyers — SHAK 327:1
until men are prepared to k. — SHAW 336:14
you must k. him — EMER 133:5
killed don't mind your being k. — KITC 215:1
kids have you k. today — ANON 11:11
like to have been k. in the war — POW 297:11
killing assert their manhood by k. — WAUGH 380:8
k. no murder briefly discourst — SEXBY 324:2
kindly KCMG ('K. Call Me God') — SAMP 319:9
king And when I am k. — SHAK 327:1
as I have served the K. — WOLS 394:3
As to the K., the laws of the land — CHAR 82:6
authority forgets a dying k. — TENN 360:4
authority of a K. is the keystone — STR 352:3

away my life to make you K.   CHAR 83:3
beat the K. ninety-nine times   MANC 249:1
benefit of the K.'s Coronation   BLUNT 49:7
blind, despised, and dying k.   SHEL 338:1
blind the one-eyed man is k.   ERAS 133:10
Cotton is K.   CHR 86:1
cuts off his k.'s head   SHAW 335:13
Did the K. sigh   SHAK 325:13
Every subject's duty is the k.'s   SHAK 326:14
For your K. and your Country   RUB 314:8
God bless the K.   BYROM 70:10
God save the k.   HOGG 181:2
government without a k.   BANC 31:11
great and mighty k.   ROCH 307:5
heart and stomach of a k.   ELIZ 130:9
If the K. asks you   ATTL 19:9
I served my k.   SHAK 327:8
I think the k. is but a man   SHAK 326:12
it is impossible for the K.   PEPYS 290:2
k. can do no wrong   BLAC 48:8
k. delighteth to honour   BIBLE 43:13
k. is a thing men have made   SELD 323:2
k. is truly *parens patriae*   JAM 189:10
k. may make a nobleman   BURKE 67:17
k. never dies   BLAC 48:6
K., observing with judicious eyes   TRAPP 367:6
K. of England cannot enter   PITT 292:9
K. of Great Britain is not   REED 302:10
K. over the Water   ANON 11:6
K., refused a lesser sacrifice   MARY 253:7
k. reigns, and the people govern   THI 363:2
K.'s life is moving peacefully   DAWS 110:5
K.'s Moll   ANON 11:7
k.'s name twenty thousand names   SHAK 333:7
K. to Oxford sent a troop   BROW 59:6
K. will get away with it   CHAN 81:5
K. will never leave   ELIZ 132:9
last K. of England   EDW 128:3
last k. to be strangled   MESL 257:6
lessened my esteem of a k.   PEPYS 290:1
loses the k. in the tyrant   MAYH 255:1
material for a constitutional k.   BAG 26:2
More of a royalist than the k.   ANON 13:3
Mrs Simpson's pinched our k.   ANON 10:5
my griefs; still am I k. of those   SHAK 334:4
neck of the last k.   DID 116:1
No bishop, no K.   JAM 189:9
no circumstances fight for its K.   GRAH 158:6
Northcliffe has sent for the K.   ANON 10:6
not so much a k. as a Monarch   SELL 323:7
our sins lay on the k.   SHAK 326:15
sang a k. out of three kingdoms   WHAR 386:4
substitute shines brightly as a k.   SHAK 332:11
such divinity doth hedge a k.   SHAK 326:4
These five kings did a k. to death   THOM 363:3
Till the K. enjoys his own again   PARK 285:4
To my true k. I offered   MAC 238:9

What is a K.?—a man   PRIOR 298:4
What must the k. do now   SHAK 334:2
whatsoever K. shall reign   ANON 10:12
when thy k. is a child   BIBLE 43:17
When you strike at a k.   EMER 133:5
you must not be a k., so long as   CHAR 82:5
Your K. and Country need you   FIELD 136:5
kingdom but to mock the k.   PYM 298:6
k. against it.   BIBLE 44:9
that of a great k.   SMITH 342:6
they become aliens to this k.   GEOR 149:4
voice of the k.   SWIFT 353:5
kingdoms king out of three k.   WHAR 386:4
kingfish can just call me the K.   LONG 232:3
kingly K. conclaves stern and cold   SHEL 338:5
kings captains and the k. depart   KIPL 212:11
commonwealths and ruin k.   DRYD 125:3
divine right of K. to fall   MACM 244:4
folly of hereditary right in k.   PAINE 281:2
good of subjects is the end of k.   DEFOE 111:11
heart's ease Must k. neglect   SHAK 326:16
heroic k. governed   BAG 25:7
k. and ministers   SMITH 341:7
k. are not only God's lieutenants   JAM 189:11
K. will be tyrants from policy   BURKE 67:2
laws or k. can cause   GOLD 157:5
laws or k. can cause   JOHN 197:7
people keep even k. in awe   D'AV 110:1
punctuality is the politeness of k.   LOU 233:4
setter up and puller down of k.   SHAK 327:4
stories of the death of k.   SHAK 333:8
there will be only five K. left   FAR 135:6
Through talk, we tamed k.   BENN 36:8
with a heavier hand than k.   FRAN 142:1
kiss cheer you, thank you, k. you   RUB 314:8
gave him the k. of death   SMITH 343:4
k. 'em one day and kick 'em   KIPL 214:1
k. my ass in Macy's   JOHN 196:8
London will be wanting to k.   MACD 240:6
kitchen get out of the k.   VAUG 373:4
Kitchener K. is a great poster   ASQ 18:10
Klondike beer of a man in K.   CHES 84:5
knave coined an epithet for a k.   MAC 237:5
in life a foolish prating k.   SHAK 325:10
man must be supposed a k.   HUME 185:2
To feed the titled k.   BURNS 68:13
Wherever a k. is not punished   HAL 166:11
knavery k. seems to be so much   GEOR 149:4
knaves grudge at k. in place   DEFOE 111:5
knees first fell upon their own k.   EVAR 134:3
live on our k.   ROOS 309:12
live on your k.   IBAR 186:6
knell k. of the Union   JEFF 193:7
knife He who wields the k.   HES 177:9
keep the k. in his hand   MACH 241:8
knight earl and a k. of the garter   ATTL 20:9

knights invincible k. of old WORD 394:5
knives night of the long k. HITL 179:4
knot political k. BIER 44:15
know do not k. what they have said CHUR 87:5
find out what you don't k. WELL 384:10
How do they k. PARK 285:3
It is better to k. nothing BILL 45:5
learnt to k. and honour CHUR 89:2
no one to k. what it is ANON 9:8
that which you yourselves do k. SHAK 330:9
what did the President k. ANON 14:12
knowledge envied kind of k. ADAMS 3:4
k. itself is power BACON 22:1
k. of everything but power HER 177:4
k. of the possible BEVAN 40:11
such a k., in its ultimate GLAD 156:3
sum of human k. REED 302:11
known safer than a k. way HASK 170:2
knows He k. nothing SHAW 336:13

label l. on the can of worms CRIT 104:8
labels l. on empty luggage BEVAN 41:7
laborious assiduity of a very l. one BAG 27:8
labour common interests of capital and l.
ATK 19:6
ever done to the L. Party TAWN 356:4
Fair shares for all, is L.'s call JAY 190:5
I did not enter the L. Party BENN 36:9
it is to live without l. TAWN 355:11
kind of leader for the L. Party BEVAN 41:5
L. council hiring taxis KINN 211:11
L. disgraces no man GRANT 160:4
L. isn't working ANON 11:8
[L. is] the natural party of WILS 390:10
L. is the party of law BLAIR 48:11
L. Party is going around stirring WHIT 387:6
L. Party owes more to Methodism PHIL 291:7
l. spread her wholesome store GOLD 157:6
leader of the L. party KINN 212:4
never visualised L. as separate WEBB 381:3
of the L. Party JENK 194:5
parliamentary L. Party DALT 108:9
they've elected a L. Government ANON 9:6
trouble with the L. Party GRIM 162:3
trying to fracture the L. party KINN 212:3
upon the brow of l. BRYAN 60:6
We l. soon, we l. late BURNS 68:13
laboured l. as his extempore WALP 377:6
labourer l. to take his pension RUSK 315:5
labouring l. children can look out CLEG 98:3
labour-intensive monarchy is a l. WILS 391:7
labours wasting the l. of the people JEFF 192:10
laceration l. of their bodies TAWN 355:8
ladder l. called 'the status quo' BENN 37:2
l. to all high designs SHAK 335:8
lowliness is young ambition's l. SHAK 328:10

ladies remember the l. ADAMS 2:1
lady in a l.'s chamber SHAK 334:9
iron l. ANON 11:2
l.'s not for turning THAT 361:2
l.'s pocket handkerchief LLOY 230:2
Said our L. of the Snows KIPL 213:1
Lafayette L., we are here STAN 348:8
lagging justice is ever l. after GLAD 154:10
laisser faire l. ARG 16:1
l. tous les acheteurs QUES 299:2
laissez-faire l. and noblesse oblige HES 178:3
principle of l. HAYEK 171:5
lamb skin of an innocent l. SHAK 327:2
lamentable dark, l. catalogue CHUR 90:6
laments forest l. in order that CHUR 86:4
lamp carrying her l. GRIF 161:7
I lift my l. beside the golden door LAZ 219:7
l. of experience HENRY 176:6
lampposts drunken man uses l. LANG 217:6
lamps l. are going out GREY 161:5
Lancashire L. merchants CHES 84:11
land abroad throughout the l. BRIG 56:4
empire of the l. RICH 305:3
ill fares the l. GOLD 157:6
It is l. reclamation WILS 391:4
l. for the people ANON 11:10
L. of Hope and Glory BENS 37:6
l. that I love BERL 38:6
l. where my fathers died SMITH 344:5
more precious than a piece of l. SADAT 317:4
new people takes the l. CHES 84:8
O'er the l. of the free KEY 207:1
splendid and a happy l. GOLD 157:7
This l. of such dear souls SHAK 333:4
woe to the l. that's governed SHAK 335:1
landing l. was made EIS 129:3
we shall fight on the l. grounds CHUR 90:7
landlord paid to the l. for the use RIC 304:4
though he were a feudal l. ATTL 19:7
lands envy of less happier l. SHAK 333:4
l. produce less by reason of MONT 265:1
Then l. were fairly portioned MAC 237:1
landslide going to pay for a l. KENN 203:8
Lang How L., O Lord BULL 61:5
language By that dear l. MAC 238:10
divided by a common l. SHAW 337:3
enemy of clear l. is insincerity ORW 279:10
He mobilized the English l. MURR 268:5
l. of priorities is the religion BEVAN 40:7
of course, l. WILDE 388:7
political l. . . . is designed ORW 279:11
riot is the l. of the unheard KING 211:3
Under the tropic is our l. spoke WALL 377:3
Lansbury conscience like L. BEVIN 42:7
lanterns show two l. REV 303:7
larger children of a l. growth CHES 83:10

lascivious l. pleasing of a lute   SHAK 334:9
lash blood drawn with the l.   LINC 226:9
   rum, sodomy, prayers, and the l.   CHUR 93:7
lass It came with a l.   JAM 190:3
last God's infinite mercy, a l. resort   O'RO 277:2
   I don't want the l. headline   HES 178:1
   l. article of my creed   GAND 147:3
   l. chance saloon   MELL 256:7
   l. great Englishman is low   TENN 359:9
   l. King of England   EDW 128:3
   l. thing I shall do   PALM 284:9
   like girls and roses: they l.   DE G 112:13
   marks of the l. person   HAIG 163:1
   people with one in the l. ditch   MACL 242:9
   today is the l. day of an era past   YELT 396:4
lasts democracy never l. long   ADAMS 4:2
late offering even that too l.   NEV 271:2
lath l. of wood painted to look   BISM 47:2
lathe could not tell a l. from   JOS 200:1
Latin learn L. as an honour   CHUR 88:12
laugh far too badly hurt to l.   LINC 225:10
laughable very l. things   JOHN 197:10
laughed honest man is l. at   HAL 166:11
   l. at in the second   NAP 269:6
   When he l., respectable senators   AUDEN 21:5
laurels l. to paeans   CIC 95:7
   Northern l. do not change   LEE 220:1
   Thy banished peace, thy l. torn   SMOL 345:3
   Whether in chains or in l.   PHIL 292:3
law books of l.   JOHN 195:8
   common l. is at a disadvantage   SCAR 321:5
   custom, that unwritten l.   D'AV 110:1
   dead-level of l. and order   TAWN 355:9
   destroy all respect for the l.   CHUR 94:14
   doctrine of liberty under the l.   HAIL 163:7
   enforce a l. not supported   HUMP 185:3
   entitled to protection by l.   JACK 189:1
   Every l. is contrary to liberty   BENT 37:10
   fig for those by l. protected   BURNS 68:11
   first is l., the last prerogative   DRYD 125:15
   For where no l. is   BIBLE 44:13
   good of the people is the chief l.   CIC 95:6
   government above the l.   SCAR 321:3
   had people not defied the l.   SCAR 320:7
   ignorance of the l. excuses no   SELD 323:1
   In civilized life, l. floats in a sea   WARR 379:1
   it is not a l. at all   ROB 306:6
   Labour is the party of l. and order   BLAIR 48:11
   l. is above you   DENN 113:6
   l. is above you   FULL 144:6
   l. is to be to restraint   MILT 260:7
   L. is whatever is boldly asserted   BURR 69:1
   L.: It has honoured us   WEBS 382:11
   l. of motion of modern society   MARX 252:8
   l. of the Medes and Persians   BIBLE 43:20
   l.'s delay   SHAK 325:8
   majestic equality of the l.   FRAN 141:2

   make a scarecrow of the l.   SHAK 332:5
   necessity hath no l.   CROM 105:11
   No man is above the l.   ROOS 311:7
   Now this is the L. of the Jungle   KIPL 212:9
   on the silence of the l.   HOBB 180:5
   People crushed by l.   BURKE 65:3
   prevail, of a common l.   JEFF 192:2
   provision in its organic l.   LINC 225:6
   right...is the child of l.   BENT 37:7
   rule of l. in England   DENN 113:7
   severity of the criminal l.   PEEL 287:9
   strict observance of the written l.   JEFF 193:2
   There's a lot of l.   WHAL 386:2
   this is the royal L.   COR 103:10
lawful instituted by 'l. authority'   MACD 240:4
lawn Get your tanks off my l.   WILS 391:1
   tell a lathe from a l. mower   JOS 200:1
laws arranges l.   MACH 241:10
   arts, of warfare, and of l.   DU B 126:4
   bad l. are the worst sort   BURKE 65:4
   best use of l. is to teach men   PHIL 291:9
   can be made so by l.   BOL 50:6
   Christianity is part of the l.   HALE 164:5
   construe the constitution or l.   LINC 225:6
   country's planted thick with l.   BOLT 51:3
   do everything the l. permit   MONT 264:8
   Do not taint pure l. with mere   AESC 6:2
   folly of human l.   SMITH 343:3
   government of l., and not of men   ADAMS 3:7
   If l. are needed, Islam   KHOM 208:9
   If l. are their enemies   BURKE 65:3
   If the l. could speak for themselves   HAL 166:1
   l. and learning die   MANN 249:5
   L. and systems of polity   MILL 259:9
   L. are generally found to be   SHEN 338:9
   L. are like cobwebs   SWIFT 353:4
   L. are silent in time of war   CIC 95:12
   L. grind the poor   GOLD 157:4
   L., like houses, lean on   BURKE 62:5
   l. of God will be suspended   SHAW 336:18
   l. of morality   BURKE 65:11
   l. of most countries   MILL 259:11
   l. of necessity, of self-preservation   JEFF 193:2
   l. of the land   CHAR 82:6
   L. were made to be broken   NORTH 275:4
   makers, and their l. approve   DRYD 126:1
   make the l. of a nation   FLET 137:8
   more numerous the l.   TAC 354:6
   neither the l. made   JOHN 195:1
   not a government of l.   WEBS 382:8
   nothing to do with the l.   HORS 183:4
   passing l. which cannot   EINS 128:7
   rather than obey the l.   TOCQ 366:3
   repeal of bad or obnoxious l.   GRANT 160:2
   That part which l. or kings   GOLD 157:5
   That part which l. or kings   JOHN 197:7
   Written l. are like spider's webs   ANAC 8:3

lawyer l. tells me I *may* do | BURKE 64:5
lawyers complain of the l. | HAL 166:1
  let's kill all the l. | SHAK 327:1
  one hundred and fifty l. | JEFF 193:10
lay that he l. down his friends | THOR 364:7
lazy His l., long, lascivious reign | DEFOE 111:8
lead easy to l., but difficult to drive | BRO 58:2
  evening l. | CHUR 89:9
leader Ah well! I am their l. | LEDR 219:8
  fanatic is a great l. | BROUN 58:3
  final test of a l. | LIPP 228:3
  great and wonderful l. | LLOY 230:8
  importance of a plebeian l. | DISR 118:18
  l. of the Labour party | KINN 212:4
  make a great l. | MONC 261:11
  one realm, one people, one l. | ANON 9:11
  Over the face of the l. | WHIT 388:5
  people may require a l. | PLATO 294:4
  political l. must keep looking | BAR 32:9
  right kind of l. for the Labour Party | BEVAN 41:5
leaders not the l. of a revolution | CONR 102:4
  up more to the political l. | HEAD 172:4
leadership crisis in American l. | BALT 31:9
  l. is not about being nice | KEAT 203:2
  l. is saying no, not yes | BLAIR 48:12
  very essence of successful l. | REAG 302:7
leak confidential briefings; you l. | LYNN 235:10
  they all l. the fact | LYNN 235:9
leaking l. is what you do | CALL 72:6
lean laws, like houses, l. on | BURKE 62:5
  l. and hungry look | SHAK 328:7
  l. and tight-lipped | JOS 199:7
leap must l. into the ocean | HUME 184:9
learned governments have never l. | HEGEL 173:12
learning in the middle age of a state, l. | BACON 23:7
  liberty without l. | KENN 205:3
  not l. from our history | BLAIR 49:2
  of light, of liberty, and of l. | DISR 120:2
  that loyal body wanted l. | TRAPP 367:6
learnt They have l. nothing | TALL 354:11
least l. government was the best | FEIN 136:3
  line of l. resistance | AMERY 7:6
  man who promises l. | BAR 32:7
leave couldn't l. without the King | ELIZ 132:9
  right to l. any country | ANON 9:13
  wiser to l. five minutes too soon | BIFF 45:2
leaving Became him like the l. it | SHAK 331:6
left l. out he would be dangerous | MELB 255:6
  l. to the politicians | DE G 112:9
  My position was on the l. | MOSL 267:2
leg like pissing down your l. | JOHN 196:12
legacies l. of empire | SAMP 319:11
legacy l. from a rich relative | SMITH 344:1

legal fact into a l. right | MILL 259:9
legality suffer from any taint of l. | KNOX 215:2
legalize l. it and it splits | BAG 24:8
legally accomplishing small things l. | BALZ 31:10
legend true l.—that of Judas | STAL 348:6
legions Varus, give me back my l. | AUG 21:7
legislation morals and l. | BENT 37:9
  There is a mania in l. | POW 297:4
legislative distinct from both the l. | ADAMS 3:12
  l. power is nominated | GIBB 151:4
  when l. power is more corrupt | MONT 264:12
legislator people is the true l. | BURKE 62:4
legislators idea of hereditary l. | PAINE 282:8
legislature l. is in session | ANON 12:10
legitimacy l. and equilibrium | KISS 214:13
legitimate l. powers of government | JEFF 193:13
legs dog's walking on his hinder l. | JOHN 197:9
  four legs good, two l. bad | ORW 278:10
  not for your bad l. | ELIZ 131:3
  walk under his huge l., and peep | SHAK 328:4
leisure increased l. | DISR 119:20
  politicians also have no l. | ARIS 16:4
  survey of conspicuous l. | VEBL 373:6
lemon as a l. is squeezed | GEDD 148:7
lend l. me your ears | SHAK 329:13
Lend-Lease assistance called L. | CHUR 92:5
Lenin L. was right | KEYN 207:5
  teaching of Marx, Engels and L. | KHR 209:1
leper here as a parliamentary l. | WILS 390:7
lesser refused a l. sacrifice | MARY 253:7
lest l. we forget | KIPL 212:11
let L. justice be done | FERD 136:4
  L. my people go | BIBLE 43:7
  L. the word go forth | KENN 204:2
letter ability to write a good l. | MACM 245:13
  huge wordy l. came from Capri | JUV 201:7
letters No arts; no l. | HOBB 180:2
level Those who attempt to l. | BURKE 66:11
levellers l. wish to level *down* | JOHN 197:8
levelling cannot bear l. *up* | JOHN 197:8
levers I shan't be pulling the l. | THAT 362:11
Leviathan that great L. | HOBB 179:9
levity I sank by my l. | SMITH 345:1
lex *salus populi suprema est l.* | CIC 95:6
  salus populi suprema l. esto | SELD 323:3
liar easy virtue and a proved l. | HAIL 163:5
  known l. should be outlawed | HAL 165:6
liars l. ought to have good | SIDN 340:1
liberal between l. concessions | BOOK 52:1
  first L. leader for over half | STEEL 348:10
  head of European l. principles | CLAY 97:4
  ineffectual l.'s problem | FRAYN 143:1
  Is either a little L. | GILB 152:6
  'L.' and 'Conservative' | RUSK 315:12
  l., emphasizing the civil | MORSE 266:7
  L. is a man who uses | ROOS 309:7
  L. party takes the rudder | BISM 47:7

L., who wishes to replace them	BIER 44:16	L. means responsibility	SHAW 336:8
particular L. Party	HERB 176:10	l. of the individual	MILL 259:2
so much harm to the l. cause	HAYEK 171:5	l. of their inhabitants	MONT 265:1
liberals l. and conservatives	MOYN 267:5	l. of the press	JUN 201:3
l. offer a mixture	MACM 245:3	l. plucks justice by the nose	SHAK 332:4
liberate l. this country	MAND 249:4	L.'s a glorious feast	BURNS 68:11
liberation l. of the human mind	GOLD 157:2	L.'s in every blow	BURNS 68:12
no organization with 'l.'	LEVIN 222:13	L. to be saucy	HAL 166:8
libertas *imperium et l.*	DISR 120:13	l. to man is eternal vigilance	CURR 107:4
Liberté *L.! Égalité! Fraternité*	ANON 11:13	L. too must be limited	BURKE 65:1
liberties L. . . . depend on silence	HOBB 180:5	L., when it begins to take	WASH 380:1
l. of its people	LINC 226:7	L. without learning	KENN 205:3
not to have l. in truth	PYM 298:6	light, of l., and of learning	DISR 120:2
O freedom, what l. are taken	GEOR 150:9	loudest yelps for l.	JOHN 198:9
people never give up their l.	BURKE 65:10	manly, moral, regulated l.	BURKE 66:6
liberty abstract l.	BURKE 63:9	men wrangle in behalf of l.	HAL 166:3
all cry 'peace, freedom, and l.!'	SHAK 329:7	new nation, conceived in l.	LINC 226:3
bulwark of continuing l.	ROOS 309:5	Next to the right of l.	TAFT 354:10
cost of l. is less than the price	DU B 126:7	Of course l. is not licence	SCAN 320:6
dangers to l. lurk	BRAN 55:3	O l.! what crimes	ROL 308:1
desires in l. anything other	TOCQ 367:2	people contend for their l.	HAL 166:7
despotism of l. against tyranny	ROB 306:8	political l. in a citizen	MONT 264:10
despotism to l. in a featherbed	JEFF 191:11	power to endanger the public l.	ADAMS 3:5
distinction between l. and slavery	CAMD 73:5	priests have been enemies of l.	HUME 185:1
divests himself of his natural l.	LOCKE 231:8	progress of things is for l. to yield	JEFF 191:8
doctrine of l. under the law	HAIL 163:7	public l.	HENRY 176:8
erecting individual l. as an idol	SAL 318:7	Real l. is neither found	HAM 167:4
Every law is contrary to l.	BENT 37:10	safeguards of l.	FRAN 141:8
extremism in the defence of l.	GOLD 157:8	seek power and to lose l.	BACON 22:10
for heavy taxes; it is l.	MONT 264:15	slogan 'L. or Death' is splendid	WOOL 394:4
give me l., or give me death	HENRY 176:5	survival and the success of l.	KENN 204:2
give up essential l.	FRAN 141:9	Sweet land of l.	SMITH 344:5
history of l.	FRAN 141:6	symptom of constitutional l.	GIBB 151:9
holy name of l. or democracy	GAND 147:5	there can be no public l.	BLAC 48:9
I desire their l. and freedom	CHAR 82:6	They believed l. to be the secret	BRAN 54:10
If none were to have l. but those	HAL 166:9	tree of l. must be refreshed	JEFF 191:7
individual l. is individual power	ADAMS 4:9	valued l. for its own sake	BERL 39:5
interfering with the l. of action	MILL 258:8	wait for l. till they become wise	MAC 237:6
I see the ardour for l. catching	PRICE 298:3	what cannot be sold—l.	GRAT 160:5
Let there be light! said L.	SHEL 338:8	Where L. is not, there is my	PAINE 283:11
l., and the pursuit of happiness	JEFF 191:1	Where l. is, there is my country	OTIS 280:2
l. and the pursuit of happiness	ANON 14:7	Where slavery is, there L. cannot	SUMN 353:1
L. *and* Union, now and forever	WEBS 382:3	**libraries** l. of the House	CHAN 81:6
L. cannot be preserved without	ADAMS 3:4	**library** spend less time in the l.	STR 352:4
l. cannot long exist	BURKE 64:18	**licence** l. to print money	THOM 363:8
L. consists in doing	MILL 259:4	love not freedom, but l.	MILT 260:8
L. does not consist merely of	BRY 60:8	Of course liberty is not l.	SCAN 320:6
l. doesn't even go to the trouble	BALZ 31:10	**lie** dost thou l. so low	SHAK 329:8
L. has never come from	WILS 391:11	fall victim to a big l.	HITL 179:3
L. is always unfinished business	ANON 11:14	honest man sent to l. abroad	WOTT 394:9
L. is l., not equality or fairness	BERL 39:1	In our country the l. has become	SOLZ 346:1
L. is precious	LENIN 221:11	know I can't tell a l.	WASH 379:5
L. is the only thing	WHITE 387:4	misleading impression, not a l.	ARMS 16:12
L. is the right to do	MONT 264:8	obedient to their laws we l.	SIM 340:6
L. is to faction what air	MAD 246:1	Then give them both the l.	RAL 300:4
L. is, to the lowest rank	JOHN 197:6	Whoever would l. usefully	HERV 177:5
L. knows nothing but victories	PHIL 292:3		

lied Therefore I l. to please the mob   KIPL 213:6
lies believing their own l.   ARB 15:8
   History, sir, will tell l. as usual   SHAW 336:1
   It produces l. like sand   ANON 14:13
   l. about the Democrats   STEV 350:1
   l., damned l. and statistics   DISR 121:15
   l. it lives on and propagates   FOSD 139:6
   make l. sound truthful   ORW 279:11
   swallowing their own l.   ARB 15:9
lieutenants God's l. upon earth   JAM 189:11
life After l.'s fitful fever he sleeps   SHAK 332:2
   all the voyage of their l.   SHAK 330:14
   best prize that l. offers   ROOS 311:6
   But all l. is about discrimination   POW 297:4
   doctrine of the strenuous l.   ROOS 310:10
   England will take away my l.   CHAR 83:3
   evidence of l. after death   SOPER 346:7
   heaven daily for your longer l.   ELIZ 131:2
   His l. was gentle   SHAK 330:16
   I gave my l. for freedom   EWER 134:5
   in the distinction of your l.   TAC 354:4
   It is not a L. at all   GLAD 155:12
   Just gave what l. required   GOLD 157:6
   lay down his friends for his l.   THOR 364:7
   l., and liberty, and the pursuit   JEFF 191:1
   l. beyond the grave   KHR 209:8
   l., liberty and the pursuit of   ANON 14:7
   l. of man, solitary, poor   HOBB 180:2
   my whole l., whether it be long   ELIZ 132:4
   nearest thing to death in l.   ANON 12:8
   Nothing in his l.   SHAK 331:6
   one l. to lose for my country   HALE 164:6
   only honour and l.   FRAN 141:4
   priceless gift of l.   ROS 313:1
   right to a dignified l.   JOHN 195:3
   should forfeit my l.   BROWN 59:3
   walk and live a Woolworth l.   NIC 272:3
light creates the l. that makes   TOCQ 366:2
   Give me a l. that I may tread   HASK 170:2
   Let there be l.! said Liberty   SHEL 338:8
   l. has gone   NEHRU 270:8
   l., of liberty, and of learning   DISR 120:2
   pay him tribute for l.   SHAK 325:2
   Put out the l.   ROOS 312:4
   radiate momentary gleams of l.   LLOY 231:1
   shaft of l. cut into the darkness   KENN 205:7
   thousand points of l.   BUSH 69:6
lighthouse great l. which stands   JENK 194:8
lighthouses those revolving l.   LLOY 231:1
lightning He snatched the l. shaft   TURG 372:7
   like writing history with l.   WILS 392:2
   loosed the fateful l.   HOWE 184:3
lights gradual dimming of the l.   NIC 272:4
like I l. Ike   SPAL 347:4
   now she is l. everyone else   DE G 112:6
   People who l. this sort of thing   LINC 227:3
   plotted to make men l.   TREV 368:3

likes privilege of doing as he l.   ARN 17:5
Lilli burlero L. bullen a la   WHAR 386:3
limit l. to our realization   ROOS 310:9
limitation history of the l.   WILS 391:11
limited revelation is necessarily l.   PAINE 283:6
limpet-like l. Prime Ministers   JENK 194:7
Lincoln am a Ford, not a L.   FORD 138:11
   shared the fate of Abraham L.   GRIGG 161:8
line Hit the l. hard   ROOS 311:1
   l. of least resistance   AMERY 7:6
   no party l.   DJIL 122:3
link last l. which keeps Ireland   PARN 286:7
lion better to serve a well-bred l.   VOLT 376:4
   globe that had the l.'s heart   CHUR 94:1
   l. to frighten the wolves   MACH 241:5
   still a living l.   SOLZ 346:3
lips my l. are not yet unsealed   BALD 29:9
   Read my l.: no new taxes   BUSH 69:7
liquid But the Thames is l. history   BURNS 68:9
liquidation l. of the British Empire   CHUR 91:9
list Examine the honours l.   BENN 37:3
   l. of two hundred and five   MCC 239:6
listen l. to their critics   GALB 146:13
literature l.'s always a good card   BENN 37:4
little It has been a splendid l. war   HAY 171:1
   l. local difficulties   MACM 244:8
   Little man, l. man   ELIZ 132:2
   l. woman who wrote the book   LINC 227:4
   makes the l. man so happy   MONC 261:10
   offering Germany too l.   NEV 271:2
   So l. done, so much to do   RHOD 304:3
   texture, as the l. creep through   SHEN 338:9
littleness ruined by the l.   BREC 55:8
live date which will l. in infamy   ROOS 310:1
   he isn't fit to l.   KING 210:9
   He shall not l.   SHAK 330:12
   l. on your knees   IBAR 186:6
   l. together as brothers   KING 211:2
   l. within your means   THAT 361:4
   l. without labour   TAWN 355:11
   make war that we may l. in peace   ARIS 16:3
   rascals, would you l. for ever   FRED 143:2
   sometimes l. apart   SAKI 317:6
   teaching nations how to l.   MILT 260:5
   unable to l. in society   ARIS 16:6
   which enable its citizens to l.   WEIL 383:5
   work and pray, l. on hay   HILL 178:8
lived better if he had never l.   CHUR 92:13
   who has not l. during the years   TALL 355:4
lively l. Oracles of God   COR 103:10
livery apparel them all in one l.   SHAK 327:1
lives All political l.   POW 297:7
   careless talk costs l.   ANON 9:7
   evil that men do l. after them   SHAK 329:13
   live our l. as though Christ   CART 77:5
living between those who are l.   BURKE 67:5
   learning from our history but l. it   BLAIR 49:2

l. to some purpose   PAINE 283:10
Vietnam was lost in the l. rooms   MCL 243:9
Lloyd George [L.] did not seem   BEAV 34:5
L. knew my father   ANON 12:2
[L.] thinks he is Napoleon   CLEM 98:5
L. would have a better rating   GRIGG 161:8
pool for the soul of L.   MASS 254:3
loaves seven halfpenny l. sold   SHAK 327:1
lobby into the l. against us   BALD 29:9
local All politics is l.   O'NE 276:8
little l. difficulties   MACM 244:8
Men enter l. politics solely   PARK 286:2
working of l. government   THAT 362:15
log Give me a l. hut   GARF 147:9
log-cabin From l. to White House THAY 363:1
London L. is a modern Babylon   DISR 118:10
parks are the lungs of L.   PITT 293:6
people of L. with one voice   CHUR 91:5
long How l. a time   SHAK 333:3
In the l. run we are all dead   KEYN 207:6
it hath very l. arms   HAL 166:2
night of the l. knives   HITL 179:4
Too l. a sacrifice   YEATS 395:7
week is a l. time in politics   WILS 390:8
longer heaven daily for your l. life ELIZ 131:2
longest l. running farce   SMITH 343:7
l. suicide note in history   KAUF 202:4
longing cast a l. eye on them   JEFF 191:14
look I l. at the senators   HALE 164:4
l. the East End in the face   ELIZ 132:8
L. to it   LINC 225:9
l. to your Moat   HAL 165:3
someone to l. down on   JOHN 195:6
looking L. for houses, Nye   ATTL 20:2
no use l. beyond   CHAM 80:1
politics is the art of l. for trouble BENN 35:8
looks If it l. like a duck   REUT 303:4
Looney misfits, L. Tunes   REAG 302:1
lord L. *is out walking*   LLOY 230:12
L.'s anointed temple   SHAK 331:9
of the coming of the L.   HOWE 184:3
we battle for the L.   ROOS 311:12
lords admiring the House of L.   BAG 26:4
Admit l., and you admit all   SHAF 324:3
And l. whose parents   DEFOE 111:9
For the l. who lay ye low   SHEL 338:3
hand of new unhappy l.   CHES 84:9
House of L., an illusion   STOP 351:7
House of L. is a perfect eventide   STOC 351:6
[House of] L. is its irrationality   CAMP 73:7
L. do not encourage wit   DISR 116:6
L. is a matter of controversy   STJ 317:5
only a wit among L.   JOHN 197:1
reform the House of L.   DANG 109:4
thither from the House of L.   NORF 275:2
lordships good enough for their l. ANON 13:11

lose be on the right side and l.   GALB 146:1
Better we l. the election   STEV 349:8
I would rather l. her as a friend   GLAD 156:1
meanly l., the last, best hope   LINC 226:1
much to hope and nothing to l.   BURKE 65:3
nothing to l. but our aitches   ORW 278:2
nothing to l. but their chains   MARX 253:4
Oh! we don't want to l. you   RUB 314:8
Or l. our ventures   SHAK 330:14
seek power and to l. liberty   BACON 22:10
take care not to l. wars   CHUR 92:12
We should never l. an occasion   DISR 118:11
loser It is a l. politically   NIXON 274:15
losers no winners, but all are l. CHAM 80:8
losing conduct of a l. party   BURKE 67:13
l. one pleased Cato   LUCAN 234:3
loss l. of a dear friend   SOUT 347:3
l. of power tends to corrupt   RUSK 315:4
losses l. to a nation   CECIL 79:8
lost France has not l. the war   DE G 112:3
Frederick the Great l. the battle   ANON 10:3
Great Britain has l. an empire   ACH 1:5
he always l. it   SMITH 344:2
L. is our old simplicity   ANON 12:3
Next to a battle l.   WELL 385:1
not see your country is l.   WILL 389:3
Vietnam was l.   MCL 243:9
we are l.   PYRR 299:1
lot Their l. forbad   GRAY 160:8
lottery prize in the l. of life   RHOD 304:2
their judgement is a mere l.   DRYD 125:1
louder l. he talked of his honour EMER 133:4
loud-mouthed l. fellow   ATTL 20:3
loudspeaker small voice and not a l. ATTL 20:7
lout It's a l.'s game   WEST 385:9
love come to l. men too little   BURKE 67:8
Greater l. hath no man   THOR 364:7
I must l. the dog   GIBB 152:1
It is the l. of the people   BURKE 64:6
land that I l.   BERL 38:6
l. of freedom itself   GLAD 154:11
l. that asks no question   SPR 348:1
l. those who l. you   VOLT 375:13
Only L. the Beloved Republic   FORS 139:5
That l. my friend   SHAK 330:8
They l. him most for the enemies   BRAGG 54:9
to save the party we l.   GAIT 145:1
will not l. his country   SHAK 329:12
You all did l. him once   SHAK 330:4
loved Not that I l. Caesar less   SHAK 329:10
prince to be feared than l.   MACH 241:3
to Washington to be l.   GRAMM 159:4
loves I have reigned with your l. ELIZ 132:1
l. what he knows   CROM 105:3
loving l. ourselves to death   PRES 298:2
low Caesar! dost thou lie so l.   SHAK 329:8
involuntary homage of the l.   DICK 115:6

low (*cont.*):
  malice is of a l. stature   HAL 166:2
lower l. than vermin   BEVAN 40:6
  never knew that the l. classes   CURZ 108:2
  they call the L. House   DISR 117:3
  while there is a l. class   DEBS 111:3
lowliness l. is young ambition's   SHAK 328:10
loyal He is l. to his own career   DALT 109:2
loyalties l. which centre   CHUR 93:6
  tragic conflict of l.   HOWE 184:2
loyalty I want l.   JOHN 196:8
  l., a principle   BOSW 53:4
  L. is a fine quality   KINN 211:7
  L. is the Tory's secret weapon   KILM 209:9
  That learned body wanted l.   TRAPP 367:6
Lucifer he falls like L.   SHAK 327:6
luck l. to be called upon   CHUR 94:1
luggage labels on empty l.   BEVAN 41:7
lunatic l. fringe   ROOS 311:13
lunatics lunatic asylum run by l.   LLOY 230:5
lunch no such thing as a free l.   ANON 13:9
luncheon do not take soup at l.   CURZ 108:5
lungs parks are the l. of London   PITT 293:6
Lupercal On the L.   SHAK 330:3
lustre bright l. of a court   CECIL 79:9
lute lascivious pleasing of a l.   SHAK 334:9
luxury republics end in l.   MONT 264:3
lying branch of the art of l.   CORN 103:9

MacArthur General M.   TRUM 372:2
Macaulay [M.] has occasional flashes
           SMITH 344:9
  Tom M.   MELB 255:10
machinery [Our] whole political m.   BALF 31:2
  political m.   CHOD 85:9
  whole m. of the State   BRO 58:1
macht *Arbeit m. frei*   ANON 8:7
mackerel stinks like rotten m.   RAND 301:1
mad half of the nation is m.   SMOL 345:2
  old, m., blind, despised   SHEL 338:1
  This m. dog of the Middle East   REAG 302:2
  Whom the m. would destroy   LEVIN 222:3
madam m. I may not call you   ELIZ 131:10
made revolutions are not m.   PHIL 291:8
madmen m. in authority   KEYN 208:6
  when we join the fashionable m.   DID 116:2
madness m. in great ones   SHAK 325:9
  sort of m. [Bolshevism]   SMITH 344:1
magic not let in daylight upon m.   BAG 25:13
  tightness of the m. circle   MACL 242:8
magistrate m. corruptible   ROB 306:7
Magna Charta M. is such a fellow   COKE 101:1
magnanimity In victory: m.   CHUR 93:5
  m. in politics   BURKE 64:7
magnet m. [Mariner's Needle]   BACON 22:2

magpie would have a m. society   CHUR 94:3
maiden bevy of m. aunts   LLOY 230:10
maids Old m. biking to Holy   ORW 278:7
mail bastard who gets the m.   KEAT 203:1
maimed m. us at the start   YEATS 396:2
main Into the m. of waters   SHAK 332:11
  with an eye to the m. chance   CECIL 79:6
Maine As M. goes, so goes Vermont   FARL 135:5
maintain m. good government   HAM 167:3
maintained plausibly m.   BURR 69:1
majestic m. equality of the law   FRAN 141:2
majesty cease of m. Dies not alone   SHAK 325:13
  This earth of m.   SHAK 333:4
  When m. falls to folly   SHAK 331:2
majority as a rule the m. are wrong   DEBS 111:2
  As for our m....one is enough   DISR 120:17
  great silent m.   NIXON 274:6
  however safe its m.   BOOK 51:8
  indifference of the m.   REST 303:3
  indifferent and self-indulgent m.   STEP 349:3
  in the opinions of the m.   PEEL 288:7
  m. is always the best repartee   DISR 118:8
  m. never has right on its side   IBSEN 186:8
  man with courage makes a m.   JACK 189:4
  minority to the m.   LENIN 221:6
  on God's side is a m.   PHIL 292:1
  vast untutored m.   HEAD 172:3
  will of the m. is in all cases   JEFF 192:5
majors m. in the party   MACM 244:9
make does not usually m.   PHEL 291:3
  king may m. a nobleman   BURKE 67:17
  to m. as much money   FRI 143:7
maker am prepared to meet my m.   CHUR 93:14
making m. the world safe for   WOLFE 393:6
malaise energy and m.   CART 77:8
malefactors m. of great wealth   ROOS 311:9
malice m. is of a low stature   HAL 166:2
  With m. toward none   LINC 227:1
malignant not m. and remove it   WAUGH 380:9
  with m. fidelity   BALF 31:3
malignity m. truly diabolical   BURKE 63:2
man affinity with the soul of m.   PARK 285:5
  Am I not a m. and a brother   WEDG 383:3
  And the M. of Blood was there   MAC 236:4
  but make a m. a woman   PEMB 289:12
  century of the common m.   WALL 376:10
  encompassed but one m.   SHAK 328:6
  every m. against every man   HOBB 179:12
  everyone has sat except a m.   CUMM 107:2
  figure of 'The Reasonable M.'   HERB 177:1
  It's that m. again   ANON 11:5
  landing a m. on the Moon   KENN 204:8
  led to *perdition* by a m.   WEST 385:8
  m. and the hour have met   YANC 395:3
  M. being...by nature all free   LOCKE 231:6
  m. for all seasons   WHIT 388:6
  M. is something to be surpassed   NIET 273:3

m. is the only animal | JEFF 191:5
M. is the only creature | ORW 278:9
M., proud man | SHAK 332:9
m. who stood at the gate | HASK 170:2
once to every m. and nation | LOW 234:1
plain, blunt m. | SHAK 330:8
right m. in the right place | JEFF 193:14
right to be obeyed than m. | JOHN 195:1
theories about the rights of m. | BURKE 66:14
this is an extraordinary m. | JOHN 198:11
this was a m. | SHAK 330:16
unpleasantness from a m. | NAP 269:5
want anything said, ask a m. | THAT 360:8
Would this m., could he see | AUDEN 21:6
managed m. or well-conducted | RADC 299:6
management m. of a balance | KISS 214:8
m. of illusions | WALD 376:7
telling British m. off | JOS 200:1
Manchester school of M. | DISR 121:14
manhood customs and its m. | ENN 133:8
They could assert their m. | WAUGH 380:8
Youth is a blunder; M. a struggle | DISR 117:8
manifesto have our m. written | BENN 36:9
manifestoes party m. | ROTH 314:2
mankind gates of mercy on m. | GRAY 160:8
M. always sets itself | MARX 252:6
m. and posterity | INGE 187:6
M. are happier | JOHN 198:13
M. must put an end | KENN 204:10
M.'s salvation lies exclusively | SOLZ 345:11
not created m. entirely | TOCQ 365:6
short way of abolishing m. | MONT 263:10
There is no history of m. | POPP 295:12
war with the rights of m. | JEFF 191:10
you shall not crucify m. | BRYAN 60:6
manners Oh, the times! Oh, the m. | CIC 95:9
Peel has no m. | WELL 384:13
manoeuvre blend force with a m. | TROT 370:10
manufacturing m. the plausible | BALD 30:1
manure It is its natural m. | JEFF 191:7
many makes so m. of them | LINC 227:5
so much owed by so m. to so few | CHUR 90:10
map Lord would use a larger m. | SAL 317:8
roll up that m. | PITT 293:11
maps m. on a small scale | SAL 317:8
Too much poring over m. | SAL 319:2
marble left it m. | AUG 21:8
March beware the ides of M. | SHAK 328:2
Do not m. on Moscow | MONT 265:3
ides of M. are come | SHAK 329:1
I intend to m. my troops | GRIM 162:1
m. as an alternative to jogging | FITT 137:6
m. of a nation | PARN 286:8
these gentlemen wish to m. | GLAD 154:16
they said, 'Let us m.' | STEV 350:13
You can m. towards it | CALL 72:9

marches forced m., battles | GAR 148:1
marching His truth is m. on | HOWE 184:3
'Tis the people m. on | MORR 266:5
mare brought him a Flanders m. | HENR 176:1
marijuana I experimented with m. | CLIN 99:5
mark Now m. me how I will undo | SHAK 334:5
market gentle m. economy | KINN 211:8
m. has no morality | HES 177:11
market-place gathered in the m. | CAV 79:2
marks bears the m. of the last | HAIG 163:1
marriage fifty times more for a m. | BAG 25:8
m. is the waste-paper basket | WEBB 381:6
married If m. life were all | MILL 259:11
like other m. couples | SAKI 317:6
marrow largest vegetable m. | ASQ 18:9
Mars possible attack from M. | SAL 319:1
marshal m.'s baton of the duke | LOU 233:3
martial become valiant and m. | BACON 23:4
m. airs of England | WEBS 382:7
martyr has the soul of a m. | BAG 24:5
I am the m. of the people | CHAR 82:6
Thou fall'st a blessed m. | SHAK 327:7
martyrdom crown of m. | WALP 377:11
torches of m. | JEFF 193:3
Marx illegitimate child of Karl M. | ATTL 20:8
M is for M. | CONN 102:1
teaching of M. | KHR 209:1
Marxism M. is now a world faith | BENN 36:7
M. is only an episode | POPP 296:1
monetarism, like M. | GILM 153:1
more to Methodism than to M. | PHIL 291:7
Marxist I am not a M. | MARX 252:10
tried to be a M. | TAYL 357:10
mask He had a m. like Castlereagh | SHEL 338:2
mass arithmetically calculable m. | WEBB 381:6
broad m. of a nation | HITL 179:3
m. meeting for a m. movement | MCG 240:8
Paris is well worth a m. | HENR 175:6
masses And Movement of M. | CONN 102:1
back the m. against the classes | GLAD 155:5
m. were calmer | TAYL 357:13
Your huddled m. yearning | LAZ 219:7
master between M. and Servant | CHUR 88:6
but one mistress, and no m. | ELIZ 131:1
dominion of the m. | HUME 184:9
I would not be a m. | LINC 224:8
m. of very little else | BEV 42:5
these forces met their m. | ROOS 309:2
master-morality m. and slave | NIET 273:4
masters educate our m. | LOWE 233:6
I have had two m. | BEAV 34:7
m. of their fates | SHAK 328:4
new m. | HAL 166:7
people are the m. | BURKE 65:5
We are the m. now | SHAW 337:4
masterships just and unjust m. | RUSK 315:10

mastiff leal and trusty m.   LLOY 229:1
mat put them under the m.   GURN 162:6
matches have a box of m.   HOME 182:1
  With that stick of m.   MAND 249:4
material tortured by m. success   MACM 245:5
Matilda since M. and Stephen   WAUGH 380:10
matter dirt is only m. out of place   GRAY 160:6
  take away the m. of them   BACON 23:1
Max If M. gets to Heaven   WELLS 385:6
maxim It is a just political m.   HUME 185:2
  only m. of a free government   ADAMS 3:5
  We have got The M. Gun   BELL 35:1
may lawyer tells me I m. do   BURKE 64:5
Mayflower here on the M.   ROOS 310:4
maypole organ and the m.   JORD 199:5
McCarthyism M. is Americanism   MCC 239:7
McKinley M. has no more   ROOS 311:2
me thee and m.   OWEN 280:5
mean citizen of no m. city   BIBLE 44:11
  even if you don't m. it   TRUM 371:16
  Happy the golden m.   MASS 254:2
  having a m. Court   BAG 25:11
  He nothing common did or m.   MARV 251:7
meanest brightest, m. of mankind   POPE 295:5
meanly nobly save, or m. lose   LINC 226:1
means cease to be a mere m.   HAYEK 171:6
  continuation of politics by other m.   CLA 96:11
  he still retains the m. of Grace   BALF 30:10
  Increased m.   DISR 119:20
  it m. just what I choose   CARR 77:1
  live within your m.   THAT 361:4
  m. by which we live   KING 211:1
  m. of rising in the world   JOHN 198:4
  political expectations to military m.
    POW 296:5
measles m. of the human race   EINS 129:1
measure assent to any political m.   PEEL 288:4
  shrunk to this little m.   SHAK 329:8
  ultimate m. of a man   KING 210:6
measures cant of 'm. not men'   CANN 74:9
  cant of *Not men, but m.*   BURKE 63:5
  Great public m.   PEEL 289:10
meat appointed to buy the m.   SELD 323:2
  keep the flies off the m.   CHUR 90:14
  teeth are in the real m.   GRIM 162:2
  Upon what m.   SHAK 328:5
mechanical m. arts   BACON 23:7
  organic rather than m.   PARK 285:9
medal m. glitters, but it also casts   CHUR 91:2
meddle m. and muddle   DERBY 114:2
  m. not with any man's conscience
    CROM 105:5
meddling m. government   MAC 236:7
media m., I tell pedants   INGH 188:1
medieval marvellous in m. politics   MACM 245:12
mediocre titles distinguish the m.   SHAW 336:10

mediocrity real m.   SMITH 342:3
meek borne his faculties so m.   SHAK 331:7
  m. shall inherit the earth   SMITH 343:9
meet prepared to m. my Maker   CHUR 93:14
meeting He mistakes a mass m.   MCG 240:8
  Winston *loves* m. people   LLOY 230:9
Melting-Pot crucible, the great M.   ZANG 396:8
members m. of the Communist   MCC 239:6
memoirs To write one's m.   PÉT 290:11
memorable Upon that m. scene   MARV 251:7
memorandum m. is written   ACH 1:7
memorial whole earth as their m.   PER 290:5
memories ought to have good m.   SIDN 340:1
memory For my name and m.   BACON 23:10
  indebted to his m. for his jests   SHER 338:13
  nation's collective m.   POW 297:15
  no force can abolish m.   ROOS 310:2
  proper m. for a politician   MORL 266:3
men all m. are created   JEFF 191:1
  all m. would be tyrants   ADAMS 2:1
  As though he had 200,000 m.   NAP 269:12
  cant of 'measures not m.'   CANN 74:9
  cant of *Not m., but measures*   BURKE 63:5
  For thyse m. don most harm   LANG 217:7
  individual m. and women   THAT 362:2
  m. and nations behave   EBAN 127:5
  m. dominating men   WEBER 381:8
  m. in great place   BACON 22:9
  m. know so little of m.   DU B 126:6
  m. lived like fishes   SIDN 340:2
  Millions of innocent m., women   JEFF 191:2
  not m. but principles   PAINE 282:10
  political question from the m.   BURKE 66:2
  state which dwarfs its m.   MILL 259:5
  stupid to deny that all m.   MILT 261:1
  wealth accumulates, and m.   GOLD 157:6
  What I want is m. who will   MELB 256:4
menace m. to be defeated   SCAR 321:3
mental and slavery are m. states   GAND 147:7
  I am haunted by m. decay   NIC 272:4
mentioned family that is never m.   TREV 368:4
Mephistopheles who is the M.   HEAL 173:1
mercantile m. projects   SMITH 343:2
merchandise arts and m.   BACON 23:7
merchandize m. candidates   STEV 350:11
merchantman monarchy is a m.   AMES 8:2
merchants m. have no country   JEFF 193:5
mercury pick up m. with a fork   LLOY 230:3
mercy As m. does   SHAK 332:7
  crowning m.   CROM 105:7
  quality of m. is not strained   SHAK 332:10
  reason to rule, but m. to forgive   DRYD 125:15
  shut the gates of m.   GRAY 160:8
merit *m.* for a bishopric   WEST 385:10
  What is m.   PALM 284:6
meritocracy true m. of talent   YOUNG 396:7

mischief execute any m.   CLAR 96:2
  In every deed of m.   GIBB 151:10
  m., thou art afoot   SHAK 330:11
miserable arise and make them m.   HUXL 186:3
miseries m. brought upon the world
    BURKE 67:7
misery certain amount of m.   LOWE 233:7
  greatest m. is a battle gained   WELL 385:1
  relation of distant m.   GIBB 151:11
  trapping of a splendid m.   ROSS 313:5
misfits strangest collection of m.   REAG 302:1
misfortunes crimes, follies, and m.   GIBB 151:6
  tableau of crimes and m.   VOLT 376:3
misguided guided missiles and m.   KING 211:1
mislead m. the people   STEV 349:8
  one to m. the public   ASQ 18:6
misplaced rise of m. power   EIS 129:8
missed he m. the bus   CHAM 81:4
mission My m. is to pacify Ireland   GLAD 154:7
missionaries free m.   MENC 256:14
Missouri God has given us M.   RAND 300:9
mistake Biggest damfool m.   EIS 129:9
  When I make a m., it's a beaut   LA G 216:3
mistaken you may be m.   CROM 105:6
mistakes All great men make m.   CHUR 86:9
  If he makes m.   CHUR 93:6
  learned from the m. of the past   TAYL 357:7
  man who makes no m.   PHEL 291:3
mistress But m. in my own   KIPL 213:1
  but one m., and no Master   ELIZ 131:1
  m. I am ashamed to call you   ELIZ 131:10
mistresses your Lordship's m.   WILK 389:1
mitre between a m. and a crown   WALP 377:11
moat look to your m.   HAL 165:3
mob amphibious ill-born m.   DEFOE 111:6
  do what the m. do   DICK 115:1
  each tyrant, every m.   KIPL 213:5
  fit object of redress by m. law   LINC 224:3
  I lied to please the m.   KIPL 213:6
  m. of their constituents   BURKE 66:3
  m., Parliament   COBB 100:2
  Our supreme governors, the m.   WALP 377:4
mock but to m. the kingdom   PYM 298:6
  How my achievements m. me   SHAK 335:11
model best m. the world ever   HAM 167:2
  m. of a modern Prime   HENN 175:2
moderate in m. government   HAM 167:4
  Iranian m. is one who   KISS 214:9
  m. income   LAMB 216:7
  white m.   KING 210:8
moderation astonished at my own m.
    CLIVE 99:9
  deviate into m.   BURKE 66:3
  M. in the affairs of the nation   JOHN 196:5
  m. in war is imbecility   MAC 237:4
modern m. Prime Minister   HENN 175:2
  thought of m. civilization   GAND 147:4

modest much to be m. about   CHUR 93:13
moll King's M. Reno'd   ANON 11:7
Moloch right of that great M.   MEYER 258:3
moment creed of the m.   BAG 23:15
  exigency of the m.   PEEL 288:2
monarch hereditary m. was insane   BAG 27:1
  merry m., scandalous   ROCH 307:6
  not so much a king as a M.   SELL 323:7
monarchical m. or popular   HOBB 180:4
monarchies In elective m.   GIBB 151:1
  m., in poverty   MONT 264:3
monarchize To m., be feared   SHAK 333:8
monarchs For righteous m.   BRO 57:7
  m., whose power seems   MONT 264:1
  schemes for persuading m.   SWIFT 353:8
monarchy characteristic of the English M.
    BAG 25:7
  constitutional m.   TROL 369:3
  constitutional m. such as ours   BAG 26:1
  discontented under m.   HOBB 180:8
  essential to a true m.   BAG 24:9
  lock a door against absolute M.   PAINE 280:8
  M. and succession   PAINE 281:3
  m. has become   ST J 317:5
  M. has no further part   PHIL 291:6
  M. is a labour-intensive industry   WILS 391:7
  m. is a merchantman   AMES 8:2
  M. is a strong government   BAG 25:5
  M. is only the string   SHEL 338:7
  of m.   PAINE 282:15
  state of m. is the supremest   JAM 189:11
monetarism m., like Marxism   GILM 153:1
money as much m. as possible   VOLT 376:1
  bad m. drives out good   ANON 8:8
  can be master of m.   BEV 42:5
  draining m. from the pockets   SMITH 342:2
  flood of m. that gushes   WHITE 387:2
  getting m.   JOHN 198:1
  Giving m. and power   O'RO 277:1
  He had m. as well   THAT 362:1
  hell of not making m.   CARL 76:4
  If you have m. you spend it   KENN 206:4
  mark of distinction with m.   BUR 69:2
  m. for their stockholders   FRI 143:7
  M. has no smell   VESP 374:2
  M. is indeed the most important   SHAW 336:11
  M. . . . is none of the wheels   HUME 184:7
  Neither is m. the sinews of war   BACON 23:3
  not spending m. alone   EIS 129:4
  sinews of war, unlimited m.   CIC 95:11
  spending other people's m.   RAND 301:3
  spending the public m.   COOL 103:6
  there shall be no m.   SHAK 327:1
  They hired the m., didn't they   COOL 103:4
  virtue does not come from m.   SOCR 345:8
  voter who uses his m.   SAM 320:1
  your own licence to print m.   THOM 363:8

moneybag Aristocracy of the M.   CARL 75:10
mongrels continent of energetic m.   FISH 137:1
monk cloistered m.   BIRCH 45:9
monkey m. looking for fleas   LASKI 218:5
   no reason to attack the m. BEVAN 41:2
monkeys politicians are like m.   LLOY 231:3
monologue m. is not a decision   ATTL 19:10
monopolies one m. commission   ANON 15:2
monopoly best of all m. profits   HICKS 178:6
   m. stage of capitalism   LENIN 221:3
   shun the temptations of m. SCOTT 322:4
Monroe M. Doctrine   ROOS 311:4
   mouth of Marilyn M.   MITT 261:8
monstrous against a m. tyranny   CHUR 90:6
Montezuma who imprisoned M.   MAC 238:6
monument left some m.   BURKE 65:9
   m. was erected by the state AUDEN 21:4
   Pentagon, that immense m.   FRAN 142:10
moon defend the m.   SAL 319:1
   I felt like the m., the stars TRUM 371:1
   landing a man on the m.   KENN 204:8
moonlight rotten mackerel by m.   RAND 301:1
moose strong as a bull m.   ROOS 310:12
moral Arthur is wicked and m.   CHUR 88:2
   government is often the most m. MENC 257:5
   It *is* a m. issue   HALEY 164:7
   m. imperative that we have it DID 116:2
   m. or intellectual damage   KRUG 215:6
   m. principles   PAINE 283:8
   scarcely a single m. action GLAD 156:3
   This party is a m. crusade WILS 390:3
morality laws of m. are the same   BURKE 65:11
   market has no m.   HES 177:11
   M. is the herd-instinct   NIET 273:2
   periodical fits of m.   MAC 237:8
   personal and national m.   SHAW 336:11
morally not m. sure   BURKE 62:9
morals either m. or principles   GLAD 155:2
   faith and m. hold   WORD 394:5
   foundation of m.   BENT 37:9
more some animals are m. equal   ORW 278:11
mores *O tempora, O m.*   CIC 95:9
morganatic m. alliance   HARD 168:4
morning It's m. again in America   RINEY 306:1
   m. had been golden   CHUR 89:9
   never glad confident m. again BROW 60:2
   they take you in the m.   BALD 28:9
   What a glorious m. is this ADAMS 5:3
mors *principis m. est*   MORE 265:7
mortality emblem of m.   DISR 121:12
mortifications m. and humiliations   WALP 377:13
Moscow Do not march on M.   MONT 265:3
Mosley Why does M. always   ATTL 19:7
mother France, m. of arts, of warfare   DU B 126:4
   m. of battles   HUSS 186:1
   m. of Parliaments   BRIG 56:7
   M. of the Free   BENS 37:6

   m. who talks about   DISR 120:3
   My m., drunk or sober   CHES 84:1
   skin of his m.   LLOY 230:16
mothers city of the best-bodied m.   WHIT 388:3
mothers-in-law m. and Wigan Pier   BRID 56:3
motion economic law of m.   MARX 252:8
   renders the m. of the wheels HUME 184:7
motivation undiscussable m.   POW 297:14
motive noble in m.   HOOV 182:7
motives two m., neither of them   BURKE 65:12
mould out-of-date m.   JENK 194:4
Mount Sermon on the M.   BRAD 54:4
mountain beauty of the m. rose   BEAV 34:2
   go up to the m.   KING 211:4
mourn M., hapless Caledonia, m.   SMOL 345:3
mourner sole m. at his own   ROS 312:6
mourning waste any time in m.   HILL 178:9
mouth m. of Marilyn Monroe   MITT 261:8
   silver foot in his m.   RICH 305:2
   subject with an open m.   STEV 351:2
mouths I stuffed their m. with gold   BEVAN 41:10
move If I could pray to m.   SHAK 329:3
moved We shall not be m.   ANON 14:8
movement mass m.   MCG 240:8
   right of free m.   JOHN 195:3
moving king's life is m. peacefully   DAWS 110:5
MP Being an M. feeds your vanity   PARR 286:11
   Being an M. is the sort of job ABB 1:1
   only quality needed for an M. MACM 245:13
MPs dull M. in close proximity   GILB 152:9
   healthy cynicism of M.   CREWE 104:2
   I've seen M. on both sides BROWN 58:5
   many M. never see   LIV 228:7
   When in that House M. divide GILB 152:8
much So little done, so m. to do   RHOD 304:3
   so m. owed by so many   CHUR 90:10
muck when to stop raking the m.   ROOS 311:8
mud builds on m.   MACH 241:4
muddle meddle and m.   DERBY 114:2
   m. through   BRIG 56:6
muddy m. understandings   BURKE 66:17
muffled with m. oars   RAND 301:2
mufflered m. men in the 1930s dole   JOS 199:7
mule like a m.   DONN 122:7
   m. of politics   DISR 117:9
   What that Sicilian m. was to me GLAD 155:10
mules m. of politics   POWER 298:1
multitude m., such as Mob   COBB 100:2
mundus *fiat justitia et pereat m.*   FERD 136:4
murder I met m. on the way   SHEL 338:2
   Killing no m. briefly discourst SEXBY 324:2
   Most sacrilegious m.   SHAK 331:9
   m. respectable   ORW 279:11
   we have m. by the throat   LLOY 230:1
   We hear war called m.   MACD 240:5
muse talked shop like a tenth m.   ANON 10:7

mushroom councillor is like a m.   MAG 247:5
music m. of our own opinions   STEV 351:3
   shriller than all the m.   SHAK 328:2
music-hall cross between a m. turn   MACM 245:4
Mussolini Hitler and M.   LOW 233:5
must Is *m.* a word to be addressed   ELIZ 132:2
mutability large republics is m.   BOL 51:1
mutamur *et nos m. in illis*   ANON 13:7
mute that of m.   MACM 244:11
mutiny rise and m.   SHAK 330:10
muzzle m. this terrible young   WALP 378:4
myself I find m. a traitor   SHAK 334:7
   never thought of thinking for m.   GILB 152:4
mystery grasped the m. of the atom   BRAD 54:4
   Its m. is its life   BAG 25:13
   m. of the king's power   JAM 190:1
   riddle wrapped in a m.   CHUR 90:1
myth 'good old days' were a m.   ATK 19:5
   m. of democracy   CROS 106:12
mythology British m.   GRIGG 161:8
myths devoid of plausible m.   BERG 38:5
   m. of the British Parliament   MAYB 254:6

nabobs n. of negativism   AGNEW 6:7
naked It is n. aggression   POW 297:13
   left me n. to mine enemies   SHAK 327:8
   n. into the conference chamber   BEVAN 41:3
   thus I clothe my n. villainy   SHAK 334:11
name For my n. and memory   BACON 23:10
   ghost of a great n.   LUCAN 234:4
   have our n. spelled wrong   SHER 339:3
   I glory in the n. of Briton   GEOR 149:1
   In the n. of God, go   AMERY 8:1
   In the n. of God, go   CROM 105:8
   Is not the king's n.   SHAK 333:7
   liberties are taken in thy n.   GEOR 150:9
   n. is Ainsley Gotto   ERWIN 134:1
   n. is neither one thing   CHUR 95:3
   n. to all succeeding ages curst   DRYD 125:4
   n. we give the people   FLERS 137:7
   whistling of a n.   POPE 295:5
names little man with three n.   CROM 106:2
Napoleon N. forgot Blücher   CHUR 86:9
   thinks he is N.   CLEM 98:5
   used to say of him [N.]   WELL 384:6
Napoleons Caesars and N.   HUXL 186:3
nastiest n. thing in the nicest way   GOLD 156:9
nasty n., brutish, and short   HOBB 180:2
nation against the rest of the n.   HAL 166:4
   against the voice of a n.   RUSS 317:1
   American n.   BAG 24:7
   AMERICA was thus clearly top n.   SELL 323:11
   bind up the n.'s wounds   LINC 227:1
   broad mass of a n.   HITL 179:3
   citizenship of the whole n.   MACD 240:7
   deprive a n. of its right to   NAM 269:1

England is a n. of shopkeepers   NAP 270:1
   existence as a n.   ADAMS 4:7
   find faith in a n. of sectaries   DISR 117:11
   fit only for a n. of shopkeepers   SMITH 341:6
   For n. shall rise against n.   BIBLE 44:9
   France…a n. of forty millions   CRILE 104:3
   geographical fragment, but a n.   PARN 286:5
   God hath sifted a n.   STO 351:12
   If a n. expects to be ignorant   JEFF 193:6
   Licensed build that n.'s fate   BLAKE 49:4
   losses to a n. may be so great   CECIL 79:8
   Maine goes, so goes the n.   FARL 135:5
   march of a n.   PARN 286:8
   n. is not governed   BURKE 64:12
   n. is only at peace   KING 211:6
   n. of differences   CART 77:6
   n. of shopkeepers are very seldom   ADAMS 5:4
   n.'s collective memory   POW 297:15
   n. shall not lift up sword   BIBLE 43:18
   N. shall speak peace unto n.   REND 303:1
   N. spoke to a Nation   KIPL 213:1
   n. which indulges toward   WASH 379:12
   new n., conceived in liberty   LINC 226:3
   No n. is fit to sit in judgement   WILS 392:3
   No n. was ever ruined by trade   FRAN 142:6
   once to every man and n.   LOW 234:1
   one-third of a n. ill-housed   ROOS 309:3
   operating instructions for a n.   O'RO 277:4
   our existence as a n.   PITT 293:9
   places the n. at his service   POMP 295:1
   public burden of the n.'s care   PRIOR 298:4
   real favours from n. to n.   WASH 379:9
   rich and lazy n.   KIPL 213:4
   should not create a n. Europe   MONN 263:2
   things which make a n. great   BACON 23:9
   Think of what our N. stands for   BETJ 40:1
   unity of the n.   KOHL 215:4
   watching a n. busily engaged   POW 296:10
   we are a n. of amateurs   ROS 312:10
   We are a n. of communities   BUSH 69:6
   what it can do for the n.   HARD 168:5
   will have to exterminate a n.   SPOCK 347:9
national n. debt   HAM 167:1
   N. Debt is a very Good Thing   SELL 323:8
   n. events are decided   MILLS 260:2
   n. home for the Jewish   BALF 30:6
   N. honour is n. property   MONR 263:3
   There is the N. flag   SUMN 353:2
nationalism N. is an infantile sickness   EINS 129:1
   N. is a silly cock crowing   ALD 6:9
nationalities smaller n. of Europe   ASQ 18:3
   squabbling n.   ROOS 311:14
nationality condense—a N.   WHIT 388:4
   what n. he would prefer   RHOD 304:1
nationalization *n. of the coal*   TAWN 355:6

nationalize n. in this country | WILS 391:9
nations acceptable to all n. | TRUM 371:4
and the people formed Two N. | DISR 118:3
characteristic danger of great n. | BAG 27:12
day of small n. has long passed | CHAM 80:6
empire is a commonwealth of n. | ROS 312:5
Europe of n. | DE G 112:10
friendship with all n. | JEFF 192:7
general association of n. | WILS 392:7
Great n. are never impoverished | SMITH 342:5
great n. have always acted | KUBR 215:7
let fierce contending n. know | ADD 5:9
n. and states draw aside | GOGOL 156:8
N. begin by forming | HAIL 163:11
N., like men, have their infancy | BOL 50:8
N. touch at their summits | BAG 26:5
n. which have put mankind | INGE 187:6
Other n. use 'force' | WAUGH 380:6
teaching n. how to live | MILT 260:5
two great n. in the world | TOCQ 365:9
two n.; between whom | DISR 118:2
native eyes of a n. | LESS 222:1
ideas about the n. | LESS 221:13
This is my own, my n. land | SCOTT 322:5
NATO N. exists for three reasons | ISMAY 188:4
nattering n. nabobs of negativism | AGNEW 6:7
natural irresistible n. laws | BON 51:4
n. effort of every individual | SMITH 343:3
n. order of things | PAINE 282:11
n. party of government | WILS 390:10
n. rights is simple nonsense | BENT 37:8
naturalized man who was n. | LODGE 232:1
nature better angels of our n. | LINC 225:8
How n. always does contrive | GILB 152:6
n. has no cure for this | SMITH 344:1
n. of all greatness | BURKE 64:14
n. of war consisteth not | HOBB 180:1
n.'s mighty feast | MALT 248:11
state that n. hath provided | LOCKE 231:4
naval decisive n. force | WASH 379:8
n. tradition | CHUR 93:7
navy head of the N. | CARS 77:3
It is upon the n. | CHAR 82:8
n. nothing but rotten timber | BURKE 64:6
royal n. of England | BLAC 48:7
thoroughly efficient n. | ROOS 311:4
Nazi N. Germany | NEV 271:2
Nazis N. wanted war | WAUGH 380:8
nearest those who are n. to him | MILL 259:10
nearly I was n. kept waiting | LOU 232:10
necessary but a n. evil | PAINE 281:1
It became n. to destroy the town | ANON 11:3
no n. evils in government | JACK 189:2
not n. to change | FALK 135:3
necessities Great n. call out | ADAMS 2:2
people's hard n. | BEV 42:1

necessity cruel n. | CROM 105:4
laws of n., of self-preservation | JEFF 193:2
n. hath no law | CROM 105:11
n. is the plea | PITT 293:7
pragmatic n. | DID 116:2
neck lest it break thy n. | SHAK 331:3
Roman people had but one n. | CAL 72:5
some chicken! Some n. | CHUR 91:7
necklace with our n. | MAND 249:4
necks throw the reins over their n. | CLAY 97:10
necromancy mere n. | WHITE 386:7
need whenever we n. them | FLERS 137:7
needle darning n. is broader | NIC 272:2
needs to each according to his n. | BAK 28:5
to each according to his n. | MARX 252:9
negation This is the n. of God | GLAD 154:2
negative prefers a n. peace | KING 210:8
negativism nattering nabobs of n. | AGNEW 6:7
negotiate never n. out of fear | KENN 204:4
negotiating n. with de Valera | LLOY 230:3
negotiation finish a difficult n. | SAL 318:2
Negro dehumanizing the N. | LINC 224:9
living with the N. | BALD 28:8
N.'s great stumbling block | KING 210:8
negroes drivers of n. | JOHN 198:9
neighbour n.'s house is on fire | BURKE 66:7
policy of the good n. | ROOS 308:9
neighbourhood narrow into a n. | JOHN 195:9
neighbouring n. state is in decline | MONT 264:7
neighbours peace to all his n. | SHAK 327:9
what is happening to our n. | CHAM 80:7
neither n. one thing nor | CHUR 95:3
Nell Pretty witty N. | PEPYS 290:4
Nelson death of N. was felt | SOUT 347:3
neo-classical post n. | BROWN 58:6
nephews Priests have n. | PEEL 289:7
Nero N. fiddled | MENC 256:13
nerve I do not lose my n. | NEHRU 270:9
nest I have no n.-eggs | LLOY 229:2
nets n. of such a texture | SHEN 338:9
neutral studiously n. | WILS 392:5
United States must be n. | WILS 392:1
neutrality armed n. is ineffectual | WILS 392:10
Just for a word 'n.' | BETH 39:8
never n. explain | FISH 137:4
n. glad confident morning again | BROW 60:2
n. had it so good | MACM 244:7
n. in the field of human | CHUR 90:10
n. was and n. will be | JEFF 193:6
new against the n. and untried | LINC 225:3
n. deal for the American people | ROOS 308:6
n. wine into old bottles | ATTL 20:5
Newcastle no more coals to N. | GEOR 149:9
New England growth of N. | PARK 286:3
New France expansion of N. | PARK 286:3
news item of n. | TALL 355:2
President who never told bad n. | KEIL 203:3

New South Wales govern N.   BELL 35:3
newspaper never to look into a n.   SHER 338:11
   n. is of necessity something   SCOTT 322:4
newspapers government without n.   JEFF 191:4
   I read the n. avidly   BEVAN 41:9
   It's the n. I can't stand   STOP 351:11
   Vietnam War, the n. nobly   BLACK 48:5
Newspeak aim of N. is to narrow   ORW 279:3
New World N. into existence   CANN 75:4
nexus n. of man to man   CARL 76:2
nice not about being n.   KEAT 203:2
nicest nastiest thing in the n. way   GOLD 156:9
nick-name every n. is a title   PAINE 282:7
niece hitting the n. of a bishop   ORW 277:10
night long dark n. of tyranny   MURR 268:5
   n. of the long knives   HITL 179:4
   show thy dangerous brow by n.   SHAK 328:11
   touch of Harry in the n.   SHAK 326:10
Nightingale Florence N.   GRIF 161:7
nightmare national n. is over   FORD 138:12
nightstick at the end of a n.   WHAL 386:2
nihil Aut Caesar, aut n.   BORG 53:1
ninety n. percent of the politicians   KISS 214:6
Ninety-two glorious N.   REV 303:6
nip n. him in the bud   ROCHE 307:4
Nixon You won't have N.   NIXON 274:2
no he can say n. in such a way   PEAR 287:6
   leadership is saying n., not yes   BLAIR 48:12
   N.! No! No   THAT 362:10
   rebel? A man who says n.   CAMUS 74:6
nobility and in others n.   PAINE 282:6
   leave us still our old n.   MANN 249:5
   n. is a graceful ornament   BURKE 67:6
   n. is the act of time   BACON 22:14
   order of n. is of great use   BAG 26:3
nobleman king may make a n.   BURKE 67:17
nobles n. by the right   MAC 237:7
noblesse laissez-faire and n. oblige   HES 178:3
noblest n. Roman of them all   SHAK 330:16
   remains the n. word   TAYL 357:1
nobly We shall n. save   LINC 226:1
nobody n. left to be concerned   NIEM 273:1
   there is n. there   KEYN 208:8
   To n.   GURN 162:6
nominated I will not accept if n.   SHER 339:4
nomination decide the n.   DAUG 109:9
nonconformist comes from the n.   TAYL 356:12
nonconformity history of N.   ORW 277:11
none With malice toward n.   LINC 227:1
nonexistence nonviolence or n.   KING 210:3
nonpolitical n. speech   NIXON 274:1
nonsense little n. now and then   POW 296:7
   n. upon stilts   BENT 37:8
non-violence n. is the first article   GAND 147:3
   n. or nonexistence   KING 210:3
   organization of n.   BAEZ 23:11

north against the people of the N.   LEE 220:6
   forth in triumph from the n.   MAC 236:3
   men and women of the N.   ANTH 15:5
   N. is determined to preserve   HOUS 183:8
North African egg of a N. Empire   GLAD 155:4
Northcliffe N. has sent for the King   ANON 10:6
northern constant as the n. star   SHAK 329:3
   N. laurels   LEE 220:1
   N. States will manage somehow   BRIG 56:6
   southern efficiency and n. charm   KENN 205:12
nose Do not run up your n.   BALD 29:12
   Had Cleopatra's n. been shorter   PASC 287:1
   liberty plucks justice by the n.   SHAK 332:4
nothing better to know n.   BILL 45:5
   desired to know n.   JOHN 198:2
   do n.   MELB 256:5
   good man to do n.   BURKE 68:7
   Having n. to construct   TROL 369:9
   n.   LOU 233:2
   n. is ever done   SHAW 336:14
   n. should ever be done for   CORN 103:8
   Thinking n. done   LUCAN 234:5
nought n. shall make us rue   SHAK 331:1
nouns n. of number, or multitude   COBB 100:2
novel be the hero of a n. yet   MAC 236:8
November remember the fifth of N.   ANON 13:2
now n. she is like everyone else   DE G 112:6
nuclear forces of n. destruction   KENN 205:7
   n. arms race has no military   MOUN 267:4
   n. freeze proposals   REAG 301:12
   n. giants and ethical infants   BRAD 54:5
nuisance not make himself a n.   MILL 259:2
   n. in time of war   CHUR 92:8
NUM against the Pope or the N.   BALD 29:12
number centre upon n. one   CHUR 93:6
   greatest n.   BENT 37:9
   nouns of n., or multitude   COBB 100:2
numbers better than n.   CROM 105:2
nurse baby beats the n.   SHAK 332:4
nursery great n. of freemen   SHIP 339:6
   not a n. of future revolutions   BURKE 66:9
nut sledgehammer to miss a n.   BOOK 52:2
nutrition n. and health   JAY 190:4

oaks hews down o. with rushes   SHAK 324:5
oars to his object with muffled o.   RAND 301:2
Obadiah O. Bind-their-kings   MAC 236:2
obedience o. to the law   ROOS 311:7
   rebellion to tyrants is o. to God   BRAD 54:8
   reluctant o. of distant provinces   MAC 238:5
obedient o. to their laws we lie   SIM 340:6
obey laws but to o. them   HORS 183:4
   not to o. the will of the people   PEEL 288:6
obeyed more right to be o.   JOHN 195:1
objections o. may be made   JOHN 197:11

obligation o. of subjects	HOBB 180:6
o. which goes unrecognized	WEIL 383:4
oblivion gets you o.	NIXON 274:16
observance o. of procedural	FRAN 141:6
strict o. of the written law	JEFF 193:2
obstinate o. little man	THOM 363:5
obstruction kind of 'consecrated o.'	BAG 25:10
obtain What we o. too cheap	PAINE 281:11
obvious in o. distress	BALF 30:8
occasion never lose an o.	DISR 118:11
occupations O let us love our o.	DICK 115:2
occurred Ought never to have o.	BENT 38:2
ocean leap into the o., and perish	HUME 184:9
Like the rolling on of o.	MORR 266:5
use the o. as their road	WALL 377:2
you had better abandon the o.	CLAY 97:2
oceans To the o. white with foam	BERL 38:6
odds o. we'll get reforms	PEROT 290:10
Odysseus Like O., the President	KEYN 207:4
off o. with his head	SHAK 335:2
offence only defence is in o.	BALD 29:6
where the o. is	SHAK 325:11
offended speak; for him have I o.	SHAK 329:12
offer not what I intend to o.	KENN 203:9
office By o. boys for o. boys	SAL 318:10
candidates for high o.	STEV 350:11
chances of getting o.	HAIL 163:4
commonplace mind high in o.	HARDY 168:7
dignity of the o.	GEOR 149:7
dog's obeyed in o.	SHAK 331:4
going to run his o.	HEND 174:6
I found myself without an o.	CHUR 89:3
in o. but not in power	LAM 217:2
insolence of o.	SHAK 325:8
lifetime in public o.	GALB 146:7
Men, if in o., seemed	PEEL 288:5
men in o.	PEEL 289:3
most insignificant o.	ADAMS 4:1
o. before honour	POW 297:6
o.-building and o.-hunting	JEFF 192:1
o. is something that builds up	BENN 36:6
o. of the Prime Minister	ASQ 18:5
o. tends to confer	LAWS 219:2
party or statesman got into o.	CHUR 93:9
price paid for o.	TOCQ 366:8
receives the seals of o.	ROS 312:9
refreshing waters of o.	TROL 369:2
second o. of government	JEFF 191:13
statesman in o.	TAYL 358:10
trusted with the o.	BROD 57:4
trying to get into o.	MCM 243:11
unfit to hold an o.	FAB 134:6
when o. is in question	PEEL 289:8
When we got into o.	KENN 204:9
Whichever party is in o.	WILS 391:6
officer art thou o.	SHAK 326:11

offices Excluded from o.	ADAMS 2:3
o. are acceptable here	JEFF 191:14
o. as public trusts	CALH 72:2
official concept of the 'o. secret'	WEBER 381:11
its duty is to augment o. power	BAG 26:10
No sane local o.	SMITH 343:6
This high o., all allow	HERB 176:9
officially o. denied	COCK 100:6
officials high appointed o.	O'RO 277:6
o. are the servants	GOW 158:5
o. sometimes take a different	ROTH 314:1
protect o.	LYNN 235:6
tell the permanent o.	HARC 168:3
offspring time's noblest o.	BERK 38:4
oil like an o. painting	INGH 188:1
o. which renders the motion	HUME 184:7
old All wars are planned by o. men	RICE 304:5
call young men instead of o. ones	PEEL 288:3
conservative when o.	FROST 144:3
'good o. days' were a myth	ATK 19:5
I name thee O. Glory	DRIV 124:9
new wine into o. bottles	ATTL 20:5
not adherence to the o. and tried	LINC 225:3
O. Age a regret	DISR 117:8
o. age is the most unexpected	TROT 370:13
O. Country must wake up	GEOR 149:5
o., mad, blind, despised	SHEL 338:1
o. man in a hurry	CHUR 86:7
o. order changeth	TENN 360:5
o., white-headed and large	BUSH 69:4
redress the balance of the o.	CANN 75:4
shaking hand of an o., wild	VICT 374:6
Too o., too bourgeois	GISC 153:6
violent Tory of the o. school	RUSK 316:4
warn you not to grow o.	KINN 211:10
older o. men declare war	HOOV 183:1
oligarchy *aristocracy*, call it o.	HOBB 180:8
extreme democracy or absolute o.	ARIS 16:9
Olympian O. bolts	DISR 118:15
omelette What a fuss about an o.	VOLT 375:12
omitted o., all the voyage	SHAK 330:14
omnibus man on the Clapham o.	BOWEN 54:1
once o. is more than enough	BIRCH 45:8
o. lead this people into war	WILS 392:14
o. to every man and nation	LOW 234:1
one encompassed but o. man	SHAK 328:6
merely o. man fewer	METT 257:8
o. as the hand	WASH 379:2
O. man shall have one vote	CART 77:9
O. realm, one people, one leader	ANON 9:11
our majority…o. is enough	DISR 120:17
win just o. for the Gipper	GIPP 153:5
one-eyed o. man is king	ERAS 133:10
only o. thing we have to fear	ROOS 308:8
open enter the o. society	CARM 76:17
If you o. that Pandora's Box	BEVIN 43:5
o. covenants of peace	WILS 392:15

open (*cont*.):
o. door   HAY 171:2
with an o. mouth   STEV 351:2
opening sending your o. batsmen   HOWE 184:1
operating o. instructions   O'RO 277:4
operative o. White House Position   ZIEG 397:3
opinion being without an o.   BAG 27:9
conforming to majority o.   SCAN 320:6
gross and scope of my o.   SHAK 325:4
man of common o.   BAG 23:14
of one o.   MILL 258:11
o. is truth filtered   PHIL 292:4
o. one man entertains   PALM 284:6
Our researchers into public o.   AUDEN 21:3
Party is organized o.   DISR 119:9
plague of o.   SHAK 335:10
poor itch of your o.   SHAK 324:4
public o. is a permeating influence   BAG 24:1
representing no o. but their own   WILS 392:9
respect public o.   RUSS 316:8
sacrifices it to your o.   BURKE 63:8
supported by popular o.   CATT 78:6
They that approve a private o.   HOBB 179:11
opinions by men's o., by blame   FAB 134:6
delivers his o.   CIC 95:5
music of our own o.   STEV 351:3
o. of the majority   PEEL 288:7
o. that are held with passion   RUSS 316:6
so bad as their o.   MACK 242:3
That he held the proper o.   AUDEN 21:3
There are as many o.   TER 360:6
opium o. of the people   MARX 252:2
touches it as with an o. wand   PAINE 282:12
opponent Never corner an o.   LIDD 223:5
o. cannot be both honest   ORW 278:12
opponents political o.   MACL 243:6
purposes of his o.   TROL 370:6
opportunism principally o.   CHUR 86:3
opportunist What is an o.   BISM 47:14
opportunities I seen my o.   PLUN 294:6
our history, one of those o.   GLAD 155:7
opportunity greatest o.   DISR 120:18
I am a product of o.   HEATH 173:10
open the gates of o.   JOHN 196:7
o. is more powerful   DISR 118:11
o. of taking decisions   PARK 286:1
uses the most favourable o.   BISM 47:14
oppose o. everything   DERBY 114:1
pleasure of the opposition to o.   MACL 243:5
opposing more in the wrong in o.   BISM 46:5
opposition duty of an O.   DERBY 114:1
every time the o. are asked   MACL 243:7
government must needs be in O.   JENK 194:10
make a figure by o.   HAL 166:5
Minister or Leader of the O.   DISR 121:9
O. is four or five years'   HATT 170:3
o. means death   TROT 370:14

O., on coming into power   BAG 26:8
o. politician must at all times   RIPP 306:3
O.'s about asking   LYNN 235:1
phrase, 'Her Majesty's O.'   BAG 24:14
phrase 'His Majesty's O.'   HOBH 180:10
pleasure of the O. to oppose   MACL 243:5
whole period in o. forgetting   RIDL 305:4
without a formidable O.   DISR 117:12
oppressed mind of the o.   BIKO 45:4
oppression there is no limit to o.   MENC 257:5
to violate would be o.   JEFF 192:5
oppressive so o. and unjust   BURKE 67:12
oppressor in the hands of the o.   BIKO 45:4
o.'s wrong   SHAK 325:8
revolutionary ends as an o.   CAMUS 74:8
opprobrium term of o.   MOYN 267:5
oppugnancy In mere o.   SHAK 335:9
opulence private o.   GALB 145:10
oracles lively o. of God   COR 103:10
orange *quoted as* '*Play the o. card*'   CHUR 86:8
orang-outang o. or the tiger   BURKE 65:9
orator I am no o., as Brutus is   SHAK 330:8
No o. ever made an impression   BAG 24:11
orators one of those o.   CHUR 87:5
oratory appetite for o.   GALB 146:9
contemporary parliamentary o.   CRIT 104:6
object of o. alone is not truth   MAC 236:5
order and a Democrat, in that o.   JOHN 195:5
custom, in all line of o.   SHAK 335:7
given me the o. of the boot   CHUR 92:7
Good o. is the foundation   BURKE 67:10
is defined by the word 'o.'   METT 258:2
keep the government in o.   SCAR 321:4
more devoted to o. than to justice   KING 210:8
old o. changeth   TENN 360:5
only war creates o.   BREC 55:7
o. destroyed by a revolution   TOCQ 367:3
o. reigns in Warsaw   ANON 13:1
party of o. or stability   MILL 259:1
renovation of the natural o.   PAINE 282:11
social progress, o., security   JOHN 195:2
ordered o. their estate   ALEX 7:1
orders I gave them their o.   WELL 384:5
ordinary behaviour of o. people   TAYL 357:13
warn you not to be o.   KINN 211:10
organ great o. of public opinion   DISR 118:15
o. grinder   BEVAN 41:2
organic committee is o.   PARK 285:9
organization o. of idolatry   SHAW 336:9
o. of non-violence   BAEZ 23:11
o. with 'Liberation'   LEVIN 222:13
systematic o. of hatreds   ADAMS 2:7
organize mourning—o.   HILL 178:9
organized party is o. opinion   DISR 119:9
organs all the other o.   GLAD 154:3
orgies emotional o.   ROB 306:12

original expect any one to be o. BAG 23:13
  none of the sound ideas is o. MACM 245:3
originality o. is taken to be a mark GALB 145:8
  pluck and some o. WEBB 381:2
originals few o. and many copies TOCQ 366:6
origins disinter the o. of those JOUB 200:6
  must have radical o. TREV 368:6
ornament o. to the civil order BURKE 67:6
orphan defeat is an o. CIANO 95:4
osprey As is the o. to the fish SHAK 325:1
ostrich America can not be an o. WILS 392:7
other guessing what was at the o. side
                                 WELL 384:10
  spending o. people's money RAND 301:3
  This o. Eden, demi-paradise SHAK 333:4
  without that o.'s consent LINC 224:6
ought didn't o. never BEVIN 43:6
  something o. to be done WELLS 385:5
  tells me I o. to do BURKE 64:5
ourselves We have done it o. LAO-T 217:8
out one that's o. ROG 307:7
  went o., like all good things DISR 121:1
out-argue we will o. them JOHN 198:7
outdoor gigantic system of o. relief BRIG 57:2
outlaw attacks from o. states REAG 302:1
outlawed known liar should be o. HAL 165:6
  o. or exiled MAGN 247:3
out of touch say he is o. DOUG 123:5
outside than o. pissing in JOHN 196:9
out-vote we cannot o. them JOHN 198:7
over oversexed, and o. here TRIN 369:1
over-bearing o. and offensive VICT 374:7
overcame He o. evil with good KING 210:4
overcome we shall o. ANON 14:9
overpaid grossly o. HERB 176:9
  o., overfed, oversexed TRIN 369:1
oversexed overpaid, overfed, o. TRIN 369:1
overstated being o. BERL 39:6
own every country but his o. CANN 75:1
  for my words are my o. CHAR 83:1
  for what they o. TAYL 357:15
Oxford king To O. sent a troop BROW 59:6
  secret in the O. sense FRAN 142:11
  To O. sent a troop of horse TRAPP 367:6
oxygen o. of publicity THAT 361:13
Ozymandias O., king of kings SHEL 337:9

pacific by p. means BRI 56:2
pacify My mission is to p. Ireland GLAD 154:7
pack can p. the cards BACON 22:5
  made the peasantry its p. animal TROT 370:11
  running with the p. BUTL 70:9
pack-horse posterity is a p. DISR 119:4
Paddington As London is to P. CANN 74:10
paeans yield to peace, laurels to p. CIC 95:7

Paganini village fiddler after P. NIC 272:5
page foot of the first p. SAND 320:2
paid Lord God, we ha' p. in full KIPL 212:10
pain gave p. to the bear MAC 239:2
pains by p. men come to greater BACON 22:11
  no gains without p. STEV 349:9
paint layer of democratic p. TOCQ 365:3
painted gilded loam or p. clay SHAK 333:1
  lath of wood p. to look like iron BISM 47:2
painting writing and p. CHUR 87:7
palace p. is not safe DISR 121:13
Palestine establishment in P. BALF 30:6
Palladium P. of all the civil JUN 201:3
palliate p. what we cannot cure JOHN 197:2
palm And bear the p. alone SHAK 328:3
  dominion over p. and pine KIPL 212:11
paltered Nor p. with Eternal God TENN 360:2
pamphleteers not the age of p. HOGB 181:1
Pandora If you open that P.'s Box BEVIN 43:5
panics Tory party never p. HOSK 183:6
Panther Black P. Party NEWT 271:3
papacy p. is not other HOBB 180:9
paper hand that signed the p. THOM 363:3
  I ran the p. [the *Daily Express*] BEAV 33:9
  just for a scrap of p. BETH 39:8
  reactionaries are p. tigers MAO 250:5
  virtue of p. government BURKE 64:3
paper-mill thou hast built a p. SHAK 327:3
papers in the p. yesterday LYNN 235:7
paradise cannot catch the bird of p. KHR 209:4
paragraphs p. and plausibilities CARL 76:5
parapet could not see a p. without CRIT 104:7
parboiled place my p. head GRAH 159:2
parchment ρ., being scribbled o'er SHAK 327:2
  rotten p. bonds SHAK 333:4
pardon God may p. you ELIZ 131:5
parens king is truly p. patriae JAM 189:10
parent poverty is the p. of revolution ARIS 16:8
  Revolution a p. of settlement BURKE 66:9
parents illegitimate p. JOS 200:5
  In peace, children inter their p. HER 177:3
  lords whose p. were DEFOE 111:9
Paris no more Hoares to P. GEOR 149:9
  P. was French TUCH 372:6
parish take his pension from his p. RUSK 315:5
parks p. are the lungs of London PITT 293:6
parliament build your house of P. WELL 385:2
  cease to be returned to P. DISR 121:17
  duty as a Member of P. BIGG 45:3
  English P. is composed PAINE 282:12
  government is a p. of whores O'RO 277:8
  In P. it should not only MACL 243:5
  most of the time by P. SCAR 321:1
  multitude, such as mob, P. COBB 100:2
  My desire to get here [P.] BOOT 52:5
  myths of the British P. MAYB 254:6
  not even p. SCAR 320:8

parliament (*cont.*):

pandered to by a supine p.	RIDL 305:7
p. can do any thing but	PEMB 289:12
P. itself would not exist	SCAR 320:7
P. speaking through reporters	CARL 76:7
prejudiced it may be, of p.	SCAR 321:5
Take P. out of the history	POW 297:8
They [p.] are a lot of hard-faced	BALD 29:1
This P. is enough to discourage	HEAD 172:3
want to have voices in P.	RUSK 315:11

parliamentarian pleasure for a p.   CRIT 104:4

parliamentary cage of the P. Labour Party

	DALT 108:9
contemporary P. oratory	CRIT 104:6
next p. opportunity	FOOT 138:9
P. government	BAG 23:12
P. Government as the noblest	DISR 119:17
P. leper	WILS 390:7
unhappy bag of p. eloquence	CARL 76:8
without party P. government	DISR 119:18

parliaments heavier hand than kings and p.

	FRAN 142:1
In p., men wrangle	HAL 166:3
mother of P.	BRIG 56:7

parson become the world's p.   HEAL 172:8
see a Whig in a p.'s gown   JOHN 197:14

part p. of the solution   CLE 98:2
play a p., any p., in its burial   MACM 244:11

partiality With neither anger nor p.   TAC 354:5

participate p. in politics   PLATO 294:3

parties All political p. die at last   ARB 15:9

both our political p. will bid	BAG 27:4
P. come to power	RIDL 305:4
P. must ever exist	BURKE 64:9
ridiculousness of the division of p.	
	RUSK 315:12
three p. there	MAYB 254:6
two p. which divide the state	EMER 133:2
warns the heads of p.	ARB 15:8

parts *dignified* p.   BAG 24:10

party best p. is but a kind   HAL 166:4

competent to judge a political p.	ROOS 310:5
conduct of a losing p.	BURKE 67:13
each p. is worse than the other	ROG 307:7
educate our p.	DISR 119:12
effects of the spirit of p.	WASH 379:11
extreme p. is most irritated	BAG 27:11
false teeth in the p. manifestoes	ROTH 314:2
fight again to save the P. we love	GAIT 145:1
great p. is not to be brought	HAIL 163:5
I always voted at my p.'s call	GILB 152:4
meanness of which a political p.	DISR 116:5
natural p. of government	WILS 390:10
necessary nature of a political p.	TROL 369:11
P. is little less	HAL 166:6
P....is not a faction or club	POW 297:5
P. is organized opinion	DISR 119:9

p. of order or stability	MILL 259:1
p. platforms are contracts	TRUM 371:9
p.'s over	CROS 106:6
p. whose mission it is	SAL 318:4
political p. in power	SCAR 321:1
prove that the other p. is unfit	MENC 257:4
put p. before country	CREWE 104:2
responsibility of a political p.	HAIL 163:4
Stick to your p.	DISR 121:3
stupidest p.	MILL 259:7
Then none was for a p.	MAC 237:1
there is no P. line	DJIL 122:3
This p. comes from the grass roots	BEV 42:1
This p. is a bit like	WILS 391:5
This p. of two	BRIG 56:9
to heaven but with a p.	JEFF 191:9
when any particular p.	CHUR 93:9
Whichever p. is in office	WILS 391:6
without a seat, without a p.	CHUR 89:3
without p.	DISR 119:18
with the majors in the p.	MACM 244:9

pass cunning men p. for wise   BACON 22:6

p. the ammunition	FORGY 139:3
They shall not p.	ANON 10:9
They shall not p.	IBAR 186:7

passer *laisser* p.   QUES 299:2

passeront *Ils ne p. pas*   ANON 10:9

passes free speech, free p.   BETJ 40:1

passion No p. so effectually robs   BURKE 62:3

opinions that are held with p.	RUSS 316:6
political p.	ANON 11:9
such a p.	SHAW 337:5

Passionaria La P. of middle-class   HEAL 173:2

passionate full of p. intensity   YEATS 395:6

passions All his p. were expressed   WALP 377:12

more powerful and more lofty p.	TOCQ 366:2
p. of men will not conform	HAM 167:6

past cannot remember the p.   SANT 320:1

controls the p.	ORW 279:2
falsely imagined p.	BORK 53:2
future but by the p.	HENRY 176:6
have their roots in the p.	TRUM 371:8
lament the p.	BURKE 62:10
last day of an era p.	YELT 396:4
no political p.	MONC 261:9
nothing but the p.	KEYN 207:9
plan the future by the p.	BURKE 67:16
remember what is p.	HAL 165:5
Utopia is a blessed p.	KISS 214:11

pasture enough p. for all the sheep   WALP 378:9

pastures green p. of the European   VERW 374:1

paternal form of p. socialism   MACM 244:1
p., or in other words   MAC 236:7

paternalism lessons of p.   CLEV 99:3

path p. of great principles   BAG 24:2

patience my p. is now at an end   HITL 179:7
not stamina but p.   MAJOR 247:8

patient I am extraordinarily p. THAT 362:4
patrie Allons, enfants de la p. ROUG 314:3
patries *europe des p.* DE G 112:10
patriot Never was p. yet DRYD 125:12
  p. on an empty stomach BRANN 55:5
  steady p. of the world CANN 75:1
  Such is the p.'s boast GOLD 157:3
  Would the honest p. JEFF 192:6
patriotism history to his p. ADAMS 4:11
  nothing but this—a larger p. ROS 312:8
  p. in the female sex ADAMS 2:3
  p. is a lively sense ALD 6:9
  p. is a sort of religion TOCQ 365:4
  p. is the last refuge JOHN 198:3
  till you knock the p. out SHAW 336:19
patriots all these country p. BYRON 71:5
  blood of p. and tyrants JEFF 191:7
  p. are in the right WAUGH 380:5
  so to be p. BURKE 63:6
  this last effort of the p. ADAMS 3:6
pattern predetermined p. FISH 136:8
pause I p. for a reply SHAK 329:12
pawns p. are men CARL 76:10
pay *Equal P. for Equal Work* ANTH 15:6
  Not a penny off the p. COOK 102:5
  p. given to a state hireling JOHN 197:3
  that we are made to p. for FRI 144:2
  ulcer Man on 4 Ulcer p. EARLY 127:4
  we shall p. any price KENN 204:2
paying p. the Dane-geld KIPL 213:4
  price worth p. LAM 216:8
peace advocates of p. upon earth GEOR 149:6
  call it p. TAC 354:3
  carry gentle p. SHAK 327:7
  cherish a just and lasting p. LINC 227:1
  Don't tell me p. has broken out BREC 55:10
  enamoured on p. CLAR 96:4
  enemies in war, in p. friends JEFF 190:6
  find the solution for world p. MARS 251:1
  for p. like retarded pygmies PEAR 287:4
  fortunes in p. and in war CHUR 93:8
  good war, or a bad p. FRAN 142:4
  hasty inordinate demand for p. PEEL 288:10
  have to take chances for p. DULL 126:9
  I believe it is p. for our time CHAM 81:1
  If p. cannot be maintained RUSS 317:2
  If you want p., prepare for war VEG 373:7
  ingeminate the word P. CLAR 96:3
  In p., children inter their parents HER 177:3
  In p.: goodwill CHUR 93:5
  In the arts of p. Man is SHAW 336:5
  in time of p. thinks of war ANON 10:4
  Let us have p. GRANT 160:1
  Let war yield to p. CIC 95:7
  make war than to make p. CLEM 98:6
  making p. is harder STEV 349:6
  may not be a just p. IZET 188:5

  merry songs of p. SHAK 327:9
  nation is only at p. KING 211:6
  nation shall speak p. unto nation REND 303:1
  not to send p., but a sword BIBLE 44:5
  only give us p. PITT 293:4
  open covenants of p. WILS 392:15
  p. at the price of NIC 272:1
  p. between equals WILS 392:8
  P., commerce JEFF 192:7
  p., easy taxes SMITH 341:1
  P., freedom, and liberty SHAK 329:7
  P. hath her victories MILT 261:3
  p. I hope with honour DISR 120:9
  P. is a very apoplexy SHAK 324:11
  P. is indivisible LITV 228:6
  P. is much more precious SADAT 317:4
  P. is nothing but slovenliness BREC 55:7
  P., *n.* BIER 44:17
  P., retrenchment, and reform BRIG 56:5
  p. with honour CHAM 81:1
  people want p. so much EIS 129:7
  plunging into a cold p. YELT 396:5
  prefers a negative p. KING 210:8
  right is more precious than p. WILS 392:13
  security and p. of each country JOHN 195:2
  shameless Warwick, p. SHAK 327:4
  taking a chance on p. BUSH 69:8
  that we may live in p. ARIS 16:3
  This is not a p. treaty FOCH 138:2
  Thy banished p. SMOL 345:3
  war is p. ORW 279:1
  we cannot live alone, at p. ROOS 310:6
  When p. has been broken ROOS 309:6
  When there was p. AUDEN 21:3
  work, my friend, is p. ROOS 310:8
  world p. or world destruction BAR 32:4
  yet it's interest that keeps p. CROM 105:10
peaceably p. if we can CLAY 97:3
peaceful p. coexistence FULB 144:4
peacefully moving p. towards DAWS 110:5
peach When a man wants a p. ASQ 18:9
peasantry But a bold p. GOLD 157:6
  made the p. its pack animal TROT 370:11
peasants cricket with their p. TREV 368:2
pecker I want his p. in my pocket JOHN 196:8
Pecunia p. non olet VESP 374:2
Peel P. has no manners WELL 384:13
peer Not a reluctant p. BENN 36:1
  p. is exalted into MAN PAINE 282:6
peerage We owe the English p. DISR 117:5
  When I want a p., I shall buy it NORT 275:6
Peers House of P. GILB 152:7
  My Lord in the P. will take BRO 57:8
  we love our House of P. GILB 152:5
Peking relations with P. NIXON 274:7
pen mightier than the p. HOGB 181:1

pendulum vibration of a p. — JUN 200:10
pennies P. don't fall from heaven — THAT 360:12
penny Not a p. off the pay — COOK 102:5
pension p. list of the republic — CLEV 99:2
P. Pay given to — JOHN 197:3
take his p. from his parish — RUSK 315:5
Pentagon P., that immense — FRAN 142:10
people About one-fifth of the p. — KENN 206:3
And a new p. takes the land — CHES 84:8
belongs to the p. — LINC 225:7
city but the p. — SHAK 324:7
common p. know — MENC 256:8
contracts with the p. — TRUM 371:9
does not suppose the p. good — ROB 306:7
enthusiasm of the p. — WELL 384:1
far more stupid than their p. — EIS 129:6
fool all the p. some of the time — LINC 227:8
fool too many of the p. — THUR 364:8
For we are the p. of England — CHES 84:7
from the interests of the p. — LINC 224:2
good of the p. is the chief law — CIC 95:6
government by the p. — CAMP 74:3
government of the p., by the p. — WYCL 395:1
great masses of the plain p. — MENC 256:11
He who builds on the p. — MACH 241:4
I am myself the p. — ROB 306:4
include the support of the p. — CLEV 99:3
indictment against an whole p. — BURKE 64:2
in favour of the p. — BURKE 62:11
land for the p. — ANON 11:10
law for rulers and p. — DAVIS 110:2
Let my p. go — BIBLE 43:7
love of the p. — BURKE 64:6
made for the p., made by the p. — WEBS 382:2
many opinions as there are p. — TER 360:6
more than half of the p. — WHITE 386:6
My faith in the p. governing — DICK 115:7
my p.'s happiness — ELIZ 131:2
of the p., by the p. — PAGE 280:7
one realm, one p., one leader — ANON 9:11
p. are never so perfectly backed — HAL 165:11
p. are the masters — BURKE 65:5
p. as a source of sovereign — SCAR 321:1
p. formed Two Nations — DISR 118:3
p. govern themselves — THI 363:2
p. is the true legislator — BURKE 62:4
p. made the Constitution — MARS 251:4
p. only know that they exist — LAO-T 217:8
p. overlaid with taxes — BACON 23:4
p.'s choice — SHER 338:12
p. strong enough — ROOS 309:5
p. that has licked — BROG 57:5
pockets of the p. — GLAD 156:2
power to the p. — ANON 13:4
'Tis the p. marching on — MORR 266:5
voice of the p. is the voice of God — ALC 6:8
wasting the labours of the p. — JEFF 192:10

We...are no petty p. — YEATS 396:1
we were to set the p. free — HEATH 173:7
What kind of a p. do they think — CHUR 91:3
worship the p. — BACON 22:3
peopled p. half the world — SEEL 322:6
Peoria It'll play in P. — ANON 11:4
perch Their p. and not their terror — SHAK 332:5
perdition led to p. by a man — WEST 385:8
pereat *fiat justitia et p. mundus* — FERD 136:4
perestroika restructuring [*p.*] — GORB 158:3
perfect entire and whole and p. — SPR 348:1
p. democracy — BURKE 67:4
perfectibility p. as a dream — MILL 258:7
perfection Ideal p. — GLAD 155:3
must function to p. — MUSS 268:8
perfidious p. Albion — XIM 395:2
Pericles what P. felt of Athens — KEYN 207:3
perils adds to our p. — MOUN 267:4
period p. of our dominion — BURKE 65:9
p. of silence on your part — ATTL 19:8
perish no vision, the people p. — BIBLE 43:15
ordained that England shall p. — ELIZ 131:6
p. together as fools — KING 211:2
though the world p. — FERD 136:4
venal city ripe to p. — SALL 319:7
permanent p. indignation — VAL 372:12
tell the p. officials — HARC 168:3
permitted if a man were p. — FLET 137:8
Whereas in England all is p. — MEG 255:3
pernicious most p. race — SWIFT 353:6
Perón had not been born P. — PERÓN 290:6
perpetual p. quarrel — BURKE 64:4
persecute p. a sect — BAG 24:8
persecuted p. minority — FRAN 141:7
persecution p. is not an original — PAINE 282:9
p. produced — MAC 238:13
persevering p. in error — PEEL 288:11
person only one p. at a time — FRAN 142:11
personal come in p. contact — TAYL 358:11
personality political p. — JENK 194:2
persons principles, rather than p. — PAINE 283:8
perspiration p. of firm confidence — FOOT 138:3
perspire Mr Gladstone may p. — CHUR 86:4
persuade p. a multitude — HOOK 182:5
persuading By p. others — JUN 200:11
persuasion in what things p. only — MILT 260:7
not truth, but p. — MAC 236:5
P. is the resource of the feeble — GIBB 151:12
pertness obliged to put up with p. — DISR 116:6
petrified p. adolescence — BEVAN 40:12
petticoat in my p. — ELIZ 130:4
petty We...are no p. people — YEATS 396:1
we p. men — SHAK 328:4
petty larceny political p. — DISR 118:13
petulance p. is not sarcasm — DISR 118:16
pews Talk about the p. and steeples — CHES 84:6

phantom p. of Lord Goderich	DISR 120:14	rising unto p. is laborious	BACON 22:11
philanthropist professed p.	TROL 369:5	**place-expectants** Gratitude of p.	WALP 378:7
Philistines barbarians, P.	ARN 17:2	**places** desire p. under one	SHIP 339:7
from the P. proper	ARN 17:4	Men in high p.	TAYL 358:13
philosopher p. may preach	GIBB 152:2	private faces in public p.	AUDEN 21:1
philosophers p. are very regardless of expense	PEEL 289:6	**plagues** of all p.	DEFOE 111:10
political p.	KEYN 208:6	**plain** p., blunt man	SHAK 330:8
some p. have not maintained	SWIFT 353:8	**plaintive** p. treble	DISR 118:15
philosophy p. quenches them	VOLT 376:2	**plan** p. the future by the past	BURKE 67:16
This barbarous p.	BURKE 66:17	p. to resist all planning	OAK 276:3
Phrases P. make history here	MAFF 246:8	rebuild it on the old p.	MILL 259:6
phylacteries fly-blown p.	ROS 312:13	rest on its original p.	BURKE 65:2
picked hastily p. himself up	CHUR 94:10	**planets** heavens themselves, the p.	SHAK 335:7
picking won't notice you're p.	JOHN 195:6	**planning** plan to resist all p.	OAK 276:3
pickle weaned on a p.	ANON 13:12	professed aims of p.	HAYEK 171:6
picnic many apples short of a p.	MAJOR 248:4	**plans** finest p. are always ruined	BREC 55:8
pictures You furnish the p.	HEAR 173:5	**plant** confidence is a p. of slow	PITT 292:10
pie You'll get p. in the sky	HILL 178:8	p. of rapid growth	WASH 380:1
piebald p. complexion	CHUR 90:13	**planted** p. thick with laws	BOLT 51:3
pies *eat one of Bellamy's veal p.*	PITT 293:12	**plateaus** no p.	KISS 214:7
pigmies built by p.	CHUR 89:5	**platforms** party p. are contracts	TRUM 371:9
pigs p. treat us as equals	CHUR 94:11	**platitude** p. is simply a truth	BALD 29:2
pike freedom for the p. is death	TAWN 356:1	**Plato** living in P.'s Republic	CIC 95:5
pilgrims Land of the p.' pride	SMITH 344:5	P. is never sullen	MAC 237:10
pillar p. of the State	SOLZ 346:1	**plausibilities** p. bring votes	CARL 76:5
pillars four p. of government	BACON 22:16	**plausibility** confer a dreadful p.	LAWS 219:2
real p. of civilization	MONN 263:1	**plausible** manufacturing the p.	BALD 30:1
pillow like the feather p.	HAIG 163:1	**play** better than a p.	CHAR 83:2
pilot daring p. in extremity	DRYD 125:5	It'll p. in Peoria	ANON 11:4
dropping the p.	TENN 359:6	Not only did we p. the race card	SHAP 335:12
replace the p.	BAG 25:3	watch the men at p.	CLEG 98:3
pin with a little p.	SHAK 333:8	yet cannot p. well	BACON 22:5
pinched Mrs Simpson's p. our king	ANON 10:5	**play'dst** Thou p. most foully for't	SHAK 331:10
pine dominion over palm and p.	KIPL 212:11	**played** always p. the game	SMITH 344:2
pinstripe have to come in a p. suit	FEIN 136:2	I p. by the rules of politics	NIXON 275:1
pips until the p. squeak	GEDD 148:7	your role is p. out	TROT 370:12
piratical p. old bruiser	HAIL 163:10	**playing** p. fields of Eton	WELL 384:11
piss worth a pitcher of warm p.	GARN 148:2	**please** am to do what I p.	FRED 143:4
pissing inside the tent p. out	JOHN 196:9	p. myself or you	HEND 174:5
p. down your leg	JOHN 196:12	To tax and to p.	BURKE 64:15
pistol found the smoking p.	CON 101:6	**pleasure** gave p. to the spectators	MAC 239:2
I reach for my p.	JOHST 198:14	what is meant by the p. of life	TALL 355:4
pitcher p. of warm piss	GARN 148:2	would afford them no p.	MILL 258:7
Pitt P. is to Addington	CANN 74:10	**pleasures** English take their p.	SULLY 352:7
pity p. never ceases to be shown	DRYD 125:10	two supreme p. in life	ROS 312:9
place All rising to great p.	BACON 22:13	**plebeian** importance of a p. leader	DISR 118:18
fought for our p. in the sun	WILH 388:9	**plot** Gunpowder Treason and p.	ANON 13:2
Get p. and wealth, if possible	POPE 295:7	This blessèd p., this earth	SHAK 333:4
In p. of strife	CAST 78:3	**plots** p., true or false	DRYD 125:3
men in great p.	BACON 22:9	**plotted** rarely p.	MACL 243:2
Observe degree, priority, and p.	SHAK 335:7	**plough** I must p. my furrow alone	ROS 312:12
our own p. in the sun	BÜLOW 61:7	Men of England, wherefore p.	SHEL 338:3
p. is given for the sake	HAL 165:12	**ploughed** have p. the sea	BOL 51:2
p., that great object	SMITH 341:2	**ploughman** even the poorest p.	CHAR 82:4
p. with power	ROS 312:7	**plowshares** swords into p.	BIBLE 43:18
right man in the right p.	JEFF 193:14	**plumage** pities the p., but forgets	PAINE 282:4

plumbers good p.	NIXON 274:11
plutocracy not a p. of wealth	YOUNG 396:7
plutocratic *like* p. government	TAWN 356:2
Plymouth pious ones of P.	EVAR 134:3
PM But he ended P.	ATTL 20:9
only P. in England	DALT 109:1
P.—whose motto	LYNN 235:4
pocket in your neighbour's p.	RUSK 315:6
in your p. or purse	WILS 390:12
put the house in his p.	GARV 148:6
want his pecker in my p.	JOHN 196:8
won't notice you're picking his p.	JOHN 195:6
pockets p. of the people	GLAD 156:2
poem p. to the glory of beating	WOLFE 393:5
poetry power corrupts, p. cleanses	KENN 205:8
writing p.	POW 297:3
You campaign in p.	CUOMO 107:3
poets p. keep our mouths shut	YEATS 395:5
point different p. of view	NAP 269:5
points thousand p. of light	BUSH 69:6
poised p. between a cliché	MACM 244:6
poising p. every weight	MARV 252:1
poison put p. in your coffee	ASTOR 19:3
strongest p. ever known	BLAKE 49:3
pole top of the greasy p.	DISR 121:5
polecat semi-house-trained p.	FOOT 138:7
police For the urban poor the p.	HARR 169:6
p. can beat you	SHAW 336:16
p. were to blame	GRANT 159:5
policeman p. is there to preserve disorder	DALEY 108:8
p.—whose utility	SAL 318:9
terrorist and the p.	CONR 102:3
world's p.	HEAL 172:8
policies but rarely p.	HURD 185:8
catastrophic, p.	BAL 31:7
impossible p.	RIDL 305:4
principles and p.	POW 297:5
policy directing their own p.	BAG 26:11
English p. is to float lazily	SAL 317:7
exercise power and determine p.	TREV 368:8
[foreign] p. is to be able	BEVIN 43:4
from your p. do not wholly	AESC 6:2
idea behind foreign p.	O'RO 277:7
If the p. isn't hurting	MAJOR 247:9
incomes p. alone	JOS 200:2
kings will be tyrants from p.	BURKE 67:2
My home p.: I wage war	CLEM 98:4
not a p. of conciliation	PARN 286:6
p. of the American government	JEFF 193:15
p. of the good neighbour	ROOS 308:9
state p., a cyclops with one eye	COL 101:3
That p. is violent	HUME 184:8
They seek a p.	WAUGH 380:7
To defend a bad p.	SAL 318:11
polite have no allies to be p. to	GEOR 150:4
p. father of his people	JAM 189:10

p. society smiles hopefully	TAWN 356:3
politeness p. of kings	LOU 233:4
politic must unavoidably be p.	PEEL 287:8
political adventurer of modern p. history	BUTL 70:2
All p. lives, unless they are cut	POW 297:7
anyone's p. prospects	HEAD 172:2
any p. doctrine	TROL 370:7
beyond p. life itself	ARIS 16:4
capacity for p. passion	ANON 11:9
death of a p. economist	BAG 24:4
distance from the p. situation	RAK 300:2
entering p. life	HEAD 172:3
expect me to have any p. future	MONC 261:9
exudes from every p. pore	FOOT 138:3
for fear of P. Economy	SELL 323:8
get hold of the p. machinery	CHOD 85:9
healthy state of p. life	MILL 259:1
in excess it fills p. graveyards	KINN 211:7
In our time, p. speech	ORW 279:9
Man is by nature a p. animal	ARIS 16:5
match p. expectations	POW 296:5
no p. or ideological difference	KENN 203:5
not a normal feature of p. life	KILM 209:10
of p. life	TROL 370:8
[Our] whole p. machinery	BALF 31:2
points clearly to a p. career	SHAW 336:13
p. campaigns	ROB 306:12
p. country is like an American	BAG 27:5
p. heads of departments	HARC 168:3
p. image is like mixing cement	MOND 262:2
p. language	ORW 279:11
p. liberty in a citizen	MONT 264:10
p. life dealing with humdrum	THAT 361:7
p. ones are insoluble	HOME 182:4
p. power grows	MAO 250:4
p. power of another	LOCKE 231:6
p. power of the sovereign	TROL 370:3
p. thought, in France	ARON 17:7
powerful p. personality	JENK 194:2
religion with no p. power	WOLFE 394:1
schemes of p. improvement	JOHN 197:10
Science of P. Economy	RUSK 316:2
social and p. problems	BAL 31:8
test of any p. decision	TREND 367:7
politically It is a loser p.	NIXON 274:15
politician achieved by a p.	LYNN 234:10
education of a p.	CHUR 89:10
Every p. ought to sacrifice	BURKE 67:11
forced to be a p.	POW 297:3
geniality of the p. who for years	MAUG 254:4
good p. is quite as unthinkable	MENC 256:10
greatest art of a p.	BOL 50:7
honest p. is one who	CAM 73:6
I am not a p., I am a citizen	STEV 349:5
like a scurvy p.	SHAK 331:5
my life as a p.	POW 297:14

nonpolitical speech by a p.	NIXON 274:1	do not go in for p.	CAMUS 74:5
nostrils of an English Tory p.	TROL 369:2	first part of p.? Education	MICH 258:4
oldest, wisest p.	THOR 364:4	first requirement of p. is not	MAJOR 247:8
opposition p. must at all times	RIPP 306:3	focus of p. on real people	HAVEL 170:5
pathetic as a p. who has	MENC 257:1	From p., it was an easy step	AUST 21:10
p. has not to revenge	BISM 46:7	give his mind to p.	SHAW 337:1
p. has to simplify	POW 297:12	great reform in p. if wisdom	CHUR 92:14
p. is a man who understands	TRUM 371:13	holy mistaken zeal in p.	JUN 200:11
p. is an arse	CUMM 107:2	I approve his p.	GIBB 151:14
p. is a person who approaches	STEV 351:2	I must study p. and war	ADAMS 3:13
p. is a statesman	POMP 295:1	in America, the p. of happiness	HUMP 185:5
p. never believes what he says	DE G 112:12	In p. if you want anything said	THAT 360:8
p. performs upon the stage	TAYL 356:10	In p. I think it is wiser	BIFF 45:2
p.'s corpse was laid away	BELL 35:5	In p. it is more blessed	POW 296:6
p. to complain about the press	POW 297:9	in p. that you are much exposed	BALD 29:11
p. was a person with whose	LLOY 230:6	in p. the middle way	ADAMS 3:8
p. who steals	PLUN 294:7	in p. there is no honour	DISR 116:5
professional p. can sympathize	POW 296:8	In p., there is no use looking	CHAM 80:1
proper memory for a p.	MORL 266:3	In p. you must keep running	BUTL 70:9
radical p.	TROL 369:9	invariably of the p. of the people	BORR 53:3
politicians conviction p., certainly	BANC 32:1	invisible hand in p.	FRI 144:1
done to death by p.	CHES 83:8	In well-framed p., innovation	BAG 27:7
don't want to die for p.	THOM 364:6	I taste no p. in boiled and roast	SMITH 344:7
fighting the p.	MONT 265:4	I think that p. is worse	MONT 265:2
great fault of our p.	TROL 369:8	I will not close my p.	FOX 140:7
If p. lived on praise and thanks	HEATH 173:9	long time in p.	WILS 390:8
left to the p.	DE G 112:9	Magnanimity in p.	BURKE 64:7
ninety percent of the p.	KISS 214:6	marvellous in medieval p.	MACM 245:12
Old p. chew on wisdom past	POPE 295:6	Men enter local p. solely	PARK 286:2
P. also have no leisure	ARIS 16:4	money that gushes into p.	WHITE 387:2
P. [are] a set of men	LINC 224:2	mule of p.	/ DISR 117:9
P. are exiles	GRIGG 161:9	My p. are based…on things	THAT 361:4
P. are like monkeys	LLOY 231:3	no consistency, except in p.	BYRON 71:1
P. are the same all over	KHR 209:6	no sympathy in p.	THAT 360:9
p. in possessing whom	TROL 369:7	Nothing in p. is ever as good	BOYLE 54:2
P. in pursuit of votes	GALB 146:10	no true friends in p.	CLARK 96:10
P. neither love nor hate	CHES 83:11	not the language of p.	DISR 119:3
P. often believe that their world	ROTH 314:1	now in the centre of p.	MOSL 267:2
P.' Syllogism	LYNN 235:11	objective of the science of p.	ARIS 16:2
p. who wanted something	BISM 46:10	Our p. seem to be increasingly	WALD 376:7
poor if p. treat them	FIELD 136:6	people who went into p.	COOK 102:7
schemes of visionary p.	BURKE 64:17	played by the rules of p.	NIXON 275:1
Seventeen unelected reject p.	RIDL 305:7	P. are, like God's infinite mercy	O'RO 277:2
tinhorn p.	WHITE 387:3	P. are now nothing more	JOHN 198:4
to do with politics or p.	CHUR 87:7	P. are too serious a matter	DE G 112:9
too many p. who believe	ADAMS 2:5	P. are usually the executive	BRIT 57:3
When the p. complain that TV	MURR 268:6	P., as a practice	ADAMS 2:7
Where would we p. be	POW 296:7	P. compels its votaries	VAL 372:12
whole race of p. put together	SWIFT 353:7	p. consists in ignoring facts	ADAMS 3:1
politics aim of practical p.	MENC 256:9	p. grease the wheels	TAWN 356:3
All p., however, are based on	REST 303:3	p. is about surviving	LYNN 235:8
All p. is local	O'NE 276:8	P. is for the present	EINS 129:2
ascertainable facts, in p.	PEEL 289:9	P. is just like show business	REAG 301:6
Being in p. is like being a football	MCC 239:5	P. is largely a matter	BUTL 70:8
confound their p.	ANON 9:9	P. is not an exact science	BISM 46:4
definition of the art of p.	ATTL 20:14	P. is not the art of	GALB 145:12
disentangle religion from p.	TREV 368:9	P. is perhaps the only profession	STEV 351:4

politics (*cont.*):

p. is present history	FRE 143:5
P. is supposed to be	REAG 301:8
P. is the art of acquiring	GAND 147:2
P. is the art of looking	BENN 35:8
P. is the art of preventing	VAL 373:1
P. is the art of the possible	BISM 46:6
P. is trying to get into office	MCM 243:11
P. is war without bloodshed	MAO 250:3
P., like religion, hold up	JEFF 193:3
P. makes strange bedfellows	WARN 378:11
p. of the left and centre	JENK 194:4
p. of Versailles	MONN 262:7
p. only one thing really counts	HEAD 172:5
p. to a spectator sport	GALB 146:4
practice of p. in the East	DISR 116:8
refusing to participate in p.	PLATO 294:3
same style of p.	OAK 276:3
second in p. gets you oblivion	NIXON 274:16
secret of p.? Make a good treaty	BISM 46:3
talking p. after dinner	DISR 120:4
theory of p. was Bismarck's	KEYN 207:3
this P. thing	ROG 307:7
times in p. when	GALB 146:1
to do with p. or politicians	CHUR 87:7
want to succeed in p.	LLOY 229:12
war is the continuation of p.	CLA 96:11
poll-taking so-called science of p.	WHITE 386:7
poll tax *of the p.*	THAT 362:15
pollution p. of democracy	WHITE 387:2
Pomeranian P. grenadier	BISM 47:10
pomp grinning at his p.	SHAK 333:8
Vain p. and glory of this world	SHAK 327:6
Pompey Knew you not P.	SHAK 328:1
Pontius Pilate Christ crucified P.	HOUS 183:7
pony piebald complexion of my p.	CHUR 90:13
poodle Gentleman's p.	LLOY 229:1
in a p. parlour	PARR 286:10
poor better to be rich than p.	CECIL 79:7
decent provision for the p.	JOHN 197:12
For the urban p. the police	HARR 169:6
Give me your tired, your p.	LAZ 219:7
help the many who are p.	KENN 204:3
laws grind the p.	GOLD 157:4
make everybody p.	SEN 323:12
My p. are happy	PAINE 283:12
no longer works for the p.	FIELD 136:6
none so p. to do him reverence	SHAK 330:5
not that men are p.	DUB 126:6
of the rich on the p.	JEFF 191:5
peasant in my kingdom so p.	HENR 175:5
p. fish	MENC 257:3
p. have cried, Caesar hath wept	SHAK 330:2
p. have no right	RUSK 315:8
p. man at his gate	ALEX 7:1
p. man loved the great	MAC 237:1
p. people in rich countries	BAUER 33:1

p. relations who are horribly	ORW 278:5
p. to sleep under bridges	FRAN 141:2
p. would be very little less	SHAW 336:21
RICH AND THE P.	DISR 118:2
rich richer and the p. poorer	NEHRU 270:11
rich wage war it's the p. who die	SART 320:5
You cannot help the p.	LINC 227:7
poorest p. he that is in England	RAIN 300:1
p. man may in his cottage	PITT 292:9
Pope against the P. or the NUM	BALD 29:12
P.! How many divisions	STAL 348:5
Popish P. liturgy	PITT 293:1
To tie a p. successor with laws	HAMP 167:9
populace keep the p. alarmed	MENC 256:9
philistines, and p.	ARN 17:2
propriety give the name of p.	ARN 17:5
When the p. is excited	LA BR 216:2
popular base, common and p.	SHAK 326:11
basis of p. government	ROB 306:11
custom supported by p. opinion	CATT 78:6
monarchical or p.	HOBB 180:4
p. feeling	TROL 369:4
regarded p. government	BAG 24:3
restrain the p. sentiments	PEEL 288:8
wars are p.	MACD 240:3
popularity I don't resent his p.	REAG 302:6
population balance of our p.	JOS 200:3
one part of the p.	LENIN 221:6
p., when unchecked	MALT 248:9
populi *salus p. suprema est lex*	CIC 95:6
salus p. suprema lex esto	SELD 323:9
voice of God [*vox p., vox Dei*]	ALC 6:8
porcupines throw a couple of p.	KHR 209:7
pore from every political p.	FOOT 138:3
poring Too much p. over maps	SAL 319:2
pornography statistics as p.	JENK 194:9
port p. is near	WHIT 387:9
portal From out the fiery p.	SHAK 334:1
portmanteau p. word of abuse	TEBB 359:3
position Every p. must be held	HAIG 163:2
positive p. peace	KING 210:8
wish that he gave more p. signs	BLUNT 49:7
possessed limited in order to be p.	BURKE 65:1
possessions All my p.	ELIZ 132:3
possibilities land of unlimited p.	GOLD 157:1
possible art of the p.	BISM 46:6
knowledge of the p.	BEVAN 40:11
not the art of the p.	GALB 145:12
p. you may be mistaken	CROM 105:6
poster Kitchener is a great p.	ASQ 18:10
posterity ancestry or hope of p.	DONN 122:7
ancestry, or hope of p.	POWER 298:1
enjoy what p. will say	FRAN 142:3
looked upon by p.	CLAR 96:5
Nation are the trustees of p.	DISR 118:6
not go down to p.	DISR 122:1
not look forward to p.	BURKE 66:10

our forefathers, and p.	ADAMS 5:2	in office but not in p.	LAM 217:2
p. is a pack-horse	DISR 119:4	jaws of p. are always opened	ADAMS 3:3
p. most in their debt	INGE 187:6	Johnson's instinct for p.	WHITE 387:1
p. will do justice	DISR 121:9	less the p., the greater the desire	LEVIN 222:12
Think of your p.	ADAMS 4:5	limitation of governmental p.	WILS 391:11
post office efficiency of the p.	SULL 352:5	lost, when the legislative p.	GIBB 151:4
postponing avoided simply by p.	CHUR 94:16	lust for p.	ROOS 309:2
postwar attitudes of p. funk	TEBB 359:2	management of a balance of p.	KISS 214:8
pot *chicken in every p.*	HOOV 182:9	men live without a common p.	HOBB 179:12
chicken in his p. every Sunday	HENR 175:5	monarchs, whose p. seems	MONT 264:1
potent p. advocates of peace	GEOR 149:6	most of the p. is in the hands	ORW 278:5
Potomac All quiet along the P.	MCCL 239:9	mystery of the king's p.	JAM 190:1
poultry lives of the p.	ELIOT 130:1	no hopes but from p.	BURKE 65:3
pound p. here in Britain	WILS 390:12	once intoxicated with p.	BURKE 67:14
pounding Hard p. this, gentlemen	WELL 384:3	only have p. over people as long	SOLZ 345:10
poverty against hunger, p.	MARS 251:2	opposition, on coming into p.	BAG 26:8
it is possible to conquer p.	JOHN 196:1	outrun our spiritual p.	KING 211:1
monarchies, in p.	MONT 264:3	paltered with Eternal God for p.	TENN 360:2
p. is the parent of revolution	ARIS 16:8	parties come to p. with silly	RIDL 305:4
setting him up in p.	NAIDU 268:9	place without p.	ROS 312:7
suffer so much p. and excess	PENN 289:13	political p. grows out of the barrel	MAO 250:4
war on p. in America	JOHN 195:10	political p. of another	LOCKE 231:6
power absolute p.	ADAMS 4:3	political p. of the sovereign	TROL 370:3
absolute p. of preventing	SAL 318:5	politics of p.	HAIL 163:9
All p., each Tyrant, every Mob	KIPL 213:5	p. can be rightfully exercised	MILL 258:10
all p. is a trust	DISR 116:3	p. corrupts, poetry cleanses	KENN 205:8
any man who has p. is led	MONT 264:9	p. elite are those who decide	MILLS 260:2
arts of p. and its minions	CLAY 97:7	p. has risen up	CALH 72:3
aspired to p. instead of influence	TAYL 357:9	p. in trust	DRYD 125:8
black p....is a call	CARM 76:16	p. is an indispensable condition	KEANE 202:5
but the act of p.	BACON 22:14	P. is not a means	ORW 279:7
candidates for p.	PAINE 283:8	P. is so apt to be insolent	HAL 166:8
civil to persons in p. under her	DERBY 114:3	P. is the great aphrodisiac	KISS 214:3
command, p., and glory	CIC 95:8	P.? It's like a Dead Sea	MACM 245:7
conception of the p.-state	TEMP 359:5	p. of decision	HEAD 172:5
constitutes the balance of p.	NIC 271:7	p. of the crown	BURKE 63:1
corridors of p.	SNOW 345:4	p. of the press	NORT 275:7
depositary of p.	DISR 117:10	p. over nothing	HER 177:4
disastrous rise of misplaced p.	EIS 129:8	p. should always be distrusted	JONES 199:2
drape over their will to p.	HUXL 186:4	p. tends to corrupt	RUSK 315:4
duty is to augment official p.	BAG 26:10	P. tends to corrupt	ACTON 1:9
enchanted chambers of p.	LAND 217:4	p. to act according to discretion	LOCKE 231:9
encroachment of those in p.	MAD 246:6	p. to endanger the public liberty	ADAMS 3:5
Everyone who desires p.	MILL 259:10	p. to tax	MARS 251:2
For also knowledge itself is p.	BACON 22:1	P. to the people	ANON 13:4
friend in p. is a friend lost	ADAMS 2:8	p. which has dotted over	WEBS 382:7
from which the sun draws its p.	TRUM 371:2	p. without conscience	BRAD 54:5
general are great toadies of p.	TREV 368:7	P. without responsibility	KIPL 214:1
generally, in the acquisition of p.	RUSS 316:5	religion with no political p.	WOLFE 394:1
Giving money and p.	O'RO 277:1	remorse from p.	SHAK 328:9
government, when it comes to p.	SNOW 345:5	responsibility without p.	STOP 351:7
greater the p.	BURKE 63:7	restless desire of p. after p.	HOBB 179:10
greed for p. normally met	LEVIN 222:11	road to p., credit	BURKE 65:8
history of political p.	POPP 295:12	standing armies of p.	RADC 299:5
holding, and wielding p.	GAND 147:2	strange desire to seek p.	BACON 22:10
individual liberty is individual p.	ADAMS 4:9	*supreme p. must be arbitrary*	HAL 165:10
inherit when we come to p.	BENN 36:4	Those who exercise p.	TREV 368:8

power (*cont.*):

Treasury is in p.	WILS 391:6
Unlimited p. is apt to corrupt	PITT 292:11
utility of monarchical p.	BOSW 53:4
What p. have you got	BENN 36:11
When p. to flattery bows	SHAK 331:2

powerful p. and free — TOCQ 365:6

rich society and the p. society	JOHN 196:2

powers accumulation of all p. — MAD 246:5

headmasters have p.	CHUR 88:11
high contracting p.	BRI 56:2
jurisdiction of two hostile p.	MAC 236:6
legitimate p. of government	JEFF 193:13
little-celebrated p. of Presidents	GALB 146:13
new p. of the executive	DENN 113:8
real separation of p.	DENN 113:7
ultimate p. of the society	JEFF 193:8
wars of the European p.	MONR 263:5

pox gallows or of the p. — WILK 389:1

practical government was a p. thing — BURKE 64:17

power of sustained p. activity	TAWN 355:7
p. men, who believe	KEYN 208:6
we look at the p.	GLAD 155:3

practice intention of putting it into p. — BISM 48:1

put into p.	GILM 153:1
wear and tear of p.	TROL 370:5

praise If politicians lived on p. — HEATH 173:9

Let us now p. famous men	BIBLE 44:2
P. the Lord and pass	FORGY 139:3
took the p. as a greedy boy	MAC 236:9

praised less happy when being p. — BALF 31:4

p., decorated, and got rid of	CIC 95:13

pray day when I did not p. for them — LEE 220:6

If I could p. to move	SHAK 329:3
I p. for the country	HALE 164:4
p., that this mighty scourge	LINC 226:9
work and p., live on hay	HILL 178:8

prayer Conservative Party at p. — ROYD 314:7

One p. absorbs all others	GLAD 155:8
people's p.	DRYD 125:7

preachers I need p. I buy 'em — LONG 232:6

preaching woman's p. is like — JOHN 197:9

precedent From precedent to p. — TENN 359:8

p. embalms a principle	STOW 352:1

precious liberty is p. — LENIN 221:11

right is more p. than peace	WILS 392:13
This p. stone set in the silver	SHAK 333:4

predictable seldom p. — BERL 39:4

pre-eminence p. in her Colonial — GEOR 149:5

preferences individual p. — MILL 259:10

pregnant like being a little p. — HEND 174:7

prejudices p. through the door — FRED 143:3

respect the p. and habits	GIBB 152:2
such of the proprietor's p.	SWAF 353:3

prelate religion without a p. — BANC 31:11

prelaty impertinent yoke of p. — MILT 260:4

Premier great P. must add — BAG 27:8

will probably be p. for years	CHAN 81:7

preparation I need a week for p. — WILS 392:18

no p. is thought necessary	STEV 351:4

prerogative English subject's sole p. — DRYD 125:14

first is law, the last p.	DRYD 125:15
p. of the harlot	KIPL 214:1
rotten as p.	BURKE 63:1
that which is called p.	LOCKE 231:9

prescience he lacked p. — DISR 119:1

prescription discards P. — DISR 117:6

presence conspicuous by its p. — RUSS 317:3

p. on the field	WELL 384:6

present know nothing but the p. — KEYN 207:9

offers no redress for the p.	DISR 117:6
politics is for the p.	EINS 129:2

preservation p. of their property — LOCKE 231:7

preserve p. contracts — MELB 256:6

p. disorder	DALEY 108:8

preserved it must be p. — JACK 188:8

Presidency close to the P. — DEAN 110:6

in the pursuit of the P.	JOHN 196:5
one heart-beat from the P.	STEV 350:8
runaway P.	SCHL 321:5
Teflon-coated P.	SCHR 321:8
wants the p. so much	BROD 57:4

President All the P. is — TRUM 371:5

America any boy may become P.	STEV 350:6
anybody could become P.	DARR 109:8
As P., I have no eyes but	LINC 227:2
candidate for P.	KENN 204:1
damned cowboy is P.	HANNA 168:1
making the P. a czar	SCHL 321:6
P. is Commander-in-Chief	STEV 349:4
P. may slip without the state	TOCQ 365:5
P. needs political understanding	TRUM 371:10
P.'s hardest task is not to	JOHN 196:6
P.'s spouse	BUSH 69:3
P. who never told bad news	KEIL 203:3
P. who thinks arms control	SCHR 321:9
problems a P. has to face	TRUM 371:8
rather be right than be P.	CLAY 97:8
republican candidate for P.	SIMP 340:7
security around the American P.	MAIL 247:7
slept more than any other P.	MENC 256:13
their P. is a crook	NIXON 274:10
We are the P.'s men	KISS 214:10
what did the P. know	ANON 14:12
When the P. does it	NIXON 274:13
who is the best P.	PET 291:1

Presidents powers of P. — GALB 146:13

press complain about the p. — POW 297:9

freedom of the p.	CHUR 94:7
freedom of the p.	JEFF 192:8
freedom of the p. in Britain	SWAF 353:3

freedom of the p. is guaranteed	LIEB 223:6
free p. is not a privilege	LIPP 228:4
liberty of the p.	JUN 201:3
lose your temper with the P.	PANK 284:11
popular p. is drinking in	MELL 256:7
power of the p. is very great	NORT 275:7
P. lives on disaster	ATTL 20:10
To the p. alone	JEFF 191:15
want not really a free p.	RADC 299:6
where the p. is free	JEFF 191:12
with the P. in a manner	MELB 255:7
with you on the free p.	STOP 351:11
pressure go out and put p. on me	ROOS 310:7
relation between p. and resistance	NIC 271:7
prestige doesn't work without p.	DE G 112:1
points of p.	MONN 262:8
pretender But who p. is	BYROM 70:10
pretending p. that people	DISR 118:4
pretexts tyrants seldom want p.	BURKE 67:15
prevarication last dyke of p.	BURKE 66:5
prevent our duty to try to p. it	MILN 260:3
way to p. war is not to fear	RAND 300:8
preventing art of p. people	VAL 373:1
p. lamentable events	SAL 318:5
prevents but in what it p.	BAG 26:3
prey to hast'ning ills a p.	GOLD 157:6
price All those men have their p.	WALP 378:6
another man's p. increase	WILS 391:3
If blood be the p. of admiralty	KIPL 212:10
love that pays the p.	SPR 348:1
p. of repression	DU B 126:7
p. worth paying	LAM 216:8
resides in the p. paid for office	TOCQ 366:8
prices contrivance to raise p.	SMITH 341:5
prick To p. the sides of my intent	SHAK 331:8
pride idleness and p. tax	FRAN 142:1
On either side it is p.	TOCQ 365:1
to save its p.	MEYER 258:3
priest guts of the last p.	DID 116:1
guts of the last p.	MESL 257:6
rid me of this turbulent p.	HENR 175:7
priests dominion of p.	PRICE 298:3
p. by the imposition	MAC 237:7
p. have been enemies	HUME 185:1
P. have nephews	PEEL 289:7
prig not too much of the p.	CROS 106:7
Prime Minister best P. we have	BUTL 70:3
buried the unknown P.	ASQ 18:7
capacity of a man...[to be P.]	TROL 370:9
Every P. needs a Willie	THAT 362:12
fresh to be our war P.	BALD 29:8
Great of Finchley, the P. herself	HEAL 173:1
I think a P. has to be a butcher	BUTL 70:5
It's no part of a P.'s duty	CHAM 81:2
model of a modern P.	HENN 175:2
more often than the P.	BIRCH 46:1
next P. but three	BELL 35:3

office of P.	MACM 245:10
office of the P. is what its holder	ASQ 18:5
power of the P.	BENN 36:12
P. and the Cabinet	SCH 322:3
P. has an absolute genius	BEVAN 41:7
P. has had a very difficult	GEOR 150:6
P. has nothing to hide	CHUR 92:9
P. has resigned and Northcliffe	ANON 10:6
P. is like the great banyan	PATIL 287:2
P. is shuffling along	HEAL 173:4
P. or Chancellor	THAT 360:7
P. or Leader	DISR 121:9
P. should be intimidating	THAT 362:14
P. should give an example	LLOY 230:11
radicals, we shall have you P.	WILDE 388:8
second time the P. has got rid	BIRCH 45:8
see a woman becoming a P.	ASQ 18:11
turned-out P.	MELB 255:5
upon the provinces of the P.	MELB 255:7
when a British P. sneezes	LEVIN 222:8
Prime Ministers Even P.	CLARK 96:6
P. are wedded to the truth	SAKI 317:6
P. can be easily disposed of	JENK 194:7
P. have never	CHUR 88:11
wild flowers, and P.	BALD 29:3
primordial p. condition of liberty	BAK 28:5
primus p. inter pares	MORL 266:1
prince constitutional king is a p.	BAG 26:2
Is in a p. the virtue	MASS 254:1
p. sets himself up above	MAYH 255:1
p. who gets a reputation	NAP 269:6
two talents invaluable to a p.	MAC 238:14
under the dominion of a p.	HUME 184:9
Prince of Wales God bless the P.	LINL 227:10
princes difficulties in p.' business	BACON 22:8
p. and lords may flourish	GOLD 157:6
p....have frequently engaged	SMITH 343:2
p. in this case	DAN 109:5
p. ought to leave	MACH 241:9
That sweet aspect of p.	SHAK 327:6
these her p. are come home	SHAK 331:1
wade into the weakness of p.	JAM 190:1
principis indignatio p.	MORE 265:7
principle approves of something in p.	BISM 48:1
call the 'falling domino' p.	EIS 129:5
citizen is influenced by p.	RAK 300:2
except from some strong p.	MELB 256:1
good men to rise above p.	LONG 232:7
He does everything on p.	SHAW 335:13
precedent embalms a p.	STOW 352:1
p. of the English constitution	BLAC 48:8
protection is not a p.	DISR 117:16
shrinks from p.	DISR 117:6
when subjects are rebels from p.	BURKE 67:2
women's rights is the basic p.	FOUR 140:2
principles begins with that of its p.	MONT 264:4
by reference to p.	TAWN 355:7

principles (*cont.*):

certain political p.	POW 297:5
Damn your p.	DISR 121:3
embrace your Lordship's p.	WILK 389:1
had either morals or p.	GLAD 155:2
moral p., rather than persons	PAINE 283:8
no retreat from the p.	MURR 268:4
not men but p.	PAINE 282:10
path of great p. is marked	BAG 24:2
p. of a free constitution	GIBB 151:4
p. that gave her birth	WILS 392:11
Their p. are the same	JOHN 198:10
We need good p.	HAYEK 171:8

print in Britain means freedom to p. SWAF 353:3

licence to p. money THOM 363:8

printing gunpowder, p. CARL 75:12

namely, p., gunpowder BACON 22:2

thou hast caused p. to be used SHAK 327:3

priorities language of p. BEVAN 40:7

priority Observe degree, p. SHAK 335:7

prison black, you're born in p. MALC 248:7

just man is also a p.	THOR 364:2
p. to which the emperor holds	CUST 108:6
soul in p., I am not free	DEBS 111:3
'Twixt a p. and a smile	WOTT 394:8

prisoner object to your being taken p.

KITC 215:1

passing on the p.'s life SHAK 332:6

thoughts of a p. SOLZ 345:9

prisoners p. of addiction ILL 187:4

privacy right of p. means anything BREN 56:1

private conduct of every p. family SMITH 342:6

economy of p. people	SMITH 341:7
exertions of p. citizens	MAC 239:3
invade the sphere of p. life	MELB 256:3
kings neglect, that p. men enjoy	SHAK 326:16
lovely in p. life	BURKE 63:6
no liberty of p. opinion	HAL 166:6
p. faces in public places	AUDEN 21:1
p. opinion	HOBB 179:11
p. opulence and public squalor	GALB 145:10
p. property	LIPP 228:2
p. property is a necessary	TAWN 355:10
p. will governs	ROB 306:5
right of p. judgement	ADAMS 5:5
system of p. property	HAYEK 171:4

privilege danger justified p. WAUGH 380:8

Englishman's heaven-born p. ARN 17:5

free press is not a p. LIPP 228:4

not a product of p. HEATH 173:10

Privileged P. and the People DISR 118:3

prize Far and away the best p. ROOS 311:6

p. in the lottery of life RHOD 304:2

prizes offer glittering p. SMITH 343:8

probabilities human p. FAIR 135:2

problem or you're part of the p. CLE 98:2

p. of the colour line DU B 126:5

p. very often for people CURR 107:6

problems government does not solve p.

REAG 301:7

Others bring me p.	THAT 362:9
p. a President has to face	TRUM 371:8
social and political p.	BAL 31:8
such p. as it can solve	MARX 252:6
Two p. of our country	CART 77:8

procedural p. standards FRAN 141:6

procedure p. is all the poor Briton PICK 292:6

process common market is a p. MONN 262:6

procreation Like the p. of eels SCH 322:3

prodigality public p. and misconduct

SMITH 342:5

produce more than they p. HAYEK 171:10

product I am not a p. of privilege HEATH 173:10

process, not a p. MONN 262:6

production purpose of p. SMITH 342:1

upon the deep river of p. CHUR 88:9

productivity increase p. HEATH 173:6

profaned desolated and p. GLAD 154:12

professed p. philanthropist TROL 369:5

profession be the second oldest p. REAG 301:8

have a second p. NIC 272:9

professional p. politician POW 296:8

professors all conscientious p. PAINE 281:9

profit no p. but the name SHAK 326:2

profited p. from public service NIXON 276:3

profits best of all monopoly p. HICKS 178:6

civilization and p. go hand COOL 103:2

p. should belong TAWN 355:11

progress basic principle of all social p.

FOUR 140:2

Congress makes no p.	LIGNE 224:1
conservatism and p.	TROL 369:7
disavows P.	DISR 121:4
emphatically the history of p.	MAC 238:3
European talks of p.	DISR 118:9
party of p. or reform	MILL 259:1
policy for promoting p.	MAO 250:6
p. is not real	GEOR 150:10
p. of evolution	ADAMS 2:10
social p., order, security	JOHN 195:2

progression Nothing in p. can rest BURKE 65:2

progressive p. country DISR 119:13

prohibited in Germany all is p. MEG 255:3

prohibition by the P. laws EINS 128:7

Communism is like p. ROG 307:8

more successful than P. BOAZ 50:2

of the '20s and '30s, P. BOAZ 50:1

P....goes beyond the bounds LINC 224:4

proletarian p. socialist state LENIN 221:4

proletariat dictatorship of the p. MARX 252:5

promise Who broke no p. POPE 295:3

Whose p. none relies on ROCH 307:5

promised As the weird women p. SHAK 331:10

I've seen the p. land KING 211:4

You never reach the p. land | CALL 72:9
promises make good their p. | BAG 26:8
p. and panaceas | ROTH 314:2
result of interviews, p. | TAYL 358:2
vote for the man who p. least | BAR 32:7
young man of p. | BALF 31:6
propaganda purely for p. | BEAV 33:9
propagandist p.'s purpose | HUXL 186:5
propensities natural p. | BURKE 68:1
proper held the p. opinions | AUDEN 21:3
property consider himself as public p.
| JEFF 192:12
degrees and kinds of p. | MAD 246:2
distinguished by rank or p. | JUN 200:12
Every man holds his p. | ROOS 311:11
from the dominion of p. | GOLD 157:2
Greedy for the p. of others | SALL 319:4
no right to the p. of the rich | RUSK 315:8
not deprived of either p. | MACH 241:6
our p. belongs to everybody | RUSK 316:1
preservation of their p. | LOCKE 231:7
preserve his p. | LOCKE 231:5
private p. is a necessary | TAWN 355:10
private p. was the original | LIPP 228:2
P. is theft | PRO 298:5
p.-owning democracy | SKEL 340:9
p. they can call their own | WASH 379:6
right of governing was not p. | FOX 140:5
right of p. is the most important | TAFT 354:10
system of private p. | HAYEK 171:4
thereby makes it his p. | LOCKE 231:4
through p. | PANK 285:1
unequal distribution of p. | MAD 246:4
Where p. is in question | SAL 318:7
prophesy never safe to p. | HEAD 172:2
prophet p. in Israel | BIBLE 43:12
prophets ceased to pose as its p. | POPP 295:10
proportions by p. true | MARV 252:1
proposal describe a p. | LYNN 235:5
propose cabinet does not p. | ATTL 20:6
p. nothing | DERBY 114:1
prose You govern in p. | CUOMO 107:3
prospect p. of bettering | MILL 259:14
prospects political p. | HEAD 172:2
prosper Treason doth never p. | HAR 169:1
prosperous nation great and p. | BACON 23:9
p. or caring society | HES 178:2
prostitutes small nations like p. | KUBR 215:7
protect to p. the writer | ACH 1:7
protection entitled to p. by law | JACK 189:1
p. is not a principle | DISR 117:16
p. is not only dead | DISR 121:11
Protestant attacked me and the P. church
| NIEM 273:1
by my shoul 'tis a P. wind | WHAR 386:3
I am the P. whore | GWYN 162:7
preservation of the P. religion | HAMP 167:9

printing, and the P. Religion | CARL 75:12
P. ethic | WEBER 381:7
P. religion | BURKE 63:10
P. with a horse | BEHAN 34:9
Protestantism All P. | BURKE 63:10
proud man being too p. to fight | WILS 392:4
prove p. anything by figures | CARL 76:1
providence never could believe that P.
| RUMB 314:9
P. has not created mankind | TOCQ 365:6
p. that protects idiots | BISM 47:12
way that P. dictates | HITL 179:5
province p. they have desolated | GLAD 154:12
provinces defending those p. | SMITH 342:3
provision decent p. for the poor | JOHN 197:12
prudence p. never to practise | TWAIN 372:9
Prussia military domination of P. | ASQ 18:3
national industry of P. | MIR 261:6
psychological p. rule | KEYN 208:3
public After a lifetime in p. office | GALB 146:7
aggrandizes the p. | HUME 184:8
All my experience in p. life | PEEL 288:3
as if I was a p. meeting | VICT 374:8
at the expense of p. interests | TAYL 358:11
besetting sin of p. men | TAYL 358:11
burn your fingers in p. life | BEAV 33:4
consult the p. good | SWIFT 353:8
debate on p. issues | BREN 55:11
does not describe holding p. office | ACH 1:4
Every p. action | CORN 103:8
excites the p. odium | CLAY 97:7
failure of a listless p. | SOLZ 346:4
fascination of a p. execution | FOOT 138:4
for the p. good | LOCKE 231:9
government and p. opinion | SHAW 336:4
Great p. measures | PEEL 289:10
He died by inches in p. | ROS 312:6
If the British p. falls for this | HAIL 163:6
loudest complainers for the p. | BURKE 62:7
may be met with, in p. life | TAYL 358:4
no p. institutions | SMITH 343:1
one to mislead the p. | ASQ 18:6
private faces in p. places | AUDEN 21:1
private opulence and p. squalor | GALB 145:10
promote the p. interest | SMITH 342:4
p. be damned | VAND 373:2
p. has to bear it | PEEL 289:6
p. liberty | HENRY 176:8
p. opinion | BAG 24:1
p. prodigality and misconduct | SMITH 342:5
p. servants, therefore | TAYL 358:12
p. service carried on | TAWN 355:6
p. welfare may require | ROOS 311:11
p. will take care | SULZ 352:8
qualities to be found in p. life | DISR 121:19
require the p. expectation | GALB 146:6
researchers into P. Opinion | AUDEN 21:3

public (*cont.*):

servants of the p.	GOW 158:5
spending the p. money	COOL 103:6
true policy in p. life	PEEL 288:16
what one pleases about p. affairs	BLACK 48:4
what the p. will not stand	HARC 168:3
When a man assumes a p. trust	JEFF 192:12
youth to the aid of p. service	TREV 368:1

publicity oxygen of p. THAT 361:13
  qualities which create p. ATTL 20:4
public relations glorified p. man TRUM 371:5
publish p. and be damned WELL 384:4
pudding Take away that p. CHUR 95:1
Pulitzer P. Prize ready to be won CHIL 85:5
pull man with a political p. PLUN 294:7
pulled time we p. our finger out PHIL 291:5
puller p. down of kings SHAK 327:4
punch p. above its weight HURD 185:9
punctuality p. is the politeness LOU 233:4
Punica *P. fide* SALL 319:8
punish God p. England FUNKE 144:7
punished knave is not p. HAL 166:11
  should be p. PENN 289:14
punishments p. which corrupt PAINE 282:5
puppet czar and making him a p. SCHL 321:6
purchasing I am not worth p. REED 302:10
pure too p. an Air for Slaves ANON 12:13
purification p. of the Whig party MAC 238:4
Puritan P. hated bear-baiting MAC 239:2
Puritanism P. MENC 257:2
Puritans My ancestors were P. KEIL 203:4
  [P.] looked down MAC 237:7
purpose far-reaching in p. HOOV 182:7
  politics of p. HUMP 185:5
purposes government's p. BRAN 55:3
pursuit politicians in p. of votes GALB 146:10
  p. of happiness ANON 14:7
  p. of happiness JEFF 191:1
put up with which I will not p. CHUR 93:4
  Willie, what p. me up to it BEVIN 43:6
pygmies for peace like retarded p. PEAR 287:4
pyramid bottom of the economic p. ROOS 308:4
pyramids summit of these p. NAP 269:3
pyre heaping up its own funeral p. POW 296:10
Pyrenees P. are no more LOU 233:1

quackocracy baleful, stages of *q.* CARL 75:8
qualification My only great q. CARS 77:3
qualifying any q. adjectives LODGE 231:10
qualities great q., the imperious will BAG 25:2
  He has many good q. WILS 391:10
  none of the q. which create ATTL 20:4
quality q. of mercy is not strained SHAK 332:10
quarrel find q. in a straw SHAK 326:3
  have therefore a perpetual q. BURKE 64:4
  only one to make a q. INGE 187:5

q. in a far away country CHAM 80:9
  suffer by a sanguinary q. BAG 28:1
quarter for the remaining q. NAP 269:7
Quebec Long Live free Q. DE G 112:14
queen dying for Q. and country THOM 364:6
  I am your anointed Q. ELIZ 130:4
  I have been to the Q. GLAD 155:10
  Q....must sign her own BAG 25:12
  Q. of Scots is this day ELIZ 130:5
queer All the world is q. OWEN 280:5
question better to debate a q. JOUB 200:7
  Irish secretly changed the q. SELL 323:10
  merits of any political q. BURKE 66:2
  q. is absurd AUDEN 21:4
questions awkward q. LYNN 235:1
quiet All q. along the Potomac MCCL 239:9
  monopoly profits is a q. life HICKS 178:6
  You'll never have a q. world SHAW 336:19
quietus might his q. make SHAK 325:8
quilt q. of jumbled crochet CHUR 89:5
quis *Sed q. custodiet ipsos* JUV 201:6
quitter you won't be backing a q. KERR 206:8
quote q. aptly HOGB 181:1

race in a r. to run second MACL 243:8
  most pernicious r. SWIFT 353:6
  no matter what their r. WILL 389:5
  Not only did we play the r. card SHAP 335:12
  Purity of r. does not exist FISH 137:1
  r. is not to the swift BIBLE 43:16
  slinks out of the r. MILT 260:6
  white r. *is* the cancer SONT 346:6
racehorses public servants, like r. TAYL 358:12
races lighter r. of men DU B 126:5
racing r. tipster TAYL 357:2
racket This is all a German r. RIDL 305:6
radical I never dared be r. FROST 144:3
  most r. revolutionary AREN 15:10
  must have r. origins TREV 368:6
  my advice is: Be as r. as you like CHAM 80:2
  Nothing commends a r. change FISH 137:2
  of the r. politician TROL 369:9
  R. is a man with both ROOS 309:7
radicalism r. and nothing else DISR 118:4
radicals I'm one of these goddam r. CAP 75:6
  to the dogs or the r. WILDE 388:8
  trouble with r. CARV 78:1
raft republic is a r. AMES 8:2
ragout in a fricassee, or a r. SWIFT 354:1
raid r. by Dr Jameson KRUG 215:6
railway by r. timetables TAYL 357:8
  dying beast lying across a r. line JENK 194:5
  miniature r. MORT 266:8
rain be able to command the r. PEPYS 290:1
  droppeth as the gentle r. SHAK 332:12

rainbow real r. coalition — JACK 189:7

raise r. others to his own level — TROL 369:6
r. the price of corn — BYRON 71:5

rank However distinguished by r. — JUN 200:12
r. is but the guinea's stamp — BURNS 68:10
That unassailable holds on his r. — SHAK 329:3

ranks closes its r. — ORW 278:5
it must first close r. — CARM 76:17

ransom Of the world's r. — SHAK 333:4

rapine march through r. — GLAD 154:16
r. and injustice — SMITH 341:2

rascals r., would you live for ever — FRED 143:2

rash r. and precipitate assent — PEEL 288:4

rat Anyone can r. — CHUR 88:5
Grey was like a r. — ANON 9:4
Mr Speaker, I smell a r. — ROCHE 307:4
not worth a r.'s squeak — RUSK 315:11

ratio increases in a geometrical r. — MALT 248:9

rational lack of r. conviction — RUSS 316:6

rats r. of my own breed — VOLT 376:4

ravished Or r. with the whistling — POPE 295:5

razor fitter instrument than a r. — PEEL 288:12
with an arse full of r. blades — KEAT 202:6

reach I r. for my pistol — JOHST 198:14
You never r. the promised land — CALL 72:9

reaction Any r. which is — TREV 368:6

reactionaries r. are paper tigers — MAO 250:5

reactionary If r. measures are to — BISM 47:7
R. is a somnambulist — ROOS 309:7
recklessly r. steps — BOOK 52:1

read Not that I ever r. them — SHER 338:11
r. my lips: no new taxes — BUSH 69:7
When I want to r. a novel — DISR 121:18
Why r. the crystal — BEVAN 40:8
You can r. — WALP 378:10

readers by Bible r. *for* Bible r. — BAIN 28:3

ready necessity of being r. — LINC 225:9

Reagan Ronald R....is attempting — SCHR 321:8

real focus of politics on r. people — HAVEL 170:5
hatreds which sound so r. — TROL 370:8

realization r. of tomorrow — ROOS 310:9

realm one r., one people, one leader — ANON 9:11
this r., this England — SHAK 333:4

reap r. the whirlwind — BIBLE 44:1

reappraisal r. of basic United States — DULL 126:8

reaps seed ye sow, another r. — SHEL 338:4

rearming Germany was r. — BALD 29:10

reason beyond the bounds of r. — LINC 224:1
by their feelings than by r. — ADAMS 5:6
Come now, let us r. together — JOHN 196:11
dictates of r. and justice — HAM 167:6
dominion of r. — PRICE 298:3
influence of mere r. — PEEL 289:10
r., and justice, tells me — BURKE 64:5
R. and the Imagination — MAC 236:6
R. herself will respect — GIBB 152:7
R. to rule, but mercy to forgive — DRYD 125:15

We know no r. why gunpowder — ANON 13:2
With reasonable men, I will r. — GARR 148:5

reasonable after r. discussion — CHUR 93:11
figure of 'The R. Man' — HERB 177:1
will to be rightful must be r. — JEFF 192:5
With r. men, I will reason — GARR 148:5

reasoning r. of tyrants — GIBB 151:8

reasons R. are not like garments — ESSEX 134:2
r. will certainly be wrong — MANS 250:1
twenty r. why I can't — BEVIN 43:1

rebel die like a true-blue r. — HILL 178:9
I am *still* a r. — BROWN 59:5
What is a r. — CAMUS 74:6

rebelled have already r. — GIBB 151:8

rebellion bring the r. to an end — WILS 390:11
if r. was the certain consequence — MANS 249:6
little r. now and then — JEFF 191:6
r. against the United States — LINC 225:11
R. lay in his way — SHAK 326:5
R. to tyrants — BRAD 54:8
rum, Romanism, and r. — BURC 62:2

rebels One final tip to r. — NIC 272:9
r. are our countrymen again — GRANT 159:8
subjects are r. from principle — BURKE 67:2

rebirth r. of the Union — WILS 392:6

rebuild no use in attempting to r. — MILL 259:6

receiver corrupts both the r. — BURKE 66:13

recession It's a r. when — TRUM 371:14
spend your way out of a r. — CALL 72:8

reclamation It is land r. — WILS 391:4

recognition We are fighting for r. — MALC 248:8

reconciliation silence and r. — MAC 238:8

recovery *green shoots of r.* — LAM 217:1

recreational r. activities — BOAZ 50:2

red better r. than dead — ANON 9:1
r. men scalped each other — MAC 239:4
We'll keep the r. flag flying here — CONN 101:7
your raiment all r. — MAC 236:3

redress r. by mob law — LINC 224:3

redtape r. talking-machine — CARL 76:8

refined most r. citizens — SHEL 338:6

reform cured by r. or revolution — BERL 39:4
fringe in all r. movements — ROOS 311:13
great r. in politics if wisdom — CHUR 92:14
party of progress or r. — MILL 259:1
r. has dished it — DISR 120:16
retrenchment, and r. — BRIG 56:5
sets about r. — TOCQ 367:3
To innovate is not to r. — BURKE 68:4

reformation plotting some new r. — DRYD 125:2
total r. is wanted in England — PAINE 282:3

reforms beneficial r. — THAT 362:15
odds we'll get r. are zero — PEROT 290:10

refuge patriotism is the last r. — JOHN 198:3

refuse thrice r.: was this ambition — SHAK 330:3
war will cease when men r. — ANON 14:6
wretched r. of your teeming shore — LAZ 219:7

register r. of the crimes | GIBB 151:6
regret Old Age a r. | DISR 117:8
regrets series of congratulatory r. | DISR 120:10
regulate r. matters of the mind | TRUM 371:6
regulations greatest avalanche of r. | BOOK 52:2
 ten thousand r. | CHUR 94:14
Reich *ein R., ein Volk, ein Führer* | ANON 9:11
 German *R.* is made | BISM 47:5
reign George VI's r. | WAUGH 380:10
 His lazy, long, lascivious r. | DEFOE 111:8
 Long to r. over us | HOGG 181:2
 prince who begins early to r. | BAG 26:2
reigned I have r. with your loves | ELIZ 132:1
reigning capable of r. if only | TAC 354:8
reigns king r., and the people | THI 363:2
reinforcement r. of the State | CAMUS 74:7
reins throw the r. over their necks | CLAY 97:10
reject To elect, and to r. | PAINE 283:7
rejoice Just r. at that news | THAT 361:6
relation No cold r. is a zealous | BURKE 67:9
 r. of men dominating men | WEBER 381:8
relations personal character and r. | NAP 269:7
 recognising the r. | MILL 259:9
 r. with Peking | NIXON 274:7
relief system of outdoor r. | BRIG 57:2
relieve chance to r. yourself | ANON 12:9
relieved are r. | SHAK 326:1
religion As to r., I hold it to be | PAINE 281:9
 black face and a different r. | EDW 128:2
 But the r. most prevalent | BURKE 63:10
 cult is a r. with no political | WOLFE 394:1
 disentangle r. from politics | TREV 368:9
 dominion of r. | GOLD 157:2
 feature of *any* r. | PAINE 282:9
 Freedom of r. | JEFF 192:8
 my r. is to do good | PAINE 283:2
 patriotism is a sort of r. | TOCQ 365:4
 politics as well as in r. | JUN 200:11
 politics, like r. | JEFF 193:3
 prefer fox-hunting—the wisest r. | HAIL 163:3
 r. is allowed to invade | MELB 256:3
 R....is the opium of the people | MARX 252:2
 r., justice, counsel | BACON 22:16
 R. may in most of its forms | RUSS 316:11
 r. of humanity | PAINE 283:9
 r. of Socialism | BEVAN 40:7
 r. without a prelate | BANC 31:11
 reproach to r. and government | PENN 289:13
religions r. considered man | TOCQ 366:5
religious all r. revolution | WEBER 381:10
relish deal closely and with r. | MACL 242:6
reluctant Not a r. peer | BENN 36:1
remedy dangerous r. | FAWK 136:1
 force is not a r. | BRIG 57:1
 prefer the grievance to the r. | PEEL 289:5
 r. our *enemies* have chosen | SHER 339:1
 Things without all r. | SHAK 332:1

'Tis a sharp r., but a sure one | RAL 300:5
remember Please to r. the Fifth | ANON 13:2
 r. what is past | HAL 165:5
 will little note, nor long r. | LINC 226:3
remembered something to be r. | ADAMS 3:6
 would you like to be r. | POW 297:11
remorse r. from power | SHAK 328:9
remove not malignant and r. it | WAUGH 380:9
render r. therefore unto Caesar | BIBLE 44:7
rendezvous r. with destiny | ROOS 308:10
renewed perpetually r. | LIPP 228:5
Reno'd king's moll R. | ANON 11:7
renounce I r. war | FOSD 139:6
renovation r. of the natural order | PAINE 282:11
renown land of just and old r. | TENN 359:8
rent r. is that portion | RIC 304:4
 tear-wrung millions—why? for r. | BYRON 71:6
repartee always the best r. | DISR 118:8
repeal r. of bad laws | GRANT 160:2
repeat condemned to r. it | SANT 320:4
repel retard what we cannot r. | JOHN 197:2
replace r. the pilot of the calm | BAG 25:3
reply I pause for a r. | SHAK 329:12
report false r., if believed | MED 255:2
reporters speaking through r. | CARL 76:7
reporting r., rather than debating | HOGG 181:3
representation taxation and r. | CAMD 73:5
 taxation without r. is tyranny | OTIS 279:14
representative being your r. | BELL 35:2
 drollery called a r. government | DISR 118:7
 Your r. owes you | BURKE 63:8
representing r. the citizenship | MACD 240:7
repression less than the price of r. | DU B 126:7
reproach leave affairs of r. | MACH 241:9
reproofs Even r. from authority | BACON 22:12
republic England is a disguised r. | BAG 27:2
 essence of the R. | ROB 306:9
 good citizen in this R. | ROOS 311:3
 great R. is a Government | FORD 138:12
 If a r. is small, it is destroyed | MONT 264:6
 more corrupt the r. | TAC 354:6
 Only Love the Beloved R. | FORS 139:5
 r., if you can keep it | FRAN 142:8
 r. is a raft | AMES 8:2
republican God is a R. and Santa | O'RO 277:3
 no Democratic or R. way | LA G 216:5
 on r. principles | SHAW 335:13
 R. candidate for President | SIMP 340:7
 R. form of Government | SPEN 347:5
 r. is the only form | JEFF 191:10
 respectable R. cloth coat | NIXON 273:6
 understood by r. government | TOCQ 365:8
Republicans If they [the R.] | STEV 350:1
 We are all R. | JEFF 192:4
 We are R. and don't propose | BURC 62:2
republics characteristic of small r. | BOL 51:1*
 R. end in luxury | MONT 264:3

R. weak   BAG 25:9
repulsive Roundheads (right but r.)   SELL 323:5
reputation Dear for her r.   SHAK 333:4
  spotless r.   SHAK 333:1
requirement first r. of politics   MAJOR 247:8
re-rat ingenuity to r.   CHUR 88:5
researchers r. into Public Opinion   AUDEN 21:3
resent I don't r. his popularity   REAG 302:6
reservations no mental r.   LINC 225:6
reserved I am r. for some end   CLIVE 99:8
residence r. within   ANON 9:13
resign says he won't r.   GALB 146:2
resignation Always threatening r.   BEAV 33:10
  by death are few; by r. none   JEFF 192:9
  Has he got a r. in him   BUTL 70:1
resigned Prime Minister has r.   ANON 10:6
resist r. authority   BAG 27:3
resistance act of intellectual r.   O'BR 276:5
  I am for r. by the *sword*   CLAY 97:1
  liberty is the history of r.   WILS 391:11
  refinement on the principle of r.   BURKE 63:10
  relation between pressure and r.   NIC 271:7
  r. of established ideas   BERL 39:6
  r. of the adversaries   STAL 348:3
resolution In war: r.   CHUR 93:5
  r. on reflection   WALP 377:10
resort God's infinite mercy, a last r.   O'RO 277:2
resources r. of civilization   GLAD 154:15
  rock of the national r.   WEBS 382:6
respect cease to r. each other   TAYL 357:15
  fail to get r.   MACH 241:7
  impartial r. for the rights   BAG 27:10
  insult their self-r.   TAWN 355:12
respected r. persons occasionally   HURD 185:8
respecter God is any r. of persons   BROWN 59:2
respond To r. to evil   HAVEL 170:6
responsibility Collective r.   LYNN 235:9
  liberty means r.   SHAW 336:8
  lively sense of collective r.   ALD 6:9
  power without r.   KIPL 214:1
  r. for action   GALB 145:5
  r. of a political party   HAIL 163:4
  r. without power   STOP 351:7
rest all the r. were little ones   ELIZ 131:9
resting history knows no r. places   KISS 214:7
restricted R. means   LYNN 235:7
restrictions finding greater r.   KEIL 203:4
restructuring idea of r. [*perestroika*]   GORB 158:3
results more for routine than for r.   BAG 26:9
  presenting the r.   ROSS 313:4
retail r. mind in a wholesale   LLOY 230:7
retaliation policy of r.   PARN 286:6
retard r. what we cannot repel   JOHN 197:2
reticence It is a r.   GLAD 155:12
retirement final r. from the stage   MACM 245:14
  there must be no r.   HAIG 163:2

retreat no r. from the principles   MURR 268:4
  not r. a single inch   GARR 148:3
retrenchment peace, r., and reform   BRIG 56:5
retrograde r. if it does not advance   GIBB 151:13
retrospective r. or utopian   ARON 17:7
return I shall r.   MAC 235:12
revelation r. is necessarily limited   PAINE 283:6
revenge Gerald Ford as his r.   ABZUG 1:2
  not to r. what has happened   BISM 46:7
  ranging for r.   SHAK 329:9
  take r. for slight injuries   MACH 241:2
revenue abundant streams of r.   WEBS 382:6
  almost the whole public r.   SMITH 342:5
  Instead of a standing r.   BURKE 64:4
  Internal R. Service   SULL 352:5
reverence mystic r.   BAG 24:9
  so poor to do him r.   SHAK 330:5
  take away the mystical r.   JAM 190:1
revolt It is a big r.   LA R 218:1
  r. by all means   MACM 244:10
revolution After a r., you see   HAL 165:8
  age of r. and reformation   JEFF 192:8
  cured by reform or r.   BERL 39:4
  day after the r.   AREN 15:10
  fear that the R., like Saturn   VERG 373:8
  I entered into this R.   BROWN 59:5
  make peaceful r. impossible   KENN 204:11
  may be fatal to a r.   TOCQ 366:9
  No, Sire, a big r.   LA R 218:1
  not the leaders of a r.   CONR 102:4
  poverty is the parent of r.   ARIS 16:8
  religion from politics in a r.   TREV 368:9
  restrained tyrants, averted r.   BENN 36:8
  r. is not the same   MAO 250:2
  r. of rising expectations   CLEV 99:4
  safeguard a r.   ORW 279:7
  served the cause of the r.   BOL 51:2
  social order destroyed by a r.   TOCQ 367:3
  time to stop a r.   STEV 350:4
  white heat of the technological r. WILS 390:5
  You've had a r.   GEOR 150:7
revolutionaries R. are more formalistic
                                                CALV 73:4
  r. are potential   ORW 278:4
revolutionary can't feel fierce and r.   LINK 227:9
  continent of r. change   BUSH 69:9
  Every r. ends as an oppressor   CAMUS 74:8
  fine r. phrases   KHR 209:8
  on the eve of r. crises   BOOK 52:1
  r. government is the despotism   ROB 306:8
  r. right to dismember   LINC 225:7
  r. will become a conservative   AREN 15:10
revolutionists age fatal to R.   DESM 114:4
revolutions collapse of the r.   ROB 307:1
  main cause of r.   INGE 187:9
  modern r. have ended   CAMUS 74:7
  not a nursery of future r.   BURKE 66:9

revolutions (*cont.*):

R. are celebrated	BOUL 53:6
R. are not made	PHIL 291:8
R. have never lightened	SHAW 336:6
R. in this country	MACL 243:2
r. never go backward	SEW 324:1
share in two r. is living	PAINE 283:10
What were formerly called r.	PAINE 282:11

reward act worthy of r.

	BROWN 59:1
should be well fed with r.	TAYL 358:12

rhetoric death, without r.

	SIEY 340:4

rhetorician sophistical r.

	DISR 120:11

Rhine you think of the R.

	BALD 29:7

riband Just for a r. to stick

	BROW 60:1

rich cannot make everybody r.

	SEN 323:12
Chief Justice was r., quiet	MAC 238:7
convenient time to tax r. people	LLOY 229:13
forbids the r.	FRAN 141:2
Great Britain is not r. enough	REED 302:10
if the incomes of the r.	SHAW 336:21
interfered in behalf of the r.	BROWN 59:1
it is better to be r. than poor	CECIL 79:7
poor by destroying the r.	LINC 227:7
poor people in r. countries	BAUER 33:1
prey of the r. on the poor	JEFF 191:5
R. AND THE POOR	DISR 118:2
r. enough to pay over 75%	HEAL 172:7
r. have no right	RUSK 315:8
r. in a more precious treasure	MAC 237:7
r. man in his castle	ALEX 7:1
r. man makes a bonny traitor	PAINE 282:2
r. men rule the law	GOLD 157:4
save the few who are r.	KENN 204:3
tend to make the r. richer	NEHRU 270:11
toward the r. society	JOHN 196:2
When the r. wage war	SART 320:5
which people can still get r.	REAG 301:11

riches best r., ignorance of wealth

	GOLD 157:6
material and spiritual r.	KHR 209:8

rid decorated, and got r. of

	CIC 95:13

riddle r. wrapped in a mystery

	CHUR 90:1

ride if you cannot r. two horses

	MAXT 254:5

ridiculous from the sublime to the r.

	NAP 269:9
no spectacle so r. as the British	MAC 237:8

Ridley Be of good comfort Master R.

	LAT 218:6

rien *r.*

	LOU 233:2

right almost always in the r.

	SMITH 344:10
as a nation being so r.	WILS 392:4
be on the r. side and lose	GALB 146:1
beyond doubt that they are r.	VAN 373:3
defend to the death your r.	VOLT 375:11
exercise their constitutional r.	LINC 225:7
folly of hereditary r. in kings	PAINE 281:2
forgive those who were r.	MACL 243:1
generalities of natural r.	CHO 85:8
God has more r. to be obeyed	JOHN 195:1
greed is r.	WEIS 383:6

half of the people are r.	WHITE 386:6
if r., to be kept r.	SCH 322:2
know what is r.	JOHN 196:6
law is demanded as a r.	ROOS 311:7
majority never has r. on its side	IBSEN 186:8
man of the r.	MOSL 267:2
my r. is retreating	FOCH 138:1
natural r. of all to the ballot	ANTH 15:7
New South Wales R.	WRAN 394:10
no r. in the circus	MAXT 254:5
no r. to strike against the public	COOL 103:1
of no government, r. by divine r.	HARR 169:7
our country, r. or wrong	DEC 111:4
our r. as well as our duty	PANK 284:10
put the r. man in the r. place	JEFF 193:14
rather be r. than be President	CLAY 97:8
r. is more precious than peace	WILS 392:13
R....is the child of law	BENT 37:7
'r.' means nothing but	PLATO 294:2
r. must unavoidably be politic	PEEL 287:8
r. of the ignorant man	CARL 76:3
r. to be consulted	BAG 26:1
r. to be heard	HUMP 185:4
r. to be let alone	BRAN 55:2
r. to do everything the laws	MONT 264:8
r. to leave any country	ANON 9:13
r. to say what one pleases	BLACK 48:4
r. which goes unrecognized	WEIL 383:4
Roundheads (R. but Repulsive)	SELL 323:5
secure of private r.	DRYD 125:11
unalienable, indefeasible, divine r.	ADAMS 3:4
When I am r., I get angry	DE G 112:5
with firmness in the r.	LINC 227:1

righteous armour of a r. cause

	BRYAN 60:4

rightful will to be r.

	JEFF 192:5

rights absolutes in our Bill of R.

	BLACK 48:3
adverse to the r. of other citizens	MAD 246:3
Bill of R. was not ordained	JORD 199:4
certain unalienable r.	ANON 14:7
equal in dignity and r.	ANON 8:4
equal r.	JOHN 195:8
extension of women's r.	FOUR 140:2
natural r. is simple nonsense	BENT 37:8
refuses to defend his r.	JACK 188:6
respect for the r. of all	BAG 27:10
r. inherent and inalienable	JEFF 191:1
r. of an Englishman	JUN 201:3
r. of the smaller nationalities	ASQ 18:3
theories about the r. of man	BURKE 66:14
trusted to safeguard human r.	SCAR 320:8
violates the inalienable r. of man	ROB 306:6
war with the r. of mankind	JEFF 191:10
Where all your r. become	CAS 78:2

ring They now r. the bells

	WALP 378:5
When we let freedom r.	KING 210:11

riot r. is at bottom

	KING 211:3

rise nation shall r. against nation | BIBLE 44:9
  people should never r. | ADAMS 3:6
  populace r. at once | WHIT 388:2
rising All r. to great place | BACON 22:13
  means of r. in the world | JOHN 198:4
  passed from r. hope | FOOT 138:8
  revolution of r. expectations | CLEV 99:4
rivalry dead there is no r. | MAC 237:10
river bridge where there is no r. | KHR 209:6
  disorderly government as in a r. | HAL 165:13
  fame is like a r. | BACON 22:15
  greatest r. of human industry | TOCQ 365:2
  guy who cleans the r. | PEROT 290:8
  Parliament upon the r. | WELL 385:2
rivers r. of blood must yet flow | JEFF 193:11
road in the middle of the r. | BEVAN 40:13
  r. to Damascus | THAT 362:7
  what is the r. to power | BURKE 65:8
roar called upon to give the r. | CHUR 94:1
roast no politics in boiled and r. | SMITH 344:7
  r. beef of old England | BURKE 63:3
rob r. those who use the money | TAWN 355:11
robber ties the r.'s bundle | SHEL 338:7
robe nor the judge's r. | SHAK 332:7
robes r. ye weave, another wears | SHEL 338:4
Robin R. and I are two honest | SHIP 339:7
robs r. Peter to pay Paul | SHAW 337:2
rock 'doggie' until you find a r. | CATL 78:5
rocked r. the system | ROB 307:3
rocket As he rose like a r. | PAINE 283:4
  every r. fired signifies | EIS 129:4
rocking r. a grown man | BURKE 65:2
rod in time the r. | SHAK 332:4
rogue no room for the r. elephant | TAYL 356:7
roi Plus royaliste que le r. | ANON 13:3
role has not yet found a r. | ACH 1:5
roll r. up that map | PITT 293:11
Rolls-Royce is a bit like a R. | BUTL 70:4
Roman effort to found the R. nation | VIRG 375:4
  Empire was neither holy, nor R. | VOLT 375:9
  I am a R. citizen | CIC 95:10
  noblest R. of them all | SHAK 330:16
  R. people had but one neck | CAL 72:5
  that would not be a R. | SHAK 329:12
Roman Empire deceased R. | HOBB 180:9
Romanism rum, R., and rebellion | BURC 62:2
Romans friends, R., countrymen | SHAK 329:13
  R. were like brothers | MAC 237:1
romantic r. Ireland's dead | YEATS 395:4
Romanus civis R. sum | CIC 95:10
  when he could say civis R. sum | PALM 284:2
Rome bishop of R. | BOOK 51:6
  but that I loved R. more | SHAK 329:10
  Cato is the voice of R. | JONS 199:3
  Men, I'm getting out of R. | GAR 148:1
  Now is it R. indeed | SHAK 328:6
  R., in the height | WEBS 382:7

R. is but a wilderness | SHAK 335:6
R., though her eagle | WALL 377:1
R. under Sulla | ADC 5:7
than second at R. | CAES 71:10
treaty [of R.] is like | DENN 113:5
you cruel men of R. | SHAK 328:1
roof beneath whose r. I sleep | BORR 53:3
roofs tiles on the r. | LUTH 234:7
room great hatred, little r. | YEATS 396:2
  is it Rome indeed and r. enough | SHAK 328:6
  just entering the r. | BROUN 58:3
  perpetual struggle for r. and food | MALT 248:10
  There is always r. at the top | WEBS 383:1
rooms boys in the back r. | BEAV 33:8
Roosevelt R....Give us the tools | CHUR 91:6
roost rules the r. | ANON 10:8
root Lay then the axe to the r. | PAINE 282:5
  motto has been 'r., hog, or die' | BROG 57:5
rooted r. in age-long traditions | BALF 30:7
rooting r. for Gary Cooper | BALD 28:6
roses like girls and r. | DE G 112:13
  smells like r. | JOHN 196:8
rotten r. in the state of Denmark | SHAK 325:6
  shines like r. wood | RAL 300:4
  stinks like r. mackerel | RAND 301:1
rottenness r. begins in his conduct | JEFF 191:14
Roundheads R. (Right but Repulsive)
                                SELL 323:5
rout r. send forth | MAC 236:3
routine more for r. than for results | BAG 26:9
royal R. authority is a great spring | MONT 264:14
  this is the r. Law | COR 103:10
  This r. throne of kings | SHAK 333:4
royaliste Plus r. que le roi | ANON 13:3
royalties entertain four r. | SAL 318:2
royalty our r. is to be reverenced | BAG 25:13
  r. is a government | BAG 25:9
  when you come to r. | DISR 121:4
rue nought shall make us r. | SHAK 331:1
ruffians all the crowned r. | PAINE 281:4
ruffle Would r. up your spirits | SHAK 330:10
rugged r. individualism | HOOV 182:8
ruin boy will r. himself | GEOR 149:10
  Resolved to r. or to rule the state | DRYD 125:6
  Thou its r. didst not share | DOD 122:5
ruined finest plans are always r. | BREC 55:8
  men that are r. | BURKE 68:1
  No nation was ever r. by trade | FRAN 142:6
rule bear r. in their kingdoms | BIBLE 44:3
  bureaucracy, the r. of no one | MCC 239:8
  Ill can he r. the great | SPEN 347:8
  other party is unfit to r. | MENC 257:4
  reason to r. | DRYD 125:15
  Resolved to ruin or to r. the state | DRYD 125:6
  rich men r. the law | GOLD 157:4
  that some should r. | ARIS 16:7
  To r. o'er freemen | BRO 57:7

rule (*cont.*):

we prefer r. by amateurs ATTL 20:12
ruled others be r. ARIS 16:7
rulers conduct of their r. ADAMS 3:4
law for r. and people DAVIS 110:2
Of the best r. LAO-T 217:8
r. have no authority from God MAYH 254:7
rules by any hypercritical r. LINC 225:6
I played by the r. of politics NIXON 275:1
man of genius r. STEP 349:3
minutes r. the roost ANON 10:8
We need fixed r., not fixers HAYEK 171:8
ruling hated the r. few BENT 37:11
in the hands of the r. class STAL 348:3
refresh their r. class TREV 368:5
rum r., Romanism, and rebellion BURC 62:2
r., sodomy, prayers CHUR 93:7
rumour this, the sound and r. MORR 266:5
rumours wars and r. of wars BIBLE 44:8
rump r. Parliament—so called SELL 323:6
run country was r. by two men ROTH 313:7
I don't r. in a race MACL 243:8
In the long r we are all dead KEYN 207:6
Now Teddy must r. KENN 206:5
They get r. down BEVAN 40:13
runner-up no second prize for the r. BRAD 54:6
running all their r. dogs MAO 250:7
can't keep on r. from labour JACK 189:8
keep r. with the pack BUTL 70:9
Rupert Prince R. DISR 117:14
R. of Debate BULW 62:1
R. of the Rhine MAC 236:4
russet-coated plain r. captain CROM 105:3
Russia action of R. CHUR 90:1
between R. and British India SAL 317:8
in R., Communism SOLZ 346:3
legislation which outlaws R. REAG 301:13
Make a good treaty with R. BISM 46:3
proletarian socialist state in R. LENIN 221:4
R. can be an empire BRZ 61:3
R. has two generals NICH 271:5
R.'s future HERZ 177:8
Whoever has really seen R. CUST 108:7
Russian not to embrace the R. CHAN 81:8
R. Ambassador CHAN 81:9
R. autocracy turned upside down HERZ 177:7
Russians keep the R. out ISMAY 188:4
R. and the Americans TOCQ 365:9

sabre keenness of his s. WALP 377:8
sack S. the lot FISH 137:3
sacked we are all s. CLARK 96:6
sacred facts are s. SCOTT 322:4
only s. thing FRAN 141:3
reserved for s. texts KAUF 202:3

sacrifice give an example of s. LLOY 230:11
great pinnacle of s. LLOY 229:6
makes undaunted the final s. SPR 348:1
people being asked to s. GING 153:3
refused a lesser s. MARY 253:7
s. to the graces BURKE 67:11
Still stands Thine ancient S. KIPL 212:11
Too long a s. YEATS 395:7
sacrificed s. to conciseness JOHN 197:5
sacrificers s., but not butchers SHAK 328:12
sacrifices s. it to your opinion BURKE 63:8
sacrilege consecrated s. DISR 119:16
sacrilegious Most s. murder SHAK 331:9
sad tell s. stories of the death SHAK 333:8
saddle put Germany in the s. BISM 46:8
saddled millions ready s. RUMB 314:9
sadly take their pleasures s. SULLY 352:7
sadness shade of s. WHIT 388:5
safe National Health Service is s. THAT 361:5
s. for democracy WILS 392:12
s. for diversity KENN 205:4
s. for hypocrisy WOLFE 393:6
s. to be unpopular STEV 350:7
safeguard one s. DEM 113:2
s. of the West WORD 394:6
safeguards destroy the juridical s. HAYEK 171:9
s. acceptable to all nations TRUM 371:4
s. of liberty have been forged FRAN 141:8
safer much s. for a prince MACH 241:3
s. than a known way HASK 170:2
safety by a politician, so has s. LYNN 234:10
every man shall eat in s. SHAK 327:9
obtain a little temporary s. FRAN 141:9
's. first' does not mean BALD 29:4
s., honour, and welfare CHAR 82:8
said if you want anything s. THAT 360:8
sailed never s. with *me* before JACK 189:3
saint seem a s. when most I play SHAK 334:11
saints Christ and His s. slept ANON 12:5
salad shit can turn to chicken s. JOHN 195:4
salmon s.'s going upstream WHITE 387:1
smoked s. and tinned s. WILS 390:4
saloon last chance s. MELL 256:7
s. keepers were Democrats GRE 161:2
salus S. *populi suprema est lex* CIC 95:6
this sentence, s. *populi* SELD 323:3
salutes see if anyone s. it ANON 11:12
salvation commence the s. of Europe PITT 293:8
mankind's s. lies exclusively SOLZ 345:11
not the s. of the Union WILS 392:3
Samaritan remember the Good S. THAT 362:1
same facing in the s. direction ROST 313:6
we must all say *the* s. MELB 256:2
sanctions financial s. WILS 390:11
sanctuary classes which need s. BALD 29:3
sandhills Everest among the s. ASQ 18:8

sang I s. a king out of three | WHAR 386:4
sanguinary suffer by a s. quarrel | BAG 28:1
sank They s. my boat | KENN 205:11
Sansculotte *bon S. Jésus* | DESM 114:4
Santa Claus going to shoot S. | SMITH 343:6
  in the dark besides S. | HOOV 182:11
  S. is a Democrat | O'RO 277:3
sat everyone has s. | CUMM 107:2
  when they have s. down | CHUR 87:5
  You have s. too long here | CROM 105:8
Satanic Among these dark S. mills | BLAKE 49:5
satirist s. may laugh | GIBB 152:2
saucepan dance like fishes in a s. | KHR 209:5
savage almost a s. | TOCQ 365:2
savaged s. by a dead sheep | HEAL 172:10
save destroy the town to s. it | ANON 11:3
  God s. the king | HOGG 181:2
  helped s. the world | KEYN 208:7
  if you want to s. yourselves | BALD 29:6
  little less democracy to s. | ATK 19:4
  nobly s., or meanly lose | LINC 226:1
  nothing will s. | WHIT 387:7
  to s. the Party we love | GAIT 145:1
  to s. the Union | LINC 226:2
  To s. your world | AUDEN 21:6
saved they only s. the world | CHES 84:10
  to be s. in this World | HAL 165:3
savings If you strike at s. | CHUR 88:8
say s. what you think | TAC 354:7
  They are to s. what they please | FRED 143:4
  we must all s. *the same* | MELB 256:2
  what they are going to s. | CHUR 87:5
saying as bad as we'd been s. | KENN 204:9
scabbard threw away the s. | CLAR 96:1
scabbards leapt from their s. | BURKE 66:15
scabs Make yourselves s. | SHAK 324:4
scaffold truth forever on the s. | LOW 234:2
scandal exposing a sewage s. | LAW 219:1
scandalous merry monarch, s. | ROCH 307:6
scarecrow not make a s. of the law | SHAK 332:5
scarlet raise the s. standard high | CONN 101:7
scene this our lofty s. | SHAK 329:6
scent whiff of s. | LLOY 230:2
sceptered this s. isle | SHAK 333:4
schedule My s. is already full | KISS 214:2
schemes most s. of political | JOHN 197:10
Schleswig-Holstein S. question | PALM 284:7
scholarship slender indications of s. | CHUR 88:10
school erecting a grammar s. | SHAK 327:3
  every fucking grammar s. | CROS 106:5
  s. of Manchester | DISR 121:14
  went to s. without any boots | BULM 61:6
schoolboy Every s. knows who | MAC 238:6
schools hundred s. of thought | MAO 250:6
science dismal s. | CARL 76:9
  founded an entire s. of Political | RUSK 316:2
  objective of the s. of politics | ARIS 16:2

politics is not an exact s. | BISM 46:4
s. of diplomacy consists | ADAMS 4:10
so-called s. of poll-taking | WHITE 386:7
stick to s. | BEVIN 42:8
typical triumph of modern s. | WAUGH 380:9
scientific Our s. power has outrun | KING 211:1
  s. revolution | WILS 390:5
scores bridge s. in his head | BUTL 70:6
scorn think foul s. that Parma | ELIZ 130:9
scorning s. the base degrees | SHAK 328:10
scotched We have s. the snake | SHAK 332:1
Scotchmen S. are to Englishmen | PEEL 288:15
Scotland grapes can be raised in S. | SMITH 342:7
  stands S. where it did | SHAK 332:3
scoundrel last refuge of a s. | JOHN 198:3
scoundrels ten obvious s. | MENC 257:3
scrap s. of paper | BETH 39:8
screaming Wild men s. through | LLOY 229:11
scribblers teenage s. | LAWS 219:4
Scripture contrary to S. | TAWN 355:11
scum glittering s. | CHUR 88:9
  mere s. of the earth | WELL 384:7
sea complaining about the s. | POW 297:9
  dominion of the s. | COV 103:11
  fed our s. for a thousand years | KIPL 212:10
  floats in a s. of ethics | WARR 379:1
  I am very much at s. | CARS 77:3
  in a s. of glory | SHAK 327:6
  revolution have ploughed the s. | BOL 51:2
  smiling surface of the s. | PLUT 294:9
  squires ride slowly towards the s. | CHES 84:8
  stone set in the silver s. | SHAK 333:4
  to the English that of the s. | RICH 305:3
  water in the rough rude s. | SHAK 333:6
  willing foe and s. room | ANON 15:3
seagreen s. Incorruptible | CARL 75:9
seals receives the s. of office | ROS 312:9
seas troubled s. of thought | GALB 145:9
seasons man for all s. | WHIT 388:6
season-ticket held a s. | AMERY 7:6
seat s. in the House of Commons | DISR 120:18
  this s. of Mars | SHAK 333:4
  without an office, without a s. | CHUR 89:3
seated wiser when he was s. | KEYN 207:4
second Finishing s. in politics | NIXON 274:16
  first in a village than s. at Rome | CAES 71:10
  have a s. profession | NIC 272:9
  in a race to run s. | MACL 243:8
  In war there is no s. prize | BRAD 54:6
  not a s. on the day | COOK 102:5
  not provide for first and s. class | WILL 389:6
  s. office of government | JEFF 191:13
  s. oldest profession | REAG 301:8
secrecy greatest aid to s. | TAYL 358:9
  s. and a free | TRUM 372:3
secret concept of the 'official s.' | WEBER 381:11
  s. in the Oxford sense | FRAN 142:11

secret (*cont.*):
s. may be sometimes best kept   TAYL 358:8
s. of happiness   BRAN 54:10
s. of politics   BISM 46:3
secretary s. stays and gets thinner   ANON 12:12
secrets not to protect s.   LYNN 235:6
sect It found them a s.   MAC 238:13
persecute a s. and it holds   BAG 24:8
sectaries nation of s.   DISR 117:11
security common s.   PAINE 282:14
freedom can make s. secure   POPP 295:11
order, s. and peace   JOHN 195:2
Our watchword is s.   PITT 293:5
s. around the American   MAIL 247:7
s. for life and property   TAWN 355:9
s. in a flock of sheep   CHUR 89:6
seditions surest way to prevent s.   BACON 23:1
see can't s. a belt without hitting   ASQ 19:2
day I was meant not to s.   THAT 361:10
go and s. General Grant   LEE 220:5
To s. the things thou dost not   SHAK 331:5
We had better wait and s.   ASQ 18:1
seed s. however broadcast   PARK 285:3
s. ye sow, another reaps   SHEL 338:4
seed-time s. of continental union   PAINE 281:5
seek desire to s. power   BACON 22:10
We still s. no wider war   JOHN 196:3
seem to s. active   LAW 218:6
seen I have s. war   ROOS 309:1
s. to be done   HEW 178:5
segregation s. now, s. tomorrow   WALL 376:9
self Infusing him with s.   SHAK 333:8
self-assertion s. abroad   WAUGH 380:4
self-censorship s. becomes   GALB 146:7
self-evident truths to be s.   ANON 14:7
self-government tyranny of s.   DISR 118:12
self-interest propelled by s.   BAG 28:2
self love their s.   SMITH 341:4
self-preservation s. in the other   JEFF 193:9
self-protection number, is s.   MILL 258:8
self-respect starves your s.   PARR 286:11
self-satisfaction smug s.   BALD 29:4
self-sufficiency s. at home   WAUGH 380:4
sell To no man will we s.   MAGN 247:4
selling s. *the family silver*   MACM 245:11
semi-house-trained s. polecat   FOOT 138:7
semi-royal s. millionairess   CHAN 81:10
semper s. *aliquid novi Africam*   PLINY 294:5
Sic s. tyrannis   BOOTH 52:3
senator make you feel like a s.   O'RO 277:5
S., you're no Jack Kennedy   BENT 38:3
United States S.   JOHN 195:5
senators I look at the s.   HALE 164:4
s. burst with laughter   AUDEN 21:5
send s. these, the homeless   LAZ 219:7
senior execution of a s. colleague   CLARK 96:9

sensation create a s.   BROWN 58:5
sense good s. and the good faith   GLAD 154:13
Let's talk s. to the American   STEV 349:9
pretensions to common s.   SHEL 337:6
s. kept breaking in   TAYL 357:14
senseless worse than s. things   SHAK 328:1
sensibilité *no word equivalent to* s.   PALM 284:8
sentenced s. to death   BEHAN 34:10
sententiae *Quot homines tot s.*   TER 360:6
sentiment interest, not s.   CHES 83:11
sentiments imaginative s.   BAG 24:9
restrain the popular s.   PEEL 288:8
separate as s. as the fingers   WASH 379:2
forever s.   GRANT 160:3
Never wholly s. in your mind   BURKE 66:2
s. and equal station   JEFF 190:7
separately all hang s.   FRAN 142:2
separation impel them to the s.   JEFF 190:7
make any real s. of powers   DENN 113:7
nor are we fighting for s.   MALC 248:8
prepare for a s.   QUIN 299:3
seraglio s. of eunuchs   FOOT 138:5
serious war is too s. a matter   CLEM 98:7
Sermon S. on the Mount   BRAD 54:4
servant born to be a s.   TOCQ 367:2
master and s.   CHUR 88:6
s. to the devil   SISS 340:8
servants s. of the public   GOW 158:5
talent of choosing his s. well   MAC 238:14
thrice s.: s. of the sovereign   BACON 22:9
serve better to s. a well-bred lion   VOLT 376:4
I love to s. my country   GIBR 152:3
s. our country   ADD 5:8
They also s. who only stand   MILT 261:5
To s. your captives' need   KIPL 213:2
will not s. if elected   SHER 339:4
served Had I but s. my God   SHAK 327:8
have them s. to him   CHUR 89:11
service aid of public s.   TREV 368:1
s. and conduct of the commonwealth
BURKE 63:6
s. of my love   SPR 348:1
s. of our great Imperial family   ELIZ 132:4
s. of the nation   POMP 295:1
servitude freedom and not s.   BURKE 64:1
session while the legislature is in s.   ANON 12:10
setter s. up and puller down   SHAK 327:4
setting against a s. sun   SHAK 335:4
settlement Revolution a parent of s.   BURKE 66:9
s. of America   ADAMS 3:2
settling without s. it   JOUB 200:7
seven Even the Almighty took s.   CHUR 92:4
have the s. minutes   COLL 101:5
please your Majesty, s. weeks   POPH 295:9
s. feet of English ground   HAR 169:4
seventy Oh, to be s. again   CLEM 98:8

sewage exposing a s. scandal   LAW 219:1
    sewer and not the s.   BIFF 44:18
sewer midst of this putrid s.   TOCQ 365:2
    s. and not the sewage   BIFF 44:18
sewing broader than a s.-needle   NIC 272:2
sex legal subordination of one s.   MILL 259:8
sexes of the two s.   GIBB 151:7
shackles s. and restraints   GOLD 157:2
shade Within its s.   CONN 101:7
shadow but it also casts a s.   CHUR 91:2
shadows s. on county [cricket]   MAJOR 248:2
shake rise up, and s. off   LINC 224:5
Shakespeare That S. spake   WORD 394:5
shaking entrusted to the s. hand   VICT 374:6
shall His absolute 's.'   SHAK 324:6
shambles accountable s.   HUNT 185:7
shame blush of s.   WHIT 388:5
    monument of s.   CHUR 89:5
    now bound in with s.   SHAK 333:4
    Tory s.   BEVAN 41:8
shameful s. conquest of itself   SHAK 333:4
shameless most s. thing   BURKE 67:4
shape our dwellings s. us   CHUR 92:3
shaped s. by this one man   CHUR 93:8
shapely It wiggles, it's s.   ERWIN 134:1
share Thou its ruin didst not s.   DOD 122:5
shares fair s. for all, is Labour's call   JAY 190:5
sharks We are all s. circling   CLARK 96:10
sharp s. remedy, but a sure one   RAL 300:5
sheath We shall never s. the sword   ASQ 18:3
shed under a s.   JOHN 198:11
sheep enough pasture for all the s.   WALP 378:9
    savaged by a dead s.   HEAL 172:10
    s. are born carnivorous   FAG 135:1
    s. in sheep's clothing   CHUR 94:17
    s. on the way to the butcher   CHUR 89:6
    s. to pass resolutions   INGE 187:5
    Your s., that were wont to be   MORE 265:5
sheet old England's winding s.   BLAKE 49:4
    turn over the s.   SAND 320:2
shepherd Wilson is the nation's s.   SPR 348:2
shepherds s. and butchers   VOLT 375:7
shift let me s. for my self   MORE 265:9
shine men who s. in a faction   HAL 166:5
shines s. brightly as a king   SHAK 332:11
ship bigger and more expensive s.   CHUR 91:1
    good old s. of the Union   LINC 225:4
    s. has weathered every rack   WHIT 387:9
    S. me somewheres east of Suez   KIPL 212:8
ships far distant, storm-beaten s.   MAHAN 247:6
    s. empty of men   NIC 271:4
shit pile of s. in a silk stocking   NAP 270:4
    s. can turn to chicken salad   JOHN 195:4
shits he knew who the s. were   CLARK 96:8
shiver s. looking for a spine   KEAT 202:9
shock And we shall s. them   SHAK 331:1
    great s. around the age of 5   BALD 28:6

shoot s., if you must   WHIT 388:5
    s. me in my absence   BEHAN 34:10
    they shout and they s.   INGE 187:8
shoots green s. of economic spring   LAM 217:1
shop in the s. window   WILS 391:10
shopkeepers for a nation of s.   SMITH 341:6
    nation of s.   NAP 270:1
    nation of s. are very seldom   ADAMS 5:4
shopocracy abuse the s.   NORTH 275:5
shore refuse of your teeming s.   LAZ 219:7
shores s. of modern Conservatism   HENN 175:1
short I shall be but a s. time tonight   BALD 29:9
    nasty, brutish, and s.   HOBB 180:2
    s. decisive war   LYND 234:9
shortage s. of coal and fish   BEVAN 40:5
shorter make you s. by the head   ELIZ 130:7
shot My God! They've s. our fox   BIRCH 45:6
shots best s.   VOLT 375:8
shoulder looking over his s.   BAR 32:9
    shifted it to another s.   SHAW 336:6
    s. to s. on a burning deck   MACL 243:6
shoulders on the s. of the saint   WEBER 382:1
shout send forth a joyous s.   MAC 236:3
    s. and they shoot   INGE 187:8
    s. with the largest   DICK 115:1
shouting tumult and the s. dies   KIPL 212:11
show politics is just like s. business   REAG 301:6
    s. it is worth s.   DANT 109:7
shriller I hear a tongue, s.   SHAK 328:2
shrimp until a s. learns to whistle   KHR 209:1
shrunk s. to this little measure   SHAK 329:8
shut Men s. their doors   SHAK 335:4
sick enterprise is s.   SHAK 335:8
side for the good or evil s.   LOW 234:1
    on the s. of the angels   DISR 119:10
sides works both s. of the street   ROOS 310:5
siege beats back the envious s.   SHAK 333:4
sight safely out of s.   GALB 146:8
signed hand that s. the paper   THOM 363:3
    I s. my death warrant   COLL 101:4
    never s. off   BEAV 33:10
significance No personal s.   LINC 225:12
signposts s. to the socialist Utopia   CROS 106:4
signs positive s. of his awareness   BLUNT 49:7
silence easy step to s.   AUST 21:10
    ensure their s.   GALB 146:13
    golden Gospel of s.   MORL 265:11
    It is my day of s.   GAND 147:6
    occasional flashes of s.   SMITH 344:9
    period of s. on your part   ATTL 19:8
    s. of the law   HOBB 180:5
silenced you have s. him   MORL 265:10
silencing justified in s. mankind   MILL 258:11
silent great s. majority   NIXON 274:6
    impossible to be s.   BURKE 66:4
    laws are s. in time of war   CIC 95:12
    Paris was French—and s.   TUCH 372:6

silent (*cont.*):
s. encroachment   MAD 246:6
s. witnesses to the desolation   GEOR 149:6
silver *and* the thirty pieces of s.   BEVAN 41:1
First of all the Georgian s. goes   MACM 245:11
Just for a handful of s. he left us   BROW 60:1
Like the s. plate on a coffin   CURR 107:5
s. foot in his mouth   RICH 305:2
simplicity elegant s.   STOW 352:2
lost is our old s. of times   ANON 12:3
s. of character is no hindrance   MORL 266:2
sweet s. of the three per cents   DISR 120:19
simplify politician has to s.   POW 297:12
simply We live very s.   CHUR 87:8
Simpson little man with 'is Mrs S.   THOM 363:5
Mrs S.'s pinched our king   ANON 10:5
sin besetting s. of public men   TAYL 358:11
By that s. fell the angels   SHAK 327:7
sincere Always be s.   TRUM 371:16
s. ignorance   KING 210:5
sinews s. of war   BACON 23:3
s. of war, unlimited money   CIC 95:11
sing s. a song in it   BELL 35:4
singeing s. of the King of Spain's   DRAKE 124:6
single to a s. country   GALB 146:3
sink raft which would never s.   AMES 8:2
sinking desert a s. ship   BEAV 34:3
sit let us s. upon the ground   SHAK 333:8
Never stand when you could s.   ANON 12:9
Though I s. down now   DISR 116:12
sitting exact their demands by s.   WELL 385:2
He struts s. down   DYKS 127:3
situation war s. has developed   HIR 179:1
situations s. as yet unforeseen   MONN 262:9
sixpence nothing above s.   BEVAN 40:3
sixties divided up the s.   LEVIN 222:5
inflation in the s.   LEVIN 222:7
s. technology   LEVIN 222:4
sixty-seven at the age of s.   DE G 112:7
skin s. of an innocent lamb   SHAK 327:2
s. of his mother   LLOY 230:16
thick s. as a first gift   TROL 370:1
thick s. is a gift from God   ADEN 6:1
skinning eels get used to s.   CHUR 90:9
skins such white s.   CURZ 108:2
slag-heap post-industrial s.   DRAB 124:5
s. 120 ft high   WILS 391:4
slain fifty thousand men s.   WALP 378:3
slanged sneered and s.   BELL 35:5
slaughter through s. to a throne   GRAY 160:8
slave giving freedom to the s.   LINC 226:5
half s. and half free   LINC 225:1
It is a s. to its animosity   WASH 379:12
I would not be a s.   LINC 224:8
millions in this s. country   BROWN 59:3
moment the s. resolves   GAND 147:7
s. of that s.   CONN 102:2

to the American s.   DOUG 123:6
without freeing any s.   LINC 226:2
slaveholders of the North are s.   ANTH 15:5
slave-morality and s.   NIET 273:4
slaveowners those of the South s.   ANTH 15:5
slavery classified as s.   CHUR 87:4
distinction between liberty and s.   CAMD 73:5
freedom and s. are mental states   GAND 147:7
I hear anyone arguing for s.   LINC 227:6
S. they can have anywhere   BURKE 64:10
Where s. is   SUMN 353:1
wise and good in s.   MAC 237:6
slaves all persons held as s.   LINC 225:11
creed of s.   PITT 293:7
Englishmen never will be s.   SHAW 336:4
freemen or s.   WASH 379:6
only freemen, are the only s.   MASS 254:2
s. become so debased   ROUS 314:6
sons of former s.   KING 210:10
too pure an Air for s.   ANON 12:13
two kinds of s.   ILL 187:4
wholly s. or wholly free   DRYD 125:16
sledgehammer s. to miss a nut   BOOK 52:2
sleek-headed s. men   SHAK 328:7
sleep deep s. of England   ORW 278:3
disturbed the s. of my generation   STEV 351:1
s. is so deep   CHAN 81:6
s. under bridges   FRAN 141:2
such as s. o' nights   SHAK 328:7
We shall not s.   MCCR 240:2
sleeps while the world s.   NEHRU 270:7
sleepwalker assurance of a s.   HITL 179:5
sleeve having a card up his s.   LAB 216:1
sleeves with its s. rolled   MCC 239:7
slept [Calvin Coolidge] s. more   MENC 256:13
Christ and His saints s.   ANON 12:5
slew as he was ambitious, I s. him   SHAK 329:11
slippery standing is s.   BACON 22:11
slob He was just a s.   LONG 232:8
slogan s. 'Liberty or Death'   WOOL 394:4
slovenliness peace is nothing but s.   BREC 55:7
slowly Let him twist s.   EHRL 128:6
slum If you've seen one city s.   AGNEW 6:5
smack s. of firm government   MCL 242:5
small day of s. nations   CHAM 80:6
I have no s. talk   WELL 384:13
s. is beautiful   SCH 321:10
that cannot reach the s.   SPEN 347:8
with s. men no great thing   MILL 259:5
smarter thought themselves s.   ATTL 20:9
smash all s. and no grab   NIC 272:8
smell Money has no s.   VESP 374:2
Mr Speaker, I s. a rat   ROCHE 307:4
smile expressed by one livid s.   WALP 377:12
I hear a s.   CROSS 106:8
nice s., but he's got iron teeth   GROM 162:4
s. we would aspire to   SHAK 327:6

solution (*cont.*):
kind of s.   CAV 79:3
total s. of the Jewish question   GOER 156:7
solutions David brings me s.   THAT 362:9
some fool s. of the people   LINC 227:8
S. chicken! Some neck   CHUR 91:7
someone fear that s., somewhere   MENC 257:2
something *s. must be done*   EDW 128:4
Step One: We must do s.   LYNN 235:11
son dumb s. of a bitch   TRUM 372:2
Earl of Fitzdotterel's eldest s.   BRO 57:8
fair s.   ELIZ 130:5
rude s. should strike his father   SHAK 335:9
s. of Saint Louis   FIRM 136:7
song ane end of ane old s.   OGIL 276:7
sing a s. in it   BELL 35:4
songs they know no s.   CHES 84:9
sons s. of bitches   KENN 205:2
sophisms string of s.   SHEL 337:7
sorrow death and s.   CHUR 90:11
sorrowed one that hath s.   CECIL 79:9
sorry for which I feel personally s.   HIR 179:2
sort s. of traitors   SHAK 334:7
soul every subject's s.   SHAK 326:14
for the s. of Lloyd George   MASS 254:3
iron has entered into his s.   LLOY 230:15
no s. to be damned   THUR 364:9
perfection of your s.   SOCR 345:7
see America save her s.   THOM 363:7
s. of a martyr   BAG 24:5
to change the s.   THAT 361:4
while there is a s. in prison   DEBS 111:3
with s. so dead   SCOTT 322:5
souls common men have s.   TAWN 355:12
in men's s.   STEV 350:5
not open windows into men's s.   ELIZ 131:7
prostration of men's s.   TAWN 355:8
stuff of other people's s.   MCGR 241:1
times that try men's s.   PAINE 281:10
sound cracking s.   CROS 106:11
none of the s. ideas   MACM 245:3
other not very s.   SMOL 345:2
s. and rumour   MORR 266:5
soup do not take s. at luncheon   CURZ 108:5
South of the S. slaveowners   ANTH 15:5
s. is avenged   BOOTH 52:3
wrest from the s.   LEE 220:6
South Africa barbarism in S.   CAMP 74:2
southern do not change to S.   LEE 220:1
s. efficiency and northern charm   KENN 205:12
sovereign he will have no s.   COKE 101:1
obligation of subjects to the s.   HOBB 180:6
people as a source of s. power   SCAR 321:1
political power of the s.   TROL 370:3
reverence and affection for a s.   BOSW 53:4
S. has, under a constitutional   BAG 26:1
s. Nation   PAGE 280:7

S. state power   KEANE 202:5
s. sway may be dissolved   DRYD 125:11
subject and a s. are clean different   CHAR 82:6
what to be a S.   ELIZ 130:6
sovereigns what s. are doing   NAP 269:8
sovereignties national s.   MONN 262:5
sovereignty By s. of nature   SHAK 325:1
I'm not against giving up s.   RIDL 305:8
national s. is ultimately vested   MONN 262:8
s. is an artificial soul   HOBB 179:9
S. is unlimited   BARK 32:3
Soviet equals S. power   LENIN 221:8
no S. domination of Eastern   FORD 139:2
Soviet Union S. and the United States   KENN 203:5
sow hath the right s. by the ear   HENR 176:2
when to s., and when to reap   JEFF 193:16
sown They have s. the wind   BIBLE 44:1
space more s. where nobody is   STEIN 349:2
spaghetti ticker tape ain't s.   LA G 216:4
Spaniards thrash the S. too   DRAKE 124:7
spare s. your country's flag   WHIT 388:5
spark-gap s. is mightier   HOGB 181:1
Spartans Go, tell the S.   SIM 340:6
spasm I call it an emotional s.   BEVAN 41:4
spawn upstream to s.   WHITE 387:1
speak If I am to s. for ten minutes   WILS 392:18
I only s. right on   SHAK 330:9
s. for England   AMERY 7:7
s. ill of everybody   PÉT 290:11
s. softly and carry a big   ROOS 311:4
truth,—one to s.   THOR 364:3
which it is difficult to s.   BURKE 66:4
You s. for Britain   BOOT 52:4
speaking first necessity for good s.   TROL 369:10
speaks He s. to Me   VICT 374:8
spectacle no s. so ridiculous   MAC 237:8
spectator politics to a s. sport   GALB 146:4
spectators anything more than s.   ASQ 18:2
spectre haunt Europe as a s.   TAYL 357:3
s. is haunting eastern   HAVEL 170:4
s. is haunting Europe   MARX 253:1
speculation not land s.   WILS 391:4
speech first is freedom of s.   ROOS 309:11
function of s. to free men   BRAN 55:1
Listening to a s. by Chamberlain   BEVAN 40:3
little other use of their s.   HAL 165:9
making a s. on economics   JOHN 196:12
no more make a good s.   BELL 35:4
nonpolitical s.   NIXON 274:1
nor utterance, nor power of s.   SHAK 330:9
precious things: freedom of s.   TWAIN 372:9
vulgar, crude and intemperate s.   MACL 242:6
speeches have its old s. burnt   SNOW 345:5
His s. were fine   WALP 377:6
spend If you have money you s. it   KENN 206:4
s. more time with my family   FOWL 140:3

state (*cont.*):

no such thing as the S.	AUDEN 21:2
Nothing doth more hurt in a s.	BACON 22:6
partnership between the s.	TAWN 355:6
pillar of the S.	SOLZ 346:1
put the s. to rights for us	ENN 133:9
reinforcement of the S.	CAMUS 74:7
Scoffing his s.	SHAK 333:8
sole employer is the S.	TROT 370:14
sovereign s. power	KEANE 202:5
S. business is a cruel trade	HAL 166:12
S. for every Star	WINT 393:3
S. is an instrument	STAL 348:3
S. is a relation of men	WEBER 381:8
S. is not 'abolished', *it withers*	ENG 133:6
s. is or can be master	BEV 42:5
S. policy, a cyclops	COL 101:3
'S.' reveals itself	POW 297:16
S. which dwarfs its men	MILL 259:5
s. without the means	BURKE 66:8
Then all were for the s.	MAC 237:1
two parties which divide the s.	EMER 133:2
wall between church and s.	BLACK 48:2
when church and s. hold hands	MITC 261:7
While the S. exists	LENIN 221:7
whole machinery of the S.	BRO 58:1
without the s. suffering	TOCQ 365:5

states free and independent S. ADAMS 3:9

indestructible S.	CHASE 83:7
In s. unborn	SHAK 329:6
many sovereign S.	PAGE 280:7
mental s.	GAND 147:2
more s. there are to suffer	BAG 28:1
number of independent s.	GIBB 151:2
peoples of the several s.	CARD 75:7
saved the Union of these S.	WHIT 388:1
S. dissevered, discordant	WEBS 382:4
sustain the rights of s.	BROWN 59:5

statesman conscience of a s. TAYL 358:3

constitutional s. is in general	BAG 23:14
first requirement of a s.	ACH 1:6
from rising hope to elder s.	FOOT 138:8
greatest gift of any s.	METT 258:1
great s.	MONN 262:9
he was a s.	LLOY 230:6
importance to a s. to make	TAYL 358:1
no gift to set a s. right	YEATS 395:5
No s., be he as discreet	TAYL 358:2
no s. who has committed	DISR 118:13
not in Washington as a s.	ASH 17:8
often a defect in a s.	TOCQ 366:9
quality of the constructive s.	TAYL 356:9
sole care of the s. in office	TAYL 358:10
s. got into office	CHUR 93:9
s. is a politician who places	POMP 295:1
s. is a politician who's been	TRUM 371:13
s....must wait until he hears	BISM 47:11

[s.] should steer	TAYL 358:7
s. who is enamoured	BIER 44:16
S., yet friend to Truth	POPE 295:3

statesmanship You call that s. BEVAN 41:4

statesmen *Advice to s.* LIDD 223:5

constitutional s.	BAG 23:15
faults of s. give birth	WALP 377:7
government of s. or of clerks	DISR 117:4

stations always know our proper s. DICK 115:2

statistic tragedy, one million is a s. STAL 348:7

statistics He uses s. as a drunken LANG 217:6

It is s. as pornography	JENK 194:9
lies, damned lies and s.	DISR 121:15

stature malice is of a low s. HAL 166:2

status quo little ladder called 'the s.' BENN 37:2

stay If they want to s. BEVIN 42:8

I kind of have to s. around	PEROT 290:10

staying s. down with him WASH 379:4

steal I come not, friends, to s. SHAK 330:8

to s. bread	FRAN 141:2

stealing not hanged for s. horses HAL 166:10

steals politician who s. is worse PLUN 294:7

s. the common from the goose	ANON 14:2

steam-engine He traces the s. DISR 118:1

like a s. in trousers	SMITH 344:8

steeds mounting barbèd s. SHAK 334:9

steeple North Church s. REV 303:7

steeples dreary s. of Fermanagh CHUR 88:4

Talk about the pews and s.	CHES 84:6

steering Washington is a s. wheel GOOD 158:1

step One s. forward two steps back LENIN 221:2

Stephen since Matilda and S. WAUGH 380:10

steps hears the s. of God BISM 47:11

sterner made of s. stuff SHAK 330:2

stick carry a big s. ROOS 311:4

first s. that he seizes	TORR 367:4
he fell like the s.	PAINE 283:4
s. to science	BEVIN 42:8

sticker it is a bad s. CHUR 89:4

stiffen it has had time to s. ORW 278:8

still conscience is a s. small voice ATTL 20:7

stilts nonsense upon s. BENT 37:8

stingy government ever was not s. TROL 370:4

stir Is not to s. SHAK 326:3

To s. men's blood	SHAK 330:9
To s. up undisputed matters	SALL 319:5

stirring s. up apathy WHIT 387:6

stock woman s. is rising CHILD 85:3

stocking hung up an empty s. SMITH 343:6

shit in a silk s.	NAP 270:4

stocks great s. of Europe YEATS 396:1

stomach army marches on its s. NAP 269:11

heart and s. of a king	ELIZ 130:9
patriot on an empty s.	BRANN 55:5
s. of the country	GLAD 154:3

stone back into the S. Age LEMAY 220:8

Can make a s. of the heart	YEATS 395:7

first s. which he [the savage]	TORR 367:4	**struts** He s. sitting down	DYKS 127:3
precious s. set in the silver sea	SHAK 333:4	**stubbornness** self-righteous s.	JENK 194:6
stones s. of Rome to rise	SHAK 330:10	**stud-horse** only a retired s.	MENC 257:1
stood Have s. against the world	SHAK 330:5	**studiously** apart, s. neutral	WILS 392:5
s. four-square to all the winds	TENN 359:11	**study** I must s. politics and war	ADAMS 3:13
stop time to s. a revolution	STEV 350:4	**stuff** made of sterner s.	SHAK 330:2
stopped s. the engine in its tracks	JENK 194:3	**stuffed** I s. their mouths with gold	BEVAN 41:10
stories tell sad s. of the death	SHAK 333:8	**stumbled** s. over the truth	CHUR 94:10
storm by the pilot of the s.	BAG 25:3	**stupid** governments are far more s.	EIS 129:6
in the west, that coming s.	GLAD 154:1	never be right that the s.	IBSEN 186:8
storms He sought the s.	DRYD 125:5	s. are cocksure	RUSS 316:12
story we shall be made a s.	WINT 393:2	**stupidest** s. party	MILL 259:7
strain Sometimes the s. is awful	MACM 245:10	**stupidity** conscientious s.	KING 210:5
stranger gratitude of a s.	TOCQ 365:10	simple explanation of s.	LEVER 222:2
strangers beaten by s.	DOS 123:2	**subject** s. and a sovereign	CHAR 82:6
strategy industrial s.	BENN 36:5	s.'s duty is the king's	SHAK 326:14
strawberry Like s. wives	ELIZ 131:9	to be a s.	ELIZ 130:6
stream watching a s. of blood	ANON 12:1	To every s. of this land	DENN 113:6
streams when crossing s.	LINC 226:6	**subjects** from the s. of government	WILS 391:11
street works both sides of the s.	ROOS 310:5	maintains among his s.	HERB 177:2
street-bred poor little s. people	KIPL 212:7	obligation of s. to the sovereign	HOBB 180:6
streetcars as common as s.	REUT 303:5	s. are rebels from principle	BURKE 67:2
streets grow in the s.	HOOV 182:10	**subjugation** conquest and s.	WEBS 382:7
grow in the s. of every city	BRYAN 60:5	**sublime** s. to the ridiculous	NAP 269:9
little children died in the s.	AUDEN 21:5	**submission** s. of men's actions	HOBB 180:7
republican way of cleaning the s.	LA G 216:5	**submit** king do now? Must he s.	SHAK 334:2
strength at length that tower of s.	TENN 359:11	**subordination** legal s. of one sex	MILL 259:8
progress which is her present s.	TROL 369:7	**subsidizes** problems; it s. them	REAG 301:7
s. of the Empire	GLAD 155:1	**subsistence** s. only increases	MALT 248:9
S. should be lord of imbecility	SHAK 335:9	**substance** persons of some s.	WIND 393:1
S. through joy	LEY 223:4	**substitute** no s. for victory	MAC 235:13
To have a giant's s.	SHAK 332:8	**subtlety** s. of intellect	MORL 266:2
strenuous doctrine of the s. life	ROOS 310:10	**subtracting** without s.	REED 302:11
stretch never s. out the hand	HES 177:10	**subversion** complaining about s.	JUV 201:5
stretched government are s.	MONT 264:13	**success** generals who gain s.	LINC 226:4
strife In place of s.	CAST 78:3	his s. is disgraceful	MENC 256:12
strike no right to s. against	COOL 103:1	judgements—s.	BURKE 67:13
s. the tent	LEE 220:7	S. or failure lies in conforming	MACH 241:11
When you s. at a king	EMER 133:5	tortured by material s.	MACM 245:5
strikes puny subject s.	SHAK 333:7	**successful** s. experiment	JEFF 192:6
string monarchy is only the s.	SHEL 338:7	whether s.	ADAMS 4:6
untune that s.	SHAK 335:9	**succession** monarchy and s.	PAINE 281:3
stringent s. execution	GRANT 160:2	**successor** tie a popish s. with laws	HAMP 167:9
stroke at a s., reduce	HEATH 173:6	**Sudeten** S. Germans	HITL 179:7
stroked if not s.	HAL 165:11	**Suez** felt as if the S. Canal	EDEN 128:1
strong Give them a s. and a just	WELL 384:1	ship me somewheres east of S.	KIPL 212:8
nor the battle to the s.	BIBLE 43:16	S.—a smash and grab raid	NIC 272:8
not to the s. alone	HENRY 176:7	**suffer** Better one s.	DRYD 125:9
those who think they are s.	BID 44:14	nobody is going to s.	KALD 201:10
stronger interest of the s. party	PLATO 294:2	not s. fools gladly	PEAR 287:5
on the side of the s.	TAC 354:9	who clamour most, s. most	PEEL 288:13
There is one thing s.	ANON 13:8	**suffering** cannot be s. very much	GALB 146:8
struggle class s. leads	MARX 252:5	loved the s. many	BENT 37:11
long twilight s.	KENN 204:6	**suffice** O when may it s.	YEATS 395:7
perpetual s. for room and food	MALT 248:10	**sufficient** not s. to keep him	LLOY 231:2
struggles history of class s.	MARX 253:2	**suggest** s. modes of taxation	PEEL 289:3

suicide did not commit s.   ADAMS 4:2
[Earl Haig] committed s.   BEAV 34:4
it is s.   MACD 240:5
longest s. note in history   KAUF 202:4
s. to avoid assassination   TRUM 371:6
sui generis hell, say that I am s.   LONG 232:5
suis J'y s., j'y reste   MACM 243:10
Sulla Rome under S.   ADC 5:7
summer if it takes all s.   GRANT 159:7
on a hot s. afternoon   ANON 13:11
summers This many s. in a sea   SHAK 327:6
summits nations touch at their s.   BAG 26:5
sun against a setting s.   SHAK 335:4
blushing discontented s.   SHAK 334:1
has the s. in his eyes   CHUR 90:2
light a candle to the s.   SIDN 340:3
our own place in the s.   BÜLOW 61:7
our place in the s.   WILH 388:9
summer this s. of York   SHAK 334:8
s. draws its power   TRUM 371:2
s. never sets   NORTH 275:3
sunk s. in a bigger   CHUR 91:1
sunset into the s. of my life   REAG 302:8
sunshine s. patriot   PAINE 281:10
superfluous s. lags the vet'ran   JOHN 196:14
superior embarrass the s.   SHAW 336:10
want no-one to be their s.   TOCQ 365:1
superiors only want it with our s.   BECQ 34:8
superman I teach you the s.   NIET 273:3
superstition forgive his s.   GIBB 151:14
s. sets the whole world   VOLT 376:2
supervision national s.   O'RO 277:6
suppliant s. for his own   BYRON 71:3
supplies bought some new s.   BREC 55:10
support depend on the s. of Paul   SHAW 337:2
men who will s. me   MELB 256:4
oath to s. the constitution   JACK 188:9
s. of the people   CLEV 99:3
s. rather than illumination   LANG 217:6
without the help and s.   EDW 128:5
supportable such as are s.   HAL 165:14
supported not s. by the people   HUMP 185:3
suppose s. what may come   HAL 165:5
suppress power of s.   NORT 275:7
suprema salus populi s. est lex   CIC 95:6
supreme But if ever the S. Court   TOCQ 365:5
s. power must be arbitrary   HAL 165:10
surface fear the smiling s.   PLUT 294:9
surplus economic s.   POTT 296:3
surprised quite s. to be taken   DE G 112:12
surrender immediate s.   GRANT 159:6
No s.   ANON 12:11
we shall never s.   CHUR 90:7
survived I s.   SIEY 340:5
suspicion against despots—s.   DEM 113:2
Caesar's wife must be above s.   CAES 71:9
democracy is the recurrent s.   WHITE 386:6

suspicions s. amongst thoughts   BACON 23:2
swap It is not best to s. horses   LINC 226:6
swayed easily s.   CLAY 97:6
sweat blood, toil, tears and s.   CHUR 90:5
spending the s. of its labourers   EIS 129:4
sweets bag of boiled s.   CRIT 104:4
s. of place with power   ROS 312:7
swift race is not to the s.   BIBLE 43:16
swim that I may s.   GRAH 159:2
swimming s. for his life   GLAD 154:8
swooped s. down upon us   ANON 9:4
sword at the point of the s.   GEOR 149:3
I gave them a s.   NIXON 274:14
lightning of his terrible swift s.   HOWE 184:3
nation shall not lift up s.   BIBLE 43:18
not to send peace, but a s.   BIBLE 44:5
power of the s.   CHAR 82:6
resistance by the s.   CLAY 97:1
s. is the axis   DE G 112:2
We shall never sheath the s.   ASQ 18:3
when he first drew the s.   CLAR 96:1
wield the s. of France   DE G 112:4
swords I thought ten thousand s.   BURKE 66:15
s. into plowshares   BIBLE 43:18
turns our s.   SHAK 330:15
sycophants s. and flatterers   HARD 168:4
syllogism politicians' s.   LYNN 235:11
sympathy Our s. is cold   GIBB 151:11
there's no s. in politics   THAT 360:9
system knocking the American s.   CAP 75:6
s. of Government   GLAD 154:2
they rocked the s.   ROB 307:3

table people at whose t. I sit   BORR 53:3
victuals from the t.   CHUR 89:11
tableau t. of crimes and misfortunes   VOLT 376:3
tact No more t.   CAMP 74:4
tail Every time it wags its t.   TOYN 367:5
which was the t.   BRIG 56:9
taint any t. of legality   KNOX 215:2
take big enough to t. away   FORD 138:10
don't t. everything away   SOLZ 345:10
If they t. you in the morning   BALD 28:9
more blessed not to t.   POW 296:6
t. away these baubles   CROM 105:9
t. up the White Man's burden   KIPL 213:2
taken t. at his word   DE G 112:12
takes if it t. all summer   GRANT 159:7
taking-off deep damnation of his t.   SHAK 331:7
talent concentration of t.   KENN 205:1
t. of our English nation   DRYD 125:2
talents career open to the t.   NAP 269:13
ministry of all the t.   ANON 12:7
t. invaluable to a prince   MAC 238:14
virtue and t.   JEFF 193:4

talk careless t. costs lives · ANON 9:7
  men who t. fluently · HOGB 181:1
  Through t., we tamed kings · BENN 36:8
talked t. for a hundred years · JOHN 195:8
  t. shop like a tenth muse · ANON 10:7
talking if you can stop people t. · ATTL 20:11
  t. politics after dinner · DISR 120:4
talking-machine redtape t. · CARL 76:8
taller may be t. than other men · HAR 169:4
tamed in one year t. · MARV 251:8
Tandy I met wid Napper T. · ANON 10:11
tanks Get your t. off my lawn · WILS 391:1
taping t. of conversations · NIXON 274:12
Tarpeian from the T. rock · ARN 17:6
Tarsus which am a Jew of T. · BIBLE 44:11
tart he is like the town t. · BAXT 33:2
tarts by the action of two t. · MACM 245:6
taste t. for freedom · TOCQ 366:11
taunted I am sometimes t. · PEEL 289:2
taunting grave, and not t. · BACON 22:12
tax idleness and pride t. · FRAN 142:1
  I pay my t. bills more readily · HOLM 181:7
  power to t. · MARS 251:3
  soon be able to t. it · FAR 135:4
  t. collector for the welfare state · GING 153:2
  time to t. rich people · LLOY 229:13
  To t. and to please · BURKE 64:15
taxation suggest modes of t. · PEEL 289:3
  t. and representation · CAMD 73:5
  t. without representation · OTIS 279:14
taxes compensation for heavy t. · MONT 264:15
  except death and t. · FRAN 142:9
  just to pay our t. · PEROT 290:7
  little people pay t. · HELM 174:4
  peace, easy t. · SMITH 341:1
  people overlaid with t. · BACON 23:4
  read my lips: no new t. · BUSH 69:7
taxi empty t. arrived · CHUR 94:9
taxing more or less of a t. machine · LOWE 233:7
taxis Labour council hiring t. · KINN 211:11
taxpayer t.—that's someone · REAG 301:14
tax-paying working, t. Americans · GING 153:3
tea take—and sometimes t. · POPE 295:2
  those damned t. parties · LODGE 232:2
teacher value of a true t. · GARF 147:9
teaching for the t. of which · SMITH 343:1
  t. nations how to live · MILT 260:5
team by the t. captain · HOWE 184:1
tear shed one English t. · MAC 238:10
  t. down this wall · REAG 302:5
tears blood, toil, t. and sweat · CHUR 90:5
  enough of blood and t. · RABIN 299:4
  Mine eyes are full of t. · SHAK 334:7
  With mine own t. I wash · SHAK 334:6
technological t. revolution · WILS 390:5
technology in relation to our t. · BERR 39:7
  into the sixties t. · LEVIN 222:4

  province of t. · POPP 296:2
Ted fond of dear T. · THAT 360:9
Teddy Now T. must run · KENN 206:5
teenage t. scribblers · LAWS 219:4
teenagers among t. · FRI 143:11
teeth but he's got iron t. · GROM 162:4
  have three or four t. taken out · HITL 179:8
  Our t. are in the real meat · GRIM 162:2
teetotaller usually a secret t. · ORW 277:11
Teflon-coated T. Presidency · SCHR 321:8
television [political] t. show · MACM 245:4
tell And t. sad stories of the death · SHAK 333:8
  Go, t. the Spartans · SIM 340:6
  I t. you that which you · SHAK 330:9
temper agreeable to their t. · BURKE 62:6
  many things including my t. · NEHRU 270:9
  Never lose your t. with the Press · PANK 284:11
  with a ruffled t. · WALP 378:8
temperament But a first-class t. · HOLM 181:8
temple lord's anointed t. · SHAK 331:9
  t. of silence and reconciliation · MAC 238:8
tempora O t., O mores · CIC 95:9
  t. mutantur, et nos mutamur · ANON 13:7
temporary force alone is but t. · BURKE 64:12
temptation always a t. · KIPL 213:4
temptations you may find t. · KITC 214:15
tempted 'Tis one thing to be t. · SHAK 332:6
ten amend the T. Commandments · BIGG 45:3
  I thought t. thousand swords · BURKE 66:15
  no T. Commandments · KIPL 212:8
tenants feudal landlord abusing t. · ATTL 19:7
tenement Like to a t. · SHAK 333:4
tent inside the t. pissing out · JOHN 196:9
  strike the t. · LEE 220:7
tenth He talked shop like a t. muse · ANON 10:7
termination law for its own t. · LINC 225:5
terminological risk of t. inexactitude · CHUR 87:4
terrible t. beauty is born · YEATS 395:8
territorial last t. claim · HITL 179:6
territory it [the t.] is worth · MAC 238:5
terror added a new t. to death · WETH 386:1
  For t., not to use, in time · SHAK 332:4
  just as great a t. · LLOY 229:3
  perch and not their t. · SHAK 332:5
  t. instituted by 'lawful authority' · MACD 240:4
  was the t. of the world · PITT 293:4
terrorist t. and the policeman · CONR 102:3
  ways to starve the t. · THAT 361:13
testators it would do well · HERB 176:10
Thames But the T. is liquid history · BURNS 68:9
thee save t. and me · OWEN 280:5
theft property is t. · PRO 298:5
  t. from those who hunger · EIS 129:4
theme glad diviner's t. · DRYD 125:7
  pudding—it has no t. · CHUR 95:1
theologians if you believe the t. · SAL 318:1

theories seldom is it that t. stand — TROL 370:5
taken up with their t. — BURKE 66:14
theory *died of a t.* — DAVIS 110:3
fate that for a t. is worse — GILM 153:1
It is sometimes t. — MAC 236:6
trickle-down t. — GALB 147:1
upon a t. — BURKE 65:7
there you were not t. — HENR 175:3
these saved the union of t. States — WHIT 388:1
thick ask the Gods for a t. skin — TROL 370:1
t. skin is a gift — ADEN 6:1
thicker history gets t. — TAYL 357:10
thigh He smote them hip and t. — BIBLE 43:9
thin those pale and t. ones — PLUT 294:8
thing only t. we have to fear — ROOS 308:8
There is one t. stronger — ANON 13:8
this the sort of t. they like — LINC 227:3
things t. fall apart — YEATS 395:6
think dare to t. 'unthinkable' — FULB 144:5
easier to act than to t. — AREN 15:11
t. alike who t. at all — PAINE 283:3
T. of your forefathers — ADAMS 4:5
you may t. what you like — TAC 354:7
You might very well t. — DOBBS 122:4
You must t. the unthinkable — ROSS 313:4
thinker Too conventional a t. — MONC 261:11
thinking All t. for themselves — GILB 152:9
columnists say 'Every t. man' — ADAMS 2:4
modes of t. are different — JOHN 198:10
never thought of t. for myself — GILB 152:4
thinks He t. too much — SHAK 328:7
t. he knows everything — SHAW 336:13
thirst man can raise a t. — KIPL 212:8
offer you hunger, t. — GAR 148:1
thirty t. pieces of silver — BEVAN 41:1
this t. happy breed of men — SHAK 333:4
t. was a man — SHAK 330:16
thorn t. in Charles's side — FOX 140:4
thorns can't have the crown of t. — BEVAN 41:1
this crown of t. — BRYAN 60:6
thought experience is the child of t. — DISR 116:4
freedom of t. — HAYEK 171:7
freedom of t. and the right — ADAMS 5:5
investigation and t. — HALD 164:2
their modes of t. — MILL 259:12
they ought to have t. — ANON 12:12
troubled seas of t. — GALB 145:9
thoughtcrime make t. literally — ORW 279:3
thoughts I am a farmer of t. — PAINE 282:1
not make t. your aim — KIPL 213:3
suspicions amongst t. — BACON 23:2
t. of a prisoner — SOLZ 345:9
thousand difference of forty t. men — WELL 384:6
end of a t. years of history — GAIT 145:2
like a t. points of light — BUSH 69:6
Rhodesia—not in a t. years — SMITH 344:4
t. generations — KINN 212:2

threatened because I t. no one — BUSH 69:4
threatening t. its own demise — BLAIR 49:1
three divided into t. parts — CAES 71:7
little man with t. names — CROM 106:2
t. corners of the world — SHAK 331:1
t. kinds of lies: lies, damned — DISR 121:15
throat frog in my t. — MAJOR 247:10
have murder by the t. — LLOY 230:1
So he has cut his t. at last — BYRON 71:4
throne esteemed worthy of the t. — GIBB 151:8
highest t. in the world — MONT 263:9
possession of a t. — GIBB 151:5
something behind the t. greater — PITT 292:12
This royal t. of kings — SHAK 333:4
t. of bayonets — INGE 187:7
T. sent word to a Throne — KIPL 213:1
t. *we* honour is the *people's* — SHER 338:12
t. will sway a little — CHAN 81:5
vacancy of the t. — GIBB 151:1
wade through slaughter to a t. — GRAY 160:8
throw t. away the dearest thing — SHAK 331:6
thrown All *this* t. away for *that* — MARY 253:6
Tiber River T. foaming — POW 297:1
T. foaming with much blood — VIRG 375:6
ticker t. tape ain't spaghetti — LA G 216:4
ticket take a t. at Victoria Station — BEVIN 43:4
tide [Rome] is like an incoming t. — DENN 113:5
t. in the affairs of men — SHAK 330:14
tiger atom bomb is a paper t. — MAO 250:5
orang-outang or the t. — BURKE 65:9
t. will turn vegetarian — BROUN 58:4
tigers but a wilderness of t. — SHAK 335:6
t. are getting hungry — CHUR 89:8
tight-lipped t. mufflered men — JOS 199:7
tightness t. of the magic circle — MACL 242:8
tigress t. surrounded by hamsters — BIFF 45:1
tiles t. on the roofs — LUTH 234:7
tilling dignity in t. a field — WASH 379:3
timber crooked t. of humanity — KANT 202:1
time ancient nobility is the act of t. — BACON 22:14
for a moment of t. — ELIZ 132:3
idea whose t. has come — ANON 13:8
like to devote more t. — FOWL 140:3
peace for our t. — CHAM 81:1
plenty of t. to win — DRAKE 124:7
rely upon a comfortable t.-lag — WELLS 385:5
sell t., which belongs to God — TAWN 355:11
spend more t. with my family — RIDL 305:5
spend more t. with your family — THAT 362:8
That's why it's t. for a change — DEWEY 114:5
t. has come — LONG 232:7
T. is on our side — GLAD 154:6
t. is out of joint — SHAK 325:7
T.'s noblest offspring — BERK 38:4
T. spent on any item — PARK 285:10
t. will come when you — DISR 116:12

too much of the t.	THUR 364:8	T. every Duchess in London	MACD 240:6
unconscionable t. dying	CHAR 83:6	**tongue** die, who speak the t.	WORD 394:5
waste of t. and effort	VEBL 373:6	eye to see, nor t. to speak	LENT 221:12
week is a long t. in politics	WILS 390:8	put a t. In every wound	SHAK 330:10
well to t. the beginnings	BACON 22:7	t. in the balance	BISM 47:13
whips and scorns of t.	SHAK 325:8	t. to persuade	CLAR 96:2
you're ahead of your t.	MCG 240:9	would not yield to the t.	BIER 44:15
times best of t.	DICK 115:4	**tongues** with their t. doom men	SHAK 335:5
conforming to the t.	MACH 241:11	**tonight** be but a short time t.	BALD 29:9
Oh, the t.! Oh, the manners	CIC 95:9	Not t., Josephine	NAP 270:3
our old simplicity of t.	ANON 12:3	**tools** give us the t.	CHUR 91:6
These are t. in which a genius	ADAMS 2:2	t. to him	CARL 75:13
t. change, and we change	ANON 13:7	**toothpaste** Once the t. is out	HALD 164:3
T. has made many ministries	BAG 25:1	**top** always room at the t.	WEBS 383:1
t. that try men's souls	PAINE 281:10	Churchill on t. of the wave	BEAV 33:5
t. that were are better	GRE 161:1	**torch** t.; be yours to hold it	MCCR 240:2
t. will not mend	PARK 285:4	t. has been passed	KENN 204:2
timetables by railway t.	TAYL 357:8	**Tories** both T.; both convinced	BOSW 53:4
timing lucky t. of your death	TAC 354:4	Mamma, are T. born wicked	ANON 12:4
real bad sense of t.	MCG 240:9	revolutionaries are potential T.	ORW 278:4
TINA acronym T.	THAT 361:1	stern and unbending T.	MAC 238:1
tincture Nature has left this t.	DEFOE 111:12	T., every election	BEVAN 40:9
tinhorn t. politicians	WHITE 387:3	T., in short, are atrophied	JOHN 196:13
tinker don't matter a t.'s cuss	SHIN 339:5	T. own no argument but force	BROW 59:6
tinned t. salmon	WILS 390:4	**tormenting** t. the people with trivia	NAP 270:2
Tippecanoe old soldier of T.	MORR 266:4	**torrent** leave it to a t. of change	CHES 84:4
T. and Tyler, too	ROSS 313:3	mere cork, dancing on a t.	BALF 30:5
tipster racing t.	TAYL 357:2	**torture-chamber** scene in a t.	MACM 245:4
tire see if he may not t. me	GEOR 149:2	**tortured** t. by material success	MACM 245:5
tired Give me your t., your poor	LAZ 219:7	**Tory** burning hatred for the T. Party	
tireless sound of t. voices	STEV 351:3		BEVAN 40:6
Titanic on the deck of the T.	MORT 267:1	Disraeli was my favourite T.	FOOT 138:6
title Who gained no t.	POPE 295:3	I may be a T.	PEEL 287:9
titles T. are but nick-names	PAINE 282:7	Let the Toryism of the T.	TROL 370:6
T. are shadows	DEFOE 111:11	loyalty is the T.'s secret weapon	KILM 209:9
T. distinguish the mediocre	SHAW 336:10	nostrils of an English T.	TROL 369:2
t. manifold	WORD 394:5	secret weapon of the T. Party	CRIT 104:9
to not freedom from, but freedom t.	BERL 39:2	T. and Whig in turns	SMITH 344:7
toadies t. of power	TREV 368:7	T. Corps d'Armée	GLAD 154:14
toast My t. would be	ADAMS 4:6	T. is someone who thinks	POW 297:10
tobacco chew of t.	LONG 232:6	T. men and Whig measures	DISR 117:7
today never jam t.	CARR 77:2	T. party never panics	HOSK 183:6
T. is the last day	YELT 396:4	T. shame	BEVAN 41:8
toga idealism is the noble t.	HUXL 186:4	violent T. of the old school	RUSK 316:4
toil blood, t., tears and sweat	CHUR 90:5	what T. Democracy is	CHUR 86:3
fifty years of unrequited t.	LINC 226:9	wise T. and a wise Whig	JOHN 198:10
horny-handed sons of t.	SAL 318:8	within the T. party	MACL 243:2
told Nobody t. us we could do this	WEBB 381:5	**Toryism** T. has always been	MACM 244:1
tolerance continuous t.	BAG 27:6	T. of the Tory	TROL 370:6
such a thing as t.	WILS 392:14	**total** t. solution	GOER 156:7
tolerate at least t. one another	TREV 368:3	**totalitarian** lead to the t. state	DENN 113:8
tolerated t. the Right Honourable	BEVAN 40:2	t. innovation	O'BR 276:5
toleration t. produced	GIBB 151:3	**totalitarianism** name of t.	GAND 147:5
Tomnoddy My Lord T. is thirty-four	BRO 57:8	**touch** Can t. him further	SHAK 332:2
tomorrow jam t. and jam yesterday	CARR 77:2	little t. of Harry in the night	SHAK 326:10
jam we thought was for t.	BENN 36:3	**tough** t. get going	KENN 206:2
limit to our realization of t.	ROOS 310:9	t.-minded	BEN 35:7

tough (*cont.*):

T. on crime and t. on	BLAIR 48:11
toughness t. doesn't have to	FEIN 136:2
tower t. of strength	TENN 359:11
town destroy the t. to save it	ANON 11:3
t. drunkard, a t. atheist	BROG 57:6
tracks stopped the engine in its t.	JENK 194:3
trade autocrat: that's my t.	CATH 78:4
great t. will always be attended	BURKE 64:14
No nation was ever ruined by t.	FRAN 142:6
none of the wheels of t.	HUME 184:7
People of the same t.	SMITH 341:5
pre-eminence in her Colonial t.	GEOR 149:5
state business is a cruel t.	HAL 166:12
There isn't any t.	HERB 176:9
war is the t. of kings	DRYD 126:2
world society is through free t.	CHOD 85:10
trades unionists t. at heart	JEV 194:11
trade Unionist British t.	BEVIN 42:6
trade unions first snarl of the t.	LLOY 229:11
tradition t. means giving votes	CHES 84:2
traditions rooted in age-long t.	BALF 30:7
tragedy first time as t.	MARX 252:4
Herein lies the t. of the age	DU B 126:6
One death is a t., one million	STAL 348:7
trahison t. *des clercs*	BENDA 35:6
train leave Powell's t.	MACL 243:3
traitor find myself a t. with the rest	SHAK 334:7
rich man makes a bonny t.	PAINE 282:2
traitors can see a sort of t. here	SHAK 334:7
hate t.	DRYD 126:1
watched the form of our t.	WEST 385:9
trample If you dare t. upon these	SHEL 338:6
trampled businessman has t.	NIC 272:6
trampling right of t. on them	CHILD 85:2
tranquillity fame and t.	MONT 263:8
transgression there is no t.	BIBLE 44:13
transient t. and embarrassed	DISR 120:14
transit t. *gloria mundi*	ANON 13:2
traps to recognize the t.	MACH 241:5
travelled care which way he t.	BEAV 34:5
travelling I am weary of t.	CHAR 83:4
t. round the world	COOK 102:6
treachery even t. cannot trust	JUN 201:2
t. of the intellectuals	BENDA 35:6
t. with a smile on its face	THAT 362:13
tread that I may t. safely	HASK 170:2
treason bloody t. flourished over us	SHAK 330:7
But t. is not owned	DRYD 125:13
condoned high t.	DISR 119:16
hate traitors and the t. love	DRYD 126:1
If *this* be t., make the most of it	HENRY 176:3
In trust I have found t.	ELIZ 130:6
none dare call it t.	HAR 169:1
no reason why gunpowder t.	ANON 13:2
state hireling for t. to his country	JOHN 197:3
That t. can but peep	SHAK 326:4

though they love the t.	DAN 109:5
t. has done his worst	SHAK 332:2
[T.] is a question of dates	TALL 355:5
treasure purest t.	SHAK 333:1
Treasury If the T. were to fill old bottles	KEYN 208:4
in this country is the T.	WILS 391:9
on our T. Bench	TROL 370:1
plaintive treble of the T. Bench	DISR 118:15
T. is in power	WILS 391:6
T. is the spring of business	BAG 24:12
treaties t., you see, are like girls	DE G 112:13
treaty hand that signed the t.	THOM 363:4
Make a good t. with Russia	BISM 46:3
This is not a peace t.	FOCH 138:2
t. [of Rome] is like	DENN 113:5
treble plaintive t.	DISR 118:15
tree t. of liberty must be refreshed	JEFF 191:7
Trelawny And shall T. die	HAWK 170:7
tremble Indeed I t. for my country	JEFF 191:3
trembles he t. as I do	WELL 383:8
trembling t. most, maintain	WALP 377:10
tres *est omnis divisa in partes* t.	CAES 71:7
trial t. by juries	JEFF 192:8
t. through which we pass	LINC 225:12
tribalism It is pure t.	FITT 137:6
t. is the strongest force	DEL 112:15
tribunes t. with their tongues	SHAK 335:5
tribute not one cent for t.	HARP 169:5
Why should we pay t.	SHAK 325:2
trickle-down t. theory	GALB 147:1
tricks frustrate their knavish t.	ANON 9:9
tried Almost everything has been t.	BENN 36:5
trifle As 'twere a careless t.	SHAK 331:6
trigger be one finger on the t.	MACM 245:2
want on the t.	ANON 15:1
trimmer This innocent word t.	HAL 165:2
Trinity God also is a T. man	BIRR 46:2
trip From fearful t. the victor ship	WHIT 387:10
look forward to the t.	STIN 351:5
triple t. cord, which no man	BURKE 68:3
trips If he t. he must be sustained	CHUR 93:6
Triton T. of the minnows	SHAK 324:6
triumph for evil to t.	BURKE 68:7
in t. from the north	MAC 236:3
meet with t. and disaster	KIPL 213:3
t. for democracy	HOPE 183:2
t. of modern science	WAUGH 380:9
t. of the embalmer's art	VIDAL 375:2
We shall not see the t.	DICK 115:5
troika like a spirited t.	GOGOL 156:8
Trojan never know what T. 'orses	BEVIN 43:5
troops march my t.	GRIM 162:1
tropic Under the t. is our language	WALL 377:3
trouble art of looking for t.	BENN 35:8
most credit with the least t.	TAYL 358:10
t. with this country	ADAMS 2:5

When in t., delegate   BOREN 52:6
when we are in bad t.   DID 116:2
troubled see that ye be not t.   BIBLE 44:8
trousers never have your best t.   IBSEN 186:9
steam-engine in t.   SMITH 344:8
trowel lay it on with a t.   DISR 121:4
true by the people as equally t.   GIBB 151:3
England to itself do rest but t.   SHAK 331:1
firm state by proportions t.   MARV 252:1
trumpet no use blowing the t.   CHAM 80:3
Now the t. summons us   KENN 204:6
trumps turn up the ace of t.   CHUR 86:8
trust absolute t.   SHAK 331:6
all power is a t.   DISR 116:3
aroused every feeling except t.   TAYL 357:12
even treachery cannot t.   JUN 201:2
exercises a public t.   CLEV 99:1
In t. I have found treason   ELIZ 130:6
man assumes a public t.   JEFF 192:12
no more than power in t.   DRYD 125:8
not property but a t.   FOX 140:5
t. no man living with power   ADAMS 3:5
you never should t. experts   SAL 318:1
trusted not to be t. with the office BROD 57:4
unfit to be t.   CHES 83:12
trustworthiness Carthaginian t.   SALL 319:8
truth committing ourselves to the t. NIXON 274:3
contaminated by the t.   RIPP 306:3
diminution of the love of t.   JOHN 197:4
economical with the t.   ARMS 16:12
economy of t.   BURKE 68:2
everybody can tell you the t.   MACH 241:7
fiction lags after t.   BURKE 64:13
fight for freedom and t.   IBSEN 186:9
Give me a grain of t.   WILK 389:2
His t. is marching on   HOWE 184:3
I just tell the t.   TRUM 371:12
innocent...To forsake this t.   ROS 313:1
In the strife of T. with Falsehood   LOW 234:1
is such a thing as t.   BAG 24:5
Ministers are wedded to the t.   SAKI 317:6
no appetite for t. in Ireland   PEEL 288:1
not maintained for t.   SWIFT 353:8
not t., but persuasion   MAC 236:5
opinion is t. filtered   PHIL 292:4
platitude is simply a t. repeated   BALD 29:2
statesman, yet friend to t.   POPE 295:3
stop telling the t. about them   STEV 350:1
stumbled over the t.   CHUR 94:10
takes two to speak the t.   THOR 364:3
trusted to speak the t.   BALF 30:4
T. against the world   LLOY 230:14
T. forever on the scaffold   LOW 234:2
T. is the first casualty   JOHN 197:4
t. is the glue   FORD 139:1
T. never yet fell dead   PARK 285:5
t. which makes men free   AGAR 6:4

unclouded face of t.   SCOTT 322:4
What is t.? said jesting Pilate   BACON 23:5
truths basic human t.   KENN 205:8
Few new t. have ever won   BERL 39:6
t. begin as blasphemies   SHAW 336:20
We hold these t. to be self-evident   ANON 14:7
We hold these t. to be sacred   JEFF 191:1
try But above all, t. something   ROOS 308:5
guiltier than him they t.   SHAK 332:6
tu *Et t., Brute*   CAES 71:13
Et t., Brute? Then fall, Caesar   SHAK 329:4
tube toothpaste is out of the t.   HALD 164:3
tumult t. and the shouting dies   KIPL 212:11
tune complain about the t.   BEVAN 41:2
turbulent rid me of this t. priest   HENR 175:7
Turkey T. is a dying man   NICH 271:4
turkeys t. have been known to vote   CALL 73:1
Turkish English, not the T. court   SHAK 326:8
Turks Let the T. now carry away   GLAD 154:12
turned if I were t. out of the Realm ELIZ 130:4
not t. the clock back   WAUGH 381:1
To be t. from one's course   FAB 134:6
turning lady's not for t.   THAT 361:2
Turning and t.   YEATS 395:6
turnip candle in that great t.   CHUR 93:3
TV politicians complain that T.   MURR 268:6
twelve bringing t. good men into a box
                                         BRO 58:1
in the sworn t. have a thief   SHAK 332:6
ruin himself in t. months   GEOR 149:10
twentieth language of the t. century
                                         BEVAN 40:10
would the t. century   SCHL 321:7
twenty given me t. reasons   BEVIN 43:1
twilight burden of a long t. struggle KENN 204:6
ever fly by t.   BACON 23:2
live in the grey t.   ROOS 310:11
twist Let him t. slowly, slowly   EHRL 128:6
two idea of the occasion in t. hours EVER 134:4
t. nations; between whom   DISR 118:2
whoever could make t. ears   SWIFT 353:7
two o'clock t. in the morning   NAP 269:10
Tyler Tippecanoe and T., too   ROSS 313:3
type highest t. of human nature   SPEN 347:5
tyrannical In all t. governments   BLAC 48:9
nothing more t.   TROL 369:4
tyrannis *Sic semper t.*   BOOTH 52:3
tyrannize t. over his bank balance   KEYN 208:2
tyrannous strength, but it is t.   SHAK 332:8
tyranny call it t.   HOBB 180:8
caused by some one's t.   BAG 24:11
despotism of liberty against t.   ROB 306:8
ecclesiastic t.'s the worst   DEFOE 111:10
grovelling t. of self-government   DISR 118:12
long dark night of t.   MURR 268:5
never lightened the burden of t.   SHAW 336:6
not consist merely of denouncing T.   BRY 60:8

tyranny (*cont.*):
submission to an unnecessary t.   RUSS 316:8
T. entrenches itself   SHEL 338:6
T. is always better organized   PÉGUY 289:11
Under conditions of t.   AREN 15:11
very definition of t.   MAD 246:5
war against a monstrous t.   CHUR 90:6
without representation is t.   OTIS 279:14
worst sort of t.   BURKE 65:4
tyrant each t., every Mob   KIPL 213:5
little t. of his fields   GRAY 160:8
loses the king in the t.   MAYH 255:1
No t. need fear till men   ARIS 16:11
When the t. has disposed   PLATO 294:4
tyrants all men would be t.   ADAMS 2:1
all men would be t.   DEFOE 111:12
argument of t.   PITT 293:7
barbarity of t.   SMITH 344:6
blood of patriots and t.   JEFF 191:7
curry favour with t.   ZAP 397:1
kings will be t. from policy   BURKE 67:2
reasoning of t.   GIBB 151:8
rebellion to t. is obedience to God   BRAD 54:8
sceptre from t.   TURG 372:7
stuff of which t. are made   BEAV 33:5
T. seldom want pretexts   BURKE 67:15
we tamed kings, restrained t.   BENN 36:8
Tyrone Fermanagh and T.   CHUR 88:4

Ulcer I am an 8 U. Man   EARLY 127:4
Ulster betrayal of U.   CAIR 72:1
U. says no   ANON 14:4
U. will fight   CHUR 86:6
unacceptable u. face   HEATH 173:8
unassailable position was u.   THAT 362:6
That u. holds on his rank   SHAK 329:3
unbearable in victory u.   CHUR 94:5
unbeatable In defeat u.: in victory   CHUR 94:5
unbribed u., there's no occasion   WOLFE 393:4
unconditional u. and immediate   GRANT 159:6
unconscionable u. time dying   CHAR 83:6
unconstitutional u. takes   KISS 214:5
uncreating before thy u. word   POPE 295:8
undecided Often u. whether to   BEAV 34:3
underachievers muscular u.   HENN 174:8
under-belly u. of the Axis   CHUR 91:11
underestimated u. for decades   KOHL 215:3
underestimating lost money by u.   MENC 256:11
underlings that we are u.   SHAK 328:4
undermined like a rat, he u. us   ANON 9:4
understand doesn't really u. the situation
          MURR 268:7
One has to u. the country   LESS 221:13
those who u. what it is   HAL 166:9
u. a little less   MAJOR 248:1
u. any other   BAG 25:5

understanding appeal to the u.   BAG 25:9
evidence against their own u.   HAL 165:9
President needs political u.   TRUM 371:10
u. between France and England   PEEL 289:1
understandings muddy u.   BURKE 66:17
understood not as it is u.   JACK 188:9
undertaking no such u.   CHAM 81:3
undo mark me how I will u. myself   SHAK 334:5
u. a man   SHAK 327:2
unearned u. increment   LLOY 229:4
u. increment of rent   MILL 259:13
uneasy u. lies the head   SHAK 326:7
You are u.; you never sailed   JACK 189:3
uneconomic not shown it to be 'u.'   SCH 322:1
uneducated government by the u.   CHES 85:1
unelected u. reject politicians   RIDL 305:7
unemployed from amongst the u.   LLOY 229:5
retired widow and an u. youth   BAG 25:4
unemployment reduce u.   HEATH 173:6
u. among teenagers   FRI 143:11
u. results   COOL 103:7
unequal u. distribution of property   MAD 246:4
u. earnings   ELL 133:1
unexpected old age is the most u.   TROT 370:13
unfathomable u. depths of insincerity
          ANON 13:10
unfinished liberty is always u.   ANON 11:14
unfit other party is u. to rule   MENC 257:4
u. to be trusted   CHES 83:12
unforeseen contingent and the u.   FISH 136:8
unfree Ireland u. shall never   PEAR 287:3
unglamorous government is too u.   O'RO 277:6
unhappily u. married   PARK 286:2
unhappy some should be u.   JOHN 198:6
u. the land that needs heroes   BREC 55:6
unheard language of the u.   KING 211:3
uniformity u. [of opinion]   JEFF 191:2
union determined to preserve this U.
          HOUS 183:8
devotion to the u.   CARS 77:4
fragments of a once glorious U.   WEBS 382:4
good old ship of the U.   LINC 225:4
knell of the U.   JEFF 193:7
Liberty *and* U., now and forever   WEBS 382:3
looks to an indestructible U.   CHASE 83:7
music of the U.   CHO 85:7
Our federal U.   JACK 188:8
our u. is perfect   DICK 115:9
perfect U., one and inseparable   PAGE 280:7
rebirth of the U.   WILS 392:6
seed-time of continental u.   PAINE 281:5
strict and indissoluble U.   HAM 167:5
struggle is to save the U.   LINC 226:2
take the key of the U.   CLAY 97:9
U., sir, is my country   CLAY 97:12
U. will be dissolved   COBB 100:1
unnatural a bond of u.   BURKE 64:16

Was saved the U. of these States WHIT 388:1
without the U. perishing TOCQ 365:5
unions there would have been no u. BALD 29:5
when Hitler attacked the u. NIEM 273:1
unite eggheads of the world u. STEV 350:15
united neither be u. at home SHEL 337:6
That these u. colonies are LEE 220:3
We must be u. CHUR 90:11
United Colonies these U. are ADAMS 3:9
United States children, and the U. of America
BISM 47:12
close to the U. DIAZ 114:6
constitution of the U. CLAY 98:1
constitution of the U. DAVIS 110:2
cowboy is President of the U. HANNA 168:1
disposition toward the U. MONR 263:6
failure of the U. BRYCE 61:2
Great Government of the U. WILS 392:9
I believe in the U. of America PAGE 280:7
in rebellion against the U. LINC 225:11
In the U. there is more space STEIN 349:2
On my arrival in the U. TOCQ 366:1
Soviet Union and the U. KENN 203:5
U.—bounded on the north FISKE 137:5
U. must be neutral in fact WILS 392:1
U. of Europe CHUR 92:11
U. themselves are essentially WHIT 387:8
uniting By u. we stand DICK 115:8
community u. peoples MONN 262:4
unity u. of our fatherland KOHL 215:5
u. of the empire BURKE 63:12
u. of the nation KOHL 215:4
universal become a u. law KANT 202:2
university u. should be a place DISR 120:2
unjust just and u. masterships RUSK 315:10
unkindest most u. cut of all SHAK 330:6
unking u. himself MAYH 255:1
unknown tread safely into the u. HASK 170:2
u. is held to be glorious TAC 354:2
u. Prime Minister [Bonar Law] ASQ 18:7
unlimited sovereignty is u. BARK 32:3
unmake people can u. it MARS 251:4
unmeritable slight u. man SHAK 330:13
unmuzzled come among you 'u.' GLAD 154:5
unnecessary u. War CHUR 92:6
unpalatable disastrous and the u. GALB 145:12
un-person abolished, an u. ORW 279:5
unpleasantness put up with u. NAP 269:5
unpolitical nearly an u. office ANON 11:9
no such thing as an u. man MAL 248:6
unpopular it is safe to be u. STEV 350:7
unselfish most u. and unsordid CHUR 92:5
unshaked u. of motion SHAK 329:3
unsoiled delicately and u. CHUR 88:3
unstable what the English call u. MACM 245:8
unthinkable dare to think 'u.' FULB 144:5
think the u., but always wear ROSS 313:4

untried against the new and u. LINC 225:3
untrue say something that is u. WALD 376:6
untying u. with the teeth BIER 44:15
unwritten that u. law D'AV 110:1
u. custom supported by popular CATT 78:6
up kicked u. stairs HAL 165:1
u. Guards and at them WELL 384:2
upmost once attains the u. round SHAK 328:10
upside turned the world u. down BIBLE 44:10
upward great one that goes u. SHAK 331:3
u. to the Great Society JOHN 196:2
urban For the u. poor the police HARR 169:6
urge u. for destruction BAK 28:4
US defeat the U. aggressors MAO 250:7
use best u. of laws is to teach PHIL 291:9
used Learn to get u. to it CHUR 90:9
useful as equally u. GIBB 151:3
usual business carried on as u. CHUR 87:6
usurper u. ought to examine MACH 241:8
usury u. is contrary to Scripture TAWN 355:11
Utopia possibly be attained in U. GLAD 155:3
principality in U. MAC 237:11
right signposts to the socialist U. CROS 106:4
U. is a blessed past KISS 214:11
utopian retrospective or u. ARON 17:7
Utopias all the static U. INGE 187:9
utterances flat, dishwatery u. ANON 13:6
U-turn catch-phrase, the U. THAT 361:2

vacancies v. to be obtained JEFF 192:9
vacancy v. of the throne GIBB 151:1
vacant no v. cover for him MALT 248:11
vae V. victis LIVY 228:8
valiant As he was v., I honour SHAK 329:11
value unique v. in her KEYN 207:3
values restore Victorian v. THAT 361:8
vanity Being an MP feeds your v. PARR 286:11
vapour I absorb the v. GLAD 155:11
street-bred people that v. KIPL 212:7
variety because it admits v. FORS 139:5
Vatican creeping about the V. MACM 245:12
vaulting v. ambition SHAK 331:8
veal more than cold boiled v. MAC 236:10
one of Bellamy's v. pies PITT 293:12
vegetarian often with v. leanings ORW 277:11
tiger will turn v. BROUN 58:4
vegetarianism in favour of v. INGE 187:5
vein not in the giving v. SHAK 335:3
venal v. city ripe to perish SALL 319:7
vengeance gods forbade v. CHUR 87:2
veni v., vidi, vici CAES 71:12
vent full of v. SHAK 324:11
venture v. to recommend them GLAD 155:6
ventures Or lose our v. SHAK 330:14
verbosity exuberance of his own v. DISR 120:11

verbs irregular v.	LYNN 235:10	**vigour** great physical v.	BROW 60:3
verdict cannot think that the v.	BIRCH 45:10	**vile** v., but viler George	LAND 217:5
verge brought to the v. of war	DULL 126:9	**village** first in a v.	CAES 71:10
vermin race of little odious v.	SWIFT 353:6	Some v.-Hampden	GRAY 160:8
they are lower than v.	BEVAN 40:6	v. fiddler after Paganini	NIC 272:5
Vermont As Maine goes, so goes V.	FARL 135:5	**villain** that v. Hitler	GEOR 150:3
Versailles politics of V.	MONN 262:7	**villany** thus I clothe my naked v.	SHAK 334:11
verse write it out in a v.	YEATS 395:8	**vine** Under his own v.	SHAK 327:9
vessel by remaining in a v.	HUME 184:9	**vintage** He is trampling out the v.	HOWE 184:3
vestry of Commons as a mere v.	DISR 120:16	**violate** to v. would be oppression	JEFF 192:5
vet'ran superfluous lags the v.	JOHN 196:14	**violence** I say v. is necessary	BROWN 58:7
vex I believe they die to v. me	MELB 255:8	legitimate v.	WEBER 381:8
vicar I will be the v. of Bray, sir	ANON 10:12	organization of v.	BAEZ 23:11
vice characteristic v. a reluctance	TAWN 355:7	outburst of crime and v.	TEBB 359:2
defence of liberty is no v.	GOLD 157:8	v. employed by well-meaning	TOCQ 367:1
in a private man a v.	MASS 254:1	**violent** policy is v.	HUME 184:8
render v. serviceable to the cause	BOL 50:7	v. revolution inevitable	KENN 204:11
vice-presidency v. isn't worth	GARN 148:2	**violently** v. if they must	QUIN 299:3
Viceroy future V. must	VICT 374:7	**violet** v. smells to him	SHAK 326:12
V. has been forgotten	NEHRU 270:12	**Virginian** I am not a V.	HENRY 176:4
vices By hating v. too much	BURKE 67:8	**virtue** from v. comes money	SOCR 345:8
judge the v. and virtues	TOCQ 366:2	fugitive and cloistered v.	MILT 260:6
victim fall v. to a big lie	HITL 179:3	grounds of this are v. and talents	JEFF 193:4
It marks a v.; denounces it	CLAY 97:7	in a prince the v.	MASS 254:1
While he felt like a v.	WALP 377:9	practise v. afterwards	HOR 183:3
victims first v. of American Fascism	ROS 313:2	serviceable to the cause of v.	BOL 50:7
They are its v.	CONR 102:4	v. does not come from money	SOCR 345:8
victis vae v.	LIVY 228:8	v. is the essence	ROB 306:9
victor to the v. belong the spoils	MARCY 250:8	v. of Englishmen	TAWN 355:7
Victoria take a ticket at V. Station	BEVIN 43:4	v. to withstand	WASH 379:7
Victorian restore V. values	THAT 361:8	wisdom, capacity and v.	SWIFT 353:8
victories few sharp v.	WAUGH 380:5	**virtues** call out great v.	ADAMS 2:2
liberty knows nothing but v.	PHIL 292:3	his v.	SHAK 331:7
peace hath her v.	MILT 261:3	in war the two cardinal v.	HOBB 180:3
victorious Make him v.	HOGG 181:2	vices and v. of mankind	TOCQ 366:2
victors written by the v.	NEHRU 270:6	**virtuous** looking upon men as v.	BOL 50:6
victory But 'twas a famous v.	SOUT 347:2	think all men v.	BURKE 63:2
In v.: magnanimity	CHUR 93:5	**visible** v. governments	RUSK 316:3
in v., Revenge	LYNN 235:4	**vision** no v., the people perish	BIBLE 43:15
in v. unbearable	CHUR 94:5	Oh, the v. thing	BUSH 69:5
knows not v. nor defeat	ROOS 310:11	To grasp and hold a v.	REAG 302:7
Let 'dig for v.' be the motto	DORM 123:1	young men's v.	DRYD 125:7
never had a v.	CHUR 93:10	**visionary** schemes of v. politicians	BURKE 64:17
no substitute for v.	MAC 235:13	**vive** V. Le Québec Libre	DE G 112:14
One more such v.	PYRR 299:1	**vocabulary** diplomatist's v.	TAYL 357:1
peace without v.	WILS 392:8	**voice** America, with the same v.	ADAMS 4:7
than to v. by a woman	WEST 385:8	prevail against the v. of a nation	RUSS 317:1
Together we shall achieve v.	EIS 129:3	saying the v. of the people	ALC 6:8
v. has a hundred fathers	CIANO 95:4	v. of Rome	JONS 199:3
victuals instead of snatching his v.	CHUR 89:11	v. of the kingdom	SWIFT 353:5
Vienna V. is nothing	METT 257:10	v. we heard	ATTL 20:1
Vietnam led to the V. War	BLACK 48:5	**voices** sound of tireless v.	STEV 351:3
To win in V., we will have to	SPOCK 347:9	want to have v. in Parliament	RUSK 315:11
V. was lost in the living	MCL 243:9	**void** against the constitution is v.	OTIS 280:1
viewpoint gives their v.	NEHRU 270:6	**volcanoes** range of exhausted v.	DISR 119:19
vigilance eternal v.	CURR 107:4	**Volk** ein Reich, ein V., ein Führer	ANON 9:11

war (*cont.*):

neither shall they learn w.	BIBLE 43:18
never to go to w.	CHAM 80:10
no declaration of w.	EDEN 127:7
no interest in a w.	WAUGH 380:5
older men declare w.	HOOV 183:1
once lead this people into w.	WILS 392:14
only w. creates order	BREC 55:7
peace is harder than making w.	STEV 349:6
possibility of a short decisive w.	LYND 234:9
prepare for the last w.	TUCH 372:4
prepare for w. like precocious giants	
	PEAR 287:4
quickest way of ending a w.	ORW 278:13
require a resort to w.	JEFF 192:11
rich wage it's the poor	SART 320:5
Second World W. the British	TAYL 357:11
silent in time of w.	CIC 95:12
since the second world w.	LEVIN 222:9
sinews of w., unlimited money	CIC 95:11
splendid little w.	HAY 171:1
squalid nuisance in time of w.	CHUR 92:8
stirring up some w. or other	PLATO 294:4
surest way to prevent w.	RAND 300:8
take a country into a w.	CHAM 81:2
tell us all about the w.	SOUT 347:1
There ain't gonna be no w.	MACM 244:5
There never was a good w.	FRAN 142:4
time of peace thinks of w.	ANON 10:4
too long without a w. here	BREC 55:7
unnecessary w.	CHUR 92:6
very well out of the w.	BALD 29:1
w. against a monstrous tyranny	CHUR 90:6
W. always finds a way	BREC 55:9
W. is a contagion	ROOS 309:4
W. is a very rough game	MONT 265:2
W. is capitalism	STOP 351:9
W. is over	GRANT 159:8
W. is peace	ORW 279:1
w. is politics with bloodshed	MAO 250:3
w. is the continuation of politics	CLA 96:11
W. is the health	BOUR 53:7
W. is the national industry	MIR 261:6
W. is the remedy our *enemies*	SHER 339:1
W. is the trade of kings	DRYD 126:2
W. is too serious a matter	CLEM 98:7
w. on a kindred nation	BETH 39:8
w. on poverty in America	JOHN 195:10
w. regarded as inevitable	KENN 203:6
w. run to show the world	BERR 39:7
w. situation has developed	HIR 179:1
w. that will end w.	WELLS 385:4
w. to 'make the world safe'	ROB 307:1
w. violates the order	HER 177:3
W. will cease when men refuse	ANON 14:6
way to win an atomic w.	BRAD 54:3
We hear w. called murder	MACD 240:5

We make w. that we may live	ARIS 16:3
We still seek no wider w.	JOHN 196:3
We've a w., an' a debt	LOW 233:8
When is a w. not a war	CAMP 74:2
when there was w., he went	AUDEN 21:3
When w. enters a country	ANON 14:13
When w. is declared	JOHN 197:4
which enable it to make w.	WEIL 383:5
witnesses to the desolation of w.	GEOR 149:6
Work at w. speed	MORR 266:6
you must take chances in w.	DULL 126:9
you want peace, prepare for w.	VEG 373:7
warfare mother of arts, of w.	DU B 126:4
w. must be preceded	ZIN 397:4
warn right to w.	BAG 26:1
w. you not to be ordinary	KINN 211:10
warning w. to all Ministers	WALP 378:10
warrant not a sufficient w.	MILL 258:10
wars All w. are planned by old men	RICE 304:5
came to an end all w.	LLOY 229:8
European and quarrels	PAINE 281:6
history is littered with the w.	POW 296:9
In the w. of the European	MONR 263:5
I see w., horrible wars	VIRG 375:6
sent into any foreign w.	ROOS 309:9
take care not to lose w.	CHUR 92:12
to the beginnings of all w.	ROOS 310:8
w. and rumours of w.	BIBLE 44:8
W. are popular	MACD 240:3
W. begin when you will	MACH 242:2
W. cannot be fought	MOUN 267:4
w. in history have been avoided	CHUR 94:16
Warsaw order reigns in W.	ANON 13:1
warship every w. launched	EIS 129:4
warts w. *and all*	CROM 105:14
w., and everything as you see	CROM 105:14
war-war better than to w.	CHUR 94:2
Warwick shameless W., peace	SHAK 327:4
wash Can w. the balm	SHAK 333:6
Washington come to W. to be loved	
	GRAMM 159:4
directed from W.	JEFF 193:16
government at W. lives	GARF 147:8
inflation is made: that's in W.	FRI 143:9
not in W. as a statesman	ASH 17:8
W. has lots of those	O'RO 277:5
W. is a city of southern efficiency	KENN 205:12
W. is a steering wheel	GOOD 158:1
what posterity will say of W.	FRAN 142:3
Washingtonian W. dignity	POTT 296:4
wasms All the 'isms are w.	ANON 8:5
wasp exceedingly agile w.	LASKI 218:3
wasps let w. and hornets	SWIFT 353:4
waste Don't w. any time	HILL 178:9
w. of goods	VEBL 373:6
waste-paper w. basket	WEBB 381:6

wasting w. the labours | JEFF 192:10
watch keeping w. above his own | LOW 234:2
watching BIG BROTHER IS W. YOU | ORW 278:14
  something out there w. over us | ALLEN 7:4
watchword Our w. is security | PITT 293:5
water Ah, on the w., I presume | LLOY 230:12
  drawers of w. | BIBLE 43:8
  feet are always in the w. | AMES 8:2
  king over the w. | ANON 11:6
  reached the calm of w. | ADAMS 2:9
  w. in the rough rude sea | SHAK 333:6
Waterloo battle of W. was won | WELL 384:11
  Every man meets his W. at last | PHIL 292:2
  Probably the battle of W. *was* won | ORW 278:6
  That world-earthquake, W. | TENN 360:1
waters bounded w. | SHAK 335:9
  By the w. of Babylon | WALP 378:2
  refreshing w. of office | TROL 369:2
wave Churchill on top of the w. | BEAV 33:5
way all the w. with LBJ | ANON 8:6
  I know really which w. I want | THAT 361:14
  not seem to care which w. | BEAV 34:5
  provided I get my own w. | THAT 362:4
  This is the w. the world ends | ELIOT 130:2
  war always finds a w. | BREC 55:9
  w. she disposed of an empire | HARL 169:3
we w. shall not be moved | ANON 14:8
  w. shall overcome | ANON 14:9
weak concessions of the w. | BURKE 64:11
  w. have one weapon | BID 44:14
weakness compassion is not w. | HUMP 185:6
  wade into the w. of Princes | JAM 190:1
  w. of their imaginations | BAG 25:6
weal according to the common w. | JAM 190:2
wealth acquisition of w. | SOCR 345:7
  get w. and place | POPE 295:7
  greater the w., the thicker | GALB 145:11
  his best riches, ignorance of w. | GOLD 157:6
  Let w. and commerce | MANN 249:5
  malefactors of great w. | ROOS 311:9
  no increase in material w. | TAWN 355:12
  O citizens, first acquire w. | HOR 183:3
  regard the w. of their master | SMITH 343:2
  w. accumulates, and men decay | GOLD 157:6
  w. is a sacred thing | FRAN 141:3
  w. piled by the bond-man's | LINC 226:9
  w. should be found everywhere | BURKE 68:8
  w. ye find, another keeps | SHEL 338:4
wealthy some people are very w. | ARIS 16:9
weaned w. on a pickle | ANON 13:12
weapon art is not a w. | KENN 205:9
  bayonet is a w. | ANON 8:10
  Loyalty is the Tory's secret w. | KILM 209:9
  most potent w. | BIKO 45:4
  weak have one w. | BID 44:14
weapons books are w. | ROOS 310:2
  fought with nuclear w. | MOUN 267:4

wearied w. me for two hours | GEOR 149:2
wearing w. o' the Green | ANON 10:11
weary I am w. of travelling | CHAR 83:4
weasel called 'w. words' | ROOS 312:1
weathercock bit like a rusty w. | BENN 37:1
webs laws are like spider's w. | ANAC 8:3
Webster Daniel W. struck me | SMITH 344:8
wedding bride at a w. | HEAD 172:1
weed ignorance is an evil w. | BEV 42:4
  w. that grows in every soil | BURKE 64:10
week w. for preparation | WILS 392:18
  w. is a long time in politics | WILS 390:8
weeks your Majesty, seven w. | POPH 295:9
weep As make the angels w. | SHAK 332:9
  Babylon we sit down and w. | WALP 378:2
weight punch above its w. | HURD 185:9
  willing to pull his w. | ROOS 311:3
weights new system of w. | NAP 270:2
weird As the w. women promised | SHAK 331:10
welfare failures of the w. state | GING 153:3
  goes with the w. of the country | WILS 389:7
  honour, and w. of this realm | CHAR 82:8
  lead to the w. state | DENN 113:8
  led to that of the w.-state | TEMP 359:5
  most anxious for its w. | BURKE 62:7
  tax collector for the w. state | GING 153:2
  w. became a term of opprobrium | MOYN 267:5
well golden crown like a deep w. | SHAK 334:3
  It is not done w.; but you | JOHN 197:9
  w.-placed business men | YOUNG 396:6
  would do very w., if they | WALP 377:5
wen fate of the great w. | COBB 100:3
west Cincinnatus of the W. | BYRON 71:2
  Go W., young man, go W. | SOULE 346:8
  political history of the W. | HAIL 163:7
  safeguard of the W. | WORD 394:6
  what is thought in the W. | SOLZ 345:11
West End farce in the W. | SMITH 343:7
western Iron Lady of the W. World | THAT 360:11
  w. world | PAINE 281:12
Westminster brothels of W. | LIV 228:7
westward w. the course of empire | BERK 38:4
whale decent beached w. | HENN 175:1
wharf sit on the w. for a day | BEAV 34:3
wharf-rat merely a grey w. | THOR 364:4
what W. did the President know | ANON 14:12
  W. is to be done | LENIN 221:1
wheel great w. runs down a hill | SHAK 331:3
wheels none of the w. of trade | HUME 184:7
when w. did he know it | ANON 14:17
where have they fixed the w. | HAWK 170:7
  w. are all the people | ATTL 20:5
Whig ascendancy of the W. party | MAC 238:4
  first W. was the Devil | JOHN 198:8
  see a W. in any dress | JOHN 197:1
  Tory and W. in turns | SMITH 344:5
  Tory men and W. measures | DISR 117:5

Whig (*cont.*):

wise Tory and a wise W.   JOHN 198:10

Whigs caught the W. bathing   DISR 117:15

For W. admit no force   BROW 59:6

while w. there is a lower class   DEBS 111:3

whim conform to our w.   REST 303:2

whimper not with a bang but a w.   ELIOT 130:2

whine thin w. of hysteria   DID 116:2

Whip [W.'s duty is] to make   CANN 75:5

whips Chamber selected by the W.   FOOT 138:5

Like most Chief W. he knew   CLARK 96:8

w. and scorns of time   SHAK 325:8

whirlwind they shall reap the w.   BIBLE 44:1

whisper w. of a faction   RUSS 317:1

whistle until a shrimp learns to w.   KHR 209:1

white acceptance of w. people   BOES 50:3

between the w. and black races   LINC 225:2

necessity of the American w. man   BALD 28:8

nor w. so very white   CANN 75:2

no 'w.' or 'coloured' signs   KENN 205:5

take up the W. Man's burden   KIPL 213:2

want to be the w. man's brother   KING 210:2

When a w. man in Africa   LESS 222:1

w. *heat of the technological*   WILS 390:5

w. moderate   KING 210:8

w. race *is* the cancer   SONT 346:6

Whitehall gentleman in W.   JAY 190:4

like a condottiere through W.   HURD 185:8

White House From log-cabin to W.   THAY 363:1

no whitewash at the W.   NIXON 274:9

on the way to the W.   STEV 350:9

operative W. Position   ZIEG 397:3

preside over the W.   BUSH 69:3

whitewash no w. at the White   NIXON 274:9

who W.? Whom   LENIN 221:9

wholesale in a w. business   LLOY 230:7

whom Who? W.   LENIN 221:9

whore I am the Protestant w.   GWYN 162:7

w. and gambler   BLAKE 49:4

whores parliament of w.   O'RO 277:8

whose w. finger do you want   ANON 15:1

why ask w.   AUDEN 21:6

wicked Arthur is w. and moral   CHUR 88:2

born w., and grow worse   ANON 12:4

not that men are w.   DU B 126:6

wickedness human w.   TAYL 357:4

w. is the root of despotism   ROB 306:9

widening in the w. gyre   YEATS 395:6

wider We still seek no w. war   JOHN 196:3

w. still and w.   BENS 37:6

widow actions of a retired w.   BAG 25:4

wields He who w. the knife   HES 177:9

wife Aids—and that is the w.   CURR 107:7

Caesar's w. must be above   CAES 71:9

If I were your w.   ASTOR 19:3

wig must grow to resemble a w.   COCK 100:9

Wigan W. Pier   BRID 56:3

wiggles It w., it's shapely   ERWIN 134:1

wild one is the w. herb   TOCQ 366:10

w., and incomprehensible man   VICT 374:6

W. men screaming through   LLOY 229:11

wilderness Rome is but a w.   SHAK 335:6

savage w. into   BURKE 63:11

send choice grain into this w.   STO 351:12

They make a w. and call it peace   TAC 354:3

wilful little group of w. men   WILS 392:9

will above all, the w.   ROOS 309:10

general w. rules in society   ROB 306:5

his w. is not his own   SHAK 325:5

not according to the common w.   JAM 190:2

not to obey the w.   PEEL 288:6

One single w. is necessary   ROB 306:10

w. of the majority   JEFF 192:5

w. to be free   LIPP 228:5

Willie Prime Minister needs a W.   THAT 362:12

willows not change to southern w.   LEE 220:1

Wilson I suppose Mr W.   HOME 182:3

W. is the nation's shepherd   SPR 348:2

[Woodrow W.] thinks   CLEM 98:5

win hope to w. by't   SHAK 327:7

spend it, and w.   KENN 206:4

To w. in Vietnam, we will have   SPOCK 347:9

way to w. an atomic war   BRAD 54:3

w. just one for the Gipper   GIPP 153:5

wind he must lie with the w.   TAYL 358:7

They have sown the w.   BIBLE 44:1

to pure w.   ORW 279:11

twist slowly, slowly in the w.   EHRL 128:6

w. in his teeth   CHUR 90:2

w. of change is blowing   MACM 245:1

winding by a w. stair   BACON 22:13

weave old England's w. sheet   BLAKE 49:4

window broken w. pane   PANK 285:2

kiss my ass in Macy's w.   JOHN 196:8

they will return through the w.   FRED 143:3

windows w. into men's souls   ELIZ 131:7

winds W. of the World, give answer   KIPL 212:7

w. that would blow then   BOLT 51:3

Windsor great W. marshes   NIC 271:8

wine new w. into old bottles   ATTL 20:5

strong w. diluted   SAL 318:1

temptations both in w. and women   KITC 214:15

wings hear the beating of his w.   BRIG 56:4

winners there are no w.   CHAM 80:8

winning He is w. through   CHAN 81:7

w. cause pleased   LUCAN 234:3

Winston has to remind W.   DALT 109:1

W. is back   ANON 15:4

W. with his hundred-horse-power   BALD 30:3

winter w. of our discontent   SHAK 334:8

wisdom contrivance of human w.   BURKE 66:12

conventional w.   GALB 145:7

Here is w.; this is the royal Law	COR 103:10
if w. could be made to spread	CHUR 92:14
Is this the w. of a great minister	JUN 200:10
their w., capacity and virtue	SWIFT 353:8
w. and truth	SOCR 345:7
with how little w. the world is	OXEN 280:6
wise cunning men pass for w.	BACON 22:6
great men are not always w.	BIBLE 43:14
known generally to the w.	DEM 113:2
never w. to appear to be	WHIT 387:5
Nor ever did a w. one	ROCH 307:5
What all the w. men promised	MELB 255:4
w. become as the unwise	LAND 217:4
wisely men and nations behave w.	EBAN 127:5
wiser guided by the w.	CARL 76:3
President looked w.	KEYN 207:4
wisest w. fool in Christendom	HENR 175:4
wish I do w. he did not look	ANON 13:12
willing to believe what they w.	CAES 71:8
wit I have neither w., nor words	SHAK 330:9
lords do not encourage w.	DISR 116:6
no free and splendid w.	MILT 260:4
only a w. among Lords	JOHN 197:1
witch You get w.-hunts and wars	MITC 241:7
withers not 'abolished', it w. *away*	ENG 133:6
withstand virtue to w.	WASH 379:7
witnesses multitude of silent w.	GEOR 149:6
wits our hopes our w. beguile	WOTT 394:8
wives divides the w.	SMITH 341:2
political leaders and their w.	HEAD 172:4
woe W. to the land	SHAK 335:1
wolf And the w. that shall keep it	KIPL 212:9
We have the w. by the ears	JEFF 193:9
w. remains of a different opinion	INGE 187:5
Wolsey W.'s Home Town	ANON 11:7
wolves lion to frighten the w.	MACH 241:5
woman dead w. bites not	GRAY 160:7
help and support of the w. I love	EDW 128:5
man a w., and a w. a man	PEMB 289:12
No w. in my time	THAT 360:7
So you're the little w. who wrote	LINC 227:4
to *victory* by a w.	WEST 385:8
want anything done, ask a w.	THAT 360:8
weak and feeble w.	ELIZ 130:9
wicked folly of 'W.'s Rights'	VICT 374:5
w. becoming a Prime Minister	ASQ 18:11
w.'s preaching is like a dog's	JOHN 197:9
w. stock is rising	CHILD 85:3
women As the weird w. promised	SHAK 331:10
temptations both in wine and w.	KITC 214:15
to claim our right as w.	PANK 284:10
w. and children could work	SELL 323:9
W.—one half the human race	BAG 25:8
w.'s rights is the basic principle	FOUR 140:2
W., then, are only children	CHES 83:10
won elections, but I w. the count	SOM 346:5
prize we sought is w.	WHIT 387:9

w. in my lifetime—by the blood	JACK 189:6
wonder to see the boneless w.	CHUR 89:1
wood hewers of w.	BIBLE 43:8
lath of w. painted to look like	BISM 47:2
wooden w. walls are the best walls	COV 103:11
Woolworth paying a visit to W.'s	BEVAN 40:3
to walk and live a W. life hereafter	NIC 272:3
word And what the w. did make it	ELIZ 131:4
But yesterday the w. of Caesar	SHAK 330:5
If you use a 'weasel w.' after	ROOS 312:1
Let the w. go forth from this time	KENN 204:2
time lies in one little w.	SHAK 333:3
'When *I* use a w.,' Humpty	CARR 77:1
words can't find the w. to clothe	CHUR 94:4
conceal a fact with w.	MACH 242:1
few w. to the Solicitor	PITT 292:8
good w. will not do	LAMB 216:6
my w. are my own	CHAR 83:1
often had to eat my w.	CHUR 94:15
say a few w. of my own	EDW 128:5
when you read the mere w.	TROL 370:8
wit, nor w., nor worth	SHAK 330:9
work got to w. five months	PEROT 290:7
people are unable to find w.	COOL 103:9
say *Equal Pay for Equal W.*	ANTH 15:6
those that w. under them	HAL 165:4
W. and pray, live on hay	HILL 178:8
W. expands so as to fill	PARK 285:8
w. hard at w. worth doing	ROOS 311:6
W. is the call	MORR 266:6
W. makes free	ANON 8:7
worker weapon with a w. at each end	
	ANON 8:10
w. can be lulled	KHR 209:8
w. is the slave of capitalist	CONN 102:2
workers organised w.	SHIN 339:5
state and the w.	TAWN 355:6
To secure for the w. by hand	ANON 14:3
w. are perfectly free	ENG 133:7
working choice of w. or starving	JOHN 197:6
Labour isn't w.	ANON 11:8
policy isn't hurting, it isn't w.	MAJOR 247:9
support of the w. man	BAG 27:4
working class capitalism of the w.	SPEN 347:7
sort of job all w. parents	ABB 1:1
That vast portion…of the w.	ARN 17:5
w. where we belong	ORW 278:2
workings w. of government	BLACK 48:5
works Greed w.	WEIS 383:6
Look on my w., ye Mighty	SHEL 337:9
seen the future; and it w.	STEF 349:1
upon your w.	GRANT 159:6
Well, it w., doesn't it	CALL 73:3
workshop nation may be its w.	CHAM 80:4
w. of the world	DISR 117:1
world and they only saved the w.	CHES 84:10
become the w.'s policeman	HEAL 172:8

y. man of promise	BALF 31:6	y. who must fight and die	HOOV 183:1
y. men's vision	DRYD 125:7	**Yugoslavia** Democratic, federal Y.	TAYL 357:6
youth invite the flower of our y.	TREV 368:1		
traitorously corrupted the y.	SHAK 327:3		
unemployed y. become	BAG 25:4	**zeal** holy mistaken z. in politics	JUN 200:11
y., beauty, graceful action	DRYD 125:10	not the slightest z.	TALL 355:3
Y. is a blunder	DISR 117:8	**zealous** z. citizen	BURKE 67:9
y. is the season of credulity	PITT 292:10	**Zionism** Z., be it right or wrong	BALF 30:7
y. of a Nation	DISR 118:6	**zip** he did not have great z.	SMITH 344:3
y. to the gallows	PAINE 283:1	**Zurich** all the little gnomes in Z.	WILS 390:1